D1761531

The Prose Works of Andrew Marvell

VOLUME I

THE PROSE WORKS OF

Andrew Marvell

VOLUME I

1672–1673

YALE UNIVERSITY PRESS

NEW HAVEN & LONDON

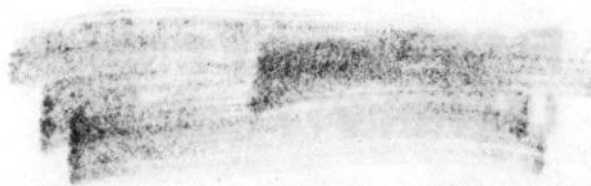

Published with assistance from the foundation established in memory of Oliver Baty Cunningham of the Class of 1917, Yale College.
Figures 1–4 are printed by permission of the Syndics of Cambridge University Library.

Designed by Nancy Ovedovitz and set in Adobe Caslon type by Keystone Typesetting, Inc. Printed in the United States of America by Sheridan Books.

Library of Congress Cataloging in Publication Data
Marvell, Andrew, 1621–1678.
[Prose works]
The prose works of Andrew Marvell /
edited by Martin Dzelzainis and Annabel Patterson.
p. cm.
Contents: v. 1. 1672–1673
Includes index.
ISBN 0-300-09935-5 (v. 1)
I. Dzelzainis, Martin. II. Patterson, Annabel M. III. Title.
PR3546.A6 2003
828′.408—dc21 2003050055

A catalogue record for this book is available from the British Library.

The paper in this book meets the guidelines for permanence and durability of the Committee on Production Guidelines for Book Longevity of the Council on Library Resources.

10 9 8 7 6 5 4 3 2 1

Editorial Committee

Contents: Volume I

Contents: Volume II

Introduction

Annabel Patterson

Andrew Marvell is known to most late-twentieth-century readers as the author of a handful of exquisite lyric poems, a smaller number of political poems provocative of much debate, and, to those few who persist in curiosity or commitment after these categories have been exhausted, some rather nasty-minded satires of the Restoration court and government. In his own time, however, Marvell was known for quite other reasons: as the author of several brilliant prose pamphlets on the subject of church government and religious toleration; and another pamphlet, less witty but more immediately influential, on the history and principles of parliamentary government in Restoration England.

Marvell made his reputation initially by publishing the *Rehearsal Transpros'd,* an electrically charged contribution to the debate on toleration. He first appeared as a polemicist (though anonymously) in support of the king's desire to grant some latitude to those who, from the left or the right of the religious spectrum, could not in conscience belong to the Established Church. Some idea of the excitement he caused is registered opposite the title page of a copy in the Folger Library, where one seventeenth-century reader wrote, "It is supposed to bee written, by Mr Marvell, A Countrey Gentleman & A Great Republican." And beneath it another reader objected, "In saying he is a great Republican you ar very much mistaken for he is one of this parliament and a conformist."[1] Since the parliament had

[1] Folger Library, Washington, D.C., M878B, copy 1.

been prorogued on April 22, 1671, not to meet again until February 4, 1673, the most likely moment for this heated little exchange, which raises so many of the issues of the day and Marvell's attitudes to them, would have been between February 4 and March 29, 1673, when the Cavalier parliament was again prorogued; for during that session it must have been apparent to all that "the first Restoration crisis"[2] was in full swing. The crisis was generated by parliament's decision in 1670 to renew the Conventicle Act of 1664 enforcing religious conformity, and its most dramatic moments were Charles II's Declaration of Indulgence on March 15, 1672, and its withdrawal, under parliamentary pressure, at the beginning of the session in question. By the time of the session, however, the *Rehearsal Transpros'd* had already caused a sensation, resulting in a second impression (no doubt timed for parliament's meeting) and a couple of pirated editions.

Today, although certain Marvell scholars still debate whether Marvell was "a great Republican" or a loyalist parliamentarian and religious conformist, very little heat can be generated by these questions, largely because the textual stimulus, along with the political context, is inaccessible. The 1670s, as an era, have struggled for notice beside those more famous moments of crisis, 1678–83 and 1688–89. And throughout the twentieth century, Marvell's prose works have been, if not forgotten, unreasonably neglected, thanks to the accidents of academic publishing. The last more or less complete edition of his works was produced in the final quarter of the nineteenth century by that indefatigable conservationist Alexander Grosart. Grosart's four-volume edition still reflected the respect paid to Marvell as a polemicist by those of his own party in the late seventeenth century, by readers of a Whiggish persuasion subsequently, and by historians who found his letters and pamphlets full of reliable and often unique information.[3] Grosart's tone and motivation partly make up for his frequent inaccuracies, lack of collation, and embryonic annotation. One might have expected a complete mid-twentieth-century edition, given the status that Marvell had acquired as a poet under the influence of H. G. Grierson, T. S. Eliot, and the New Critics. But while the poems were often reedited, and the letters became more reliably and completely available in H. M. Margoliouth's splendid *Poems and Letters,* the prose pamphlets, with

[2] The phrase is Gary de Krey's, in "The First Restoration Crisis: Conscience and Coercion in London, 1667–73," *Albion* 25 (Winter 1993), pp. 565–80.

[3] *Complete Works in Verse and Prose of Andrew Marvell M.P.,* ed. Alexander B. Grosart, 4 vols. (Blackburn, 1872–75; reprinted AMS Press, 1966.)

one major exception, were allowed to stand as they did in Grosart's text, by modern standards archaic.[4] That major exception was, of course, the two parts of the *Rehearsal Transpros'd*, which were edited by D. I. B. Smith for the Clarendon Press in 1971.[5] The *Rehearsal Transpros'd* was picked for survival, one can surmise, by virtue of its literary qualities, its parodic relation to Restoration comedy in general and to Buckingham's *Rehearsal* in particular, along with its high density of other literary allusions. But the four tracts that formed Grosart's fourth volume, *Mr. Smirke; or, the Divine in Mode*, its appended *Short Historical Essay Concerning General Councils*, the *Remarks Upon a Late Disingenuous Discourse*, and the famous *Account of the Growth of Popery and Arbitrary Government*, were allowed to slide into the territory of the arcane. Thanks to the generosity of Yale University Press, which committed itself, for principle's sake, to a venture unlikely to be commercially profitable, the time has now come to give all of Marvell's prose the recognition that Milton's has in our time enjoyed, again thanks to Yale University Press. Marvell's reinstatement as a prose writer of great style and important substance thus comes too late for the twentieth century, but not for the twenty-first; and just how important that substance can still be to modern secular democracies will emerge as, it is to be hoped, this edition becomes part of the standard equipment for seventeenth-century studies.

MARVELL'S CAREER

Andrew Marvell was born in Yorkshire in the spring of 1621, at the end of which year James I would famously rip out of the Journal of the House of Commons a parliamentary declaration of its privileges and right to debate matters of foreign policy. In the spring of 1659 Marvell was elected to parliament for Hull, a position he maintained with one brief electoral gap and some periods of absenteeism until his death in August 1678. Two-thirds of his relatively short life, therefore, were committed to parliamentary service (not counting the several periods when parliament was not in session), and his letters to his constituents in Hull constitute an exemplary record of patience and attention to detail. Earlier in 1678 Marvell had published, anonymously, his *Account of the Growth of Popery and Arbitrary*

[4] *Poems and Letters of Andrew Marvell*, ed. H. M. Margoliouth, 2 vols. (Oxford, 1927, 1952; rev. Pierre Legouis, 1971).

[5] *The Rehearsal Transpros'd and the Rehearsal Transpros'd: The Second Part*, ed. D. I. B. Smith (Oxford, 1971).

Government, which in its last act (Marvell's own word) describes how Charles II had abused his parliament, rewarding them "for their itch of perpetual sitting and acting" by declaring them refractory in the *Gazette* and allowing the Speaker of the House, Sir Thomas Seymour, to adjourn them summarily, "(trampling upon, and treading under foot, . . . the privileges and usage of Parliament)" (2:371). Framed by these two moments of monarchical contempt for monarchy's traditional restraints, Marvell's life can be seen as a robust story of increasingly liberal views and ameliorative effort, generated first by the traumas of the execution of Charles I and the creation of a republic, consolidated by loyalty to Oliver Cromwell, and maintained by the taking of considerable risks during the first eighteen years of renewed Stuart government.[6]

Marvell's childhood was spent in Hull as the son of a Puritan minister, who must have been ambitious for his son's education. At age thirteen he left the Hull grammar school and matriculated at Trinity College, Cambridge, where he continued his education for eight years. In the spring of 1639, just as Charles I's government was collapsing, he took his bachelor's degree, and the civil war had already begun when, rendered suddenly independent by his father's death by drowning in January 1641, Marvell left Cambridge for London. This might have been the moment for him to have written those famous opening lines of the *Horatian Ode,* invoking the forward youth to emerge from the shades of academe into the world of history in the making, but instead, presumably using his patrimony, Marvell went abroad and traveled through Europe, returning toward the end of 1647. He was thus safely out of the way of the civil war. The official sign of his return to public life is his printed signature attached to two poems, "To his noble Friend Mr. Richard Lovelace," and "Upon the Death of Lord Hastings," both published in 1649, after the king's execution. *Then* comes the *Horatian Ode,* initiating a decade of increasingly close relationships

[6] For Marvell's career as a whole, see Pierre Legouis, *André Marvell poète, puritain, patriote 1621–1678* (Paris, 1928); abridged and translated as *Andrew Marvell, Poet, Puritan, Patriot, 1621–78* (Oxford, 1965); John M. Wallace, *Destiny His Choice: The Loyalism of Andrew Marvell* (Cambridge, 1968); Warren Chernaik, *The Poet's Time: Politics and Religion in the Work of Andrew Marvell* (Cambridge, 1983). For a more psychologically inflected account of the career, see Annabel Patterson, *Marvell: The Writer in Public Life* (London and New York, 1999). And see also two collections of essays: *The Political Identity of Andrew Marvell,* ed. Conal Condren and A. D. Cousins (Aldershot, 1990), and *Marvell and Liberty,* ed. Warren Chernaik and Martin Dzelzainis (London, 1999), and Hilton Kelliher, *Andrew Marvell: Poet and Politician 1628–1678* (London, 1978).

with the leaders of the revolution, first as tutor to Sir Thomas Fairfax's daughter, next as tutor to Cromwell's ward William Dutton, next Latin Secretary to John Thurloe, a post for which Milton had recommended him four years earlier, and finally, in January 1659, member of parliament for Hull in Richard Cromwell's short-lived parliament. On February 11 he wrote to George Downing at the Hague an account of the opposition mounting against Richard by Haslerig, Vane, Ashley Cooper (later to become the earl of Shaftesbury), Lambert, and others. "They have much the odds in speaking," he wrote, "but it is to be hoped that our justice our affection and our number which is at least two thirds will weare them out in the long runne" (*P&L* 2:308). This was not to be. The destabilization that followed Oliver Cromwell's death in September 1658, an event that had elicited from Marvell an extremely moved (rather than moving) elegy for the Protector, was inevitably to result in the restoration of Charles II.

During the decade of his increasing alignment with the revolution Marvell had, it is usually assumed, written most of his lyric poetry; but since the eulogy for Lovelace and the elegy for Hastings he had published nothing over his name. The only poem he *had* published, the *First Anniversary* of Cromwell's Protectorate, was anonymous.[7] It was conceivably this fact that allowed him to regain his seat in the first Restoration parliament in April 1660. This seat he held for the rest of his life. And although we know that he wrote more anonymous poems—now in the genre that is lyric's polar opposite, political satire—the next work that appeared over his name was the *Second Part* of the *Rehearsal Transpros'd*, a signature that retrospectively acknowledged also the first part. For the last five years of his life, then, from 1672 to 1677, Marvell reconstituted himself as a public spokesman for causes that could not be called lost because they had never yet been won.

To focus on these last five years (and what followed his death) is to recognize Marvell as one of the most original political writers of his day—as important as Milton, if we think in terms of the influence each had at the time. Milton's *Defense of the English People*, commissioned by the new

[7] Despite its anonymity and its excision from the 1681 *Miscellaneous Poems*, the poem's authorship was known to Samuel Parker, who in his *History of his own Time*, written in the 1680s, inserted into his attack on Marvell a hostile but knowledgeable account of it as "a Satire against all Monarchs, legally established . . . [which] said, that Kings were slow Bodies; slower than Saturn in their Revolutions." See *Bishop Parker's History: or, the Tories Chronicle* (London, 1730), p. 215.

republic as a legitimation of the king's deposition and execution, brought him international fame and reproach, and with the regime behind it it ran to more than a dozen editions in the first two years after its publication; but the first part of Marvell's *Rehearsal Transpros'd,* a gesture in what looked like a local quarrel and initially published illegally, ran to five editions, two of them pirated, a sign of popularity as a writer that Milton never achieved.[8] Each had parts of his work republished to serve the Williamite Revolution, and into the eighteenth century. As Milton's *Areopagitica* was reprinted in 1737 in an attempt to ward off the Stage Licensing Act, Marvell's *Essay* was reprinted in 1709 in the context of Tory attempts to prevent what was called occasional conformity, that is, minimal churchgoing by Dissenters in order to enable them to hold public office and avoid financial penalties. The *Account of the Growth of Popery and Arbitrary Government* was cited as an ethical authority in John Oldmixon's *Secret History of Europe* (1712), written in the immediate aftermath of the trial of Henry Sacheverell, and in Charles McCormick's *Secret History of the Courth and Reign of Charles the Second* (1792), in which late Stuart history is used to anatomize and critique the reign of George III.[9] And none of Milton's pamphlets became, as did Marvell's *Account of the Growth of Popery and Arbitrary Government,* a primary resource for *modern* accounts of seventeenth-century politics or parliamentary history. One finds quotations from the *Account* in William Cobbett's eighteenth-century parliamentary history, in the *Cambridge Modern History,* and in the old *Dictionary of National Biography*'s sketch of George Villiers, second duke of Buckingham.

With Marvell's prose in our sights, we can see how important were the 1670s in laying the intellectual groundwork for Whig and liberal policy thereafter; an insight until now rather obscured by the vast scholarly investment in the Popish Plot and the Williamite Revolution of the 1680s.

[8] There were two issues of the first edition of the *Rehearsal Transpros'd,* followed by one called "The Second Impression with Additions and Amendments," but in fact a second edition, plus two pirated editions, one in 1672 and another in 1673. See *HMC* Report 4, p. 234. There were two editions of the *Second Part.* There were three editions of *Mr. Smirke* and the *Essay* in 1676, and evidence of organized distribution by a group of Nonconformists. One of these editions, probably the first, was intended to be fifteen hundred copies. See *HMC,* Report 4, p. 234 and Coventry mss., vol. III, f. 128. There were two editions of the *Account of the Growth of Popery,* followed by a posthumous folio edition.

[9] See Patterson, "Marvell and Secret History," in *Marvell and Liberty,* ed. Chernaik and Dzelzainis, pp. 37–47.

THE 1670S IN ENGLAND AND EUROPE

Dividing history into slices ten years long is an artificial process at best, and can be seriously misleading. Yet in the case of Marvell's career it can actually be a tool of clarification. In the 1650s, indeed from the year 1650 itself, Marvell was a commonwealthman, and then a Cromwellian. In the 1660s, two phases of Restoration culture and politics deeply affected him: the first when the Cavalier parliament was steadily enacting the restrictive and intolerant legislation of what is now known as the Clarendon Code: the Corporation Act of December 1661, the Act of Uniformity of 1662, resulting in the expulsion of the nonconforming ministers from their pulpits on St. Bartholomew's Day, August 24, 1662, the Conventicle Act (1664), and the Five Mile Act (1665). These five years were also the period of Clarendon's control over the king's agenda. But during these same years, Charles was already drawing closer to Louis XIV of France, by virtue of the marriage (1661) of his sister Henrietta to Louis's brother, the duke of Orleans, and his own marriage to the French candidate among eligible princesses, Catherine of Braganza. The sale of Dunkirk to France, at the urging of Albemarle and Sandwich, tightened the connection. As Charles moved closer to France, his relations with the Dutch worsened, in part by quarrels over trade and foreign possessions, in part because of the exclusion of his nephew from the statholdership. The death of Philip of Spain in September 1665 helped to shift the balance of power away from Spain to France, as also did Charles's alliance with Portugal.

In the second half of the 1660s, these shifts resulted in the Second Dutch War, which galvanized Marvell into becoming a satirist in verse. The diplomatic, behind-the-scenes story is too complex to rehearse here, but it included Charles's private treaty with France to be complicit in Louis's long-term attack on the Spanish Netherlands—the War of Devolution whereby Louis recovered his wife's Spanish possessions and effectively isolated Spain. On July 31, 1667, in the Treaty of Breda, the Second Dutch War came to an ignominious end for England, after the disaster at Chatham (explored at length in Marvell's *Last Instructions to the Painter*). English shame and parliamentary outrage resulted in Charles's dismissal of Clarendon from the chancellorship, and a new phase of foreign policy began, at least on the surface. John de Witt, leader of the Dutch republic, unable to withstand the military power of France as it overran the Spanish Netherlands, began to look for a coalition between himself, England, and Sweden. The result was the famous Triple Alliance (April 1668), brilliantly negotiated by Sir William Temple, immediately undermined by Charles's private agreements with Louis, and mourned by Marvell in the *Account of the Growth of Popery*.

The decade of the 1670s also falls into two halves. The first saw a new phase of policy for both Charles and Louis XIV. For both, it was initiated by the secret Treaty of Dover of April 1670, whereby Charles agreed to become a pensioner of France in return for neutrality in Louis's new war against the Dutch Republic, and his own promise to return his country to Roman Catholicism and to rule without parliamentary interference. On April 6, 1672, Louis declared war on the Dutch, and his land invasion was prevented only when the Dutch broke their dykes and flooded the country. England, despite the Triple Alliance, began its own war against them. John de Witt was murdered by a mob in August 1672, and Dutch leadership devolved on the newly powerful figure of William, prince of Orange. Although the Franco-Dutch war continued through 1679, beyond Marvell's death, the Anglo-Dutch war was concluded in 1674. In 1673 relations between king and parliament were overtly strained over the marriage of the duke of York to the Catholic Mary Beatrice, duchess of Modena; but through 1675 Charles was able to keep on proroguing parliament by counting on his financial subsidies from Louis.

Domestically, also, the 1670s could be said to begin with the renewal of the Conventicle Act, which reignited parliamentary and national disputes over religious conformity. To this period belong not only the Declaration of Indulgence and its forced withdrawal, but also parliament's reactionary Test Act against Catholics (March 1673), which drove all sincere Catholics from office. The result was that James, duke of York, was forced to appear as an overt Romanist, and Clifford resigned as treasurer. This disintegration of the Cabal—the group of powerful ministers who had run the government since Clarendon's departure in 1668—was completed when Charles dismissed Shaftesbury from the chancellorship on November 9, 1673, precipitating Shaftesbury's move into the Opposition and heralding the regime of Thomas Osborne, later earl of Danby.

In the second half of the 1670s, therefore, Charles had acquired an extremely able minister, with three goals: financial consolidation of the king's revenue; the undermining of parliament by bribery and pensions; and the reinforcement of the Anglican church as a religious monopoly. The last of these goals meant that Charles had abandoned his personal goal of returning the country to Catholicism. There would be no further truckling to Catholicism or to France if Danby could help it; but the nascent Whig party did not necessarily believe this, and the new policies seemed to be insidiously coherent. In July 1675 Marvell wrote a long letter to his nephew William Popple describing a conspiratorial situation: "In order to make their Episcopal Cavalier Party, they contrived beforehand a politic Test to be enacted, and then taken by all Members of Parliament, and all Officers. Among other Chimaeras, they discoursed of none having any beneficial Offices but Cavaliers, or Sons of Cavaliers. . . . But principally the Laws were to be severely executed, and reinforced against Fanaticks and Papists."[10]

For Marvell, this was the period of his widely circulated parody of Charles's speeches to parliament, of the *Dialogue between the two Horses* and two other "statue" poems motivated by London displays of royalist statuary, and of his decision to enter the tolerationist battle again, this time in defense of Bishop Herbert Croft. The reference above to the "politic Test" applied to Danby's project for a new "Non-Resisting" Test Act, which was entered early in the session of April 1675, passed the Lords despite the resistance of Shaftesbury, Buckingham, and Wharton, and was finally avoided only by the delaying tactics of the Shirley-Fagg case of privilege. The next stage was the Long Prorogation, from November 1675 to February 1677, a possible strategy for Charles because he was still being paid a substantial allowance for remaining neutral in the Franco-Dutch war. The Long Prorogation would then become one of the strongest signs for Marvell of an actual conspiracy at work, the opening premise of his 1677/78 *Account.*

The notorious *Letter from a Person of Quality to His Friend in the Country,* the most important tract in the propaganda war waged by Shaftesbury, which was ordered to be burned by the hangman on November 8, 1675, not only closely matches this letter of Marvell to Popple, but also anticipates the *Account of the Growth of Popery.* The author of the *Letter* begins with a review of "a project of several years standing" to establish absolute monarchy in England. Sharing the conspiracy are "the great churchmen" and some newly created ministers, for which read Danby. Their goal is "to make a distinct party from the rest of the nation of the high and episcopal men and the old cavaliers. . . . Next, they design to have the government of the church sworn to as unalterable; and so tacitly owned to be of divine right; and allow monarchy, as well as episcopacy, to be jure divino, and not to be

[10] *P&L,* 2:341–42. For Danby's program, see Mark Goldie, "Danby, the Bishops and the Whigs," in T. Harris, P. Seaward, and M. Goldie, eds., *Religion and Politics in Restoration England* (Oxford, 1990), pp. 75–105.

bounded or limited by any human laws."[11] Given the similarity of tone and purpose, it is clear that Marvell and Shaftesbury shared by now at least an identical target. And since we now know that Shaftesbury collaborated with the earl of Anglesey in preventing the suppression of the *Rehearsal Transpros'd,* they may have been somewhat more closely associated.[12]

THE CHARACTER OF MARVELL'S PAMPHLETS

In a mere five years (as compared to the twenty-year period of Milton's career as a polemicist), Marvell reinvented the idea of prose persuasion at least twice. Starting in the genre of animadversions, the two parts of the *Rehearsal Transpros'd* may try the patience of readers taught to expect consecutive argument. Following his prey, Marvell treads an uneven path, often circling back to the same spot, jumping to the heights of idealist political theory, and landing in the swamps of scatology. But his brilliant adaptation of Buckingham's satirical method in *The Rehearsal* (which had mocked Dryden for the high-flown absurdities of his heroic dramas) to an ecclesiastical "high-flyer," as the high church Anglicans came to be called, created a new vogue for religious debate carried on in a comic, satirical style rather than a solemn one. *Mr. Smirke* was also in the animadversions mode, and also played off Restoration comedy in its allusion to George Etherege's *The Man of Mode.* The *Short Historical Essay* attached to it, however, was another innovation, completely different in style and effect. Gone are the ad hominem attacks on a particular churchman and his writing, replaced by an amazingly bold attack on the history of intolerance within Christianity initiated by the Council of Nicaea. The *Essay* follows the time-honored method of chronological arrangement, beginning in the days of the apostles, passing through late antiquity Roman emperor by Roman emperor, and bringing matters up to their Restoration date at the end. The *Account of the Growth of Popery* is also rigorously chronological, but it substitutes for retold (translated) narrative history a scrupulous and quite original documentary and oral history of Charles II's parliaments and foreign policy, including texts of bills and painstaking accounts of debates, with the arguments on both sides reported in the same neutral tone of voice; these

[11] For the *Letter,* Maurice Cranston, *John Locke: A Biography* (London and New York, 1957), pp. 158–59; Richard Ashcraft, *Revolutionary Politics and Locke's Two Treatises of Government* (Princeton, 1986), pp. 117–23.

[12] For the documents that bring Shaftesbury's name into the publication history of *RT,* see below, pp. 26–27.

became primary documents for subsequent parliamentary historians. The *Remarks Upon a Late Disingenuous Discourse,* by contrast, returns to the narrow path of tracking another person's argument, phrase by phrase, but with very little of the merriment that made Marvell a hero over Samuel Parker. The statements of John Howe on the subject of free will and some of its central conundrums are minutely (and favorably) compared with those of his opponent, the rigid Calvinist Thomas Danson. The *Remarks* is, however, necessary reading to get a full picture of Marvell and confirm that on this central issue in theology Marvell and Milton were both left-wing Arminians, however self-contradictory those terms might seem.

What, then, holds these very different works together? What makes them a canon? What are the signs of Marvell's authorship? The most obvious proposition, to be confirmed only by reading the pamphlets themselves, is the unmistakably Marvellian wit, which gained him the reputation of being, in Gilbert Burnet's words, "the liveliest droll of the age."[13] This wit, though preeminent in the *Rehearsal Transpros'd,* and somewhat toned down in *Mr. Smirke,* mutates in the *Essay* into very saucy translations of the early ecclesiastical historians; it can still be heard even in the *Remarks,* not least in Marvell's interpretation of the initials *T.D.* as standing only for *The Discourse,* out of mock concern for Danson's reputation. All the pamphlets explicitly promote a set of qualities related to wit as Marvell understands it—modesty, moderation, ingeniousness, civility; and they equally inveigh against cruelty, virulence, ill-nature, when deployed in the public sphere. The list of negative attributes that Marvell ascribes to the higher clergy of the past and present, "Covetousness, Ambition, Pride, Ignorance, Formality and Contentions" (*RT2,* p. 330), a list that will be echoed in the *Essay,* implies that the institutional rewards dangled before the clergy, rather than genuine differences of conviction, are the cause of civil strife. This near-allegorical seizure of the moral high ground is characteristic of Marvell; and he manages to prevent it from sounding priggish by displays, hilarious or sardonic, of the low ground occupied by his antagonists. This theme of ethical behavior or misbehavior has a fully articulated rhetorical or stylistic component. Perhaps nothing more firmly places the *Remarks* in Marvell's canon than its opening distinction between the styles of Howe and Danson, the first "direct and coherent, his style perspicuous and elegant . . . in short, a manly discourse, resembling much, and expressing the humane perfection"; whereas Danson's "immodest and hectoring

[13] Burnet, *History of his own Time,* ed. Osmund Airy, 2 vols. (Oxford, 1897), 1:467.

Discourse . . . may remain as a mark (the best use it can be put to) of what ought to be avoided in all writing of controversies" (pp. 420–21).

If his concern with the ethics of style goes back to Cicero and Quintilian, the pamphlets also evince an up-to-the-minute awareness of the prevailing conditions of writerly production, the material life of books and printers. It is not merely a convention when, at the end of *Mr. Smirke,* Marvell remarked, "But the Printer calls: the press is in danger," a phrase that could mean merely that he was holding up the process by continuing his attack on Turner longer than the process of press scheduling, casting off, and dividing up the work permitted. It could also be a double entrendre, suggesting the real political danger experienced by scofflaw printers. Unlike Milton, who argued rationally but unsuccessfully against licensing, Marvell played a game with censorship of the press and won; engaging the king on his side, with the help of Shaftesbury and Lord Anglesey, in relation to the *Rehearsal Transpros'd,* to the extent that he could publish its second part under his own name and oversee its printing with impunity; outsmarting Sir Roger L'Estrange, the rabidly Tory Licenser of the Press, who was forced to release the *Rehearsal Transpros'd,* who evidently lost the battle to suppress *Mr. Smirke* and the *Essay,* and who was still searching for the author of the *Account* when Marvell died prematurely.[14] But Marvell was not only engaged with censorship as a game of wits; he addressed with verve the theoretical problem of state censorship, a matter to which he returns again and again in the *Rehearsal Transpros'd,* in *Mr. Smirke,* and especially in the *Account of the Growth of Popery,* where at least part of his motive is to make available parliamentary materials, such as the all-too-revealing speech of Lord Keeper Orlando Bridgeman, that would otherwise have been suppressed.

Another remarkable aspect of Marvell's practice as a polemicist becomes visible only when the pamphlets and their reconstructed printing history are placed in a very detailed chronology, such as follows this introduction. What this chronology reveals is how fast Marvell worked, and how closely his work was geared to the events just passed or expected. Marvell almost certainly depended on parliamentary recesses to get his research and writing done, but the first part of the *Rehearsal Transpros'd* and the *Account* were

[14] L'Estrange's interference with the *Rehearsal Transpros'd* seems, ironically, to have been caused by a printers' rivalry, whereby Nathaniel Ponder asked L'Estrange's help in securing his copyright against John Winter; this, however, drew L'Estrange's attention to an unlicensed work, which he was then reluctantly persuaded to license by Anglesey. See below, pp. 23–32.

both surely aimed at the upcoming sessions a few months later. In addition, the first part of the *Rehearsal Transpros'd,* though it may have been begun early in 1672, includes in its targets a work of Parker's that was not licensed until September 7; Marvell's riposte was selling in November. Similarly, though Marvell probably began work on the *Short Historical Essay* as soon as parliament was prorogued on November 22, 1675, the reply to Francis Turner to which the *Essay* would be attached could not have been begun before February 23, 1676, when Turner's *Animadversions* was licensed, and must have been finished before April 29, when Henry Oldenburg turned in his license as a stationer. The *Account* was probably begun during the April-May recess of 1677, and it was written up to the moment when Charles, having postponed the next session to April 4, 1678, suddenly changed his mind and called it for January 15. That is, the *Account* records the king's message of December 3 in its closing paragraphs. By February 8, the *Account* was printed and ready for stitching. Perhaps in December, while parliament was still not in session, Marvell would have started work on the *Remarks,* in response to Danson's *De Causa Dei,* licensed on November 26, 1677, the *Remarks* itself being licensed on April 17. These scenarios indicate extraordinary speed, efficiency, and cooperation between author and printer, not least because all but the last of his pamphlets were underground productions.

MARVELL AND THE PRACTICE OF PRINT

The printing history of his works, so far as it can be reconstructed, is evidence of how Marvell was able to negotiate with the underground printers and risk-taking publishers of the Restoration so as to produce an operation as clever as, and more financially successful than, that which had kept the Marprelate pamphlets circulating several generations earlier.

The modern reader needs to grasp from the outset that only the last of Marvell's pamphlets, the *Remarks,* was properly licensed. It was printed by Christopher Hussey, a printer/bookseller with no history of illegal work. The *Remarks* appears to have been his first production. By contrast, the first part of the *Rehearsal Transpros'd* was initially published surreptitiously and anonymously, and though L'Estrange was eventually persuaded by Anglesey to give the second impression a license, it was never entered in the Stationers' Register. Neither was the *Second Part,* which seems to have been given a tacit allowance and appeared over Marvell's name. *Mr. Smirke* and the *Essay,* as a joint publication, were both unlicensed and anonymous, though Marvell's authorship was an open secret. As for the *Account of the Growth of Popery,* it too was unlicensed and anonymous, and on February 19, 1678, a warrant was issued for the discovery and arrest of those responsible. Again, all except the *Remarks* appeared in two editions, the second showing some signs of being a corrected version. It is these second editions that the Yale edition uses as its copy-texts. The first part of the *Rehearsal Transpros'd, Mr. Smirke* and the *Account* all share the unusual feature of being specified by their titles in the Wardens' Accounts, where the expenses relating to the searches for them are detailed, whereas most of the wardens' records of searches have unspecified targets.[15] This suggests that they were regarded as especially provocative or dangerous, perhaps because unusually successful as business propositions.

The printer of the first edition of the first part of the *Rehearsal Transpros'd,* identified on the title page as *A.B.,* was possibly Ann Brewster, the widow of the Thomas Brewster who had been official printer to the Council of State under Cromwell until the end of 1653. He had been tried at the Old Bailey in 1661 for shared responsibility in publishing the speeches of the executed regicides and *The Phoenix,* a commonwealth cry of defiance. He died in Newgate, for another offense, in 1671. His widow continued his work, in the full ideological sense. She would reappear in 1678, when L'Estrange tracked her to "the house of a former officer under Cromwell" who worked as an underground scrivener and suspected she was involved in the production of the *Account.*[16] On the other hand, *A.B.* may have been dummy initials, to conceal the involvement of printers and publishers we know were involed: John Darby, Sr., Nathaniel Ponder, and perhaps also Nathaniel Thompson, the partner of Thomas Ratcliffe.

Brewster was said to be in league with John Darby, Sr., much later

[15] See *Wardens' Accounts 1663–1728, Records of the Worshipful Company of Stationers,* ed. Robin Myers (Cambridge, 1985), published as microfilm, Chadwyck Healey 8520, part 7, reel 76. Exceptions to the above statement are *The Poor Whores' Petition,* printed by John Darby in 1667/68 (a satire on Charles II's affair with the countess of Castlemaine), and the work which inspired Marvell's defense in 1676, Bishop Herbert Croft's *The Naked Truth.*

[16] See *CSPD,* 23 August. 1678, pp. 372–73: "One may fairly presume that all those delicate copies, which Brewster carried to the press, were written by her landlord, and copied by him from the author. Besides, it is very probable that the late libels concerning the *Growth of Popery* and the *List of the Members of Parliament* passed through the same hands . . . If she be questioned, probably she will cast the whole on Mr. Marvell, who is lately dead, and there the enquiry ends."

described by John Dunton as "the religious printer . . . and a true assertor of English liberties."[17] Darby had been involved in the *Phoenix* but was released on the adjournment of parliament in November 1661. He was again investigated (under the alias Randolph Malpub) in connection with *The Poor Whores' Petition,* a satire on the king's affair with Lady Castlemaine, and was paid two pounds "for confessing the printers and dispensers" of that and other pamphlets. His illegal press at Blue Anchor Alley in Little Britain was dismantled at this time, but he was back in business in January 1671, for he shows up in the report made by the stationers to Secretary of State Arlington according to his order of the fifteenth of that month. In January 1673 Darby was deposed by Secretary Coventry in the case of the *Rehearsal Transpros'd,* whose second impression was actually advertised as his work, but he shared the immunity granted to that work as a result of Anglesey's intervention. In 1676 he was again arrested and examined for *Mr. Smirke* but released in the hope that he would turn informer again. In February 1684 he was convicted of printing *Lord Russell's Speech* at his trial for treason. He seems to have been remarkably dextrous in maintaining a long career of defiant oppositional publishing despite all odds, even making a little government money on the side.

For the second impression of the *Rehearsal Transpros'd,* Darby seems to have been in competition with the printer John Winter. It was at his establishment that two sheets of an edition of the *Rehearsal Transpros'd* were seized in December/January 1672. J. Hetet has argued that this was the first pirated edition, and that Darby's interest was in having it suppressed.[18] Winter was reported deceased in the report of March 29, 1675, and so could have played no part in Marvell's subsequent pamphlets.[19] But Nicholas von Maltzahn has discovered that Darby was also involved in the early stages of printing the *Account.*

[17] John Dunton, *Life and Errors* (London, 1705), p. 328.

[18] J. Hetet, "A Literary Underground in Restoration England: Printers and Dissenters in the Context of Constraints 1660–1689" (Ph.D. thesis, Cambridge University, 1987, pp. 180–82.

[19] George Kitchin, *Sir Roger L'Estrange: A Contribution to the History of the Press in the Seventeenth Century* (London, 1913), provides scattered information about illegal presses. For broader and more coherent accounts of the underground presses in the Restoration, see N. H. Keeble, *The Literary Culture of Nonconformity in Latter Seventeenth-Century England* (Leicester and Athens, Ga., 1987), pp. 93–126; and Richard Greaves, *Enemies under his Feet: Radicals and Nonconformists in Britain, 1664–1677,* (Stanford, 1990) pp. 167–90.

The other highly visible figure in Marvell's printing history was Nathaniel Ponder, the publisher of all authorized (that is, nonpirated) editions of both parts of the *Rehearsal Transpros'd.* Ponder was the son of a Nonconformist mercer, and he began his publishing career with a work of John Owen, whose patron was the earl of Anglesey. Ponder published a steady stream of Owen's work during the 1670s, all of which was licensed and advertised in the Term Catalogues. In 1672, after the king's Declaration of Indulgence, he was busily helping the Nonconformist clergy to acquire the new licenses to preach that the Declaration permitted. In 1678 he would publish the first edition of Bunyan's *Pilgrim's Progress,* which turned out to be a best-seller. In 1676 he was indicted and imprisoned, however, for his role in *Mr. Smirke* and the *Essay,* and on this occasion Anglesey was overruled by other members of the Privy Council. It may have been Owen who introduced Ponder to Marvell in 1672, since Owen was deeply interested in having Samuel Parker refuted, having published in 1669 his own response to Parker's *Discourse of Ecclesiastical Politie,* which far from silencing him had only provoked him into new outbursts.

Marvell did not count only on the outstanding loyalty of opposition printers and publishers; he was also invested in the practical and theoretical issues of typography. He paid an unusual degree of attention to the print features of the work of his opponents. He criticizes Parker, for example, for failing to place part of a biblical quotation in italics, thereby creating ambiguity as to whether it was a part of the privileged text (*RT2,* p. 340). This helps to explain his own scrupulosity in italicizing quotations and in the partial repairs performed on both parts of the *Rehearsal Transpros'd* when the printer failed to follow instructions. He deployed black letter in the *Second Part* to highlight Parker's egregious mimicry of Charles's Declaration of Indulgence; and he complains that Danson has discovered a new way of "rearing up pillar's to men's infamy" by excerpting sections of Howe's *Letter* and its various postscripts so as to "post them up in Columns" (p. 473). By similar token, Marvell was obviously stung by Parker's complaints that in the first part he had failed to cite chapter and verse of Parker's books. In the *Second Part* he not only became pedantically concerned to cite page references, but mimicked his opponent's strategy in the *Reproof to the Rehearsal Transpros'd* of having these page numbers cited in the margin. The effect is rendered comic, however, by Marvell's including marginal references also to Buckingham's *Rehearsal,* usually rendered as *Reh.Com.* By similar token, he responded to Parker's gibe that he had miscounted the epistles of Augustine to Marcellinus by reading him a lecture several pages long on where to find the fifth epistle in the "Edition Lugduni. Anno 1561" and suggesting that the fault lay in Parker's relying on the Index (both reader's aide and digit), whereas if he had used the Pollex, the thumb used for actually turning pages, he might not have been so careless (p. 426). But these skirmishes are not just about scholarly rigor and integrity. Marvell was increasingly sensitive to what we might call the politics of quotation, and one can follow the twists he gives it from his duel with Parker through his rejection in the *Remarks* of his own earlier strategies. There Marvell praises Howe because he does *not* "raise the spectres of ancient authors, or conjure their venerable names, to frighten men out of their senses and understanding" (p. 420). By the time he needed to write the *Account* Marvell had developed an entire theory of typographical display for ideological purposes. It is remarkable how competent the Restoration printers were in following his instructions.

MARVELL'S SOURCES OF INFORMATION

To achieve the success he did, while flaunting his evasion of the rules that governed the press, Marvell needed connections. Unlike Milton, who during the Restoration was, by choice or necessity, a private person, Marvell appears to have been a member of a communications network. He was, after all, a member of parliament, a role for which networking was then, as now, a prerequisite. He had known Oliver Cromwell and Richard Cromwell personally and maintained connections with old Cromwellians. Among his close friends were Sir Jeremy Smith, the naval commander who had featured as one of the heroes of his Dutch war satires, and whose will Marvell witnessed in November 1675;[20] John Rushworth, the old parliamentary historian and lawyer who had sat in Richard Cromwell's parliament and dedicated his *Historical Collections* to the new Protector in 1659, with whom Marvell talked "very deliberately and fasting" in January 1675;[21] and, according to Aubrey, James Harrington, Milton's friend and organizer of the Rota. These were all old men now, but they must have been mines of information.

Marvell also had powerful contacts within the new regime. For a year and a half he had been in Russia, Sweden, and Denmark as secretary to the

[20] *P&L*, 2:363.

[21] *P&L*, 2:335. In *RT*, Marvell would make substantial use of Rushworth's *Collections*, both the parts published in 1659 and those not published until after his death. This implies collaboration.

king's ambassador extraordinary, the earl of Carlisle, who "as plain Charles Howard had served Oliver Cromwell faithfully," as Pierre Legouis reminds us.[22] Lord Anglesey (and Shaftesbury) intervene between Ponder and L'Estrange about the *Rehearsal Transpros'd,* and Anglesey attempts the same for *Mr. Smirke.* In 1675/76 Marvell seems to be collaborating with the Shaftesbury/Buckingham entente, writing a parodic "King's speech" about the 1675 sessions of parliament and a scandalous poem, "The Royal Buss," about the duchess of Portsmouth's role in persuading Charles to prorogue the parliament on November 22.[23] He is in correspondence with Sir Edward Harley, a Presbyterian squire of great standing in Herefordshire, and Philip, Lord Wharton, an old Cromwellian aristocrat. According to Thomas Cooke, Marvell was "often conversant, and to a great Degree of Intimacy, with the late Duke of Devonshire";[24] that is, William Cavendish, first duke, who had decisively entered the Opposition in 1676, and to whose young son Cooke would eventually dedicate his edition of Marvell's poems. He also, evidently, had close connections with such leading Nonconformists as John Owen and John Howe.

But Marvell also had a street life, or more probably a coffeehouse life. In 1673 people bring him rumors of Parker's off-the-record conversations, and three years later he hears the details of how Francis Turner, the butt of *Mr. Smirke,* and the bishop of London who had licensed it reacted to their own copies. He has read, in manuscript, Rochester's *Satire against Reason and Mankind* and quotes it in *Mr. Smirke,* knowing the annoyance this would cause Edward Stillingfleet, one of the royal chaplains, who had recently aimed one of his sermons at it. He cruises the bookshops, keeping his finger on the pulse of London publishing and looking for material he can use. He is able to read the unbound sheets of Parker's *Reproof to the*

[22] Legouis, *Andrew Marvell,* p. 129.

[23] See *POAS: Augustan Satirical Verse, 1660–1714,* ed. George de F. Lord (New Haven and London, 1963), 1:263–65. This poem was entered in the records as a "seditious and traitorous libel" by Secretary of State Williamson (*CSPD,* May 3, 1676). It was ascribed to Marvell by John Phillips, Milton's nephew, in *The Secret History of the Four Last Monarchs* (1691), p. 85.

[24] Thomas Cooke, *The Works of Andrew Marvell, Esq.* (London, 1726), p. 14. This assertion is supported by several appearances of Cavendish in Marvell's correspondence, including the description of him to Sir Edward Harley as leading the attack on the legality of the Long Prorogation. See *P&L,* 2:353–54: "But my L. Cavendish modestly moved in few words . . . that they might have the Order read whereby they were last Adjourned."

Rehearsal Transpros'd at the printer's shop.[25] In particular, he must have known John Starkey,[26] the Whig bookseller who distributed Milton's *Tetrachordon* and *Accidence of Grammar,* along with the 1672 translation of Suetonius that Marvell quotes in detail in the *Rehearsal Transpros'd* and that (we have now pretty well established) he had close at hand because he had written it himself![27] Both Marvell and Starkey belonged to the Green Ribbon Club, the meeting place of the Whigs.[28] But while the anecdotal richness of Marvell's earlier pamphlets might partly be attributed to his moving in these circles and keeping his ears open, the scholarly density of his work gives us a far less casual author, one who could clearly differentiate between a good joke and an authority with impeccable credentials.

MARVELL'S READING

This brings us to the question of Marvell's reading. We tend to forget what scholarship must have been like in the early modern period, before the establishment of great public or academic libraries. Marvell must have had access to a large library or libraries, much larger than he could afford. For the first part of the *Rehearsal Transpros'd,* he drew extensively on literary resources, especially in comedy, satire, and mock-heroic: Aesop, Horace, Juvenal, Heliodorus; Montaigne, Bacon, Jonson's *Volpone, Don Quixote,* Guarini, Davenant's *Gondibert,* Butler's *Hudibras;* nothing unexpected. But these flashes of elegance are grounded by his having read, reread, collated, and made detailed notes on all of Samuel Parker's works for the occasion, along with such pertinent classics in the field as John Hales's *Tract concerning Schism* (1642), Richard Hooker's *Laws of Ecclesiastical Policy,* John Foxe's *Acts and Monuments,* and the nonconformist works of John Owen. He had even tracked down a copy of Archbishop Matthew Parker's *De Antiquitate Britannicae Ecclesiae,* published in 1572, for the sake of inserting a long Latin

[25] See his letter to Sir Edward Harley of May 3, 1672: "Dr. Parker will be out the next weeke. I have seen of it already 330 pages and it will be much more." *P&L,* 2:329.

[26] Starkey fled to Amsterdam in 1683 to avoid prosecution for having attempted to republish Nathaniel Bacon's antimonarchical *Historical Discourse.*

[27] See Patterson, "A Restoration Suetonius: A new Marvell text?" *Modern Language Quarterly,* 61 (2000), 463–80.

[28] For the Green Ribbon Club and Starkey's membership, see Melinda Zook, *Radical Whigs and Conspiratorial Politics in Late Stuart England,* (University Park, Penn., 1999), pp. 7–18, 27. In 1675 the satirical *Duke of Buckingham's Litany* listed Marvell as a member of the club.

diatribe against the massacre of the monks of Bangor, encouraged, some said, by Augustine, for refusing to accept Roman ceremonials. Like his researches into other earlier Parkers, Marvell's researches here were strategically narrow and nominal.

The *Second Part,* however, shows sustained recourse to more varied and scholarly materials: Martin Del Rio, *Disquisitionum Magicarum* (1633), one of the very few of his sources to which Marvell draws attention in his own marginal notes; the biblical commentaries of Hugo Grotius; Paoli Sarpi's *History of the Council of Trent,* in Nathaniel Brent's 1620 translation; Ammianus Marcellinus's *Rerum Gestarum,* the obscure works of the emperor Julian, the letters of Synesius, one of Rastell's collections of English statutes, travel books and geographies by Peter Heylyn, George Sandys, Sebastian Münster, Samuel Purchas, and R. Knolles; Talmudic materials about Jewish rituals; the old ecclesiastical historians Sozomen and Socrates Scholasticus; European histories by Philip de Commines and Lieuw van Aitzema; ancient religious polemic by Augustine, Nazianzus, Chrysostom, and recent ecclesiastical polemic by Heylyn, Milton, and Grotius (again); a manuscript source for Thomas Cranmer's "Seventeen Questions concerning the Sacraments"; not to mention standard classical works like Pliny, Strabo, Juvenal, Martial, Plautus, Virgil, Horace, and Tacitus. He read for polemical purchase, and he read for witty ammunition. He evidently scoured the compendia he read for potentially anti-Parker anecdotes.

As Sir Edward Dering remarked in a speech in parliament on November 22, 1641, "£600 is but a mean expense in books and will advance but a moderate Library." Clearly, Marvell had access to a great one. In an article separately published in the *Historical Journal,* we identified that library as the famous collection of the earl of Anglesey, whose holdings, as catalogued for sale in 1686, can account for almost everything that Marvell read for the two parts of the *Rehearsal Transpros'd.*[29] Our reasoning consisted in three major points: the striking connection between Marvell and Anglesey over the publication of the *Rehearsal Transpros'd*; the greatness (and geographical convenience) of the latter's library, whose contents we know from the sale catalogue published in 1686;[30] and the legend of Marvell's poverty, installed by Cooke in his 1726 edition of Marvell's poetry. Despite the

[29] See Patterson and Dzelzainis, "Marvell, Locke, and the earl of Anglesey: A chapter in the history of reading," *Historical Journal* 44 (2001), 703–27.

[30] *Bibliotheca Angleseiana, sive catalogus variorum librorum* (1686). The catalogue originally included 6,505 books and 178 bundles of pamphlets.

unwillingness of modern readers to accept the legend, with its Whig emphasis, nobody has found any evidence that Marvell had any means of subsistence other than his parliamentary wages from Hull (six shillings and eightpence for each day's presence in parliament). After his death, his disappointed landlady, posing as his wife, complained in a deposition that all she found in his lodgings were "but a few Bookes & papers of a small value."[31] And the legend of Marvell's poverty has now been confirmed by new research by Art Kavanagh, who discovered a deposition by Ponder of 1682 to the effect that from about 1673 Marvell was never "worth one hundred pounds besides his bookes and furniture" and owed his publisher money.[32]

It is also likely that a few texts he read that do not appear in the Anglesey catalogue were lent to him by Owen, who read the manuscript of the *Rehearsal Transpros'd,* whose own library catalogue also exists[33] and who owned, for example, not only the 1633 edition of Del Rio, not in Anglesey's collection, but copies of both *Gondibert* and *Certain Verses Written by several of the Authors Friends; to be reprinted with the Second edition of Gondibert* (1653), both of which Marvell cites. Marvell also indicates several times in *RT* and *RT2* that he scoured the booksellers' shops, making use of the privilege of leafing through texts recently published. In default of other evidence, this might account not only for his reference to Anthony Sparrow's *Rationale upon the Book of Common-Prayer,* which he tells us he "observe[d] by chance . . . t'other day," (*RT2,* p. 194), but also Alexander Ross's *Pansebeia,* entered in the Term Catalogues for Michaelmas 1671, and J. Welsch's *Popery Anatomized,* reissued in 1672. In order to make available to the modern reader some sense of Marvell's resourceful research practices, his sources in the editions he probably used, rather than modern ones, are given in square brackets in the notes to both parts of the *Rehearsal Transpros'd.*

For whatever reason, Marvell became a great deal more frugal with authorities in his later pamphlets. In *Mr. Smirke,* rather than introducing his own anecdotes, he mocks the learned allusions of Francis Turner, as in the Antiochus/Popilius story from classical history, or the rhetorical battle between Demosthenes and Aeschines, or the "learned P. Aerodius" who

[31] See Kelliher, *Andrew Marvell: Poet and Politician,* pp. 90, 120, 124.

[32] Art Kavanagh, "Andrew Marvell 'in want of money': The evidence in *John Farrington v. Mary Marvell,*" *Seventeenth Century* 17 (2002), 206–12.

[33] *Bibliotheca Oweniana* (1684).

furnished Turner with an ancient Roman legislative precedent for the Conventicle Act. His authorities are mainly Scripture, with an occasional gesture to Tertullian, Chrysostom, or Jeremy Taylor's civil war tract, *The Liberty of Prophecying*. This move continues, less surprisingly, into the *Short Historical Essay*, in which the authorities are, first and foremost, Scripture, the early Church historians, Eusebius, Sozomen, and Socrates Scholasticus, with occasional tactical recourse to the Church Fathers, such as Gregory Nazianzus or Hilary, who spoke to his purpose. By the time we reach the *Remarks* of 1678, it is exceedingly hard to discern if Marvell is currently reading anything other than the text he is attacking and the one he is defending. And as for the *Account of the Growth of Popery and Arbitrary Government*, the only books it cites, apart from contemporary propaganda pamphlets like the *Packet of Advice to the Men of Shaftesbury*, are the *De jure belli et pacis* of Hugo Grotius (the standard text on just war theory) and the edition of the old medieval *Modus Tenendi Parliamentum* edited by William Hakewill and published by order of the Long Parliament in 1641. (All three, by the way, were in Anglesey's library.)

MARVELL'S LARGER AGENDA

The subject of Marvell's beliefs, concerns, and motives, in the prose pamphlets and in toto, deserves analysis in several monographs. Some of these have already been written. Any student of his prose should begin with one of Pierre Legouis's two versions of his biography, preferably in its French *thèse* version, and follow it with the studies of Wallace, Chernaik, and Patterson. Despite comparatively superficial differences of emphasis, most of them produced by what look like irresolvable contradictions among Marvell's own statements, all these studies acknowledge the importance of the pamphlets in completing the trajectory of his career. His assessors vary as to whether politics or religion concerned him most deeply. To Wallace, who does not deal with *Mr. Smirke* and the *Essay*, Marvell was essentially a constitutional monarchist, who adapted his principles as best he could during the civil war and Protectorate. For Chernaik, he was a political thinker of republican or Miltonic tendencies, if not actually a political theorist like Locke. For Patterson, he became far more of a Cromwellian than he had ever expected to be in 1650 and remained so at heart during the 1660s and 1670s. He was particularly attached to that aspect of Cromwell's character expressed in the 1675 satire a *Dialogue between the two Horses*, in which the horse upon which Charles II's statue belongs remarks,

> I freely declare it, I am for old Noll.
> Though his Government did a Tyrants resemble,
> Hee made England great and it's enemies tremble.[34]

There is evidence of a strong and increasingly detailed interest in foreign policy and diplomacy in Marvell's career, from his early poems on the First Dutch War and Cromwellian embassies, through the personal letters to Harley and Sir Henry Thompson of 1674–76, to the *Account* itself, in which the last sections of the narrative are devoted to attempts by the Commons to persuade Charles II to embark on a league with the Dutch and a war against France.

But the *Account* is the only one of the six major pamphlets with politics at its center. Even though we align it with his Dutch war satires of the later 1660s and the statue poems and other satires of the 1670s, we must not let it overshadow the career. For Legouis, whose biography only improves with time, religious motivation was crucial to Marvell. In the *Essay* he "seriously sets out to undermine the foundations of Anglican intolerance" (p. 204), though he could best be understood, finally, as "still a Protestant while already a free-thinker," probably not a deist, and not as far down the road of rationalism as his nephew William Popple (pp. 222–23). But working closely with the prose reveals how deeply and frequently Marvell relied on Scripture to make his points for him and confirm his principles. This is not a practice that normally leads to rationalism or deism. There are moments in the *Essay* when his position verges on radical anti-institutionalism in religion, but even then he falls back on a great historical truth that seemed to have gotten lost in Restoration England: "'Twas the Bible brought in the Reformation" (2:144). In the two parts of the *Rehearsal Transpros'd,* in *Mr. Smirke* and the *Essay,* and in the *Remarks* in defense of John Howe (which, it must be remembered, is his last work) the subject is, literally, ecclesiastical polity and practice; he argues in different styles and with different emphases the basic premise he quoted from Francis Bacon at the end of the *Second Part* of

34 *P&L,* 1:212. For an argument about the importance of an aggressive foreign policy to Marvell, both in the poems of the revolutionary and Cromwellian era and during the Restoration, see Patterson, "Andrew Marvell and the Revolution," in *Cambridge Companion to Writing of the English Revolution,* ed. N. H. Keeble (Cambridge, 2001), pp. 107–23.

the *Rehearsal Transpros'd:* "We ought to remember that the ancient and true Bounds of Unity are, one Faith, one Baptism, and not one Ceremony or Policy. . . . The diversities of Ceremonies do set forth the Unity of Doctrine" (p. 432). His father was a clergyman, after all, and Marvell probably meant what he said in the *Remarks:* that he entered the dispute between Danson and Howe only to "hinder one Divine from offering violence to another" (2:482). Quarreling within the church embarassed him. On the other hand, he certainly showed an animus against bishops, past and present, which exceeds or conflicts with a peace-making enterprise. Direct echoes of Milton's antiprelatical tracts are among the new evidence that now needs to be taken into account.

Was Marvell an early tolerationist, making an important bridge between Milton's *Areopagitica* and Locke's *Letter concerning Toleration?* Yes, if one acknowledges that a theory of toleration between Protestants was, for all three of these writers, quite compatible with politically motivated anti-Catholicism. How closely did he work with Shaftesbury after that flexible character had abandoned hope in the king as the agent of toleration and been dismissed from the chancellorship in November 1673? It is impossible to tell from Marvell's own statements, but what he wrote matched Shaftesbury's agenda so closely that it presupposes communication between them. Did Marvell himself cease trying to trust Charles II, while pretending in public to do so? and if so, when? In what sense do terms like *republican, loyalist, Dissenter, Socinian, deist* help or hinder our task, especially that part of the task which requires paying attention to everything Marvell wrote, no matter whether or not it helps our hypothesis or fits our preconceptions? It is the hope of the editors that the appearance of *The Prose Works of Andrew Marvell* will keep such questions alive into the new century.

THE EDITORIAL TRADITION

It would be disingenuous to pretend that this edition does not have an agenda itself, in addition to the presumably meritorious one of making available important old texts and new information. That agenda is to continue and complete, as far as completion is ever possible, the work of those in the past who saw that Marvell's prose was at least as important to civilization as his poetry and did their best to persuade others.

Thomas "Hesiod" Cooke did not, of course, edit Marvell's prose; but he hoped to persuade others to do so. A journalist and literateur who had come to London in 1722 and attached himself to the Whig writers John Dennis, Thomas Tickell, Richard Steele, and Ambrose Philips, Cooke notoriously attacked Alexander Pope. Later in life he took over the *Craftsman,* succeeding Nicholas Amhurst, and in 1742 he published, anonymously, a letter "concerning Persecution for Religion and Freedom of Debate," which he dedicated to the third earl of Shaftesbury. His small octavo edition of 1726, however, he dedicated, as noted, to the young son of William Cavendish, first duke of Devonshire, remarking that his father's virtues "recommended him and Mr. Marvell to each other."[35] This friendship would have been based on Cavendish's strong move, in 1676, into the parliamentary opposition, to his arguing that the Long Prorogation was in fact a dissolution, and his moving to lay on the table in the opening debates of 1677 the relevant act of Edward III. After Marvell's death, Cavendish had plotted to bring over William of Orange, and was one of the signatories of the letter of June 30, 1688. Later still, and importantly perhaps for the reprinting of Marvell's *Essay* in the context of attacks on occasional conformity in the first decade of the next century, Cavendish had been chief manager for the Lords in 1702–03 in resisting that attempt. Unfortunately, a six-year-old heir was hardly the sponsor Cooke required in making his plea for a further Marvell edition: "Nor will it, I believe, be ever said, that his other Pieces, in Prose, were not revived, for Want of sufficient Encouragement. Ever far be such a Reproach from any English man!" (xi–xii).

It is one of the few flaws of Legouis's biography that he pours scorn on Captain Edward Thompson, the first editor of Marvell's prose. The three-volume edition, which appeared in 1776, "provided the occasion," wrote Legouis, "for a so-called democratic demonstration of the Whigs, excluded from power by George III's policy." (p. 230). And, he continued, "A noisy and not overscrupulous Opposition did not hesitate to call up memories of the Civil War, . . . or even to glorify, rather against logic, the tyrant Cromwell. The list of the 146 subscribers thus presents an interest more political than literary." Of these subscribers Legouis mentions only "the notorious Duke of Cumberland," and "the Burke of the *Reflections on the Causes of the Present Discontents* and of the speeches in favour of the American Whigs." And his final comment on Thompson's edition is as follows: "What had become, amidst all this dust of the Forum, of those delicate poems of Marvell's in praise of the countryside?"

[35] Cooke, *Works of Andrew Marvell,* Dedication.

But Thompson's edition deserves better than this. In the first instance, it was in part the legacy of Thomas Hollis, whose grandfather, also Thomas Hollis, had been a huge benefactor to Harvard. Hollis, having inherited a fortune from a family of manufacturers and merchants, Old Whigs and Dissenters in character, took upon himself the mission of preserving for posterity (and for the American colonies) the canon of Whig political thought. Among his many selfless projects was an edition of all Marvell's prose, based on the pamphlets that Hollis himself had collected. He had already sent an edition of Milton's prose works to President Edward Holyoke of Harvard, suggesting in a letter that the very existence of Harvard College was a result of the principles of political liberty and government by consent articulated by Milton and endorsed by the Williamite Revolution. When Hollis died with this project stalled, his adoptive heir Brand Hollis passed over to Thompson a treasury of Marvell materials, from which the new edition was constructed.[36]

Seventeen seventy-six was not an accidental moment for the edition's appearance. This was a period of intense Whig activity in the press and elsewhere–of Edmund Burke's *Cause of the Present Discontents* (1770), the *Letters of Junius* (1769–72), the 1771 parliamentary furor over the right to print parliamentary debates, with John Wilkes again at the center of the hurricane, and the war with the American colonies, ending with the Declaration of Independence in July 1776. In this climate, the appearance of Thompson's edition would certainly have been seen as an eloquent contribution to the current political debates. He had placed at the beginning of all three volumes the same nine lines from James Thomson's *Liberty,* a poem written in 1735–36 as a critique of the corruption of the Walpole Whigs. While the first volume was dedicated to the Hull Corporation, which had evidently supported this publishing project, the second, dated March 29, 1776, was dedicated to Sir George Savile, a leading Whig who was strongly opposed to British policy in North America and who on May 18, 1775, had introduced in the Commons a bill calling for the repeal of the Quebec Act. "May you be the happy instrument to heal those wounds now bleeding in our distracted empire," wrote Thompson to Savile, "and reconcile her to

[36] For Thomas Hollis's editorial and publishing projects, see Francis Blackburne, *The Memoirs of Thomas Hollis,* 2 vols. (London, 1780); Caroline Robbins, "The Strenuous Whig, Thomas Hollis of Lincoln's Inn," *William and Mary Quarterly* 7 (1950), 405–53; and Patterson, *Early Modern Liberalism* (Cambridge, 1997), pp. 27–61.

her brave, though distressed children" (A3v). And as for the list of subscribers, to which Legouis seemed to take such objection, it included not only Burke but also Wilkes, who among his other revolutionary activities had recently delivered a long speech opposing the king's position on the American colonies. It included two leaders of the American Revolution, Samuel Adams, one of the chief movers of the Declaration of Independence, and John Hancock, who had been excluded from the offer of amnesty made by the British. And it was headed not only by the "notorious" duke of Cumberland, but also by Hugh Percy, duke of Northumberland, who had opposed the Stamp Act, and William Petty, earl of Shelburne, another inveterate critic of the government's policy on America. Among the 165 subscribers were also Thomas Brand Hollis, who subsequently donated a copy of the edition to Harvard College; Thomas Erskine, due to become the greatest legal defender of free speech of his era; David Garrick, the age's preeminent actor; the Whig historian Catherine Macaulay; Archdeacon Francis Blackburne, who would edit the memoirs of Thomas Hollis with their tributes to Marvell, Milton, and Locke; and a raft of members of parliament who names can continually be found in the lists of minority or Rockingham voters in both houses.[37]

A century later, Alexander Grosart recognized the Whig or liberal legacy represented by Thompson's edition and extended its historical sweep in the preface to his own. Making his own, late-Victorian, case for the importance of Marvell's prose, Grosart wrote, "In *The Rehearsal Transpros'd,* and *Mr. Smirke,* and the *Defence of John Howe,* and the *Growth of Popery,* Andrew Marvell in 'evil days' stood forward in behalf of principles of civil and religious liberty, that were being traduced and trampled on."[38] The half-hidden allusion to Milton's *Paradise Lost* (book 7, ll. 24–26) is telling, for Grosart was recalling Milton's refusal to be silenced by the Restoration: "More safe I Sing with mortal voice, unchang'd / To hoarse or mute, though fall'n on evil days, / On evil days though fall'n, / And evil tongues." But rather than assume the victim position, Grosart saw his own time as an

[37] See *The Parliamentary History of England* (London, 1813), vols. 18 and 19, for speeches and votes of the earls of Shelburne, Grafton, Effingham, Tankerville; of Richard Oliver, the London alderman, David Hartley, MP for Hull, Sir Robert Clayton, James and Temple Luttrell, Jacob Wilkinson, James Scawen, Lord Richard Cavendish, Captain Boyle Walsingham, Major Ralph Gowland, and Crisp Molineux.

[38] Marvell, ed. Grosart, *Complete Works,* 2:xxxviii–xxxix.

age of fulfillment of Marvell's principles. He dedicated his edition to Lord John Russell, author of the Reform Bill of 1832, then in his eighties. As Edward Thompson had cited James Thomson's Whig critique of Whig decadence, Grosart now cleverly cited the Victorian poet laureate, Alfred Lord Tennyson, as if everyone now agreed that England's evil days were gone forever:

It is the Land that freemen till,
That sober-suited Freedom chose;
That Land where, girt with friends or foes,
A Man may speak the things he will.
A Land of settled government,
A Land of just and old renown;
Where freedom broadens slowly down
From precedent to precedent. (2:xl)

What Grosart did not acknowledge was that Tennyson wrote these lines (in a poem entitled "You ask me, why, tho' ill at ease") as an expression of *distaste* for the reforms of 1832 and an appeal to hold off legislative change in favor of *slow* mutation of custom through the common law (which cannot produce constitutional change). Instead, Grosart made Tennyson one of Marvell's late beneficiaries: "I claim therefore for the Prose of Andrew Marvell a too little recognized place in History, as one of the pioneers of literatures, civil and religious freedom, and as himself one of the elect few to whom England owes it, that her living Laureate could truthfully write [those] household words [just cited]" (2:xl).

THE YALE EDITION

Our own claims are somewhat less orotund. We hope in this new edition of his prose to consolidate the place of Marvell in the center of early modern studies. Recently, conversations and collaborations between those trained as historians and those trained as literary scholars have sparked new interest and produced new knowledge, especially about England and Europe in the seventeenth century. We hope that the project will be seen, moreover, as one of Anglo-American collaboration, which indeed it has been.

In these two volumes, we offer the first complete edition of Marvell's prose; that is, published pamphlets (as distinct from his letters or what sketchy record survives of his speeches in parliament). For the pamphlets that had never previously been edited, as distinct from being reprinted, establishing a text is important, but even more vital today is the task of annotating and explaining Marvell's allusions and the political and social contexts to which they bear witness.

On this count, perhaps the most neglected of the works was *Mr. Smirke; or, the Divine in Mode.* This was originally assigned to Jeremy Maule, whose extraordinary knowledge of the 1670s had sharpened all our early discussions of the edition and its protocols, as his kindness and intellectual generosity had warmed them. But Jeremy died suddenly in November 1998. The loss to our project, as to his friends and colleagues everywhere, was incalculable. *Mr. Smirke* therefore became reattached, as it had been originally, to the *Short Historical Essay Concerning General Councils,* my own assignment. Fortunately Jeremy had already laid down the outline of their context: the parliamentary events of 1675–76, the tolerationist efforts of Bishop Herbert Croft, and the collaboration therein of Marvell's friend Sir Edward Harley. He and his student, Beth Lynch, had also assembled some striking details about the actively hostile reception of these pamphlets by the Restoration government.

The *Account of the Growth of Popery and Arbitrary Government* has been available in facsimile since 1971, but the history of its publication and reception has never been fully explained.[39] Nor has its *assembly* from contemporary parliamentary diaries and pamphlets been understood, a process that Nicholas von Maltzahn has cleverly unpacked. He also discovered the hitherto unknown second and more correctly printed edition of the *Account* and deduced how the printing history of the work was coordinated with Charles II's mercurial and changing plans for the parliamentary session of 1678, in the tense aftermath of the 1677 session when the Long Prorogation was challenged and the four great lords, including Shaftesbury and Buckingham, were sent to the Tower. While waiting for the new session, Marvell may have begun his *Remarks Upon a Late Disingenuous Discourse* (1678), which refuted a work by Thomas Danson that was entered in the Stationers' Register late in November 1677. The *Remarks* were attributed to Marvell by James Yonge (ca. 1678) and Edmund Calamy (1724) and were first added to the canon in Grosart's edition, though Grosart provided no rationale. These statements are supported by evidence from library catalogues. As N. H. Keeble demonstrates, copies of the *Remarks* were owned

[39] *Account,* ed. G. Salgado (Farnborough, 1971).

by John Owen, who was closely connected with Marvell during their joint battles with Samuel Parker, and, still more tellingly, by John Locke, who entered it in his section of Marvell books in his personal library catalogue. Keeble also shows how the *Remarks* are attached to the earlier pamphlets by several shared features and references.

The decision to reedit the two parts of the *Rehearsal Transpros'd* was made on two grounds, the first and most practical being that Smith's edition has been long out of print. The second was that, though extremely learned (especially considering that it began as a Ph.D. dissertation) and for the most part textually meticulous, the edition can be improved upon.[40] Smith evidently misconstrued the publication history and censorship of the first part of the *Rehearsal Transpros'd,* about which Martin Dzelzainis has made important archival discoveries. Moreover, Smith's version provides little of the information about the political context of the pamphlets as a whole—Charles II's Declaration of Indulgence, announced in 1672 and then withdrawn under pressure—that today's readers expect. Both pamphlets, but especially the second, now need a different style of introduction and annotation, one that alerts the reader not just to the sources of particular allusions but also to their rationale. We judged, also, that today's readers would be grateful for translations of Latin and more frequent glossing of uncommon terms. It would have been a serious loss to the reader, however, if the great harvest of Smith's detective scholarship had disappeared from view. The texts have been reedited from first principles, and a new account of the publication history supplied by Dzelzainis. For both parts we have used as copy-text not the first edition used by Smith, but the second, which contains, in each case but for different reasons, Marvell's revisions. In reannotating, many of Smith's valuable contributions have been retained and credited to him; others have been considerably shortened or corrected; and the information in the notes is now, as it was not in Smith's edition, accessible via the index.

As an appendix, and to show how widely his style varied in different circumstances, we include examples of Marvell's prose that do not fit the definition of a prose work in the sense used above, that is, of an original work written for publication:

1. A selection from Marvell's longest autograph manuscript, "The Justice

[40] It is unfortunate that, of the very few typographical errors or mistranscriptions, seven involve the misreading of the archaic long S.

of the Swedish Cause," a 1658 translation of a Latin tract attributed to the Swedish envoy in England, Johann Frederick von Friessendorff.

2. A substantial sample of the 1672 translation of Suetonius whose attribution to Marvell has now been, we hope, established.

3. The mock-speech supposed to have been delivered by Charles II and attributed to Marvell in the 1704 edition of *Poems on Affairs of State,* where it is dated April 13, 1675. It was noted, however, on March 1 by Girolamo Alberti, Venetian secretary to the Doge and Senate, in a long letter on the church politics of the day.[41] Widely attested in manuscript, it clearly circulated rapidly at the time.

[41] *CSPD Venetian* 1675, p. 366.

Editorial Protocols

Because Marvell's interest in the world of print production and dissemination is so clear throughout this last phase of his life, the new *Prose Works* aims to retain as much of the visual effect of his pamphlets as is consistent with modern readerly expectation. The original spelling and punctuation have been retained throughout, subject of course to collation, and italics have been retained for all quotations and words that Marvell apparently wished to emphasize. The original italicization of proper names and places has, however, been dropped, on the grounds that it distracts from the ideological intentions of italicization as a debating practice. Marginal notes have been replicated (which helps to distinguish Marvell's own system of reference from an editor's, not the case in Smith's edition of the *Rehearsal Transpros'd*). Alterations achieved by censorship or revision have been made visible on the page rather than needing to be deduced from the apparatus. On the grounds that Marvell was *not* a verbatim quoter, far from it, we have not included in the apparatus the differences between his version of a text and its original, since a theory of intention in such differences is less probable than that Marvell often used his memory or transcribed hastily and carelessly.

Each of the major works has its own complicated printing history (the *Remarks* excluded), to be detailed in the individual introductions. The evidence of would-be interference by the authorities, and its largely successful evasion, is clear and entertaining enough to crowd out what might have been expected in a bibliographer's edition—the complex narrative of different *states* of the texts as produced by press corrections, and so on. Instead we concentrate on the broad differences between *editions,* looking for what can therefore be inferred about the number of printers involved, the reasons for reprinting, and the strategies used by the printers both to evade the censor and to keep Marvell's pamphlets on the market. There was clearly a pattern of first and second authorially sponsored editions in the case of all the major works, the *Remarks* again being an exception; and an important part of the strategy of Marvell and his printers was to match the second edition to the first on a page-by-page basis, presumbly so that readers of a later edition would be able to refer to the same page numbers as their friends!

Chronology: Marvell in the Restoration

1660	
April 2	Marvell reelected to Convention parliament for Hull
April 4	Declaration of Breda
May 25	Charles II lands at Dover
October	Executions of regicides
December 17	Marvell speaks in parliament to urge Milton's release from prison
December 24	Dissolution of Convention parliament
1661	
January 30	Exhumation and disgrace of Cromwell's body
May 8	Meeting of Cavalier parliament, with Marvell as member for Hull
June 27	Marvell writes to Hull about imminent passage of Act of Uniformity
June 30	Bishops restored to House of Lords
December 19	Corporation Act
1662	
February 24	Roger L'Estrange becomes Surveyor of the Press
March	Act of Uniformity debated in parliament
March 20	Marvell quarrels with Clifford in the House
May 19	Parliament prorogued until February 18, 1663; Act of Uniformity and Licensing Act become law

June	Marvell leaves for Holland on unspecified political mission
1663	
April 2	Marvell writes to Hull to announce his return to his seat (*P&L*, 2:34–35)
July 20	Marvell accompanies Carlisle on embassy to Russia, Sweden, and Denmark
1664	
April 27	Outbreak of Second Dutch War
	Conventicle Act (expired 1668)
1665	
January	Marvell returns to parliament
June	Battle of Lowestoft
October 9	Five Mile Act
1666	
April	Self-dating of *Second Advice*
June 1–4	Four Days' battle with Dutch
September 2–6	Great Fire of London
October 1	Self-dating of *Third Advice*
October 2	Marvell added to parliament committee to investigate Fire of London
1667	
Spring	Locke joins Shaftesbury as his personal physician
June 10	Naval disaster at Chatham
September 4	Self-dating of *Last Instructions*
October 13	Marvell speaks in defense of Peter Pett re Chatham disaster
November 19	Clarendon flees the country
1668	
February 15	Marvell speaks intemperately against Arlington
March 13, 30	Marvell attacks proposal to renew Conventicle Act
	Buckingham speaks in the Lords for toleration
July 24	John Darby and John Winter listed in violation of Press Act
1669	
February	Buckingham attacks Sir William Coventry in *The Country Gentleman*
November 22	Samuel Parker's *Discourse of Ecclesiastical Politie* advertised for sale

December	John Owen's *Truth and Innocence Vindicated* answers Parker
1670	
March	Conventicle Act renewed
May 22	Secret Treaty of Dover signed by Clifford and Arlington
June	Samuel Parker promoted to archdeaconship of Canterbury
July	Charles sends Buckingham to negotiate cover treaty with Louis XIV
August 18	John Dryden appointed Poet Laureate and Historiographer Royal
November 21	Marvell speaks for James Hayes, prosecuted under Conventicle Act
November 22	Parker's *Defence and Continuation* advertised for sale
December/January	John Locke, James Tyrrell, and others discuss Parker's *Discourse*
1671	
February 27	Speech of Lord Lucas in Commons against government (*P&L*, 2:322–23)
April 22	Parliament prorogued; Marvell perhaps begins translation of Suetonius
October	Charles cancels Buckingham's commission and transfers it to Monmouth and Ossory
December 7	First performance of Buckingham's *Rehearsal*
1672	
January 1	Stop of the Exchequer
	Marvell (?) writes *The Kings Vowes*
February	Search of all printing houses
February 7	Dryden's *Conquest of Granada,* dedicated to James, attacking commonwealth and anticipating Third Dutch War, advertised for sale
March 15	Charles's Declaration of Indulgence
March 17	Declaration of war against the Dutch
June 24	Buckingham's *Rehearsal* advertised in Term Catalogue
	Parker's *Preface* advertised in Term Catalogue; Marvell begins *RT.*
September 7	Parker's *Preface* listed in Stationers' Register

November 17	Shaftesbury becomes Lord Chancellor
December 2	Wardens of Stationers' Company search for *RT*
	Two sheets seized by Mearne at Winter's press; Anglesey and Shaftesbury intervene
December 10	Benjamin Woodroffe writes of *RT,* "It has been stopped from spreading, but is now again allowed to be bought."
December 16	Court of Assistants orders that *RT* not be entered in Stationers' Register
1673	
January 15	Arlington summons Wardens to account for several printers
January 21	John Darby promises Wardens to take down one of his presses
January 23	Henry Coventry deposes L'Estrange about first edition of *RT*
January 24	Wardens report three visits to Whitehall about *RT*
January 25	Coventry deposes Ponder
	Second impression of *RT,* intended for new session of parliament?
February 4	Parliament reconvenes; supply requested for Dutch war; Shaftesbury's *delendo est Carthago* speech
	Milton writes *Of true religion, haeresie, schism, toleration*
March 7	Anglesey drafts bill to exempt Protestant dissenters from legal penalties
March 8	King's speech withdraws Declaration of Indulgence
March 29	Parliament prorogued
April 22	Anglesey becomes Lord Privy Seal
May 3	Marvell reads Parker's *Reproof* in press and declares his intention to answer it (in letter to Harley)
July 15	Thomas Blount writes to Wood concerning "great searching of the Printhouses for Marvel's Reply to Parker"
November 3	Marvell publishes *Rehearsal Transpros'd: the Second Part*
	Shaftesbury learns of secret clauses in Treaty of Dover

November 9	Shaftesbury dismissed from chancellorship and Council of Charles, partly at request of James, and goes over to the Opposition
1674	
January 13	Buckingham attacked in Commons, dismissed from Council
February 19	Treaty of Westminster ends Third Dutch War
Summer	Marvell mentioned by government spies as member of a Dutch fifth column in England
November	Marvell writes *Upon his Majesty's being made free of the City*
1675	
Spring	Buckingham returns to London and begins alliance with Country party
March 1	Girolamo Alberti describes Marvell's parody of king's speech to Doge
April 13	Parliament reconvenes; Croft and five other bishops meet to discuss religious comprehension; Croft writes *Naked Truth* and has four hundred copies printed to distribute to MPs
April 22	Marvell reports to Hull on Danby's proposed Test (*P&L,* 2:148–49)
May 29	*Gazette* announces setting up of king's statue in Stock Market
June 9	Parliament prorogued
July 24	Marvell describes Danby's Test in a letter to Popple and comments on Buckingham's mockery of the bishops (*P&L,* 2:341–43)
Summer	Marvell writes "statue" poems (?)
October 13	Parliament reconvenes.
November 8	*Letter from a person of quality* ordered by Lords to be burned by the common hangman
November 9	Marvell reports this to Hull (*P&L,* 2:171–72)
November 12	Locke leaves England in haste
November 16	Buckingham drafts bill for relief of Protestant dissenters
November 18	Marvell reports, "To morrow . . . a great Lord brings in a Bill into the Lords for care of dissenters"

November 22	Parliament prorogued; beginning of Long Prorogation
December	Marvell writes *The Royal Buss* (?) (*CSPD*, May 3, 1676)
1676	
February 7	Francis Turner's *Animadversions* on *Naked Truth* advertised in *Gazette* (no. 1066)
February 18	Evelyn reports Gunning's and Turner's answers
March 3	Wardens paid about "another search for *Naked Truth*"
March 11	Etherege's *Man of Mode* first produced at Dorset Garden
March 17	Wardens send list of printers to Henry Compton, bishop of London
April 29	Henry Oldenburg turns in his Licenser's license. Marvell must have already finished *Mr. Smirke*
May 8–18	Wardens search for "Ponders Pamphlett, being part of *Mr. Smirke*"
May 10	Ponder indicted; Anglesey intervenes unsuccessfully
May 18	John Darby examined by Coventry
June 6	Thomas Blount comments on sales of *Mr. Smirke*
July 1	Marvell writes to Harley about reception of *Mr. Smirke* (*P&L*, 2:344–46)
1677	
February 15	Parliament reconvenes; Buckingham's speech declares dissolution
February 16	Four lords sent to the Tower by Danby
March 27	Lords bill for educating royal children; Marvell speaks against it; named to the committee to consider it
March 29	Marvell's scuffle in the House with Sir Philip Harcourt
April	Marvell probably begins work on *Account of Growth of Popery*
July 16	Marvell in his seat; parliament adjourned to December 3
October 28	Royal proclamation postponed session to April 4

November 26	Danson's *De Causa Dei* entered in Stationers' Register
December 3	Charles moved session up to January 15
December	Premiere of Dryden's *All for Love*
	Trial of John Harrington
1678	
January 31	Wardens attend king and Council at Whitehall with L'Estrange
February 8	Loose sheets of *Account* taken for stitching
February 19	Warrant for the arrest of those responsible for *Account*
February 14	Wardens seize a porter with twelve copies of *Account*
March 1	William Leach gives information about Packer's involvement
March 21	Dryden's *All for Love* appears in print, with an anti-republican dedication to Danby
March 21–25	*Gazette* advertises *All for Love* and offers a reward for the discovery of those responsible for the *Account*
April 17	Marvell's *Remarks* vs. Danson licensed
May 14	L'Estrange's *Account of the Growth of Knavery* advertised for sale
June 10	Marvell writes to Popple describing search for *Account* (*P&L*, 2:357)
August 16	Marvell dies
September	Titus Oates gives first depositions about Popish Plot
1679	
March	Parliament refuses to renew Licensing Act
May	First Exclusion Bill
	Folio edition of the *Account*
May 27	Parliament prorogued, never to meet again
	Monmouth sent into exile in Holland
July 18	Wakeman acquitted; first doubts about Popish Plot
October 7	Exclusion Bill parliament prorogued before it met
November 17	Settle's antipopish pageant
1680	
Summer	Monmouth's unauthorized progress
October 15	Mary "Marvell's" dating of *Miscellaneous Poems*

October 21	Parliament reconvened
November 11	Exclusion Bill fails to pass the Lords
1681	
January 10	Parliament prorogued; Narcissus Luttrell bought a copy of *Miscellaneous Poems. By Andrew Marvell . . . Late Member of the Honourable House of Commons.*
March 21	Oxford parliament convened and dissolved on March 28
April 8	Charles' *Declaration*
June	Dryden's *His Majesties Declaration Defended* refers to Marvell as "their deceased Judas"
July 1	Fitzharris executed
July 2	Shaftesbury arrested on charge of treason
1682	
June 28	Ponder's deposition about Marvell's poverty for about the last five years

Abbreviations

Account	Marvell, *An Account of the Growth of Popery and Arbitrary Government in England* ("Amsterdam") (1677)
CPW	John Milton, *The Complete Prose Works,* gen. ed., D. M. Wolfe, 8 vols. in 10 (New Haven, 1953–80)
CSPD	*Calendar of State Papers Domestic*
Censure	Samuel Parker, *A Free and Impartial Censure of the Platonick Philosophie* (Oxford, 1666)
Defence	Samuel Parker, *A Defence and Continuation of the Ecclesiastical Politie. By way of a letter to a friend in London. Together with a letter from the author of the Friendly debate* [Simon Patrick] (London, 1671)
DNB	*The Dictionary of National Biography founded in 1882 by George Smith*
Discourse	Samuel Parker, *A Discourse of Ecclesiastical Politie, Wherein The Authority of the Civil Magistrate over the Consciences of Subjects in Matters of External Religion is Asserted; The Mischiefs and Inconveniences of Toleration are Represented, And all Pretenses Pleaded in Behalf of Liberty of Conscience are Fully Answered* (London, 1669).
Essay	Marvell, *A Short Historical Essay, concerning General Councils, Creeds, and Imposition, in Matters of Religion* (London, 1676)

Grosart	*The Complete Works in Verse and Prose of Andrew Marvell M.P.,* ed. Alexander B. Grosart, 4 vols. (London, 1872–75)
Henning	Basil Duke Henning, *The House of Commons 1660–1690,* 3 vols. (1983)
HMC	Historical Manuscripts Commission
JHC	*Journal of the House of Commons, 1547–1800,* 55 vols. (1983)
JHL	*Journals of the House of Lords, beginning anno primo Henrici octavi,* 79 vols. (1771)
P&L	Andrew Marvell, *Poems and Letters,* ed. H. M. Margoliouth, 3rd ed. rev. Pierre Legouis, with the collaboration of E. E. Duncan-Jones, 2 vols. (Oxford, 1971)
POAS	*Poems on Affairs of State: Augustan Satirical Verse, 1660–1714,* vol. 1, ed. George de F. Lord (New Haven and London, 1963)
Preface	Samuel Parker, *Bishop Bramhall's Vindication of himself and the episcopal clergy, from the Presbyterian charge of popery . . . together with a preface shewing what grounds there are of Fears and Jealousies of Popery* (London, 1672).
PRO	Public Record Office
Remarks	Marvell, *Remarks Upon a Late Disingenuous Discourse, Writ by one T. D. Under the pretence De Causa Dei . . . By a Protestant.* (London, 1678)
Reproof	Samuel Parker, *A Reproof to the Rehearsal Transpros'd* (London, 1673)
RT	Marvell, *The Rehearsal Transpros'd: Or, Animadversions Upon a late Book, Intituled, A Preface Shewing what grounds there are of Fears and Jealousies of Popery* (London, 1672)
RT2	*The Rehearsal Transpros'd: The Second Part* (London, 1673)
Smirke	Marvell, *Mr. Smirke: Or, The Divine in Mode: Being Certain Annotations, upon the Animadversions on the Naked Truth.* (London, 1673)
Smith	Andrew Marvell, *The Rehearsal Transpros'd and the Rehearsal Transpros'd: The Second Part,* ed. D. I. B. Smith (Oxford, 1971)
Thompson	*The Works of Andrew Marvell, esq., Poetical, Controversial, Political, containing many Original Letters, Poems, and Tracts, never before printed. With a new life of the author, by Capt. Edward Thompson* (London, 1776)
Wood	Anthony à Wood, *Athenae Oxonienses,* ed. Philip Bliss, 5 vols. (Oxford, 1813–15)

The Prose Works of Andrew Marvell

VOLUME I

REHEARSAL TRANSPROS'D

1672

Introduction

Martin Dzelzainis and Annabel Patterson

THE REHEARSAL TRANSPROS'D

In *Gregory, Father-Greybeard* (1673), Edmund Hickeringill relates how

> at the *Rainbow-Coffee house* the other day, taking my place at due distance, not far from me, at another Table sat a whole *Cabal* of wits; made up of Virtuoso's, Ingenioso's, young Students of the Law, two Citizens, and to make the Jury full, *vous avez*, one old Gentleman . . . they all laughing heartily and gaping . . . I was tickled to know the cause of all this mirth, and presently found, it was a *Book* made all this sport; the Title of it, *The Rehearsal transpros'd*. Look you here, says one of them, do not you see, p. 309. how smartly he *ferrets* the old *Foxes*, the Fathers of the Church? (as in biting *Irony*, he calls the old Bishops:).[1]

Intrigued by these exchanges, Hickeringill "resolv'd, though it cost me a shilling, to see what I could find in this *marvellous Book* . . . readily finding one at the next *Stationers*."[2] Fictitious though it may be, the scene in the Rainbow (an actual coffehouse near the Inner Temple gate on Fleet Street) is nevertheless revealing.[3] Hickeringill's repeated puns on Marvell's name

[1] Edmund Hickeringill, *Gregory, Father-Greybeard* (London, 1673), p. 5.

[2] Ibid., p. 28.

[3] According to B. Lillywhite, *London Coffee Houses* (London, 1963), p. 467, the Rainbow premises also housed the bookseller Samuel Speed, who was charged with publishing and selling seditious books in May 1666. For the proximity between coffee-

confirm that his authorship of the *"marvellous" Rehearsal Transpros'd*, published anonymously in 1672, was an open secret (its sequel, *The Rehearsal Transpros'd: The Second Part* (1673), bore his name on the title page). It is also clear that the book was popular and—despite censorship, as we shall see—widely and cheaply available; that it was communally read and discussed in coffeehouses, a milieu often associated with Marvell;[4] and that it was noted for its mordant antiepiscopal wit. Marvell's prose début, like that of his friend John Milton thirty years earlier, thus took the form of a tract directed against the bishops as the embodiment of a persecuting spirit. The circumstances, however, were very different; whereas Milton's antiprelatical tracts swam with the tide of root-and-branch reform inside and outside the Long Parliament, Marvell faced a resurgent episcopate that was "arguably more confident and more powerful than at any time since the Reformation" and in tune with the instincts of "an Anglican Parliament which believed that Calvinism had destroyed the civil peace and the Book of Common Prayer and should never be allowed the opportunity to do so again."[5] Furthermore, Milton had written against the bishops as prepublication censorship collapsed, whereas Marvell was working in the shadow of the 1662 Press Act that reinstated it.[6]

CONTEXT

In the Declaration of Breda (April 1660) Charles II promised "liberty to tender consciences," to be confirmed by legislation once he was restored. No such bill was forthcoming. Instead, between 1661 and 1665 the Cavalier parliament passed a series of repressive laws subsequently known as the Clarendon Code. By imposing political and religious tests, the Corporation Act (1661) barred all but Anglican royalists from municipal office, while the Act of Uniformity (1662) removed from their livings any clergy-

houses and bookshops, see Adrian Johns, *The Nature of the Book: Print and Knowledge in the Making* (Chicago and London, 1998), pp. 111–13; for their political importance, see Steven Pincus, "'Coffee Politicians Does Create': Coffeehouses and Restoration Political Culture," *Journal of Modern History* 67 (1995), 807–34.

[4] See [Samuel Butler,] *The Transproser Rehears'd* (Oxford, 1673), pp. 35–36; for the attribution to Butler, see Nicholas von Maltzahn, "Samuel Butler's Milton," *Studies in Philology* 92 (1995), 482–95.

[5] Mark Goldie, "John Locke and Anglican Royalism," *Political Studies* 31 (1983), 76–7.

[6] See Johns, *Nature of the Book*, pp. 230–48.

men who would not subscribe to all the Thirty-Nine Articles and give their "unfeigned consent to all and every thing" in the revised Book of Common Prayer.[7] These measures in themselves left the ejected ministers and the lay population free to worship outside the Church of England. Another act passed in 1662 did prohibit more than five persons (other than the members of a household) from meeting for unauthorized religious purposes, but this applied only to Quakers. It was also unclear whether earlier legislation like the 1593 statute outlawing conventicles of any kind was still in force.[8] Matters were put beyond doubt by the Conventicle Act of August 1664, which universalized the prohibition against Quaker meetings, and the Five Mile Act of October 1665, which banned ejected clergy from coming within five miles of any parish where they had ministered or of any corporate town whatsoever. England was now manifestly a persecuting state, seeking to achieve religious uniformity through coercion.

The Anglican hegemony was less secure than it appeared. Since the Conventicle Act was due to expire three years from the end of the session in which it was passed plus another session (in the event, opinion differed as to whether this meant it lapsed in August 1668 or in March 1669), and the Five Mile Act would arguably fall with it, further legislation was needed.[9] However, the leading ministers in the new government formed after the fall of Clarendon in 1667—Clifford, Arlington, Buckingham, Ashley Cooper (earl of Shaftesbury from 1672), and Lauderdale, whose initials formed the acronym Cabal—were all patrons either of dissent or Catholicism. Among those most closely involved in schemes for modifying the Restoration church settlement from the autumn of 1667 on were George Villiers, Duke of Buckingham (1628–87), widely thought of as "the head of all those parties, that were for liberty of Conscience," and John Owen (1616–83), formerly Cromwell's chaplain and now spokesman for the Independents.[10]

[7] J. P. Kenyon, ed., *The Stuart Constitution 1603–1688* (Cambridge, 1976), pp. 358, 380.

[8] See John Miller, *After the Civil Wars: English Politics and Government in the Reign of Charles II* (Harlow, 2000), pp. 150, 183.

[9] See ibid., pp. 205–06, and Richard Tuck, "Hobbes and Locke on Toleration," in *Thomas Hobbes and Political Theory,* ed. Mary G. Dietz (Lawrence, Kansas, 1990), p. 156.

[10] M. Sylvester, ed., *Reliquiae Baxterianae* (London, 1696), 3:21; on Buckingham, see Maurice Lee, *The Cabal* (Urbana, Ill., 1965), pp. 161–201, Tim Harris, "Introduction: Revising the Restoration," in *The Politics of Religion in Restoration England,* ed. Tim Harris, Paul Seaward, and Mark Goldie (Oxford, 1990), pp. 7, 11, and, for a more skeptical account, Bruce Yardley, "George Villiers, Second Duke of Buckingham, and

Early in 1668, Buckingham sponsored discussions between the moderate Anglican John Wilkins and the Presbyterian divine Richard Baxter (1615–91) about bills for "comprehension" (relaxing the requirements for conformity to the Church of England) and toleration or, as it was more often called, "indulgence" (relief from legal penalties for dissenters who remained outside the Church of England). Sir Matthew Hale drafted a comprehension bill, while the question of indulgence was referred to Owen. In February, however, the Commons blocked the proposals before the king could even ask them to "think of some course to beget a better union and composure" in religion and turned instead to trying to renew the Conventicle Act.[11]

The lobbying outside Parliament was intense. John Humfrey initiated the debate in June 1667 with *A Proposition for the Safety & Happiness of the King and Kingdom both in Church and State,* followed by John Corbet's *Discourse of the Religion of England* (1667) and two contributions from Owen, *A Peace-Offering in an Apology and Humble Plea for Indulgence and Liberty of Conscience* and *Indulgence and Toleration Considered* (both 1667). Sir Charles Wolseley further developed the dissenting case in *Liberty of Conscience upon its True and Proper Grounds* and *Liberty of Conscience, the Magistrates Interest* (both 1668).[12] The response from Anglican divines was immediate: Thomas Tomkins replied to Humfrey, Richard Perrinchief attacked Corbet and Owen, and Herbert Thorndike composed a reply to Corbet as well as a critique of Baxter's proposals for comprehension.[13]

---

the Politics of Toleration," *Huntington Library Quarterly* 55 (1992), 317–37; on Owen, see Peter Toon, *God's Statesman. The Life and Work of John Owen: Pastor, Educator, Theologian* (Exeter, 1971).

[11] See Norman Sykes, *From Sheldon to Secker* (Cambridge, 1959), pp. 72–73; R. Thomas, "Comprehension and Indulgence," in *From Uniformity to Unity,* ed. G. F. Nuttall and O. Chadwick (London, 1962), pp. 198–202; John Spurr, "The Church of England, Comprehension and the Toleration Act of 1689," *English Historical Review* 104 (1989), 933–35.

[12] On Humfrey, Owen, and Wolseley, see Gary S. de Krey, "Rethinking the Restoration: Dissenting Cases for Conscience, 1667–1672," *Historical Journal* 38 (1995), 53–83; see also Blair Worden, "Toleration and the Cromwellian Protectorate," in *Persecution and Toleration,* ed. W. J. Sheils, Studies in Church History, vol. 21 (Oxford, 1984), pp. 229–33.

[13] See Thomas Tomkins, *The Inconveniencies of Toleration* (1667); Richard Perrinchief, *A Discourse of Toleration* (1668 but actually 1667) and *Indulgence Not Justified* (1668); Herbert Thorndike, "The True Principles of Comprehension" and "The Plea of

Orchestrating the campaign was Gilbert Sheldon, archbishop of Canterbury since 1663.[14] While there *was* an intellectually coherent theory of persecution based on Augustine's teachings,[15] Sheldon's views on dissent were more visceral: "Tis only a resolute execution of the law that must cure this disease, all other remedies serve and will increase it; and it's necessary that they who will not be governed as men by reason and persuasions should be governed as beasts by power and force, all other courses will be ineffectual, ever have been so, ever will be."[16] Persecution was necessary, and it worked. Accordingly, Sheldon approved of Simon Patrick's *Friendly Debate* series (1668, 1669, 1670), which, in defiance of its title, savaged the nonconformists. But the most extreme version of the case for persecution was articulated by Samuel Parker (1640–88), who, like Tomkins, was a chaplain to Sheldon and who, in common with Patrick, sought to thwart comprehension and indulgence and to promote measures against dissent.[17] In rapid succession, Parker produced a trio of Sheldonian polemics: *A Discourse of Ecclesiastical Politie: Wherein the Authority of the Civil Magistrate Over the Conscience of Subjects in Matters of Religion is Asserted; The Mischiefs and Inconveniences of Toleration are Represented. And All Pretenses*

Weakness and Tender Consciences," in *The Theological Works of Herbert Thorndike,* 6 vols. (Oxford, 1844–56), 5:309–80 (neither was published at the time). The second edition of Humfrey's *Proposition* (1667) included a reply to Tomkins while Corbet replied to Perrinchief's *Discourse* in *A Second Discourse* (1668).

[14] See W. G. Simon, "Comprehension in the Age of Charles II," *Church History* 31 (1962), 446–48.

[15] See Mark Goldie, "The Theory of Religious Intolerance in Restoration England," in *From Persecution to Toleration,* ed. O. P. Grell, J. Israel, and N. Tyacke (Oxford, 1989), pp. 331–68, and John Coffey, *Persecution and Toleration in Protestant England, 1558–1689* (Harlow, 2000), pp. 21–46.

[16] Bodleian Library, MS Carte 45, f. 151, quoted in John Spurr, *The Restoration Church of England, 1646–1689* (New Haven, 1991), p. 47.

[17] On Parker, see the following: Gordon G. Schochet, "Between Lambeth and Leviathan: Samuel Parker on the Church of England and Political Order," in *Political Discourse in Early Modern Britain,* ed. Nicholas Phillipson and Quentin Skinner (Cambridge, 1993), pp. 189–208, and "Samuel Parker, Religious Diversity and the Ideology of Persecution," in *The Margins of Orthodoxy: Heterodox Writing and Cultural Response, 1660–1750,* ed. R. D. Lund (Cambridge, 1995), pp. 119–48; Jon Parkin, "Liberty Transpros'd: Marvell and Samuel Parker," in *Marvell and Liberty,* ed. Warren Chernaik and Martin Dzelzainis (Basingstoke, 1999), pp. 269–89, and "Hobbism in the Later 1660s: Daniel Scargill and Samuel Parker," *Historical Journal* 42 (1999), 85–108.

Pleaded in behalf of Liberty of Conscience are Fully Answered (1670, actually 1669), which as its title suggests was a kind of *summa* of the debate to this point; *A Defence and Continuation of the Ecclesiastical Politie* (1670); and an edition of *Bishop Bramhall's Vindication of Himself and the Episcopal Clergy From the Presbyterian Charge of Popery, As it is managed by Mr. Baxter in his Treatise of the Grotian Religion. Together with a Preface Shewing What Grounds there are of Fears and Jealousies of Popery* (1672). As soon as the *Discourse* appeared, John Locke made a set of hostile notes.[18] Owen urged Baxter to reply to it and when he declined did so himself in *Truth and Innocence Vindicated* (1669). The prolific John Humfrey meanwhile took on both the *Discourse* and Patrick's *Friendly Debate* in *A Case of Conscience* (1669) before addressing the *Preface* to Bramhall in *The Authority of the Magistrate, About Religion* (1672). And then there was Andrew Marvell's *The Rehearsal Transpros'd; Or, Animadversions Upon a late Book, Intituled, A Preface Shewing What Grounds there are of Fears and Jealousies of Popery* (1672).

From one angle, Marvell was just a late contributor to a debate that had already run for five years. But in the meantime the ideological landscape had been transformed by two events. The first was the renewal of the Conventicle Act in 1670, this time on a permanent footing. In Marvell's brutal phrase, it was "the Price of Money"; that is to say, extorted from the king by the Cavalier parliament and the bishops in return for supply. The Lords tried to mitigate the bill's provisions and make it temporary and also inserted a controversial clause (subsequently watered down) to the effect that nothing in the act should invalidate the king's ecclesiastical supremacy or indeed any of his or his predecessors' prerogatives. Like Baxter, Marvell suspected that, since "it is & will be in his M^tys^ power to dispose with the execution of the whole bill," the intention was to reduce dissenters to a state of dependence on royal favor, and, as if to drive this message home, the legislation was promptly followed by a bout of persecution.[19]

The second event was the king's exercise of his supremacy in issuing the Declaration of Indulgence on 15 March 1672, two days before the Third Dutch War began. This suspended legal penalties against nonconformists and Catholics, though only the former had the right (under license) to public worship.[20] The older generation of Presbyterians still sought com-

18 See Mark Goldie, ed. *Locke: Political Essays* (Cambridge, 1997), pp. 211–15.

19 Marvell, *Poems & Letters,* 2:315, 104; see Miller, *After the Civil War,* pp. 204, 208–10.

20 See Kenyon, *Stuart Constitution,* pp. 407–8.

prehension within the national church rather than a sectarian existence outside it, while the Quakers would have nothing to do with indulgence at all. Nevertheless, hundreds—including Baxter—applied for licenses, while Marvell's bookseller, Nathaniel Ponder, was active in procuring them for nonconformist clergy in Northamptonshire and elsewhere.[21] Others were uneasy at sharing indulgence with Catholics, an anxiety heightened by the strident Anglican campaign against popery, though Marvell for one was completely unimpressed (see p. 174). Reservations were also voiced about the legality of exercising the prerogative in this way. As Richard Tuck has observed, however, the readiness of the Cabal "to elevate monarchical power, if by doing so they undermined the power of the Church" made political sense given that "throughout the seventeenth century in England there was an Anglican, Tory majority in the country, and anyone who wanted toleration would be pretty sceptical about Parliaments."[22] The policy of using royal power to break the Anglican hegemony was both coherent and attractive, and "a constellation of Puritans and future Whigs backed the crown," including Owen, John Locke, Algernon Sidney, and Marvell.[23]

ARGUMENT AND LITERARY STRATEGY

The Rehearsal Transpros'd is the Cabal's literary memorial: the most brilliant defense of its keynote policy of religious toleration. Like the regime itself, Marvell's work is a hybrid. Its most visible generic debt is to Buckingham's burlesque play *The Rehearsal*, performed in December 1671 and published

[21] See N. H. Keeble, *The Literary Culture of Nonconformity in Later Seventeenth-Century England* (Athens, Ga., 1987), pp. 59, 121; Frank Mott Harrison, "Nathaniel Ponder: The Publisher of *The Pilgrim's Progress,*" *The Library*, 4th ser., 15 (1934), 261–62.

[22] Richard Tuck, *Hobbes* (Oxford, 1989), pp. 36–37.

[23] Mark Goldie, "Priestcraft and the Birth of Whiggism," in *Political Discourse*, ed. Phillipson and Skinner, p. 229; for Sidney, see Jonathan Scott, *Algernon Sidney and the English Republic, 1623–1677* (Cambridge, 1988), pp. 167–68. Marvell's support for this policy is confirmed by Nicholas von Maltzahn's recent discovery of a document in Marvell's handwriting dating from May 1668. It consists of a draft address (never delivered), jointly prepared with Philip Lord Wharton (1613–96), inviting Charles II to by-pass Parliament and modify the church settlement by exercising 'the Power inherent in You in Ecclesiasticall affairs by the Prerogatiue annext to Your Imperiall Crown': see Nicholas von Maltzahn, "Marvell's Constant Mind," *Times Literary Supplement*, 21 June 2002, pp. 14–15.

in the summer of 1672.[24] Marvell partly took his cue from an exchange between Parker and Owen on the propriety of the dialogue form used in Patrick's *Friendly Debate.* When Owen adduced Aristophanes' attack on Socrates in *The Clouds* to illustrate the destructive use of comedy for "personating" an opponent, Parker replied that Jonson's anti-Puritan satires in *The Alchemist* and *Bartholomew Fair* would have been a more apt—though still inapplicable—comparison. Appended to the *Defence* was an unsigned twenty-six-page letter from Patrick rebutting Owen's account of Aristophanes and dismissing his threat of retaliation in kind; indeed, had Owen replied "in the same form of writing that I used, it had, in my poor judgment, been more for his reputation."[25] Marvell, however, eschewed canonical works in favor of Buckingham's successful assault on the conventions of heroic drama, the chief exponent of which, John Dryden, was satirized as Bayes.

In showing how Bayes and Parker "do very much Symbolize" each other (p. 51), Marvell aimed to demonstrate that, as N. H. Keeble puts it, "Parker's priestcraft is of a piece with Bayes' stagecraft; his pronouncements on ecclesiastical policy deserve no more respect than do Bayes' pronouncements on dramatic technique."[26] More than this, Marvell's text was a tissue of often fragmentary allusions to *The Rehearsal,* an act of appropriation which allowed him to couch ecclesiastical controversy in an idiom that would accommodate it to a variety of milieux otherwise unsympathetic to it: coffeehouses, theaters, the Inns of Court, and the Court itself. Above all, it was a signal that Marvell might expect the patronage and protection of Buckingham, one of a group of influential peers sympathetic to nonconformity, including Anglesey, Shaftesbury, Carlisle, and Wharton, on whom Marvell could and did rely.

The "animadversions" of Marvell's subtitle was the workhorse genre of seventeenth-century religious and political controversy. It typically consisted of point-by-point refutation in the form of quotations from the adversary's text followed by commentary. The main drawback of the method

[24] Buckingham's probable collaborators were his protégé Thomas Sprat (1633–1713), his secretary, Martin Clifford (d. 1677), and Samuel Butler (1612–80), the author of *Hudibras,* to whom Marvell respectfully alludes in *RT* (p. 66); see George Villiers, Duke of Buckingham, *The Rehearsal,* ed. D. E. L. Crane (Durham, 1976), p. vii.

[25] Parker, *Defence,* pp. 732; see also pp. 173–75, and *Discourse,* ppp. xv–xix; Owen, *Truth and Innocence Vindicated,* pp. 46–50.

[26] N. H. Keeble, "Why Transprose *The Rehearsal?*" in *Marvell and Liberty,* ed. Chernaik and Dzelzainis, p. 256.

was its inflexibility in that those replying to a given work had to accept its arrangement of topics and arguments as a template for their own. Complaints about being forced to attend to the vagaries of the opposing case were a conventional feature of the genre, as were various ploys for evading this obligation. One of the most important of these was to search out contradictions between the work under scrutiny and the author's other writings and play off these texts against each other. Alternatively, one could stick to the text in question but focus on seemingly incidental features of it such as solecisms, unwitting innuendoes, and stylistic mannerisms, the aim being to demonstrate that these lapses were in fact indicative of larger intellectual and moral failings. Finally, the point of the attack could be switched entirely from the text to its author, seeking to destroy his ethical standing and with it his case. Marvell could hardly avoid being familiar with this repertoire of techniques given their ubiquity as a way of conducting arguments in print, but he was particularly aware of the models provided by his friend John Milton in his antiprelatical tracts and Latin defenses. Also like Milton, he turned for guidance on the ethics of literary controversy to Francis Bacon's influential *Wise and Moderate Discourse, Concerning Church-Affaires* (1641). And, in fitting out Parker with a mock-heroic persona, he was specifically indebted to Owen's *Truth and Innocence Vindicated* for a number of tactics.[27]

Like most animadverters, Marvell complains of being yoked to his opponent's chaotic discourse ("there being no method at all in his wild rambling talk; I must either tread just on in his footsteps, or else I shall be in a perpetual maze" [p. 124]), while he is actually organizing things behind the scenes. Marvell informally divides his work into three sections, of which the first (pages 1–87) and the third (pages 161–326) are devoted to Parker's *Preface.* The opening section explores the anti-Calvinist implications of Bramhall's grandiose scheme "to reconcile all the Churches to one Doctrine and Communion" (p. 58) while the third examines the theme of "Episcopal Ambition" (p. 133), culminating in an extended historical essay on church-state relations during the reign of Charles I (see below). In the middle section, Marvell addresses Parker's notorious *Discourse of Ecclesiastical Politie* and its *Defence and Continuation.* Remarkably, Marvell reduces the 56 pages of preface and 326 pages of text in the *Discourse* to just six "Aphorisms or Hypotheses," which he rehearses in turn even though, as he

[27] See Annabel Patterson, *Marvell: The Writer in Public Life* (Harlow, 2000), pp. 111–16, 126–27.

himself admits, this is "but collateral to my work of examining the Preface" (p. 96). He then demonstrates how what Parker says in the *Discourse* about the unlimited power of the magistrate is contradicted in the *Defence* before contriving a three-way conversation on the page between both these books and Owen's *Truth and Innocence.*

In formal terms, this "collateral" part of the book is the nearest Marvell comes to producing a standard set of animadversions, and the nearest he gets to a direct confrontation with Parker's "grand Thesis" that the magistrate must have an absolute "Power to govern and conduct the Consciences of Subjects in affairs of Religion" if social order is to be maintained (pp. 91–92). And even here he makes Parker do the work of confuting himself by citing his other writings. Elsewhere the business of replying to Parker tends to resolve into ingenious displays of wit and virtuoso flights of fancy. Parker's ponderous circumlocution "the present juncture of Affairs" becomes hilarious through repetition (see pp. 44, 52, 58, 89, 97, 122). The vacuousness of "comfortable importance" allows Marvell to construe it as a reference to Parker's wife (see pp. 47, 65, 86, 102, 108, 135). Parker's slip in locating Geneva on the south side of Lake Leman rather than at its western end becomes the subject of a competitive exchange between coffeehouse wits; sets off another variation on the theme of Calvin; and finally comes to rest in the mock imprint on the title page of the first edition (fig. 1): "Printed by *A.B.* for the Assigns of *John Calvin* and *Theodore Beza*, at the sign of the Kings Indulgence, on the South-side of the *Lake Lemane*" (see pp. 68–71). The scholarly norms of the genre are further subverted by the eclecticism of the reading Marvell chooses to display, which ranges from the absurdly recondite to the absolutely trivial by way of such canonical writers as Montaigne and Shakespeare. The outcome of these diversionary tactics was not to hand the initiative to his opponents, but rather to leave them looking flat-footed.

Mindful of his readership, Marvell plays up the topicality and immediacy of his work whenever he can. His transcription of the title page of the 1672 reprint of "A *Rationale upon the Book of Common-Prayer of the Church of England by A. Sparrow, D.D. Bishop of Exon. With the Form of Consecration of a Church or Chappel, and of the place of Christian Burial. By Lancelot Andrews late Lord Bishop of Winchester. Sold by Robert Pawlet at the Sign of the Bible in Chancery Lane*" risked dying on the page, so he prefaced it with the nonchalant remark that he "could not but observe by chance the Title page of a Book t'other day" and signed off with a jibe at "the Fathers of the Church" (p. 194). (It worked: this was the page that Hickeringill imagined

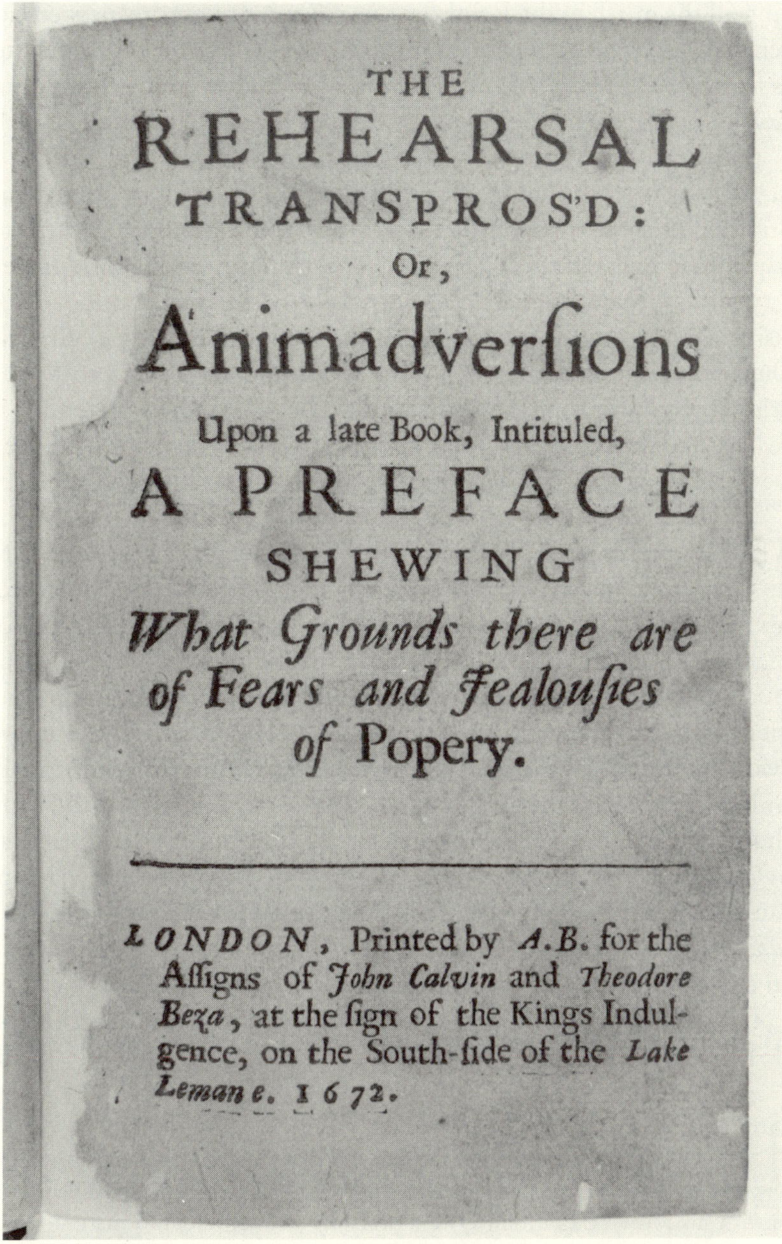

THE

REHEARSAL

TRANSPROS'D:

Or,

Animadverſions

Upon a late Book, Intituled,

A PREFACE

SHEWING

What Grounds there are of Fears and Jealouſies of Popery.

LONDON, Printed by *A.B.* for the Aſſigns of *John Calvin* and *Theodore Beza*, at the ſign of the Kings Indulgence, on the South-ſide of the *Lake Lemane*. 1672.

Fig. 1. Title page of the first edition (first issue).

causing all the mirth in the Rainbow.) As *RT* went to press, a new edition of Davenant's *Works* was advertised in the *London Gazette*—hence the quotations from *Gondibert* with which Marvell concludes.[28] He repeatedly buttonholes the reader, confiding what "I have heard" or what "I have been told" (see, for example, pp. 65, 182, 189, 190, 192, 195). His sources were good. When Marvell mockingly recites (p. 154) the epitaph that Herbert Thorndike (1598–1672) composed for himself, it was copied not from an inscription on his grave (as one might expect), but from his will, proved on July 15, 1672.[29] Such nuggets of information were highly valued in "this diffusive age, greedy of intelligence and public affairs," as Evelyn called it. Deflating ecclesiastical pretensions was moreover bound to appeal to Charles II, who was fond of "showing the cheat of such as pretended to be more holy and devout than others, and said they were generally the greatest knaves," singling out bishops from "some eminent men of the present age."[30]

Whereas the king could name names freely, Marvell has to be careful. He declines to identify Archbishop Alexander Burnet (1614–84), forced to resign the see of Glasgow in 1667 for opposing Lauderdale's policy of indulgence: "I have not been curious after his name nor his crime, because as much as possible I would not expose the nakedness of any person so eminent formerly in the Church" (p. 111).[31] When sarcastically citing works by two "of our present Bishops" (p. 79), Marvell never identifies Peter Gunning (1614–84) as the author of *The Holiness of Lent,* while the name of Anthony Sparrow (1612–85) appears only as cited on the title page of the *Rationale.* Only by implication is Simon Patrick (1626–1707), rector of St Paul's, Covent Garden, revealed as "the Ingenious Writer of the *Friendly Debates*"; otherwise, the book stands in for its author (pp. 55, 177). Marvell could be less circumspect with the deceased. Even so, because the "Dignitary of Lincoln" whom he accuses of cheating at cards is "not long since dead, I will save his name" (p. 182). Doctor Thorndike was not so lucky.

[28] See *London Gazette,* 729, November 14–18, 1672.

[29] The epitaph is also inscribed on the flyleaf of a 1672 volume belonging to Thomas Barlow, former librarian of the Bodleian. Barlow, a Calvinist who remained on good terms with his former pupil John Owen, probably gleaned the information from *The Rehearsal Transpros'd.* Thorndike was a senior fellow at Trinity College, Cambridge, when Marvell forfeited his place in 1641. See *Works of Herbert Thorndike,* 6:175, 257, 284; Hilton Kelliher, *Andrew Marvell: Poet and Politician 1621–78* (London, 1978), p. 26.

[30] Spurr, *England in the 1670s,* pp. 165, 229.

[31] See Lee, *Cabal,* pp. 60–61.

Peter Heylyn (1600–62) is named as an exponent of "new-fangled Divinity" in opposition to the Calvinist John Prideaux (1578–1650) (p. 79). When it comes to Archbishop William Laud (1573–1645), Marvell professes himself reluctant to reproduce extracts from a narrative in which Laud featured, written by Archbishop George Abbot (1562–1633), another Calvinist, and published in John Rushworth's *Historical Collections* (1659): "I shall only in the way demand excuse, if contrary to my fashion, the names of some eminent persons in our Church long since dead, be reviv'd here under no very good character; and most particularly that of Arch-bishop Laud, who, if for nothing else, yet for his learned Book against Fisher, deserved far another Fate than he met with, and ought not now to be mentioned without due honour. But those names having so many years since escaped the Press, it is not in my power to conceal them" (p. 181). Having entered this disclaimer, he goes on the offensive. Bishop John Cosin (1579–1672) is named under the aegis of Abbot's narrative, but otherwise referred to anonymously as "a great Prelate in the last King's time" or by the title of his book on the sacraments (pp. 112, 151, 186). Notwithstanding Marvell's caution, as we shall see, these materials were still subject to censorship.

The aim of *RT,* however, was not so much to shame individuals as to expose a clerical obsession with "the Reputation, the Interest, the secular grandure of the Church" (p. 196). In attacking Parker and similar "*Politick would-be's* of the Clergy," Marvell was attacking "men that have a mind to be Bishops, and that will do any thing in the World to compass it" (p. 161). Conversely, in praising James Ussher (1581–1656), the Calvinist archbishop of Armagh, he was praising one who "undertook to abate of our Episcopall *Grandeur,* and condescended indeed to reduce the Ceremonious Discipline in these Nations to the Primitive Simplicity" (p. 57).[32] Reducing "Episcopall *Grandeur*" was also Marvell's objective, but instead of appealing to primitive times, he told a story about how the Church of England had been captured by ideologues in the 1620s and 1630s.

How to categorize these ideologues was—and is—a matter of controversy. A convenient point of departure is the title of Bramhall's *Vindication of himself and the Episcopal Clergy, from the Presbyterian Charge of Popery, As it is managed by Mr. Baxter in his Treatise of the Grotian Religion.* Baxter had published *The Grotian Religion Discover'd* in 1658 in order to expose what he

[32] Marvell is clearly alluding to Ussher's *Reduction of Episcopacie unto the Forme of Synodical Government received in the Antient Church* (1656).

saw as a conspiracy to deliver the Church of England over to Rome—"Grotian" because it had been the ambition of the Dutch scholar and theologian Hugo Grotius (1583–1645) and his English acolytes to reunify Christendom on the basis of renouncing the extremes of the Reformation and the Counter-Reformation.[33] Baxter was about to reply to the *Vindication,* in which he thought Bramhall aimed at "the Uniting of Christendom under the old Patriarchs of the Roman Imperial Church, and so under the Pope," when he was warned off by Roger L'Estrange, Surveyor of the Press.[34] By this time, however, Baxter no longer thought of Grotius as the *éminence grise.* Instead, alarmed by Heylyn's posthumously published biography of Laud, *Cyprianus Anglicanus* (1668), he now saw "Laudians" where before he saw "Grotians."[35]

Marvell defended Baxter ("Mr. B.") in *RT* (see pp. 79–83); he also agreed that "that incomparable Person Grotius did yet make a Bridge for the Enemy to come over" (p. 63); and his targets, like Baxter's, included Gunning, Sparrow, and Thorndike as well as Bramhall, Parker, and the dangerous Heylyn. But Marvell's preferred term was "Arminian" rather than "Grotian" or "Laudian." Jacobus Arminius (1560–1609) was a professor of theology at Leiden who rejected the Calvinist teaching on salvation according to which God had predestined from all time those who would be saved and those who would be damned, arguing instead that individuals were free to accept or reject God's universal offer of saving grace. The ensuing dispute between the Arminians, backed by the republicans under the leadership of Grotius and Jan van Oldenbarnevelt, and their Calvinist opponents, backed by the House of Orange, brought the United Provinces to the brink of civil war.[36] In 1619, the Calvinists triumphed at the Synod of Dort, an international gathering of divines, but the English Arminians prospered under the patronage of Laud, a key figure in the Caroline regime. What followed was the "Arminianisation of the Church of England," in return for which the Arminians offered unswerving support to royal abso-

[33] See Geoffrey F. Nuttall, "Richard Baxter and *The Grotian Religion,*" in *Reform and Reformation: England and the Continent c1500–c1750,* ed. Derek Baker, Studies in Church History (Oxford, 1979), 2: 245–50.

[34] See Keeble, *Literary Culture of Nonconformity,* p. 105.

[35] See William Lamont, "Arminianism: The Controversy that Never Was," in *Political Discourse,* ed. Phillipson and Skinner, pp. 45–66.

[36] See Richard Tuck, *Philosophy and Government 1572–1651* (Cambridge, 1993), pp. 180–84.

lutism.[37] However, when the king and archbishop tried to impose canons and a liturgy upon the Presbyterian Scots, they provoked a rebellion that ended Charles I's personal rule and led to civil war in England.

Marvell was not alone in subscribing to this version of events. His friend James Harrington alluded to it in *Oceana* (1656), while Thomas Hobbes offered a witty summary in *The Questions Concerning Liberty, Necessity, and Chance, Clearly Stated and Debated, Between Dr. Bramhall Bishop of Derry, And Thomas Hobbes of Malmesbury* (1656), a work Marvell would have come across in researching Bramhall.[38] More important, Marvell—as so often—had access to inside information. During his time at Eton College in the early 1650s he met John Hales (1584–1656) and "convers'd a while with the living *remains* of one of the clearest heads and best prepared brests in Christendom" (p. 130). The implied contrast here is between the living man known to Marvell and the posthumously published *Golden remains of the ever memorable Mr Iohn Hales* (1659) through which the less privileged knew him, a volume which did, however, make public the revealing letters sent by Hales to Sir Dudley Carleton from the Synod of Dort.[39] Hales had become Laud's chaplain in 1639 but, though theologically an Arminian, disliked Laudian clericalism.[40] For Marvell, he represented the human face of the Church of England. Furthermore the provost of Eton at the time, Francis Rous the elder (1579–1659), was a veteran anti-Arminian campaigner. He had been prominent in the attack on Roger Manwaring (a royal chaplain who had delivered two controversial sermons on *Religion and Allegiance*) during the 1628 parliamentary session; led the debate on Arminianism with his stepbrother John Pym in 1629; and, in 1641, presented the articles impeaching John Cosin for his Arminianizing pol-

[37] Nicholas Tyacke, "Puritanism, Arminianism and Counter-revolution," in *The English Civil War,* ed. Richard Cust and A. Hughes (London, 1997), p. 149; see also Hugh Trevor-Roper, *Catholics, Anglicans and Puritans* (London, 1987), pp. 40–119; K. Fincham, "William Laud and the Exercise of Ecclesiastical Patronage," *Journal of Ecclesiastical History* 51 (2000), 69–93.

[38] See James Harrington, *The Commonwealth of Oceana and A System of Politics,* ed. J. G. A. Pocock (Cambridge, 1992), p. 56; Thomas Hobbes, *The Questions Concerning Liberty, Necessity, and Chance* (London, 1656), pp. 1–2. For Marvell's knowledge of this work, see below, p. 301 and n.425.

[39] Another edition of *Golden remains* was published in 1673, also edited by Peter Gunning; there was a competition going on over the legacy of Hales.

[40] See Trevor-Roper, *Catholics, Anglicans and Puritans,* pp. 59–60, 207–208.

icies.[41] It was with some confidence therefore that Marvell launched his thirty-seven-page offensive against the Arminians (pages 274–311; 178–95 below)—in many ways, the most important part of the work.

The immediate occasion is Parker's claim in the *Preface* that the nonconformists served the interests of popery "by creating disturbances in the State" and his supporting assertions that "the late War was wholly upon a Fanatical Cause, and the dissenting party do still go big with the same Monster" (pp. 178, 181). Parker had also spent sixteen pages in the *Defence* discussing the origins of the Civil War and refuting the view, attributed to Owen among others, that "the Cause of Religion was not pretended or engaged in that Quarrel, but that it was a meer Contest about Civil Rights and Priviledges."[42] Unexpectedly, however, Marvell does not deploy his narrative directly in support of Owen's position. Instead he adopts Parker's premise about the importance of religion but turns the tables by arguing that it was in fact Arminian clerics who had caused the war and continued to disturb the state. Their "design" had not been to defect to Rome outright, but (as Baxter had suggested) "rather to set up a new kind of Papacy of their own here in England. And it seemed they had to that purpose, provided themselves of a new Religion in Holland. It was Arminianism, which though it were the *Republican* Opinion there, and so odious to King James, that it helped on the death of Barnevelt, yet now they undertook to accommodate it to Monarchy and Episcopacy" (p. 189). The first step in this process of ideological accommodation was the campaign on behalf of the Forced Loan of 1626 by Samuel Harsnet, Robert Sibthorpe, and Manwaring, which Marvell retells as far as possible in the words of Abbot (pp. 183–88). The clerical grip on power was consolidated through patronage whereby "the Calvinists were all studiously discountenanced, and none but an Arminian was judg'd capable and qualified for imployment in the Church" (p. 190). Once they had gained the "Ascendent" upon the king himself, they "made the whole business of State their Arminian Jangles, and the Persecution for Ceremonies, [and] did for recompence assign him that imaginary absolute Government, upon which Rock we all ruined" (p. 191). Finally, Marvell blames Laud alone for the "dangerous Experi-

[41] See Conrad Russell, *The Fall of the British Monarchies 1637–1642* (Oxford, 1991), pp. 105, 231, 278.

[42] Parker, *Defence*, p. 612; see Owen, *Truth and Innocence*, pp. 146–48.

ment" of imposing the liturgy on the Scots, so making him personally responsible for the Civil War (ibid.).

Marvell begins his summing up—perhaps the most famous passage in the book—by stepping back from the point at issue between Parker and Owen:

> Whether it were a War of Religion, or of Liberty, is not worth the labour to enquire. Which-soever was at the top, the other was at the bottom; but upon considering all, I think the Cause was too good to have been fought for. Men ought to have trusted God; they ought and might have trusted the King with that whole matter. The *Arms of the Church are Prayers and Tears,* the Arms of the Subjects are Patience and Petitions. The King himself being of so accurate and piercing a judgment, would soon have felt where it stuck. For men may spare their pains where Nature is at work, and the world will not go the faster for our driving. Even as his present Majesties happy Restauration did it self; so all things else happen in their best and proper time, without any need of our officiousness. (p. 192)

For the author of *A Common-place Book Out of the Rehearsall Transpros'd* (1673) there was only one way to read the crucial phrase about the "Cause . . . too good to have been fought for": "according to Natural Logick, whatsoever is too good, is good enough, and more to spare."[43] Samuel Butler, knowing of Marvell's friendship with Milton, saw "nothing but *Iconoclastes* drawn in Little, and *Defensio Populi Anglicania* [*sic*] in Miniature."[44] What makes the whole passage genuinely disconcerting is the semantic slippage between the Good Old Cause and natural causes. In writing human agency out of the story ("men may spare their pains where Nature is at work"), Marvell sounds like a thoroughgoing determinist who believes that everything that happens is the necessary effect of antecedent causes.[45] However, the advantage of this way of putting things is that it serves both to depoliticize Marvell's counsel and to make it absolutely compelling. For if events are always the necessary effects of causes, then, as Marvell puts it in the very next sentence, "all the fatal consequences of that

[43] Anon., *A Common-place Book Out of the Rehearsall Transpros'd* (1673), p. 51.

[44] [Butler,] *The Transproser Rehears'd,* p. 72.

[45] See Vere Chappell, ed., *Hobbes and Bramhall on Liberty and Necessity* (Cambridge, 1999), p. xi.

Rebellion . . . can only serve as Sea-marks unto wise Princes to avoid the Causes" (p. 192). The moral of the story for Charles II is that he should keep his distance from the bishops and so avoid a repetition of his father's mistake of colluding with the Arminians.

As well as telling the king what to avoid, Marvell had earlier set out the principles that should positively inform his actions (and, in the process, offered a magisterial summary of the nonconformist case for conscience as this had developed between 1667 and 1672):

> That men therefore are to be dealt with reasonably: and conscientious men by Conscience. That even Law is force, and the execution of that Law a greater Violence; and therefore with rational creatures not to be used but upon the utmost extremity. That the Body is in the power of the mind; so that corporal punishments do never reach the offender, but the innocent suffers for the guilty. That the Mind is in the hand of God, and cannot correct those perswasions which upon the best of its natural capacity it hath collected: So that it too, though erroneous, is so far innocent. (pp. 166–67)

Yet the question of which path—persecution or toleration—the king would choose remained open. The trade-off between persecution and financial supply that marked the passage of the Conventicle Act in 1670 looked to Marvell very much like a rerun of the Forced Loan (see pp. 182–87, 195). Yet in issuing the Declaration of Indulgence in 1672, Charles appeared to have broken with the ecclesiastical politicians of the Church of England, a breach that Parker was anxious to close and Marvell to widen and, if possible, make permanent. However, by the time *The Rehearsal Transpros'd: The Second Part* appeared late in 1673, the king had already canceled the Declaration and begun to realign himself with the Anglican interest.

THE AFTER-LIFE OF *THE REHEARSAL TRANSPROS'D*

RT was instantly and hugely successful and established Marvell's reputation as—in the first instance—a prose writer. Gilbert Burnet (not distinguishing between *RT* and *RT2*) thought they were "the wittiest books that have appeared in this age" and reported that the king, who "was not a great reader of books, read them over and over again."[46] The first response to *RT* in print was entirely positive too, though it came from a surprising quarter

[46] Gilbert Burnet, *A Supplement to the History of My Own Time*, ed. H. C. Foxcroft (Oxford, 1902), p. 216.

given the usual assumptions about Marvell's anti-Catholicism. Roger Palmer, earl of Castlemaine (1634–1705), was the leading Restoration spokesman for Catholics, and in his polemics he drew repeatedly on *RT* (and, in due course, *RT2*) as a suitably Protestant stick with which to beat his Anglican opponents. In his view, Marvell was "that witty, Masculine, and most judicious Author," while *RT* was simply "incomparable."[47] That such an informal literary alliance should have formed at all tells us a great deal about the reconfiguration of religion and politics in the period of the Cabal. And the contrast between the warmth with which Castlemaine greeted *RT* and the hostility he showed to Milton's *Of True Religion, Haeresie, Schism, Toleration, And what best means may be us'd against the growth of Popery* (1673) is also instructive, for what Milton was displaying was some older-style partisan reflexes from which Marvell seems to have been free. As far as Marvell was concerned, Parker would have done better to write "A Preface showing the CAUSELESNESS of the Fears and Jealousies of POPERY" (p. 174).

What was more important still was that *RT,* by successfully introducing wit and fantasy into an arena in which brute intellectual force was hitherto dominant, had transformed the rules of the discursive game. In 1674, William Lloyd, one of the king's chaplains, replying to Castlemaine, complained of this new way of writing that "I cannot think our Religion and Laws, our Liberties and Lives, are so trivial a Prize, as to be carried by a Mastery in fooling."[48] But the lesson Marvell had taught a generation of Restoration and Augustan writers in his destruction of Parker was that "a Mastery in fooling" was the most potent weapon in the armory of the controversialist.

We can see some of his pupils at work in the spring of 1687, just after James II had issued his own Declaration of Indulgence and Dryden had published *The Hind and the Panther,* a defense of Catholic doctrine written with the aim of getting Anglicans to agree to the repeal of the Test Act.[49] This prompted one of Dryden's enemies to print some manuscript letters criticizing Dryden's *Conquest of Granada* originally written and circulated

[47] Roger Palmer, Earl of Castlemaine, *A Full Answer and Confutation of a Scandalous Pamphlet, Called, A Seasonable Discourse* ([Antwerp], 1673), p. 10, quoted in Martin Dzelzainis, "Marvell and the Earl of Castlemaine," in *Marvell and Liberty,* ed. Chernaik and Dzelzainis, p. 304.

[48] William Lloyd, *A Reasonable Defence of the Seasonable Discourse* (London, 1674), p. 46.

[49] See James Anderson Winn, *John Dryden and His World* (New Haven and London, 1987), p. 423.

by Martin Clifford (a coauthor of *The Rehearsal*) in 1672. To these were now added a set of hostile *Reflections* on Dryden's recent poem, possibly by Tom Brown.[50] For long stretches, however, Brown's text is virtually a cento of quotations from *RT*.[51] Though unacknowledged, these borrowings were not meant or expected to go unrecognized, as Brown signals in an authentically Marvellian self-reflexive fashion; his accusation of plagiarism against Dryden—"to speak the truth, there is very little *of his own* in any Book that he hath published, but the Arrogance and unparallel'd Censoriousness, which he exercises over all other Writers"—is itself lifted from Marvell![52]

THE TWO EDITIONS

Wherever Marvell was in the weeks between July 4, 1672, when he wrote from Westminster to Trinity House in Hull, and October 29, when he found a reply from the society "at my returne to towne," he was busy writing *RT*.[53] Publication may originally have been planned to coincide with the session of parliament due to begin on October 30, but on September 17 the session was further prorogued until February 4, 1673.[54] Despite this, clandestine printing of the work, which was neither licensed nor entered in the Stationers' Register, went ahead. Although liable to search and seizure by the authorities and piracy by competitors, the first edition (*72*), an octavo of 326 pages, was printed without any apparent interference.

By contrast, the second edition (*72a*), a page-for-page resetting of the first (except for sheet X, the forms of which had been kept standing), was beset by problems. When it eventually appeared it was prefaced by an

[50] See ibid., p. 614.

[51] See *Notes upon Mr. Dryden's Poems in Four Letters. By. M. Clifford, late Master of the Charter House, London. To which are annexed some Reflections upon the Hind and Panther. By another Hand.* (London, 1687), esp. pp. 17–19, 37–39 (misnumbered: should be 33–35).

[52] [Brown], *Notes . . . To which are annexed some Reflections,* p. 32; *RT2,* p. 263.

[53] *Poems and Letters,* 2: 275; Smith suggests (p. xii), without giving any evidence, that *RT* appeared in September 1672. This is unlikely; since *RT* sold very well, and most copies of the first edition had still not been sold at the start of December (see below, p. 29), its publication must have been nearer that time. Parker's *Preface* to Bramhall, upon which Marvell was animadverting, was entered in the Stationers' Register only on September 7, having been advertised in the Term Catalogue for June 24—as was Buckingham's *Rehearsal*: Term Catalogues, 1: 111.

[54] See *CSPD* 1672, p. 626.

"Advertisement from the Bookseller" in which Ponder complains, *"This Book having wrought it self thorow many difficulties, it hath newly incountred with that of a Counterfeit Impression in* 12° *under the Title and pretence of* the 2d Edition Corrected. *Whereas in truth that Impression is so far from having been Corrected, that it doth grossly and frequently corrupt both the Sence and Words of the Coppy"* (sig. A2v; p. 37). Ponder is frank about the last-minute commercial threat posed by the pirated "2d Edition Corrected," a duodecimo in 184 pages that forced him to describe his own second edition on its title page as "The second Impression, with Additions and Amendments." But he leaves the reader in the dark about the nature of the earlier *"difficulties."* In fact, as we now know, *72a* had been seized in the press and censored. These events and their aftermath, up to and including the composition of *The Rehearsal Transpros'd: The Second Part,* form a complex narrative. The key to this, and part of the story in its own right, is a series of depositions taken by Secretary of State Henry Coventry in January 1673, of which full and accurate transcripts have never been published hitherto.

The first, endorsed "Mr Lestranges Examinacon concerning a Book called the Rehearsall Transposed, taken by the Right Honble. Mr Secretary Coventry Jan: 23. 167[3]," is not a minute of the interview as such but a full statement in a neat hand, with supporting documentation (since lost) and signed by L'Estrange (the "Examinate").

> L'Estrange declareth, that he neither knew, nor heard of the Rehearsall Transpros'd, till the first Impression was distributed, and that Enquiring of one Brome, a Bookseller, about it, he told this Examinate, that it was printed for Ponder, who own'd the thing, and sayd that if the Book were Questioned, there were those would Justify it, and bring him off. Before this Examinate could meet with Ponder, there were two sheets of a second Impression seised at the Presse, by Mr Mearn, one of the Wardens of the Company of ~~th~~ Stationers; and thereupon, Ponder came to L'Estrange, and told him of it and withall, that the Earle of Anglesey desired to speake with him; who took Ponder along with him Immediately to his Lord.^{spp} at his house in Drury Lane: where the Earle was pleased to speak to the Examinate (in the presence, and (as he beleeves,) in the hearing of Mr Ponder) in these or the like words. Look you M^{r} L'Estrange there is a Book come out, (the Rehearsall Transpros'd) I presume you have seen it.) I have spoken to his Ma:^{ty} about it, and the King says he will not have it supprest, for Parker has

done him, wrong, and this man has done him Right: and I desired to speak with you to tell you this. And since the King will have the Book to passe, Pray give M[r] Ponder your License to it, that it may not bee printed from him. To which, this Examinate Reply'd, that since it was his Ma:[ty's] pleasure, he would not meddle to give it any Interruption, but that there were some things in it not fit to be Licensed, Instancing in two Passages: viz: the Roman Emperour's receiving a Dagger Pag: 24[4] and the Wisdome of the King and Parliament Exposed: Pag: 310 whereupon his Lord:[spp] took the Book of Ponder, and upon perusall of those places agreed with this Examinate, that they were better out, then In, advising him withall, to Alter those places, letting the body of the discourse remayne. To which, This Examinate made answere that he did not love to tamper with other mens Copyes, without the Privity and Allowance of the Author. His Lord.[spp] reply'd that he could not say any thing of the Author, but that such alterations might be made without him. And so this Examinate took Leave of the Earle and departed with Ponder in his Company, who upon the way, desired L'Estrange to give him a note under his hand, of signification to Printers, what direction his Lord.[spp] had given him, from his Ma:[ty] concerning this Book, which he did Accordingly.

The next work was to reade over the Book, in Order to a License, which was done, (all but two or three sheets) in the presence of Ponder to whome, this Examinate, at the same time, declared, that it was intended only for the saving of his Propriety, and not at all to Authorise the Publication of it. This Examinate's first Exception was to the bottome of the Title-Page [Printed by the Assignes of John Calvin &c. And upon reading the discourse over, he changed and struck out severall sharp Reflexions upon B.[pp] Laud, and D[r] Parker, and others also of a more Generall Prospect: which beeing done hee this Examinate gave his license to the Book, and to the End aforesayd. Which License beeing signed by a Warden of the Company, and delivered to the Clark to Enter it, according to Custome, for the behoofe of the Proprietor, and hee refusing to do it, This Examinate wrote to him, at the Instance of Ponder, to know upon what Consideration it was that he Refused it: Declaring in his Letter, that hee this Examinate disliked the thing as much as any body, but that beeing overruled himselfe, hee expected the Company's officer should Likewise conform. This as he remembers was the sence of the Letter. Hereupon, Ponder told him that the Earle of Anglesey had sent for one of the Wardens~~A~~ and the Stationers Clarke about ∧^{it} ~~this busynesse~~[?], and that if he did not receive Satisfaction, His Lord.^{spp} would bring the businesse before the King and Counsell, desiring and prevailing with this Examinate, to go along with him to the Earle, who was then Ill of the Gout. His Lord.^{spp} was pleased to discourse with this Examinate about the Methodes of the Company of Stationers, in the matter of Licenses, and Entryes; and to direct particular Enquiry as to the poynt in Question: whereupon, this Examinate desired his Lord.^{spp} to honour him with a Signification of his pleasure under his hand, which would carry a great deale more Credit and Authority with it, then any thing by word of mouth from this Examinate. And his Lord.^{spp} had the Goodnesse to write a Letter unto this Examinate accordingly, which Letter is annexed ~~to~~ unto this his Examin∧^{a}tion.

L'Estrange sayth moreover, that the Book in Question was not printed according to ye Corrections and Emendations of the Copy licensed by this Examinate; and so in Equity, not Imputable to the Licensor. And whereas, the first License being withdrawn from the Clarke of the Stationers, a second license was desired by Ponder upon another Title-Page; the sayd License was granted expressly under the Limitations of the Former, and with condition of Applying that second Title-page, to the Former Corrected Copy, w:^{ch} Ponder promised unto this Examinate, should be faithfully performed.[55]

The following day, Joan Darby, the wife of Ponder's printer, was deposed and signed the following minute:

Jan: 24. 167[3]. John Darby's wife
Saith, that in December ∧^{last} her husband being Constable went with Mr Lestranges man & Mr Ponder to the house of [blank space] Winter a Printer in Cocklane in an Alley neare Sepulchres Church, and there seized upon some sheets of a book called the Rehearsall Transprosed which were printed by the said Printer.[56]

[55] Leicestershire Record Office, Finch MSS, DG7, Box 4985, Bundle IX, p. 9/2. There is a partial transcript in Kelliher, *Andrew Marvell*, p. 108. See also HMC, *Report on the Manuscripts of the Late Allan George Finch, Esq.*, II, pp. 9–10; HMC *Appendix to Seventh Report*, pp. 517b–518a.

[56] Longleat House, Coventry MSS, vol. 11, f. 10.

Finally, Ponder was reexamined on the basis of his previous testimony (of which there is no known record) and evidence given by others and signed the following minute:

> Jan: 25. 167[3]. Mr Ponder being againe examined whether he knew of nobody but Dr Owen that had those proofs in their hands, saith that he knowes of nobody. M^{r}. Brome asked whether he did not say to a Bookseller that he might sell the Book, for he had those that would bring him off & justify it: he answers, that he ~~thou~~ said he ∧^{thought} had those that would bring him off. Being asked who these were, he named the Lord Chancellor & Earle Anglesey; and gaue this reason for it, because (as he said) they liked the Book; and the E. of Anglesey said, that the King was well pleased with it, and found no fault with it. Being asked whether he did not tell Mr Lestrange that if the Warden & Clerk of the Company would not enter the Book, the E. of Anglesey would cause them to be brought before the King & councell; he answers, that he doth not remember that he said such words, hauing no reason to use them. He confesses that Mr Lestr. ordered seuerall words in the Book to be altered, but that afterwards Lestrange allowed some of them at the request of one Mr Tomson & the said Ponder.[57]

These depositions, in conjunction with other documents, permit us to reconstruct the printing history of *RT.* The raid by Samuel Mearne took place on or about December 2, 1672, when the accounts kept by the wardens of the Stationers' Company record that £1.5s. "was spent on a Search for ye Rehearsall transposed [*sic*]."[58] Since the company had been in dispute with Ponder for several years over his printing of the *Protestant Almanack* and had incurred legal expenses as recently as September 1672, it is possible that the raid was a punitive strike aimed at Ponder's business and not at Marvell's book as such.[59] By the time of the raid, according to L'Estrange, "the

[57] LRO, Finch MSS, HMC, vol. 2, p. 10/1. See also HMC, *Report on the Manuscripts of the Late Allan George Finch, Esq.*, II, pp. 10–11.

[58] Stationers' Hall, Wardens' Accounts, December 2, 1672 (*Wardens' Accounts 1663–1837, Records of the Worshipful Company of Stationers,* ed. Robin Myers [Cambridge: Chadwyck-Healey, 1985], part VII, reel 76: unfoliated).

[59] Archbishop Sheldon ordered the company to stop Ponder's impression of the almanac in December 1667: see John Hetet, "A Literary Underground in Restoration England: Printers and Dissenters in the Context of Constraints, 1660–1689" (Ph.D. diss., University of Cambridge, 1987), p. 78; Stationers' Hall, Wardens' Accounts, "Sept: 3d [1672] Item given to the Comon Sergeant about Ponder &c 001 01 06."

first Impression [i.e., edition]" of *RT* had already been printed and "distributed" to booksellers so that what Mearne "seised at the Presse" was "two sheets of a second Impression [i.e., edition]."[60] The two sheets, T and X, were at different stages of production. After *72* went through the press, the forms of sheet X had been kept standing in case they were needed for a new edition. Now that X had been reprinted for *72a,* the forms were being dismantled so that the type could be reused, and all that was left was the pages of type from the outer form, individually tied awaiting distribution. Sheet T had been reset for *72a,* though printing had only just started, to judge from the rarity of surviving examples. The forms of T and the tied pages of X were stored, pending the outcome of negotiations at the earl of Anglesey's house in Drury Lane and at Stationers' Hall.

The parties involved all knew each other.[61] Ponder was banking on the support of Anglesey as well as Shaftesbury (lord chancellor as of November 17, 1672) when he made it part of his pitch for *RT* to one "Bookseller that he might sell the Book, for he had those that would bring him off & justify it." He had earlier published two works addressed to Anglesey by Sir Charles Wolseley, *The Unreasonableness of Atheism* (1669) and *The Reasonablenes of Scripture-Belief* (1672). L'Estrange had first come across Anglesey as a patron of dissent in 1662, when the printer of two seditious tracts by Anglesey's chaplain, Edward Bagshaw, confessed that "*he delivered* five hundred Copies *of each, into Mr. Bagshaw's own hand, in the house of the Earl of Anglesy.*"[62] In the matter of *RT,* however, Anglesey was speaking for the

[60] D. I. B. Smith mistakenly insists (pp. xxi–xxii) that what was seized was "two sheets of the second issue." This antedates the raid in the printing history of *RT* as a result of confusing an "issue" or "reissue" (composed of sheets printed from the original setting of type) with an "edition" (a separate printing of the work from a new setting of type); in the age of the hand press, an edition was usually the same thing as an "impression" (all the copies printed at any one time from a setting of type). For these terms, see P. Gaskell, *A New Introduction to Bibliography* (Oxford, 1972), pp. 315–16.

[61] Ponder, however, appears not to have known Marvell much before the publication of *RT.* In June 1682 Ponder deposed that he "knew & was acquainted with him the said Andrew Marvell for the space of five years or thereabouts before his decease [in August 1678]," Public Record Office C24/1069 [Part 2, No. 36], transcribed in Art Kavanagh, "Andrew Marvell 'in want of money:' The Evidence in *John Farrington v Mary Marvell,*" *Seventeenth Century* 17 (2002), 206–12. I am very grateful to Kavanagh for allowing me to cite from his article. It could have been Owen (several of whose works had been published by Ponder), Anglesey, or even Wolseley who introduced Marvell to Ponder.

[62] Roger L'Estrange, *Truth and Loyalty Vindicated, From the Reproches and Clamours*

king himself, who thought so well of the work that "he will not have it supprest."[63] While L'Estrange had to comply, he pointed out two passages on pages 244 and 310 reflecting on the king that were "not fit to be Licensed," and Anglesey allowed him "to Alter those places, letting the body of the discourse remayne." When L'Estrange probed further, professing dislike of changes made "without the Privity and Allowance of the Author," Anglesey cut him short with the assurance that while "he could not say any thing of the Author . . . such alterations might be made without him." Despite the narrowness of Anglesey's remit for censorship, L'Estrange made a series of changes immediately after leaving Drury Lane with Ponder. They were intended to take the sting out of Marvell's attack on the Anglican establishment, most notably when "he changed and struck out severall sharp Reflexions upon B.pp Laud, and Dr Parker" (see pp. 43, 97, 101, 121, 123, 144–45, 158, 175, 177, 183, 184, 193). Not only did these interventions lack Anglesey's approval, but they also crossed the king's view that "Parker has done him wrong, and this man has done him Right."

Anglesey and L'Estrange agreed that the license was to protect Ponder's commercial interest in *RT* "and not at all to Authorise the Publication of it." It was thus simply a prerequisite for having *RT* entered in the Stationers' Register. The day after the raid, the license was signed by a warden and delivered to the clerk, George Tokefield, at which point the plan broke down.[64] Tokefield refused to make the entry, persisting even after L'Estrange wrote on Ponder's behalf.[65] Anglesey also interviewed Tokefield and

---

of Mr. Edward Bagshaw. Together with A Further Discovery of the Libeller Himself, and his Seditious Confederates (London, 1662), p. 8. For Anglesey as "Friend" of the Baptist bookseller Francis Smith, see the letter to Smith from his wife, Elizabeth, October 10, 1661, PRO SP29/43/42, cited by Hetet, "A Literary Underground," p. 27.

63 Anglesey had discussed press issues with the king earlier in the year. On April 21, Anglesey recorded in his diary that he "heard Dr Tillotsons excellent sermon at Whitehall agt. ye papists" and the next day "moued" Charles to have it printed, "but I had long dispute wth ye king wch I will not mention he giuing no direction for ye printing" (British Library, Additional MS, 40860, f. 27).

64 Mearne later told the Lords Libels Committee that "The next day ^ after I had seized the Rehearsall transprosed Mr Le Estrange licensed it." HLRO, Committee Book, H.L., April 6, 1677, f. 197; see also HMC, *Ninth Report,* Appendix 2 (House of Lords MSS), p. 78b.

65 Mearne later produced the letter "to Mr Tokesfield from Mr L Estrange concning Licensing ye sd Booke," HLRO, Committee Book, H.L., April 6, 1677, f. 197.

one of the wardens and threatened to bring the whole matter before the king in council, and agreed to supply L'Estrange with "a Signification of his pleasure under his hand." But the pressure proved counterproductive; on December 16 the Court of Assistants placed the weight of the Stationers' Company behind its clerk: "Ordered, that the Book or Coppie Intituled the Rehearsall Transprosed be not Entered in the Register Booke of this Company to Mr Ponder, And that the Clerke to this Company be found harmless and Indempnified in his not entering the same."[66]

In the meantime Ponder was flouting the terms of the license. The effect of the censorship was to render the stock of *72* already "distributed" to booksellers potentially unsaleable. Rather than scrap most of *72* and take a heavy loss, Ponder opted for subterfuge, printing censored title pages (the imprint read simply, "*London,* Printed in the Year, 1672" [fig. 2]) to be collated with existing sheets, inserted as a cancel, or, as in the case of one bound copy, pasted over the old title page.[67] A manuscript note in a Folger copy of *RT* registers the speed of the operation: "The Preface of this book, or, Title of it, was altered, within one weeke after It was printed And the following words left out Printed for the Assignes of John Calvin, And Theodore Beza, and to bee sold At the Signe of the Kings last Indulgence."[68] This chimes with a newsletter, postmarked December 11, in which Benjamin Woodroffe informed the earl of Huntingdon that a book which "every one reades . . . called the *Rehearsall transprosed* . . . hath beene stopt from spreading, but is againe allowed to be bought."[69]

The ploy worked, up to a point. Within days, seemingly censored copies of *RT* were on sale. L'Estrange had only to glance at the text, however, to discover it "was not printed according to ye Corrections and Emendations of the Copy licensed," and the license was accordingly "withdrawn from the

66 Stationers' Hall, Court Book D, March 5, 1654, to October 24, 1679, f. 208v (part III, reel 56); see also Waste Books, Draft Minutes, July 8, 1668, to February 22, 1674, f. 93v (part III, reel 45).

67 Bodleian Library: 8°. C.118. Linc.: of the twenty-three copies collated by Smith and the present editor, only ten bear uncensored title pages.

68 Folger Library copy of *RT,* M878B, leaf facing title page. There is a residual ambiguity: was the title page printed one week after it was altered, or was the title page altered one week after it ("this book") was printed?

69 Huntington Library, R. R. Hastings MSS, HA 13627–13648. I owe this information to Tracey Tomlinson. See HMC, *Report on the Manuscripts of the late Reginald Rawdon Hastings, Esq.,* 2:160, where the letter is incorrectly dated November 1672.

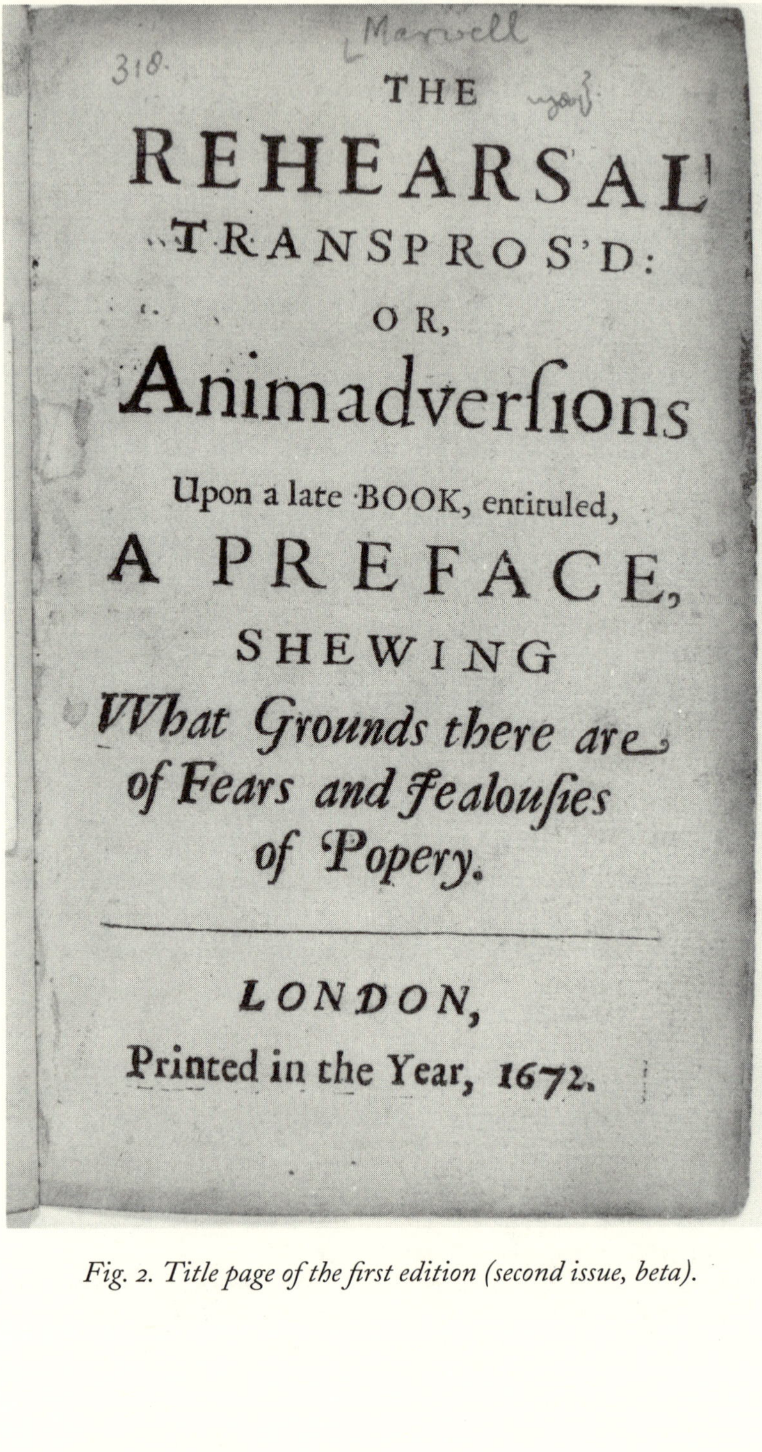

THE

REHEARSAL

TRANSPROS'D:

OR,

Animadversions

Upon a late BOOK, entituled,

A PREFACE,

SHEWING

What Grounds there are of Fears and Jealousies of Popery.

LONDON,

Printed in the Year, 1672.

Fig. 2. Title page of the first edition (second issue, beta).

Clarke of the Stationers," probably after the assistants met on 16 December.[70] Yet L'Estrange could not remain intransigent for long without displeasing his political masters, who favored the book. Ponder for his part could not presume further upon his patrons, having already placed Anglesey, who had agreed to some censorship, in a false position. Furthermore, now that *72* had been cleared off the shelves, Ponder was ready to proceed with *72a*, particularly since any delay would encourage piracy. Accordingly, when "a second license was desired by Ponder upon another Title-Page; the sayd License was granted expressly under the Limitations of the Former, and with condition of Applying that second Title-page, to the Former Corrected Copy."

A new title page was needed to differentiate the actually censored *72a* from the seemingly censored second issue of *72* and to allow Ponder to assert ownership. Adding the printer's initials and the bookseller's name and address to the place and date of publication would have sufficed, yet when *72a* appeared the imprint reintroduced the wording which L'Estrange had originally found offensive: "*London*, Printed by *J.D.* for the Assigns of *John Calvin* and *Theodore Beza*, at the sign of the *King's Indulgence*, on the South-side the Lake-*Lemane*; and sold by *N. Ponder* in *Chancery-Lane*, 1672" (see fig. 3). Since it is unlikely that Ponder had again defied L'Estrange, the latter must have relented when the second license was agreed or soon after. The likelihood is that this is what Ponder was referring to when he deposed that "M[r] Lestr. ordered seuerall words in the Book to be altered, but that afterwards Lestrange allowed some of them at the request of one M[r] Tomson & the said Ponder."[71]

This does not tell us when the printing of *72a* recommenced. What we do know is that John Darby's workers picked up exactly where they had left off. They began with sheet T, making the required changes in the forms with minimal resetting. Thus an allusion identifying Simon Patrick as the butt of a joke was cut from page 273. A reflection on the "pickthankness of the Clergy" on page 284 was softened by the insertion of "some of." And,

[70] This can be inferred from the fact that the entering or not of *RT* in the Stationers' Register was still a live issue when the assistants met, whereas entry would automatically have been precluded by lack of a license; see Johns, *Nature of the Book,* pp. 216–18; for earlier practice, see Cyndia Susan Clegg, *Press Censorship in Elizabethan England* (Cambridge, 1997), p. 27.

[71] It is likely that "Tomson" was not (as Smith suggests, p. xxiv, n.2) "perhaps one of the family of Thompsons with whom Marvell was friendly," but the printer Nathaniel Thompson (see below, p. 36).

finally, a tart observation on Laud's involvement in court politics on page 286 was replaced by an anodyne phrase and a series of dashes to fill out the space. Next they turned to sheet X, reusing the tied pages of the outer form, which were entirely unaffected by censorship. The required changes to pages 306 and 310 of the inner form were made as they were reset. L'Estrange's other changes were implemented as the sheets were reset page for page; some created minimal difficulties, such as the cutting of a word or two (for example, on pages 2 and 163), while others involved disruption spread over several pages (for example, the changes to page 204, which affected all page breaks and most paragraph breaks from pages 198 to 205). Ponder also retrieved the sheets of T and X seized by Mearne.[72] Since these were then mixed with those produced after censorship, the outcome was that many copies of *72a* went into circulation only partially censored. Among them, by a notable irony, was the one belonging to Simon Patrick; since gathering T was in its uncensored state he was able to read Marvell's joke at his expense![73]

Although *RT* had been relicensed, it still lacked an entry. Not being obliged to protect Ponder's copy from piracy, the stationers did nothing when a cheaper duodecimo edition, printed in smaller type on inferior paper, stole the market from his forthcoming *72a*. Ponder therefore turned to L'Estrange: not only had he expressly licensed the copy so that "it may not bee printed from him," but the pirated text was that of the uncensored *72*. According to Joan Darby, "Mr Lestranges man"—his deputy, Richard Jefferys—lent the surveyor's authority to a raid that seized "some sheets" of the pirated edition at John Winter's printing house in the latter part of December.[74]

[72] This was probably prior to the resumption of printing, since many fewer sheets of censored X were printed than would otherwise have been required for the second edition, to judge from the ratio of uncensored to censored gatherings in surviving copies: of the twenty copies collated by Smith and the present editor, only eight feature censored X.

[73] Cambridge University Library: Ely e.55, signed "S: [or J:] Patrick" on leaf opposite the title page (John Patrick often obtained books for his brother Simon).

[74] Hetet claims, on the basis of unspecified "indications," that Mearne had "a special interest in confiscating Ponder's edition because he had taken steps to pirate the popular work for his own pecuniary reasons," and personally "organised the illegal printing" by Winter: "A Literary Underground," p. 180. While the grandees of the Stationers' Company were certainly capable of such illicit practices (as Hetet has amply documented in "The Wardens' Accounts of the Stationers' Company," in *Economics of the*

That should have been an end of the matter. In January 1673, however, the case was reopened, in the process generating the depositions on which this narrative is based. Some tightening of press regulation was to be expected in advance of the parliamentary session due in February, but much of the activity was focused on Marvell's book. The Wardens' Accounts record the cost of "Coach-hire three times to whitehall & expenses about the Rehearsall transposed."[75] While Arlington pressured the wardens,[76] the assistants turned the screws on Marvell's collaborators; on January 15, Darby had to promise to take down one of his three presses, while six days later Ponder was threatened with prosecution "this next Hillary Tearme for Recovery of the debt due from him to this Company and the English Stock."[77] The action was stayed only on May 5, on condition that Ponder pay £28.2s. 6d, plus all legal costs.[78] Marvell too was targeted. When Ponder was asked "whether he knew of nobody but Dr Owen that had those proofs in their hands," it was a leading question aimed at flushing out the author of *RT.* The point is not that the authorities did not know who had written it—they almost certainly knew it was Marvell. What they wanted was for someone to go on the record to that effect. This may throw some light on Marvell's later allegation that "the License of my Book was recall'd, and the *Rehearsal Transprosed* was dubb'd a Theological Book, only to bring it under the verge of that Jurisdiction, on purpose that it might be prohibited," and that Parker "procured that I should be asked by good Authority whether the *Rehearsal Transpros'd* were of my doing, which I under my hand avowed" (*RT2,* pp. 250–51). But while it is probable there was an Anglican-inspired campaign against Marvell's book in January 1673, such an assault may possibly have been launched after mid-March, when the king cancelled the Declaration and so abandoned the policy of which Marvell had been the most conspicuous defender.

British Book Trade 1605–1939, ed. R. Myers and M. Harris [Cambridge, 1985], pp. 32–59), his reliance on Smith's chronology undermines his claims. Another pirated edition, also in duodecimo but this time passing itself off as "The second Impression, with Additions and Amendments," appeared in 1673. Neither of these pirated versions has featured in the preparation of the present edition.

[75] Stationers' Hall, Wardens' Accounts, January 24, 1673.

[76] Stationers' Hall, Wardens' Accounts, January 16, 1673: "Item paid wth Warden Roper Mr Roycroft to goe to the Lord Arlington about the Printers 000 12 06."

[77] Stationers' Hall, Court Book D, January 15 and 21, 1673, ff. 210v–211.

[78] Stationers' Hall, Court Book D, May 5, 1673, f. 215; see also Waste Books, Draft Minutes, May 5, 1673, f. 99v.

FIRST EDITION (FIRST ISSUE)

Title Page

THE/REHEARSAL/TRANSPROS'D:/Or,/Animadversions/Upon a late Book, Intituled,/A PREFACE/SHEWING/*What Grounds there are/ of Fears and Jealousies/ of* Popery.//*LONDON,* Printed by *A.B.* for the/Assigns of *John Calvin* and *Theodore Beza,* at the sign of the Kings Indul-/ gence, on the South-side of the *Lake/ Lemane.* 1672.

Collation

8°[A][1], B–X[8], Y[3] [[A] and Y1 separate leaves]. 164 leaves pp: [*2*] 1–189, 191, 192, 192–326 [=326]

Signatures

$(4)(-Y3, Y4)

Contents

[A]1r: T.P.; [A]1v: blank; B1r: Half title under a row of type ornaments: *Animadversions upon the/ Preface to Bishop* Bram-/hall's *Vindication &c./* Text; Y3v; FINIS.//ERRATA.[with list]

Copies Examined

B1	British Library: C.131.b.22
C1	Cambridge University Library: Williams 509[1]
H	Hull University, Brynmor Jones Library: sPR3456R3
S1	Sion College Collection, Lambeth Palace Library: A69.3/M.36.4
S2	Sterling Library, University of London: [S.L.] I.[Marvell, A.-1672]
U	Ushaw College, Durham: XIX.E.11.16
W1	Worcester College Library, Oxford: GG.7.7

There are two states of the title page: the first with the spelling *Leman* (copies S1, S2, and W1), and the second with the spelling *Lemane* (copies B1, C1, H, and U).

FIRST EDITION (SECOND ISSUE)

Title Page α

THE/REHEARSAL/TRANSPROS'D:/Or,/Animadversions/Upon a late Book, Intituled,/A PREFACE/SHEWING/*What Grounds there are*/*of Fears and Jealousies*/*of* Popery.//*LONDON,*/Printed in the Year, 1672.

Title Page β

THE/REHEARSAL/TRANSPROS'D:/OR,/Animadversions/Upon a late BOOK, entituled,/A PREFACE,/SHEWING/*What Grounds there are*/*of Fears and Jealousies*/*of Popery.*//*LONDON,*/Printed in the Year, 1672.

Collation, Signatures, Pagination, and Contents

Identical to the first issue.

Copies Examined

B2	Bodleian Library: 8°.C.118 Linc.
B3	British Library: Cup.406.j.5
C2	Cambridge University Library: Keynes P.1.13
D1	Dr Williams's Library: 1024.E.5
E	Emmanuel College Library, Cambridge: S14.4.15
K	Kingston upon Hull Local Studies Library: Marvell Collection
L	Lambeth Palace Library: H5136
O1	Oxford English Faculty Library: XK13.1[Reh](formerly Rar.D234)
P	Pepys Library, Magdalene College, Cambridge: PL.710

Title page α was used for L and O1; title page β for B2 (pasted over the second state of the title page of the first issue), B3, C2, D1, E, K, and P. Smith (p. xxvii) notes two significant variants in gathering Y at pp. 323 and 324, the second of which (the omission of "his," as in B1, B2, C1, D1, H, and U) was transmitted to *72a*.

Smith states (p. xxi and n. 2) that *72* was probably printed by Anne Brewster, largely on the strength of the phrase "Printed by *A.B.*" in the mock imprint of the first issue (even though these are no less likely to be dummy initials), and her later connection with Marvell's *Account of the*

Growth of Popery.[79] Yet the only printers we know worked for Ponder in 1672 are John Darby, who put his initials to *72a,* and Nathaniel Thompson and Thomas Ratcliffe (partners from 1672–78), who printed the other two books published by Ponder that year: Henry Danvers, *Theopolis, or the City of God,* and Wolseley, *The Reasonablenes of Scripture-Belief.* It was probably Thompson who helped Ponder to persuade L'Estrange to relax the censorship of *RT,* while Ratcliffe was later suspected of involvement in the printing of *Mr. Smirke.*[80] Smith also assumes (p. xxiv, n. 3) that when Ponder deposed that Owen alone handled the proofs of *RT* he was referring to *72a,* when it is just as likely to have been *72.* In either case, Owen was presumably acting for Marvell so as to preserve his anonymity. It is a striking fact that, while *RT* provides one of the best-documented cases of early-modern censorship, Marvell's name is absent from the record.[81]

SECOND EDITION ("SECOND IMPRESSION")

Title Page α

THE/REHEARSAL/TRANSPROS'D;/Or,/Animadversions/Upon a late Book, Intituled,/A PREFACE/SHEWING/ *What Grounds there are/ of Fears and Jealousies/ of* Popery.//The second Impression, with Additions/and Amendments.// *London,* Printed by *J. D.* for the Assigns of/ *John Calvin* and *Theodore Beza,* at the sign/of the *King's Indulgence,* on the South-side/the Lake-*Lemane*; and sold by *N. Ponder* in/ *Chancery-Lane,* 1672.

[79] Hetet insists that Smith is wrong about Brewster's involvement, though without explaining why: "A Literary Underground," p. 180. Since it was usual for those who printed the first edition to print subsequent ones (see *An Exact Narrative of the Tryal and Condemnation of John Twyn for Printing and Dispersing of a Treasonable Book* [London, 1664], p. 43), the presumption must be that Darby was responsible for both editions, especially since he had the standing forms of X.

[80] On February 23, 1677, the Lord Libels Committee were informed that "Thomas Ratcliff and Nathaniel Thompson, copartners in printing, might be persons much to be suspected for printing unlicensed books and pamphlets." HMC, *Ninth Report,* Appendix 2 (House of Lords MSS), p. 73a.

[81] A deposition by John Darby, in which he "Saith, as he understood Ponder said Mr Marvel was the Author of the Book," that Smith (p. xxiii, n.2, citing HMC, *Fourth Report,* p. 234) took to refer to *RT,* actually relates to Marvell's *Mr. Smirke* four years later; Longleat House, Coventry MSS, vol. 11, f. 128 (May 18, 1676).

Title Page β

THE/REHEARSAL/TRANSPROS'D;/OR,/Animadversions/Upon a late BOOK,/INTITULED,/*A* PREFACE, *shewing/what Grounds there are/ of Fears and Jealousies of/ Popery.*//The second Impression, with Additions/and Amendments.//*LONDON,* Printed by *J.D.* for the Assigns of/ *John Calvin* and *Theodore Beza* at the sign of/the *King's Indulgence* on the South-side of/the Lake *Lemane*; and Sould by *N. Ponder*/in *Chancery Lane,* 1672.

Collation

8°: $[A]^2$, B-X^8, Y^4; 166 leaves pp. [*4*] 1-229, 219, 232–64, 165, 266–326. [=326] (pp. 161–240 and 257–72 in round, the rest in square brackets.)

Signatures

$ (4) (-Y3, Y4)

Contents

[A]1: Blank; [A]2r: Title; [A]2v: "An Advertisement from/the Bookseller," signed "N.P." between rows of type ornaments: *This Book having wrought it self thorow/many difficulties, it hath newly incoun-/tred with that of a Counterfeit Impression in* 12°/*under the Title and pretence of* the 2d Edition/ Corrected. *Whereas in truth that Impression/is so far from having been Corrected, that it doth/grossly and frequently corrupt both the Sence and/Words of the Coppy.*; B1r: Half title, under a row of type ornaments: *Animadversions upon the/Preface to Bishop* Bram-/hall's *Vindication, &c.*/Text; Y3v: // *FINIS.*//

Copies Examined

B4	Bodleian Library: Ashm.1591
B5	Bodleian Library: Vet.A3.f.531
B6	Bodleian Library: Vet.A3.f.628
B7	British Library: G.19514
B8	British Library: 1485.k.17
B9	British Library: 1019.e.12
C3	Cambridge University Library: F.12.10
C4	Cambridge University Library: Ely e.55
D2	Dean and Chapter Library, Durham Cathedral: K.III.47
D3	Dr Williams's Library: 5614.G.9

D4	Durham University Library, Archives and Special Collections: Routh XV.C.29
D5	Durham University Library, Archives and Special Collections: uncatalogued duplicate, bequest of Professor C. E. Whiting
O2	Oxford English Faculty Library: XK13.1[Reh] (formerly Rar.D123)
S3	Sion College Collection, Lambeth Palace Library: A69.3/M.36.(4)
S4	Sterling Library, University of London: [S.L.] I.[Marvell, A.-1672]
W2	Worcester College Library, Oxford: FF.1.21
W3	Wren Library, Trinity College, Cambridge: I.5.68

Title page α was used for B5, B7, B9, C4, D2, S4, W2, and W3; title page β for B4, B6, B8, C3, D3, D4, D5, O2, and S3. The type ornaments used for Ponder's "Advertisement" on the verso of the title page differ as between the two states. Smith noted the variants in gatherings E (p. 53, but overlooking p. 60), F (p. 67), G (p. 83), K (pp. 134, 135, 138, 142, 143), M (p. 161), and Q (pp. 228, 237, 240).

As we have seen, gatherings T and X each exist in two states. Uncensored T—of which Smith was unaware—can be seen in copies C4, D4, Edinburgh University Library: B.248.83 (=the copy microfilmed in *Early English Books, 1641–1700,* reel 1235:1), and Princeton: Ex 3850.3.375. Uncensored X can be seen in B4, B5, B8, B9, C3, C4, D2, D4, O2, S4, and W2. Although not subjected to censorship, gathering Y, which consists of a half sheet of eight pages (the last two of them blank), still shows signs of considerable disruption in the press. The evidence suggests that the pages were imposed in two forms rather than one.[82] But in both cases, while the pages of type remained relatively stable, the skeletons of the forms were, for whatever reason, modified during printing.[83]

[82] For the difference between a half sheet imposed for work and turn and two half sheets worked together, see Gaskell, *New Introduction,* p. 83.

[83] The outer form of Y (pp. 321, 324, 325) features two different settings of the page numbers; in one of these settings (copies B5, D2, and D5), p. 321 is also misnumbered 312. (To complicate matters further, the signature letter Y on p. 321 can be found in three different positions and the catchword in two, but the incidence of these does not fully correlate with the settings of the page numbers.) Only B6 has the stop-press corrections on Y2v–Y3 (pp. 324–25). The inner form of Y (pp. 322, 323, 326) also features two

The cancel of M8 (pp. 175–76) found in some copies (B5, D3, S4) baffled Smith, who (p. xxix) could find "no political reason" why the pages should have been reset. But he missed the obvious typographical explanation. Halfway down p. 176 in both editions, Marvell begins the extensive quotations from John Hales's *Tract Concerning Schisme and Schismaticks* which continue through to p. 183. In *72*, these are set in double quotation marks with diples. The compositor for *72a* decided to set the material in italics, but these took up less space and by the time he reached the bottom of the page material was being pulled across from p. 177, the start of sheet N. Even so he set the first two lines of p. 177 in italic (as in copies B4, B6, B8, C3, C4, D2, D4, and W2; overlooked by Smith) before realizing that there would not be enough italic type to set a quotation of this length and that the pagination of the sheet, and hence of the volume, would be disrupted. The top of p. 177 was corrected, reverting to quotation marks. The Hales material was now partly in italics and partly not, so M8 was also reset with quotation marks and diples replacing italics. Copies B5, D3, and S4 feature both the cancel and the corrected state of p. 177; B7, B9, D5, O2, S3, and W3 feature the latter but not the former.

The attention to aesthetic detail implicit in the cancel is one sign that the printers were no longer working under pressure now that the book was licensed. Another is that Marvell was prepared to insert material in sheet N, which was otherwise undisturbed by censorship, despite the extra work this created for the compositors. In this case, creating space for the new copy added to p. 192, involved the elimination of a paragraph break and changes to page breaks from p. 188 onward. The purely voluntary nature of Marvell's intervention underpins the rationale for adopting *72a* rather than *72* for the present edition. We have registered additions as between # #, and deletions as between ⟨ ⟩.

All editors are indebted to their predecessors—in my case, this means principally D. I. B. Smith, whose heroic labors on the Clarendon Press edition in turn lightened the burden for Keith Walker and Frank Kermode in their Oxford Authors edition of the first part of *The Rehearsal Transpros'd.* Collaborating with Annabel Patterson on this edition as well as other

settings of the page numbers; additionally, in one setting (copies B4, B7, C3, and O2), the rule above "FINIS." on p. 326 is straight while in the other setting it is uneven. There is only one minor textual variant, at Y2 (p. 323), but the incidence of this does not correlate with the settings of the page numbers.

Marvell projects has been a pleasure and an intellectually rewarding—at times, exhilarating—experience. I have also incurred many obligations to my fellow students of Marvell: Warren Chernaik, Neil Keeble, the late Jeremy Maule, Nicholas von Maltzahn, and Nigel Smith. For archival and other forms of assistance, I am very grateful to Ian Doyle, Mark Goldie, Paul Hammond, Art Kavanagh, Peter Lindenbaum, James Loxley, Richard Maber, Paul Mathole, Robin Myers, and Tracey Tomlinson. I owe a particular debt to my former colleague at Royal Holloway, John Creaser, who read and commented on an early draft of the introduction with his characteristic scrupulousness. I also benefited greatly from the response to my findings from audiences at the conference on the Republic of Letters 2000 held at St Catherine's College, Oxford, the History and Theory Seminar at the University of Sussex, the Early Modern Group at the University of Durham, and the London Renaissance Seminar at Birkbeck College.

Various institutions have supported and encouraged me in my work. The English Department at Royal Holloway, University of London, has been generous both in terms of sabbatical leave and in providing computing facilities. Most of all, however, I must thank the Leverhulme Trust for the award of a Research Fellowship which allowed me spend the whole of 1999 working on the project. Finally, the staff at several libraries and archives have been unfailingly helpful: the Bodleian Library, Oxford; the British Library, London; the rare books room of the Cambridge University Library; Dr Williams's Library, London; the Dean and Chapter Library, Durham Cathedral; Archives and Special Collections, Durham University Library; Emmanuel College Library, Cambridge; the House of Lords Record Office, London; the Brynmor Jones Library, Hull University; Kingston-upon-Hull Local Studies Library; Lambeth Palace Library, London; the Leicestershire Record Office; the palaeography room at the University of London Library; Oxford English Faculty Library; the Pepys Library, Magdalene College, Cambridge; the Public Record Office, London; Worcester College Library, Oxford; and the Wren Library, Trinity College, Cambridge.

THE REHEARSAL TRANSPROS'D;

Or,

Animadversions

Upon a late Book, Intituled,

A PREFACE
SHEWING
What Grounds there are
of Fears and Jealousies
of Popery.

The Second Impression, with Additions
and Amendments.

London, Printed by J. D. for the Assigns of
John Calvin and *Theodore Beza,* at the sign
of the *King's Indulgence,* on the South-side
the Lake-*Lemane*; and sold by *N. Ponder* in
Chancery-Lane, 1672.

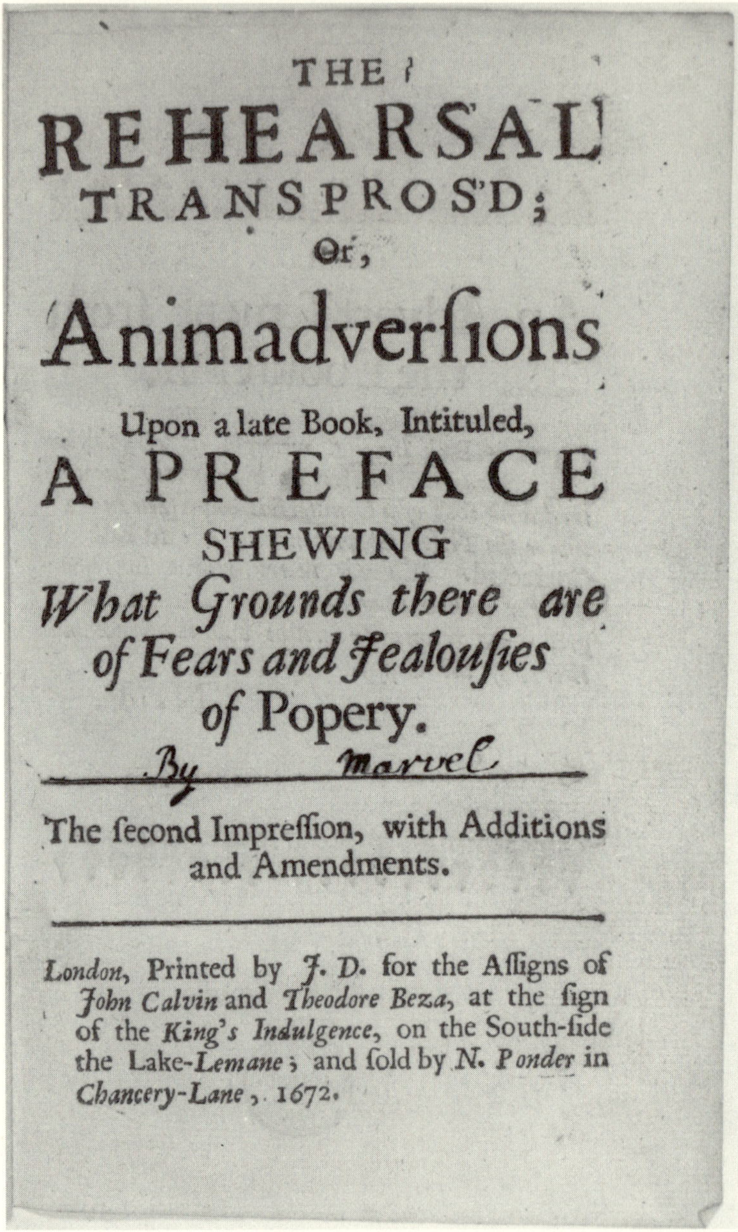

THE
REHEARSAL TRANSPROS'D;
Or,
Animadverſions
Upon a late Book, Intituled,
A PREFACE
SHEWING
What Grounds there are of Fears and Jealouſies of Popery.

By Marvel

The ſecond Impreſſion, with Additions and Amendments.

London, Printed by *J. D.* for the Aſſigns of *John Calvin* and *Theodore Beza*, at the ſign of the *King's Indulgence*, on the South-ſide the Lake-*Lemane*; and ſold by *N. Ponder* in *Chancery-Lane*, 1672.

Fig. 3. Title page of the second edition, or "second Impression" (alpha).

Animadversions upon the Preface to Bishop Bramhall's Vindication, &c.

THe Author of this Preface had first writ a *Discourse of Ecclesiastical Policy*; after that, *A Defence and Continuation of the Ecclesiastical Policy*; and there he concludes his Epistle to the Reader in these words: *But if this be the Penance I must undergo for the wantonness of my Pen, to answer the impertinent and slender Exceptions of every peevish and disingenuous Caviller; Reader, I am reformed from my incontinency of Scribling, and do here heartily bid thee an Eternal Farewel.*[1] Now this Expression lyes open to his own *Dilemma* against the Nonconformists confessing in their prayers to God such heinous Enormities. For if he will not accept his own Charge, his Modesty [1] is all impudent and counterfeit: or, if he will acknowledg it, why then he had been before, and did still remain upon Record, the same ⟨lewd,⟩ wanton and incontinent Scribler.

But however, I hop'd he had been a Clergy-man of Honour, and that when herein the World and he himself were now so fully agreed in the censure of his Writings, he would have kept his word; or at least that his Pen would not so soon have created us a disturbance of the same nature, and so far manifested how indifferent he is as to the business either of Truth or Eternity. But the Author, alas, instead of his own, was fallen now into Amaryllis's Dilemma:[2] (I perceive the Gentleman hath travelled by his remembring *Chi lava la testa al asino perde il sapone*,[3] and therefore hope I may without Pedantry quote the words in her own *whining*[4] Italian,)

S'il peccar è si dolce e'l non peccar si necessario,
O troppo imperfetta Natura che ripugni a la Legge. [2]
O troppo dura Legge che Natura offendi.

If to scrible be so sweet, and not to scrible be so necessary;
O too frail Inclination, that contradictest[5] *Obligation:*
O too severe Obligation, that offendest Inclination.[6]

[1] *But if . . . Farewel:* Parker, *Defence,* Preface, A8.

[2] Amaryllis's Dilemma: *Defence,* p. 196. Amarylli is the heroine of Guarini's pastoral tragicomedy, *Il Pastor Fido* (A, 1602; p. 96, #140).

[3] *Chi lava . . . sapone:* Italian proverb: "Who washes the ass's head wastes soap." This appears, with the appropriate illustration, in the *Proverbi Figurati* of Guiseppe Maria Mitelli (Bologna, 1678). Marvell is quoting Parker, *Discourse,* xii.

[4] *Preface,* A2v.

[5] *contradictest* 72a] *contradicteth* 72.

[6] *Il Pastor Fido,* 3.4.19–24: "If to sin is so sweet, and not to sin is so necessary, O too frail Nature that rejects the Law, O too severe Law that offends against Nature."

For all his Promise to write no more, I durst alwaies have laid Ten pound to a Crown on Natures side. And accordingly he hath now blessed us with, as he calls it, *A Preface, shewing what Grounds there are of Fears and Jealousies of Popery.*

It will not be unpleasant to hear him begin his Story. *The ensuing Treatise of Bishop Bramhall's*[7] *being somewhat superannuated, the* Bookseller *was very sollicitous to have it set off with some Preface that might recommend it to the Genius of the Age, and reconcile it to the present Juncture of Affairs.*[8] A pretty task indeed: That is as much as to say, To trick up the good old Bishop in a yellow Coif[9] and a Bulls-head,[10] that he [3] may be fit for the Publick, and appear in Fashion. In the mean time 'tis what I alwayes presaged: From a Writer of Books, our Author is already dwindled[11] to a Preface-monger, and from Prefaces I am confident he may in a short time be improved to endite Tickets for the Bear-garden.[12] But the Bookseller I see was a cunning Fellow, and knew his Man. For who so proper as a young Priest to sacrifice to the Genius of the Age; yea, though his Conscience were the Offering? And none more ready to nick a juncture of Affairs than a malapert[13] Chaplain; though not one indeed of a hundred but dislocates them in the handling. And yet our Author is very maidenly, and condescends to his Bookseller not without some reluctance, as being, forsooth, first of all *none of the most zealous Patrons of the Press.*[14]

Though he hath so lately forfeited his Credit, yet herein I dare believe him: For the Press hath ought[15] him a shame a long time, and is but now beginning to pay off the Debt. The Press [4] (that *villanous*[16] Engine)

[7] *Bishop Bramhall:* John Bramhall (1594–1663), archbishop of Armagh, a conservative, as indicated by his *Vindication of himself... from the Presbyterian Charge of Popery,* published posthumously in 1672, probably at Parker's instigation, with the offending *Preface.*

[8] *The ensuing... Affairs: Preface,* A2.

[9] yellow Coif: a coif was a close-fitting cap, or ecclesiastical headdress. Perhaps Parker wore a yellow one, since Marvell mentions one in *RT2,* p. 232 below.

[10] Bulls-head: false frizzled hair, usually worn by women.

[11] dwindled Ed.] dwinled 72, 72a.

[12] Bear-garden: Bear-baiting, made illegal in 1642, was revived at the Restoration. The chief bear-garden was on the south side of the Thames.

[13] malapert: presumptuous, impudent.

[14] *none... Press: Preface,* A2.

[15] ought: owed.

[16] *villanous: Preface,* A4; *Discourse,* p. 137.

invented much about the same time with the Reformation, that hath done more mischief to the Discipline of our Church, than all the Doctrine can make amends for. 'Twas an happy time when all Learning was in Manuscript, and some little Officer, like our Author, did keep the Keys of the Library. When the Clergy needed no more knowledg than to read the Liturgy, and the Laity no more Clerkship than to save them from Hanging.[17] But now, since Printing came into the World, such is the mischief, that a Man cannot write a Book but presently he is answered. Could the Press but once be conjured to obey only an *Imprimatur,*[18] our Author might not disdain *perhaps*[19] to be one of its most zealous Patrons. There have been wayes found out to banish Ministers, to fine not only the People, but even the Grounds and Fields[20] where they assembled in Conventicles:[21] But no Art yet could prevent these seditious meetings of Letters. Two or three brawny Fellows in a Corner,[22] with meer Ink and [5] Elbow-grease, do more harm than an *hundred Systematical*[23] *Divines*[24] with their *sweaty Preaching.*[25] And, which is a strange thing, the very Spunges,[26] which one would think should rather deface and blot out the whole Book, and were antiently used to that purpose, are become now the Instruments to make things legible. Their ugly Printing-Letters, that look but like so many rotten-Teeth, How oft have they been pull'd out by B. and L. the Publick-

[17] Clerkship . . . Hanging: a reference to the notorious neck-verse, usually the opening of Psalm 51, which accused men would recite to claim benefit of clergy and hence save themselves from execution.

[18] *Imprimatur:* "Let it be printed"; the formal notification that a book had been licensed as fit to print.

[19] *perhaps: Defence,* p. 160.

[20] Grounds and Fields: cf. Marvell's letter of March 10, 1670, to Mayor Tripp describing the new penalties in the revised Conventicle Act: "Whoever wittingly & willingly suffer such meeting in his house barn woods or grounds [shall be fined] 50 li." (*P&L,* 2:102).

[21] Conventicles: forbidden religious meetings, especially of dissenters; the Conventicles Act of 1664 defined a conventicle as any meeting of more than five persons beyond the members of one family. The penalties, as made harsher in 1670 (see *P&L,* 2:102), were fines (including fines for constables, jailors, etc. who failed to do their duty), imprisonment, and, for a third offense, banishment to the American colonies.

[22] Corner: a slang word for an illegal printing shop.

[23] *Systematical* 72 Errata, 72a] *Schismatical,* 72.

[24] *hundred . . . Divines: Discourse,* p. 253.

[25] *sweaty Preaching: Defence,* p. 188.

[26] Spunges: inking pads.

Tooth-drawers![27] and yet these rascally Operators of the Press have got a trick to fasten them again in a few minutes, that they grow as firm a Set, and as biting and talkative as ever. O *Printing!* how hast thou disturb'd the Peace of Mankind! that Lead, when moulded into Bullets, is not so mortal as when founded into Letters! There was a mistake sure in the Story of Cadmus;[28] and the Serpents Teeth which he sowed, were nothing else but the Letters[29] which he invented. The first Essay that was made towards this Art, was in single Characters upon Iron, where-[6]with of old they stigmatized Slaves and remarkable Offenders; and it was of good use sometimes to brand a Schismatick. But a *bulky*[30] Dutchman[31] diverted it quite from its first Institution, and contriving those innumerable *Syntagmes*[32] of Alphabets, hath pestred the World ever since with the *gross Bodies of their German Divinity.*[33] One would have thought in Reason that a Dutchman at least might have contented himself only with the Wine-press.

But, next of all, our Author, beside his aversion from the Press, alledges, that *he is as much concerned as De-Wit,*[34] *or any of the High and Mighty Burgomasters, in matters of a Closer and more Comfortable Importance to himself and his own Affairs.*[35] And yet who ever shall take the pains to read over his Preface, will find that it intermeddles with the King, the Succession, the Privy-Council, Popery, Atheism, Bishops, Ecclesiastical Govern-

[27] B. and L.: a cropped marginal MS note in B7 identifies them as "[B]erkenhead L'strange"; i.e., Sir John Birkenhead (1616–79), pamphleteer and satirist, employed after the Restoration to search out unlicensed printers (*CSPD,* Jan. 6. 1662, p. 237); and Sir Roger L'Estrange (1616–1704), Tory propagandist and Surveyor of the Press from 1662. [S]

[28] Cadmus: the legendary founder of Thebes. See Ovid, *Metamorphoses,* 3:101–30.

[29] Serpents Teeth . . . Letters: Marvell owed this analogy to Milton, *Areopagitica;* "I know [books] are as lively, and as vigorously productive, as those fabulous Dragons teeth; and being sown up and down, may chance to spring up armed men." (*CPW,* 2:492).

[30] *bulky: Preface,* A6.

[31] Dutchman: Laurens Koster (c. 1370–1440), a Dutch printer, recognized as one of the inventors of the art. [S]

[32] *Syntagmes:* systematically arranged treatises; see *Preface,* A6.

[33] *gross . . . Divinity: Defence,* p. 312.

[34] *De-Wit:* John de Witt (1625–72), leader of the Dutch Republican party against the princes of the House of Orange. In August 1672, he and his brother Cornelius were murdered by a mob at the Hague, thereby rendering Parker's sneer especially distasteful. Marvell reported the event to William Popple (*P&L,* 2:327).

[35] *he is . . . own Affairs: Preface,* A2.

ment, and above all with Nonconformity, and J.O.[36] A man would wonder what this thing should be of a *Closer Importance*; But being *more comfor-*[7]*table* too, I conclude it must be one of these three things; either his Salvation, or a Benefice, or a Female. Now as to Salvation he could not be so much concern'd: for that care was over; there hath been a course taken to insure all that are on his bottom. And he is yet surer of a Benefice; or else his Patrons must be very ungrateful. He cannot have deserved less than a Prebend[37] for his first Book, a *Sine-cure*[38] for his second, and for his third a Rectorship, although it were that of Malmsbury.[39] Why, then of necessity it must be a Female. For, that I confess might have been a sufficient excuse from writing of Prefaces, and against the importunity of the Book-seller. 'Twas fit that all business should have given place to the work of Propagation. Nor was there any thing that could more closely import him, than that the Race and Family of the Railers should be perpetuated among Mankind. Who could in reason expect that a man should in the same moments undertake the labour of an Author and a Father? *Ne-*[8]*vertheless, he saith, he could not but yield so far as to improve every fragment of time that he could get into his own disposal, to gratify the Importunity of the Bookseller.* Was ever Civility graduated up and inhanc'd to such a value! His Mistris her self could not have endeared a Favour so nicely, nor granted it with more sweetness.

Was the Bookseller more Importunate,
or the Author more Courteous?
The Author was the Pink of Courtesie, the
Bookseller the Bur of Importunity.

And so, not being able to shake him off, *this,* he saith, *hath brought forth this Preface, such an one as it is; for how it will prove, he himself neither is, nor (till 'tis too late) ever shall be a competent Judge, in that it must be ravish'd out of his hands before his thoughts can possibly be cool enought to review*[40] *or correct the Indecencies either of its stile or contrivance.*[41] He is now growing a very

[36] J.O.: John Owen (1616–83), dissenting minister, leader of the Independents, theological controversialist. In 1669, he answered Parker's *Discourse* with *Truth and Innocence Vindicated.* See Introduction.

[37] Prebend: ecclesiastical stipend.

[38] *Sine-cure:* an ecclesiastical office with no duties attached to it.

[39] Malmsbury: birthplace of Thomas Hobbes, author of *Leviathan* (1651), with whom Marvell liked to ally Parker.

[40] *review* Ed., Parker] *revive* 72, 72a.

[41] *hath . . . contrivance: Preface,* A2v.

Enthusiast himself. No Nonconformist-Minister, as it seems, could have spoke more *extempore.* I see he is not so civil to his Readers as he was to his Bookseller: [9] and so A.C. and James Collins[42] be gratified, he cares not how much the rest of the World be disobliged. Some Man that had less right to be fastidious and confident, would, before he exposed himself in publick, both have cool'd his Thoughts, and corrected his Indecencies: or would have considered whether it were necessary or wholesom that he should write at all. Forasmuch as one of the Antient Sophists (they were a kind of Orators of his Form) kill'd himself with declaming while he had a Bone in his Throat,[43] and J.O. was still in being. *Put up your Trumpery good noble Marquess.*[44] But there was no holding him. Thus it must be and no better, when a man's Phancy is up, and his Breeches are down; when the Mind and the Body make contrary Assignations, and he hath both a Bookseller at once and a Mistris to satisfie: Like Archimedes,[45] into the Street he runs out naked with his Invention. And truly, if at any time, we might now pardon this Extravagance and Rapture of our Author; when he was pearch'd upon [10] the highest Pinacle of Ecclesiastical Felicity, being ready at once to asswage his Concupiscence, and wreck his Malice.

But yet he knows not which way his Mind will work it self and its thoughts.[46] This is Bayes[47] the Second.—*'Tis no matter for the Plot—The Intrigo was out*

[42] A.C. and James Collins: Andrew Clark was a printer in Aldersgate, and James Collins a bookseller at the King's Head, Westminster Hall. [S] Marvell is quoting from the title page of Parker's *Preface.*

[43] one of the . . . Throat: The sophist Niger, sophisteuein in Galatia, having heard another sophist speak, choked on a bone but insisted on delivering his own speech in reply. A doctor removed the bone, but Niger died later as a result of the operation. See Plutarch, *Moralia* 131A, "De tuenda sanitate praecepta." [CW]

[44] *Put . . . Marquess:* originally "Put up thy wife's trumpery, good noble Marquis," from *The Session of Poets,* c. 1668, attributed to Buckingham or Rochester. The marquis was William Cavendish, duke of Newcastle, who is mocked for his much-published wife, Margaret Cavendish. Marvell must have seen the poem in manuscript. See *POAS,* vol. 1, ed. George de F. Lord (New Haven, 1965), p. 333.

[45] Archimedes: mathematician of Syracuse (287–212 B.C.), employed by King Hiero to solve many mechanical problems. In his bathtub, he discovered hydrostatics, or how to measure bulk by water displacement (the Archimedes principle), hence the anecdote of his running naked through the streets of Syracuse shouting *Eureka.*

[46] *which way . . . thoughts: Preface,* A2v.

[47] Bayes: the foolish playwright in Buckingham's *Rehearsal* (1672). See Introduction. The apt nickname, originally intended for Dryden, stuck to Parker irrevocably.

of his head—But you'l apprehend it better when you see't.[48] Or rather, he is like Bayes his Actors, *that could not guess what humour they were to be in: whether angry, melancholly, merry, or in Love.*[49] Nay, insomuch that he saith, *he is neither Prophet nor Astrologer enough to foretell.*[50] Never Man certainly was so unacquainted with himself. And, indeed, 'tis part of his discretion to avoid his acquaintance, and tell him as little of his mind as may be: for he is a dangerous fellow. But I must ask his pardon if I treat him too homely. It is his own fault that misled me at first, by concealing his quality under such vulgar comparisons as *De-wit* and the *Burgomasters.* I now see it all along; This can be no less a man than Prince [11] Volscius[51] himself, in dispute betwixt his Boots which way his mind will *work it self*; whether Love shall detain him with his *Closer Importance, Parthenope, whose Mother, Sir, sells Ale by the Town-wall*: or Honour shall carry him *to head the Army that lies concealed for him at Knightsbridge,*[52] and to encounter J.O.

> *Go on cryes Honour: tender Love saith Nay.*
> *Honour aloud commands, Pluck both Boots on.*
> *But safer Love doth whisper, Put on none.*[53]

And so now when it comes that he is *not Prophet nor Astrologer enough to foretell* what he will do, 'tis just,

> *For as bright Day, with black approach of Night,*
> *Contending, makes a doubtful puzzling Light;*
> *So does my Honour and my Love together,*
> *Puzzle me so, I am resolv'd on neither.*[54] [12]

Yet no Astrologer could possibly have more advantage and opportunity to make a Judgment. For he knew the very minute of the Conception of his Preface, which was immediately upon His Majesties issuing his Declaration of Indulgence to Tender Consciences. Nor could he be ignorant of the moment when it was brought forth. And I can so far refresh his memory, that it came out in the Dog-dayes,

[48] *The Intriguo . . . see it: Rehearsal* (1672), act 1, scene 1, pp. 3, 6.

[49] *that could not . . . Love: Rehearsal,* p. 5.

[50] *he is . . . foretell: Preface,* A2v.

[51] Prince Volscius: the mock-heroic protagonist of the play that Bayes rehearses.

[52] *Parthenope . . . Town-wall: Rehearsal,* act 3, scene 2, p. 29.

[53] *Go on . . . none: Rehearsal,* act 3, scene 2, p. 29.

[54] *For as . . . neither: Rehearsal,* p. 30.

—the Season hot, and She too near:
O mightly Love! J.O. will be undone.[55]

According to the Rule in Davenant's *Ephemerides*;[56] *But the heads which at this moment, and under the present Schemes and Aspects of the Heavens he intends to treat of* (pure Sidrophel)[57] *are these two: First, Something of the Treatise it self. Secondly, of the seasonableness of its publication: and this, unless his Humour jade him* ('tis come to a Dog-trot already) *will lead him further into the Argument as it relates to the present state of things, and from thence 'tis odds but he shall take occasion to bestow some Animadversions upon one J.O.*[58] There's no trusting him. [13] He doubtless knew from the beginning what he intended. And so too all his story of the Bookseller, and all the *Volo Nola's,* and *shall-I, shall-I's* betwixt them, was nothing but fooling: And he now all along owns himself to be the Publisher, and alledges the slighter and the main reasons that induced him. Would he had told us so at first; for then he had saved me thus much of my labour. Though, as it chances, it lights not amiss on our Author, whose delicate stomach could not brook that J.O. should say, *he had prevailed with himself, much against his inclination, to bestow a few (and those idle) hours upon examining his Book*:[59] and yet he himself stumbles so notoriously upon the very same fault at his own threshold.

But now from this Preamble he falls into his Preface to Bishop Bramhall: though indeed like Bayes his Prologue, that would have serv'd as well for an Epilogue, I do not see but the Preface might have past as well for a Postscript, or the Headstall[60] for a Crooper.[61] And our Authors *Divinity*

[55] *the Season . . . undone:* Marvell is parodying Sir William Davenant's epic poem *Gondibert* (1651), 1.2.42: "But were his season hot, and she but neer, / O mighty Love!) his Hunters were undone." [S]

[56] *Ephemerides:* a book of prognostications. Davenant wrote no such work, although in 1672 John Gadbury published *Ephemerides of the celestial motions for X. years. beginning anno 1672 . . . and ending in 1681.* The allusion to Davenant is probably to his *Preface to Gondibert* (1650), addressed to Thomas Hobbes, which predicts that the new republic, if it denies its citizens poetry and entertainment, will not survive.

[57] Sidrophel: William Lilly (1602–81), a notorious astrologer. He is nicknamed thus in Samuel Butler's *Hudibras,* part 2, canto 3, ll. 105ff. [S]

[58] *But . . . J.O.: Preface,* A2v.

[59] *he had . . . Book:* Owen, *Truth and Innocence Vindicated,* p. 4.

[60] Headstall: part of the bridle or halter that fits around the horse's head.

[61] Crooper: crupper, the leather strap that passes under the horse's tail.

might have gone [14] to *Push-Pin*[62] with the Bishop, which of their two Treatises was the *Procatarctical Cause*[63] of both their Edition. For, as they are coupled together, to say the truth, 'tis not discernable, as in some Animals, whether their motion begin at the head or the tail; whether the Author made his Preface for Bishop Bramhall's *dear sake,* or whether he published the Bishop's Treatise for sake of his *own dear Preface.* For my own part I think it reasonable that the Bishop and our Author, should (like fair Gamsters at Leap-frog) stand and skip in their turns; and however our Author got it for once, yet, if the Bookseller should ever be sollicitous for a Second Edition, that then the Bishops Book should have the Precedence.

But before I commit my self to the dangerous depths of his Discourse, which I am now upon the brink of, I would with his leave make a motion: that, instead of Author, I may henceforth indifferently call him Mr. Bayes as oft as I shall see occasion. And that, first, because he hath no Name, or [15] at least will not own it, though he himself writes under the greatest security, and gives us the first Letters of other Mens Names before he be asked them. Secondly, because he is I perceive a lover of Elegancy of Stile, and can endure no mans Tautologies but his own, and therefore I would not distaste him with too frequent repetition of one word. But chiefly, because Mr. Bayes and he do very much Symbolize; in their understandings, in their expressions, in their humour, in their contempt and quarrelling of all others, though of their own Profession. Because our Divine the Author, manages his contest with the same Prudence and civility, which the Players and Poets have practised of late in their several Divisions. And, lastly, because both their Talents do peculiarly lie in exposing and personating the Nonconformists. I would therefore give our Author a Name, the memory of which may perpetually excite him to the exercise and highest improvement of that Virtue. For, our Cicero doth not [16] yet equal our Roscius,[64] and one turn of Lacy's[65] *face* hath more *Ecclesiastical Policy* in it, than all the Books of our Author put together. Besides, to say Mr. Bayes is more *civil* than to say *Villain* and *Caitiff,* though these indeed are more *tuant.*[66] And,

[62] Push-pin: a children's game; Parker introduced the term, which becomes a motif for Marvell, in *Preface,* A8v.

[63] *Procatarctical Cause:* the immediate cause of anything; Parker, *Defence,* pp. 139–40.

[64] Roscius: Quintus Roscius (c. 134–c. 62 B.C.), Roman comedian who taught Cicero elocution and was subsequently defended by him in a property suit.

[65] Lacy's: John Lacy (d. 1681), dramatist and comedian, a great success in the role of Bayes.

[66] *tuant:* trenchant, cutting. Used in *Rehearsal,* act 4, scene 1, p. 36.

to conclude; The Irrefragable Doctor[67] of School-Divinity, pag. 460 of his *Defence;* determining concerning Symbolical Ceremonies, hath warranted me *that not only Governors, but any thing else, may have power to appropriate new names to things, without having absolute authority over the things themselves.*[68] And therefore henceforward, seeing I am on such sure ground, *Author,* or Mr. Bayes, whether I please. Now, having *had our Dance, let us advance to our more serious Counsels.*[69]

And first, Our Author begins with a Panegyrick upon Bishop Bramhal; a Person whom my age had not given me leave to be acquainted with, nor my good fortune led me to converse with his Writings: but for whom I had collected a deep Reverence from the gene-[17]ral Reputation he carried, beside the Veneration due to the Place he filled in the Church of England. So that our Author having a mind to shew us some proof of his Good Nature, and that his Eloquence lay'd not all in Satyr and Invectives, could not, in my opinion, have fixed upon a fitter subject of commendation. And therefore, I could have wished for my own sake, that I had missed this occasion of being more fully informed of some of the Bishop's Principles, whereby I have lost part of that pleasure which I had so long enjoyed in thinking well of so considerable a Person. But however, I recreate my self with believing that my simple judgment cannot, beyond my intention, abate any thing of his just value with others. And seeing he is long since dead which I knew but lately, and now learn it with regret, I am the more obliged to repair in my self whatsoever breaches of his Credit, by that additional Civility which consecrates the Ashes of the Deceased. But by this means I am come to discern [18] how it was possible for our Author to speak a good word of[70] any man. The Bishop was expired, and his Writings jump[71] much with our Author. So that if you have a mind to die, or to be of his Party, (there are but these two Conditions) you may perhaps be rendred capable of his Charity. And then write what you will, he will make you a *Preface that shall recommend you and it to the* Genius *of the Age, and reconcile it to the Juncture of Affairs.*[72] But truly he hath acquitted himself herein so

[67] Irrefragable Doctor: Alexander of Hales (c. 1185–1245), medieval theologian, called Doctor Irrefragibilis or the Unrefutable. His *Summae Universae Theologica* was published in 1622.

[68] *that . . . themselves* 72a] set in roman in 72.

[69] *had . . . Counsels* 72a] set in roman in 72; from *Rehearsal,* act 5, scene 1, p. 45.

[70] of 72a] for 72.

[71] jump: suit, coincide with.

[72] *Preface . . . Affairs* 72a] set in roman in 72.

ill-favourdly to the Bishop, that I do not think it so much worth to gain his approbation; and I had rather live and enjoy mine owne opinion than be so treated. For, beside his reflexion on the Bishop, and the whole Age he lived in; that *he was, as far as the prejudice of the Age would permit him, an acute Philosopher*[73] (which is a sufficient taste of Mr. Bayes his Arrogence, that no Man, no Age can be so perfect but must abide his Censure, and of the officious virulence of his Humour which infuses it self, by a malignant [19] remark, that (but for this acuter Philosopher) no man else would have thought of, into the Praises of him whom he most intended to celebrate) if, I say, beside this, you consider the most elaborate and studious Periods of his Commendation, you find it at best very ridiculous. By the Language he seems to transcribe out of the *Grand-Cyrus*[74] and *Cassandra,*[75] but the Exploits to have borrowed out of the *Knight of the Sun,*[76] and *King Arthur.*[77] For in a luscious and effeminate Stile he gives him such a *Termagant*[78] Character, as must either fright or turn the stomach of any Reader; *Being of a brave and enterprising temper, of an active and sprightly mind, he was alwayes busied either in contriving or performing great Designs.*[79] Well, Mr. Bayes, I suppose by this that he might have been an over-match to the Bishop of Cullen[80] and the Bishop of Strasburg.[81] In another place, *He finished all the glorious Designs that he undertook.*[82] This might have become

[73] *he was . . . Philosopher: Preface,* A3.

[74] *Grand-Cyrus: Artamenes, or The Grand Cyrus,* a roman à clef about the Fronde by Madeleine de Scudéry (1649–53), translated in 1653 by F.G.

[75] *Cassandra: Cassandre,* a romance by Costes de la Calprenède, published 1644–45, translated in 1652 by Sir Charles Cotterell, reissued 1661, 1667. These talkative romances were highly popular in royalist circles during the "interregnum."

[76] *Knight of the Sun:* Ortunez de Calahorra, *The First Part of the Mirrour of Princely deedes and knighthood, Wherein is shewed the Knight of the Sunne,* translated M. Tyler (1579). Marvell is contrasting the earlier action-oriented romances with the later more courtly and rhetorical ones.

[77] *King Arthur:* Malory's *Morte D'Arthur* (1485) was for the English the source of Arthurian romance in its most bloodthirsty mode.

[78] *Termagant:* an imaginary deity held in medieval Christianity to be worshiped by Mohammedans; hence in the mystery plays a violent and overbearing character.

[79] *Being . . . Designs: Preface,* A3v.

[80] Bishop of Cullen: Henry Maximilian (1621–88), archbishop and elector of Cologne.

[81] Bishop of Strasburg: Franz Egon Fürstenberg (1625–82). Both men were aggressive supporters of Louis XIV and frequently mentioned in the *London Gazette* during 1672. [S]

[82] *He finished . . . undertook: Preface,* A3v.

the Bishop of Munster[83] before had rais'd the Siege from Groningen. *As he was* [20] *able to accomplish the most gallant attempts, so he was alwayes ready not only to justifie their Innocence, but to make good their Bravery.*[84] I was too prodigal of my Bishops at first, and now have never another left in the Gazette, which is ⟨too⟩ our Authors Magazin. *His Reputation and Innocence were both Armor of Proof against Toryes and Presbyterians.*[85] But me-thinks Mr. Bayes having to do with such dangerous Enemies, you should have furnished him too with some weapon of Offence, a good old Fox, like that of another Heroe, his Contemporary in *Action upon the Scene of Ireland,*[86] of whom it was sung,

> *Down by his side he wore a Sword of price;*
> *Keen as a Frost, glaz'd like a new made Ice:*
> *That cracks men shell'd in Steel in a less trice,*
> *Than Squirrels Nuts, or the Highlanders Lice.*[87]

Then he saith; *'Tis true, the Church of* [21] *Ireland was the largest Scene of his Actions; but yet there, in a little time, he wrought out such wonderous Alterations, and so exceeding all belief, as may convince us that he had a mind large and active enough to have managed the Roman Empire at its greatest extent.*[88] This indeed of our Author's is *Great*: and yet it reacheth not a strain of his fellow-*Pendets*[89] in the History of the Mogol;[90] where he tells Dancehment Kan, *That when he put his*[91] *foot in the Stirrop, and when he march'd*[92] *upon*

[83] Bishop of Munster: Christoph Bernard von Galen (1606–78), a warlike prelate who aided Charles II against the Dutch in 1665 and in 1672 was fighting for Louis XIV. He raised the siege of Groningen on August 27. (*London Gazette,* no. 707.) [S]

[84] *As he . . . Bravery: Preface,* A3v.

[85] *His Reputation . . . Presbyterians: Preface,* A4.

[86] *Action . . . Ireland: Preface,* A3v.

[87] *Down . . . lice:* According to a MS note in Aubrey's copy of *RT* (Bodley, Ashmolean 1591), these lines are from John Ogilby's *Character of a Trooper,* a work written by him when he was in Ireland with Bramhall and Wentworth. [S] There are no known surviving copies of the poem.

[88] *'Tis true . . . extent: Preface,* A3v.

[89] *Pendets:* Hindu Brahmins learned in Sanskrit; the original of our term *pundit,* wise man.

[90] history of the Mogol: François Bernier, *A Continuation of the Memories of Monsieur Bernier concerning the Empire of the Great Mogul . . . ,* tr. H.[enry] O.[ldenburg?], 1672, p. 76 (A, p. 36, #102).

[91] Kan, *That when he put his* 72a] Kan, *when you put your* 72.

[92] *he march'd* 72a] *you march* 72.

Horseback in the front of the Cavalry, the Earth trembled under his[93] *feet, the eight Elephants that hold it on their heads not being able to support it.* But enough of this Trash.

Beside that it is the highest *Indecorum* for a Divine to write in such a stile as this [part Play-Book and part Romance] concerning a Reverend Bishop; these improbable *Elogies* too are of the greatest disservice to their own design, and do in effect diminish alwayes the Person whom they pretend to magnifie. Any worthy Man may pass through the World unquestion'd [22] and safe with a moderate Recommendation; but when he is thus set off, and bedawb'd with Rhetorick, and embroyder'd so thick that you cannot discern the Ground, it awakens naturally (and not altogether unjustly) Interest, Curiosity, and Envy. For all men pretend a share in Reputation, and love not to see it ingross'd and monopoliz'd, and are subject to enquire, (as of great Estates suddenly got) whether he came by all this honestly, or of what credit the Person is that tells the Story? And the same hath happened as to this Bishop, while our Author attributes to him such Atchievements, which to one that could believe the Legend of Captain Jones,[94] might not be incredible. I have heard that there was indeed such a Captain, an honest brave fellow: but a Wag that had a mind to be merry with him, hath quite spoil'd his History. Had our Author epitomiz'd the Legend of sixty six Books *de Virtutibus Sancti Patricii*[95] (I mean not the Ingenious Writer of the *Friendly Debates,*[96] but St. Patrick the Irish Bishop) he [23] could not have promis'd us greater Miracles. And 'tis well for him that he hath escaped the fate of Secundinus, who (as Josselin relates it) acquainting Patrick that he was inspired to compose something in his Commendation, the Bishop foretold the Author should die as soon as 'twas perfected. Which so done, so happened.[97] I am sure our Author had died no other death but of this his own *Preface,* and a surfeit upon Bishop Bramhall, if the swelling of

[93] *trembled under his* 72a] *trembles under your* 72.

[94] *Legend of Captain Jones:* David Lloyd, *The Legend of Captain Jones* (1648, 1671) (A, p. 51, #70).

[95] *Virtutibus . . . Patricii:* St. Patrick (373–463) brought Christianity to Ireland. See Jocelyn, *Vita S. Patricii,* ed. T. Messingham (Paris, 1624), chapter 186, p. 81. [S]

[96] Ingenious Writer: Simon Patrick (1626–1707), bishop of Ely, author of *A Friendly Debate between a Conformist and a Nonconformist* (1669), supporting conformity (A, p. 15, #188).

[97] Secundinus: bishop of Armagh (c. 373–448), one of St. Patrick's chief assistants, who wrote a hymn in his praise. For the anecdote, see Jocelyn, *Vita,* chapter 177, p. 77 [S]

Truth could have choak'd him. He tells us, I remember somewhere, that this same Bishop of Derry said, the Scots had a civil expression for these *Improvers of verity,* that they are[98] *good Company;*[99] and I shall say nothing severer, than that our Author speaks the language of a Lover, and so may claim some pardon, if the habit and excess of his Courtship do as yet give a tincture to his discourse upon more ordinary Subjects. For I would not by any means be mistaken, as if I thought our Author so sharp set, or so necessitated that he should make a dead Bishop his [24] Mistress; so far from that, that he hath taken such a course, that if the Bishop were alive, he would be out of love with himself. He hath, like those frightfull Looking-glasses, made for sport, represented him in such bloated lineaments, as I am confident, if he could see his face in it, he would break the Glass. For, hence it falls out too, that men seeing the Bishop furbish'd up in so martial accoutrements, like another Odo Bishop of Baieux,[100] and having never before heard of this prowess, began to reflect what *Giants* he defeated, and what *Damsells* he rescued. Serious Men consider whether he were ingaged in the conduct of the Irish army, and to have brought it over upon England, for the Imputation of which the Earl of Strafford[101] his Patron so undeservedly suffered. But none knows any thing of it. Others think it is not to be taken literally, but the wonderfull and unheard-of Alterations that he wrought out in Ireland, are meant of some Reformation that he made there in things of his own Function. But [25] then men ask again, how he comes to have all the honour of it, and whether all the while that great Bishop Usher,[102] his Metropolitan, were unconcerned? For even in Ecclesiasticall Combates how instrumental soever the Captain hath been, the General usually carries away the honour of the Action. But the good *Primate* was engaged in Designs of lesser moment, and was writing his *de Primordiis Ecclesiae Britanicae,* and the Story of Pelagius[103] our Countryman. He

[98] are 72] had 72a.

[99] *good Company: Defence,* p. 230.

[100] Odo Bishop of Baieux: (d. 1097) earl of Kent, half-brother of William the Conqueror.

[101] Thomas Wentworth (1593–1641), lord deputy of Ireland for Charles I, impeached and executed by the Long Parliament.

[102] Bishop Usher: James Ussher (1581–1656), archbishop of Armagh. His *Britannicarum Ecclesiarum Antiquitates,* better known as the *De Primordiis* (Dublin, 1639), was one of the major sources for Milton's *History of Britain.*

[103] Pelagius: British theologian of the fifth century, author of the Pelagian heresy.

Honest man, was deep gone in *Grubstreet*[104] and *Polemical Divinity,* and troubled with fits of *Modern Orthodoxy.* He satisfied himself with being *admired by the blue and white Aprons,*[105] and *pointed at by the more judicious Tankard-bearers.*[106] Nay, which is worst of all, he undertook to abate of our Episcopall *Grandeur,* and condescended indeed to reduce the Ceremonious Discipline in these Nations to the Primitive Simplicity. What then was this that Bishop Bramhal did? Did he, like a Protestant Apostle, in one day convert thousands of the Irish Papists? The contrary is [26] evident by the Irish Rebellion[107] and Massacre, which, notwithstanding his *Publick Employment and great Abilities,*[108] happened in his time. So that after all our Authors bombast, when we have search'd all over, we find our selves bilk'd in our expectation: and he hath erected him, like a St. Christopher[109] in the Popish Churches, as big as ten Porters, and yet only imploy'd to sweat under the burden of an *Infant.*

All that appears of him is, first, that he busied himself about a *Catholick Agreement among the Churches of Christendom.*[110] But as to this, our Author himself saith, that he was not *so vain, or so presuming as to hope to see it effected in his dayes.*[111] And yet but two pages before he told us, that *the Bishop finish'd all the glorious Designs which he undertook.* But this Design of his he draws out in such a circuit of words, that 'tis better taking it from the Bishop himself, who speaks more plainly alwayes, and much more to the purpose. And he saith, pag. 87 of his Vindication, *My design is rather to reconcile the Popish Party to* [27] *the Church of England, than the Church of England to the Pope.* And how[112] he manages it, I had rather any man would learn by

[104] *Grubstreet:* a street in London near Moorfields, the locale of many hack writers.

[105] *white Aprons: Preface,* a4.

[106] *Tankard-bearers: Preface,* A7v.

[107] Irish Rebellion: the Ulster rebellion against English rule of October 1641.

[108] *Publick . . . Abilities: Preface,* A3.

[109] St. Christopher: a martyr, probably of the third century; in the Greek legend he was born a pagan, of extraordinary strength and size. Having vowed to serve only the strongest lord, he was baptized by a hermit and accepted the work of carrying travelers across a raging river. One day, carrying across a child, it seemed to him that he was carrying the weight of the whole world on his shoulders; and when the child revealed himself as Christ, he acquired the name *kristopheros,* Christ-bearer.

[110] *a Catholick . . . Christendom: Preface,* A4v.

[111] *so vain . . . dayes: Preface,* A4v.

[112] how 72] now 72a.

reading over his own Book, than that I should be thought to misrepresent him, which I might, unless I transcribed the whole. But in summe it seems to me that he is upon his own single judgment too liberal of the Publick, and that he retrenches both on our part more than he hath Authority for, and grants more to the Popish than they can of right pretend to. It is however indeed a most glorious Design, to reconcile all the Churches to one Doctrine and Communion (though some that meddle in it do it chiefly in order to fetter men straiter under the formal bondage of fictitious Discipline); but it is a thing rather to be wished and prayed for, than to be expected from these kind of endeavours. It is so large a Field, that no man can see to the end of it; and all that have adventured to travel it, have been bewildred. That Man must have a vast opinion of his own sufficiency, that can think he may [28] by his Oratory or Reason, either in his own time, or at any of our Author's *more happy Junctures of Affairs,* so far perswade and fascinate the Roman-Church, having by a regular contexture of continued Policy for so many Ages interwoven it self with the Secular Interest, and made it self necessary to most Princes, and having at last erected a Throne of Infallibility over the Conscience,[113] as to prevail with her to submit a Power and Empire so acquired and established in Compromise to the Arbitration of an humble Proposer. God only in his own time, and by the inscrutable methods of his Providence is able to effect that *Alteration*: though I think too he hath signified in part by what means he intends to accomplish it, and to range so considerable a Church, and once so exemplary, into Primitive Unity and Christian Order. In the mean time such Projects are fit for Pregnant Scholars that have nothing else to do, to go big with for forty years, and may qualifie them to discourse with Princes and [29] States-men at their hours of leisure; but I never saw that they came to Use or Possibility: No more than that of Alexanders Architect,[114] who proposed to make him a Statue of the Mountain Athos (and that was no Molehill); and among other things, that Statue to carry in its hand a great habitable City. But the Surveyor was gravell'd,[115] being asked whence that City should be supplied with Water.[116] I would only have ask'd the Bishop, when he had carv'd and hammer'd the

[113] the Conscience 72a] the Consciences 72; their Consciences 72 Errata.

[114] Alexanders Architect: Deinocrates, who proposed to carve Mount Athos into a statue of Alexander. See Strabo, *Geography,* 14.1.23 (A, p. 37, #4).

[115] gravell'd: perplexed, nonplused.

[116] An extended, comic version of this anecdote is told by George Puttenham, *Arte of English Poesie* (1589), pp. 140–41.

Romists and Protestants into one Colossian-[117]Church, how we should have done as to matter of Bibles. For the Bishop, p. 117. complains that *unqualified people should have a promiscuous Licence to read the Scriptures*:[118] and you may guess thence, if he had moreover the Pope to friend, how the Laity should have been used. There have been attempts in former Ages to dig through the Separating Istmos of Peloponnesus;[119] and another to make communication between the Red-Sea and the Mediterranean:[120] both more easie than to cut this *Ecclesiastick Canal*; and yet [30] both laid by, partly upon the difficulty of doing it, and partly upon the inconveniences if it had been effected. I must confess freely, yet I ask pardon for the presumption, that I cannot look upon these undertaking Church-men, however otherwise of excellent Prudence and Learning, but as men struck with a Notion, and craz'd on that side of their head. And so I think even the Bishop had much better have busied himself in Preaching in his own Diocess, and disarming the Papists of their Arguments, instead of rebating[121] our weapons; that in taking an *Oecumenical*[122] care upon him, which none called him to, and, as appears by the sequel, none conn'd him thanks for.

But[123] if he were so great a Politician as I have heard, and indeed believe him to have been, methinks he should in the first place have contrived how we might live well with our Protestant Neighbours, and to have united us in one Body under the King of England, as Head of the Protestant Interest, which might [31] have rendred us more considerable, and put us into a more likely posture to have reduced the Church of Rome to Reason. For the most leading Party of the English Clergy in his time retained such a Pontifical stiffness towards the Foreign Divines, that it puts me in mind of Austin the Monk[124] when he came into Kent, not deigning to rise up to the Brittish, or

[117] Colossian: colossal, huge.

[118] *unqualified . . . Scriptures* 72a] set in roman in 72.

[119] Istmos of Peloponnesus: The idea of cutting through the Isthmus of Corinth occurred to Periander (Diogenes Laertes, 1.99), Julius Caesar (Suetonius, *Caesar,* 44), and Nero (Suetonius, *Nero,* 19). [S]

[120] Red Sea . . . Mediterranean: the first attempt is credited to Sesostris (Strabo, *Geography,* 1.2.31).

[121] rebating: blunting.

[122] *Oecumenical:* representing the whole Christian world.

[123] But: new paragraph 72a.

[124] Austin the Monk: St. Augustine, first archbishop of Canterbury (d. 604). At the meeting in 603 at Aust on the Severn, he refused to rise at the approach of the bishops from Bangor. See Bede, *Historia Ecclesiastica,* 2.2 (A, p. 26 #244).

give them the hand, and could scarce afford their Churches either Communion or Charity, or common Civility. So that it is not to be wondred if they also on their parts looked upon our Models of Accommodation with the same jealousie that the British Christians had of Austin's Design, to unite them first to (that is, under) the Saxons, and then deliver them both over bound to the Papal Government and Ceremonies. But seeing hereby our hands were weakned, and there was no probability of arriving so near the end of the work, as to a consent among Protestants abroad; had the Bishop but gone that step, to have reconciled the Ecclesiastical Differences in [32] our own Nations, and that we might have stood firm at home before we had taken such a Jump beyond-Sea, it would have been a Performance worthy of his Wisdom. For at that time the Ecclesiastical Rigours here were in the highest ferment, and the Church in being arrayed it self against the peaceable Dissenters only in some points of Worship. And what great Undertaking could we be ripe for abroad, while so divided at home? or what fruit expected from the labour of those Mediating Divines in weighty matters, who were not yet past the Sucking-bottle; but seem'd to place all the business of Christianity in persecuting men for their Consciences, differing from them in smaller matters? How ridiculous must we be to the Church of Rome to interpose in her Affairs, and force our Mediation upon her; when, besides our ill correspondence with the Foreign Protestants, she must observe our weakness within our selves, that we could not, or would not step over a straw, though for the perpetual settle-[33]ment and security of our Church and Nation? She might well look upon us as those that probably might be forced at some time by our folly to call her in to our assistance (for with no weapons or Arguments but what are fetch'd out of her Arsenals can the Ceremonial-Controversie be rightly defended) but never could she consider us as of such Authority or wisdom, as to give Ballance to her Counsels.

But[125] this was far from Bp. Bramhall's thoughts; who, so he might (like Caesar) *manage the Roman Empire at its utmost extent,*[126] had quite forgot what would conduce to the Peace of his own Province and Country. For p. 57. he settles this Maxime as a Truth, *That second Reformations are commonly like Metal upon Metal, which is false Heraldry.* Where, by the way, it is a wonder that our Author in enumerating the Bps perfections in Divinity,

[125] But: new paragraph 72a.

[126] *manage . . . extent: Preface,* A6.

Law, History, and Philosophy, neglected this peculiar gift he had in Heraldry; and omitted to tell us that his Mind was large enough to have animated the Kingdoms of Garter[127] and Cla-[34]rencieux[128] at their greatest dimensions. But, beside what I have said already in relation to this Project upon Rome, there is this more, which I confess was below Bishop Bramhall's reflexion, and was indeed fit only for some vulgar Politician, or the Commissioners of Scotland about the late Union:[129] Whether it would not have succeeded, as in the consolidation of Kingdoms, where the Greatest swallows down the less; so also in Church-Coalition, that though the Pope had condescended (which the Bishop owns to be his Right) to be only a Patriarch, yet he would have swoop'd up the Patriarchate of Lambeth to his Mornings-draught, like an egg in Muscadine.[130] And then there is another Danger always when things come once to a Treaty, that, beside the debates of Reason, there is a better way of tampering to bring Men over that have a Power to conclude. And so who knows in such a Treaty with Rome, if the Alps (as it is probable) would not have come over to England, as the Bishop designed it, England might not have been ob-[35]liged, lying so commodious for Navigation, to undertake a Voyage to *Civita Vecchia*?[131] But what though we should have made all the Advances imaginable, it would have been to no purpose: and nothing less than an intire and total resignation of the Protestant Cause would have contented her. For the Church of Rome is so well satisfied of her own sufficiency, and hath so much more wit than we had in Bishop Bramhall's days, or seem to have yet learned; that it would have succeeded just as at the Council of Trent.[132] For there, though many Divines of the greatest Sincerity and Learning, endeavoured a Reformation, yet no more could be obtained of Her than the

[127] Garter: the highest order of English knighthood.

[128] Clarencieux: an English dukedom; the second King of Arms.

[129] Union: In October 1669 Charles proposed joint commissions of England and Scotland to negotiate a formal union between the two kingdoms, a project first mooted unsuccessfully by James I. Marvell discussed this in letters to Hull and William Popple (*P&L*, 2:86, 313).

[130] egg in Muscadine: *Preface*, B4; muscadine was a musky wine.

[131] *Civita Vecchia:* the ancient city; Rome.

[132] Council of Trent: Initially summoned by Pope Paul III to define doctrine and reform abuses in the church, in order to counter the Reformation, the council met in three stages, 1545–47, 1551–52, and 1562–53. The attempts at reformation from within were largely nugatory.

Nonconformists got of those of the Church of England at the Conference of Worcester House.[133] But on the contrary, all her Excesses and Errors were further rivited and confirmed, and that great Machine of her Ecclesiastical Policy there perfected.

So that this Enterprise of Bishop Bramhalls, being so ill laid and so unseasonable, deserves rather an Excuse [36] than a Commendation. And all that can be gathered besides out of our Author concerning him is of little better value; for he saith indeed, that *he was a zealous and resolute Assertor of the Publick Rites and Solemnities of the Church.*[134] But those things, being only matters of external neatness, could never merit the Trophies that our Author erects him. For neither can a Justice of Peace for his severity about Dirt-baskets deserve a Statue.[135] And as for *his expunging some dear and darling Articles from the Protestant Cause,*[136] it is, as far as I can perceive, onely his substituting some Arminian Tenets,[137] (which I name so, not for reproach, but for difference) instead of the Calvinian Doctrines. But this too could not challenge all these Triumphal Ornaments in which he installs him: For, I suppose these were but meer *mistakes on either side, for want of being* (as the Bishop saith, pag. 134.) *scholastically stated; and that he, with a distinction of School-Theologie, could have smoothed over and plained away these knots though they had been much harder.* [37]

For the rest, which he leaves us to seek for, and I meet casually with in the Bishop's own Book; I find him to have been doubtless a very good-

[133] Conference of Worcester House: Charles II himself, with several lords and bishops, met with Baxter and Calamy and other leading presbyterians at Worcester House, Clarendon's residence, on October 23, 1660. This brief conference, which resulted in the Worcester House Declaration of October 25 outlining a comprehensive church settlement acceptable to the Presbyterians, was followed by the Savoy Conference, in the residence of Gilbert Sheldon, bishop of London, in the Strand, which sat by royal warrant from April 15 to July 14. Consisting of twelve bishops and twelve presbyterian divines, this was a more extensive but even less successful attempt to arrive at a compromise. See Daniel Neal, *History of the Puritans,* ed. Edward Parsons, 2 vols. (London, 1811), 2:498–506, and John Miller, *After the Civil Wars: English Politics and Government in the Reign of Charles II* (Harlow, 2000), pp. 174–75. Marvell often mentions these events, sometimes seeming to merge the two conferences.

[134] *he was . . . Church: Preface,* A6.

[135] Justice . . . Statue: cf. Montaigne, *Essais,* 3:10: "Of husbanding your will."

[136] *his expunging . . . Cause: Preface,* A6.

[137] Arminian tenets: the doctrines of Jacob Arminius (1560–1609), Dutch Protestant theologian, opposed to Calvin on the issues of free will and predestination. See Introduction, p. 16.

natur'd Gentleman. Pag. 160. *He hath much respect for poor Readers*; and pag. 161. He judges *that if they come short of Preachers in point of Efficacy, yet they have the advantage of Preachers as to point of Security.* And pag. 163. He commends the care taken by *the Canons that the meanest Cure of Souls should have formal Sermons at least four times every year.* Pag. 155. He *maintains the Publick Sports on the Lords day by the Proclamation to that purpose, and the Example of the Reformed Churches beyond-Sea*; and *for the Publick Dances of our Youth upon Country-Greens on Sundayes, after the duties of the day, he sees nothing in them but innocent and agreeable to that under-sort of people.* And pag. 117. (which I quoted before) he *takes the promiscuous licence to unqualified persons to reade the Scriptures, far more prejudicial, nay, more pernitious, than the over-rigorous restraint of the Romanists.* And [38] indeed, all along he complies much for peace-sake, and judiciously shews us wherein our separation from the Church of Rome is not warrantable. But although I cannot warrant any man who hence took occasion to traduce him of Popery, the contrary of which is evident, yet neither is it to be wondred, if he did hereby lye under some imputation, which he might otherwise have avoided. Neither can I be so hard-hearted as our Author in the Nonconformists case of Discipline, to think it were better that *he, or a hundred more Divines of his temper should suffer, though innocent* in their Reputation,[138] *than that we should come under a possibility of losing our Religion.* For as they (the Bishop, and I hope most of his Party) did not intend it so, neither could they have effected it. But he could not expect to enjoy his Imagination without the annoyances incident to such as dwell in the middle story: the Pots from above, and the Smoak from below. And those Churches which are seated nearer upon the Frontire of Popery, did natural-[39]ly and well if they took Alarm at the March. For, in fact, that incomparable Person Grotius[139] did yet make a Bridge for the Enemy to cover over; or at least laid some of our considerable Passes open to them and unguarded: a crime something like what his Son De Groot (here's Gazette again for you) and his Son-in-law Mombas[140] have been charged with. And, as to the Bishop

[138] in . . . Reputation 72a] in italics in 72.

[139] Grotius: Hugo Grotius (De Groot) (1583–1645), renowned Dutch scholar. He was a Remonstrant or Arminian who gradually moved further toward the Roman Catholic position.

[140] De Groot . . . Mombas: The *London Gazette,* no. 698, July 25–29, 1672, carried information about the defeats of the younger De Groot and his brother-in-law de Mombas in the struggle between De Witt and the prince of Orange. [S]

himself, his Friend, an Accusatory Spirit would desire no better play than he gives in his own Vindication. But that's neither my business nor humour: and whatsoever may have glanced upon him, was directed only to our Author; for publishing that Book, which the Bishop himself had thought fit to conceal, and for his impertinent efflorescence of Rhetorick upon so mean Topicks, in so choice and copious a Subject as Bishop Bramhal.

Yet though the Bishop prudently undertook a Design, which he hoped not to accomplish in his own dayes, our Author, however, was something wiser, and hath made sure to obtain his end. [40] For the Bishop's Honour was the furthest thing from his thoughts, and he hath managed that part so, that I have accounted it a work of some Piety to vindicate his Memory from so scurvy a commendation. But the Author's end was only railing. He could never have induc'd himself to praise one man but in order to rail on another. He never oyls his Hone but that he may whet his Razor; and that not to shave, but to cut mens throats. And whoever will take the pains to compare, will find, that as it is his only end; so his best, nay his only talent is railing. So that he hath, while he pretends so much for the good Bishop, used him but for a Stalking-horse till he might come within shot of the Forreign Divines and the Nonconformists. The other was only a copy of his countenance: But look to your selves, my Masters; for in so venomous a Malice, Courtesie is always fatal. Under colour of some mens having taxed the Bishop, he flyes out into a furious Debauch, and breaks the Windows, if he could, would raze [41] the foundations of all the Protestant-Churches beyond Sea: but for all men at home of their perswasion, if he meet them in the dark he runs them thorow. He usurps to himself the Authority of the Church of England, who is so well bred, that if he would have allowed her to speak, she would doubtless have treated more civilly those over whom she pretends no Jurisdiction: and under the names of Germany and Geneva, he rallies and rails at the whole Protestancy of Europe. For you are mistaken in our Author (but I have worn him thread-bare) if you think he designs to enter the Lists where he hath but one man to combate. Mr Bayes, ye know, *prefers that one quality of fighting single with whole Armies, before all the moral Vertues put together.*[141] And yet I assure you, he hath several times obliged moral Vertue so highly, that she ows him a good turn whensoever she can meet him. But it is a brave thing to be the Ecclesiastical

[141] *prefers . . . together: Rehearsal,* act 4, scene 1, p. 35.

Draw-Can-Sir;[142] He kills whole Nations, he kills Friend and Foe; Hungary, Transylvania, Bohe-[42]mia, Poland, Savoy, France, the Netherlands, Denmark, Sweden, and a great part of the Church of England, and all Scotland (for these, besides many more, he mocks under the title of Germany and Geneva) may perhaps rouse our Mastiff, and make up a Danger worthy of his Courage. A man would guess that this Giant had promised his *Comfortable Importance* a Simarre[143] of the beards of all the *Orthodox Theologues* in Christendom.

But[144] I wonder how he comes to be Prolocutor[145] of the Church of England! For he talks at that rate as if he were a *Synodical Individuum*;[146] nay, if he had a fifth Council[147] in his belly he could not dictate more dogmatically. There had been indeed, as I have heard, about the dayes of Bishop Bramhal, a sort of Divines here of that Leaven, who being dead, I cover their names, if not for healths sake, yet for decency, who never could speak of the first Reformers with any patience; who pruned themselves in the peculiar Virulency of their Pens, and so they might say a tart thing concerning the [43] Forreign Churches, cared not what obloquy they cast upon the History or the profession of Religion. And those men undertook likewise to vent their Wit and their Choler under the stile of the Church of England; and were indeed so far owned by her, that what preferments were in her own disposal she rather conferr'd upon them. And now when they were gone off the Stage, there is risen up this Spiritual Mr. Bayes; who having assumed to himself an incongruous Plurality of Ecclesiastical Offices, one the most severe, of Penitentiary-Universal to the Reformed-Churches; the other most rediculous, of Buffoon-General to the Church of England, may be henceforth capable of any other Promotion. And not being content to enjoy his own folly, he has taken two others into Partnership,[148] as fit for his design, as those two that clubb'd with Mahomet in

[142] Draw-Can-Sir: "a fierce Hero, that frights his Mistriss, snubs up Kings, baffles Armies, and does what he will, without regard to good manners, justice or numbers." *Rehearsal,* act 4, scene 1, p. 34.

[143] Simarre: *Cymar,* a loose robe or undergarment for women; also a bishop's gown.

[144] But: new paragraph 72a.

[145] Prolocutor: spokesman.

[146] *Synodical Individuum:* a whole council in one individual.

[147] fifth Council: Protestants recognized only four ecumenical councils: Nicaea (A.D. 325), Constantinople (A.D. 381), Ephesus (A.D. 431), and Chalcedon (A.D. 451). [S]

[148] two others: A marginal MS note in B7 identifies them as "Drs Patrick & Crad-

making the Alchoran:[149] who by a perverse Wit and Representation might travesteere the Scripture, and render all the carefull and serious part of Religion odious [44] and contemptible. But, lest I might be mistaken as to the Persons I mention, I will assure the Reader that I intend not Huddibras:[150] For he is a man of the other Robe, and his excellent Wit hath taken a flight far above these Whiflers: that whoever dislikes the choice of his Subject, cannot but commend his Performance, and calculate if on so barren a Theme he were so copious, what admirable sport he would have made with an Ecclesiastical Politician. But for a *Daw-Divine* not only to foul his own Nest in England, but to pull in pieces the Nests of those beyond Sea, 'tis that which I think undecent, and of very ill example.

There[151] is not indeed much danger, his Book, his Letter, and his Preface being writ in English, that they should pass abroad: but, if they be printed upon incombustible Paper, or by reason of the many Avocations of our Church they may escape a Censure, yet 'tis likely they may dye at home the common fate of such Treatises amongst the more judicious Oylmen and Grocers. Unless Mr. Bayes [45] be so far in love with his own Whelp, that, as a Modern Lady,[152] he will be at the charge of translating his Works into Latin, transmitting them to the Universities, and dedicating them in the Vaticane. But, should they unhappily get vent abroad (as I hear[153] some are already sent over for curiosity) what scandal, what heart-burning and animosity must it raise against our Church: unless they chance to take it right at first, and limit the Provocation within the Author. And then, what can he expect in return of his Civility,[154] but that the Complement which passed betwixt Arminius and Baudius[155] should concenter upon him, that

---

dock"; i.e., Simon Patrick, author of *The Friendly Debate,* and Zachary Craddock (1633–95), fellow of Eton College in 1671 and chaplain in ordinary to Charles II.

[149] those two: Sergius and Abdallah, "A Nestorian monk of Constantinople and a paynime Jew," *Purchas his Pilgrimages* (1613), p. 200 [S] (A, (1625) p. 27, #155).

[150] Huddibras: Samuel Butler (1612–80), whose mock-epic *Hudibras* satirizing the dissenters appeared in three parts: 1663, 1664, 1678.

[151] There: new paragraph 72a.

[152] Modern Lady: Margaret, duchess of Newcastle. According to Antony à Wood, in 1667 she commissioned James Bristow of Corpus Christi, Oxford, to translate her philosophy into Latin, but the task proved beyond him. See *Athenae Oxonienses,* ed. Philip Bliss, 4 vols. (Oxford, 1813–20), 4:281 (*Fasti*). See also n. 44 above.

[153] hear 72] here 72a.

[154] Civility 72] Civililty 72a.

[155] Baudius: Dominick Baudius (1516–1613), Flemish scholar and poet. For the

he is both *Opprobrium Academiae,* and *Pestis Ecclesiae.*[156] For they will see at the first that his Books come not out under Publick Authority, or recommendation: but only as things of Buffoonery do commonly, they carry with them their own *Imprimatur*; (But I hope he hath considered Mr. L.[157] in private, and payed his Fees:) Neither will the Gravity therefore of their Judgments take the measures, I hope, [46] either of the Education at our Universities, or of the Spirit of our Divines, or of the Prudence, Piety, and Doctrine of the Church of England, from such an Interloper. Those Gardens of ours use to bear much better fruit. There may happen sometimes an ill Year, or there may be such a Crab-stock[158] as cannot by all ingrafting be corrected. But generally it proves otherwise. Once perhaps in a hundred years there may arise such a Prodigy in the University (where all Men else learn better Arts and better manners) and from thence may creep into the Church (where the Teachers at least ought to be well instructed in the knowledge and practice of Christianity) so prodigious a Person I say may even there be hatch'd, as shal neither know or care how to behave himself to God or Man; and who having never seen the receptacle of Grace or Conscience at an Anatomical Dissection, may conclude therefore that there is no such matter, or no such obligation among Christians; who shall persecute the Scripture it self, unless it [47] will conform to his Interpretation; who shall strive to put the World into Blood, and animate Princes to be the Executioners of their own Subjects for well-doing. All this is possible; but comes to pass as rarely and at as long periods in our Climate, as the birth of a false Prophet. But unluckily, in this fatal Year of Seventy two, among all the Calamities that Astrologers foretel, this also hath befaln us. I would not hereby confirm his vanity, as if I also believed that any Scheme of Heaven did influence his actions, or that he were so considerable as that the Comet,[159] under which they say we yet labour, had fore-boded the appearance of his Preface. No, no: though he be a creature most noxious, yet

---

"Complement," see James Howell, *Familiar Letters,* ed. Jacobs, 1890, p. 32: "Thou Baudius disgracest our University, and thou Arminius our Religion."

[156] *Opprobrium . . . Ecclesiae:* an embarrassment to the academy and a plague to the church.

[157] Mr. L.: Sir Roger L'Estrange; see n. 27 above.

[158] Crab-stock: a young crab-apple tree used as a stock to graft on, with a pun on *crabbed,* sour.

[159] Comet: Wood notes a comet, December 16, 1664, which was followed the next year by plague, "prodigious births, great inundations and frosts, warr with the Dutch, sudden deaths." See *Life and Times,* ed. Andrew Clarke, 4 vols. (Oxford, 1892), 2:24, 53–54.

he is more despicable. A Comet is of far higher quality, and hath other kind of imployment. Although we call it an Hairy-Star, it affords no prognostick of what breeds there, but the Astrologer that would discern our Author and his business, must lay by his Telescope, and use a Microscope. You may find him [48] still in Master[160] Calvin's head.

Poor[161] Mr. Calvin and Bp.[162] Bramhall, what crime did you dye guilty of, that you cannot lye quiet in your graves, but must be conjured up on the stage as oft as Mr. Bayes will ferret you? And which of you two are most unfortunate I cannot determine; whether the Bishop in being alwayes courted, or the Presbyter in being alwayes rail'd at. But in good earnest I think Mr. Calvin hath the better of it. For, though an ill man cannot by praising confer honour, nor by reproaching fix an ignominy; and so they may seem on equal terms; yet there is more in it: for at the same time that we may imagine what is said by such an Author to be false, we conceive the contrary to be true. What he said[163] of him indeed in this place did not come very well in: for Calvin writ nothing against Bishop Bramhall, and therefore here it amounts to no more than that his Spirit forsooth had propagated an original *Waspishness* and false *Orthodoxy* amongst all his Followers. But if you look in other pages of his Book, and particularly pag. 663 of [49] his *Defence*, you never saw such a Scarcrow as he makes him. *There sprang up a mighty Bramble on the South side the Lake Lemane, that (such is the rankness of the soil) spread and flourished with such a sudden growth, that partly by the industry of his Agents abroad, and partly by its own indefatigable pains and pragmaticalness, it quite over-ran the whole Reformation.*—You must conceive that Mr. Bayes was all this while in an extasy in *Dodona's Grove*;[164] or else here is strange work, worse than *explicating a Post*, or *examining a Pillar*.[165] A *Bramble* that had *Agents abroad*, and it self an *indefatigable Bramble*. But straight our Bramble is transformed to a Man, and he *makes a Chair of Infallibility for himself*,[166] out of his own Bramble Timber. Yet all this while we know not his Name. One would suspect it might be a Bp. *Bramble*. But then *he made himself both Pope and Emperor too*

[160] Master 72a] Mr. 72.

[161] Poor: new paragraph 72a.

[162] Bp. 72a] Bishop 72.

[163] said 72a] saith 72.

[164] *Dodona's Grove:* James Howell's Royalist political allegory (1640) in which all the participants in the civil war were represented as different kinds of trees (A, p. 35 #74).

[165] *explicating . . . Pillar: Defence*, p. 102.

[166] *Chair . . . himself: Defence*, p. 662.

of the greatest part of the Reformed World.[167] How near does this come to his Commendation of Bishop Bramhall before? For our Author seems copious, but is indeed very poor of Ex-[50]pression: and, as smiling and frowning are performed in the face with the same muscles very little altered; so the changing of a line or two in Mr. Bayes at any time, will make the same thing serve for a Panegyrick or a Philippick.[168] But what do you think of this Man? Could Mistris Mopsa[169] her self have furnished you with a more pleasant or[170] worshipful tale? It wants nothing of perfection, but that it doth not begin with *Once upon a time?* which Mr.[171] Bayes, according to his Accuracy, if he had thought on't, would never have omitted.

Yet[172] some critical People, who will exact Truth in Falshood, and tax upon an[173] old-wife's fable to the punctuality of History, were blaming him t'other day for placing this Bramble on the South-side of the Lake Lemane. I said, it was well and wisely done that he chose a South Sun for the better and more sudden growth of such a Fruit-tree. Ay, said they, but he means Calvin by the Bramble; and the *rank soyl on the South-side the Lake Lemane* is the City of Geneva, situate (as he would have it) on the South-[51]side of that Lake. Now it is strange that he having travell'd so well, should not have observ'd that the Lake lies East and West, and that Geneva is built at the West end of it. Pish, said I, that's no such great matter, and, as Mr. Bayes hath it upon another occasion, *Whether it be so or no, the fortunes of Caesar and the Roman Empire are not concerned in't.*[174] One of the Company would not let that pass, but told us, if we look'd in Caesar's Commentaries,[175] we should find their fortunes were concerned, for it was the Helvetian Passage, and many mistakes might have risen in the marching of the Army. Why then replyed I again, Whether it be East, West, North or South, there is

[167] *he made himself . . . Reformed World: Defence,* p. 664.

[168] Panegyrick or Philippic: praise or invective; *philippic* derives from the hostile orations of Demosthenes against Philip of Macedon.

[169] Mistress Mopsa: the vulgar shepherd's daughter in Sir Philip Sidney's *Arcadia,* who, in book 2, chapter 15, tries to join in the story-telling game, but her contribution is so ludicrous it has to be cut short.

[170] or 72a] and 72.

[171] Mr. 72a] Master 72.

[172] Yet: new paragraph 72a.

[173] upon an 72a] up an 72.

[174] *Whether . . . in't: Defence,* p. 337; Parker misremembered an anecdote about Demosthenes that Marvell quotes correctly in *Mr. Smirke.* See vol. 2, p. 89.

[175] Caesar's Commentaries: Julius Caesar, *De Bello Gallico.*

neither *Vice* nor *Idolatry* in it, and the Ecclesiastical Politican may command you to believe it, and you are bound to *acquiesce* in his judgment, whatsoever may be *your private Opinion.*[176] Another, to continue the mirth, answered, That yet there might be some Religious Consideration in building a Town East and West, or North and South, and 'twas not a thing [52] so indifferent as men thought it; but because in the Church of England, where the Table is set Altar-wise,[177] the Minister is nevertheless obliged to stand at the North-side (though it be the North-end of the Table) it was fit to place the Geneva Presbyter in diametrical opposition to him upon the *South-side of the Lake.* But this we all took for a cold conceit, and not enough matured. I, that was still upon the doubtful and excusing part, said, That to give the right situation of a Town, it was necessary first to know in what position the Gentlemans head then was when he made his Observation, and that might cause a great diversity, as much as this came to. Yes, replyed my next Neighbour; or, perhaps some roguing Boy that managed the Puppets, turned the City wrong, and so disoccidented[178] our Geographer. It was grown almost as good as a Play among us: and at last they all concluded that Geneva *had sold Mr. Bayes a Bargain,* as the *Moon* serv'd the *Earth*[179] in the *Rehearsal,*[180] and in good sooth had *turn'd her breech on him.* [53]

But[181] this, I doubt not, Mr. Bayes will bring himself off with Honour: but that which sticks with me is, that our Author having undertaken to make Calvin and Geneva ridicule, hath not pursued it to so high a point as the Subject would have afforded. First, he might have taken the name of the beast Calvinus, and of that have given the Anagram, Lucianus.[182] Next, I would have turned him inside outward, and have made him Usinulca.[183]

[176] *acquiesce . . . Opinion: Discourse,* p. 312.

[177] Altar-wise: In 1633 Archbishop Land ruled that the communion table should be placed in the East end of all churches.

[178] disoccidented: confused the sense of where the west was; the *OED* cites Marvell's as the only usage.

[179] *Earth* 72 Errata, 72a] Sun 72, 72a (B5, B7, B9, D5).

[180] *Rehearsal:* i.e., in act 5, scene 1, p. 50.

[181] But: new paragraph 72a.

[182] Lucianus: i.e., the Roman satirist Lucian, known for his scurrility. According to Tallemant des Reaux, the anagram was invented by Rabelais. See *Les Historiettes* (Paris, 1862), p. 222.

[183] Usinulca: an anagram found in Barclay's *Argenis,* trans. Robert Le Grys (1630), pp. 92–96 (A, p. 47, #121).

That was a good Hobgoblin name to have frighted Children with. Then he should have been a *Bramble* still, ay, an *indefatigable Bramble* too: but after that he should have continued (for in such a Book a passage in a Play is clear gain, and a great loss[184] if omitted) and upon that Bramble *Reasons grew as plentiful as Blackberries,*[185] but both unwholesome, and they stain'd all the *white aprons* so, that there was no getting of it out. And then to make a fuller description of the place, he should have added; That near to the City of *roaring Lions* there was a Lake, and that Lake was [54] all of Brimstone, but stored with over-grown Trouts, which Trouts *spawned*[186] Presbyterians, and those *spawned* the *Millecantons* of all other Fanaticks. That the[187] Shoal of Presbyterians *landed at* Geneva and devoured all the Bishop of Geneva's Capons, which are of the greatest size of any in the Reformed-World. And ever since their mouths have been so in relish that the Presbyterians are in all parts the very Canibals of Capons: insomuch that if Princes do not take care, the race of Capons is in danger to be totally extinguished. But that the River Rhosne was so *sober* and *intelligent,* that its Waters would not mix with this *Lake perilous,* but ran sheer thorow without ever touching it: nay, such is its apprehension lest the Lake should overtake it, that the River dives it self under ground till the Lake hath lost the scent: and yet when it rises again, imagining that the Lake is still at its heels, it runs on so impetuously that it chuseth rather to pass through the *roaring Lions,* and never thinks it self safe, [55] till it hath taken sanctuary at the Popes Town of Avinion.[188] He might too have proved that Calvin made himself *Pope and Emperour,* because the City of Geneva stamps upon its Coyn the two-headed Imperial Eagle. And, to have given us the utmost Terror, he might have considered the Alliance and Vicinity of Geneva to the Canton of Bern, the Arms of which City is the Bear, (and an Argument in Heraldry, even Bishop Bramhall himself being Judge, might have also held in Divinity) and therefore they keep under the Town-house constantly a whole den of Bears. So that there was never a more dangerous situation, nor any thing so carefully to be avoided by all Travellers in their wits, as Geneva: the *Lions* on one side, and the *Bears* on the other.

[184] loss 72] less 72a.

[185] *Reasons . . . Blackberries:* Shakespeare, I *Henry IV,* 2.4.242–43.

[186] *spawned: Discourse,* p. 23: "Sect was spawn'd out of sect."

[187] the 72a] this 72.

[188] Avinion: Avignon.

This[189] Story would have been Nuts to Mother Midnight,[190] and was fit to have bin imbellish'd with Mr. Bayes his Allegorical Eloquence. And all that he saith either by fits and girds of Calvin, or in his justest Narratives, hath less foundation in Nature: and is indeed twice [56] incredible, first in the matter related, and then because Mr. Bayes it comes from: or, to express it shorter, because of the Tale and the Tales-man. He is not yet come to that Authority but that his Dogmatical *Ipse Dixits*[191] may rather be a reason why we should not believe him. If Mr. Bayes will speak of Controversy; let him enter into a regular Disputation concerning these Calvinian Tenets, and not write an History. Or, if he will give us the History of Calvin, let him at the same time produce his Authors. And whether History or Controversy, let him be pleas'd so long to abate of the exuberancy of his Fancy and Wit; to dispense with his Ornaments and superfluencies of Invention and Satyre, and then a man may consider whether he may believe his Story, and submit to his Argument. But in the mean time (for all he pleads in pag. 97. of his *Defence*) it looks all so like subterfuge and inveagling; it is so nauseating and tedious a task, that no man thinks he ows the Author so much service as to [57] find out the reason of his own *Categoricalness* for him. One may beat the Bush a whole day; but after so much labour shall, for all game, onely spring a Butterfly, or start an Hedghog. Insomuch that I am ever and anon disputing with my self whether Mr. Bayes be indeed so ill-natured a person as some would have him, and do not rather innocently write things (as he professes, pag. 4.[192] of his *Preface*) so *exceeding all belief*, that he may make himself and the Company merry. I sometimes could think that he intends no harm either to Publick or Private, but onely rails contentedly to himself and his Muses; That he seeks onely his own diversion, and chargeth his Gun with Wind but to shoot at the Air. Or that, like Boyes, so he may make a great Paper-Kite of his own *Letter* of 850 pages,[194] and his *Preface* of an hundred, he hath no further design upon the Poultry of the Village. But he takes care that I shall never be long deceived with that pleasing imagination: and though his Hyperboles and Impossibilities can have onely a ri-[58]diculous effect, he

[189] This: new paragraph 72a.

[190] Nuts . . . Mother Midnight: Mother Midnight was slang for a midwife, frequently a bawd; nuts were treats.

[191] *Ipse Dixits:* he himself (the master) said it: dogmatic statements.

[192] pag. 4: actually A3v.

[193] 850 pages: actually 750 pages.

will be sure to manifest that he had a felonious intention. He would take it ill if we should not value him as an Enemy of mankind: and like a raging Indian (for in Europe it was never before practised) he runs a *Mucke*[194] (as they call it there) stabbing every man he meets, till himself be knockt on the head.

This here is the least pernicious of all his mischiefs; though it be no less in this and all his other Books, than to make the German Protestancy a reproachful Proverb, and to turn Geneva and Calvin into a Common-Place of Railing. I had alwayes heard that Calvin was a good Scholar, and an honest Divine. I have indeed read that he spoke something contemptuously of our Liturgy: *Sunt in illo Libro quaedam tolerabiles ineptiae.*[195] But that was a sin which we may charitably suppose he repented of on his death-bed. And if Mr. Bayes had some just quarrel to him on that or other account, yet for *Divinity's sake* he needed not thus have made a constant Pissing-place of his Grave. And as [59] for Geneva, I never perceiv'd before but that it was a very laudable City, that there grew an excellent Grape on the South-side of the Lake Lemane, that a man might make good chear there, and there was a *Pall-mall,* and one might shoot wth[196] the *Arbalet,*[197] or play at *Courte boule* on Sundaies. What was here to inrage our Author so that he must raze the Fort of St. Katherine,[198] and attempt with the same success a second *Escalade*?[199] But the difficulty of the Enterprize doubtless provoked his Courage, and the honour he might win made the justice of his quarrel. He knew that not only the Common-wealth of Switzerland, but the King of France, the King of Spain, and the Duke of Savoy would enter the lists for[200] the common preservation of the place: and therefore, though it be otherwise but a petty Town, he disdain'd not where the Race was to be run by Monarchs, to exercise his footmanship.

[194] a *Mucke:* dangerously mad. *OED* gives Marvell's as the earliest use.

[195] *Sunt . . . ineptiae:* "There are in that book certain tolerable awkwardnesses." Smith found the phrase in a letter from Calvin to Francford, in his *Epistolae,* ed. T. Beza, 2d ed. (1576), p. 158.

[196] wth 72a] with 72, 72a (B5, B7, B9, D5).

[197] *Arbalet:* the crossbow.

[198] Fort of St. Katherine: a fort erected by Charles Emmanuel, duke of Savoy, southeast of Geneva.

[199] *Escalade:* a failed attack on Geneva by the duke of Savoy, December 11, 1602; the name marks an annual festival celebrating the city's survival.

[200] for 72, 72a] of 72a (B5, B7, B9, D5).

But[201] is it not a great pity to see a man in the flower of his age, and the vigor of his studies, to fall into such a distra-[60]ction, That his head runs upon nothing but Roman Empire and Ecclesiastical Policy? This happens by his growing too early acquainted with *Don Quixot,*[202] and reading the Bible too late: so that the first impressions being most strong, and mixing with the last, as more novel, have made such a medly in his brain-pan that he is become a mad Priest, which of all the sorts is the most incurable. Hence it is that you shall hear him anon instructing Princes, like Sancho, how to govern his Island:[203] as he is busied at present in vanquishing the Calvinists of Germany and Geneva. Had he no friends to have given him good counsel before his Understanding were quite unsetled? or if there were none near, why did not men call in the neighbours, and send for the Parson of the Parish to perswade with him in time, but let it run on thus till he is fit for nothing but Bedlam[204] or Hogsdon?[205] However though it be a particular damage, it may tend to a general advantage: and young students will, I hope, by his example learn to beware hence-[61]forward of over-weening Presumption and preposterous Ambition.

For this Gentleman, as I have heard, after he had read *Don Quixot* and the Bible, besides such School-books as were necessary for his age, was sent early to the *University*: and there studied hard, and in a short time became a competent Rhetorician, and no ill Disputant. He had learnt how to erect a *Thesis,* and to defend it *Pro* or *Con* with a serviceable distinction: while the Truth #is# (as his Camarade Mr. Bayes hath it on another occasion)

Before a full Pot of Ale you can swallow,
Was here with a Whoop and gone with a Holla.[206]

And so thinking himself now ripe and qualified for the greatest Undertakings, and highest Fortune; he therefore exchanged the narrowness of

[201] But: new paragraph 72a.

[202] *Don Quixot:* Cervantes's *Don Quixote* (1605, 1615) trans. Thomas Shelton (1620), had become the referent for the absurdities of the medieval and early sixteenth-century romances, despite the fact that the novel itself parodies romance extremism.

[203] Sancho . . . Island: *Don Quixote,* part 2, chapter 17: "Of the advice that Don Quixote gave Sancho Panza before he should go to governe the Island." [S]

[204] Bedlam: The hospital of St. Mary of Bethlehem, originally in Bishopsgate, was used as a mental asylum.

[205] Hogsdon: Hoxton, synonymous with Bedlam as a place for lunatics.

[206] *Holla* 72a] *Hollow* 72; the quotation is from *Rehearsal,* act 5, scene 1, p. 45.

the University for the Town; but coming out of the confinement of the Square-cap[207] and the Quadrangle into the open Air, [62] the World[208] began to turn round with him: which he imagined, though it were his own giddiness, to be nothing less than the *Quadrature* of the *Circle.*[209] This accident concurring so happily to increase the good opinion which he naturally had of himself, he thenceforward apply'd to gain a-like reputation with others. He follow'd the Town life, haunted the best companies; and, to polish himself from any Pedantick roughness, he read and saw the Plaies, with much care and more proficiency than most of the Auditory. But all this while he forgot not the main chance, but hearing of a vacancy with a Noble-man,[210] he clap'd in, and easily obtain'd to be his Chaplain. From that day you may take the Date of his Preferments and his Ruine. For having soon wrought himself dexterously into his Patrons favour, by short Graces and Sermons, and a mimical way of drolling upon the Puritans, which he knew would take both at Chappel and Table; he gained a great Authority likewise among all the do-[63]mesticks. They all listened to him as an Oracle: and they allow'd him by common consent, to have not onely all the *Divinity,* but more wit too than all the rest of the family put together. This thing alone elevated him exceedingly in his own conceit, and raised his *Hypocondria*[211] into the Region of the Brain: that his head swell'd like any Bladder with wind and vapour. But after he was stretch'd to such an height in his own fancy, that he could not look down from top to toe but his Eyes dazled at the Precipice of his Stature;[212] there fell out, or in, another natural chance which push'd him headlong. For being of an amorous Complexion, and finding himself (as I told you) the *Cock-Divine* and the *Cock-Wit* of the Family, he took the priviledge to walk among the Hens:

207 Square-cap: mortarboard.

208 World 72] Wold 72a.

209 *Quadrature . . . Circle:* How to square the circle was one of the mathematical conundrums of the age, tackled by, among others, Thomas Hobbes. Cf. Marvell, *Upon Appleton House,* ll. 45–46: "Let others vainly strive t'immure / The *Circle* in the *Quadrature*"; and see *RT2,* p. 282.

210 Noble-man: Gilbert Sheldon (1598–1677), archbishop of Canterbury. Parker became his chaplain in 1667.

211 *Hypocondria:* melancholy, vapours.

212 Precipice . . . Stature: Marvell used this conceit in "A Dialogue between the Soul and Body," in which the Body complains of being so "stretcht upright" by the Soul "That mine own Precipice I go" (ll.13–14).

and thought it was not impolitick to establish his new-acquired Reputation upon the Gentlewomens side. And they that perceiv'd he was a Rising-man,[213] and of pleasant Conversation, dividing his Day among them into Canonical hours,[214] of reading [64] now the Common-prayer, and now the Romances, were very much taken with him. The sympathy of Silk began to stir and attract the Tippet[215] to the Pettycoat and the Pettycoat toward the Tippet. The innocent Ladies found a strange unquietness in their minds, and could not distinguish whether it were Love or Devotion. Neither was he wanting on his part to carry on the Work; but shifted himself every day with a clean Surplice, and, as oft as he had occasion to bow, he directed his Reverence towards the Gentlewomens Pew. Till, having before had enough of the Libertine, and undertaken his Calling only for Preferment; he was transported now with the Sanctity of his Office, even to extasy: and like the Bishop over Maudlin Colledge Altar,[216] or like Maudlin de la Croix,[217] he was seen in his Prayers to be lifted up sometimes in the Air, and once particularly so high that he crack'd his Scul against the Chappel Ceiling. I do not hear for all this that he had ever practised upon the Honour of the Ladies, but [65] that he preserved alwayes the Civility of a *Platonick Knight-Errant.* For all this Courtship had no other operation than to make him stil more in love with himself: and if he frequented their company, it was only to speculate his own Baby in their Eyes.[218] But being thus, without Competitor or Rival, the Darling of both Sexes in the Family and his own Minion; he grew beyond all measure elated, and that crack of his Scull, as in broken Looking-Glasses, multiply'd him in self-conceit and imagination.

Having fixed his Center in this Nobleman's House, he thought he could

[213] Rising-man: a pun: a man on the way up, and tumescent.

[214] Canonical hours: prescribed hours of the day appointed for prayers.

[215] Tippet: a band of silk worn round the neck with the two ends pendent from the shoulders in front; worn by ecclesiastics.

[216] Bishop . . . Altar: The altarpiece of Magdalen College Chapel, Oxford, painted by Isaac Fuller (1606–72) shows a bishop suspended in air. It was described by Addison in his poem *Resurrection* (1718) [E.D.J.]

[217] Maudlin de la Croix: an abbess of Cordova (c. 1545) supposedly in league with the devil and given to elevation. See Martin Del Rio, *Disquisitionum Magicarum* (1633), book 4, ch. 1, p. 509. [E.D.J.] Marvell would cite this work, in this edition, several times in *RT2*. John Owen owned this edition (p. 16, #23).

[218] speculate . . . Eyes: gaze on his image in their eyes.

now move and govern the whole Earth with the same facility. Nothing now would serve him but he must be a madman in print, and write a Book of *Ecclesiastical-Policy.* There he distributes all the *Territories of Conscience*[219] into the Princes Province, and makes the *Hierarchy* to be but Bishops of the *Air*; and talks at such an extravagant rate in things of higher concernment,[220] that the Reader will avow that in the whole [66] discourse he had not one *lucid interval.*[221] This Book he was so bent upon, that he sate up late at nights, and wanting sleep, and drinking sometimes Wine to animate his Fancy, it increas'd his Distemper. Beside that too he had the misfortune to have two Friends,[222] who being both also out of their wits, and of the same though something a calmer phrensy, spurr'd him on perpetually with commendation. But when his Book was once come out, and he saw himself an Author; that some of the Galants of the Town layd by the new Tune, and the *Tay, tay, taree,* to quote some of his impertinencies; that his Title-page was posted and pasted up at every avenue next under the Play for that afternoon at the Kings or the Dukes House: the Vain-Glory of this totally confounded him. He lost all the little remains of his understanding, and his *Cerebellum*[223] was so dryed up, that there was more brains in a Walnut and both their Shells were alike thin[224] and brittle. The King of France[225] that lost his wits, had not near so many [67] unlucky circumstances to occasion it: and in the last of all there is some Similitude. For, as a negligent Page that rode behind and carried the Kings Lance, let it fall on his head, the King being in Armour, and the day hot, which so disordered him that he never recovered it: so this Gentleman, in the Dog-dayes, stragling by

[219] *Territories of Conscience: Discourse,* p. 90.

[220] concernment 72] concernments 72a.

[221] *lucid interval: Defence,* p. 473 (discussing the madness of the Elizabethan Robert Brown).

[222] Smith suggested Simon Patrick and Thomas Tomkins; but B7 gives a cross-reference to "P.44," where it had already glossed the two friends as "Drs. Patrick & Craddock."

[223] *Cerebellum:* the smaller or hinder brain.

[224] thin 72, 72a] thine 72a variant reported by Smith in Harvard EC65.M2685.672b (A), and Yale IjM368.672b.

[225] King of France: Charles VI (1368–1422) was frightened out of his wits when a page let his spear fall on his companion's helmet. See Froissart's *Chronicle,* trans. Lord Berners, ed. W. P. Ker (1903), 6:68. (Anglesey possessed "Froissarts Chronicle 1525," p. 26, #94.)

Temple-bar, in a massy Cassock[226] and Surcingle,[227] and taking the opportunity at once to piss and admire the Title-page of his Book; a tall Servant of his, one J.O. that was not carefull as he should be, or whether he did it of purpose, lets another Book of four hundred leaves fall upon his head; which meeting with the former fracture in his *Cranium,* and all the concurrent Accidents already mentioned, has utterly undone him. And so in conclusion his Madness hath formed it self into a perfect *Lycanthropy.*[228] He doth so verily believe himself to be a Wolf, that his speech is all turn'd into howling, yelling, and barking: and if there were any Sheep here, you should see him pull out their throats and suck [68] the blood. Alas, that a sweet Gentleman, and so hopeful, should miscarry! For want of Cattel here, you find him raving now against all the Calvinists of England, and worrying the whole Flock of them. For how can they hope to escape his chaps and his paws better than those of Germany and Geneva; of which he is so hungry, that he hath scratch'd up even their dead bodies out of their Graves to prey upon? And yet this is nothing if you saw him in the height of his fits: but he hath so beaten and spent himself before, that he is out of breath at present; and though you may discover the same fury, yet it wants of the same vigour. But however you see enough of him, my Masters, to make you beware, I hope, of valuing too high, and trusting too far to your own Abilities.

It were a wild thing for me to *Squire* it after this *Knight,* and accompany him here through all his Extravagencies against our Calvinists. You find nothing but *Orthodoxy, Systems,* and *Syntagms, Polemical Theology, Subtilties* [69] and *Distinctions. Demosthenes; Tankard-bearers; Pragmatical; Controversial*: General terms without foundation or reason assigned. That they seem like words of Cabal,[229] & have no significance till they be decipher'd. Or, you would think he were playing at *Substantives* and *Adjectives.* All that rationally can be gathered from what he saith, is that the man is mad. But if you would supply his meaning with your imagination, as if he spoke sense and to some determinate purpose; it is very strange that, conceiving himself to be the Champion of the Church of England, he should bid such a generall defiance to the Calvinists. For, he knows, or perhaps I may better say he did know before this Phrensy had subverted both his Understanding

226 Cassock: long clerical garment, worn under a surplice.

227 Surcingle: a girdle or belt which confines the cassock.

228 *Lycanthropy:* a madness in which the sufferer imagines himself a wolf.

229 Cabal: Cabbala, the Jewish tradition of biblical exegesis; hence, any secret system of interpretation.

and Memory, that most of our ancient, and many of the later Bishops nearer our times, did both hold and maintain those Doctrines which he traduces under that by-word. And the contrary Opinions were even in Bishop Prideaux's[230] time accounted so [70] novel, that, being then publick Professor of *Divinity,* he thought fix to tax Doctor Heylin[231] at the Commencement for his new-fangled Divinity: *Cujus,* saith he, in the very words of promotion, *te Doctorem creo.* He knew likewise that of our present Bishops, though one had leisure formerly to write a *Rationale*[232] of the *Ceremonies* and *Lyturgie,* and another a Treatise of the *Holiness of Lent*;[233] yet that most of them, and 'tis to be supposed all, have studied other Controversies, and at another rate than Mr. Bayes his Lead can fathom. And as I know none of them that hath published any Treatise against the Calvinian tenets, so I have the Honour to be acquainted with some of them who are intirely of that judgment, and differ nothing, but (as of good reason) in the point of *Episcopacy.* And as for that, Bishop Bramhal, page 61. hath proved that Calvin himself was of the *Episcopal* perswasion. So that I see no reason why Mr. Bayes should here and every where be such an enemy to *Controversial*[234] *skill,* or the Calvinists. [71]

But[235] I perceive 'tis for Bp Bramhall's sake here that all the Tribe must suffer. This Bayes is not a good dog: for he runs at a whole flock of sheep, when Mr. B.[236] was the Deer whom he had in view from the beginning. However having foil'd himself so long with every thing he meets, after him

230 Bishop Prideaux: John Prideaux (1578–1650), bishop of Worcester, Regius Professor of Divinity at Oxford, 1615–41.

231 Doctor Heylin: Peter Heylyn (1600–62), royalist and high church polemicist, who appears frequently in both parts of *RT.* For the story of how Heylyn was examined by Prideaux for his B.D. in April 1627 and gave several unacceptable answers, see Wood, *Athenae Oxonienses,* 3:553.

232 *Rationale:* Anthony Sparrow (1612–85), bishop of Norwich, wrote, while still under Cromwell's government, *A Rationale upon the Book of Common Prayer of the Church of England* (1657). This was republished in 1672, and Marvell comments on its reappearance. See below, p. 194.

233 *Holiness of Lent:* Peter Gunning (1614–84), bishop of Ely, an ardent royalist and high churchman, published *The Paschal or Lent Fast, Apostolical and Perpetual* (1662) (A, p. 7, #149).

234 *Controversial* 72] *Controversal* 72a.

235 But: new paragraph 72a.

236 Mr. B.: Richard Baxter (1615–91), famous and long-lived Presbyterian controversialist. Bramhall replied to him in his *Vindication.* For Baxter's theology, see N. H. Keeble's Introduction to the *Remarks,* vol. 2, pp. 388–91.

now he goes, and will never leave till he hath run him down. Poor Mr. B. I find that when he was a Boy he pluck'd Bishop Bramhall's *Sloes* and *ate his Bullice*;[237] and now, when he is as superannuated as the Bishop's Book, he must be whipt for't, there is no remedy. And yet I have heard, and Mr. Bayes himself seems to intimate as much, that how-ever he might in his younger years have mistaken, yet that even as early as Bishop Bramhall's Discourse, he began to retract: and that as for all his sins against the Church of England, he hath in some late Treatises cryed *Peccavi*[238] with a Witness. But Mr. Bayes, doth not this now look like *Sorcery* and *Extortion*, which of all crimes you purge your self from so often without an Accuser? For [72] first; whereas the old Bishop was at rest, and had under his last Pillow laid by all cares and contests of this lower World; you by your *Necromancy* have disturb'd him, and rais'd his Ghost to persecute and haunt Mr B. whom doubtless at his death he had pardoned. But if you called him up to ask some Questions too concerning your Ecclesiastical Policy, as I am apt to suppose, I doubt you had no better Answer than in the Song:

Art thou forlorn of God, and com'st to me?
What can I tell thee then but miserie?[239]

And then, as for Extortion; who but such an Hebrew Jew as you, would, after an honest man had made so full and voluntary Restitution, not yet have been satisfied without so many pounds of his flesh over into the bargain?[240] Though J.O. be in a desperate condition, yet methinks Mr. B. not *being past Grace*, should not neither *have been past Mercy*.[241] Are there no terms of Pardon, Mr. Bayes? is there no time for Expiation? but, after so ample a Confession as he [73] hath made, must he now be hang'd too to make good the Proverb?[242] It puts me in mind of a Story in the time of the

[237] *Bullice:* a wild plum, larger than the sloe.

[238] *Peccavi:* I have sinned.

[239] *Art . . . miserie:* from an anonymous paraphrase of 1 Samuel 28:8–20, entitled "In Guilty Night" or "The Witch of Endor." The earliest MS version seems to be in a pre-1650 songbook in the Bodleian Library (Don C.57), with a setting by Robert Ramsay, organist of Trinity College, Cambridge, from 1628 to 1644. Marvell could have heard it when a student at Trinity. [S]

[240] Hebrew . . . bargain: an allusion to Shylock's bargain for a pound of flesh in Shakespeare's *Merchant of Venice.*

[241] *being . . . Mercy: Preface,* C4.

[242] the Proverb: "Confess and be hanged"; cf. Shakespeare, *Othello,* 4.1.38.

Guelphs and Ghibilines, whom I perceive Mr. Bayes hath heard of:[243] They were two Factions in Italy, of which the Guelphs were for the Pope, and the Ghibilines for the Emperour; and these were for many years carried on and fomented with much animosity, to the great disturbance of Christendom. Which of these two were the Nonconformists in those days, I can no more determin, than which of our Parties here at home is now *schismatical.* But so *nonconformable* they were to one another, that the Historian said they took care to differ in the least circumstances of any humane action: and, as those that have the Masons Word, secretly discern one another; so in the peeling or cutting but of an Onion, a Guelph and *vice versa* would at first sight have distinguished a Ghibiline. Now one of this latter sort coming at Rome to Confession upon Ash-wednesday, the Pope or the Penitentiary sprinkling Ashes on the Man's head [74] with the usual ceremony instead of pronouncing *Memento homo quod Cinis es & in Cinerem revertêris,*[244] changed it to *Memento homo quod Ghibilinus es &c.*[245] And even thus it fares with Mr. B. who though he should creep on his knees up the whole Stairs of *Scholastick Penitence,*[246] I am confident neither he, nor any of his Party, shall by Mr. Bayes his good will ever be absolved. And therefore truly if I were in Mr. B's case, if I could not have my Confession back again, yet it should be a warning unto me not without better grounds to be so coming and so good-natured for the future.

But[247] whatever he do, I hope others will consider what usage they are like to find at Mr. Bayes's hand, and not suffer themselves by the touch of his *Penitential Rod* to be transformed into Beasts, even into *Rats,* as here he hath done with Mr. B. I have indeed wondred often at this Bayes his insolence, who summons-in all the World, and *preacheth* up only this *Repentance*: and so frequently in his Books he calls for *Testimonies, Signal*

[243] Mr. Bayes hath heard of: *Defence,* p. 645.

[244] *Memento . . . reverteris:* Genesis 3:19: "Remember, o man, that dust thou art and unto dust shall return."

[245] Now one . . . *Ghibilinus es:* Though Marvell's "Historian" cannot be precisely identified, the story is told frequently. See, for example, Platina, *Historia De Vitis Pontificum Romanorum* (1610), p. 246. The pope was Boniface VIII, or Benedict Caetani (c. 1235–1303), the Ghibelline Porchetus Spinola, Franciscan archbishop of Genoa. The incident took place on February 22, 1300. [S]

[246] Stairs . . . Penitence: doubtless the flight of stairs in the chapel Sancta Sanctorum in the Piazza di San Giovanni, Rome. Leo IV granted an indulgence of nine years for every step climbed by the pilgrim on his knees. [S]

[247] But: new paragraph 72a.

Marks, Publick Ac-[75]*knowledgment, Satisfaction, Recantation,* and I know not what. He that hath made the passage to Heaven so easie that one may fly thither without Grace (as Gonzales to the Moon only by the help of his *Gansa's*);[248] he that hath *disintricated* its narrow paths from those *Labyrinths*[249] which J.O. and Mr. B. have planted; this Overseer of God's Highwayes, (if I may with reverence speak it) who hath paved a broad Causway with Moral Virtue thorow his Kingdom; he me-thinks should not have made the *process of Loyalty* more difficult than that of *Salvation.* What *Signal Marks,* what *Testimonies* would he have of this Conversion? Every man cannot, as he hath done, write an *Ecclesiastical Policy,* a *Defence,* a *Preface*: and some, if they could, would not do it after his manner; lest in stead of obliging thereby the King and the Church, it should be a Testimony to the contrary. Neither, unless men have better Principles of Allegiance at home, are they likely to be reduced by Mr. Bayes his way of perswasion. He is the [76] first Minister of the Gospel that ever had it in his Commission *to rail at all Nations.* And, though it hath been long practised, I never observed any great success by reviling men into *Conformity.* I have heard that *Charms* may even invite the Moon out of Heaven,[250] but I never could see her moved by the *Rhetorick* of *Barking.* I think it ought to be highly penal for any man to impose other conditions upon his Majesties good Subjects than the King expects, or the Law requires. When you have done all, you must yet appear before Mr. Bayes his Tribunal, and he hath a new Test yet to put you to. I must confess at this rate the Nonconformists deserve some Compassion: that after they have done or suffered legally and to the utmost, they must still be subjected to the *Wand* of a *Verger,* or to the wanton lash of every *Pedant*; that they must run the *Ganteloop,*[251] or down with their breeches as oft as he wants the prospect of a more pleasing *Nudity.* But I think they may chuse whether they will submit or no to his [77] Jurisdiction. Let them but (as I hope they do) fear God, honour the

[248] as Gonzales . . . *Gansa's*: F. Godwin, *The Man in the Moone: or a discourse of a voyage thither by Domingo Gonsales the speedy Messenger* (1638). Gonsales trained wild swans to carry him and called them his "Gansas" (p. 25).

[249] *disintricated . . . Labyrinths:* see *Defence,* p. 665, for the accusation that Calvin and his followers "intricated the way to Heaven with their own new Labyrinths."

[250] *Charms* . . . Heaven: Virgil, *Eclogues,* 8:70: "carmina vel caelo possunt deducere Lunam."

[251] run the *Ganteloop:* run the gauntlet: military punishment in which the culprit had to run between two rows of men who struck at him with knotted cords or sticks.

King, preserve their Consciences, follow their Trades, and look to their Chimnies; and they need not fear Master Bayes and all his Malice. But after he hath sufficiently insulted over Mr. B's ignorance and vanity, with other Complements of the like nature, in recompence of that *candor and civility* which he acknowledges *him to have now learnt towards the Church of England,*[252] Mr. Bayes (forgetting what had past long since betwixt him and the Bookseller) saith, in excuse of his severity, that *this Treatise was not published to impair Mr. B's esteem in the least, but for a correction of his scribling humour, and to warn their Rat-Divines that are perpetually nibling and gnawing other mens Writings.*[253] Now I must confess Mr. Bayes this is a very handsome Welcome to Mr. B. that was come so far to see you, and doubtless upon this encouragement he will visit you often. This is an admirable dexterity our Author hath (I wish I could learn it) *to correct a man's scribling hu-*[78]*mour without impairing in the least his reputation.* He is as courteous as Lightning, and can melt the Sword without ever hurting the Scabbard. But as for their *Rat-Divines,* I wonder they are not all poysoned with nibling at his Writings, he hath strewed so much *Arsenick* in every leaf. But however methinks he should not have grudged them so slender a sustenance. For though there was a Sow in Arcadia so fat and insensible that she suffered a Rats nest in her buttock,[254] and they had both Dyet and Lodging in the same Gammon; yet it is not every *Rats* good fortune to be so well provided. And for *Pushpin-Divinity* I confess it is a new term of Art, and I shall henceforward take notice of it, but I am afraid in general it doth not tend much to the reputation of the Faculty.

And now, though he told us at the beginning, that the Bookseller was the main reason of publishing this Book of the Bishop and his own Preface, he tels us that the main reason of its publication was to give some check to their pre-[79]sent disingenuity, that is to say to that of J.O. And J.O. be it at present. He is come so much nearer however to the Truth, though we shall find ere we have done that there is still a mainer reason.

When I first took notice of this misunderstanding betwixt Mr. Bayes and J.O. I considered whether it were not Execution-day with the whole *Latine Alphabet*: whether all the Letters were not to suffer in the same manner,

[252] *candor . . . England: Preface,* A8.

[253] *this Treatise . . . Writings: Preface,* A8.

[254] Sow in Arcadia: see Pliny, *Natural History,* trans. Philemon Holland (1634) 11.85 (A, p. 25, #53; p. 29, #215).

except *C* only, which (having been the mark of Condemnation) might have a pardon to serve for the Executioner. I began to repent of my Undertaking, being afraid that the Quarrel was with the whole *Cris-cross-Row,*[255] and that we must fight it out through all the Squadrons of the *Vowels,* the *Mutes* the *Semi-vowels* and the *Liquids.* I foresaw a sore and endless labour, and a battel the longest that ever was read of; being probable to continue as long as one Letter was left alive, or there were any use of Reading. Therefore, to spare mine own pains, and prevent *Ink-shed,* I was advising the Letters to go before [80] Mr. Bales,[256] or any other his Majesties Justices of Peace, to swear that they were in danger of their Lives, and desire that Mr. Bayes might be bound to the *Good-behaviour.* But after this I had another Phancy, and that not altogether unreasonable; that Mr. Bayes had, onely for health and exercise-sake, drawn J.O. by chance out of the number of the rest, to try how he could rail at a Letter, and that he might be well in breath upon any occasion of greater consequence. For, how perfect soever a man may have been in any Science, yet without continual practice he will find a sensible decay of his faculty. Hence also, and upon the same natural ground, it is the wisdome of Cats to whet their Claws against the Chairs and Hangings, in meditation of the next *Rat* they are to encounter. And I am confident that Mr. Bayes by this way hath brought himself into so good railing-case, that pick what Letter you will out of the Alphabet, he is able to write an Epistle upon it of 723 pages (I have now told them right) to [81] the Author of the *Friendly Debates.*

Now though this had very much of probability, I had yet a further Conjecture; that this J.O. was a *Talisman,* signed under some peculiar influence of the heavenly bodies, and that the Fate of Mr. Bayes was bound up within it. Whether it be so or no I know not: but this I am assured of, without the help either of *Syderal*[257] *Magick* or *Judicial Astrologie,* that when *J* and *O* are in *Conjunction* they do more certainly than any of the *Planets* forebode that a great *Ecclesiastical Politician* shall that Year run mad. I confess after all this, when I was come to the dregs of my phansie (for we all

[255] *Cris-cross-Row:* the alphabet, from the figure of the cross attached to it in hornbooks.

[256] Mr. Bales: Thomas Bales was one of the commissioners entrusted with regulating building and traffic in the City of London, evidently a byword for tiresome regulation. Wood, *Life and Times,* 2:395, reported in December 1677 that "divers would be asking the king 'who should be archbishop': who to put off and stop their mouths would tell them '*Tom Bailles.*' He is a drunken leacherous Justice of Peace of Westminster."

[257] *Syderal:* caused by the stars.

have our infirmities, and Mr. Bayes his *Defence* was but the *blew-John*[258] of his *Ecclesiastical Policy,* and this *Preface* the Tap-droppings of his *Defence*) I reflected whether Mr. Bayes having no particular cause of indignation against the Letters, there might not have been a mistake of the Printer, and that they were to be read in one word *Io* that uses to go before *Paean*:[259] that is in English a Triumph Before the Vi-[82]ctory. Or whether it alluded to Io that we read of at School, the Daughter of Inachus; and that as Juno persecuted the Heifer, so this was an *He-Cow,* that is to say a *Bull* to be baited by Mr. Bayes the *Thunderer.* But these being Conceits too trivial, though a *Ragoust*[260] fit enough for Mr. Bayes his palate, I was forced moreover to quit them, remarking that it was an *J* Consonant. And I plainly at last perceived that this J.O. was a very Man as any of us are; and had a Head, and a Mouth with Tongue and Teeth in it, and Hands with Fingers and Nails upon them: nay, that he could read and write, and speak as well as I or Mr. Bayes, either of us. When I once found this, the business appear'd more serious, and I was willing to see what was the matter that so much exasperated Mr. Bayes, who is *a Person,* as he saith himself, *of such a tame & softly humour, & so cold a complexion, that he thinks himself scarce capable of hot and passionate impressions.*[261] I concluded[262] that necessarily there must be some extraordinary Accident & [83] Occasion that could alter so good a Nature. For I saw that he pursued J.O. if not from *Post to Pillar,* yet from *Pillar to Post,* and I discerned all along the footsteps of a most inveterate and implacable Malice. As oft as he does but name those two first Letters, he is, like the Island of Fayal,[263] on fire in three-score and ten places.

You see, Mr. Bayes, that I too have improved my wit with reading the *Gazetts.* Were you of that Fellows diet[264] here about Town, that epicurizes upon burning Coals, drinks healths in scalding Brimstone, scraunches the

[258] *blew-John:* the second run of beer.

[259] *Io . . . Paean:* a Greek exclamation of joy or triumph; for Io, daughter of Inachus, who was raped by Jupiter and turned into a heifer to hide the crime from jealous Juno, see Ovid, *Metamorphoses,* 1:590–667.

[260] *Ragoust:* stew, medley.

[261] *a Person . . . Impressions: Discourse,* Preface, iii.

[262] concluded 72, 72a (B5, C3, W2)] conclude 72a.

[263] Fayal: an island belonging to Portugal, formerly noted for volcanoes.

[264] Fellows diet: Richardson, the famous fire-eater. Evelyn saw him at Lady Sunderland's on October 8, 1672, "who before us devourd *Brimston* on glowing coales . . . he also mealted a beere glasse & eate it quite up." See *Diary,* ed. E. S. de Beer (Oxford, 1955), 3:626–27. [S]

Glasses for his *Dessert,* and draws his breath through glowing Tobacco pipes. Nay, to say a thing yet *greater*; had you never tasted other sustenance than the Focus of *burning Glasses,* you could not shew more *flame* than you do alwayes upon that subject. And yet one would think that even from the *little sports,* with your *comfortable importance* after supper, you should have learnt when J.O. came into play, to *love your Love* with an J, because he is *Judi-*[84]*cious,* though you *hate your Love with an* J, because he is *jealous*: and then to *love your Love with an O,* because he is *Oraculous,* though you *hate your Love with an O,* because he is *Obscure*: Is it not strange, that in those most benign minutes of a Man's life, when the Stars smile, the Birds sing, the Winds whisper, the Fountains warble, the Trees blossom, and universal Nature seems to invite it selfe to the *Bridal*; When the Lion pulls in his Claws, and the Aspick layes by its Poyson, and all the most noxious Creatures grow amorously innocent: that even then, Mr. Bayes alone should not be able to refrain his Malignity? As you love your self *Madam,* let him not come near you. He hath been fed all his life with Vipers instead of Lampreys,[265] and Scorpions for Crayfish: and if at any time he eat Chickens they had been cramb'd with Spiders, till he hath so invenomed his whole substance that 'tis much safer to bed with a Mountebank[266] before he hath taken his Antidote. But it cannot be any vulgar fur-[85]nace that hath chafed so *cool* a Salamander.[267] 'Tis not the strewing of *Cow-itch*[268] in his *Genial-bed*[269] that could thus disquiet him the first night. And therefore let's take the Candle and see whether there be not some body underneath that hath cut the Bed-Cords.

There[270] was a worthy Divine, not many years dead, who in his younger time being of a facetious and unlucky humour, was commonly known by the name of Tom Triplet.[271] He was brought up at Pauls School, under a severe Master, Dr. Gill,[272] and from thence he went to the University. There he took liberty (as 'tis usual with those that are emancipated from

[265] Lampreys: eels.

[266] Mountebank: literally, "Mount-on-bench"; an itinerant quack who sold "remedies" from a platform, sometimes by claiming to take poison and then its antidote.

[267] Salamander: a lizard supposed to live in fire.

[268] Cow-itch: cowage, the stinging hairs of the pod of a tropical plant.

[269] *Genial-Bed:* marriage bed.

[270] There: new paragraph 72a.

[271] Tom Triplet: Dr. Thomas Triplet (1603–70), a wit of Christ Church College, Oxford. See Wood, *Fasti Oxonienses,* ed. Bliss (1815), 2:255. [S]

[272] Dr. Gill: Alexander Gill, the elder (1565–1635), master of St. Paul's School.

School) to tel Tales, and make the Discipline ridiculous under which he was bred. But, not suspecting the Doctor's intelligence, comming once to Town, he went in full School to give him a Visit, and expected no less than to get a *Play-day* for his former acquaintance. But, instead of that, he found himself hors'd up in a trice; though he appeal'd in vain to the Priviledges of the Universi-[86]ty, pleaded *Adultus,* and invoked the mercy of the Spectators. Nor was he let down till the Master had planted a Grove of Birch in his back-side, for the Terrour and publick Example of all Waggs that divulge the Secrets of Priscian,[273] and make merry with their Teachers. This stuck so with Triplet, that all his life-time he never forgave the Doctor, but sent him every New-years-tide an Anniversary Ballad to a new Tune, and so in his turn avenged himself of his jerking Pedagogue.[274]

Now when I observed that of late years Mr. Bayes had regularly *spawned* his Books; in 1670 the *Ecclesiastical Policy*; in 1671 the *Defence of the Ecclesiastical Policy*; and now in 1672 this *Preface* to Bishop Bramhal, & that they were writ in a stile so vindictive and poynant, that they wanted nothing but rime to be right Tom Triplet; and that their edge bore alwayes upon J.O. either in broad meanings or in plain terms; I began to suspect that where there was so great resemblance in the Effects, there might be some parallel in [87] their Causes. For though the Peeks[275] of Players among themselves, or of Poet against Poet, or of a Conformist-Divine against a Nonconformist, are dangerous, and of late times have caused great disturbance; yet I never remarked so irreconcileable and implacable a spirit as that of Boyes against their Schoolmasters or Tutors. The quarrels of their Education have an influence upon their Memories and Understandings for ever after. They cannot speak of their Teachers with any patience or civility; and their discourse is never so flippant, nor their Wits so fluent as when you put them upon that *Theme.* Nay, I have heard old Men, otherwise, sober, peaceable and good-natured, who never could forgive Osbolston,[276] as the younger are still inveighing against Dr. Busby.[277] It were well that both old and young would reform this vice, and consider how easie a thing it is upon particular grudges, and as they conceive out of a just censure, to slip either

[273] Priscian: famous Roman grammarian of the late fifth century.

[274] There he took . . . Pegagogue: A brief and ruder version of this story appears in John Aubrey, *Brief Lives,* ed. Andrew Clark (Oxford, 1898), 1:262.

[275] Peeks: piques, quarrels.

[276] Osbolston: Lambert Osbolston (1594–1659), master of Westminster School.

[277] Busby: Richard Busby (1606–95), later master of Westminster School, noted for his severity.

into juvenile petulancy or inveterate uncharitableness. And had [88] there not been something of this in his own case, I am confident Mr. Bayes in his *Ecclesiastical Policy,* in order to the publick Peace and security of the Government, could not have failed to admonish Princes to beware of this growing Evil, and to brandish the *Publick Rods*[278] if not *the Axes*[279] against the Boyes, to teach them better manners. And he would have assured them that they might have done it with all safety, notwithstanding that there were in proportion an hundred Boyes against one *Preceptor.*[280] But therefore is it not possible that J.O. and Mr. Bayes have known one another formerly in the University;[281] and that (as in Seniority there is a kind of Magistracy) Bayes being yet young, J.O. conceiv'd himself in those dayes to be his Superiour, and exercised an Academical Jurisdiction or Dominion over him. Now whether J.O. might not be too severe upon him there (for all men are prone to be cogent and supercilious when they are in Office) or whether Mr. Bayes might not make some little escapes and excursions there [89] (as young men are apt to do when they are got together) that I know not, and rather believe the contrary. But that is certain that the young Wits in the Universities have alwayes an animosity against the Doctors, and take a peculiar felicity in having a lucky hit at any of them. I rather suppose that after Mr. Bayes had changed the place, and his condition, to be the Noblemans Chaplain, ⟨that⟩ he might commit some exorbitance in J.O.'s opinion, or preach or write something to J.O.'s reproach, and published the Secrets of the *Holy Brother hood*:[282] and that J.O. having got him within his reach, did therefore (figuratively speaking)

—Instead of Maid Jillian
Take up his Malepillian,
And whipt him like a baggage—[283]

[278] *Publick Rods: Preface,* d6v.

[279] *Axes: Defence,* p. 219; rods and axes were *Fasces,* bundles of rods of elm or birchwood, and a single-headed axe, carried by Roman lictores as signs of magisterial authority.

[280] *Preceptor:* teacher.

[281] J.O. . . . University: John Owen was vice-chancellor of Oxford University, 1652–58.

[282] *Holy Brother hood: Preface,* A8v, c6v, d3; in Spain the Santa Hermandad was a high-level police force.

[283] *Instead . . . baggage:* The more scurrilous original of these lines was quoted by Aubrey in his life of Triplet, where they read, "He took up the Male Pillion / Of his bouncing maid Gillian / And sowc'd her like a Baggage." A pillion is usually a woman's

as Tom Triplet expresses it. This might well raise Mr. Bayes his Choler, who, considering himself to be now in Holy Orders, and conceiving that he had been as safe as in a Sanctuary under his Patrons protection, must needs take it ill to be handled so irreverently. If it [90] were thus in Fact, and that J.O. might presume too much upon his former Authority to give him Correction; yet it is the more excusable, if Mr. Bayes had on his part been guilty of so much disingenuity. For though a man may be allowed once in his life to change his Party, and the whole Scene of his Affairs, either for his Safety or Preferment; nay, though every man be obliged to change an hundred times backward and forward, if his Judgement be so weak & variable; yet there are some drudgeries that no man of Honour would put himself upon, and but few submit to if they were imposed. As suppose one had thought fit to pass over from one Perswasion of the Christian Religion unto another, he would not chuse to spit thrice at every Article that he relinquished, to curse solemnly his Father and Mother for having educated him in those Opinions, to animate his new Acquaintances to the massacring of his former Camarades. These are businesses that can only be expected from a Renegade[284] of [91] Argier or Tunis; to over-doe in expiation, and gain better credence of being a sincere Musulman. And truly, though I can scarcely believe that Mr. Bayes hath so mean and desperate intentions, which yet his words seem too often to manifest; the Offices however which he undertakes are almost as dishonourable. For he hath so studied and improved their *Jargon*[285] as he calls it, heard their Sermons and Prayers so attentively, searched the Scriptures so narrowly, that a man may justly suspect he had formerly set up of J.O.'s Profession, and having the language so perfectly, hath upon *this juncture of affairs* betaken himself to turn *Spy* and *Intelligencer*; and 'tis evident that he hath travell'd the Country for that purpose. So that I cannot resemble him better than to that Politick Engine who about two years ago was employed by some of Oxford as a *Missionary* amongst the Nonconformists of the adjacent Counties; and upon design, either gathered a Congregation of his own, or preach'd amongst others, till having got all their [92] Names, he threw off the Vizard, and appear'd in his own Colours, an honest *Informer.*[286] But I would not have any man take

---

light saddle or a cushion attached to the hinder part of an ordinary saddle for a second person, usually a woman.

284 Renegade: an apostate, especially a Christian who becomes a Mahommedan.

285 *Jargon: Defence*, pp. 163, 343.

286 Politick . . . Informer: probably the notorious informer John Poulter. In May 1670

Mr. Bayes his *Fanatical Geography* for authentick, lest he should be as far misled, as in the situation of Geneva. It suffices that Mr. Bayes hath done therein as much as served to his purpose, and mixed probability enough for such as know not better, and whose eares are of a just bore for his fable.

But I.O. being of age and parts sufficient either to manage or to neglect this Quarrel, I shall as far as possible decline the mentioning of him, seeing I have too (upon further[287] intelligence and consideration) found that he was not the person whom Mr. Bayes principally intended. For the truth of it is, the King was the Person concern'd from the beginning.

His Majesty before his most happy and miraculous Restauration, had sent over a Declaration of his Indulgence to tender Consciences in Ecclesiastical matters.[288] Which, as it was doubtless the real Result of the last Advice left [93] Him by his glorious Father, and of his own consummate Prudence and natural Benignity; so at his Return he religiously observed and promoted it as far as the Passions and Influences of the contrary Party would give leave. For, whereas among all the decent Circumstances of his welcom Return, the Providence of God had so cooperated with the duty of his Subjects, that so glorious an Action should neither be soiled with the blood of Victory, nor lessened by any capitulations of Treaty, so not to be wanting on his part in courtesy, as I may say, to so happy a conjuncture, He imposed upon himself an Oblivion of former offences, and this Indulgence in Ecclesiastical affairs. And to royal and generous minds no stipulations are so binding as their own voluntary promises: nor is it to be wondred if they hold those Conditions that they put upon themselves the most inviolable. He therefore carried the Act of Oblivion and Indempnity thorow:[289]

Dr. Mews, the vice-chancellor of Oxford, wrote to Secretary Williamson, "John Poulter, who, from having mixed himself up with the fanatics, made some discoveries which . . . might have been improved upon." He was discovered by the dissenters, and his efficacy as a spy therefore ceased. See *CSPD,* 1670, p. 235. [S]

[287] too (upon further Ed.] too upon (further 72, 72a.

[288] Declaration . . . Ecclesiastical matters: *His Majesties most Gracious Declaration from his court at Breda April 14. 1660:* "We do declare a liberty to tender Consciences, and that no man shall be disquieted or called in question for differences of opinion in matters of Religion, which do not disturb the peace of the Kingdom" (pp. 7–8).

[289] Act . . . Indemnity: The Bill of Indemnity received royal assent on August 29, 1660; Marvell is being ironic here; on June 27, 1661, he wrote to Hull, "To morrow the kings Counsell is to be heard at our barr to lay out evidence against the kings dead & living judges & the other persons whom the Act of Indemnity has left to pains & penaltyes" (*P&L,* 2:33–34).

that Party who had suffered so vastly in the late Combustions not refusing to imi-[94]tate his Generosity, but throwing all their particular Losses & Resentments into the Publick Reckoning. But when it came to the Ecclesiastical Part, the accomplishment of which onely remain'd behind to have perfected his Majesty's felicity, the business I warrant you would not go so, (as I shall have occasion to say more particularly.) For, though I am sorry to speak it, yet it is a sad truth, that the Animosities and Obstinacy of some of the Clergy have in all Ages been the greatest Obstacle to the Clemency, Prudence and good Intentions of Princes, and the Establishment of their Affairs. His Majesty therefore expected a better season, and having at last rid himself of a great Minister of State[290] who had headed this Interest, he now proceeded plainly to recommend to his Parliament effectually and with repeated instances, the Consideration of tender Consciences. After the Kings last representing of this matter to the Parliament, Mr. Bayes took so much time as was necessary for the maturing of so [95] accurate a Book which was to be the standard of Government for all future Ages, and he was happily delivered in 1670 of his *Ecclesiastical Policy.*[291] And, though he thought fit in this first Book to treat his Majesty more tenderly than in those that followed, yet even in this he doth all along use great liberty and presumption. Nor can what he objects, page 282, to weak Consciences, take place so justly[292] upon them as upon himself: *who, while his Prince might expect his Compliance, doth give him Council, advises him how to govern the Kingdom, blames and corrects the Laws, and tells him how this and the other might be mended.*[293] But that I may not involve the thing in generals, but represent undeniably Mr. Bayes his performance in this undertaking, I shall without Art write down his own Words and his own *quod Scripsi Scripsi,*[294] as they ly naked to the view of every Reader.

The grand Thesis upon which he stakes not onely all his own Divinity and Policy, his Reputation, Prefer-[96]ment and Conscience, (of most of

[290] Minister of State: Edward Hyde (1600–74), earl of Clarendon, whom the dissenters regarded as responsible for the Act of Uniformity and other penal statutes. A villain in Marvell's Dutch War satires, in 1667 he was held responsible for the miscarriages of the war and arraigned for high treason by Parliament. He fled to Calais and lived the rest of his life in exile, writing his *History of the Great Rebellion.*

[291] *Ecclesiastical Policy* Ed.] in roman 72, 72a.

[292] justly 72] justily 72a.

[293] *who, while . . . mended* 72a] set in roman 72.

[294] *quod Scripsi Scripsi:* "What I have written, I have written"; the notorious statement of Pontius Pilate on delivering Christ up to execution. See John 19:22.

which he hath no reason to be prodigal)[295] but even the Crowns and Fate of Princes, and the Liberties, Lives and Estates, and, which is more, the Consciences of their Subjects, (which are too valuable to be trusted in his disposal,)[296] is this, pag. 10. *That it is absolutely necessary to the peace and government of the World, that the supream Magistrate of every Commonwealth should be vested with a Power to govern and conduct the Consciences of Subjects in affairs of Religion.* And pag. 12. he explains himself more fully: that *Unless Princes have Power to bind their Subjects to that Religion that they apprehend most advantagious to publick peace and tranquillity, and restrain those religious mistakes that tend to its subversion, they are no better then Statues and Images of Authority.* pag. 13. *A Prince is endued with a Power to conduct Religion, and that must be subject to his Dominion as well as all other Affairs of State.* P. 27. *If Princes should forgoe their Soveraignty over mens Consciences in matters of Religion, they leave themselves less power than* [97] *is absolutely necessary, &c.* And in brief: *The supream Government of every Commonwealth, where-ever it is lodged, must of necessity be universal, absolute, and uncontroulable in all affairs whatsoever that concern the Interests of Mankind and the ends of Government.* P. 32. *He in whom the Supream Power resides, having Authority to assign to every Subject his proper function, and among others these of the Priesthood; the exercise thereof as he has power to transfer upon others, so he may if he please reserve it to himself.* P.33. *Our Saviour came not to unsettle the Foundations of Government, but left the Government of the World in the same condition he found it.* P. 34. *The Government of Religion was vested in Princes by an antecedent right to Christ.*— This being the Magisterial and main Point that he maintains, the rest of his Assertions may be reckoned as Corollaries to this *Thesis,* and without which indeed such an unlimited Maxime can never be justified. Therefore, to make a Conscience fit for the nonse,[297] he sayes, p. 89. *Men may think of things according to their own* [98] *perswasions, and assert the freedom of their judgments against all the Powers of the Earth. This is the Prerogative of the Mind of Man within its own Dominions, its Kingdom is intellectual, &c. Whilst Conscience acts within its proper sphere, the Civil Power is so far from doing it violence, that it never can.* P. 92. *Mankind have the same natural right to Liberty of Conscience in matters of Religious Worship as in Affairs of Justice and Honesty; that is to say, a Liberty of Judgment, but not of Practice.* And in the same page he determines *Christian*

[295] parenthesis added 72a.

[296] parenthesis added 72a.

[297] for the nonse: for the nonce, just for the occasion.

Liberty to be *founded upon the Reasonableness of this Principle.* P. 308. *In cases and disputes of Publick concernment, Private men are not properly* sui Juris, *They have no power over their own actions: they are not to be directed by their own judgments, or determined by their own wills, but by the commands and determinations of the Publick Conscience; and if there be any sin in the Command, he that imposed it shall answer for it, and not I whose whole duty it is to obey. The Commands of Authority will warrant my Obedience, my Obedience will* [99] *hallow, or at least excuse my action, and so secure me from sin, if not from error: and in all doubtful and disputable cases, 'tis better to err with Authority than to be in the right against it: not only because the danger of a little error (and so it is if it be disputable) is outweighed by the importance of the great duty of Obedience, &c.*

Another of his Corollaries is, *That God hath appointed* (p. 80.) *the Magistrates to be his Trustees upon Earth, and his Officials to act and determine in Moral Virtues and Pious Devotions according to all accidents and emergencies of affairs: to assign new particulars of the Divine Law; to declare new bounds of right and wrong, which the Law of God neither doth nor can limit.* P. 69. *Moral Virtue being the most material and useful part of all Religion, is also the utmost end of all its other duties.* P. 76. *All Religion must of necessity be resolved into Enthusiasm or Morality. The former is meer Imposture; and therefore all that is true must be reduced to the latter.* Having thus enabled the Prince, dispensed with Conscience, and fitted up a Moral Religion for that Conscience; [100] to show how much those Moral Virtues are to be valued, P. 53. of the Preface to his *Ecclesiastical Policy* he affirms, that *'tis absolutely necessary to the Peace and happiness of Kingdoms, that there be set up a more severe Government over Mens Consciences and Religious Perswasions, than over their Vices and Immoralities.* And, pag. 55. of the same, that *Princes may with less hazard give liberty to mens Vices and Debaucheries than their Consciences.* But for what belongs particularly to the use of their Power in Religion; he first (p. 56 of his Book) saith, that *the Protestant Reformation hath not been able to resettle Princes in their full and natural rights in reference to its concerns*: & 58. *most Protestant Princes have been frighted, not to say hector'd out of the exercise of their Ecclesiastical jurisdiction.* P. 271. *If Princes will be resolute (and if they will govern so they must be) they may easily make the most stuborn Conscience bend to their resolutions.* P. 221.[298] *Princes must be sure to bind on at first their Ecclesiastical Laws with the straitest knot, and afterward keep them in force by the severity of their execution.* 223. [101] speaking of honest and well meaning men: *So easy*

[298] 221 72, 72a] actually *Discourse*, p. 21.

is it for men to deserve to be punished for their Consciences, that there is no Nation in the World, in which were Government rightly understood and duly managed, mistakes and abuses of Religion would not supply the Galleys with vastly greater numbers than Villany. Pag. 54. of the Preface to Ecclesiast. Policy. *Of all Villains the well meaning Zealot is the most dangerous.* P. 49.[299] *The Fanatick-Party in Country Towns and Villages ariseth not (to speak within compass) above the proportion of one to twenty. Whilst the publick peace and settlement is so unluckily defeated by quarrels and mutinies of Religion, to erect and create new Trading Combinations, is only to build so many Nests of Faction and Sedition,* &c. *For it is notorious that there is not any sort of people so inclinable to seditious practices as the Trading part of a Nation.* And now though many as material passages might be heap'd up out of his Book on all these and other as tender Subjects, I shall conclude this imperfect enumeration with one Corollary more, to which [102] indeed his grand Thesis and all the superstructures are subordinate and accommodated. P. 166. *Princes cannot pluck a pin out of the Church, but the State immediately shakes and totters.* This is the *Syntagm* of Mr. Bayes his Divinity, and *System* of his Policy: The Principles of which confine upon the *Territories* of Malmsbury,[300] and the stile, as far as his Wit would give him leave, imitates that Language: But the Arrogance and Dictature with which he imposes it on the world, surpasses by far the presumption either of *Gondibert*[301] or *Leviathan.*[302] For he had indeed a very Politick fetch[303] or two that might have made a much wiser man then he, more confident. For he imagined first of all, that he had perfectly secured himself from any mans answering him: not so much upon the true reason, that is, because indeed so paltry a Book did not deserve an Answer; as because he had so confounded the Question with differing terms and contradictory expressions, that he might upon occasion affirm whatsoever he denyed, or deny [103] whatsoever he affirmed. And then besides, because he had so intangled the matter of Conscience with the Magistrates Power, that he supposed no man could handle it thorowly without bringing

[299] *Of all . . . dangerous:* actually, *Discourse,* liii.

[300] Malmsbury: i.e., of Thomas Hobbes; see n. 39 above.

[301] *Gondibert:* see n. 56 above.

[302] *Leviathan:* Hobbes's famous work of political theory, justifying obedience to an absolute sovereign power as the only protection against human aggression. It was written while Hobbes took refuge in France and was published in London in 1651.

[303] fetch: a contrivance, stratagem.

himself within the Statute of treasonable words,[304] and at least a *Premunire.*[305] But last of all, because he thought that whoseover answered him must for certain be of a contrary Judgment; and he that was of a contrary Judgment should be a Fanatick; and if one of them presumed to be medling, then Mr. Bayes (as all Divines have a *Non-obstante*[306] to the *Jejunium Cecilianum,*[307] and to the Act of Oblivion and Indempnity) would either burn that, or tear it in pieces. Being so well fortified on this side, upon the other he took himself to be impregnable. His Majesty must needs take it kindly that he gave him so great an accession of *Territory*: and, lest he should not be thought rightly to understand Government, nay lest Mr. Bayes by virtue of P. 271. should not think him fit to govern, he could not in prudence and safety but submit to [104] his Admonition and Instructions. But if he would not, Mr. Bayes knew, ay that he did, how to be even with him, and would write another Book that should do his business. For, the same Power that had given the Prince that Authority, could also revoke it.

But let us see therefore what success the whole Contrivance met with, or what it deserved. For, after things have been laid with all the depth of humane Policy, there happens lightly some ugly little contrary accident from some quarter or other of Heaven, that frustrates and renders all ridiculous.

And here, for brevity and distinction sake, I must make use of the same priviledge by which I call him Mr. Bayes, to denominate also his several Aphorisms or Hypotheses: and let him take care whether or no they be significant.

First, The *Unlimited Magistrate.*
Secondly, *The Publick Conscience.*
Thirdly, *Moral Grace.*
Fourthly, *Debauchery Tolerated.*
Fifthly, *Persecution recommended.*
And lastly, *Pushpin-Divinity.* [105]

[304] Statute of treasonable words: see p. 274 below.

[305] *Premunire:* a special legal writ applied to those accused of asserting papal jurisdiction in England or of denying the monarch's control of the church.

[306] *Non-obstante:* notwithstanding: the opening of a legal clause which conveyed the monarch's license to do something notwithstanding any statute to the contrary.

[307] *Jejunium Cecilianum:* Cecil's fast: an act of February 1562 for the observance of Wednesday as a fast (fish) day, drawn up by William Cecil, Lord Burghley, to increase the national consumption of fish. See William Rastell, *A Collection of the English Statutes now in force* (1591), fol. 408v (A, 1618, p. 69, #6; 1621, #5).

And now, though I intend not to be longer than the nature of *Animadversions*[308] requires, (this also being but collateral to my work of examining the Preface, and having been so abundantly performed already) yet neither can I proceed well without some Preface. For, as I am obliged to ask pardon if I speak of serious things ridiculously; so I must now beg excuse if I should hap to discourse of ridiculous things seriously. But I shall, so far as possible, observe *decorum*,[309] and, whatever I talk of, not commit such an Absurdity, as to be grave with a Buffoon. But the principal cause of my Apology is, because I see I am drawn in to mention Kings and Princes, and even our own; whom, as I think of with all duty and reverence, so I avoid speaking of either in jest or earnest, lest by reason of my private condition & breeding, I should, though most unwillingly, trip in a word, or fail in the mannerliness of an expression. But Mr. Bayes, because Princes sometimes hear men of his quality play their Part, or preach a Ser-[106]mon, grows so insolent that he thinks himself fit to be their Governour. So dangerous it is to let such creatures be too familiar. They know not their distance, and like the Ass in the Fable,[310] because they see the Spaniel play with their Masters Leggs, they think themselves priviledged to paw and ramp[311] upon his Shoulders. Yet though I must follow his track now I am in, I hope I shall not write after his Copy.

As for his first Hypothesis of the *Unlimited Magistrate,* I must for this once do him right, that after I had read in his 12th page,[312] that *Princes have power to bind their subjects to that Religion they apprehend most advantagious to publick Peace and Tranquility*; a long time after, not as I remember till pag. 82. when he bethought himself better, he saith, *No Rites nor Ceremonies can be esteemed unlawful in the Worship of God, unless they tend to debauch men either in their practices or their conceptions of the Deity.* But no man is in Ingenuity obliged to do him that service for the future; neither yet doth that limitati-[107]on bind up or interpret what he before so loosly affirmed. However, take all along the Power of the Magistrate as he hath stated it; I am confident if Bishop Bramhall were alive (who could no more forbear

[308] *Animadversions:* a form of polemical correction in which the answerer rebuts or mocks his adversary's argument point by point.

[309] *decorum:* in writing and rhetorical theory, that which is proper to person, place, time, or subject.

[310] Ass in the Fable: see John Ogilby, *The Fables of Aesop Paraphrased in Verse* (1665), pp. 59–60, where the fable is brilliantly illustrated (A, p. 24, #8).

[311] ramp: to rear up, trample with forelegs.

[312] 12th page: *Discourse,* Preface, xii.

Grotius, than Mr. Bayes could the Bishop, notwithstanding their friendship) he would bestow the same Censure upon him that he doth upon Grotius, p. 18.[313] *When I read his Book of the Right of the Sovereign Magistrate in Sacred things,*[314] *he seem'd to me to come too near an Erastian,*[315] *and to lessen the power of the Keys*[316] *too much, which Christ left as a Legacy to his Church. It may be he did write that before he was come to full maturity of judgment: and some other things, I do not say after he was superannuated,*[317] *but without that due deliberation which he useth at other times;* (wherein a man may discern[318] Mr. Bayes in Mr. Bayes) *Or it may be some things have been changed in his* Book, *as I have been told by one of his nearest friends, and that we shall shortly see a more Authentick Edition of all his Works. This is certain, that some of those things which I dislike, were not his own* [108] *judgment after he was come to maturity in Theological matters.* And had Mr. Bayes (as he ought to have done) carryed his Book to any of the ⟨present⟩ Bishops, #to whom it belongs,# or their Chaplains, for a Licence to print it, I cannot conceive that he could have obtained it in better terms than what I have collected out of the 108 page of his Answerer: *Notwithstanding the old Pleas of the* Jus Divinum *of Episcopacy, of Example and Direction Apostolical, of a Parity of Reason between the condition of the Church whilst under Extraordinary Officers, and whilst under Ordinary, of the power of the Church to appoint Ceremonies for Decency and Order, of the patern of the Churches of old*;[319] (all which under Protestation are reserved till the first opportunity;) I have upon reading of this Book, found that it may be of use for the *present Juncture of Affairs,* and therefore let it be printed. And, as I think, he hath disobliged the Clergy of England in this matter; so I believe the favour that he doth his Majesty is not equivalent to that damage. For (that I may, with Mr. Bays his leave, [109] prophane Ben. Johnson,)[320] *though the gravest Divines should be*

[313] p. 18: Bramhall, *Vindication,* pp. 18–19.

[314] *Book . . . things:* i.e., Grotius, *De Imperio Summarum Potestatum circa Sacra* (Paris, 1647).

[315] Erastian: one who maintains the supremacy of the state in ecclesiastical government.

[316] *the power of the Keys:* ecclesiastical jurisdiction, based on Christ's mandate to Peter (Matthew 16:19): "And I will give unto thee the keys of the kingdom of heaven"; often taken to refer specifically to the power of excommunication.

[317] *superannuated:* too old.

[318] wherein . . . desire 72] in italics in 72a; discern 72 (B2, D1, H, S2), 72a] desire 72.

[319] *old Pleas . . . old:* Owen, *Truth and Innocence Vindicated,* p. 108.

[320] parenthesis added 72a; see *Discourse,* Preface, xxiii.

his Flatterers;[321] he hath a very quick sense, and (shall I prophane Horace too in the same period?)

Hunc male si palpere recalcitrat undique tutus.[322]

If one stroke him ilfavouredly, he hath a terrible way of kicking, and will fling you to the Stable door; but is himself safe on every side. He knows it's all but that you may get into the Saddle again; and that the Priest may ride him, though it be to a Precipice. He therefore contents Himself with the Power that He hath inherited from his Royal Progenitors Kings and Queens of England, and as it is declared by Parliament: and is not to be trepann'd[323] into another kind of Tenure of Dominion to be held at Mr. Bayes his pleasure, and depend upon the strength only of his Argument. But (that I may not offend in Latin too frequently) he considers that by not assuming a Deity to himself, he becomes secure and worthy of his Government. There are lightly [110] about the Courts of Princes a sort of Projectors for Concealed Lands,[324] to which they entitle the King, to begg them for themselves: and yet generally they get not much by it, but are exceedingly vexatious to the Subject. And even such an one is this Mr. Bayes with his Project of a *Concealed Power,* that most Princes, as he said,[325] *have not yet rightly understood*; but whereof the King is so little enamour'd, that I am confident, were it not for prolling[326] and molesting the People, his Majesty would give Mr. Bayes the Patent for it, and let him make his best on't, after he hath paid the Fees to my Lord-Keeper.[327]

But one thing I must confess is very pleasant, and he hath past an high Complement upon his Majesty in it: that he may, if he please, reserve the Priesthood and the Exercise of it to himself. Now this indeed is surprising; but this onely troubles me, how his Majesty would look in all the Sacerdotal

[321] *though . . . Flatterers:* set in roman in 72; Marvell is quoting Jonson, *The Alchemist,* 2.2.59–60.

[322] *Hunc . . . tutus:* "This one, if you touch him uncautiously, will protect himself by kicking in all directions"; Horace, *Satires,* 2.1.20.

[323] trepann'd: trapped, snared.

[324] Projectors . . . Lands: "Concealed land" is that held privately from the king by a person having no title to it; used especially of land that had been monastic property before the Reformation and, after the Restoration, of state land given away during Cromwell's regime. Projectors informed against the holders of such lands. [S]

[325] said 72a] saith 72.

[326] prolling: prowling (for gain).

[327] Lord Keeper: Sir Orlando Bridgeman (1606–74), Lord Keeper 1667–72; one of Marvell's butts in the *Account of the Growth of Popery.* See vol. 2, pp. 244–50.

habiliments, and the Pontifical Wardrobe. I am afraid the King would find himself incommoded with all that furniture up-[111]on his back, and would scarce reconcile himself to wear even the Lawn-sleeves and the Surplice. But what? even Charles[328] the fifth, as I have read, was at his Inauguration by the Pope, content to be vested, according to the Romane Ceremonial, in the habit of a Deacon:[329] and a man would not scruple too much the formality of the dress in order to Empire.

But one thing I doubt Mr. Bayes did not well consider; that, if the King may discharge the Function of the Priesthood, he may too (and 'tis all the reason in the world) assume the Revenue. It would be the best Subsidy that ever was voluntarily given by the Clergy. But truly otherwise, I do not see but that the King does lead a more unblamable Conversation,[330] and takes more care of Souls than many of them, and understands their Office much better, and deserves something already for the pains he hath taken.

The next is *Publick Conscience.* For as to mens private Consciences he hath made them very inconsiderable, and, [112] reading what he saith of them with some attention, I only found this new & important Discovery & great Priviledge of Christian Liberty, that *Thought is free.*[331] We are however obliged to him for that, seeing by consequence we may think of him what we please. And this he saith a man may assert against all the Powers of the Earth: And indeed with much reason and to great purpose; seeing, as he also alledges, the Civil Power is so far from doing violence to that liberty, that it never can. But yet if the freedom of thoughts be in not lying open to discovery, there have been wayes of compelling men to discover them; or, if the freedom consist in retaining their judgments when so manifested, that also hath been made penal. And I doubt not but beside *Oaths* and *Renunciations,* and *Assents* and *Consents,* Mr. Bayes, if he were searched, hath twenty other tests and picklocks in his pocket. Would Mr. Bayes then perswade men to assert this against all the Powers of the Earth? I would ask in what manner? To say the truth I do [113] not like him, and would wish the Nonconformists to be upon their guard, lest he trepan them first by this means into a Plot,

[328] Charles 72] Charls 72a.

[329] Charles . . . Deacon: Emperor Charles V (1500–58) was crowned by Pope Clement VII in Bologna on February 24, 1530. See J. Sleidan, *A Famous Cronicle of oure time,* trans. J. Daus (1560), fol. xxv (A, p. 27, #138).

[330] Conversation: behavior or mode of life; Marvell is being ironic, especially since *conversation* can mean sexual congress.

[331] *Thought is free:* a common saying; cf. Shakespeare, *The Tempest,* 3.2.123, as sung by Trinculo.

and then peach,[332] & so hang them: If Mr. Bayes meant otherwise in this matter, I confess my stupidity, and the fault is most his own who should have writ to the capacity of vulgar Readers. He cuts[333] indeed and faulters in this discourse, which is no good sign, perswading men that they may, and ought to practise against their Consciences, where the Commands of the Magistrate intervenes. None of them denies that it is their duty, where their Judgements or Consciences cannot comply with what is injoyned, that they ought in obedience patiently to suffer; but further they have not learned. I dare say that the Casual Divinity of the Jesuites is all thorow as Orthodox as this Maxime of our Authors: and, as the Opinion is brutish, so the Consequences are devilish. To make it therefore go down more glibly, he saith, that *'tis better to err with Authority, than to be in the right against it* [114] *in all doubtful and disputable cases, because the great duty of Obedience outweighs the danger of a little error, (and little it is if it be disputable.)*[334] I cannot understand the truth of this reasoning; that whatsoever is disputable is little; for even the most important matters are subject to controversie: And besides, things are little or great according to the Eyes or Understandings of several men; and however, a man would suffer something rather than commit that little error against his Conscience, which must render him an Hypocrite to God, and a Knave amongst Men. *The Commands* (he saith) *and Determinations of the publick Conscience ought to carry it; and if there be any sin in the Command, he that imposed shall answer for it, and not I whose duty it is to obey;* (And mark) *the Commands of Authority will warrant my Obedience, my Obedience will hallow, or at least excuse my action, and so secure me from sin if not from error*;[335] and so you are welcome Gentlemen. Truly a very fair and conscionable Reckoning! So far is this from hallowing the Action, [115] that I dare say it will, if followed home, lead only to all that *sanctified Villany*, for the invention of which we are beholden to the Author. But let him have the honour of it: for he is the first Divine that ever taught Christians how another man's sin could confer an *Imputative Righteousness*[336] upon all Mankind that shall follow & comply with it. Though the Subject made me serious, yet I could not reade the expression without laughter: *My Obedience will hallow, or at least excuse my Action.* So inconsiderable a difference he

[332] peach: to give incriminating evidence against, to betray.

[333] cuts: shapes, trims, avoids committing himself.

[334] *'tis better . . . disputable: Discourse,* p. 308.

[335] *The Commands . . . from error: Discourse,* p. 308.

[336] *Imputative Righteousness: Defence,* p. 352.

seems to make betwixt those terms, That if ever our Author come for his merits #in election for# to be a Bishop, a man might almost adventure instead of *Consecrated* to say that he was *Excused.*

The third is *Moral Grace.* And whoever is not satisfied with those passages of his concerning it, before quoted, may find enough where he discourseth it at large, even to surfeit. I cannot make either less or more of it than that he overturns the whole fabrick of Christianity, and Power of Religion. [116] For my part, if Grace be resolv'd into Morality, I think a man may almost as well make God too to be only a Notional and Moral Existence.

And white-apron'd Amaryllis was of that opinion:

Ma tu Sanctissima Honestà che sola sei
D'alma ben nata inviolabil Nume.[337]

But thou most holy Honesty, that only art the inviolable Deity of the well-born Soul.

And so too was the Moral Poet:[338] (for why may not I too bring out my Latin shreds as well as he his,

Quaesitum ad fontem solos deducere verpos)[339]
Nullum Numen abest si sit Prudenti—[340]

There is no need of a Deity where there is Prudence; or, if you will, where there is *Ecclesiastical Policy.*

But so far I must do Mr. Bayes right, that, to my best observation, if Prudence had been God, Bayes had been a [117] most damnable Atheist. Or, perhaps only an Idolater of their number, concerning whom he adds in the next line

—sed te
Nos facimus Fortuna Deam Coeloque locamus.

But we make thee Fortune a Goddess, and place thee in Heaven.

[337] *Ma . . . Nume:* Guarini, *Il Pastor Fido,* 3.4.28–29.

[338] the Moral Poet: Juvenal, whose Satires 14 and 10 Marvell proceeds to quote (like Parker, inaccurately) over the next few lines.

[339] *quaesitum . . . verpos:* Juvenal, Satire 14:105: "conducting none but the circumcised to the desired fountain"; cited by Parker, *Discourse,* viii.

[340] *Nullum numen . . . Prudentia:* The whole quotation, continued below, is the close of Juvenal's Satire 10:365–66: "Thou wouldst have no divinity, O Fortune, if we had but wisdom; it is we that make a goddess of thee, and place thee in the skies."

However I cannot but be sorry that he hath undertaken this desperate vocation, when there are twenty other honest and painful wayes wherein he might have got a *Living,* and made Fortune propitious. But he cares not upon what Argument or how dangerous he runns to shew his ambitious Activity: whereas those that will dance upon Ropes, do lightly some time or other break their necks. And I have heard that even the Turk,[341] every day he was to mount the High-Rope, took leave of his *Comfortable Importance* as if he should never see her more. But this is a matter forreign to my Judicature, and therefore I leave him to be tryed by any Jury of Divines: and, that he may have all right done him, let half of [118] them be *School-Divines* and the other moity *Systematical,* and let him except against as many as the Law allows, and so God send him a good deliverance. But I am afraid he will never come off.

The fourth is *Debauchery tolerated.* For supposing, as he does, that 'tis better and *safer to give a Toleration to mens Debaucheries than to their Religious Perswasions,*[342] it amounts to the same reckoning. This is a very ill way of discoursing; and that a *greater severity ought to be exercised over mens Consciences than over their Vices and Immoralities.*[343] For it argues too much indiscretion, by avoiding one evil to run up into the contrary extream. And Debauch'd Persons will be ready hence to conclude, although it be a perverse way of reasoning, That where the Severity ought to be less, the Crime is less also; nay, even that the more they are debauch'd, it is just that the Punishment should still abate in proportion; but however, that it were very imprudent and unadvisable to reform and erre on [119] the Religious hand, lest they should thereby incur the greater penalties. Mr. Bayes would have done much better had he singled out the Theme of Religion. He might have loaded it with all the truth which that subject would bear; I would allow him that *Rebellion is as the sin of Witch-craft,*[344] though that text of Scripture will scarce admit his interpretation. He could not have declamed more sharply than I, or any honest man else, would upon occasion against all those who under pretence of Conscience raise War, or create publick

[341] the Turk: On September 15, 1657, Evelyn saw "a famous *Rope-dancer* call'd the *Turk* . . . walking bare foote, & taking hold by his toes onely, of a rope almost perpendicular . . . also dauncing blindfold on the high-roope." *Diary,* 3:197. [S]

[342] *safer . . . Perswasions: Discourse,* Preface, liv–lv.

[343] *greater . . . Immoralities: Discourse,* Preface, lii–liii.

[344] *Rebellion . . . Witchcraft: Preface,* d1; from 1 Samuel 15:23; the phrase was much used in early modern political theory.

Disturbances. But Comparisons of Vice are dangerous, and though he should do this without design, yet, while he aggravates upon Religion, and puts it in ballance, he doth so far alleviate and encourage Debauchery. And moreover (which to be sure is against his design) he doth hereby more confirm the austerer sort of Sinners, and furnishes them with a more specious Colour and stronger Argument. It had been better Policy to instruct the Magistrate that there is no [120] readier way to shame these out of their Religious Niceties than by improving Mens Morals. But, as he handles it, never was there any Point more unseasonably exposed; at such a time, when there is so general a depravation of Manners, that even those who contribute towards it do yet complain of it; and though they cannot reform their practice, yet feel the effects, and tremble under the apprehension of the Consequences. It were easie here to shew a man's reading, and to discourse out of History the causes of the decay and ruine of Mr. Bayes his Roman Empire; when-as the Moralist has it,

—saevior armis
Luxuria incubuit, Victumque ulciscitur Orbem.[345]

And descending to those Times since Christianity was in the Throne, 'tis demonstrable that for one War upon a Fanatical or Religious account, there have been an hundred occasioned by the thirst of Glory and Empire that hath inflamed some great Prince to invade his Neighbours. And more have [121] sprung from the Contentiousness and Ambition of some of the Clergy; But the most of all from the Corruption of Manners, and alwayes fatal Debauchery. It exhausts the Estates of private persons, and makes them fit for nothing but the High-way or an Army. It debases the spirits and weakens the vigor of any Nation; at once indisposing them for War, and rendring them uncapable of Peace. For, if they escape intestine troubles, which would certainly follow when they had left themselves by their prodigality or intemperance, no other means of subsistence but by preying upon one another; then must they either, to get a maintenance, pick a quarrel with some other Nation, wherein they are sure to be worsted; or else (which more frequently happens) some neighbouring Prince that understands Government takes them at the advantage, and, if they do not like ripe Fruit fall into his lap, 'tis but shaking the Tree once or twice, and he is

345 *saevior . . . Orbem:* Juvenal, *Satires,* 6:292: "Luxury, more deadly than any foe, has laid her hand upon us, and avenges a conquered world." This was a favorite text of political moralists.

sure of them.[346] Where the Horses are, like those of the Sybarites, taught to [122] dance, the Enemy need only learn the Tune and bring the Fiddles.[347] But therefore (as far as I understand) his Majesty to obviate and prevent these inconveniencies in his Kingdoms, hath on the one hand never refused a just Warre; that so he might take down our Grease and Luxury, and keep the English Courage in breath and exercise; and on the other, (though himself most constantly addicted to the Church of England) hath thought fit to grant some liberty to all other Sober People, (and longer than they are so God forbid they should have it) thereby to give more temper and allay to the common and notorious Debauchery.

But Mr. Bayes nevertheless is for his fifth; *Persecution recommended*: and he does it to the purpose. Julian[348] himself, who I think was first a Reader, and held forth in the Christian Churches before he turned Apostate and then Persecutor, could not have outdone him either in Irony or Cruelty. Only it is God's mercy that Mr. Bayes is not Emperour. You have seen how he in-[123]veighs against Trade: *That whilst mens Consciences are acted by such peevish and ungovernable Principles, to erect Trading-Combinations is but to build so many Nests of Faction and Sedition.*[349] Lay up your Ships, my Masters, set Bills on your Shop-doors, shut up the Custom-house; and why not adjourn the Term, mure up Westminster-hall, leave Plowing and Sowing, and keep a dismal Holy-day through the Nation; for Mr. Bayes is out of humour. But I assure you it is no jesting matter. For he hath in one place[350] taken a List of the Fanatick Ministers, whom he reckons to be but about an hundred *Systematical Divines*: though I believe the Bartlemew-Register[351]

[346] Debauchery . . . sure of them: In this passage Marvell gives his true opinion of the Restoration state, the causes of the Second Dutch War, and Charles II's dealings with Louis XIV.

[347] Horses . . . Fiddles: The inhabitants of Sybaris, a Greek town, were noted for their luxury. For the dancing horses, see Athenaeus, *Diepnosophistae,* 12.520 [S] (A, p. 47, #110). Marvell echoes this allusion in his *Short Historical Essay,* vol. 2, p. 167.

[348] Julian: Flavius Claudius Julianus (331–63), Roman emperor, known as the Apostate because though born a Christian he converted to paganism in 351. For the three years of his tenure as emperor, he persecuted the Christians with peculiar ingenuity.

[349] *That . . . Sedition: Discourse,* Preface, xlix.

[350] in one place: *Discourse,* p. 253.

[351] Bartlemew-Register: The Act of Uniformity came into force on St. Bartholomew's Day, August 24, 1662, when the dissenters en masse gave up their pulpits rather than conform.

or the March-Licences[352] would make them about an hundred and three or an hundred and four, or so: But this is but for rounder number and breaks no square. And then for their People, either *they live in greater Societies of men*[353] (he means the City of London and the other Cities and Towns-Corporate, but expresses it so to prevent some inconvenience that might betide him) [124] *but there their noise is greater than their number.*[354] Or else in *Country Towns and Villages, where they arise not above the proportion of one to twenty.*[355] It were not unwisely done indeed if he could perswade the Magistrate that all the Fanaticks have but one neck,[356] so that he might cut off Nonconformity at one blow. I suppose the Nonconformists value themselves tho upon their Conscience and not their Numbers: but they would do well to be watchful, lest he have taken a List of their Names as well as their Number, and have set Crosses upon all their Doors against there should be occasion.[357] But till that *happy juncture,* when Mr. Bayes *shall be fully avenged of his new Enemies the wealthy Fanaticks*[358] (which is soon done too, for he saith *there are but few of them men of Estates or Interest*) he is contented that they should only be exposed (they are his own expressions) to the *Pillories, Whipping-posts, Galleys, Rods,* and *Axes*; and moreover and above, to all other Punishments whatsoever, provided they be of a severer nature than [125] those that are inflicted on men for their immoralities. O more then humane Clemency! I suppose the Division betwixt Immoralities and Conscience is universal, and whatsoever is wicked or penal is comprehended within their *Territories.* So that although a man should be guilty of all those heinous enormities which are not to be named among Christians,

[352] March-Licences: the licenses to preach, applied for by nonconformists after the Declaration of Indulgence, March 15, 1672. Approximately 1,508 licenses were issued. Evelyn, *Diary,* 3:608n. [S]

[353] *they live . . . men: Discourse,* Preface, xlix.

[354] *but . . . number: Discourse,* Preface, xlix.

[355] *Country . . . twenty: Discourse,* Preface, xlix.

[356] all . . . one neck: The emperor Caligula wished that all the Romans had only one neck. Suetonius, *Caligula,* 30. For Marvell's extensive use of Suetonius, especially in *RT2,* and his own translation thereof, see Patterson, "A Restoration Suetonius: A New Marvell Text?" *Modern Language Quarterly* 61 (2000), 463–80.

[357] set Crosses . . . occasion: The houses of Protestants were marked with a white cross for the original St. Bartholomew Massacre of 1572 in Paris. [S]

[358] *wealthy Fanaticks: Discourse,* Preface, li.

beside all lesser Peccadillo's[359] expresly against the ten Commandments, or such other part of the Divine Law as shall be of the Magistrates making, he shall be in a better condition and more gently handled, then a *well-meaning Zelot*:[360] For this is the man that Mr. Bayes saith *is of all Villains the most dangerous*: (even more dangerous it seems then a malicious and ill-meaning Zelot) this is he whom in *all Kingdoms where Government is rightly understood*,[361] he would have condemned *to the Galleys for his mistakes and abuses of Religion*. Although the other punishments are more severe, yet this being more new and unacquainted, I cannot pass it by without some reflexi-[126]on. For I considered what Princes make use of Gallyes. The first that occurred to me was the Turk, who according to Bayes his maxim, hath established Mahometism among his subjects, as the *Religion that he apprehends most advantagious to publick peace and settlement*.[362] Now in his Empire the Christians onely are guilty of those *Religious Mistakes that tend to the subversion of Mahometism*: So that he understands Government rightly in chaining the Christians to the Oar. But then in Christendom, all that I could think of were the King of France, the King of Spain, the Knights of Malta, the Pope, and the rest of the Italian princes. And these all have bound their Subjects to the Romish religion as most advantagious. But these people their Galleys, with Immoral Fellows and Debauchees: whereas the Protestants, being their Fanaticks and mistakers in Religion, should have been their *Ciurma*.[363] But 'tis to be hoped these Princes will take advice and understand it better for the future. And then at last I [127] remembered that his Majesty too hath one Gally lately built, but I dare say it is not with that intention; and our Fanaticks, though few, are so many, that one will not serve. But therefore if Mr. Bayes and his partners would be at the charge to build the King a whole Squadron for this use, I know not but it might do very well (for we delight in Novelties) and it would be a singular obligation to Sir John Baptist Dutel,[364] who might have some pretence to be General of his Majesties Gallies. But so much for that.

359 Peccadillo's: little sins, minor offenses.

360 *well-meaning Zelot: Discourse,* Preface, liii.

361 *Kingdoms . . . understood: Discourse,* p. 223.

362 *Religion . . . settlement: Discourse,* p. 12.

363 *Ciurma:* galley slaves.

364 Dutel: Sir John Duteil, appointed commander in 1671 of an English galley in the Strait of Gibraltar. In 1671 Duteil wrote to Secretary Arlington, "Requesting him to have letters dispatched from the King to the Kings of France and Spain, the Viceroys of Sicily, Naples and Sardinia, the Grand Duke of Tuscany, the Republic of Genoa, and

Yet[365] in the mean time I cannot but admire at Mr. Bayes his courage; who knowing how dangerous a Villain a well-meaning Zelot is, and having calculated to a man how many of them there are in the whole Nation, yet dares thus openly stimulate the Magistrate against them, and talk of nothing less, but much more, than *Pillories, Whipping-posts, Galleys,* and *Axes* in this manner. It is sure some sign (and if he knew not so much he would scarce adventure) of the peaceableness of their Principles, and [128] of that restraint under which their tender Consciences hold them, when nevertheless he may walk night and day in safety; though it were so easie a thing to deifie the Divine after the antient manner, and no man be the wiser. But that which I confess would vex me most, were I either an ill or a well-meaning Zealot, would be, after all to hear him (as he frequently does) sneering at me in an ironical harangue, to perswade me, forsooth, to take all patiently for Conscience-sake, and the good example of Man-kind: Nay, to wheedle one almost to make himself away to save the Hangman a labour. It was indeed near that pass in the Primitive times, and the tyred Magistrates ask't them, whether they had not Halters, and Rivers, and Precipices, if they were so greedy of Suffering?[366] But, by the good leave of your Insolence, we are not come to that yet. *Non tibi sed Petro*: or rather, *sed Regi.*[367] The Nonconformists have suffered as well as any men in the World, and could do so still if it were his Majesty's plea-[129]sure. Their *Duty to God hath hallowed,* and their *Duty to the Magistrate hath excused* both their Pain and Ignominy. To dye by a Noble hand is some satisfaction: But when his Majesty, for Reasons best known[368] to Himself, hath been graciously

---

the Grand Master of Malta, asking leave for him to levy officers and soldiers and to buy slaves in their territories to arm the two galleys that the King has had built at Leghorn to serve against the common enemy of Christendom" (*CSPD,* 1671, p. 351). [S] Marvell's list, above, suggests that he learned the contents of this letter.

365 Yet: new paragraph 72a.

366 the tyred . . . Suffering: The anecdote is told by Tertullian, "Ad Scapulam," *Opera,* ed. Ricault (Paris, 1634), p. 71 [S] (A, p. 2, #44).

367 *Non tibi sed Petro:* "Not to you but to St. Peter." This derives from an anecdote told by Peter Heylyn, *Cosmographie* (1657), book 1, p. 108 (A, p. 25, #51). In 1177 Pope Alexander III excommunicated the Emperor Frederick I and defeated him militarily. When Frederick prostrated himself before the pope, he trod on his neck: "And when the Emperor, to put the better colour on his disgrace, meekly replyed, *Non tibi sed Petro:* the Pope, not willing to lose his part of so great a glory, subjoyned as angerly *Et mihi et Petro.*" [S]

368 known 72] know 72a.

pleased to abate of your Rigors, I hope Mr. Bays that we shall not see when you have a mind to junket with your *Comfortable Importance* that the *Entremeses*[369] shall be of a Fanaticks Giblets: nor that a Nonconformists head must be wip'd off as oft as your nose drivles. 'Tis sufficient, Sir, we know your Inclination, we know your Abilities, and we know your Lodging: And when there is any further occasion you will doubtless be sent for. For, to say the truth, this Bayes is an excellent Tool, and more useful than ten other men. I will undertake that he shall rather then fail, be the Trepanner, the Informer, the Witness, the Atturney, the Judg; and, if the Nonconformist need the benefit of his Book, he shall be Ordinary too, and say he is *an ignorant fellow*,[370] *non legit*:[371] and then, [130] to do him the last Christian office, he would be his Hangman. In the mean time, let him enjoy it in speculation, secure of all the Imployments when they shall fall. For I know no Gentleman that will take any of them out of his hands, although it be an age wherein men cannot well support their quality, without some accession from the publick: and for the ordinary sort of People, they are I know not by what disaster besotted and abandon'd to Fanaticism. So that Mr. Bayes must either do it himself in person, or constitute the chief[372] Magistrate to be his Deputy. But Princes do indeed understand themselves better most of 'm, and do neither think it so safe to intrust a Clergy-man with their Authority, nor decent for themselves to do the drudgery of the Clergy. That would have past in the Dayes of Saint Dominick:[373] but when even the Inquisition hath lost its edge in the Popish Countryes, there is little appearance it should be set up in England. It were a worthy Spectacle, were it not? to see his Majesty [131] like the Governor in Synesius,[374] busied in his Cabinet among those Engines whose very names are so hard that it is some

[369] *Entremeses:* something served between the main courses of a banquet.

[370] *an . . . fellow* 72a] set in roman 72a.

[371] *non legit:* He cannot read and therefore cannot plead benefit of clergy.

[372] chief Ed.] cheif, 72, 72a.

[373] Saint Dominick: Dominic de Guzman (1170–1221), the founder of the Dominican order, then believed to have been the founder of the Inquisition and the first inquisitor, in Languedoc; the charge is denied by Catholic historians today.

[374] Synesius: Greek writer, bishop of Ptolemais (d. c. 430). Marvell is here citing one of his letters (no. 58), an encyclical against Andronicus of Berenice: "Not because of his instruments of torture to which I allude, that crush the fingers [*Dactylethrae*] and feet, [*Podostrabae*], compress the limbs, tweak the nose, [*Rhinolabides*], and deform the ears [*Otagrae*] and lips, [*Cheilostrophia*]." See *The Letters of Synesius of Cyrene,* trans. A. Fitzgerald (1926), pp. 140–41. [S]

torture to name them; the *Podostrabae*, the *Dactylethrae*,[375] the *Otagrae*, the *Rhinolabides*, the *Cheilostrophia*, devising, as they say there are particular Diseases, so a peculiar Rack for every Limb and Member of a Christians body. Or, would he (with all Reverence be it spoken) exchange his Kingdom of England for that of Macassar?[376] where the great *Arcanum* of Government is the cultivating of a Garden of venimous[377] Plants, and preparing thence a Poyson, in which the Prince dips a Dart, that where it does but draw blood, rots the person immediatly to pieces; and his Office is with that to be Executioner of his Subject. God be prais'd his Majesty is far of another temper: and he is wise, though some men be malicious.

But Mr. Bayes his sixt, is that which I call his *Push-Pin Divinity*. For he would perswade Princes that *there cannot a Pin be pull'd out of the Church but* [132] *the State immediatly totters.*[378] That is strange. And yet I have seen many a Pin pull'd out upon occasion, and yet not so much as the Church it self hath wagg'd. It is true indeed, and we have had sad experiments of it, that some Clergy-men have been so opiniastre[379] that they have rather exposed the State to ruine, than they would part with a Pin, I will not say out of their Church, but out of their Sleeve. There is nothing more natural than for the Ivy to be of opinion that the Oak cannot stand without its support: or, seeing we are going into Ivy, that the Church cannot hold up longer than It underprops the Walls: whereas it is a sneaking insinuating Imp, scarce better than Bindweed, that sucks the Tree dry, and moulders the building where it catches. But what, pray Mr. Bayes, is this Pinne in Pallas's buckler?[380] Why 'tis some Ceremony or other, that is *indifferent in its own nature*, that *hath no antecedent necessity*, but *only as commended*,[381] that *signifies nothing in it self, but what the Commander pleases*,[382] that even by the Church [133] which commands it, is *declared to have nothing of*

375 *Dactylethrae* 72 Errata] *Dactylethree* 72; *Dactylethreae* 72a.

376 Macassar: The poisons of Macassar were notorious. In March 1665 the scientists of Gresham College experimented with "the great Poyson of Macassa" on a dog, to no effect! See Pepys, *Diary*, ed. Robert Latham and William Matthews, 11 vols. (Berkeley and Los Angeles, 1979), 6:57.

377 venimous 72a] Poysonous 72.

378 *there cannot . . . totters: Discourse*, p. 166.

379 opiniastre: stubborn, opinionated.

380 Pallas's buckler: cf. *Rehearsal*, act 4, scene 1 (p. 37), where Pallas has a buckler made of cheese.

381 *indifferent . . . commanded: Discourse*, p. 94.

382 *signifies . . . pleases: Discourse*, p. 108.

Religion in it,[383] *and that is in it self of no great moment or consequence, only it is absolutely necessary that Governours should enjoyn it to avoid the evils that would follow if it were not determined.*[384] Very well, Mr. Bayes. This I see will keep cold: anon perhaps I may have a stomach. But I must take care lest I swallow your Pin.

Here we have had the Titles, and some short Rehearsal of Mr. Bayes his six Playes. Not but that, should we disvalise[385] him, he hath to my knowledg a hundred more as good in his budget: but really I consult mine own repose. But now among friends, was there ever any thing so monstrous? You[386] see what a man may come to with Divinity and High-feeding. There is a scurvy disease, which though some derive from America, others tell a story that the Genoueses in their Warrs with Venice took some of their Noblemen, whom they cut to pieces and barrel'd up like Tunny, and so maliciously vented it to the Venetians, who eating it ignorant-[134]ly, broke out in those nasty botches and ugly symptoms, that are not curable but by Mercury.[387] What I relate it for is out of no further intention, not is there any more similitude than that the Mind too hath its Nodes[388] sometimes, and the Stile its Buboes,[389] and that I doubt before Mr. Bayes can be rid of 'm, he must pass through the Grand Cure and a dry Diet.

And now it is high time that I resume the thread of my former History concerning Mr. Bayes his Books in relation to his Majesty. I do not find that the *Ecclesiastical Policy* found more acceptance than could be expected from so judicious a Prince: nor do I perceive that he was ever considered of at a Promotion of Bishops, nor that he hath the reversion of the Arch-Bishoprick of Canterbury. But if he have not by Marriage barr'd his way;[390]

[383] *declared . . . it: Discourse,* p. 99.

[384] *and that . . . determined: Discourse,* pp. 322–23.

[385] disvalise: to strip someone of his baggage; from Fr. *desvaliser.*

[386] You 72, 72a] Yet 72a variant reported by Smith in Harvard EC65.M3685.672rb (A).

[387] scurvy disease . . . Mercury: The scurvy disease is syphilis. The anecdote conflates two told by George Sandys, *A Relation of a Journey* (1627), pp. 238–39: one tells how certain merchants supplied the French army at the siege of Naples with human flesh dressed as tuna, hence spreading syphilis among them; the other tells how the Genoese avenged themselves on the Venetians by barreling up the captured Venetian nobility as tuna and sending it to Venice. [S]

[388] Nodes: knotty swellings on the skin.

[389] Buboes: inflamed swellings in the glandular parts of the body, as in bubonic plague.

[390] way 72, 72a] was 72a variant reported by Smith in Harvard EC65.M3685.67rb (A).

and it should ever fall to his lot, I am resolved instead of *his Grace* to call him alwayes *his Morality*. But as he got no Preferment that I know of at Court (though his Patron doubtless having many [135] things in his gift, did abundantly recompence him) so he mist no less of his aim as to the Reformation of Ecclesiastical-Government upon his Principles. But still, what he complains of, pag. 20.[391] *the Ecclesiastical Laws were either weakened through want of Execution, or in a manner cancell'd by the opposition of Civil Constitutions*. For, beside what in England, where all things went on at the same rate, in the neighbouring Kingdom of Scotland there were[392] I know not how many *Mas Johns*[393] restored in one day to the work of their Ministry, and a door opened whereby all the rest might come in for the future, and all this by his Majesty's Commission. Nay, I think there was (a thing of very ill example) an Arch-Bishop[394] turn'd out of his See for some Misdemeanor or other. I have not been curious after his name nor his crime, because as much as possible I would not expose the nakedness of any person so eminent formerly in the Church. But henceforward the King fell into disgrace with Mr. Bayes, and any one that had eyes might discern [136] that our Author did not afford his Majesty that Countenance and Favour which he had formerly enjoy'd. So that a Book[395] too of J.O's happening mischievously to come out at the same season, Upon pretence of answering that, he resolved to make his Majesty feel the effects of his displeasure. He therefore set[396] pen to paper again, and having kept his Midwife of the *Friendly Debate* by him all the time of his pregnancy for fear of miscarrying, he was at last happily delivered of his second Child, the *Defence of the Ecclesiastical Policy*, in the year 1671. It was a very lusty Baby, and twice as big as the former, and (which some observed as an ill sign, and that if it lived it would prove a great Tyrant) it had, when born, all the Teeth,[397] as perfect as

[391] pag. 20; i.e., *Discourse*, p. 20.

[392] were 72] where 72a.

[393] *Mas Johns:* Presbyterian preachers; this alludes to Lauderdale's policy of indulgence in 1669, which led to Burnet's resignation. See Maurice Lee, *The Cabal* (Urbana, Ill., 1965), pp. 60–61.

[394] Arch-Bishop: Alexander Burnet (1614–84), archbishop of Glasgow, forced to resign his see in 1669. He was noted for his severity toward Presbyterians. [S] See Introduction, p. 14.

[395] Book: i.e., *Truth and Innocence Vindicated.*

[396] He therefore set 72a] So that he set 72.

[397] Tyrant . . . all the Teeth: an allusion to Richard III, born with "all his teeth and haire to his shoulders," William Camden, *Remaines* (1614), p. 282 [S] (A, p. 30, #19).

ever you saw in any mans Head. But I do not reckon much upon those ominous criticismes. For there was partly a natural cause in it, Mr. Bayes having gone so many months, more than the Civil Law allows for the utmost term of legitimation, that it was no won-[137]der if the Brat were at its birth more forward than others usually are. And indeed Mr. Bayes was so provident against abortion, & careful for some reasons that the Child should cry, that the only question in Town (though without much cause, for truly 'twas very like him) was, whether it was not spurious or suppositious. But Allegories and Raillery and Hard Words apart:[398] In this his second Book, ⟨and⟩ what I quoted before out of Bishop Bramhal, p. 18. with allusion to our Author, is here faln out as exactly true as if it had been expresly calculated for Bayes his Meridian.[399] He finds himself to have come too near, nay to have far out-gone an Erastian, That he had writ his Ecclesiastical Policy before he was come to maturity of Judgment, that one might desire Mr. Bays in Mr. Bays, that something had been changed in his Book. That a more authentick Edition was necessary, that some things which he had said before, were not his Judgment after he was come to maturity in Theological matters. [138]

I will not herein too much insist upon his Reply; where his Answerer asks him pertinently enough to his grand Thesis, what was then become of their old plea of *Jus Divinum*?[400] Why, saith he, must you prescribe me what I shall write? Perhaps my next Book shall be of that Subject. For, perhaps he said so only for evasion, being old excellent at parrying and fencing. Though I have good reason to believe that we may shortly see some Piece of his upon that Theme, and in defence of an Aphorism of a great Prelate in the last King's time, *That the King had no more to do in Ecclesiastical Matters, than Jack that rubb'd his Horses heels.*[401] For Mr. Bayes

[398] apart 72 Errata, 72a] appear 72.

[399] Meridian: noon; the sun's highest point.

[400] *Jus Divinum:* divine right; a tendentious phrase in ecclesiastical history. In James's reign, Archbishop Bancroft articulated a theory of *jure divino* prelacy; in the 1630s this doctrine was reiterated by Archbishop Laud; and in the 1640s a group of presbyterians resisted the growing Erastianism of the Long Parliament by arguing that presbyterianism was laid down in Scripture. Marvell could have read the *Jus Divinum of Presbytery* (1655) in Anglesey's library (p. 12, #78).

[401] great Prelate . . . *heels:* The prelate was John Cosin (1594–1692), bishop of Durham. The quotation is of one of the articles of impeachment against Cosin read by Francis Rous in the House of Commons on March 15, 1641. See John Rushworth, *Collections,* part III (1692), 1:10. [S] Marvell, who could have met Rous at Eton, would

is so enterprising[402] you know, *Look to't, I'le*[403] *doo't.*[404] He has face enough to say or unsay any thing, and 'tis his priviledge, what the School-Divines deny to be even within the power of the Almighty, to make Contradictions true. An evidence of which (though I reserve the further instances to another occasion that draws near) does plainly appear in what I now principally urge, to [139] show how dangerous a thing it is for his Majesty and all other Princes to lose Mr. Bayes his favour. For whereas he had all along in his first Book treated them like a company of Ignorants, and that did not understand Government, (but that is pardonable in Mr. Bayes) in this his second, now that they will not do as he would have them, when he had given them Power and Instructions how to be wiser for the future, He casts them quite off like men that were desperate. He had, you know, p. 35. of his first Book and in other places, vested them with an universal and unlimited Power, and uncontroulable in the Government of Religion (that is, over mens Consciences) but now in his second, to make them an example to all incorrigible and ungrateful persons, he strips and disrobes them again of all those Regal Ornaments that he had superinduced upon them, and leaves them good Princes in *querpo*[405] as he found 'm, to shift for themselves in the wide World as well as they can. Do but read his own words, p. 237. of his *De*-[140]*fence,* parag. 5. and sure you will be of my mind. *To vest the Supreme Magistrate in an unlimited and uncontroulable Power, is clearly to defeat the Efficacy and Obligatory force of all his Laws, that cannot possibly have any binding vertue upon the minds of men, when they have no other inducement to obedience*[406] *but only to avoid the penalty. But if the Supream Power be absolute and unlimited, it doth for that very reason remove and evacuate all other Obligations, for otherwise it is restrained and conditional; and if men lye under no other impulsion than of the Law it self, they lye under no other obligation than that of prudence and self-interest, and it remains intirely in the choice of their own discretion whether they shall or shall not obey, and then there is neither Government nor Obligation to obedience; and the Principle of mens Complyance with the mind of their Superiours, is not the declaration of their*

---

also have had access to the documents collected by his friend Rushworth before their posthumous publication.

[402] enterprising 72] interprising 72a.

[403] *I'le* Ed.] *Ile* 72, 72a.

[404] *Look . . . doo't:* Buckingham, *Rehearsal,* act 1, scene 1, p. 10.

[405] in *querpo:* naked (from Spanish); picked up from Parker, *Discourse,* p. 204.

[406] *obedience* 72] *obedients* 72a.

will and pleasure, but purely the determination of their own judgments; and therefore 'tis necessary for the security of Government, though for nothing else, to set bounds to its jurisdiction; Otherwise, like [141] *the Roman Empire,* &c. I know it would be difficult to quote twenty lines in Mr. Bayes but we should encounter with the Roman Empire. But observe how laboriously here he hath asserted and proved that all he had said in his first Book was a meer mistake before he were come to years of discretion. For as in Law a Man is not accounted so till he hath compleated 21, and 'tis but the last minute of that time that makes him his own Man, (as to all things but Conscience I mean, for as to that he saith men are never *sui Juris*) so though the distance of Bayes his Books was but betwixt 1670 and 1671, yet a year, nay an instant at any time of a man's life may make him wiser, and he hath, like all other fruits, his annual maturity. It was so long since as 1670 p. 33.[407] that this *universal Unlimited and Uncontroulable Power was the natural right of Princes antecedent to Christ, firmly established by the unalterable Dictates of Natural Reason, Universal Practice, and Consent of Nations, that the Scripture rather supposes than asserts the Ecclesiasti-*[142]*cal* (and so the Civil) *Jurisdiction of Princes.* 'Twas in 1670, p. 10.[408] That it was *absolutely necessary*; and p. 12. *that Princes have that power to bind their Subjects to that Religion that they apprehend most advantagious to Publick Peace, &c.* So that they derive their title from Eternal Necessity, which the Moralists say the Gods themselves cannot impeach. His Majesty may lay by his *Dieu* and make use onely of his *Mon Droit*:[409] He hath a Patent for his Kingdom, under the Broad Seal of Nature, and next under that, and immediately *before* Christ, is over all Persons, and in all Causes as well Ecclesiastical as Civil (and over all mens Consciences) within his Majesty's Realms and Dominions Supream Head and Governour.

'Tis[410] true, the Author sometimes for fashion-sake speaks in that Book of Religion and of a Deity, but his Principles do necessarily, if not in terms, make the Princes Power *Paramount* to both those, and if he may by his uncontroulable and unlimited universal Authority introduce what Religion, he may of con-[143]sequence what Deity also he pleases. Or, if there

[407] p. 33: In fact, Marvell selects from a number of pages around p. 33.

[408] p. 10. 72, 72a] p. 19. 72a variant reported by Smith in Harvard EC65.M3685.67rb (A).

[409] *Dieu . . . Mon Droit:* "by God and my right"; originally spoken by Richard I at the battle of Gisons (1198), meaning that he was no vassal of France but owed his crown to God alone; adopted as the motto of England by Henry VI.

[410] 'Tis: new paragraph 72a.

were no Deity, yet there must be some Religion, that being an Engine most advantagious for Publick Peace and Tranquillity. This was in 1670. But by 1671. you see the case is altered. Even one night hath made some men gray.[411] And now p. 238. of his second Book, #besides what before, p. 237.# he hath made Princes accountable, ay and to so severe an Auditor as God himself. *The Thrones of Princes are established upon the Dominion of God.* And p. 241. *'Tis no part of the Princes concernment to institute rules of Moral Good and Evil, that is the care and the Prerogative of a Superiour Law-giver.* And p. 260. He owns, that if the Subjects can plead a clear[412] and undoubted preingagement to that higher Authority, they have a liberty to *remonstrate* to the equity of their Laws. I do not like this Remonstrating nor these Remonstrants.[413] I wish again that Mr. Bayes would tell us what he means by the term, and where it will end, whether he would have the Fanaticks remonstrate: but they are wary, and a-[144]shamed of what they have done in former times of that nature: or whether he himself hath a mind to remonstrate, because the Fanaticks are tolerated. That is the thing, that is the business of this whole Book: and knowing that there is a clear and undoubted preingagement to the higher Authority of Nature and necessity, if the King will persist in tolerating these people, who knows after remonstrating, what Mr. Bayes will doe next? But now in sum what shall we say of this man, and how had the King been served if he had followed Bayes's advice,[414] and assumed the power of his first Book? He had run himself into a fine *Premunire,* when now after all he comes to be made accountable to God, nay even to his Subjects. And by this means it happens, though it were beyond Mr. Bayes his forecast, and I dare say he would rather have given the Prince again a power antecedent to Christ, and to bring in what Religion he please; he hath obliged him to as tender a Conscience as any of his Christian subjects, and then good-[145]night to *Ecclesiastical Policy.* I have herein indeavoured the utmost ingenuity toward Mr. Bayes, for he hath laid himself open but to too many disadvantages already, so that I need not, I would not press him beyond measure, but to my best understanding, and if I faile I even ask him pardon, I do him right.

[411] Even . . . gray: see Thomas Fuller, *The Holy State* (1651), p. 211: "One Palevizine an Italian Gentleman, and kinsman to Scaliger, had in one night all his haire chang'd from black to gray." [S]

[412] clear 72] clean 72a.

[413] Remonstrants: the Arminian party at the Synod of Dort, who objected to the strict predestinarianism of the doctrine there adopted.

[414] Bayes's advice 72] Baye's advise 72a.

'Tis true, that being distracted betwixt his desire that the Consciences of men should be persecuted, and his anger at Princes that will not be advised, he confounds himself every where in his reasonings, that you can hardly distinguish which is the *Whoop* and which is the *Holla,* and he makes Indentures on each side of the way wheresoever he goes. But no man that is sober will follow him, lest som Justice of Peace should make him pay his five shillings, besides[415] the scandal; and it is apparent to every one what he drives at. But were this otherwise, I can spare it, and 'tis sufficient to my purpose that I do thus historically deduce the reason of his setting forth his Books, and shew that it was plainly to *remon*-[146]*strate* against the power of his Prince, and the measures that he hath taken of governing; to set his Majesty at variance not only with his Subjects, but with himself, & to raise a Civil-war in his *Intellectual Kingdom,* betwixt his controulable & his uncontroulable Jursidiction.

And[416] because, having to do with a wise man, as Mr. Bayes is, one may often gather more of his mind out of a word that drops casually, than out of his whole watchful and serious discourse, when he is talking of matters of Policy and that require caution; I cannot slight one passage of Mr. Bayes, page 656. Where raging bitterly against all the Presbyterians and other Sects, and as much against the allowing them any Tenderness, Liberty, Toleration or Indulgence, he concludes thus, *Tenderness & Indulgence to such men, were to nourish Vipers in our own Bowels, & the most sottish neglect of our own quiet & security, and we should deserve to perish with the dishonour of Sardanapalus.*[417] Now this of Sardanapalus I remember some little thing ever since [147] I read, I think it was my Justine;[418] and I would not willingly be such a Fool as to make a dangerous Similitude that has no foundation.

[415] besides 72a] beside 72.

[416] And: new paragraph 72a.

[417] *Sardanapalus:* the last king of the Assyrian monarchy, so excessively luxurious that his captains, according to the mythical account of Ctesias, conspired to kill him, which he prevented by burning himself alive with all his treasures, including his many wives and concubines. In *A Dialogue between the Two Horses* Marvell had the bronze horse state, "I had rather Bare Nero than Sardanapulus," i.e., Charles I rather than Charles II (*P&L* 1:212). When he accused Parker of making "a dangerous Similitude," therefore, he knew what he was about.

[418] my Justine: Marcus Junianus Justinus, Latin historian, second century A.D. The story of the conspiracy against Sardanapalus appears there. See *The History of Justin. Taken out of the four and fourty Books of Trogus Pompeius,* trans. R. Codrington (1664), book 1, p. 4.

For if Mr. Bayes in the Preface of his *Defence,* to excuse his long teeming before it were brought forth, places it partly upon his recreations: I know not why much more a Prince should not *be willing to enjoy the innocent comforts of this life, as well as to do the common drudgeries.*[419] But I am thinking what Mr. Bayes meant by it; for every Similitude must have, though not all, yet some likeness: Now I am sure there were no Nonconformists and Presbyterians in Sardanapalus his dayes, I am sure also that Sardanapalus was no Clergyman, that he was no subject; but he was one of the *Uncontroulable* Creatures, that instead of exercising his Ecclesiastical Power delighted in spinning; till some body came[420] in on the sudden, and catching him at it, cut his thred. Come 'tis better we left this Argument and the Company too, for you see the Crime, you see the Sentence: and who ever [148] it be, there is some Prince or other whom Mr. Bayes will have to perish. That p. 641. is indeed not so severe, but 'tis prety well; where, on the same kind of Subject, whetting the Prince against those People, he saith, *That Prince that hath felt the pounces of these ravening Vultures, if after that he shall be perswaded to regard their fair speeches at such time as they want power, without other evident and unquestionable tokens of their conversion,*[421] *deserves to be King of the Night.* Now for this matter, I believe Mr. Bayes knows that his Majesty hath received such evident & unquestionable tokens of Loyalty[422] from the Nonconformists; otherwise his own Loyalty would have hindred him from daring to use that expression.

And now I should continue my History to his third Book in hand, the Preface to Bishop Bramhal. But having his second Book stil before me, I could not but look a little further into it, to see how he hath left matters standing betwixt himself and his Answerer. And first I lighted on that place where he [149] strives to disintangle himself from what he had said about Trade in his former Book. Here therefore he defies the whole Fanatick world to discover one Syllable that tends to its discouragement. Let us put it upon that issue, and by this one example take the pattern of his ingenuity in all his other contests. *Whoop* Mr. Bayes, pag 49. *with what conscience does the Answerer tell the people that I have represented all Tradesmen as seditious,*

[419] *drudgeries* Ed.] *drugeries* 72, 72a; *Drudgeries,* Parker, *Defence,* A6r-v.

[420] came Ed.] come 72, 72a.

[421] *conversion* 72] *conversation* 72a.

[422] tokens of Loyalty: In 1670, Charles tried to borrow sixty thousand pounds from the City of London. The City could raise only twenty thousand, so the nonconformists "under Persecution, served his Majesty" with the other forty. See Marvell's letter to William Popple, November 28, 1670 (*P&L,* 2:318).

when 'tis so notorious I only suppose that some of them may be tainted with Seditious Principles? If I should affirm that when the Nobility or Clergy are possest with Principles that incline to Rebellion and disloyal practices, they are of all Rebels the most dangerous, should I be thought to impeach them of Treason and Rebellion? Holla Mr. Bayes! But in the 49th page[423] of your first Book you say expresly, *For 'tis notorious that there is not any sort of people so inclinable to Seditious Practices as the Trading part of a Nation.* Is this the same thing now? and how does this Defence take off the Objection? And yet he tears and insults [150] and declaims as if he had the Truth on his side. At last he strives to bring himself off and salve the matter in the same page 49. With, *In brief it is not the rich Citizen, but the Wealthy Fanatick that I have branded for an ungovernable Beast, and that not as Wealthy but as Fanatick.* Subtle Distinguisher! I see if we give him but Rope enough what he will come to. Mr. Bayes, many as proper a man as your self hath march'd up Holborn[424] for distinguishing betwixt the Wealth and the Fanatick: and moreover let me tell you, Fanatick Money hath no Ear-mark.

So concerning the Magistrates power in Religion, wherein his Answerer had remark'd some unsafe passages: *Whoop* Mr. Bayes! P. 12. of his first Book before quoted: *Unless Princes have power to bind their Subjects to what Religion they apprehend most advantagious,* &c. *they are no better than Statues of Authority. Holla* Bayes. Pag. 467. of the second Book: *This bold Calumny I have already I hope competently enough discovered & detested. Yet he repeats this* [151] *Fundamental Forgery in all places, so that his whole Book is but one huge Lye* 400 *pages long.* Judge now who is the Forger; And yet he roars too here as if he would mix Heaven and Earth together. But you may spare your raving, you will never claw it off as long as your name is Bayes.

So his Answerer it seemes having *p.* 85. said, that Bayes confines the whole Duty of Conscience to the inward thoughts and perswasions of the mind, over which the Magistrate hath no power at all: *Whoop* Bayes page 89. of his first Book, *Let all matters of mere Conscience, whether purely moral or religious, be subject to Conscience only, i.e. Let men think of things according to their own perswasions, and assert the Freedom of their Judgments against all the Powers of the Earth. This is the Prerogative of the mind of man within its own Dominions, its Kingdom is intellectual,* &c. *P.* 91. *Liberty of Conscience is internal and invisible, and confined to the minds and judgments of men; and*

[423] 49th page: *Discourse,* Preface, xlix.

[424] march'd up Holborn: i.e., to Tyburn, for execution.

while Conscience acts within its proper sphere, [152] ⟨*the*⟩[425] *Civil power is so far from doing it Violence, that it never can. Holla* Bayes. *p.* 229. of his Second Book, *This in down right English is a shameless Lye. Sir, you must pardon my rudeness, for I will assure you, after long Meditation, I could not devise a more pertinent answer to so bold an one at this.* I believe you Mr. Bayes: you meditated long, some twelve months at least; and you could not devise any other answer, and in good earnest he hath not attempted to give any other answer. *I confess 'tis no extraordinary Conceit, but 'tis the best Repartee my barren Fancy was able to suggest to me upon so rude an occasion.*[426] Well, Mr. Bayes! I see it must come to a quarrel; for thus the Hectors[427] use to do, and to give the Lye at adventure, when they have a mind to try a mans Courage. But I have often known them dye on the spot.

So his Answerer *p.* 134. having taxed him for his speaking against an expression in the Act of Parliament of 5*to* Eliz. concerning the Wednesday Fast. *Whoop,* Bayes, *pag.* 59. of his [153] first Book. *The Act for the Wednesday Fast the Jejunium Cecilianum* (our Ecclesiastical Politician is the better States-man of the two by far, and may make sport with Cecil when he pleases) *was injoynd with this clause of Exception, That if any person should affirm it to be imposed with an intention to bind the Conscience, he should be punished as spreader of false News.* So careful was the supreme Magistrate in those dayes not to impose upon the Conscience; and the Wisdom of it is confirmed by the experience of our time: When so eminent a Divine,[428] as I mentioned before, thought fit to write a whole Volumne concerning the Holiness of LENT; though, if I be not deceived, this Doctrine too is prohibited by Act of Parliament, under the same Penalty. But, saith Bayes there, *The matter indeed of this Law was not of any great moment, but this Declaration annexed to it proved of a fatal and mischievous Consequence.*[429] 'Tis very well worth reading at large: but in short the Consequence (or the occasion 'tis no [154] matter when I have to do with Bayes) was, that *"Princes how peremptory soever they have been in asserting the Rights of their " Supreme Power, in Civil Affairs, they have been forced to seem modest and*

[425] *the:* omitted in 72a, even though catchword on p. 152 is *the Civil.*

[426] *I confess . . . occasion: Defence,* p. 229.

[427] Hectors: Hector, son of Priam, was, of course, the great defender of Troy; the word declined to mean blusterer, bully.

[428] so eminent a Divine: Peter Gunning, bishop of Ely. See p. 79 and n. 233 above.

[429] *The matter . . . Consequence: Discourse,* p. 60.

" *diffident in the exercise of their Ecclesiastical Supremacy.*"[430] Now, *Holla,* Bayes. *p.* 298. of his Second Book. "*To what purpose does he so briskly taunt* " *me for thwarting mine own principles, because I have censured the imperti-* " *nency of a needless Provision in an Act of Parliament?*"[431] Observe, these are not the Answerers but Bayes his own Words; whereby you may see with what Reverence and Duty he uses to speak of his Superiours and their Actions, when they are not so happy as to please him. "*I may obey the Law,* " *though I may be of a different Perswasion from the Law-givers in an Opinion* " *remote and impertinent to the matter of the Law it self: nay, I may condemne* " *the wisdom of enacting it, and yet at the same time think my self to lie under* " [155] *an indispensable Obligation to obey it: for the formal reason of its* " *obligatory power (as any Casuist*[432] *will inform him) is not the Judgment and* " *Opinion of the Law-giver, but the Declaration of his Will and Pleasure.*"[433] Very good and sound Mr. Bayes: but here you have opened a passage; and this is as impertinent in you and more dangerous than what you blamed in that Act, that the Nonconformists may speak against your Ecclesiastical Laws; for their Casuists then tell them that, they lying under an indispensable obligation not to confirm to some of them, do fulfil and satisfie their Obedience in submitting to the penalty.

I looked further into what he saith in defence of the Magistrates assuming the Priesthood; what for his Scheme of moral Grace; what to palliate his irreverent expressions concerning our Blessed Saviour and the Holy Spirit; what of all other matters objected by his Answerer: and if you will believe me; but I had much rather the Rea-[156]der would take the pains to examine all himself, there is scarce any thing but slender trifling unworthy of a Logician, and beastly railing unbecoming any man, much more a Divine. At last, having read it all through with some attention, I resolved, having failed so of any thing material, to try my fortune whether it might be more lucky, and to open the Book in several places as it chanced. But, whereas they say that in the *Sortes Virgilianae,*[434] wheresoever you light you will find somthing that will hit and is proper to your intention; on the contrary here, there was not any leaf that I met with but had something

[430] *Princes . . . Supremacy:* set in roman and diples in 72.

[431] *To . . . Parliament:* set in roman and diples in 72.

[432] *Casuist:* one who studies and resolves cases of conscience.

[433] *I may obey . . . Pleasure:* set in roman and diples in 72.

[434] *Sortes Virgilianae:* a method of divination by choosing a passage from Virgil at random.

impertinent, so that I resolved to give it over. This only I observed upon the whole, that he does treat his Answerer the most ⟨basely and⟩ ingratefully that ever man did. For, whereas in his whole first Book there was not one sound Principle, and, scarce any thing in his second, but what the Answerer had given him occasion to amend and rectifie if he had understanding; after so great an obligation he handles him [157] with more rudeness than is imaginable. I know it may be said in Mr. Bayes his defence, that in this his second Book he hath made his matters in many places much worse then they were before. But I say that was Bayes his want of understanding, and that he knew not how to take hold of so charitable an opportunity as was offered him, and 'twas none of the Answerers fault. There are amongst men some that do not study alwayes the true Rules of Wisdom and Honesty, but delight in a perverse kind of Cunning, which somtimes may take for a while & attain their design, but most usually it fails in the end & hath a foul farewel. And such are all Mr. Bayes his Plots. In all his Writings he doth so confound terms, he leaps cross, he hath more doubles[435] (nay triples and quadruples) than any Hare, so that he thinks himself secure of the Hunters. And in this second Book, even the length of it was some Policy. For you must know it is all but an Epistle[436] to the Author of the *Friendly Debate*; and thought he with himself, who [158] hath so much leisure from his own affairs that he will read a Letter of another mans business of eight hundred pages? But yet, thought he again, (and I could be content they did read it) in all matters of Argument I will so muddle my self in Ink, that there shall be no catching no finding me; and besides I will speak alwayes with so Magisterial a Confidence, that no modest man (and most ingenious persons are so) shall so much as quetch[437] at me, but be beat out of Countenance: and plain men shall think that I durst not talk at such a rate but that I have a Commission. I will first, said he in his heart, like a stout Vagrant, beg, and, if that will not do, I will command the Question; and as soon as I have got it *I* will so alter the property and put on another Periwig,[438] that I defie them all for discovering me or ever finding it again. This, beside all the lock and advantage that I have the Nonconformists upon since the late

[435] doubles: A hare to confuse the hounds doubles back on his own track.

[436] all but an Epistle: This is not stated on the title page of Parker's *Discourse,* though it is a reasonable inference. As often, Marvell may have had inside information.

[437] quetch: to make a sound.

[438] Periwig Ed.] Periweg 72, 72a; a periweg, corruption of *peruke,* was a short, newly fashionable wig.

times; and though they were born since, and have taken more sober Principles, it shall be all one for [159] that matter. And then for Oratory and Railing, let Bayes alone. This contrivance is indeed all the strength of Mr. Bayes his Argument, and, as he said, (how properly let the Reader judge) *p.* 69. before quoted, *that Moral Virtue is not onely the most material and useful part of all Religion, but the ultimate end of all its other Duties*: So, Railing is not onely the most material and useful part of his Religion, his Reason, his Oratory, and his Practise; but the ultimate end of this and all his other Books. Otherwise he is neither so strongly fortified nor so well guarded, but that without any Ceremony of Trenches or Approaches, you may at the very first march up to his Counters-scarp[439] without danger. He put me in minde of the incorrigible Scold,[440] that though she was duck'd over head and ears under water, yet stretched up her hands with her two Thumb-nails in the Nit-cracking posture, or with two fingers divaricated,[441] to call the man still in that Language Lousy Rascal and Cuckold. But in-[160]deed, when I consider how miserable a Wretch his Answerer has rendred him, and yet how he persists still, and more to rail and revile him; I can liken it to nothing better betwixt them, than to what I have seen with some pleasure the Hawking at the Mag-py. The poor bird understands very well the terrible pounces of that Vulture: but therefore she chatters amain most rufully, and spreads and cocks her tail, so that one that first saw and heard the sport[442] would think that she insulted over the Hawk in that chatter, and she huff'd her train in token of Courage and Victory: when, alas, 'tis her fear all, and another way of crying the Hawk mercy, and to the end that the Hawk finding nothing but tail and feather to strike at she may so perhaps shelter her body.

Therefore I think there is nothing in my way that hinders me, but that I may now go on to the History of this Mr. Bayes his Third Book, the Preface to Bishop Bramhall, and to what *Juncture of Affairs* it was reconciled. His [161] Majesty (perhaps upon Mr. Bayes his frequent Admonitions both in

[439] Counters-scarp: in fortification, the outer wall or slope of the ditch that supports the covered way.

[440] incorrigible Scold: Montaigne, *Essais,* 2.32 (A: "Mountaignes Essays, Moral, Politick, and Military," i.e., in John Florio's translation [1632], p. 27, #120). Marvell refers to Montaigne several times in *RT.*

[441] divaricated: stretched apart; two fingers stretched apart, however, is an obscene gesture, whereas the "Nit-cracking" gesture would require them to be tightly closed.

[442] sport 72, 72a] sporr 72a (B4, B7, B8, C3, C4, D5, S3, W2).

his first and second Book, that Princes should be more attentive and confident in exercising their Ecclesiastical Jurisdiction, though, I rather believe, he never deign'd[443] to read a Line in him, but what he did herein, was onely the result of his own good understanding) resolved to make some clear tryal how the Nonconformists could bear themselves under some Liberty of Conscience. And accordingly he issued on March the 15th 1671.[444] His Gracious *Declaration of Indulgence,* of which I wish His Majesty and the Kingdom much joy, and, as far as my slender judgement can divine, dare augurate and presage mutual Felicity, and that what ever humane Accident may happen (I fear not what Bayes fore-sees) they will, they can never have cause to repent this Action or its Consequences.[445] But hereupon Bayes finding that the King had so vigorously exerted his Ecclesiastical Power, but to a purpose quite contrary to what [162] Mr. Bayes had always intended; he grew terribly[446] angry at the King and his Privy Council: So that hereupon *he started,* as himself sayes, *into many warm and glowing Meditations: his heart burnt and the fire kindled, and that heated him into all this wild and rambling talk (as some will be forward enough to call it)*[447] *though he hopes it is not altogether idle, and whether it be or be not, he hath now neither leisure nor patience to examine.*[448]

This[449] he confesses upon his best recollection, in the last page of this preface:[450] whereupon I cannot but animadvert, as in my first page, that this too lies open to his *Dilemma* against the Nonconformists Prayers: For if he will not accept his own Charge, his Modesty is all impudent and[451] counterfeit: If he does acknowledge it, he is an hot-headed Incendiary; and a wild rambling talker, and in part, if not altogether, an idle Fellow. Really I cannot but pity him, and look upon him as under some great disturbance ⟨and dispondency⟩ of mind: that this with ⟨some⟩ other scattering passages [163] here and there, argues him to be in as ill a case as Tiberius was in his

443 deign'd 72a, 72 Errata] design'd 72.

444 1671: old style dating; actually 1672.

445 never . . . Consequences: These brave remarks were rendered deeply ironic when Charles was forced to withdraw the Declaration. See Introduction and Chronology.

446 terribly 72a] terrible 72.

447 *as . . . it* 72a, Parker] set in roman in 72.

448 *many warm . . . examine: Preface,* e8.

449 This: new paragraph 72a.

450 preface 72a] Preface 72.

451 and 72a] & 72.

distracted Letter to the Senate:[452] There wants nothing of it but the *Dii Deaeque me perdant* wishing, Let the Gods and the Goddesses confound him worse than he finds himself to be every day confounded. But that I may not lose my thred. Upon occasion of this his Majesties Gracious Declaration, and against it, he writes this his third Book the *Preface to Bishop Bramhall,* and accordingly was unhappily delivered of it in June (I have forgot) or July, in 1672.[453] For he did not goe his full time of it, but miscarried; partly by a #new# fright from J.O. and partly by a fall he had upon a *Closer Importance.* But of all his three Bolts this was the soonest shot, and therefore 'tis no wonder if he miss'd his mark, and took no care where his Arrow glanced. But what he saith of his Majesty and his Council, being toward the latter end of his Discourse, I am forced to defer that a little, because, there being no method at all in his wild rambling [164] talk; I must either tread just on in his footsteps, or else I shall be in a perpetual maze, and never know when I am come to my journeys end.

And here I cannot altogether escape the mentioning of J.O. again, whom (though I have shown that he was not the main cause of publishing Bayes his Books) yet he singles out, and on his pretence runs down all the Nonconformists; this being, as he imagined, the safest way by which he might proceed first to undermine, and then blow up his Majesties gracious Declaration. And this indeed is the least immethodical part of the whole Discourse. For first he undertakes to defend, that Railing is not onely lawful, but expedient. Secondly, that though he had Railed, the person he spoke of ought not to have taken notice of it. And Thirdly, that he did not Rail. As to these things I do not much trouble my self, nor interest my self in the least in J.O.'s Quarrel: no otherwise than if he were *John a Nokes* and I heard him rail'd at by *John a Styles*:[454] Nor yet [165] would I concern my self unnecessarily in any mans behalf; Knowing that 'tis better being at the

[452] Tiberius . . . Senate: Tiberius Claudius Nero, Roman emperor A.D. 14–37; the story of his letter to the Senate is told by Suetonius (*Tiberius,* 67), quoting the letter: "quid scribam vobis, p.c., aut quo modo scribam, aut quid omnino non scribam hoc tempore, dii me deaeque peius perdant quam cotidie perire sentio si scio." In his *History of the Twelve Caesars,* Marvell translated as follows: "At length being weary of his own wickedness, he made as it were a Confession of his ill life, in the beginning of this Epistle to the Senate; *What shall I write to you, most Reverend Fathers, or in what manner? or rather what shall I not write at this time? may the Gods afflict me worse then I daily find myself afflicted, if I know.*"

[453] June . . . July: Parker's *Preface* was licensed on June 24, 1672.

[454] *John a Nokes . . . John a Styles:* fictitious names for the parties in a legal action.

beginning of a Feast, than to come in at the latter end of a Fray. For if so I should, as often it happens in such Rencounters,[455] not onely draw Mr. Bayes, but J.O. too upon my back, I should have made a sweet business on't for my self.

Now as to the Lawfulness and Expedience of Railing; were it not that I do really make Conscience of using Scripture with such a drolling Companion as Mr. Bayes, I could overload him thence both with Authority and Example. Nor is it worth ones while to teach him out of other Authors, and the best precedents of the kind, how he, being a Christian and a Divine, ought to have carried himself. But I cannot but remark his Insolence and how bold he makes upon this Argument, p. 88. of his Second Book, with the Memories of those great Persons there enumerated, several of whom, and particularly my Lord Verulam,[456] I could quote to his confusion, upon a con-[166]trary and much better Account. *So far am I from repenting my severity towards them, that I am tempted rather to applaud it by the glorious Examples of the greatest Wits of our Nation, King James, Arch-Bishop Whitgift, Arch-Bishop Bancroft, Bishop Andrews, Bishop Bilson, Bishop Mountegue,*[457] *Bishop Bramhall, Sir Walter Rawleigh, Lord Bacon, &c.* and he might have added Mr. Tarlton[458] with as good pretence to this[459] Honour as himself. The *Niches* are yet empty in the Old Exchange;[460] pray let us

[455] Rencounters: conflicts, skirmishes.

[456] Lord Verulam: Sir Francis Bacon (1561–1626), lord chancellor under James I, writer, scientist, and philosopher. Marvell will eventually, at the end of *RT2*, make good his threat, which is to quote Bacon's cautionary remarks on religious controversy, written in 1589. See pp. 432–34 below.

[457] *Arch-Bishop Whitgift . . . Bishop Mountegue:* Parker's list does not prove his point about "Wits," but it does assemble some of the greatest ecclesiastical conservatives or high churchmen: Elizabeth I's archbishop, John Whitgift (1530–1604), James I's archbishop, Richard Bancroft (1544–1610), Lancelot Andrewes (1555–1626), the only one famous for eloquence, Thomas Bilson (1547–1616), "a learned but commonplace mind" [S], and Richard Montague (1577–1641), bishop of Norwich, whom Marvell excoriates for his Arminianism. See below, pp. 129, 186, 190.

[458] Mr. Tarlton: Richard Tarlton (d. 1588), the famous Elizabethan clown.

[459] this 72] his 72a.

[460] *Niches* . . . Old Exchange: The Old Exchange displayed twenty-four niches, most of which contained statues of the kings and queens of England. In 1649, however, that of Charles I was removed. See Hobbes, *Behemoth,* ed. F. Tonnies (Chicago and London, 1990), p. 169: "Also they pulled down the late King's statue in the Exchange, and in the niche where it stood, caused to be written these words: *Exit Tyrannus, Regum ultimus, etc.*"

speak to the Statuary that next to King James's[461] we may have Bayes his Effigies. For such great Wits are Princes Fellows, at least when dead. At this rate there is not a Scold at Billingsgate[462] but may defend her self by the patern of King James and Arch-Bishop Whitgift, &c: Yet this is passable, if you consider our man. But that is most intolerable p. 17. of the preface to his first Book, where he justifies his debauched way of writing by paralel to our Blessed Saviour. And I cannot but with some aw reflect how near the punishment was to [167] the offence; when having undertaken so profane an Argument, he was in the very instant so infatuated as to say that Christ was not onely *in an hot fit of Zeal, but in a seeming Fury too, and transport of Passion.*[463] But however, seeing he hath brought us so good Vouchers, let us suppose what is not to be suppos'd, that Railing is lawful. Whether it be expedient or no, will yet be a new question. And I think Mr. Bayes, when he hath had time *to cool his thoughts,* may be trusted yet with that consideration and to compute whether the good that he hath done by Railing do countervail the damage which both he in particular and the Cause he labours, have suffered by it. For in my observation, if we meet with an Argument in the Streets, both Men, Women and Boys, that are the Auditory, do usually give it on the modester side, and conclude, that she that rails most has the least reason.

For the second, Where he would prove that though he had railed, yet his Answerer J.O. ought not to have [168] taken notice of it, nor those of the Party who are under the same condemnation, but that he should have abstracted and kept close to the Argument, I must confess it is a very secure and wholsom way of railing. And allowing this, he had[464] good reason to find fault with his Answerer, as he does, for turning over his Book, though without turning it over, I know not how he could have answered him, but with his *Hat,* or with *Mum.*[465] But for ought I can see in that onely answer which is to his first Book, he hath been obedient and abstracted the Argument sufficiently; and if he hath been any where severe upon him, he hath done it more cleanly and much more like a Gentleman, and it hath been onely in showing the necessary inferences that must follow upon the Au-

[461] James's 72] Jame's 72a.

[462] Billingsgate 72] Billins-gate 72a; Billingsgate was the fishmarket near the gate of that name, noted for vituperative language.

[463] *in an hot . . . Passion: Discourse,* Preface, vii.

[464] had 72a] hath 72.

[465] *Hat . . . Mum:* by raising his hat in greeting or keeping his mouth shut.

thors Maximes, and unsound principles. But as to any answer to Bayes his second Book or this third, for ought I can see J.O. sleeps upon both ears.[466]

To this[467] third undertaking, to show that he hath not rail'd; I shall not [169] say any thing more, but let it be judged by the Company, and to them let it be refer'd. But in my poor opinion I never saw a man thorow all his three Books in so high a Salivation.[468]

And therefore, till I meet with something more serious, I will take a walk in the Garden and gather some of Mr. Bayes his Flowers.[469] Or I might more properly have said I will go see Bedlam, and pick straws with our Mad-man. First he saith, that some that pretend a great interest in the holy Brotherhood, upon every slight accident are beating up the Drums against the Pope and Popish Plots; they descry Popery in every common and usual Chance, and a Chimney cannot take fire in the city or Suburbs but they are immediately crying Jesuites and Firebals.[470] I understand you, Sir. This, Mr. Bayes, is your Prologue, that is to be spoke by *Thunder* and *Lightning. I am loud Thunder, brisk Lightning I. I strike men down. I fire the Town–Look too't. Wee'l doo't.*[471] Mr. Bayes, it is something dangerous medling with those matters. As inno-[170]cent persons as your self, have felt the fury of the wild multitude, when such a Calamity hath disordered them. And after your late Severity against Tradesmen, it had been better you had not touched the fire. Take heed lest the Reasons which sparkle, forsooth, in your discourse have[472] not set their Chimneys on fire. None accuses you, what you make sport with, or burning the Ships at Chatham,[473] much less of blowing up the Thames. But you ought to be careful, lest having so newly distinguished betwixt the Fanatick and his Wealth, they should say, That you are distinguishing now betwixt the Fanaticks and their Houses.

466 sleeps . . . ears: proverbial, for "sleeps very soundly."

467 this 72a] his 72.

468 in so high a Salivation: doing so much spitting.

469 Flowers: choice remarks.

470 that some . . . Jesuites and Firebals: *Preface,* A8v. Both Parker and Marvell refer to revival of "the old Talk" that the Fire of London (1666) was set by Roman Catholics, the revival being caused by several fires in London during 1672. See Marvell's letter to Popple of June 1672 (*P&L,* 2:327–28).

471 *I am loud Thunder . . . doo't: Rehearsal,* act 1, scene 1, p. 10.

472 have 72] hath 72a.

473 burning . . . Chatham: In June 1667, the Dutch fleet sailed up the Medway and burned the English ships moored at Chatham. Marvell devoted a long section of his satire *Last Instructions to a Painter,* ll. 523–760, to this humiliation. See *P&L,* 1:160–66.

These things are too edged to be jested with: if you did but consider that not onely the *Holy Brother-hood,* but the *Sober and intelligent Citizens* are equally involved in these sad Accidents. And in that lamentable Conflagration (which was so terrible that though so many years ago, it is yet fresh in mens memories, and besides, is yearly by Act of Parlia-[171]ment observed with due Humiliation and Solemnity.)[474] It was not Trade onely and Merchandise suffered, which you call their Diana, and was not so much to be considered; but Saint Pauls[475] too was burnt, which the Historians tell us was Diana's Temple.[476]

The next thing was[477] more directly levell'd at J.O. for having in some later Book used those words, *We cannot conform to Arminianism or Socinianism*[478] *on the one hand, or Popery on the other.*[479] What the Answerer meant by those words, I concern not my self. Onely I cannot but say, That there is a very great neglect somewhere, wheresoever the Inspection of Books is lodged, that at least the Socinian Books are tolerated and sell as openly as the Bible. But Bayes turns all into Mirth; *He might as well have added all the -isms in the Old Testament, Perizzitism, Hivitism, Hittitism, Jebuzitism,*[480] &c.

No, Mr. Bayes, that need not; and though this indeed is a very pretty Conceit, and 'twere pity it should [172] have been lost; yet I can tell you a better way. For, if rhiming be the business, and you are also[481] good at *tagging*[482] *of points in a Garret,* there is another word that will do it better, and for which, I know not how truly, you tax your Answerer too here, as if

[474] Conflagration . . . Solemnity: On October 10, 1666, Parliament "ordered a general Fast throughout the Nation, to humble us on the late dreadful conflagration." See Evelyn, *Diary,* 2:261; and *JHC,* September 24, 1666, 8:627. [S]

[475] Pauls 72] Paul 72a.

[476] Diana's Temple: According to tradition, the first church on the site of St. Paul's was erected on the site of a temple dedicated to Diana. See W. Dugdale, *The History of St. Pauls Cathedral in London* (1658), p. 3 [S] (A, p. 26, #94).

[477] was 72a] is 72.

[478] *Socinianism:* the anti-Trinitarian doctrines of Faustus Socinus (1539–1604), from which modern Unitarianism developed.

[479] *We cannot . . . other:* John Owen, *Discourse concerning Evangelical Love, Church-Peace and Unity* (1672), p. 18.

[480] *Perizzitism . . . Jebuzitism: Preface,* A1; this passage, which parodically lists the various enemies of the Hebrews in Canaan, caused Marvell's printers some problems; *Hivitism, Hittitism, Jebuzitism* 72a] *Hivitism, Jebuzitism, Hivitism* 72; *Hivitism, Jebuzitism, Hittitism* 72 Errata.

[481] also 72a] so 72.

[482] *tagging:* supplying blank verse or prose with rhymes.

he said, *The Church of England were desperately Schismatical, because the Independents are resolved one and all, to continue separate from her Communion.*[483] Therefore let *Schism,* if you please, rhime to *ism.* And though no man is obliged to produce the Authority of the greatest Wits of the Nation to justify a Rhime, yet for your *dear sake,* Mr. Bayes, I will this once supererogate.[484] The first shall be your good friend Bishop Bramhall, who among many other memorable Passages, which I believe were the reason that he never thought fit to print his own book; p. 101. teaches us, not absurdly, that *It was not the erroneous Opinions of the Church of Rome, but the obtruding them by Laws upon other Churches, which warranted a Separation.* But if this [173] will not doe, *Vous avez* Doctor Thorndikes Deposition in print,[485] for he, I hear, is lately dead. *The Church of England in separating from the Church of Rome, is guilty of Schism before God.*[486] I have not the Book by me, but I am sure 'tis candidly recited as I have read it. Then (to show too that there is a King on this side) his present Majesty's Father in his Declaration 4*to* Caroli, 1628.[487] Affirms that a Book, entituled, *Appello Caesarem* or *an Appeal to Caesar,* and *published in the year* 1625. *by Richard Mountague*[488] *then Batchelor of Divinity, and now Bishop of Chichester, had opened the way to those Schisms and Divisions which have since ensued in the Church, and that therefore for the Redress and remedy thereof, and for the satisfaction of the Consciences of his good People, he had not onely by publick Proclamation called in that Book, which ministred matter of Offence, but to prevent the like Danger for the future, reprinted the Articles of Religion, established in the time of Queen Elizabeth of Famous Memory: and by a Declaration, before those Articles, did re-*[174]*strain all Opinions to the Sense of those Articles, that nothing might be left for private Fancies and Innovations,* &c. And if this will not amount

483 *The Church . . . Communion: Preface,* a3.

484 supererogate: do more than is commanded or required.

485 Doctor Thorndikes . . . print: Herbert Thorndike (1598–1672), Anglican divine, died on July 11. His "Deposition in print" must be the *Discourse of the Forbearance or the Penalties which a Due Reformation requires* (1670) (A, p. 11, #14).

486 *The Church . . . before God:* roughly quoted from Thorndike, *Discourse,* p. 19.

487 *Declaration . . . 1628:* see *CSPD,* January 17, 1629. Charles was on the defensive. On March 4 he issued the proclamation that dissolved parliament and was followed by eleven years of personal rule.

488 *Mountague* 72a] *Montague* 72; for Montague, see p. 125 above and pp. 186, 190 below. His *Appello Caesarem* (1625), arguing for the king's prerogative in religious matters, caused a scandal. Archbishop George Abbott complained of it, and the House of Commons voted that the book be burned and its author punished.

fully, I shall conclude with a Villanous *Pamphlet*[489] that I met with t'other day; but of which a *great Wit* indeed was the Author. And, whereas[490] Mr. Bayes is always defying the Nonconformists with Mr. Hookers *Ecclesiastical Polity,*[491] and the[492] *Friendly Debate*; I am of opinion,[493] though I have a great Reverence for Mr. Hooker, who in some things did answer himself,[494] That this little Book, of not full eight leaves, hath shut that *Ecclesiastical Polity,* and Mr. Bayes's too out of doors: But for the *Friendly Debate,* I must confess, that it is[495] unanswerable. 'Tis one Mr. Hales of Eaton,[496] a most learned Divine, and one of the Church of England, and most remarkable for his Sufferings in the late times, and his Christian patience under them. And I reckon it not one of the least Ignominies of that Age, that so eminent a Person should have been by[497] the Iniquity of the times reduced to those necessities under which he lived; as I account it [175] no small honour to have grown up into some part of his Acquaintance, and convers'd a while with the living *remains* of one of the clearest heads and best prepared brests in Christendom. That which I speak of is his little *Treatise of Schism,* which though I have[498] read many years ago, was quite out of my mind till I occasionally light upon't at a Book-seller's stall. I hope it will not be tedious, though I write of some few (and yet whatsoever I omit, I shall have left behind more) material passages.

[489] Villanous *Pamphlet:* Marvell is being ironic. This introduces one of his most important witnesses, John Hales's *Tract Concerning Schisme and Schismaticks* (1642) (A, p. 45, bundle 5; p. 47, bundle 31; p. 48, bundle 35).

[490] whereas 72a] wher as 72a cancel.

[491] Hookers *Ecclesiastical Polity:* Richard Hooker (1554–1660), Elizabethan theologian who defended the established church against the puritans, especially Thomas Cartwright, in the 1950s.

[492] and the 72a cancel] italicized 72, 72a. For the cancel, see Introduction, p. 39.

[493] of opinion 72a cancel] of the opinion 72, 72a.

[494] answer himself: perhaps a reference to the fact that book 8 of *Ecclesiastical Polity,* not published until 1651, was more tolerant of dissent than the first four books, published in 1594.

[495] that it is 72a cancel] that is 72, 72a.

[496] Mr. Hales of Eaton: John Hales (1584–1656), theologian and philosopher, at one time chaplain to Archbishop Laud. Marvell must have met him in 1653 when tutoring Cromwell's ward William Dutton in the house of John Oxenbridge at Eton. Hales's "Sufferings in the late times" included being deprived by parliament of his fellowship at Eton College and a canonry of Windsor. See Wood, *Athenae Oxonienses,* 3:411.

[497] should have been by 72, 72a] should by 72a cancel.

[498] have 72a cancel] had 72, 72a.

"Schism[499] is one of those Theological Scare-crows[500] with which they
" who use to uphold a party in Religion, use to fright away such, as making
" inquiry into it are ready to relinquish and oppose it, if it appear either
" erroneous or suspitious.[501] Schism is, if we should[502] define it, an unnec-
" essary separation of Christians from that part of the Visible Church of
" which they were once Members. Some reverencing Antiquity more than
" needs, have suffered[503] [176] themselves to be scared with imputation of
" Schism more than needs.[504]

" Nothing[505] absolves men from the guilt of Schism, but true and unpre-
" tended Conscience. But the Judgements of the Ancients many times (to
" speak most gently) are justly to be suspected. Where the Cause of Schism
" is necessary, there not he that separates, but he that is the cause of
" Separation is the Schismatick.

" Where[506] the occasion of Separation is unnecessary, neither side can be
" excused from guilt of Schism. But who shall be the Judg? That is a point
" of great difficulty, because it carries fire in the Tail of it: for it brings with
" it a piece of Doctrine which is seldom pleasing to Superiours. You shall
" find that all Schisms have crept into the Church by one of these three
" ways, either upon matter of Fact, or upon matter of Opinion, or point of
" Ambition. For the first, I call that matter of Fact, when something is re-
" [177]quired to be done by us, which either we know or strongly suspect to
" be unlawful." Where he instances in the old great Controversie about
EASTER, "For it being upon error taken for necessary that an Easter must
" be kept, and upon worse than error (for it was no less than a point of
" Judaism forc'd upon the Church) thought further necessary that the
" ground of the time for the Feast, must be the Rule left by Moses to the
" Jews: there arose a stout Question, Whether 'twas to be celebrated with
" the Jews on the fourteenth Moon, or #on# the Sunday following. This
" caused as great a Combustion as ever was; the West separating and
" refusing Communion with the East for many years together. Here I

[499] Schism 72, 72a cancel] *Shism* 72a. New paragraph introduced here in 72a cancel.

[500] Scare-crows 72a cancel] Scar-crows 72; *Scare-crows* 72a.

[501] suspitious 72a cancel] suspicious 72; *suspitious* 72a.

[502] should 72a cancel] would 72; *would* 72a.

[503] Schism . . . suffered 72, 72a cancel] set in italics and without diples in 72a.

[504] themselves . . . needs 72, 72a (B5, B7, B9, D3, D5, O2, S3, S4, W3)] set in italics and without diples in 72a.

[505] Nothing: new paragraph in 72a.

[506] Where: new paragraph in 72a.

" cannot see but all the World were Schismaticks, excepting onely that we " charitably suppose to excuse them from it, that all parties did what they " did out of Conscience. A thing which befell them by the ignorance, for I " will not say the [178] malice, of their guides; and that through the just " judgment of God, because, through sloth and blind obedience, men " examined not the things they were taught, but like beasts of burthen " patiently couched down, and indifferently under-went all whatsoever " their Superiours laid upon them. If the discretion of the chiefest guides of " the Church did, in a point so trivial, so inconsiderable, so mainly fail " them: Can we without the imputation of great grossness and folly, think " so poor-spirited persons competent Judges of the Questions now on foot " betwixt the Churches? Where, or among whom, or how many the " Church shall be, it is a thing indifferent: What if those to whom the " Execution of the publick Service is committed, do something, either " unseemly or suspitious, or peradventure unlawful; what if the Garments " they wear be censured, nay, indeed be suspitious; What if the gesture or " adoration to be used to the Al-[179]tars, as now we have learned to speak? " What if the Homilist have preached or delivered any Doctrine, of the " truth of which we are not well perswaded, (a thing which very often falls " out) yet, for all this, we may not separate, except we be constrained " personally to bear a part in it our selves. Nothing can be a just cause of " refusing Communion in Schism, that concerns Fact, but onely to require " the execution of some unlawful or suspected Act. For, not onely in Rea- " son, but in Religion too, that Maxim admits of no release; *Cautissimi* " *cujusque praeceptum, quod dubitas ne feceris*: That whatsoever you doubt of, " that you in no case do."[507] He instances then in the Second Council of Nice,[508] where, saith he, the "*Synod* it self was the Schismatical party in " the point of using the Images, which, saith he, all acknowledge unneces- " sary, most do suspect, and many hold utterly unlawful: Can then the " enjoyning of such a thing be ought else but an abuse? Can the [180] " refusal of Communion here be thought any other thing than Duty? Here, " or upon the like occasion to separate, may peradventure bring personal

[507] *Cautissimii . . . feceris:* Pliny, *Epistles,* I.18.5. The full sentence reads, "au si tutius putas illud cautissimi cuiusque praeceptum 'Quod dubites, ne feceris,' id ipsum rescribe" (If you still think there is more safety in the warning given by all cautious folk, 'When in doubt do nothing,' you can write and tell me.) Hales is putting a different stress on the maxim than was Pliny.

[508] Second Council of Nice: This council, called in A.D. 787, focused on the problem of religious icons, reversing the iconoclasm of the church hitherto.

" trouble or danger, against which it concerns any honest man to have
" *Pectus praeparatum.*"[509] Then of Schism of Opinion. "Prayer, Confession,
" Thanksgiving, Reading of Scripture, Administration of Sacraments in
" the plainest and the simplest manner, were matter enough to furnish out
" a sufficient Liturgy, though nothing either of private Opinion or of
" Church Pomp, of Garments, of prescribed Gestures, of Imagery, of Mu-
" sick, of matter concerning the Dead, of many Superfluities which creep
" into the Church, under the name or Order and Decency, did interpose it
" self. To charge Churches and Liturgies with things unnecessary, was the
" first beginning of Superstition. If the Fathers and special Guides of the
" Church would be a little sparing in incumbring Churches with Super-
" fluities, or not over-[181]rigid either in reviving obsolete customs, or
" imposing new: there would be far less cause of Schism or Superstition;
" and all the inconvenience likely to ensue, would be but this, They should
" in so doing yield a little to the imbecility[510] of their inferiours; a thing
" which Saint Paul would never have refused to do. It is alike unlawful to
" make profession of known or suspected falshood, as to put in practice
" unlawful or suspected Actions. The third thing I named for matter of
" Schism was Ambition, I mean, Episcopal Ambition; One head of which,
" is one Bishops claiming Supremacy over another, which, as it hath been
" from time to time a great Trespass against the Churches Peace, so it is
" now the final ruine of it. For they do but abuse themselves and others,
" who would perswade us that Bishops by Christs institution have any
" Superiority over other men further than that of Reverence, or that any
" Bishop is Superiour to another further than positive Order agreed upon
" among [182] Christians had prescribed.[511] Time hath taken leave, some-
" times, to fix this name of CONVENTICLES[512] upon good and honest Meet-
" ings. Though open Assemblies are required yet, at all times while men
" are really pious, all Meetings of men for mutual help of Piety and Devo-
" tion, wheresoever, and by whomsoever celebrated, were permitted with-
" out exception. In times of manifest Corruption and Persecution, wherein
" Religious Assembling is dangerous, Private Meetings, howsoever besides
" Publick Order, are not onely lawful, but they are of Necessity and Duty.

[509] *Pectus praeparatum:* "a well-prepared breast"; from Horace, *Odes,* 2.10.15. Marvell had just used the phrase, in English, to describe Hales himself. See p. 130 above.

[510] imbecility: weakness of mind.

[511] had 72a] hath 72.

[512] CONVENTICLES: Marvell added this capitalization, not in Hales.

" All pious Assemblies, in times of Persecution and Corruption, howso-
" ever practised, are indeed, or rather alone, the Lawful Congregations:
" and Publick Assemblies, though according to form of Law, are, indeed,
" nothing else but RIOTS and CONVENTICLES,[513] if they be stained with
" Corruption and Superstition." Do you not see now, Mr. Bayes, that you needed not #to# have gone so #far# for a [183] word, when you might have had it in the Neighbourhood? If there be any Coherence left in your Scull, you cannot but perceive that I have brought you Authority enough to prove that *Schism* (for the reason we may discourse another time) do's at least rhime to *Ism.* But you have a peculiar delight and felicity, (which no man envies you) in Scripture-Drollery, nothing less will taste to your Palate: whereas otherwise you have travelled so far in Italy, that you could not escape the Titles of some Books which would have served your turn as well, *Cardinalism, Nepotism, Putanism,*[514] if you were in a *Paroxism* of the *Ism's.*

When I had writ this, and undergon so grateful a Penance for no less than that I had transcribed before out of our Author; I could not upon comparing them both together but reflect most seriously upon the difference of their two ways of Discoursing. I could not but admire that Majesty and Beauty which sits upon the Forehead of masculine Truth and generous Honesty: but no [184] less detest the Deformity of Falshood disguised in all its Ornaments. How much another thing it is to hear him speak, that hath cleared himself from froth and growns,[515] and who suffers neither Sloth nor Fear, nor Ambition, nor any other tempting Spirit of that nature to abuse him, from one, who as Mr. Hales expresseth it, makes Christianity Lacquey[516] to Ambition; how wretchedly, the one to uphold his *Fiction,* must incite Princes to Persecution and Tyranny, degrade Grace to Morality, debauch Conscience against its own Principles, distort and mis-interpret the Scripture, fill the World with Blood, Execution, and Massacre; while the other needs and requires no more but a peaceable and unprejudicat Soul and the native Simplicity of a Christian-spirit! And me-thinks, if our

[513] RIOTS and CONVENTICLES: Marvell added this capitalization also.

[514] *Cardinalism . . . Putanism:* Marvell refers to the titles of three anticlerical works by Gregorio Leti, *Il Cardinalismo di Santa Chiesa* (1668), trans. G.H. (1670); *Il Nipotismò di Roma* (1667), trans. W.A. (1669) with an explanatory subtitle, "The History of the Pope's Nephews" (A, p. 95, #115); and *Il Putanismo Romano* (1668), that is, "Roman Prostitution."

[515] cleared . . . froth and growns: cleared his discourse from the froth that rises to the surface and the grounds or dregs that sink to the bottom.

[516] Lacquey 72a] Laquey 72 Errata; lackque 72.

Author had any spark of Vertue unextinguished, he should, upon considering these together, retire into his Closet, and there lament and pine away for his desperate folly; for the disgrace he hath, as far as in him is, brought upon the [185] Church of England by such an undertaking, and for the eternal shame to which he has hereby condemned his own Memory.

I ask you heartily pardon, Mr. Bayes, for treating you against *Decorum* here, with so much gravity. 'Tis possible I may not trouble you above once or twice more in the like nature; but so often at least, I hope one may in the writing of a whole Book, have leave to be serious. Your next Flower, and that indeed is a sweet one, *Dear Heart, how could I hug and kiss thee for all this Love and Sweetness?*[517] Fy, fy, Mr. Bayes, Is this the Language of a Divine, and to be used, as you sometimes express it, in the face of the Sun? Who can escape from thinking that you are adream'd of your *Comfortable Importance*? These are (as the *Moral Satyrist* calls them in the cleanliest manner the thing would bear) *Words left betwixt the Sheets*:[518] Some body might take it ill that you should misapply your Courtship to an Enemy. But in the Roman Empire it was the [186] Priviledge of the Hangman to deflour a Virgin before Execution.[519] But, sweet Mr. Bayes, (for I know you do nothing without a precedent of some of the greatest Wits of the Nation) Whose example had you for this *seeming Transport* of a gentler *Passion*?

Then comes, *Welfare poor Macedo for a modest Fool.*[520] This I know is matter of *Gazette*; which is as Canonical as *Ecclesiastical Policy*. Therefore I have the less to say to't. Only, I could wish that there were some severer Laws against such Villains who raise so false and scandalous reports of worthy Gentlemen; and that those Laws were put in execution: And that men might not be suffered to walk the streets in so confident a garb, who commit those Assassinats upon the reputation of deserving persons.

Here follows a sore Charge: that the Answerer had *without any provocation, in a publick and solemn way, undertaken the defence of the Fanatick*

[517] *Dear Heart . . . Sweetness: Preface,* A2.

[518] *Words . . . Sheets:* "Modo sub lodice relictis uteris in turba" (You are using in public the language of the bedchamber), Juvenal, *Satires,* 6.195–96.

[519] Hangman . . . Execution: see Suetonius, *Tiberius,* 61.

[520] *Welfare . . . Fool:* Parker (*Preface,* a2) had referred to a local case of character assassination. In 1672 an accusation was brought by Sir Henry Mildmay against Sir John Bramston, before the Privy Council, of being a papist. The chief witness was a Portuguese, Ferdinand de Macedo, whose evidence showed unmistakable signs of being forged. See Sir John Bramston, *Autobiography,* ed. Braybrooke (1845), pp. 134ff; and *CSPD,* May 16, 1672. [S]

Cause.[521] Here, indeed, Mr. Bayes, you have Reason, And you might have had as just a quar-[187]rel against whosoever had undertaken it. For, your design and hope was from the beginning, that no man would have answered you in a publick and solemn way; and, nothing would vex a wise man, as you are, more than to have his intention and Counsel frustrated. When you have rang'd all your forces in Battel, when you have plac'd your Canon, when you have sounded a charge, and given the Word to fall on upon the whole Party; if you could then perswade every particular person of 'm, that you gave him no Provocation, I confess, Mr. Bayes, this were an excellent and a new way of your inventing, to conquer single, ('tis your Moral Vertue) whole Armies.[522] And so the *admiring Drove* might stand gaping, till one by one, you had cut all their throats. But, Mr. Bayes, I cannot discern but that you gave him as much Provocation in your first Book, as he has you in his *Evangelical Love, Church-Peace and Unity,*[523] which is the pretence of your issuing this Preface. For,[524] having for your *Dear sake* (be-[188]side many other troubles that I have undertaken, without your giving me any Provocation) sought out and perused that Book too, I do not find you any where personally concern'd, but as you have, it seems upon some conviction, assumed to your self some vices or errours against which he speaks onely in general, and with some modesty. But for the rest, you say upon full perusal, *you find not one Syllable to the purpose, beside a perpetual Repetition of the old out-worn Story of Unscriptural Ceremonies, and some frequent whinings, and sometimes ravings,* &c.[525] Now to see the Dulness of some mens Capacities above others. I upon this occasion, begun, I know not how it came, at p. 127. And thence read on to the end of his Book. And from thence I turn'd to the beginning and continued to p. 127. and could not all along, observe any thing but what was very pertinent to the matter in hand. But this is your way of excusing your self from replying to things that yet you will be medling with, and nibling at: and 'tis besides a pretty knack (the Noncon-[189]formists have it not alone) of frighting or discouraging sober people from reading those dangerous Treatises which

521 *without . . . Cause: Preface,* a2v.

522 conquer . . . Armies: *Rehearsal,* act 5, scene 1, p. 35.

523 *Evangelical . . . Unity:* John Owen, *A Discourse concerning Evangelical Love, Church-Peace and Unity* (1672).

524 For: new paragraph removed 72a.

525 *you find . . . ravings: Preface,* a2v.

might contribute to their better information. I cannot but observe, Mr. Bayes, this admirable way (like fat Sir John Falstaffe's singular dexterity in sinking)[526] that you have of answering whole Books and[527] Discourses, how pithy and knotty soever, in a line or two, nay sometimes with a word. So it fares with this Book of the Answerers. So with a Book or Discourse of his, I know not, of the *Morality of the Lords Day*;[528] which is answered by a *Septenary Portion* in the *Hebdomadal Revolution*.[529] So, whether Book or Discourse I also know not of the *Self-evidencing light of the Scripture*,[530] where Bayes offers (and it seems strange) to produce as good proofs for it out of the Alcoran. So I show'd you where he answers demonstration with the Lye. And one thing more comes into my mind; where after he has blunder'd a great while to bring himself off the Magistrates exercising the Priesthood in his own person, he con-[190]cludes with an irresistable defence against his Answerer, *This is suitable to the Genius of his ingenuity, and betrayes him as much as the word* INTANGLEMENT, *which is the Shiboleth of all his Writings*.[531] So he defeats all the *gross bodies of Orthodoxy* with calling them *Systemes and Syntagmes*. So you know he answers all the Controversial Books of the Calvinists that ever have been written, with the Tale of Robin Hood, and the *mighty Bramble on the South side of the Lake Leman*. Mr. Bayes, you cannot enough esteem and cherrish this Faculty. For, next to your single beating whole Armies, I do not know any Virtue that you have need of so often, or that will upon tryal be found more useful.

And to this succeeds another Flower, I am sure, though I can scarce smell out the sense[532] of it. But it is printed in a distinct Character, & that is always a certain sign of a flower. For our Booksellers have many Arts to make us *yield to their importunity*: and among the rest, they promise us, that it shall be printed in fine Paper, and in a very large and fair [191] letter; that it shall be very well examined that there be no Errata; that wheresoever there is a pretty Conceit, it shall be marked out in another Character#; that the

526 Sir John Falstaffe's . . . sinking: Shakespeare, *The Merry Wives of Windsor*, 3.5.9–11.

527 and 72a] or 72.

528 *Morality . . . Day:* John Owen, *Exercitationes concerning the Name, Original Nature, Use and Continuance of a Day of Sacred Rest* (1671).

529 *Septenary . . . Revolution: Preface*, a4.

530 *Self-evidencing . . . Scripture:* John Owen, *Of the Divine, Originall Authority, Self-Evidencing Light and Power of the Scriptures* (1659).

531 *This is . . . Writings: Defence*, p. 274.

532 sense Ed.] Sense 72; sence 72a.

Sentences shall be boxed up in several paragraphs, and more Drawers than in any Cabinet; that the Books shall all be bound up in Calves Leather#.[533] But my greatest care was, that when I quoted any sentence or word of our Author's, it might be so discernable, lest I should go for a Plagiary. And I am much offended to see that in several places he hath not kept touch with me. The Word of Mr. Bayes's that he[534] has here made #more# notorious, is *Categoricalness*: and I observe that wheresoever there comes a word of that termination, he shows it the same honour; as if he had a mind to make Bayes a Collar of *Nesses*.[535] What the mystery is, I cannot so easily imagine; no more than of *Shiboleth*[536] and *Intanglement*. But I doubt Mr. Bayes is sick of many complicated Diseases; or to keep to our rhime, *Sicknesses*. He is troubled not onely with the *Isms* but the *Nesses*. He might, if [192] he had pleased, here too to have shown[537] his wit, as he did in the others, and have told us of Sheerness, Dongioness, Inverness[538] and Cathness.[539] But he ⟨might very well have⟩ omitted it #perhaps# in this place, knowing how well he had acquitted himself in another, and out of the Scripture too, which gives his Wit the highest relish. 'Tis p. 72. of his first Book, where, to prove that the fruits of the Spirit are no more than Morality, he quotes Saint Paul, Gal. 5. 22. Where the Apostle enumerates them; *Love, Joy, Peace, Patience, Gentleness, Goodness, Faith, Meekness* and *Temperance*: but our Author translates Joy to *Chearfulness*, Peace to *Peaceableness*, and Faith to *Faithfulness*: What Ignorance, or rather, what Forgery is this of Scripture and Religion? Who is there of the *Systematical, German, Geneva, Orthodox Divines*, but could have taught him better? Who is there of the *Sober*,

[533] This passage, and Marvell's addition, add to our knowledge of his familiarity with the techniques of printing and publication. His reference to the "Sentences [being] boxed up in several paragraphs" surely relates to the greatly improved paragraphing in 72a.

[534] he: Parker's printer? The antecedents of "he" in this passage are unclear. Is the "he" who "hath not kept touch" Marvell's printer, Parker, or Parker's printer?

[535] Collar of *Nesses:* The "collar of ss" was worn by the two chief justices and the chief baron of England. See E. Foss, *The Judges of England* (1864), 7:17ff. [S] But Marvell probably also puns on the legendary shirt of Nessus—dipped in the blood of Nessus the Centaur—that when put on by Hercules drove him mad with burning pain.

[536] *Shiboleth:* The Hebrew word used by Jephthah as a test to distinguish the fleeing Ephraimites, who could not pronounce it, from his own men, the Gileadites (Judges 12:4–16); subsequently a custom or formula which distinguishes a party or sect.

[537] shown 72a] show'd 72.

[538] Inverness Ed.] Innerness 72, 72a.

[539] Sheerness . . . Cathness: These are all place-names.

Intelligent, Episcopal Divines of the Church of England but would abhor this Interpretation? Yet, when his Answerer, I see, objects this to him, [193] p. 220. Bayes, like a dexterous Scholastical Disputant, it being told him, That Joy is not Chearfulness, but that *Spiritual Joy which is unspeakable*; that Peace is not peaceableness in his Sense, but *that Peace of God which through Jesus Christ is wrought in the hearts of Believers by the Holy Ghost*; and that *Faith in God* is there intended, not *faithfulness in our Duties, Trusts or Offices*: What does he do? p. 337.[540] He very ingenuously and wisely, when he is to answer, quite forgets that Faith was once named: and having supprest that, as to the rest he wipes his Mouth, and rubs his Forehead, and saith, the *Cavil is but a little one, and the Fortune of Caesar and the Roman Empire depends not upon it, and therefore he will not trouble the Reader with a Critical Account of the reason of his Translation.* No, don't Mr. Bayes, 'Tis very well; let it alone. But, though not the Fortunes of Caesar and the Roman Empire, I doubt there is something more depends upon it, if it be matter of Salvation. And I am afraid besides, that there may a Curse [194] too belong to him who shall knowingly add or diminish in the Scripture. Do you think Bishop Bramhal himself, if he had seen this, could have abstained (p. 117. before quoted,) from telling our Author, *That the promiscuous Licence given to people qualified or unqualified, not onely to read but to interpret the Scriptures according to their private Spirits or particular Fancies, without regard either to the Analogy of Faith, which they understand not, or to the Interpretation of the Doctors of former Ages, is more prejudicial (I might better say) pernicious both to particular Christians, and to whole Societies, than the over-rigorous restraint of the Romanists.*

The next is a piece of Mirth, on occasion of some discourse of the Answerers, about the Morality of the Lords-day: Where it seems, he useth some hard words, which I am naturally an Enemy to; but might be done of purpose to keep the Controversie from the White-aprons, within the white Surplices, to be more learnedly debated. But this fares no better [195] than all the rest. There is no kind of *Morality,* I see, but Bayes will try to debauch it: *Oh, what edifying Doctrine, saith he, is this to the White-Aprons! and doubtless they would with the Jews, sooner roast themselves, than a small joynt of Mutton upon the Sacred day of Rest.*[541] Now, I do not, neither, I believe, does Bayes himself know any of them that are thus superstitious. So that Mr. Bayes might, if he had pleased, have spared his jibing at that day, which

[540] p. 337; i.e., *Defence,* p. 337.

[541] *Oh, what . . . Rest: Preface,* a4.

hath more sacredness in it by far than many, nay than any of those things he pleaded[542] for. But when men are once *Adepti*[543] and have attain'd Bayes his height, and *Divinity* at least *is rightly understood,* they have a Priviledge, it seems, not onely to play and make merry *on* the Sabbath day, but *with* it.

After this I walked a great way through bushes and brambles before I could find another Flower: but then I met with two upon one stalk; on occasion of his Answerers having said some thing of the day of Judgment when men should be accountable. *Oh,* saith he, *We* [196] *shall be sure to be accounted with at that*[544] *day of Judgment*;[545] and again, *Ah sweet day, when these people of God shall once for all, to their unspeakable Comfort and Support, wreak their eternal Revenge upon their reprobat Enemies.*[546] This puts me in mind of another expression of our Authors alluding too this way. *'Tis an easie matter by this dancing and capering humour to perpetuate all the Controversies in the world, how plainly soever determinable, to the coming of Elias: and after this rate shall the Barbers bason remain Mambrino's helmet; and the Asses Pannel a furniture for the Great Horse*[547] *till the day of Judgment.* Now, good Mr. Bayes, I am one that desire to be very well resolved in these things; and though not much indeed, yet I attribute something to your judgment. Pray tell us in good earnest, what you think of these things, that we may know how to take our measures of living accordingly. For, if indeed there be no Judgment, no account for what is done here below, I have lost a great deal of precious time, that I might have injoyed [197] in one of the fruits of your Spirit, that is *Chearfulness.* How many good jests have I balk'd, even in writing this Book, lest I should be brought to answer for every profane and idle word! How frequent opportunities have I mist in my life of geniality and pleasure, and fulfilling Nature in all its ends! How have you frighted the Magistrate in vain, from exercising his uncontrolable Ecclesiastical Power, with the fear of an after-reckoning to God Almighty? And how have you, p. 238 defeated the obligatory force of all his Laws, and set his Subjects at liberty from all obligations to the duty of Obedience? for they lie under no Obligation, you say then, but of prudence and Self-

[542] pleaded 72a] pleads 72.

[543] *Adepti:* men skilled in all the secrets of anything; originally, of alchemy.

[544] *that* 72a] *the* 72.

[545] *shall . . . Judgment: Preface,* a4.

[546] *Ah sweet . . . Enemies: Preface,* a8.

[547] *Barbers bason . . . Horse:* Parker (*Defence,* p. 479) had introduced an episode from *Don Quixote* to mock the nonconformists. See *Don Quixote,* trans. Shelton, book 3, chapter 7.

interest. But unless there hath been some error in our education, and we have been seasoned with ill Books at first, so that we can never lose the Impression, there is some such matter, and the Governour had reason, when he trembled to hear Saint Paul discoursing of that Subject. The Fanatical *Book of Martyrs*[548] (for we will not with some call the Bible [198] so) tells us some old stories of persons that have been cited by some of them to appear at such a day, and that by dying at the time prefixed, they have saved their Reconnoissances. And in the Scotch History[549] we read of a great Cardinal[550] that was so summoned by poor Mr. Guichard,[551] and yet could not help it, but he must take that long and sad journey of Death to answer at the Grand Assizes. If therefore there be such a thing, I would not for fear; and if there be not, yet I would not for good luck sake, set that terrible day at defiance, or make too merry with it. 'Tis possible that the Nonconformists many of them may be too censorious of others, and too confident of their own Integrity. Others of them are more temperate, and perhaps destitute of all humane redress against their sufferings: Some of those make rash Challenges, and the other just appeals to appear at that dreadful Tribunal. In the mean time, 'tis not for you to be both the Enemy and their Judge. Much less do's it befit you, because perhaps they speak [199] too sillily or demurely of it, or too braving and confidently, therefore to make a meer mockery of the whole business of that Supreme Judge and Judicature. And one thing I will say more, though slighter; that though I am not so far gone as Campanella[552] was in the efficacy of words, and the Magick of the face, and pronunciation, yet I marked how your Answerer look'd when he spoke of the day of Judgment. Very gravely, I assure you, and yet without any dressing or adorning[553] his *Superciliums*:[554] And I have

548 *Book of Martyrs:* John Foxe, *The Actes and Monuments of these latter and perillous dayes, touching matters of the Church* (1563). Anglesey possessed the two-volume edition of 1610 (A, p. 3, #133).

549 Scotch History: i.e., the section called "Persecution in Scotland" in Foxe (1610), 2:1154 ff.

550 great Cardinal: David Beaton (1494–1546), archbishop of St. Andrews, a zealous persecutor, eventually brutally murdered. [S]

551 Mr. Guichard: George Wishart (1513–46), Scottish reformer, executed for his beliefs on March 7, 1546.

552 Campanella: Tommaso Campanella (1568–1639), Italian philosopher, noted for making faces when he spoke.

553 dressing or adorning 72a] depressing or exalting 72.

554 *Superciliums:* eyebrows.

most often observed that serious words have produced serious Effects. I[555] have by this time me-thinks, gather'd enow: nor are there many more left, unless I should go for a Flower to the *Dunghil*, which, he saith, *is his only Magazin.*[556] And this being an expression which he has several times used (for no Nonconformist repeats so often) I cannot but remark, that besides his natural Talent, Mr. Bayes hath been very industrious, and neglected no opportunity of acquiring a perfection of railing. For this is a phrase borrow-[200]ed from a modern Author lately dead,[557] and I suppose Mr. Bayes had given him a Bond for repayment at the day that he spoke of so lately. There[558] are indeed several others at which I am forc'd to stop my nose. For by the smell, any man may discern they grew upon a ranker soil, than that on the South side of the Lake Lemane, even upon the bank of the Thames in the Meadow of Billingsgate:[559] as that of the Lye, which, he saith, no Gentleman, much less a Divine, ought to put up. Now if this were to be tryed by a Court Martial of the Brothers of the Blade,[560] 'tis to be considered whether it were the down-right Lye, or whether it were ⟨only⟩ the Lye by Interpretation. For in the disputes of the Schools there is nothing more usual, than *Hoc est Verum, Hoc est falsum.*[561] But this passes without any blemish of Honour on either side, and so far it is from any obligation to a Challenge or a Duel, that it never comes to be decided, so much as by the Study-door key. But *quod restat probandum*[562] do's the business without demanding other satisfaction. [201]

Then[563] if it were the down-right Lye; it is to be examined who gave the Lye first: for that alters the case. And last of all (but which is indeed upon a

[555] I: new paragraph removed in 72a.

[556] *Dunghil . . . Magazin: Preface,* a1.

[557] modern Author lately dead: This could be Sir John Denham (d. 1669), Davenant (d. 1668), or Cowley (d. 1667); but compare *Upon Appleton House,* ll. 339–40: "The Nursery of all things green / Was then the only *Magazeen.*"

[558] There: new paragraph removed in 72a.

[559] Billingsgate 72] Billins-gate 72a.

[560] Brothers of the Blade: Gentlemen who duel and skirmish with swords, a problem in Restoration London. In 1670 Marvell reported to Popple how "seven or eight gentlemen [including the duke of Monmouth] fought with the Watch, and killed a poor Bedle" (*P&L,* 2:323). But cf. the pamphlet, *Brothers of the Blade answerable to the Sisters of the Scabberd* (1641) (A, p. 52, bundle 89).

[561] *Hoc . . . falsum:* "This is true, this false."

[562] *quod . . . probandum:* "That remains to be proved."

[563] Then: new paragraph 72a.

quarrel the least material point, yet, it too comes under some consideration) which of the two was in the right, and which of them spoke truth, and which lyed. These are all things to be discussed in their proper places. For I do not observe that the Answerer gave Bayes the down-right Lye. But I find that Bayes gave him the Lye first in terms. And as to the Truth of the things controverted and alledg'd, there needs no more than the depositions that I formerly transcribed concerning Bayes his ⟨own⟩ words. But all this is onely a Scene out of Bayes his *Rehearsal.*

> *Villain, thou liest,—*
> *—Arm, arm, Valerio arm,*
> *The Lie no flesh can bear I trow.*[564]

And[565] then as to the success of the Combate,—*They fly, they fly*
Who first did give the Lye.[566]

For that of *Caitife,* and other Provocations that are proper for the same Court, I will not meddle further. And [202] for the being *past Grace and so past Mercy;*[567] I shall only observe that the Church of England is much obliged to Mr. Bayes for having proved that Nonconformity is the Sin against the Holy Ghost.

There remains but one Flower more that I have a mind to; but that indeed is a Rapper.[568] 'Tis a *Flower of the Sun,* and might alone serve both for a Staff and a Nose-gay for any Noble mans Porter. *Symbolicalness is the very Essence of Paganism, Superstition and Idolatry. They will and ought sooner to broyl in Smithfield*[569] *than #to# submit to such Abomination of the Strumpet and the Beast. 'Tis the very Potion wherewith the Scarlet-Whore made drunk the Kings of the Earth.*[570] *Heliogabalus*[571] *and Bishop Bonner*[572] *lov'd it like Clary*[573] *and Eggs, and always made it their Mornings-draught*

564 *Villain . . . trow: Rehearsal,* act 5, scene 1, p. 48; this was itself a parody of Davenant's *The Siege of Rhodes* (1656), "The First Entry."

565 And: new paragraph 72a.

566 *They . . . Lye: Rehearsal,* act 5, scene 1, p. 49.

567 *past . . . Mercy: Preface,* c4r.

568 Rapper: an arrant lie, a downright falsehood.

569 *Smithfield:* one of the sites in London where heretics were burned at the stake.

570 *Scarlet-Whore . . . Earth:* Revelation 17:2.

571 *Heliogabalus:* Elagabalus (205–22), Roman emperor notorious for excess.

572 *Bishop Bonner:* Edmund Bonner (1500–69), bishop of London during the reign of Mary Tudor, a ferocious persecutor of Protestants.

573 *Clary:* a sweet liquor made of wine, honey, and spices.

upon burning days; and it is not to be doubted but the seven Vials of Wrath[574] *that were to be poured out upon the Nations of the Earth under the Reign of Antichrist were filled with Symbolical Extracts and Spirits*:[575] ⟨with more such stuff which I omit.⟩ This is I confess a pretty Posie for the Nose of such a Di-[203]vine. Doctor Baily's Romance of the *Wall-Flower*[576] had nothing comparable to't. And I question, whether, as well as Mr. Bayes loves preferment, yet though he had lived in the Primitive Church, he would not as Heliodorus Bishop of Trissa, I take it, that renounced his Bishoprick rather than his Title to the History of Theagenes and Chariclia, have done in like manner: nay, and have delivered up his Bible too into the bargain, before he would quit the Honour of so excellent a piece of Drollery.[577] This is surely the Bill of Fare, not at the ⟨*Ordination—Dinner* at the⟩ *Nags-Head*[578] but ⟨of the *Excusation-Dinner*⟩ at the *Cock*,[579] and never did Divine make so good Chear of Owen's Pease-porridge and Scripture. #I know no Dainty wanting, or that could have pleased his Tooth so well, except the Leg of a

[574] *seven Vials of Wrath:* Revelation 15:7.

[575] *Symbolicalness . . . Spirits: Preface,* b3v–b4.

[576] Doctor Bailey's . . . *Flower:* Thomas Bayley (d. 1657) was a royalist divine and later a Roman Catholic controversialist. While in Newgate prison for one of his works, he wrote *Herba Parietis: or The Wall-Flower . . . Being a history which is partly true, partly romantick, morally Divine* (1650).

[577] Heliodorus . . . Drollery: Marvell's source is probably Montaigne, "Of the affection of fathers for their children," *Essais,* book 2, no. 8. In Florio's translation, "Heliodorus that good Bishop of Tricea, loved rather to lose the dignity, profit and devotion of so venerable a Prelateship, than to forgoe his daughter, a young woman to this day commended for her beautie, but haply somwhat more curiously and wantonly pranked-up than beseemed the daughter of a churchman and a Bishop, and of over-amorous behaviour." The daughter here was the Greek romance *Ethiopica,* in Marvell's day thought to have been written by Heliodorus, bishop of Tricca in the late fourth century A.D.

[578] *Ordination . . . Nag's Head:* A reference to the disreputable story that the Anglican succession originated at the Nags Head Tavern in Cheapside. Bramhall had attempted to erase it in his *Consecration and Succession of Protestant Bishops Justified* (The Hague, 1658). [S] Marvell's revival of it was one of the spots marked out for censorship by L'Estrange; but Marvell substituted for the original scandal another joke about Parker and a diet of Pheasant, which was the maiden name of Parker's new wife.

[579] *Excusation . . . Cock:* An equally disreputable story reported by Wood, *Life and Times,* 2:243: "Dr. Guy Carleton consecrated bishop of Bristow at Westminster Feb. 11, Sun; kept his consecration dinner at a victualling house in Suffolk Street called 'the Cock.'" [S]

Pheasant at the *Dog* and *Partridge*; for he is of Thomas a Becket's[580] Dyet; who eat, he said, *Phaesianum sicut alij Muluellum,*[581] and can mortifie himself upon Pheasant, as well as others with Salt-fish.#

Good[582] Mr. Bayes, or Mr. Thunder, or Mr. Cartwright[583] (not the Noncon-[204]formist Cartwright,[584] that was you say (as some others too of your acquaintance) converted: but the Player in the Rehearsal) this *Divinity* I doubt was the Bacchus of your Thigh, and not the Pallas of your Brain.

Here it is that after so great an excess of Wit, he thinks fit to take a Julep[585] and resettle his Brain, and the Government. He grows as serious as 'tis possible for a Madman, and pretends to sum up the whole state of the Controversie with the Nonconformists. And to be sure he will make the story as plausible for himself as he may: but therefore it was that I have before so particularly quoted and bound him up with his own Words as fast as such a Proteus[586] could be pinion'd. For he is as waxen as the first matter, and no Form comes amiss to him. Every change of Posture[587] does either alter his opinion or vary the expression by which we should judge of it: and sitting he is of one mind, and standing of another. Therefore I take my self the less concern'd, to fight with a Wind-mill like Don Quixote:[588] [205] or to whip a Gig[589] as Boyes do, or with the Lacquies at Charing-Cross or Lincolns-Inne-fields to play at the *Wheel of Fortune,*[590] lest I should fall into

580 Thomas à Becket: archbishop of Canterbury (1118?–70); murdered in his cathedral by servants of Henry II, he was made a saint, and many stories were attached to his life.

581 *Phaesianum . . . Muluellum:* "[He could eat] pheasant as others ate cod."

582 Good: new paragraph in 72a.

583 Mr. Cartwright: the actor who played Thunder in *Rehearsal,* act 1, scene 1, p. 10.

584 Nonconformist Cartwright: Thomas Cartwright (1535–1603), famous puritan divine who in 1563 was chosen to debate the subject of church discipline at Cambridge before Queen Elizabeth. In 1570 John Whitgift, later to become archbishop of Canterbury, had him removed from his new position as Lady Margaret Professor, and he fled to Geneva. Returning, he wrote the *Second Admonition to Parliament* in 1572, to which Whitgift himself replied.

585 Julep: a cooling drink.

586 Proteus: a god of the sea famous for changing his shape.

587 Posture: a joke; *posture* is an anagram of *Proteus.*

588 fight with a Wind-mill like Don Quixote: see *Don Quixote,* 1:7.

589 whip a Gig: whip a top.

590 *Wheel of Fortune:* a revolving wheel with sections indicating bets to be placed.

the hands of my Lord Chief Justice,[591] or Sir Edmond Godfrey.[592] The truth is in short, and let Bayes make more or less of it if he can; Bayes had at first built up such a stupendious Magistrate, as never was of Gods making. He had put all Princes upon the Rack to stretch them to his dimension.[593] And, as a streight line continued grows a Circle, he had given them so infinite a Power that it was extended unto Impotency. For though he found it not, till it was too late in the Cause; yet he felt it all along (which is the understanding of Brutes) in the Effect. For, hence it is that he so often complains, that Princes knew not aright that Supremacy over Conscience, to which they were so lately, since their deserting the Church of Rome, restored. That in most Nations Government was not rightly understood, and many expressions of that Nature: Whereas indeed the matter [206] is that Princes have alwayes found that uncontrolable Government over CONSCIENCE to be both unsafe and impracticable. He had run himself here to a stand, and perceiv'd that there was a God, there was Scripture; the Magistrate himself had a Conscience, and must *take care that he did not enjoyn things apparently evil.*[594] Being at a stop here, he would therefore try how he could play the Broker on the Subjects side: and no Pimp did ever enter into a more serious disputation[595] to vitiate an innocent Virgin, than he to debauch their Consciences. And to harden their unpractis'd modesty, he imboldens them by his own Example, showing them the experiment upon his own Conscience first. But after all, he finds himself again at the same stand here, and is run up to the Wall by an Angel.[596] God, and Scripture, and Conscience will not let him go further: but he owns, that if the Magistrate enjoyns things apparently evil, the Subject may have liberty to remonstrate. What shall he do then? For it is too glori-[207]ous an Enterprize to be abandoned at the first rebuffe. Why he gives us a new Translation of the Bible, and a new Commentary. He saith that Tenderness of Conscience might be allowed in a Church to be constituted, not in a Church constituted already. That tenderness of Conscience and Scandal are Ignorance, Pride and Obstinacy. He saith, the Nonconformists should communicate

[591] Lord Chief Justice: Sir Mathew Hale (1609–76) became chief justice in 1671.

[592] Sir Edmond Godfrey: Sir Edmund Berry Godfrey (1621–78), justice of the peace for Westminster. In 1678 his murder precipitated the Popish Plot.

[593] Rack . . . dimension: an allusion to Procrustes, the legendary Greek robber who would seize passersby and stretch them on a rack.

[594] *take care . . . apparently evil: Preface,* biv.

[595] into a more serious disputation 72a] into seriouser disputation 72.

[596] by an Angel: see Numbers 22:25.

with him till they have clear evidence that it is evil. This is a civil way indeed of gaining the question, to perswade men that are unsatisfied, to be satisfied till they be dissatisfied. He threatens, he rails, he jeers them, if it were possible, out of all their Consciences and Honesty; and finding that will not do, he calls out the Magistrate, tells him, these men are not fit to live, there can be no security of Government while they are in being: Bring out the Pillories, Whipping-posts, Gallies, Rods, and Axes, (which are *Ratio ultima Cleri,* a Clergy-mans last Argument, ay and his first too:) and pull in pieces[597] all the [208] Trading Corporations those Nests of Faction and Sedition. This is a faithful account of the summ and intention of all his undertaking, for which I confess, he was as pick'd a man as could have been employ'd or found out in a whole Kingdome: but it is so much too hard a Task for any man to atchieve, that no Goose but would grow giddy with it.

For whereas he reduces the whole Controversy to a matter of two or three Symbolical Ceremonies (and if there be nothing else, more the shame of those that keep such a pudder[598] for them) it is very well worth observing how he hath behaved himself, and how come off in this Dispute. It seems that the Conformists define a Sacrament to be an Outward visible sign of an Inward Spiritual Grace. It seems that the Sacraments are usually called in the Greek *Symbola.* It seems further that some of the Nonconformists, under the name therefore of Symbolical Ceremonies, dispute the lawfulness of those that are by our Church enjoy-[209]ned, whereby the Nonconformists can onely intend that these Ceremonies are so applyed, as if they were of a Sacramental nature and institution, and that therefore they are unlawful. Our Authors Answerer handling this Argument, does among other things make use of a pertinent Passage in St. Austin, *Signa quum ad res divinas pertinent Sacramenta appellantur.*[599] What does Mr. Bayes in this Case? for it went hard with him. Why, as good luck would have it, not being willing that so great a Politician, to the irreparable Damage of the Church, should yet be destroyed, J.O. had forgot to quote the Book and the Page. Now though you send a man the length of your Weapon, and name

597 pieces 72] peices 72a.

598 pudder: commotion.

599 Passage . . . *appellantur:* This citation is the beginning of a struggle between Parker and Marvell over the accuracy of each other's scholarship. Originally cited by Owen in *Truth and Innocence Vindicated,* p. 280, the Latin phrase, which means "Signs that pertain to divine matters are called sacraments," derives, as Marvell points out later (see p. 425 below) from a letter of St. Augustine to Marcellinus. See Augustine, *Opera,* 17 vols. (Lugduni, 1561–53), vol. 2, "Epistolae," p. 19. (A, p. 10 #1).

your Second; Yet Mr. Bayes being, as you see often, admirably read in the Laws of Duelling, knew that unless the Time and Place be appointed, there is no danger. He saith therefore, p. 452. of his second Book, that he *should have advantage on his side, if he should lay odds with him, that there is no such passage in* [210] *all the Volumns of Saint Austin.*—But however, that it is neither civil nor ingenuous to trouble him with such Objections, as he cannot answer without reading over eight or ten large Volumns in Folio. It was too much to expect from one of so much business, good Augustulus:

Quum tot sustineas & tanta negotia solus;
Res Sacras Armis tuteris, Moribus ornes,
Legibus emendes—[600]

Which may be thus translated: When you alone have the Ceremonies to defend with Whipping-posts, Rods and Axes; when you have Grace to turn into Morality; when you have the Act of Oblivion and Indemnity, and the Ecclesiastical Declaration of March to tear in pieces; it were unreasonable and too much to the dammage of the publick to put you on such an imployment. I ask your Pardon, Mr. Bayes, for this Paraphrase and Digression: for [211] I perceive I am even hardned in my Latine, and am prone to use it without fear or reverence. But Mr. Bayes, there might have been a remedy for this, had you pleased. Where then were all your *Leaf-turners*? a sort of poor Readers *that you, as well as Bishop Bramhal, ought to have some Reverence for,* having made so much use of them to gather materials for your Structures and Superstructures. I cannot be perswaded, for all this, but that he knows it well enough, the passage being so remarkable in it self, and so dirtyed with the Nonconformists thumbs, that he could not possibly miss it: and I doubt he does but laugh at me now, when, to save him a labour, I tell him in the simplicity of my heart, that even I my self met with it in *Ep. 5ta. ad Marcellinum,* and the words these, *Nimis autem longum est convenienter disputare de varietate signorum quae cum ad res divinas pertinent Sacramenta appellantur.*[601] But whether there be such a place or no, he hath no mind that his Answerer should make use of it: nor of the Schoolmen, [212] whom before he had owned for the Authors of the Church of En-

[600] *Quum . . . emendes:* "Since you sustain alone many great affairs, protect the sacred things with your arms, refine our morals, correct the laws . . ." This is the opening of Horace's verse epistle to Augustus, *Epistles,* 2.1.1–3. Marvell's "translation" is, of course, ironic.

[601] *Nimis . . . appellantur:* "It would take too long to argue about the variety of signs, which when they pertain to divine things are called sacraments."

gland's Divinity; but would bind up the Answerer to the Law onely and the Gospel. And now Mr. Bayes saith he will be of the School-mens opinion *as long as they speak Sense* and no longer, (and so I believe of Saint Austin's) that is to say, so long as they will serve his turn: for all Politicians shake men off when they have no more use of 'm, or find them to thwart the design. But, Mr. Bayes, why may not your Answerer or any man else quote Saint Austin, as well as you may the Scripture? I am sure there is less danger of perverting the place, or of mis-interpretation. And though perhaps a Non-conformist may value the Authority of the Bible above that of the Fathers, #and# yet the Welch have a Proverb; that the Bible and a Stone do well together:[602] meaning perhaps, that if the one miss the other will hit. You, that are a Duellist, know how great a bravery 'tis to gain an[603] enemies Sword, and that there is no more home-thrust in disputation, than the *Argu-*[213]*mentum ad hominem.*[604] So that if your Adversary fell upon you with one of your own Fathers, it was gallantly done on his part; and no less wisely on yours, to fence in this manner, and use all your shifts to put it by. For you too, Mr. Bayes, do know, no man better, that it is not at all times safe nor honourable to be of a *Fathers* opinion.[605]

Having escaped this danger, he grows, nor can I blame him, exceeding merry: and insults heavily over *Symbolical*[606] wheresoever he meets with it, for in his Answerer I find it not. But whatsoever 'twas, it serves to good purpose. For no man would imagin that he could have received so universal a Defeat, and appear in so good humour. A terrible Disputant he is, when he has set up an hard word to be his Opponent; 'Tis a very wholsome thing he knows, and prolongs life: for all the while he can keep up this Ball, he may decline the Question. But the poor Word is sure to be mumbled and mowsled[607] to purpose, and to be made an Example. But let us, with Mr. Bayes his leave, ex-[214]amine the thing for once a little closer. The Nonconformists, as I took notice before, do object to some of the Rites of the Church of England, under the name of Symbolical or significant

[602] Proverb . . . together: "Da yw'r main gyda't Efengel." [Grosart]

[603] an 72a] your 72.

[604] *Argumentum ad hominem:* An argument directed at the character or circumstances of the opponent.

[605] *Fathers* opinion: Marvell alludes only briefly here to a thrust he will make at length in *RT2:* that Parker's father, John Parker, published a republican tract in 1650, *The Government of the People of England.* See below, pp. 291–92.

[606] *Symbolical: Preface,* b3v ff.

[607] mowsled: pulled about.

Ceremonies. They observe the Church of England does in the discourse of Ceremonies printed before the Common Prayer Book, declare that the retaining of those Ceremonies, is not onely *as they serve for decent Order and godly Discipline; but as they are apt to stir up the dull mind of Man to the remembrance of his Duty to God, by some special and notable significancy whereby he may be edified.* They further observe the Church of England's definition of a Sacrament: That it is *an outward visible sign of an inward spiritual Grace.* They find these Ceremonies, so constituted, impos'd upon them by Authority; and moreover, according to our Authors principle, made a new part of the Divine Law. They therefore quarrel and except against these under the notion of Sacraments, and insist that the Church is not impowered to institute such Cere-[215]monies under such obligations and penalties as they are imposed. Or if you will, in stead of Church you may say rather the Magistrate: for as much as our Author hath *pro hac vice*[608] delivered the Keyes and the whole power of the House into his hands.

Now the Author having got them at this lock cries Victory. Nothing less will serve him than a three dayes Triumph, as if he had conquered Europe, Asia and Africa, and let him have a fourth day added, if he please, over the *Terra incognita*[609] of Geneva. There is no end of his Ostentation and Pageantry: and the dejected Nonconformists follow the wheels of his Chariot, to be led afterwards to the Prison and there executed. He had said p. 446. of his Second Book, *Here Cartwright begun his Objection, and here he was immediately check'd in his Carriere*[610] *by Whitgift* (you might Mr. Author, for respect's sake have called him at least Mr. if not Arch-bishop Whitgift) *who told him plainly, he could not be ignorant that to the making of a Sacrament, besides the ex-*[216]*ternal Element, there is required a Commandment of God in his Word that it should be done, and a promise annexed to it, whereof the Sacrament is a Seal.* And in pursuance hereof, p. 447. our Author saith, *Here then I fix my foot, and dare him to his teeth, to prove that any thing can be capable of the nature or office of Sacraments that is not established by Divine Institution and upon Promise of Divine Acceptance.* Upon the confidence of this Argument 'tis that he Hectors and Achillizes all the Nonconformists out of the pit in this preface. This is the Sword that was consecrated first upon the Altar, and thence presented to the Champions of the Church in

[608] *pro hac vice:* "for his office."

[609] *Terra incognita:* unknown land.

[610] *Carriere* 72a] *Carrear* 72.

all Ages. This is that with which Arch-bishop Whitgift gave Cartwright *his death's wound*:[611] *and laid the Puritan Reformation a gasping.* This is the weapon wherewith Master Hooker *gained those lasting and eternal Trophies over that baffled Cause.* This is that with which Bishop Bramhal *wrought those wonderful things that exceeded all belief.*[612] This hath been transmitted successively to the [217] Writer of the *Friendly Debate,* and to this our Author. It is in conclusion the *Curtana*[613] of our Church. 'Tis Sir Salomon's Sword,[614] Cock of as many men as it hath been drawn against. Wo worth the man that comes in the way of so dead doing a tool, and when wielded with the arm of such a Scanderbag[615] as our Author. The Nonconformists had need desire a Truce to bury their dead. Nay there are none left alive to desire it: but they are slain every mothers Son of them. Yet perhaps they are but stounded[616] and may revive again. For I do not see all this while, that any of them have written, as a great Prelate of ours, a Book of *Seven Sacraments*:[617] or attempted to prove that these Symbolical Ceremonies are indeed Sacraments. Nothing less. 'Tis that which they most labour against, and they complain that these things should be imposed on them with so high Penalty, as want nothing of a Sacramental nature but Divine Institution. And because an Human Institution is herein made of equal force to a Divine Institution, therefore [218] it is that they are agrieved. All that they mean, or could mean, as far as I or any man can perceive, is onely that these Ceremonies are a kind of *Anti-Sacraments,* and so obtruded upon the

[611] Whitgift . . . *wound:* Whitgift's answer to Cartwright's *Second Admonition,* in the *Answere to a Certen Libel* (1572).

[612] *wrought . . . belief: Preface,* A3v.

[613] *Curtana:* the ritual sword, supposedly that of Edward the Confessor, borne before English kings at their coronation; mention of it was usually associated with radically contractual theories of monarchy, as by Milton in the *First Defence of the English People.* See Janelle Greenberg, *The Radical Face of the Ancient Constitution* (Cambridge, 2001), p. 237.

[614] Sir Salomon: the foolish hero of John Caryll's *Sir Salomon; or the Cautious Coxcomb* (1671).

[615] Scanderbag: George Castriot (1403–67), the national hero of Albania, famed for his victories against the Ottoman Turk. [S]

[616] stounded: astonished, stunned.

[617] Prelate . . . *Seven Sacraments:* another reference to John Cosin, bishop of Durham (see p. 112 above), whose reinvention of seven sacraments rather than five will be mentioned again in Marvell's citations from Archbishop Abbot (see p. 186 below). Cosin's *Collection of Private Devotions* (1627), the source of this reactionary doctrine, was heavily criticized in the 1628 parliament.

Church, that without condescending to these additional Inventions, no man is to be admitted to partake of the true Sacraments which were of Christ's appointing. For, without the Sign of the Cross, our Church will not receive any one to Baptism, ⟨as⟩ also without kneeling no man is suffer'd to come to the Communion. So that methinks our Author and his Partners have wounded themselves onely with this Argument: and have had as little occasion here to sing their *Te Deums,* as the Roman Emperour had to triumph over the Ocean, because he had gathered Periwinkles and Scallop shells on the Beach.[618] For the Author may transform their reasonings as oft as he pleases (even as oft as he doth his own, or the Scriptures:) but this is indeed their Fort out of which I do not see they are likely to be beat with all our Authors Cannon: that no [219] such new Conditions ought to be imposed upon Christians by a less than Divine Authority, and unto which if they do not submit though against their Consciences, they shall therefore be depriv'd of Communion with the Church. And I wonder that our Author *could not observe any thing in the Discourse of Evangelical love, that was to the purpose, beside a perpetual repetition,* of the outworn story of unscriptual Ceremonies,[619] and a peculiar uncouthness and obscurity of stile; when as this Plea is there for so many pages distinctly and vigorously insisted on. For it is a childish thing (how high soever our Author magnifies himself in this way of reasoning) either to demand from the Nonconformists a patern of their Worship from the Scripture, who affect therein a simplicity free from all exterior circumstances, but such as are natural or customary: or else to require of them some particular command against the Cross, or kneeling, and such like Ceremonies, which in the time of the Apostles and many ages after were not[620] thought [220] of. But therefore general and applicable Rules of Scripture they urge as directions to the Conscience; unto which our Author gives no satisfactory Solution, but by superseding and extinguishing the Conscience, or exposing it to the severest penalties. But here I say then is their main exception, that things indifferent, and that have no proper signature, or significancy to that purpose, should by command be made necessary conditions of Church-Communion. I have many times

[618] Roman Emperour . . . Beach: an anecdote from Suetonius, *Caligula,* 46. Marvell translated it as follows: "[Having marched his army down to the seashore, Caligula] commanded them on a sudden to fall a gathering of Cockles, and to fill their laps, and head-pieces with them, calling them *the spoils of the Ocean.*"

[619] *could not* . . . Ceremonies: *Preface,* a2v; last phrase not italicized in 72 or 72a.

[620] not 72a] never 72.

wished for peaceableness-sake, that they had a greater latitude; but if unless they should stretch their Consciences till they tear again, they cannot conform, what remedy? For I must confess that Christians have a better Right and Title to the Church, and to the Ordinances of God there, than the Author had[621] to his Surplice. And that Right is so undoubted and ancient, that it is not to be innovated upon by humane restrictions and capitulations.

Bishop Bramhall p. 141. saith, *I do* [221] *profess to all the World, that the transforming of indifferent Opinions into necessary Articles of Faith, hath been that* Insana Laurus, *or cursed Bay tree, the cause of all our brawling and contention.* That which he saw in matter of Doctrine he would not discern in Discipline, whereas this among us, the transforming of things, at best indifferent, into necessary points of practice, hath been of as ill consequence. And (to reform a little my seriousness) I shall not let this pass without taking notice that you Mr. Bayes, being the most extravagant person in this matter that ever I heard of, as I have shown, you are mad, and so the *Insana Laurus*;[622] so I wish you may not prove *that cursed Bay-tree too,* as the Bishop translates it. If you had thought of this, perhaps we might have missed both the Bishops Book and your Preface; for you see that sometimes no man hath a worse friend than he brings from home.

It is true, and very piously done, that our Church does declare that the [222] kneeling at the Lords Supper is not injoyned for adoration of those Elements, and concerning the other Ceremonies as before. But the Romanists (from whom we have them, and who said of old, we would come to feed on their Meat, as well as eat of their Porridge) do offer us here many a fair declaration, and distinction in very weighty matters, to which nevertheless the Conscience of our Church hath not complyed. But in this particular matter of kneeling, which came in first with the Doctrine of Transubstantiation, the Romish Church do reproach us with flat Idolatry, in that we not believing the real presence in the Bread and Wine, do yet pay to something or other the same adoration. Suppose the Antient Pagans had declared to the Primitive Christians, that the offering of some grains of Incense was only to perfume the room, or that the delivering up of their Bibles, was but for preserving the Book more carefully. Do you think the Christians would have palliated so far, and collu-[223]ded with their Consciences? Men are too prone to erre on that hand. In the last King's time,

[621] had 72a] hath 72.

[622] *Insana Laurus:* for the "mad laurel" overshadowing King Amycus's tomb, see Pliny, *History of the World,* trans. Philemon Holland (1634), 1.16.44 (A, p. 25, #53).

some eminent Persons of our *Clergy* made an open defection to the Church of Rome.[623] One, and he yet certainly a Protestant, and that hath deserved well of that cause, writ the Book of *Seven Sacraments.*[624] One in the Church at present, though certainly no less a Protestant, could not abstain from arguing the *Holiness of Lent:*[625] Doctor Thorndike[626] lately dead, left for his Epitaph, *Hic jacet corpus Herberti Thorndike Praebendarij hujus Ecclesiae qui vivus veram Reformatae Ecclesiae rationem & modum precibus studiisque prosequibatur,* and nevertheless he adds, *Tu Lector requiem ei & beatam in Christo resurrectionem precare.*[627] Which things[628] I do thus sparingly set down, onely to shew the danger of inventive Piety; and if men once come[629] to add new devices to the Scripture, how easily they slide on into Superstition. Therefore, although the Church do consider her self so much as not to alter her Mode unto the fancy of others, yet I can-[224]not see why she ought to exclude those from Communion, whose weaker consciences cannot for fear of scandal step further. For the Non-conformists, as to those[630] Declarations of our Church against the Reverence to the Creatures of Bread and Wine, and concerning the other Ceremonies as before, will be ready to think they have as good a Plea as that so much commended by our Author against the clause, *that whosoever should affirm the Wednesday Fast to be imposed with an intention to bind the Conscience,* should be punished *like the spreaders of false News*; which is, saith *a Learned Prelate plainly to them that understand it, to evacuate the whole Law. For all humane Power being*

[623] eminent Persons . . . Rome: Among clerical converts to Catholicism in the 1630s were Thomas Vane, who converted c. 1645 and dedicated his *A Lost Sheep Returned* to Queen Henrietta Maria; Stephen Goffe (1605–81), an active royalist, converted 1651, and one of Charles II's chaplains; Thomas Bailey (see p. 144 and n. 576 above) and Hugh de Cressy (1605–74), converted 1646, one of Queen Catherine's servants. Their names headed a list of fifty-three converts prefixed to D.Y., *Legenda Lignea* (1653).

[624] One . . . *Sacraments:* John Cosin. See n. 617 above.

[625] One . . . *Lent:* Peter Gunning. See p. 79 and n. 233 above.

[626] Doctor Thorndike: Herbert Thorndike. See p. 129 and n. 485 above.

[627] *Hic jacet . . . precare:* "Here lies the body of Herbert Thorndike, Prebendary of this church, who when living sought out with prayer and study the true doctrine and mode of the Reformed Church . . . Reader, pray for his peace and blessed resurrection in Christ." Thorndike was a prebend of Canterbury Cathedral; yet Marvell found the epitaph not in the cathedral, but in Thorndike's will. See Introduction, p. 14.

[628] things 72a] thing 72.

[629] once come 72a] come once 72.

[630] those 72a] these 72.

derived from God, and bound upon our Consciences by his power, not by Man, he that saith it shall not bind the Conscience, saith it shall be no Law, it shall have no Authority from God, and then it hath none at all; and if it be not tyed upon the Conscience, then to break it is no sin, and then to keep it is no Duty. So that a Law without such an intention is a contradicti-[225]*on. It is a Law onely which binds if we please, and we may obey when we have a mind to it, and to so much we are tyed before the Constitution. But then if by such a Declaration it was meant, that to keep such Fasting-days was no part of a direct Commandment from God, that is, God hath not required them by himself immediately, & so it was abstracting from that Law no Duty Evangelical, it had been below the wisdom of the Contrivers of it, for no man pretends it, no man saith it, no man thinks it, and they might as well have declared that that Law was none of the ten Commandments,* p. 59. of his first Book. So much pains does that learned Prelate of his take (whoever he was)[631] to prove a whole Parliament of England Coxcombs. Now I say that these Ecclesiastical Laws, with such Declarations concerning the Ceremonies by them injoyned, might *mutatis mutandis,*[632] be taxed upon the same *'Topick.* But I love not that task, and shall rather leave it to Mr. Bayes to paraphrase his learned Prelate. For he is very good at correcting the impertinence of Laws and [226] Lawgivers: and though this work indeed be not for his turn at present, yet it may be for the future. And I have heard a good Engineer say, That he never fortified any place so, but that he reserv'd a feeble point, whereby[633] he knew how to take it, if there were occasion.

I know a medicine for Mr. Bayes his Hiccough (it is but naming J.O.) but I cannot tell certainly, though I have a shrew'd guess what is the cause of it. For indeed all his Arguments here are so abrupt and short, that I cannot liken them better, considering too that frequent and perpetual repetition. Such as this, *Why may not the Soveraign Power bestow this Priviledge upon Ceremony, as well as Use and Custom, by vertue of its Prerogative? What greater Immorality*[634] *is there in them when determined by the Command and Institution of the Prince, than when by the consent and institution of the people?* This #is# the Tap-lash[635] of what he said, p. 110. *When the Civil Magistrate*

[631] learned Prelate . . . he was: Neither have the editors succeeded in identifying him.

[632] *mutatis mutandis:* having made the necessary changes.

[633] whereby 72a] by which 72.

[634] *Immorality,* Ed., Parker] *Immortality* 72, 72a.

[635] Tap-lash: dregs of liquor.

takes upon him to determine any particular Forms of outward Wor-[227]*ship, it is*[636] *of no worse Consequence than if he should go about to define the signification of all #the# words used in the worship of God.*[637]

And[638] page[639] 108. of his first Book: *So*[640] *that all the Magistrates power of instituting significant Ceremonies, &c. can be no more Usurpation upon the* CONSCIENCES *of Men, than if the Soveraign Authority should take upon it self, as some Princes have done, to define the signification of words.*[641]

And afterwards, *the same gesture, and actions are indifferently capable of signifying either Honour or Contumely: And so words; and therefore it is*[642] *necessary #that# their signification should be determined, &c.*[643]

This is[644] all very well worth reading. Page[645] 441. of his Second Book. *It is*[646] *no other Usurpation upon their Subjects Consciences than if he should take upon him to refine their Language, and determine the proper signification of all Phrases imployed in Divine Worship, as well as in #all# trades, Arts, and Sciences.*[647] [228]

Page[648] 461.[649] of the same; *Once we will so far gratifie the tenderness of their Consciences and curiosity of their Fancies, as to promise never to ascribe any other significancy to things than what himself is here content to bestow upon words.*[650]

And 462 of the same. *So that you see, my Comparison between the signification of Words and Ceremonies stands firm as the Pillars of the Earth, and the Foundations of our Faith.*[651]

636 *it is* 72a] *'tis* 72.

637 *When . . . God* 72a] When . . . God 72; set in roman with quotation marks and diples.

638 This and the following seven short paragraphs were newly set off as such in 72a.

639 page 72a] p. 72.

640 *So* 72a (B5, D5, S3, W2)] *Shewing* 72a; So 72.

641 *So . . . words* 72a (B5, D5, S3, W2)] So . . . words 72; set in roman with quotation marks and diples.

642 *it is* 72a] 'tis 72.

643 *the . . . &c.* 72a] The . . . &c. 72; set in roman with quotation marks and diples.

644 This is 72a] 'tis 72.

645 Page 72a] P. 72.

646 *It is* 72a] 'Tis 72.

647 *It . . . Sciences* 72a] 'Tis . . . sciences 72; set in roman with quotation marks and diples.

648 Page 72a] P. 72.

649 461 Ed.] 1461 72, 72a.

650 *Once . . . words* 72a] Once . . . words 72; set in roman with quotation marks and diples.

651 *So . . . Faith* 72a] So . . . Faith 72; set in roman with quotation marks and diples.

Mr. Bayes might, I see, have spared Sir Salomon's Sword of the Divine Institution of the Sacraments. Here is the terriblest Weapon in all his Armory; and therefore I perceive, reserved by our Duellist for the last Onset.

And, I who am a great Well-wisher to the Pillars of the Earth, or the eight Elephants,[652] lest we should have an Earth-quake; and much more a Servant to the King's Prerogative, lest we should ⟨all⟩ fall into confusion; and perfectly devoted to the Foundations of our Faith, lest we ⟨should⟩ run out into Popery or Paganism; have no heart to this incounter, lest if I should [229] prove that the Magistrates absolute unlimited and uncontrolable Power doth not extend to define the signification of all words, I should thereby not onely be the occasion of all those mischiefs mentioned, but, which is of far more dismal Importance, the loss of two or three so significant Ceremonies. But though I therefore will not dispute against the[653] Flower of the Princes Crown; yet I hope that without doing much harm, I may observe that for the most part they left it to the People, and seldom themselves exercised it. And even Augustus Caesar, though he was so great an Emperour, and so valiant a man in his own person, was[654] used to fly from a new word[655] though it were single, as studiously as a Mariner would avoid a Rock for fear of splitting. The difference of one Syllable in the same word hath made as considerable a Controversy as most have been in the Church, betwixt the *Homousians* and the *Homoiousians*.[656] One letter in the name of Beans in Languedoc, one party calling them *Faves,* and the other *Haves*;[230][657] as the transposition onely of a letter a[658] another time in the name of a Goat, by some call'd *Crabe,* and by others *Cabre,*[659] was the loss of

[652] eight Elephants: an allusion back to the flattery of Dancehment Kan; see p. 54 above.

[653] the 72a] that 72.

[654] was 72] who 72a.

[655] Augustus Caesar . . . new word: see Suetonius, *Augustus,* 86.

[656] *Homousians . . . Homoiousians:* the names of the two factions in the Arian controversy, temporarily settled by the first Council of Nicaea (A.D. 325) in favor of the orthodox Trinitarians. *Homousians* believed that Father and Son were of the same essence or substance, *homoiousians* that they were not. Marvell would return to this issue at length in his *Short Historical Essay.* See vol. 2, pp. 139, 150, 153.

[657] 230 72] 214 72a.

[658] a 72, 72a: The letter required to make sense of the joke about goats is *r;* presumably the compositor having the copy read out to him mistook the sound of *r* as *a.*

[659] *Cabre* 72] *Crabre* 72a; *Crabe* is the Languedoc variant, *Cabre* the Gascon. [S]

more men's lives than the distinguishing but by an Aspiration in *Shiboleth*[660] upon the like occasion. So that if a man would be learnedly impertinent, he might enlarge here to show that 'tis as dangerous to take a man by the tongue, as a Bear by the tooth. And had I a mind to play the Politician, like Mr. Bayes, upon so pleasant and copious a Subject, I would demonstrate that though the imposition of Ceremonies hath bred much mischief in the world, yet (shall I not venture too on a word once for tryal) such a Penetration or Transubstantiation of Language would throw all into Rebellion and Anarchy, would shake the Crowns of all Princes, and reduce the World into a second Babel. Therefore Mr. Bayes I doubt you were not well advised to make so close an Analogy betwixt imposing of significant words and significant Ceremonies: for I fear the Argument may be improved against [231][661] you, and that Princes finding that of words so impracticable, and of ill consequence, will conclude that of Ceremonies to be no less pernicious. And the Nonconformists (who are great Traders, you know, in Scripture, ⟨and therefore thrown out of the Temple)⟩ will be certainly on your back. For they will appropriate your pregnant Text of *Let all things be done decently and in order,*[662] to preaching or praying in an unknown Tongue, which such an imposition of words would be: and then, to keep you to your Similitude, they will say too, that yours are all Latine Ceremonies, and the Congregation does not understand them. But were not this Dominion of words so dangerous, (for how many millions of men did it cost your Roman Empire to attain it!) Yet it was very unmannerly in you to assign to Princes, who have enough beside, so mean a trouble. When you gave them leave to exercise ⟨the⟩ Priesthood in person, that was something to the purpose; That was both Honorable, and some-[232][663] thing belongs to it that would have help'd to bear the charge. But this Mint of words will never quit cost,[664] nor pay for the coynage. This is such a drudgery; that, rather than undergo it, I dare say, there is no Prince but would resign to you so pedantical a Soveraignty. I cannot but think how full that Princes head must be of Proclamations. For, if he published but once a Proclamation to that purpose, he must forthwith set out another to stamp and declare the significa-

[660] *Shiboleth:* see p. 138 and n. 536 above.

[661] 231 72] 219 72a.

[662] *Let . . . order:* 1 Corinthians 14:40; a central text for high church Anglicans since the 1640s.

[663] Because of the censorship, this page has only twenty-six lines rather than the usual twenty-seven.

[664] quit cost: give a return on investment.

tion of all the words contained in it, and then another to appoint the meaning of all the words in this, and so on: that here is work cut out in one Paper of State for the whole Privy Council, both Secretaries of State, and all the Clerks of the Council, for one Kings Reign, and *in infinitum.* But, I cannot but wonder, knowing how ambitious Mr. Bayes is of the power over words, and jealous of his own Prerogative of refining Language, how he came to be so liberal of it to the Prince: Why, the same thing that induced him to give the Prince a [233] power antecedent and independent to Christ, and to establish what Religion he pleased, &c. Nothing but his spight against the Non-conformists. I know not that thing in the world, except a Jest, that he would not part with to be satisfied in that particular. He hoped doubtless by holding up this Maxim, to obtain that the words of the Declaration of the 15th March should be understood by contraries. You may well think he expected no less an equivalent, he would never else have permitted the Prince even to define the signification of all words used in the Worship of God, and to determine the proper signification of all Phrases imploy'd in Divine Worship. Nay Mr. Bayes, if it be come to that, and you will surrender your Liturgy to the Prince, I know not what you mean; for 'tis bound up with your Bible. Was it ever heard that that Book so sacred, and in which there could not one errour be found by all the Presbyterians at the Worster-House-Conference,[665] should, upon so uncertain a prospect, [234] be now abandon'd so far, as that every word and Phrase in it may receive a new and contrary signification! But the King for ought I see likes it well enough as it is (and therefore I do so too.) Yet in case his Majesty should ever think fit to reform it, and because such kind of work is usually refer'd back to some of the Clergy; I would gladly put in a *Caveat,* that our Author may in no case be one of them. For 'tis known that Mr. Bayes is subject to a distemper; and who knows but when he is in a fit, as he made such mad alterations of the fruit of the Spirit in the Epistle for the day, he may as well insert in some other part of the *Service, welfare poor Macedo for a modest Fool*;[666] and then, *Oh how I hug thee, Dear Heart, for this!*[667] and pretend that the Supreme Magistrate should stamp upon it a signification sacred and serious. I would not have spoken so severely of him, but that his *more laboured periods,* as he calls them, are so often fill'd with much bolder and more unwholesome translations. But however that he may not [235] at his

[665] Worster-House-Conference: see p. 62 and n. 133 above.

[666] *welfare . . . Fool: Preface,* a2.

[667] *Oh how . . . this:* ibid.

better intervals be wholly unemploy'd in the work of Uniformity, ⟨I⟩ should recommend to him rather to turn the *Liturgy* and the *Rationale*[668] into the Universal Language, and so in time the whole World might come to be of his Parish.

When he was drawn thus low, did not he, think you, stand need of tilting? He had done much more service to the Cause, had he laid by all those cheating Argumentations, and dealt candidly, like the good Arch Deacon[669] not long since dead; who went about both Court and Countrey, preaching upon the *Cloke left at Troas, and the Books, but especially the Parchments.*[670] The honest Man had found out there the whole Liturgy, the Canonical Habits, and all the Equipage of a Conformist. This was something to the matter in hand, to produce Apostolical Example and Authority: And much more to the purpose than that beaten Text of *doing all things decently and in order.*

One Argument I confess remains still behind, and that will justifie any [236] thing. 'Tis that which I call'd lately *Rationem ultimam Cleri*; Force, Law, Execution, or what you will have it. I would not be mistaken, as though I hereby[671] meant the body of the English Clergy, who have been ever since the Reformation (I say it without disparagement to the Foraign Churches) of the most Eminent for[672] Divinity and Piety in all Christendom. And as far am I from censuring, under this Title, the Bishops of England, for whose Function, their Learning, their Persons I have too deep a veneration to speak any thing of them irreverently. But those that I intend onely, are a particular bran of persons, who will in spight of Fate be accounted the Church of England, and to shew they are Pluralists, never write in a modester Stile than *We, We*; nay, even these, several of them, are men of parts sufficient to deserve a Rank among the Teachers and Governors of the Church. Onely what Bishop Bramhall saith of Grotius, his defect in School Divinity;[237]

[668] *Rationale:* Sparrow, *Rationale upon the Book of Common Prayer* (1657); see p. 79 and n. 232 above.

[669] good Arch Deacon not long since dead: This was probably Nathaniel Hardy (d. June 1, 1670), archdeacon of Lewes and dean of Rochester, a frequent preacher before the king and elsewhere. See Wood, *Athenae Oxonienses,* 4:898–89.

[670] *Cloke . . . Parchments:* 2 Timothy 4:13.

[671] I hereby 72a (B5, D5, S3, W2)] thereby 72a; I hereby 72.

[672] the most Eminent for 72a] the Eminentest for 72.

Unum hoc maceror & doleo tibi deesse.[673]

I may apply to their excess and rigour in matter of Discipline. They want all consideration, all moderation in those things; and I never heard of any of them at any time, who, if they got into Power or Office, did ever make the least experiment or overture towards the peace of the Church and Nation they lived in. They are the *Politick would-be's*[674] of the Clergy. Not Bishops, but men that have a mind to be Bishops, and that will do any thing in the World to compass it. And, though Princes have always a particular mark upon these Men, and value them no more than they deserve, yet I know not very well, or perhaps I do know, how it oftentimes happens that they come to be advanced. They are Men of a fiery nature that must always be uppermost, and so they may increase their own Splendor, care not though they set all on flame about them. You would think the same day that they [238] took up Divinity they devested themselves of humanity, & so they may procure & execute a Law against the Nonconformists, that they had forgot the Gospel. They cannot endure that Humility, that Meekness, that Strictness of Manners and Conversation, which is the true way of gaining Reputation and Authority to the Clergy; much less can they content themselves with the ordinary and comfortable provision that is made for the Ministry: But, having wholly calculated themselves for preferment, and Grandeur, know or practise no other means to make themselves venerable but by Ceremony and Severity. Whereas the highest advantage of promotion is the opportunity of condescention, and the greatest dignity in our Church can but raise them to the Title of *Your Grace,* which is in the Latine *Vestra Clementia.*[675] But of all these, none are so eager & virulent, as some, who having had relation to the late times, have got access to *Ecclesiastical Fortune,*[676] and are resolved to make their best of her. For so, [239] of all Beasts, none are so fierce and cruel as those that have been taught once by hunger to prey upon their own kind; as of all Men, none are so inhumane as the *Canibals.* But whether this be the true way of ingratiating themselves with a

[673] *Unum . . . deesse:* cited by Bramhall, *Vindication,* p. 20; a line from a fragment of a poem by Julius Caesar on Terence: "I torment myself and grieve that you lack this one thing." [S]

[674] *Politick would-be's:* Sir Politick Would-be was an absurdly Machiavellian figure in Ben Jonson's *Volpone.*

[675] *Vestra Clementia:* Your Mercy.

[676] *Fortune* 72] *Fortunes* 72a.

generous and discerning Prince, I meddle not; nor whether it be an ingenuous practice towards those whom they have been formerly acquainted with: but whatsoever they think themselves obliged to for the approving of their new Loyalty I rather commend. That which astonishes me, and onely raises my indignation is, that of all sorts of Men, this kind of Clergy should always be, and have been for the most precipitate, brutish, and sanguinary Counsels. The former Civil War cannot make them wise, nor his Majesties Happy Return, good natured; but they are still for running things up unto the same extreams. The softness of the Universities where they have been bred, the gentleness of Christianity in which they have been nurtured, hath [240] but exasperated their nature; and they seem to have contracted no *Idea* of wisdom, but what they learnt at School, the Pedantry of Whipping. They take themselves qualified to Preach the Gospel, and no less to intermeddle in affairs of State: Though the reach of their Divinity is but to persecution, and an Inquisition is the height of their Policy.

And you Mr. Bayes, had you lived in the dayes of Augustus Caesar (be not scandalized, for why may you not bring sixteen hundred years, as well as five hours into one of your Playes?) would not you have made, think you, an excellent Privy Counsellour? His Father[677] too was murdered. Or (to come nearer both to our times, and your resemblance of the late War, which you trumpet alwaies in the Ear of his Majesty) had you happen'd in the time of Henry the fourth of France,[678] should not you have done well in the Cabinet? His Predecessor[679] too was assassinated. No, Mr. Bayes, you would not have been for their purpose: They took o-[241]ther measures of Government, and accordingly it succeeded with them. And His Majesty, whose Genius hath much of both those Princes, and who derives half of the Blood in his Veins from the latter,[680] will in all probability not be so forward to hearken to your advice as to follow their Example. For these Kings, Mr. Bayes, how negligent soever or ignorant you take 'em to be, have I doubt, a shrewd understanding with them. 'Tis a Trade, that God be thanked, neither you nor I are of, and therefore we are not so competent Judges of their Actions. I my self have often times seen them, some of

[677] His Father: Julius Caesar, who had adopted Octavian, later Augustus Caesar, as his son.

[678] Henry IV of France was assassinated by a Roman Catholic schoolmaster, François Ravaillac, on May 14, 1610.

[679] Predecessor: Henry III of France was assassinated by a Dominican friar, Jacques Clement, on August 1, 1589. [S]

[680] latter: Charles II's mother, Henrietta Maria, was the daughter of Henry IV.

them, do strange things, and unreasonable in my opinion, and yet a little while, or sometimes many years after, I have found that all the men in the world could not have contrived any thing better. 'Tis not with them as with you. You have but one Cure of Souls, or perhaps two, as being a Noblemans Chaplain, to look after: And if you make Conscience of discharging them as you ought, you [242] would find you had work sufficient, without writing your *Ecclesiastical Policies*. But they are the Incumbents of whole Kingdoms, and the Rectorship of the Common people, the Nobility, and even of the Clergy, whom you are prone to *affirm when possest with Principles that incline to Rebellion and disloyal practises, to be of all Rebels the most dangerous*, p. 49. the Care I say of all these rests upon them. So that they are fain to condescend to many things for peace-sake, and the quiet of Mankind, that your proud heart would break before it would bend to. They do not think fit to require any thing that is impossible, unnecessary, or wanton, of their people; but are[681] fain to consider the very temper of the Climate in which they live, the Constitution and Laws under which they have been formerly bred, and upon all occasions to give them good words, and humour them like Children. They reflect upon the Histories of former times, and the present Transactions to regulate themselves by in every cir-[243]cumstance. ⟨They have heard that one of your Roman Emperours, when his Captain of the Life-Guard came for the Word, by giving it unhandsomely, received a Dagger.[682]⟩ They observe how the Parliament of Poland[683] will be their King's Taylor, and among other Reasons, because he would not wear their Mode, have suffered the Turk to enter, as coming nearer their Fashion. Nay, that even Alexander the Great had almost lost all he had conquered by forcing his Subjects to conform to the Persian habit.[684] That the King of Spain, when upon a Progress he enters Biscay, is pleased to ride with one

[681] are 72] as 72a.

[682] one of your Roman Emperours . . . Dagger: Caligula, assassinated in A.D. 41. The captain was Cassius Charea. The story is told by Suetonius (*Caligula*, 58). Its offensiveness to the censors led to its removal; but Marvell reiterated it in *RT2*. See p. 307 and n. 462 below.

[683] Parliament of Poland: The control the Polish Diet exerted over its kings at this time was well known. For one source, see Heylyn, *Cosmographie* (1657), book 2, p. 537: "Yet when they once became *elective*, they lost much of that power . . . that at the last one King is counted little better than a *Royal Shadow; Stat magni nominis umbra*, in the Poet's language." The poet is Lucan, in his description of the decline of Pompey.

[684] Alexander . . . habit: see Quintus Curtius, *Life of Alexander the Great*, 6.2.2–4, 6.6.7–9 (Anglesey possessed the 1650 Amsterdam edition, p. 52, #353).

Leg naked, and above all to take care that there be not any Bishop in his Retinue.[685] So their people will pay their Taxes in good Gold and Silver, they demand no Subsidy of so many bushel of Fleas, lest they should receive the same answer with the Tyrant,[686] that the Subject could not furnish that quantity; and besides they would be leaping out still before they could be measured; and should they fine[687] the people for non-payment,[688] they reckon there would be little got by distraining. They have been told that a certain Queen being [244][689] desired to give a Town-Seal to one of her Cities, lighting from Horse, sate down naked on the Snow,[690] and left them that Impression; and though it caused no disturbance, but all the Town-Leases are Letters-Pattents; Kings do not approve the Example. That the late Queen of Sweden did her self no good with saying, *Io non voglio governar le Bestie,*[691] but afterwards resigned.[692] That the occasion of the revolt of Swizzerland from the Emperour, and its turning Commonwealth, was onely the imposing of a Civil Ceremony by a Capricious Governour, who set up a Pole in the high-way with a Cap upon the top of it, to which he would have all Passengers be uncover'd, and #to# do obeysance. One sturdy Swiss, that would not conform, thereupon overturn'd the Government, as 'tis at large in History.[693] That the King of Spain lost Flan-

[685] King of Spain . . . Retinue: see Heylyn, *Cosmographie* (1657), book 1, pp. 255–56.

[686] the Tyrant: Ivan IV ("the Terrible"), tzar of Muscovy (1530–84).

[687] fine 72] finde 72a.

[688] Fleas . . . non-payment: Ivan demanded the tribute of fleas for medicinal purposes from the citizens of Moscow and fined them seven hundred rubles when they failed to supply it. A marginal MS note in B7 identifies the original source as the *Life* of Johannes Basilides. Marvell's source was again Heylyn, *Cosmographie* (1657), book 2, p. 523. Marvell has evidently been scouring Heylyn for anecdotes.

[689] Because of the censorship of the dagger passage, this page has only twenty-six lines instead of the usual twenty-seven.

[690] Queen . . . Snow: a marginal MS note in B7 identifies her as "The Queen of Sweden"; i.e., Queen Christina (1626–89). Marvell wrote a Latin poem about her, *A Letter to Doctor Ingelo* (*P&L* 1:104–07, 314–19), which was probably shown to her by Bulstrode Whitlocke, ambassador to Sweden in 1653. She abdicated the following year.

[691] *Io . . . bestie:* "I don't wish to rule over beasts."

[692] late Queen . . . resigned: This certainly refers to Christina.

[693] revolt of Swizzerland . . . History: This refers to the legend of William Tell, who supposedly initiated the revolt of the Swiss from Austrian domination in the fourteenth century by refusing to salute the hat with Austrian colors erected in the square of Altdorf. The governor was Gessler.

ders[694] chiefly upon introducing the Inquisition. And you now Mr. Bayes will think these and an hundred more that I could tell you, but [245][695] idle stories, and yet Kings can tell how to make use of 'em.[696] And hence 'tis that in stead of assuming your unhoopable jurisdiction, they are so satisfied with the abundance of their power, that they rather think meet to abate of its exercise by their discretion. The greater their fortune is, they are content to use the less extravagancy.

But[697] because I see, Mr. Bayes, you are a little deaf on this ear, I will talk somewhat closer to you. In this very matter of Ceremonies, which you are so bent upon, that your mind is alwayes running on't when you should be hearkning to the Sermon; do not you think that the King knows every word you said, although he never gave your Book the reading? That you say, that the Clause 5° Eliz. of the Wednesday-Fast has been the Original of all the Puritan-Disorders. That the Controversy is now reduced onely to two or three Symbolical Ceremonies. That these Ceremonies are things indifferent in their own nature, [246][698] and have no antecedent necessity, but only bind as they are commanded. That they signify nothing in themselves but what the Commander pleases. That the Church it self declares that there is nothing of Religion or adoration in them. That they are no parts of Religious Worship. That they are only Circumstances. That the imposing of a significant Ceremony, is no more than to impose significancy upon a word. That there is not a word of any of these Ceremonies in the Scriptures. That they are in themselves of no great moment and consequence, but 'tis absolutely necessary that Government should injoyn them, to avoid the evil that would follow if they were not determined: and that there cannot be a Pin pull'd out of the Church, but the State immediately totters. Do not you think that the King has considered all these things? I believe he has; and perhaps, as you have minced the matter, he may well think the Nonconformists have very nice Stomachs, that they cannot digest such chopp'd hay:

[694] Spain . . . Flanders: In the 1560s, constitutional resistance to Spanish rule in the Netherlands was turned into a patriotic war for independence as a direct result of the cruelty of Fernando Alvarez de Toledo, duke of Alva (1507–82), Philip II's governor, appointed in 1567. He set up the so-called Council of Blood, the apparatus of centralized absolutism and religious persecution.

[695] This page has only twenty-six lines instead of the usual twenty-seven.

[696] 'em 72a] 'm 72.

[697] But: new paragraph in 72a.

[698] This page has only twenty-six lines instead of the usual twenty-seven.

[247] But on the other side, he must needs take you to be very strange men, to cram these in spite down the throats of any Christian. If a man have an Antipathy against any thing, the Company is generally so civil, as to refrain the use of it, however not to press it upon the person. If a man be sick or weak the Pope grants a Dispensation from Lent, or Fasting daies: ay, and from many a thing that strikes deeper in his Religion. If one have got a cold, their betters will force them to be covered. There is no end of Similitudes: but I am led into them by your calling these Ceremonies, Pins of the Church. It would almost tempt a Prince that is curious, and that is setled (God be praised) pretty fast in his Throne; to try for experiment, whether the pulling out of one of these Pins would make the State totter. But, Mr. Bayes, there is more in it. 'Tis matter of Conscience: and if Kings do, out of Discretion, connive at the other infirmities of their People; If great persons do out of civility condescend to their inferiours; and if all [248] men out of common humanity do yield to the weaker; Will your Clergy only be the men, who, in an affair of Conscience, and where perhaps 'tis you are in the wrong, be the only hard-hearted and inflexible Tyrants; and not only so, but instigate and provoke Princes to be the ministers of your cruelty?

But,[699] I say, Princes, so[700] far as I can take the height of things so far above me, must needs have other thoughts, and are past such boyes-play to stake their Crowns against your Pins. They do not think fit to command things unnecessary, and where the Profit cannot countervail the hazard. But above all they consider, that God has instated them in the Goverment of Mankind, with that incumbrance (if it may so be called) of Reason, and that incumbrance upon Reason of Conscience. That he might have given them as large an extent of ground and other kind of cattle for their Subjects; but it had been a melancholy Empire to have been only Supreme Grasiers and Soveraign Shepherds. And therefore, though the la-[249]ziness of that brutal magistracy might have been more secure, yet the difficulty of this does make it more honourable. That men therefore are to be dealt with reasonably: and conscientious men by Conscience. That even Law is force, and the execution of that Law a greater Violence; and therefore with rational creatures not to be used but upon the utmost extremity. That the Body is in the power of the mind; so that corporal punishments do never reach the offender, but the innocent suffers for the guilty. That the Mind is in the hand of God, and cannot correct those perswasions which upon the

[699] But: new paragraph in 72a.

[700] so 72a] as 72.

best of its natural capacity it hath collected: So that it too, though erroneous, is so far innocent. That the Prince therefore, by how much God hath indued him with a clearer reason, and by consequence with a more enlightned judgment ought the rather to take heed lest by punishing Conscience, he violate not only his own, but the Divine Majesty.

But[701] as to that Mr. Bayes, which you [250] still inculcate of the late War, and its horrid Catastrophe, which you will needs have to be upon a religious account: 'Tis four and twenty years ago, and after an Act of Oblivion; and for ought I can see, it had been as seasonable to have shown Caesars bloody Coat,[702] or Thomas a Becket's bloody Rochet.[703] The chief of the offenders have long since made satisfaction to Justice; & the whole Nation hath been swept sufficiently of late years by those terrible scourges of Heaven:[704] So that methinks you might in all this while have satiated your mischievous appetite. Whatsoever you suffered in those times, his Majesty who had much the greater loss, knowing that the memory of his Glorious Father will alwayes be preserved, is the best Judge how long the Revenge ought to be pursued. But if indeed out of your superlative care of his Majesty and your *Living*, you are afraid of some new disturbance of the same nature, let me so far satisfy you as I am satisfied. The Nonconformists say that they are bound in [251] Conscience to act as far as they can, and for the rest to suffer to the utmost. But because though they do mean honestly, 'tis so hard a Chapter for one that thinks himself in the right to suffer extremities patiently, that some think it impossible; I say next, that it's very seldom seen that in the same age, a Civil War, after such an interval, has been raised again upon the same pretences: But Men are all so weary, that he would be knock'd on the head that should raise the first disturbance of the same nature. A new War must have, like a Book that would sell, a new Title. I am asham'd Mr. Bayes that you put me on talking thus impertinently (for Policy in us is so). Therefore to be short, the King hath so indulged and obliged the Non-conformists by his late mercy, that if there were any such Knave, there can be no such Fool among them, that would

[701] But: new paragraph 72a.

[702] Caesars bloody Coat: After Julius Caesar's assassination, Mark Antony displayed his blood-stained garment to the Roman populace in order to incite them against the conspirators led by the republican Brutus. Shakespeare devoted a famous speech to this event. See *Julius Caesar*, 3.2.169–96.

[703] Rochet: A linen vestment worn by bishops and abbots. For Becket, see p. 145 and n. 580 above.

[704] scourges of Heaven: the plague and the Great Fire.

ever lift up an ill thought against him. And for you Mr. Bayes he is assured of your Loyalty, so that I think you may enjoy your *Living* very peaceably, [252] which I know is all your business. 'Twas well replyed of the English man in Edward the fourths time, to the French man that ask'd him insulting, When they should see us there again? *When your Sins are greater than ours.*[705] There are as many occasions of War, as there are Vices in a Nation; and therefore it concerns a Prince to be watchful on all hands. But should Kings remember an injury as long as you implacable Divines do, or should we take up Arms upon your Peeks,[706] because your Ecclesiastical Policy is answered to revenge your quarrel, the World would never be at quiet. Therefore Mr. Bayes let all those things of former times alone, and mind your own business; for Kings, believe me, as they have Royall understandings, so have Gentlemens memories.

And now Mr. Bayes I think it is time to take my leave, having troubled you with so long a visit. Only before I quit this matter, because I do not love to be accounted singular in my opinion, I will add the judgment of one [253] Author, and that as pertinent as I could pick out to our purpose. I have observed that not onely other Princes, but Queen Elizabeth too hath the misfortune to be much out of your favour. But for what reason I cannot possibly imagine; for none ever deserved better as to the thing of Uniformity, unless it be the ill luck she had to pass that *impertinent Clause* in the Act 5° Eliz. of the *Jejunium Cecilianum.* You cannot, for her sake, indure the Wit or Learning of her times, but say, p. 94. of your second Book, *Though this trifling Artifice of sprinkling little fragments of Wit and Poetry might have passed for Wit and Learning in the daies of Queen Elizabeth, yet to men of Learning, Reading and Ingenuity, their vulgar use has sullied their lustre, and abated their value.* This is indeed, Mr. Bayes, a very laboured period, and prepared by you, I believe, on purpose as a model of the Wit and Eloquence of your daies. But not only so; but p. 483. of the same Book, I think you call her in derision and most spightfully and unmannerely, plain [254] *Old Elsibeth.* And those that knew her humour, think you could not have disobliged her more than in stiling her so; both as a Woman, which Sex never love to be thought old, and as a Queen, who was jealous lest Men should therefore talk of the succession. Besides the irreverent nick-name you give her, that you might as well have presumed to call her Queen Bess, or Bold

[705] English man . . . *ours:* The story is told by William Camden, *Remaines* (1629), p. 238 (A, p. 30, #19).

[706] Peeks: piques, irritations.

Betrice. Now to the end that that Queen of famous Memory may have a little female revenge upon you, and to give you a taste of the Wit and Learning even of her times; I will *sprinkle* here one *fragment,* which not being a *Scholar-like saying of antient Poet or Philosopher,* but of a Reverend Divine, I hope, Mr. Bayes, may be less displeasing to you. The Man is Parker. Not Robert Parker,[707] who writ another Treatise of Ecclesiastical Policy, and the Book *de Cruce,* for which if they had catch'd him, he had possibly gone to the Gallows, or at least the Gallyes. For he was one of those well-meaning Zealots, that are of all Villains the [255] most dangerous. But it is the Arch-bishop of Canterbury, Parker,[708] (For if I named him before without addition, 'twas what I learned of you; speaking of Whitgift). He in his Book *de Antiquitatibus Ecclesiae Britannicae,* p. 47. speaking of the slaughter of the Monks of Bangor,[709] and so many Christians more, upon the instigation of Austin the Monk, who stirred up Ethelbert[710] King of Kent against them, because they would not receive the Romish Ceremonies;[711] useth these words, *Et sane illa prima de Romanis Ritibus inducendis per Augustinum tunc excitata contentio, quae non nisi clade & sanguine innocentium Britannorum poterat extingui; ad nostra recentiora tempora, cum simili pernicie caedeque*[712] *Christianorum pervenit. Cum enim illis gloriosis ceremoniis a purâ Primitivae Ecclesiae simplicitate recesserunt, non de vitae sanctitate, de Evangelii praedicatione, de spiritûs sancti vi & consolatione multum laborabant; sed novas indies altercationes de novis ritibus per Papas singulos additis, qui neminem tam excelso gradu dignum qui* [256]

[707] Robert Parker (1564–1614), puritan divine. His treatise *De cruce* (1607), protesting the enforced use of the sign of the cross in baptism, resulted in James I's proclamation for his arrest, and he was forced to flee the country. He also wrote *De Politeia ecclesiastica* (posthumously published 1616) (A, p. 8, #176).

[708] Parker: Matthew Parker, archbishop of Canterbury (1504–75). His history of the English church, *De Antiquitate Britannicae Ecclesiae* was published in 1572. Marvell used the 1605 edition, published in Hanover (A, p. 4, #139, p. 26, #247).

[709] Monks of Bangor: In the early seventh century the monks of Bangor Abbey refused to cooperate with St. Augustine's mission of conversion in England. In punishment, he predicted that, as they refused to convert the English, they would suffer death at the hands of the English. Perhaps as a result of this prophecy, Ethilbert or Ethilfred of Northumbria, who defeated the Britons at the battle of Chester in 613, put twelve hundred of the monks to death.

[710] Ethelbert 72a] Ethilbert 72.

[711] Romish Ceremonies: The Welsh church differed from the Roman usage in the date of the celebration of Easter, the rituals of baptism, etc. [S]

[712] *caedeque* 72] *caedaeque* 72a.

aliquid, ceremoniosi non dicam, monstrosi inauditi & inusitati non adjecisset; instituebant. Suggestaque & scholas fabulis rixisque suis implebant. Nam prima Ecclesiae species simplicior & integro & interno Dei cultu, ab ipso Verbo *praescripto, nec vestibus splendidis, nec magnificis structuris decorata, nec auro, argento, gemmisque fulgens fuit: Etsi liceat his exterioribus uti modo animum ab illo interiori & integro Dei cultu non abducant; Curiosis & morosis ritibus ab illa primaeva & recta simplicitate Evangelica degeneravit. Illa autem in Romana Ecclesia rituum multitudo ad immensum illius magni Augustini Hipponensis Episcopi temporibus creverat: ut questus sit Christianorum in Ceremoniis & ritibus duriorem tunc fuisse conditionem quam Judaeorum, qui etiamsi tempus Libertatis non agnoverint, Legalibus tamen sarcinis non humanis praesumptionibus subjiciebantur; nam paucioribus in divino cultu quam Christiani Ceremoniis utebantur. Qui si sensisset quantus deinde per singulos Papas coacervatus cumulus*[713] *accessit, modum Christianum credo ipse statuisset; qui hoc malum* [257] *tunc in Ecclesia viderat. Videmus enim ab illa ceremoniarum contentione nedum Ecclesiam esse vacuam; quin homines alioquin docti atque pii de vestibus & hujusmodi nugis adhuc, rixoso magis & militari,*[714] *quam aut Philosophico aut Christiano more inter se digladiantur.* These words do run so direct against the Genius of some men that contributed not a little to the late Rebellion, and, though so long since writ, do so exactly describe that evil spirit with which some men are even in these times possest, who seem desirous upon the same grounds to put all things in combustion, that I think them very well worth the labour of translating. (And indeed, that first contention then raised by Augustine about the introducing of the Romish Ceremonies, which could not be quenched but by the blood and slaughter of the innocent Brittains; hath been continued e'n[715] to our later times, with the like mischief and murder of Christians. For when once by those glorious Ceremonies they forsook the pure simplicity of the Primitive Church, they did not [258] much trouble themselves about Holiness of Life, the preaching of the Gospel, the efficacy and #the# comfort of the Holy Spirit: but they fell every day into new squabbles about new fangled Ceremonies added by every Pope, who reckoned no man worthy of so high a degree but such as invented somewhat, I will not say Ceremonious, but monstrous, unheard of, and before unpractised; and they fill'd the Schools and the Pulpits with their Fables and brawling of such

[713] *cumulus* 72] *camulus* 72a.

[714] *militari* 72] *militare* 72a.

[715] e'n 72, 72a: even.

matters. For the first beauty of the Church had more of simplicity and plainness; and was neither adorned with splendid Vestments, nor magnificent structures, nor shin'd with gold, silver and precious stones; but with the intire and inward worship of God, as it was by Christ himself prescribed. Although it may be lawful to use these external things, so they do not lead the mind astray from that more inward and entire worship of God; by those curious and crabbed Rites it degenerated from that antient and right Evangelical Simplicity. But that mul-[259]titude of Rites in the Romish Church had unmeasurably increased in the times of that great Augustine the Bishop of Hippo, in so much that he complained that the Condition of #the# Christians as to Rites and Ceremonies, was then harder than that of the Jews; who although they did not discern the time of their Liberty, yet were onely subjected to Legal burthens, instituted first by God himself, not to humane presumptions. For they used fewer Ceremonies in the Worship of God than Christians. Who, if he could have foreseen how great a heap of them was afterwards piled up, and added by the several Popes, he himself doubtless would have restrained it within Christian measure, having already perceived this growing evil in the Church. For we see, that even yet the Church is not free from that contention: but men, otherwise learned and pious, do still cut and slash about Vestments and such kind of trifles, rather in a Swash buckler and Hectoring way, than either like Philosophers or like Christians.)[260]

Now Mr. Bayes, I doubt you must be put to the trouble of writing another Preface against this Arch-bishop. For nothing in your Answerers Treatise of *Evangelical Love*[716] does so gird[717] or aim at you, for ought I can see, or at those whom you call the Church of England, as this Passage. But the last period does so plainly delineate you to the life, that what St. Austine did not presage, the Bishop seems to have foreseen most distinctly. 'Tis just your way of writing all along in this matter. You bring nothing sound or solid. Onely you think you have got the *Great Secret*, or the *Philosophers Stone* of Railing, and I believe it, you have so multiplied it in *Projection*:[718] and as they into Gold, so you turn every thing you meet with into Railing.

[716] Answerers . . . *Love:* John Owen, *Discourse of Evangelical Love* (1672) (A, p. 13, #97).

[717] gird: Strike, cut at.

[718] *Great Secret . . . Projection:* These are all alchemical terms relating to the search for the legendary philosopher's stone. Projection is the casting of the powder of philosopher's stone upon a metal in fusion to transmute it into gold or silver.

And yet the Secret is not great, nor the *Process* long or difficult, if a man would study it, and make a Trade on't. Every Scold hath it naturally. It is but crying Whore first, and having the last word, and whatsoever t'other sayes, cry, Oh these are your Nonconfor-[261]mists tricks, Oh you have learnt this of the Puritans in Grubstreet. Oh you *White-apron'd Gossip.*[719] For indeed, I never saw so provident a fetch; you have taken in before hand all the Posts of railing, and so beset all the Topicks of just crimination, foreseeing where you are feeble, that if this trick would pass, it were impossible to open ones mouth to find the least fault with you. For in your first Chapter of your second Book, beside what you do always in an hundred places when you are at a loss, you have spent almost an hundred pages upon *a Character of the Fanatick deportment towards all Adversaries.* And then on the other side, you have so ingrossed and bought up all the Ammunition of Railing, search'd every corner in the Bible, and *Don Quixot* for Powder, that you thought, not unreasonably, that there was not one shot left for a Fanatick. But truth, you see, cannot want words: and she will laugh too sometimes when she speaks, and rather than all fail too, be serious. But what wil you say to that of the Arch-bishops, *than either like Phi-*[262]*losophers or like Christians*? For the excellency of your Logick, Philosophy and Christianity in all your Books, is either, as in *Conscience,* to take away the subject of the question: or, as in the *Magistrate,* having gotten one absurdity, to raise a thousand more from it. So that, except the manufacture and labor of your periods, you have done no more than any School-boy could have done on the same terms. And so, Mr. Bayes, Good night.

And[720] now Good-morrow, Mr. Bayes; For though it seems so little a time and that you are but now gone to bed, it hath been a whole live-long night, and you have toss'd up and down in many a troublesome Dream, and are but just now awaked at the Title Page of your Book:

A Preface shewing what Grounds there are
of Fears and Jealousies of Popery.[721]

It[722] is something artifically couch'd, but looks, as if it did allow, that there are some Grounds of Fears and Jealousies of that nature. But here he words it;[263]

[719] *White-apron'd Gossip:* set in roman in 72.

[720] Paragraph follows blank line introduced in 72a.

[721] *A . . . Popery:* title newly inset and centered in 72a.

[722] It: new paragraph in 72a.

A Consideration what likelihood, or how much danger there is of the return of Popery into this Nation.[723]

Had[724] he not come to this at last, I should have thought I had been all this while reading a Chapter in Mountagne's[725] *Essayes*; where you find sometimes scarce one word in the discourse of the matter held forth in the Title. But now indeed he takes up this Argument and debates it to purpose. For I had before begun to shew that he had writ not only his two former Books, but especially too this Preface, with an evil eye and aim at his Majesty, and the Measures he had taken of Government. And whoever will take the pains to read here, will soon be of my mind. His Majesty had I said 15*th* of March 1671. issued his Declaration of Indulgence to tender Consciences. He, on the Contrary, issues out thereupon, all in haste and as fast as he could write, this his Remonstrance or Manifesto against Indulgence to tender Consciences: and to make his Majesties proceedings more [264] odious, stirs up this seditious matter, of what probability there is of Popery.

And[726] this he discourses, to be sure, in his own imagination very cunningly. For he knows that there was an Act of Parliament in this Kings Reign with a greater penalty than that of 5°[727] Eliz. of spreading false News,[728] against reports of this nature. And therefore, he resolvs to handle it so warily, that he himself might escape, but might draw others that should answer him, within the danger of that Act, and that he might lay the crime at their doors. But, notwithstanding all his slights[729] and *Legerdemain*[730] it doth enough detect his malice and ill intention to his Majesties Government, that he should take this occasion, altogether foreign and

[723] *A . . . Nation:* title newly inset and centered in 72a.

[724] Had: new paragraph in 72a.

[725] Mountagne's 72] Mountagues 72a.

[726] And: new paragraph in 72a.

[727] 5° 72] 50 72a.

[728] spreading false News: see *CSPD,* June 12, 1672: "Proclamation forbidding the spreading of false news, and licentious talking of State and government." Marvell wrote ironically of this to William Popple in June 1672: "There was . . . a severe Proclamation issued out against all who shall vent false News, or discourse ill concerning Affairs of State. So that in writing to you I run the Risque of making a Breach in the Commandment" (*P&L,* 2:328).

[729] slights: sleights, tricks.

[730] *Legerdemain:* deceitful quickness of the hand, especially in conjuring.

unseasonable, to raise a publick and solemn discourse through the whole Nation, concerning a matter the most odious and dangerous that could be exposed. So that now, no man can look at the wall, no man can pass by a Book-sellers stall, but he must see *A Preface showing what* GROUNDS *there are for* FEARS *and* JEA-[265][731]LOUSIES *of* POPERY. It[732] had been something a safer and more dutiful way of writing, A Preface showing the CAUSELESSNESS of the Fears and Jealousies of POPERY. For I do not think it will excuse a Witch to say, That she conjur'd up a Spirit onely that she might lay it: nor can there be a more dexterous and malicious way of calumny, than by making a needless Apology for another, in a criminal Subject. As, suppose I should write a Preface showing what Grounds there are of Fears and Jealousies of Bayes his being an Atheist. But this is exactly our Authors method and way of contrivance; whereby, more effectually by far than by any flying Coffee-house tattle, he traduces the State, and by printing so pernicious a question fills all mens mouths, & beats out all mens eyes with the probability of the return of POPERY. Had he heard any that malignly and officiously talk'd to such a purpose, it had been the part of one so prudent as he is, not to have continued the Discourse. Had [266] he (as he hath a great gift that way) pick'd up out of any mans talk or writing, matter whereof to make an ill story; there was a better and #a# more regular way of proceeding, had he meant honestly to his Majesties Government, to have prevented the evil, and to have brought the offender to punishment. He should have gone to one of the Secretaries of State, or to some other of his Majesties Privy Council, and have given them Information. But, instead of that, I am afraid that in the survey of this business, we shall find, that even some of them are either accused, or shrowdly mark'd out with a Character of our Authors displeasure. Therefore, I will now come nearer to his matter in hand, although it concerns me to be careful of coming too near, nor shall I dwell too long upon so jealous and impertinent a subject.

To consider what likelihood or how much danger there is of the return of Popery into this Nation. The very first word is; *For my part, I know none.*[733] Very well considered. Why then, Mr. Bayes, I [267] must tell you, that if I had printed a Book or Preface upon that Agreement, I should have thought my self, at least a Fool for my labour. The next considerer is mine Enemy; I

[731] 265 72] 165 72a.

[732] It: new paragraph removed in 72a.

[733] *To consider . . . none: Preface,* c4v.

mean he is an Enemy to the State, whoever shall foment such discourses without any likelihood or danger. Yet Mr. Bayes, you know, I have for a good while had no great opinion of your Integrity; neither here. I doubt you prevaricate a little with some body. For, I suppose you cannot be ignorant that some of your superiours[734] of your Robe did, upon the publishing that Declaration, give the Word, and deliver Orders through their Ecclesiastical Camp, to beat up the Pulpit drums against Popery.[735] Nay, even so much that there was care taken too for arming the *poor Readers, that though they came short of Preachers in point of efficacy, yet they might be inabled* to do something *in point of* common *Security*. So that, though for so many years, ⟨those⟩ #some of# your Superiours had forgot there was any such thing in the Nation as a Popish Recusant though [268] *Polemical* and *Controversial Divinity* had for so long been hung up in the Halls, like the rusty obsolete Armour of our Ancestors, for monuments of Antiquity; and for derision rather than service; all on a sudden (as if the 15*th* of March had been the 5*th* of November) happy was he that could climb up first to get down one of the old Cuirasses,[736] or an Habergeon[737] that had been worn in the dayes of Queen Elizabeth. Great variety there was, and an heavy doo. Some clapp'd it on all rusty as it was, others fell of oyling and furbishing their Armour:[738] Some piss'd in their Barrels, other spit in their pans, to scowr them. Here you might see one put on his Helmet the wrong way: there one buckle on a Back in place of a Breast. Some by mistake catched up a Socinian or Arminian Argument, and some a Popish to fight a Papist. Here a Dwarf lost in the accoutrements of a Giant: there a Don Quixot in an equipage of differing pieces, and of several Parishes. Never was there such Incongruity and Nonconformity in their [269] furniture. One ran to borrow a Sword of Calvin. This man for a Musket from Beza:[739] that for a Bandeleers[740] even

[734] some of your superiours: Marvell will identify several of these shortly.

[735] Ecclesiastical . . . Popery: See Butler, *Hudibras,* part 1, canto 1, 10–11: "to battle sounded / And pulpit, drum ecclesiastic." See p. 127, where the phrase is embedded in an unitalicized quotation from Parker, *Preface,* A8v.

[736] Cuirasses: breastplates, originally of leather.

[737] Habergeon: a sleeveless coat of mail.

[738] oyling . . . Armour: Cf. *An Horatian Ode:* "'Tis time to / . . . oyl th'unused Armours rust: / Removing from the Wall / The Corslet of the Hall" (*P&L,* 1:91). During the Restoration Marvell frequently echoed his heroic Cromwellian poetry.

[739] Beza: Théodore de Bèze (1519–1605), French Protestant theologian.

[740] Bandeleers: Bandoleers were broad gun belts worn across the shoulders.

from Keckerman.[741] But when they came to seek for Match,[742] and Bullet, and Powder, there was none to be had. The Fanaticks had bought it all up, and made them pay for it most unconscionably, and through the Nose. And no less sport was it to see their Leaders. Few could tell how to give the word of Command, nor understood to drill a Company: They were as unexpert as their Soldiers aukward: and the whole was as pleasant a spectacle, as the exercising of the Train'd-bands in—*shire.* But Mr. Bayes (for I believe you do nothing but upon common advice) either this was all intended but for a false alarum, and was onely for a pretence to take arms against the Fanaticks (which you might have done without raising all this din and obloquy against the State, and disquieting his Majesties good Subjects): or else you did really think (and who can help misapprehensions?) that you did know some likelihood or dan-[270]ger of the return of Popery. I crave you mercy, Mr. Bayes, I took you a little short. *For my part I know none,* you say, *but the Nonconformists boysterous and unreasonable opposition to the Church of England.*[743]

This I confess hath some weight in it. For truly before *I knew none* too, I was of your Opinion Mr. Bayes, and believed that Popery could never return into England again, but by some very sinister accident. This expression of mine is something uncouth, and therefore because I love to give you satisfaction in all things, Mr. Bayes, I will acquaint you with my reason of using it. Henry the fourth of France, his Majesties Grandfather, lived (you know) in the days of Queen Elizabeth. Now the wit of France and England, as you may have observed, is much of the same mode, and hath at all times gone much after the same current Rate and Standard; onely there hath been some little difference in the alloy, and advantage or disadvantage in the exchange according to mens occasions. Now Henry the fourth, was (you know [271] too) a Prince like Bishop Bramhall, *of a brave and enterprizing temper, and had a mind large and active enough to have managed the Roman Empire at its utmost extent; and* particularly (*as far as the prejudice of the age (Old Elsibeths* Age*) would permit him*) he was very witty and facetious, and the Courtiers strove to humor him always in it, and increase the mirth. So one night after Supper he gave them a Subject (which recreation did well enough in those times, but were now insipid) upon which like Boyes at Westminster, they should make a French Verse extempore. The

[741] Keckerman: Bartholomeus Keckerman (1571–1609), German Protestant theologian.

[742] Match: wick or cord used for lighting cannon.

[743] *For my part . . . England: Preface,* c4v.

Subject was, *Un Accident sinistre.* Straight answers, I know not whether 'twas Bassompierre[744] or Aubigne:[745]

> *Un sinistre Accident & un Accident sinistre;*
> *De veoir un Pere Capuchin chevaucher un Ministre.*[746]

For when I said, to see Popery return here, would be a very sinister accident; I was just thinking upon that story #of# [272] the Verses, to humour them in translation, being only this,

> *O what a trick unlucky, and how unlucky a trick,*
> *To see friend Doctor Patrick,*[747] *bestrid by Father Patrick!*[748]

Which seem'd to me would be the most improbable and preposterous spectacle that ever was seen; ⟨and more ridiculous for a sight, than the *Friendly*[749] *Debate is* for a Book.⟩[750] And yet if Popery come in, this must be and worse.

But[751] now I see there is some danger by the Nonconformists opposition to the Church of England. And now your business is all fixed. The Fanaticks are ready at hand to bear the blame of all things. Many a good job have I seen done in my time upon pretence of the Fanaticks. I do not think Mr. Bayes ever breaks[752] his shins, but it is by stumbling upon a Fanatick. And how shall they bring in Popery? why thus, three wayes. *First,* By

[744] Bassompierre: François de Bassompierre (1599–1646), marshal of France and favorite of Henry IV.

[745] Aubigne 72a] Obignè 72; Théodore Agrippa d'Aubigné (1552–1630), counselor of Henry IV, was the author of *Les Tragiques* (1616), an epic poem about the French religious wars.

[746] *Un sinistre . . . Ministre:* "A sinister mishap and accident sinister / To see a Capuchin father bestriding a Minister"; source untraced; but both lines are false verses, with too many syllables. Either Marvell mistranscribed them or he got them from a corrupt source.

[747] *Doctor Patrick:* Simon Patrick, author of *The Friendly Debates.*

[748] *Father Patrick:* Father Patrick McGinn (d. 1683), one of the Catholic priests attendant on Queen Catherine. [S]

[749] *Friendly* 72 a (C4, D4)] *Frienly* 72.

[750] and more ridiculous . . . for a Book: Material between < and > is present in 72 and in copies of 72a such as C4 and D4 in which gathering T (pp. 273–88 in the original) is in its uncensored state; hereafter designated 72aT; the censored state is hereafter designated 72aTc. Material between # and # is present in 72aTc but absent from 72 and 72aT.

[751] But: A blank line separates this paragraph from the preceding one in 72aTc.

[752] breaks 72] brake 72a.

creating disorders and disturbances in [273][753] *the State.*[754] *Secondly, By the assistance of Atheism and Irreligion.*[755] *Thirdly, By joyning with crafty and Sacrilegious Statesmen in confederacy.*[756] Now here I remark two things. One, that however you do not find that the Fanaticks are inclinable to Popery, only they may accommodate it by creating disturbances in the State. Another is, that I see these Gentlemen, the Fanaticks, the Atheists, and the Sacrilegious Statesmen are not yet acquainted; but you have appointed them a meeting (I believe it must be at your Lodgings or no where;) and I hope you will treat them handsomly. But I think it was not so wisely done, nor very honestly, Mr. Bayes, to lay so dangerous a Plot as this; and instruct men that are strangers yet to one another, how to contrive together such a Conspiracy. But first to your first.

The *Fanaticks you say may probably raise disturbance in the State.* For they *are so little friends to the present Government, that their enmity to that is one of the main grounds of their quarrel to the Church.*[757] [274] But now, though I must confess it is very much to your purpose, if you could perswade men so, I think you are clear out, and misrepresent here the whole matter. For I know of no enmity they have to the Church it self, but what it was in her power alwayes to have remedied, and so it is still. But such as you it is that have alwayes strove by your leasing[758] to keep up a strangeness and misunderstanding betwixt the King and his people; and all the mischief hath come on't does much lye[759] at your door. Whereas they, as all the rest of Man-kind, are men for their own ends too: And no sooner hath the King[760] shown them his[761] late favour, but you Mr. Bayes, and your Partners reproach them for being too much friends to the Prerogative. And no less would they be to the Church, had they ever at any age in any time found her in a treatable temper. I know nothing they demand, but what is so far from doing you any harm, that it would only make you better. But that indeed is the harm, that is the thing you are [275] afraid of. Here our Author divides the discourse into a great Elogy of the Church of England; that if he were

753 Catchword *State,* 72, 72aT; *the* 72aTc.
754 *First . . . State: Preface,* c6.
755 *By . . . Irreligion: Preface,* d7v.
756 *By joyning . . . confederacy: Preface,* e4.
757 *so little . . . Church: Preface,* c6.
758 leasing 72a] leasings 72; i.e., falsehoods.
759 much lye 72a] lye much 72.
760 King 72, 72a (B7 only)] Ling 72a.
761 his 72a] this 72.

making her Funeral Sermon, he could not say more in her commendation; and a contrary invective against the Nonconformists, upon whom (as if all he had said before had been nothing) he unloads his whole Leystall[762] and dresseth them up all in *Sambenitas,*[763] painted with all the flames & Devils in hell, to be led to the place of Execution, & there burnt to ashes. Nevertheless I find on either side only the natural effect of such Hyperboles and Oratory, that is, not to be believed. The Church of England (I mean as it is by Law established, lest you should think I equivocate) hath such a stock of solid and deserved reputation, that it is more than you (Mr. Bayes) can spoil or deface by all the Pedantry of your commendation. Only there is that partie of the Clergy, that I not long ago described, and who will alwaies presume to be the only Church of England, who have been a perpetual Eye-sore, that I may [276] not say a Canker and Gangreen in so perfect a beauty. And, as it joyes my heart to hear any thing well said of her; so, I must confess, it stirs my choler,[764] when I hear those men pride and boast[765] themselves under the Mask of her Authority. Neither did I therefore approve of an expression you here use: *The Power of Princes would be a very precarious thing without the assistance of Ecclesiasticks, and all Government do's and must ow its quiet and continuance to the Churches Patronage.*[766] That is as much as to say, That but for the assistance of your *Ecclesiastical Policy,* Princes might go a begging: and that the Church, that is you, have the *Jus Patronatus*[767] of the Kingdom, and may present whom you think fitting to the Crown of England. This is indeed something like the return of Popery; and right

Petra dedit Petro, Petrus Diadema Rudolpho.[768]

The Crown were surely well help'd up, if it were to be held at your conveni-[277]ence, and the Emperour must lead the Patriarchs Ass[769] all his life-

[762] Leystall: A laystall is where stable dung is piled.

[763] *Sambenitas:* black garments ornamented with flames and devils worn by impenitents burned by the Inquisition.

[764] choler 72, 72aT] choer 72aTc.

[765] boast 72, 72aT] bast 72aTc.

[766] *The Power . . . Patronage: Preface,* c7.

[767] *Jus Patronatus:* the sum of rights of a patron over his freedmen.

[768] *Petra dedit . . . Rudolpho:* "Peter gave stones to Peter, a diadem to Rudolph"; lines engraved on a crown sent by Pope Gregory VII to Rudolph of Swabia in 1077, referring to his previously duplicitous treatment of Henry IV.

[769] Emperour . . . Patriarchs Ass: The ceremony in which the czar leads the pa-

time. And little better do I like your *We may rest satisfied in the present Security of the Church of England, under the Protection of a wise and gracious Prince: especially when besides the impregnable Confidence that we have from his own Inclination, it is so manifest, that he never can forsake it either in Honour or Interest.*[770] This is a prety way of cokesing[771] indeed, while you are all this while cutting the grass under his feet, and animating the people against the exercise of his Ecclesiastical Supremacy. Men are not so plain-hearted, but they can see through this oblique Rhetorication and Sophistry. If there be no danger in his time of taking a *Pin out of the Church* (for that it is you intend) why do you then speak of it in his time, but that you mean mischief? but here you do not only mow the grass under his feet, but you take the pillow from under his head. *But should it ever happen that any King of England should be prevail'd with to deliver up the Church, he had as* [278] *good at the same time resign up his Crown.*[772] This is pretty plain dealing, and you have doubtless secur'd hereby that Princes Favour: I should have thought it better Courtship in a Divine, to have said, O King, Live for ever. But I see Mr. Bayes, that you and your Partners are very necessary men, and it were dangerous disobliging you. But as in this imprudent and nauseous discourse, you have all along appropriated or impropriated all the Loyalty from the Nobility, the Gentry and the Commonalty, and dedicated it to the Church; So, I doubt, you are a little too immoderate against the body of the Nonconformists. You represent them, to a man, to be all of them of Republican Principles, most pestilent, and *eo nomine,*[773] enemies to Monarchy; Traytors and Rebels; such miscreants as never was in the world before, and fit to be pack'd out of it with the first Convenience. And, I observe, that all the Argument of your Book[774] is but very frivolous and trivial; onely the memory of the late War serves for de-[279]monstration, and the detestable sentence and execution of his late Majesty, is represented again upon the Scaffold; and you having been, I suspect, better acquainted with Parliament Declarations formerly upon another account, do now ap-

---

triarch's ass after attending Easter mass. Marvell would have seen this ceremony when he accompanied the earl of Carlisle on his embassy to Russia and Sweden, 1662–65. See Guy de Miège, *A Relation of Three Embassies* (1669), p. 298.

770 *We may . . . Interest: Preface,* d7.

771 cokesing: To coax or cokes was originally to make a fool of, to persuade by flattery.

772 *But should . . . Crown: Preface,* d7.

773 *eo nomine:* as such, from the name alone.

774 Book 72a] Books 72.

ply and turn them all over to prove that the late War was wholly upon a Fanatical Cause, and the dissenting party do still go big with the same Monster. I grew hereupon much displeased with my own Ignorance of the occasion of those Troubles so near our own times, and betook my self to get the best Information concerning them, to the end that I might, if it appeared so, decline the dangerous acquaintance of the Nonconformists, some of whom I had taken for honest men, nor therefore avoided their Company. But I took care nevertheless, not to receive Impressions from any of their party; but to gather my lights from the most impartial Authorities that I could meet with. And I think I am now partly prepared to give you, Mr. Bayes, some better satisfaction in this [280] matter. And because you are a dangerous person, I shall as little as possible, say any thing of my own, but speak too before good Witnesses. First of all therefore, I will without farther Ceremony, fall upon you with the but end of another Arch-bishop. 'Tis the Arch-bishop of Canterbury, Abbot, in the Narrative[775] under his own hand concerning his disgrace at Court in the time of his late Majesty. I shall only in the way demand excuse, if contrary to my fashion, the names of some eminent persons in our Church long since dead, be reviv'd here under no very good character; and most particularly that of Arch-bishop Laud, who, if for nothing else, yet for his learned Book against Fisher,[776] deserved far another Fate than he met with,[777] and ought not now to be mentioned without due honour. But those names having so many years since escaped the Press, it is not in my power to conceal them; and I believe Arch-bishop Abbot did not write but upon good Consideration. [281]

This I have premised for mine own Satisfaction; and I will add one thing

[775] Abbot . . . Narrative: George Abbot (1562–1633), archbishop of Canterbury. In 1626–27 he clashed with William Laud, then bishop of Bath and Wells, over whether an offensively political sermon by Robert Sibthorpe should be licensed. Abbot was sequestered from his office, and during his sequestration wrote a personal narrative of the affair, which Marvell quotes at length below. His source was John Rushworth, *Historical Collections, 1618–1629* (1659), pp. 434–44. Marvell also quotes material from between pp. 436 and 455. Anglesey owned this, importantly, in the "not castrated" edition dedicated to Richard Cromwell (A, p. 26, #83).

[776] learned Book against Fisher: John Fisher (1569–1641), a Jesuit, had been instrumental in the conversion of the countess of Buckingham, and in 1622 James I had employed Laud to hold a series of public conferences with Fisher to refute his arguments. The third of these was published. (See Anglesey, *Bp. Lauds Relation of the Conference with Fisher the Jesuit,* 1639, p. 1, #30.)

[777] Fate than he met with: Laud was beheaded in 1645.

more, Mr. Bayes, for yours. That whereas the things now to be alledged relate much to some Impositions of Money[778] in the late Kings time, that were carried on by the Clergy; I know you will presently be ready to carp at that, as if the Nonconformists had, and would be alwayes enemies to the Kings supply. Whereas, Mr. Bayes, if I can do the Nonconformists no good, I am resolv'd I will do them no harm, nor desire that they should lye under any imputation on my account. For I write by my[779] own advice, and what I shall alledge concerning the Clergies intermedling with supplies, is upon a particular aversion, that I have upon good reason, against their disposing of our Money. And Mr. Bayes, I will acquaint you with the Reason, which is this. 'Tis not very many years ago that I used to play at *Picket*;[780] and there was a Gentleman of your robe a *Dignitary of Lincoln,*[781] very well known and remembred in the Ordinaries,[782] but [282] being not long since dead, I will save his name. Now I used to play *Pieces,*[783] and this Gentleman would alwayes go half a Crown[784] with me, and so all the while he sat on my hand he very honestly *gave the Sign,*[785] so that I was alwayes sure to lose. I afterwards discovered it, but of all the money that ever I was cheated of in my life, none ever vexed me so, as what I lost by his occasion. And ever since, I have born a great grudge against their fingring of any thing that belongs to me. And I have been told, and show'd the place where the man dwelt in the late King's time near Hampton Court, that there was one that used to rob on the highway, in the habit of a Bishop,[786] and all his

[778] Impositions of Money: the "Forced Loan" of 1626–27, Charles I's expedient for raising money without going through parliament.

[779] my 72a] mine 72.

[780] *Picket:* piquet, a card game played by two persons. Marvell's history as a piquet player was much insisted upon by Parker subsequently.

[781] *Dignitary of Lincoln:* The most plausible candidate is John Worthington, who was given the prebend of Asgarby in Lincoln Cathedral specifically by Sheldon. He died on November 30, 1671, and Tillotson preached his funeral sermon. Educated at Emmanuel College, Cambridge, he graduated M.A. in 1639, the same year that Marvell graduated B.A. He spent 1660–66 in London and later, despite the prebend, taught in the parish church in Hackney.

[782] Ordinaries: taverns.

[783] *Pieces:* English gold coins, worth twenty-two shillings in 1612. [S]

[784] half a Crown: two and sixpence; in other words, he pretended to share Marvell's stake.

[785] *gave the sign:* cheated, by indicating to Marvell's opponent what he held in his hand.

[786] one that used to rob . . . Bishop: untraced, but Marvell stresses the oral nature of his source.

fellows rid too in Canonical Coats. And I can but fancy how it madded those, that would have perhaps been content to relieve an honest Gentleman in distress, or however would have been less griev'd to be robb'd[787] by such an one, to see themselves so *Episcopally* pillag'd. Neither must it be less displeasing alwaies to the Gentry and Commonalty [283] of England, that the Clergy (as you do Mr. Bayes) should tell them that they are never *sui Juris*,[788] not only as to their Consciences, but even as to their Purses; and you should pretend to have this *power of the Keyes* too, where they lock their Money. Nay, I dare almost aver upon my best observation, that there never was, nor ever will be a Parliament in England, that could or can refuse the King supplies proportionable to his occasions, without any need of recourse to extraordinary wayes; but for the pickthankness[789] of #some of#[790] the Clergy, who will alwayes presume to have the thanks and honour of it, nay, and are ready alwayes to obstruct the Parliamentary Aids, unless they may have their own little project pass too into the bargain, and they may be gratified with some new *Ecclesiastical Power*, or some new Law against the *Fanaticks*. This is the naked truth of the matter. Whereas English men alwayes love to see how their money goes, and if there be any Interest or Profit to be got by it, to receive it themselves. Therefore Mr. [284] Bayes I will go on with my business, not fearing all the mischief that you can make of it.

"There was, *saith he*,[791] one Sibthorp,[792] who not being so much as
" Batchelor of Arts, by the means of Doctor Pierce[793] Vice-Chancelor of
" Oxford, got to be confer'd upon him the title of Doctor. This Man was
" Vicar of Brackley in Northamptonshire, and hath another Benefice. This
" Man preaching at Northampton, had taught, that Princes had power to
" put Poll-money upon their Subjects heads. He being a Man of a low
" fortune, conceiv'd the putting his Sermon in Print might gain favour at
" Court, and raise his fortune higher."[794] It was at the same time that the

787 robb'd 72] rob'd 72a.

788 *sui Juris:* "under their own law."

789 pickthankness: sycophancy, flattery.

790 #some of#: 72aTc only.

791 *saith he:* Archbishop Abbot. See n. 775 above.

792 Sibthorp: Robert Sibthorpe (d. 1662), published his sermon as *Apostolike Obedience, Shewing the Duty of Subjects to pay Tributes and taxes to their Princes* (1627).

793 Doctor Pierce: William Pierce (1598–1670), bishop of Bath and Wells, vice-chancellor of Oxford 1621–24.

794 There was . . . higher: Rushworth, p. 436.

business of the Loan was on foot. In the same Sermon "he called that Loan " a Tribute, Taught that the Kings dutie is first to direct and make Laws. " That nothing may excuse the Subject from active obedience, but what is " against the Law of God or Nature, or impossible; that all Antiquity was " absolutely for absolute o-[285]bedience in all civil and temporal things."[795] And the imposing of poll-mony by Princes, he justifi'd *out of* St. *Matthew*:[796] And in the matter of the *Loan, What a speech is this,* saith the Bishop, *he observes the forwardness of the Papists to offer double.*[797] For this Sermon was sent to the Bishop from Court, and he required to Licence it, not under his Chaplain, but his own hand. But he, not being satisfi'd of the Doctrine delivered, sent back his reasons why he thought not fit to give his Approbation ⟨, and unto these Bishop Laud, who was in this whole business, and a Rising Man at Court, *undertook an answer.*⟩[798]#; whereupon Bishop Laud, who understood the whole business, went to answer them in Writing.-------#[799] "His life in Oxford, saith Arch-bishop Abbot, was to " pick quarrels in the Lectures of publick Readers, and to advertise them to " the Bishop of Durham[800] that he might fill the Ears of King James with " discontent against the honest men that took pains in their places, and " setled the Truth (which he called Puritanism) in their Auditors. He made " it his work to see what Books were in the Press, [286] and to look over " Epistles Dedicatory, and Prefaces to the Reader, to see what faults might " be found. 'Twas an observation what a Sweet man this was like to be, that " the first observable Act he did, was the marrying of the Earl of D. to the " Lady R. when she had another Husband a Nobleman, and divers Chil- " dren by him."[801] Here he tells how, for this very cause, King James would not a great while endure him, till he yielded at last to Bishop Williams[802] his Importunity, whom notwithstanding he straight strove to undermine,

[795] "he called . . . temporal things": Rushworth, p. 443.

[796] justified *out of* St. *Matthew:* Inevitably, Matthew 22:21, "Render therefore unto Caesar the things which are Caesar's; and unto God the things that are God's."

[797] *What a speech . . . offer double:* Rushworth, p. 438.

[798] and unto these . . . *undertook an answer:* 72, 72aT.

[799] whereupon . . . in Writing: 72aTc.

[800] Bishop of Durham: Richard Neile (1562–1640), partly responsible for Laud's advancement. [S]

[801] marrying . . . Lady R.: In 1605, Laud, then chaplain to Charles Blount, earl of Devonshire, married his patron to the divorced wife of Lord Rich. [S] Marvell is again quoting Rushworth, p. 440.

[802] Bishop Williams: John Williams (1582–1650), chancellor and archbishop of York.

and did ⟨it⟩ at last to purpose: for, saith the Arch-bishop, "Verily, such is his " undermining nature, that he will under-work any Man in the World, so " he may gain by it. *He call'd in the Bishop of Durham, Rochester,*[803] *and* " *Oxford,*[804] tryed men for such a purpose, to the answering of my Reasons, " and the whole stile of the Speech, runs We, We. In my memory, Doctor " Harsnet[805] then Bishop of Chichester, and now of Norwich (*as he came* " *afterward to be Arch Bishop of* [287] *York*) preach'd at White-hall upon " *Give unto Caesar the things that are Caesar's*; a Sermon that was afterwards " burned, teaching that Goods and Money were Caesars, and so the Kings: " Whereupon King James told the Lords and Commons that he had failed " in not adding According to the Laws and Customs of the Country " wherein they did live. But Sibthorp was for absolutely absolute. So that if " the King had sent to me for all my Money and Goods, and so to the " Clergy, I must by Sibthorp's proportion send him all. If the King should " send to the City of London to command all their Wealth, they were " bound to do it. I know the King is so gracious he will attempt no such " matter; but if he do it not, the defect is not in these flattering Divines."[806] Then he saith, (reflecting again upon the Loan which Sibthorp called a Tribute) "I am sorry at heart, the Kings Gracious Majesty should rest so " great a Building on so weak a Foundation, the Treatise being so slender, " and [288] without substance, but that proceeded from an hungry Man."[807] Then he speaks of his own case as to the licensing this Book, in parallel to the Earl of Essex his Divorce,[808] which to give it more authority, *was to be ratified judicially by the Arch-bishop.* He concludes how finally he refused his approbation to this Sermon, and saith, "It was thereupon carried to the " Bishop of London,[809] who gave a great and stately allowance of it, the " good Man not being willing that any thing should stick with him that " came from Court, as appears by a Book commonly called the seven " Sacraments, which was allowed by his Lordship with all the errours,

[803] Rochester: John Buckeridge (1562–1631), Laud's tutor.

[804] Oxford: John Howson (1557?–1632).

[805] Doctor Harsnet: Samuel Harsnet (1561–1631).

[806] Verily . . . Divines: Rushworth, pp. 440–43.

[807] I am sorry . . . hungry Man: Rushworth, p. 443.

[808] Earl of Essex his Divorce: Robert Devereux, 3d earl of Essex (1591–1646), married Frances Howard. In 1613 the marriage was nullified, against his will, so that she could marry James's favorite, Robert Carr, earl of Somerset. The remarriage was the great scandal of James's reign.

[809] Bishop of London: George Montaigne (1569–1628), an ally of Laud.

" which have been since expunged."[810] And he adds a pretty story of one Doctor Woral,[811] the *Bishop of London's Chaplain, Scholar good enough, but a free fellow-like man, and of no very tender Conscience,* who before it was Licensed by the Bishop, Sibthorp's Sermon being brought to him, *hand over head approved it, and subscribed his name.* But afterwards hearing more of it, went [289] to a Counsel at the Temple,[812] who told him, that by that Book *there was no* Meum *nor* Tuum[813] *left in England; and if ever the Tide turn'd, he might come to be hang'd for it*: and thereupon Woral *scraped out his name again,*[814] and left it to his Lord to License. Then the Arch-Bishop takes notice of the *instructions for that Loan.*[815] "Those that refused, to be " sent for Souldiers to the King of Denmark.[816] Oaths to be administred " with whom they had conference; and who disswaded them, such persons " to be sent to prison, &c. He saith that he had complained thrice of " Mountagues Arminian Book[817] to no purpose: Cosins put out his Book " of seven Sacraments[818] (strange things) but I knew nothing of it, but as it " pleased my Lord of Durham and the Bishop of Bath,[819] *so it went.*"[820] In conclusion, the good Arch-Bishop for refusing this License of Sibthorps Sermons, was, by the underworking of his adversaries, first commanded from Lambeth, and confined to his house in Kent, and [290] afterwards sequestred, and a Commission passed to exercise the Archiepiscopal Jurisdiction to the Bishops of London, Durham, Rochester, Oxford, and Bishop Laud (who from thence arose in time to be the Arch-Bishop.) If I had leisure, how easy a thing it were for to extract out of this Narrative a just parallel of our Author, even almost upon all points: but I am now upon a more serious subject, and therefore shall leave the Application to his own ingenuity, and the good intelligence of the Reader.

810 It was . . . expunged: Rushworth, p. 448.

811 Doctor Woral: Thomas Worral (c. 1589–1639), canon of St. Paul's.

812 Counsel at the Temple: John Selden (1584–1654), the great jurist.

813 Meum *nor* Tuum: "neither mine nor yours"; conventional terms in property and constitutional law.

814 *Scholar . . . name again:* Rushworth, p. 444.

815 *instructions . . . Loan:* Rushworth, p. 455.

816 King of Denmark: Christian IV (1577–1648), currently at war with the Holy Roman Emperor.

817 Mountagues . . . Book: *Appello Caesarem;* see p. 129 and n. 488 above.

818 Cosins . . . Sacraments: see p. 151 and n. 617 above.

819 Bishop of Bath: Laud, then bishop of Bath and Wells.

820 Those that refused . . . *so it went:* Rushworth, pp. 453–54.

About the same time (for I am speaking within the circle of 2°, 3°, and 4° Caroli) that this Book of Sibthorps, called *Apostolical Obedience,* was printed, there came out another of the same stamp, intitled *Religion and Allegiance,* by one Doctor Manwaring.[821] It was the substance of two Sermons preached by him at Whitehall, beside what of the same nature at his own parish of Saint Giles. Therein he delivered for truth, "That the King is " not bound to observe the Laws of the Realm concerning [291] the Sub- " jects rights and liberties, but that his Royal Word and Command in " imposing Loans and Taxes without common consent in Parliament, does " oblige the Subjects Conscience upon pain of eternal Damnation. That " those who refused to pay this Loan offended against the Law of God, and " the Kings supream Authority, and became guilty of Impiety, Disloyalty, " and Rebellion. That the Authority of Parliament was not necessary for " the raising of Aids and Subsidies, and the slow proceedings of such great " Assemblies were not fitted for the supply of the States urgent necessities, " but would rather produce sundry impediments to the just designs of " Princes." And after he had been questioned for this doctrine, nevertheless he preached again, "That the King had right to order all as to him should " seem good, without any mans consent. That the King might, in time of " necessity, demand Aid, and if the Subject did not supply him, the King " might justly avenge it. That the [292] Propriety of Estate and Goods was " ordinarily in the Subject, but extraordinarily in the King: that in case of " the King's need, he hath right to dispose them." He had besides, entring into comparison, called the refusers of the Loan "Temporal Recusants, and " said, the same disobedience that they (the Papists as they then called " them) practise in Spirituals, that or worse, some of our side, if ours they " be, dare to practice in Temporals." And he aggravated further upon them under the resemblance of Turks, Jews, Corah, Dathan, and Abiram.[822] "Which last, said he, might as well liken themselves to the three Children; " or Theudas and Judas,[823] the two Incendiaries in the daies of Caesar's

[821] Doctor Manwaring: Roger Manwaring (1590–1653), bishop of St. David's, appointed chaplain to Charles I in 1626, in which capacity he preached before the king two sermons subsequently combined in his treatise, published 1627. The House of Commons protested, unsuccessfully. Marvell's quotations are freely paraphrased from *Religion and Allegiance,* pp. 24–33, 19–20, 49 (A, p. 59, bundle 28 contains "Serm. before K.Charls the 1st . . . by . . . Maynwaring").

[822] Corah, Dathan and Abiram: see Numbers 16:1.

[823] Theudas and Judas: see Acts 5:36–37.

" tribute, might as well pretend their Cause to be like that of the Mac-
" cabees,[824] as what the Refusers alledged in their own defence."

I should not have been so large in these particulars, had they been onely single and volatile Sermons, but because this was then the Doctrine of those persons that pretended to be the [293] Church of England. The whole Quire sung that Tune, and in stead of the Common Law of England, and the Statutes of Parliament, that part of the Clergy had invented these *Ecclesiastical Laws,* which according to their predominancy, were sure to be put in execution. So that between their own Revenue, which must be held *Jure Divino,*[825] as every thing else that belong'd to them; and the Prince's, that was *Jure Regio,*[826] they had not left an inch of propriety for the Subject. It seem'd that they had granted themselves *Letters of Reprisal*[827] against the Laity, for the losses of the Church under Henry the Eighth, and that they would make a greater havock upon their Temporalities in retaliation. And indeed, having many times since ponder'd with my greatest and earnest impartiality, what could be the true reason of the spleen that they manifested in those daies, on the one hand against the *Puritans,* and on the other against the *Gentry,* (for it was come, they tell me, to *Jack Gentleman*) I could not devise any [294] cause, but that the Puritans had ever since the Reformation, obstructed that laziness and splendor which they injoyed under the Popes Supremacy, and the Gentry had (sacrilegiously) divided the *Abby-Lands,* and other fat morsels of the Church at the Dissolution, and now was the time to be revenged on them.

While therefore the Kingdom was turned into a Prison, upon occasion of this *Ecclesiastical Loan,* and many of the eminentest of the Gentry of England were under restraint, they thought it seasonable to recover once again their antient Glory; and to *Magnificate*[828] the Church with triumphal Pomp and Ceremony. The three Ceremonies that have the Countenance of Law, would not suffice, but they were all upon new Inventions, and happy was he that was endued with that capacity, for he was sure before all others to be preferr'd. There was a *Second* Service, the *Table* set *Altar-wise,* and to be

[824] the Maccabees: The Maccabees rebelled against the Romans in the second century B.C.

[825] *Jure Divino:* by divine law.

[826] *Jure Regio:* by royal law.

[827] *Letters of Reprisal:* official warrants authorizing an aggrieved subject to exact forcible reparation from the subjects of another state.

[828] *Magnificate:* glorify.

called the *Altar*; *Candles, Crucifixes, Paintings, Images,*[829] *Copes, bowing to the East, bowing* [295] *to the Altar,* and so many several Cringes & Genuflections, that a man unpractised stood in need to entertain both a Dancing-Master and a Remembrancer. And though these things were very uncouth to English Protestants, who naturally affect a plainness of fashion, especially in sacred things; yet if those Gentlemen could have contented themselves with their own Formalitie, the Innovation had been more excusable. But many of these Additions, and to be sure, all that had any colour of Law, were so imposed and prest upon others, that a great part of the Nation was e'n put as it were to fine and ransom upon this account. What Censures, what Excommunications, what Deprivations, what Imprisonments? I cannot represent the misery and desolation, as it hath been represented to me. But wearied out at home, many thousands of his Majesties Subjects, to his and the Nations great loss, thought themselves constrained to seek another habitation; and every Country, even though it were among Savages and Caniballs, [296] appear'd[830] more hospitable to them than their own.

And, although I have been told by those that have seen both, that our Church did even *then* exceed the Romish in Ceremonies and Decorations; and indeed, several of our Church did thereby frequently mistake their way, and from a Popish kind of Worship, fell into the Roman Religion; yet I cannot upon my best judgment believe, that that party had generally a design to alter the Religion so far, but rather to set up a new kind of Papacy of their own here in England. And it seemed they had to that purpose, provided themselves of a new Religion in Holland. It was Arminianism,[831] which though it were the *Republican* Opinion there, and so odious to King James that it helped on the death of Barnevelt,[832] yet now they undertook to accommodate it to Monarchy and Episcopacy. And the choice seemed not imprudent. For on the one hand, it was removed at so moderate a distance

[829] *Images* 72a] *Imagery* 72.

[830] appear'd Ed.] pear'd 72, 72a; the catchword at the bottom of p. 296 is ap-.

[831] Arminianism: See p. 62 and n. 137 above; Marvell's understanding of Arminianism was rather different from that of Arminius himself, focusing not on the issue of free will versus predestination but on ceremonies, which could loosely fall under the doctrine of good works.

[832] Barnevelt: John van Olden Barneveldt (1547–1619), grand pensionary of Holland, a republican, and a supporter of the Arminians. Following the Synod of Dort, which reasserted the centrality of predestination, he was arrested and executed.

from Popery, that they should not disoblige the Papists more than [297] formerly, neither yet could the Puritans with justice reproach these men as Romish Catholicks: and yet, on the other hand, they knew it was so contrary to the antient reformed Doctrine of the Church of England, that the Puritans would never imbrace it, and so they should gain this pretence further to keep up that convenient and necessary Quarrel against Nonconformity. And accordingly it happened, so that here again was a new *Shiboleth.* And the Calvinists were all studiously discountenanced, and none but an Arminian was judg'd capable and qualified for imployment in the Church. And though the King did declare, as I have before mentioned, that Mountague's Arminian[833] Book had been the occasion of the Schisms in the Church, yet care was immediately taken, by those of the same robe and party, that he should be the more rewarded and advanced. As also it was in Manwarings Case: who though by Censure in Parliament made incapable of any Ecclesiastical preferment, was straight made Rector of [298] Stamford-Rivers in Essex, with a Dispensation to hold too his Living in St Giles's. And all dexterity was practised to propagate the same Opinions, and to suppress all Writings or Discourses to the contrary.

So that those who were of understanding in those dayes, tell me, that a man would wonder to have heard their kind of preaching.[834] How instead of the practical Doctrine which tends to the reforming of Mens Lives and Manners, all their Sermons were a very Mash of Arminian Subtilties, of Ceremonies, and Decency, and of Manwaring and Sibthorpianism brew'd together; besides that in their conversation they thought fit to take some more license the better to *dis-Ghibeline*[835] themselves from the Puritans. And though there needed nothing more to make them unacceptable to the sober part of the Nation, yet moreover they were so exceeding *pragmatical,* so intolerably ambitious, and so desperately proud, that scarce any Gentleman might come near the Tayle of their [299] Mules. And many things I perceive of that nature do even yet stick upon the stomachs of the *Old Gentlemen* of those times. For the English have been always very tender of their Religion, their Liberty, their Propriety, and (I was going to say) no less of their Reputation. Neither yet do I speak of these things with passion, considering at more distance how natural it is for men to desire to be in

[833] Arminian 72a] (Arminian) 72.

[834] preaching 72a] preachings 72.

[835] *dis-Ghibeline:* that is, to distinguish themselves from them as enemies; see p. 81 and n. 245 above.

Office, and no less natural to grow proud and intractable in Office; and the less a Clergy-man is so, the more he deserves to be commended. But these things before mentioned, grew yet higher, after that Bishop Laud was once not only exalted to the See of Canterbury, but to be chief Minister. Happy had it been for the King, happy for the Nation, and happy for himself, had he never climbed that Pinacle. For whether it be or no, that the Clergy are not so well fitted by Education, as others for Political Affairs, I know not; though I should rather think they have advantage a-[300]bove others, and even if they would but keep to their Bibles, might make the best Ministers of State in the world; yet it is generally observed that things miscarry under their Government. If there be any Counsel more precipitate, more violent, more rigorous, more extreme than other, that is theirs. Truly I think the reason that God does not bless them in Affairs of State, is, because he never intended them for that imployment. Or if Government, and the preaching of the Gospel, may well concur in the same person, God therefore frustrates him, because though knowing better, he seeks and manages his greatness by the lesser and meaner *Maxims.* I am confident the Bishop studied to do both God and his Majesty good service, but alas how utterly was he mistaken. Though so learned, so pious, so wise a Man, he seem'd to know nothing beyond *Ceremonies,* Arminianism, and Manwaring. With that he begun, and with that ended, and thereby deform'd the whole reign of the best [301] Prince that ever wielded the English Scepter.

For his late Majesty being a Prince truly Pious and Religious, was thereby the more inclined to esteem and favour the Clergy. And thence, though himself of a most exquisite understanding, yet thought he could not trust it better than in their keeping. Whereas every man is best in his own Post, and so the Preacher in the Pulpit. But he that will do the Clergies drudgery, must look for his reward in another World. For they having gained this Ascendent upon him, resolv'd whatever became on't to make their best of him; and having made the whole business of State their Arminian Jangles, and the Persecution for Ceremonies, did for recompence assign him that imaginary absolute Government, upon which Rock we all ruined.

For now was come the last part of the *Archbishops* indiscretion; who having strained those strings so high here, and all at the same time, which no wise man ever did; he moreover had [302] a mind to try the same dangerous Experiment in Scotland, and sent thither the Book of the English *Liturgy* to be imposed upon them. What followed thereupon, is yet within the compass of most Mens memories. And how the War broke out, and then to be sure Hell's broke loose. Whether it were a War of Religion, or of Liberty, is not worth the labour to enquire. Which-soever was at the top, the other was at the bottom; but upon considering all, I think the Cause was too good to have been fought for. Men ought to have trusted God; they ought and might have trusted the King with that whole matter. The *Arms of the church are Prayers and Tears*,[836] the Arms of the Subjects are Patience and Petitions. The King himself being of so accurate and piercing a judgment, would soon have felt where it stuck. For men may spare their pains where Nature is at work, and the world will not go the faster for our driving. Even as his present Majesty's happy Restauration did it self; so all [303] things else happen in their best and proper time, without any need of our officiousness.

But after all the fatal consequences of that Rebellion, which can only serve as Sea-marks unto wise Princes to avoid the Causes, shall this sort of Men still vindicate themselves as the most zealous Assertors of the Rights of Princes? They are but at the best *well-meaning Zealots.* Shall, to decline so pernicious Counsels, and to provide better for the quiet of Government, be traduced as the Author does here, under these odious terms of *forsaking the Church, and delivering up the Church*?[837] Shall these Men always presume to usurp to themselves that venerable stile of the Church of England? God forbid. The Independents at that rate would not have so many distinct Congregations as they. There would be Sibthorps-Church, and Manwarings-Church, and Mountagues-Church, and a whole Bed-roll[838] more, whom for decencies-sake I abstain from naming. And every Man that could invent a [304] new Opinion, or a new Ceremony, or a new Tax, should be a new Church of England.

Neither, as far as I can discern, have this sort of the Clergy since his Majesties return, given him better incouragement to steer by their Compass. I am told, that preparatory to that, they had frequent meetings in the City, I know not whether in Grubstreet,[839] with the Divines of the other party, and that there in their Feasts of Love, they promised to forget all former Offences, to lay by all Animosities, that there should be a new

[836] *The Arms . . . Tears:* Marvell is quoting, shrewdly, from Charles I's posthumous self-defense, *Eikon Basilike,* 1649.

[837] *forsaking . . . Church: Preface,* d7.

[838] Bed-roll: bead-roll; a list of those to be mentioned at prayers, hence any long list of names.

[839] Grubstreet Ed.] Grubstret 72, 72a.

Heaven, and a new Earth, all Meekness, Charity, and Condescention. His Majesty I am sure sent over his Gracious Declaration of *Liberty to tender Consciences,*[840] and upon his coming over, seconded it with his Commission under the broad Seal, for a Conference betwixt the two parties, to prepare things for an Accommodation, that he might confirm it by his Royal Authority. Hereupon what do they? Notwithstanding this happy Conjuncture of his [305] Majesties[841] Restauration, which had put all Men into so good a humour, that upon a little moderation and[842] temper of things, the Nonconformists[843] could not have stuck out; some of these Men so contriv'd it, that there should not be the least abatement to bring them off with Conscience, and (which insinuates into all men) some little Reputation. But on[844] the contrary; several unnecessary additions were made, ⟨only because⟩ they knew ⟨they⟩ #which# would be more ingrateful and[845] *stigmatical* to the Nonconformists. I remember one in the *Letany,* where to *False Doctrine and Heresie,* they added *Schism,* though it were to spoil the *Musick* and cadence of the period; but these things were the best. To show that they were Men like others, even cunning Men, revengeful Men, they drill'd things on, till they might procure a Law, wherein besides all the Conformity that had been of former-times enacted, there might be some new Conditions imposed on those that should have, or hold any Church-Livings, such as they assur'd themselves, [306] that rather than swallow, the Nonconformists would disgorge all their Benefices. And accordingly it succeeded; several thousands of those Ministers being upon one memorable day outed of their subsistence. His Majesty in the meantime, although they had thus far prevailed to frustrate his Royal Intentions, had reinstated the Church in all its former Revenues, Dignities, and Advantages, so far from the Authors mischievous aspersion of ever thinking of converting

[840] Declaration . . . Consciences: the Declaration of Breda, 1660. See p. 90 and n. 288 above.

[841] Majesties 72a (B6, B7, D3, D5, S3, W3), copies in which gathering X (pp. 305–20 in the original) was censored, hereafter designated 72aXc] Ma$^{\text{stie's}}$ 72, and copies of 72a (B4, B5, B8, B9, C3, C4, D2, D4, O2, S4, W2) in which gathering X is uncensored, hereafter designated 72aX. Material between < and > is present in 72 and 72aX but absent from 72aXc. Conversely, material between # and # is present in 72aXc but absent from 72 and 72aX.

[842] and 72aXc] & 72, 72aX.

[843] Nonconformists 72aXc] Nonconforminsts 72, 72aX.

[844] on 72aXc] to 72, 72aX.

[845] and 72aXc] & 72, 72aX.

them to his own use, that he restored them free from what was due to him by Law upon their first admission. So careful was he, *because all Government must owe its quiet and continuance to the Churches Patronage,*[846] to pay them, even what they ought. But I have observed, that if a Man be in the Churches debt once, 'tis very hard to get an acquittance: And these men never think they have their full Rights, unless they Reign. What would they have had more? They rowl'd on a flood of wealth, and yet in matter of a Lease, would make no difference be-[307]twixt a Nonconformist, and one of their own fellow sufferers, who had ventur'd his life, and spent his Estate for the King's service. They were restor'd to Parliament, and to take their places with the King and the Nobility. They had a new *Liturgy* to their own hearts desire; And to cumulate all this happiness, they had this new Law against the *Fanaticks.* All they had that could be devised in the World to make a Clergy-man good natur'd.

Nevertheless after all their former sufferings, and after all these new enjoyments and acquisitions, they have proceeded still in the same track. The matter of Ceremonies, to be sure, hath not only exercised their ancient rigour & severity, but hath been a main ingredient of their publick Discourses, of their Sermons, of their Writings. I could not (though I do not make it my work after a great example, to look over *Epistles*[847] *Dedicatory*) but observe by chance the Title page of a Book t'other[848] day, as an *Emblem* how much some of them do neglect the Scripture in re-[308]spect to their darling Ceremonies.[849] A *Rationale upon the Book of Common-Prayer of the Church of England by A. Sparrow, D.D. Bishop of Exon. With the Form of Consecration of a Church or Chappel, and of the place of Christian Burial. By Lancelot Andrews late Lord Bishop of Winchester. Sold by Robert Pawlet at the Sign of the Bible in Chancery Lane.* These surely are worthy cares for the Fathers of the Church.

But to let these things alone; How have they of later[850] years demean'd themselves to his Majesty, although our Author urges their immediate dependance on the King to be a great obligation he hath upon their Loyalty and Fidelity? I have heard that some of them, when a great Minister of

[846] *because . . . Patronage: Preface,* C7.

[847] *Epistles* 72a] *Episties* 72; the only correction to the outer form of X.

[848] t'other Ed.] 'tother 72, 72a.

[849] Ceremonies Ed.] Ceremonis 72, 72a.

[850] later 72a] late 72.

State[851] grew burdensome to his Majesty and the Nation, stood almost in defiance of his Majesties good pleasure, and fought it out to the uttermost in his defence. I have been told that some of them in a matter of *Divorce,* wherein his Majesty desired that Justice might be done to the party agriev'd, [309] opposed him vigorously, though they made bold too with a point of Conscience in the case, and went against the Judgment of the best Divines of all parties. It hath been observed, that whensoever his Majesty hath had the most urgent occasions for supply, others of them have made it their business to trinkle[852] with the *Members of Parliament,* for obstructing it, unless the King would buy it with a new Law against the Fanaticks. ⟨And hence it is that the Wisdom of his Majesty and the Parliament must be exposed to after ages for⟩#And this is that which of late years hath caused# such a *Superfoetation*[853] *of Acts* ⟨in his Reign⟩ about the same business. And no sooner can his Majesty upon his own best Reasons try to obviate this Inconvenience, but our Author, who had before out-shot Sibthorp and Manwaring in their own Bows, is now for retrenching his Authority, and moreover calumniates the State with a likelyhood, and the reasons thereof of *the return of Popery* into this Nation. And this hath been his first Method by the *Fanaticks raising disturbance*: whereupon, if I [310] have raked farther into things than I would have done, the Author's Indiscretion will, I hope, excuse me, and gather all the blame for reviving those things which were to be buried in oblivion. But, by what appears, I cannot see that there is any probability of disturbance in the State, but by men of his spirit and principles.

The Second way whereby the Fanatick party, he saith, may at last work the ruin of the Church, is *by combining with the Atheists, for their Union is like the mixture of Nitre and Charcoal, it carries all before it without mercy or resistance.*[854] So it seems, when you have made Gun-powder of the Atheists and Fanaticks, we are like to be blown up with Popery. And so will the Larks too. But his zeal spends it self most against the *Atheists,* because they

[851] Minister of State: Edward Hyde, earl of Clarendon. See p. 91 and n. 290 above. Samuel Pepys commented on the rumor that the bishops at large refused to speak out against Clarendon, and that Charles said he had only one bishop on his side, Herbert Croft, bishop of Hereford. See Pepys, *Diary,* November 16, 1667.

[852] trinkle: intrigue with.

[853] *Superfoetation* Ed.] *Superfoe ation* 72, 72aX; *Superfetation* 72aXc; this pompous word, so troublesome to the printers, originally meant "the formation of a second foetus in an already-pregnant uterus"; hence, more activity than one needs.

[854] *Union . . . resistance: Preface,* e4.

use to *jear the Parsons.*[855] That they may do, and no Atheists neither. For really, while Clergy men will, having so serious an office, play the *Drols* and the Boon-companions, and make merry [311] with the Scriptures, not onely among themselves, but in Gentlemen's company, 'tis impossible but that they should meet with, at least, an unlucky Repartee sometimes, and grow by degrees to be a tayle,[856] and contempt to the people. Nay, even that which our Author[857] always magnifies, the Reputation, the Interest, the secular grandure of the Church, is indeed the very thing which renders them ridiculous to many, and looks as improper and buffoonish, as to have seen the Porter lately in the good *Doctors Cassock* and Girdle. For, so they tell me, that there are no where more Atheists than at Rome, because men seeing that Princely garb and Pomp of the Clergy, and observing their life and manners, think therefore the meaner of Religion. For certainly, the Reputation and Interest of the Clergy, was first gained by abstracting themselves from the world, attending their Callings, Humility, strictness of Doctrine, and the same strictness in Conversation; and things are best preserved by the same means they were at [312] first attained. But if our Author had been as concern'd against Atheisme, as he is against their disrespect of his function, he should have been content that the Fanatick Preachers might have spent some of their *Pulpit-sweat* upon the Atheists, and made a noise in their ears, about *Faith, Communion with God, attendance upon Ordinances,*[858] which he himself jears at so pleasantly. Neither do I like upon the same reasons his manner of Discourse with the Atheists, where he complains that ours are not like those good Atheists of former times, who never did thrust themselves into publick cares and concerns, "minding " nothing but Love, Wine, and Poetry."[859] Nor in another place, "Put the " case the Clergy were Cheats and Juglers, yet it must be allowed they are " necessary Instruments of State to aw the Common People into fear and " obedience, because nothing else can so effectually inslave them" ('tis this it seems our Author would be at) "as the fear of invisible powers, and the " dismall apprehensions of the world to [313] come: and for this very rea- " son, though there were no other, it is fit they should be allowed the same

[855] *jear the Parsons: Preface,* e1.

[856] a tayle: a story, legend; i.e., to become a matter of common talk.

[857] Author Ed.] Athour, 72, 72a.

[858] *Pulpit-sweat . . . Ordinances: Preface,* d1v.

[859] minding . . . Poetry: *Preface,* d8.

" honour and respect, as would be acknowledged their due, if they were " sincere and honest men."[860] No Atheist could have said better. How mendicant a cause has he here made of it; they will say, They see where the shoo wrings him, and that though this be some ingenuity in him, yet it is but little Policy. Nay, perhaps they will say, That they are no Atheists neither, but only, I know not by what Fate, every day one or other of the Clergy does, or saith, some so ridiculous and foolish thing, or some so prity accident befals them, that in our Authors words a *man must be very splenetick that can refrain from laughter.*[861] I would have quoted the page here, but that the Author has, I think for evasion sake, omitted to number them in his[862] whole Preface. But whether there be any Atheists or no, which I question more than Witches, I do not for all this take our Author to be one, though some would conclude [314] it out of his Principles, others out of his Expressions. Yet really, I think he hath done that sort of men so much service in his Books by his ill handling, and while he personates one party, making all Religion ridiculous, that they will never be able to requite him but in the same manner. He hath opened them a whole Treasury of words and sentences universally applicable, where they may rifle or chuse things, which their pitiful wit, as he calls it, would never have been able to invent and flourish. But truly, as the simple *Parliament* 5° Eliz. never imagined what consequence that clause in the Wednesday Fast would have to Puritanism: neither did he what his *Periods* would have to Atheism; and yet though he is so more excusable, I hope I may have the same leave on him, as he on that *Parliament,* to censure his Impertinence. To close this; I know a Lady that chid her Master of the Horse for correcting the *Page* that had sworn a great Oath. For, saith she, *The Boy did therein show only the Generosity of his Cou-*[315]*rage, and his acknowledgement of a Deity.* And indeed, he hath approv'd his Religion, and justified himself from Atheism much after the same manner.

The third way and last (which I being tired, am very glad of) by which the Fanaticks may raise Disturbances, and so *introduce Popery,* is by joyning crafty and sacrilegious States-men into the Confederacy.[863] But really here he doth speak concerning King, and Counsellors, at such a rate, and

[860] "Put the case . . . honest men": *Preface,* e2v–e3.

[861] *man . . . laughter: Preface,* c5v.

[862] his 72Xc] this 72, 72aX.

[863] joyning . . . Confederacy: *Preface,* e4.

describe and characterize some men so, whomsoever he intends, that though I know there are no such, I dare not touch, it is too hazardous. 'Tis true he passes his Complement ill-favouredly enough. "The Church has at present " an impregnable affiance in the wisdom, &c. of so gracious a Prince, that " is not capable of such Counsels, should they be suggested to him: though " certainly no man that is worthy to be admitted to his Majesties Favour or " Privacy; can be supposed so fool-hardy or presumptuous as to offer such " weak and dishonourable Advice to so wise and [316][864] able a Prince; Yet " Princes are mortal, and if ever hereafter, (and some time or other it must " happen) the Crown should chance to settle upon a young and unexperi- " enced head, this is usually the first thing in which such Princes are abused " by their Keepers and Guardians,[865] &c." But this Complement is no better at best, than if discoursing with a man of another, I should take him by the Beard. Upon such occasions in company, we use to ask, Sir, *Whom do you mean?* I am sure our Author takes it alwayes for granted, that his Answerer intends him upon more indefinite and less direct provocations. But our Author does even personate some men as speaking at present against the Church, "They will intangle your affairs, indanger your safety, " hazard your Crown. All the reward you shall have to compensate your " misfortunes, by following Church Counsels, shall be that a few Church- " men, or such like people, shall cry you up for a Saint or a Martyr." Still *your, your,* as if it were a close [317][866] discourse unto His Majesty himself. Though if this were the worst that they said, or that the Author fathers upon them, I wish the King might never have better Counsellors about him. But if the Author be secure, for the present, in his Majesties Reign, fears not Popery, not forsaking the Church, not assuming the Church Revenues, why is he so provident? why put things in men's heads they never thought of? why stir such an odious, seditious, impertinent, unseasonable discourse? why take this very minute of time, but that he hath mischief, to say no worse, in his heart? He had no such remote conceit (for all his talk) of an *Infant* coming to the Crown. He is not so weak but knows too much, and is too well instructed, to speak to so little purpose. That would have been like a set of *Elsibeth Players,* that in the Country having worn out and over-acted all the Playes they brought with them from London, laid their

[864] 316] misnumbered 320 in D3.

[865] at present . . . Guardians: *Preface,* e7.

[866] 317] misnumbered 713 in B6, B7, D5, S3, W3.

wits together to make a new one of their own. No less man than Julius Caesar was the Argu-[318]ment; and one of the chief parts was Moses perswading Julius Caesar not to make War against his own Countrey, nor pass Rubicon.[867] If our Author did not speak of our present times (to do which nevertheless had been sufficiently false and absurd) but writ all this meerly out of his Providence for after-ages, I shall no more call him Bayes, for he is just such a *second* Moses. I ask pardon, if I have said too much, but I shall deserve none, if I meddle any further with so improbable and dangerous a business.

To conclude, the Author gives us one ground more, and perhaps more *seditiously* insinuated than any of the former; that is, if *it should so prove,* that is, if the *Fanaticks by their wanton and unreasonable opposition to the ingenious and moderate Discipline of the Church of England, shall give their Governors too much reason to suspect that they are never to be kept in order by a milder, and*[868] *more gentler*[869] *Government than that of the Church of Rome, and force them at last*[870] *to scourge them into better man-*[319]*ners, with the Briars and Thorns of their Discipline.*[871] It seems then that the Discipline contended about, is worth such an alteration. It seems that he knows something more than I did believe of the Design in the late times before the War. Whom doth he mean by *our Governours*? the King; No, for he is a single person. The Parliament, or the Bishops.

I have now done, after I have (which is I think due) given the Reader, and the Authour, a short account how I came to write this Book, and in this Manner. First of all, I was offended at the presumption and arrogance of his stile; whereas there is nothing either of Wit, or Eloquence in all his Books, worthy of a Readers, and more unfit for his own, taking notice of. Then his infinite *Tautology* was burdensome, which seem'd like marching a Company round a Hill upon a pay-day so often, till if the Muster-master were not attentive, they might receive the pay of a Regiment. All the variety of

[867] Julius Caesar . . . Rubicon: In 49 B.C. Julius Caesar, alarmed by the opposition of Pompey and the Senate to his maintaining his office as proconsul, crossed the Rubicon into Italy and initiated the first civil war. Crossing the Rubicon subsequently became proverbial for any irreversible major decision. The absurd play, however, seems to be Marvell's invention.

[868] *and* 72aXc] *&* 72, 72aX.

[869] *gentler* 72aXc] *genle* 72, 72aX.

[870] *last* 72, 72aX] *least* 72aXc.

[871] *by their . . . Discipline: Preface,* e8.

his Treat is *Pork* (he [320] knows the story)[872] but so little disguised by good Cookery, that it discovers the miserableness, or rather the penury of the Host. When I observed how he inveighs against the *Trading-part* of the Nation, I thought he deserved to be within the *five mile Act,* and not to come within that distance of any Corporation.[873] I could not patiently see how irreverently he treated Kings and Princes, as if they had been no better then King Phyz, and King Ush of Brandford.[874] I thought his profanation of the Scripture intolerable; For though he alledges that 'tis only in order to shew how it was misapplyed by the Fanaticks, he might have done that too, and yet preserved the Dignity and Reverence of those Sacred Writings, which he hath not done; but on the contrary, he hath in what is properly his own, taken the most of all his Ornaments, and Imbellishments thence in a scurrilous and sacrilegious stile; insomuch that were it honest, I will undertake out of him to make a better, that is a more ridiculous and [321][875] profaner Book, than *all the Friendly Debates* bound up together. Methought I never saw a more bold and wicked attempt, than that of reducing *Grace,* and making it a meer *Fable,* of which he gives us *the Moral.* I was sorry to see that even Prayer could not be admitted to be a Virtue, having thought hitherto it had been a *Grace,* and a peculiar gift of the Spirit; But I considered, that that Prayer ought to be discouraged, in order to prefer the *Liturgy.* He seem'd to speak so little like a Divine in all those matters, that the *Poet*[876] might as well have pretended to be the *Bishop* Davenant,[877] and that description of the Poets of *Prayer* and *Praise* was better than our Authors on the same Subject. *Canto* the 6th, where he likens Prayer to the Ocean;

[872] *Pork . . .* story: Marvell will reveal the source of this allusion in the *Second Part;* that is, Philemon Holland's translation of Livy. See below, p. 412 and n. 1005.

[873] *five mile Act . . .* Corporation: Marvell is alluding both to the Five Mile Act (1665), which made it penal for any nonconformist minister to go within five miles of any city where he had preached before the Act of Uniformity, and to the Corporation Act (1661), which made it illegal for any nonconformist to hold office in any corporation.

[874] King Phyz, and King Ush of Brandford: the two usurping kings in Buckingham's *Rehearsal,* act 2, scene 1.

[875] 321] misnumbered 312 in B5, D2, D5.

[876] the *Poet:* Sir William Davenant, author of *Gondibert.* See p. 50 and n. 55 above.

[877] *Bishop* Davenant: John Davenant (1576–1641), bishop of Salisbury. A moderate Calvinist, he represented the Church of England at the Synod of Dort. [S]

For[878] *Prayer the Ocean is where diversly*
Men steer their course each to a several coast.
Where all our interests so discordant lye,
That half beg winds, by which the rest are lost. [322][879]

And Praise he compares to the Union of Fanaticks and Atheists,[880] *&c.* that is[881] *Gunpowder*; *Praise is Devotion fit for mighty minds,*[882] &c.

Its utmost force, like Powder, is unknown.
And though weak Kings excess of praise may fear,
Yet when 'tis here, like Powder, dangerous grown,
Heavens vault receives, what would the Palace tear.[883]

Indeed all Astragon[884] appear'd to me the better *Scheme of Religion.*[885] But it is unnecessary here to recapitulate all, one by one, what I have in the former Discourse taken notice of. I shall only add, what gave, if not the greatest, yet the *last* impulse to my writing. I had observed in his first Book, p. 57. that he had said "Some pert and pragmatical Divines, had filled the world with a Buzze and noise of the Divine Spirit;" which seemed to me[886] so horribly irreverent, as if he had taken ⟨his⟩[887] similitude from the *Hum and Buz* [323] of the *Humble-Bee* in the *Rehearsal.*[888]

In the same Book, I have before mentioned, that most unsafe passage of[889] our *Saviour, being not only in an hot fit of zeal, but in a seeming fury and*

[878] Ocean; *For* 72a] Ocean; [322] *For* 72; this arrangement in 72 leaves seven blank lines at the bottom of the page, possibly related to some delay in obtaining a text of Davenant's recently published works.

[879] *For Prayer . . . lost:* Davenant, *Gondibert* (1651), 2.6.85.

[880] Union of . . . Atheists: *Preface,* e4.

[881] is 72, 72a] *is* 72a (B6, C4, D3, D4, S3, W3); this is the only textual variant in the inner form of Y in 72a.

[882] *Praise . . . minds:* Davenant, *Gondibert,* 2.6.84.

[883] *Its utmost . . . tear:* Davenant, *Gondibert,* 2.6.87.

[884] Astragon 72] Astragen 72a.

[885] Astragon . . . scheme of religion: Astragon is a holy man in *Gondibert* who explains to the hero the temples of Prayer, Praise, and Penitence.

[886] to me 72] to to me 72a.

[887] his 72, except B1, B2, C1, D1, H, U.

[888] *Hum . . . Humble-Bee: Rehearsal,* act 4, scene 1, pp. 35–36.

[889] of 72, 72a (B6)] omitted elsewhere.

transport of Passion.[890] And striving to unhook himself hence. p. 152. of his Second Book, #he# swallows it deeper, saying, *Our blessed Saviour did in that action take upon him the Person and Priviledge of a Jewish Zealot.*[891] Take upon him the Person, that is *Personam induere.* And what part did he play? Of a *Jewish Zealot.*[892]

The Second Person of the Trinity (may I repeat these things without offence) to take upon him the person of a Jewish Zealot, that is, of a notorious Rogue and Cut-throat.

This seemed to proceed from too slight an Apprehension and knowledge of the duty we owe to our Saviour. And last of all, in this Preface, as before[893] quoted, he saith, the *Nonconformist Preachers do spend most of their Pulpit-sweat in making a noise about Communion with God.*[894] So that there is not one Person of the Trinity that he hath not [324] done despight[895] to: and lest he should have distinct Communion with the Father, the Son and the Holy Ghost, for which he mocks his Answerer;[896] he hath spoken evil distinctly of the Father, distinctly of the Son, and distinctly of the Holy Ghost. That only remain'd behind, wherein our Author might surpass the Character given to Aretine,[897] a famous man of this faculty,[898]

Qui giace il[899] *Aretino*
Chi de tutti mal disse fuor d'Iddio
Ma di questo si scusa perche no'l conobbe.[900]
Here lies Aretine,
Who spoke evil of all, except God only;
But of this he beggs excuse, because he
did not know him.

[890] *hot fit . . . Passion: Discourse,* Preface, vii.

[891] *Zealot* 72, 72a (B6)] *Zelot* 72a.

[892] *Zealot* 72, 72a (B6)] *Zelot* 72a.

[893] before 72, 72a (B6)] befoe 72a.

[894] *spend most . . . God: Preface,* dlv.

[895] despight 72, 72a (B6)] despighe 72a.

[896] distinct Communion . . . Answerer: see *Defence,* p. 108, where Parker ridicules John Owen, *Saints Distinct Communion* (Oxford, 1657), p. 6.

[897] Aretine: Pietro Aretino (1492–1556), Italian poet noted for his scurrility.

[898] this faculty, 72a (B6)] his Faculty. 72; this faculty- 72a.

[899] *il* 72] *ill* 72a.

[900] *Qui . . . conobbe:* A legend attributes these lines to Paolo Giovio (1483–1552). See Carlo Bertani, *Pietro Aretino e le sue opere* (Sondrio, 1901), p. 181n. [S] There were in fact other versions of this epitaph, which identified Aretino as "poeta tosca."

And now I have done. And I[901] shall think my self largely recompensed for this trouble, if any one that hath been formerly of another mind, shall learn by this Example, that it is not impossible to be merry [325] and angry as long time as I have been writing, without profaning and violating those things which are and ought to be most sacred.

FINIS. [326]

901 I 72, 72a (B4, B5, B7, C3, D2, D5)] erroneously reported by Smith as omitted from 72a.

THE REHEARSAL TRANSPROS'D: THE SECOND PART

1673

The Rehearsal Transpros'd: The Second Part

Edited by Martin Dzelzainis and Annabel Patterson

CONTEXT

Few editors receive a gift such as Marvell left us in relation to the second part of the *Rehearsal Transpros'd:* a dated personal letter describing the hostile responses to the first part and what he proposed to do about them. In a letter of May 3, 1673, to Sir Edward Harley, his ally in the cause of toleration and comprehension, Marvell wrote,

> I find here at my returne a new booke against the Rehearsall intitled: St, to him Bayes: writ by one Hodges. But it is like the rest onely something more triviall. Gregory Gray-beard is not yet out. Dr. Parker will be out the next weeke. I have seen of it already 330 pages and it will be much more. I perceive by what I have read that it is the rudest book, one or other, that ever was publisht (I may say) since the first invention of printing. Although it handles me so roughly yet I am not at all amated by it. But I must desire the advice of some few friends to tell me whether it will be proper for me and in what way to answer it. However I will for mine own private satisfaction forthwith draw up an answer that shall have as much of spirit and solidity in it as my ability will afford & the age we live in will indure. I am (if I may say it with reverence) drawn in, I hope by a good Providence, to intermeddle in a noble and high argument wch therefore by how much it is above my capacity I shall use the more industry not to disparage it. (*P&L,* 2:328)

The letter tells us three important things: first, that Marvell has been reading the counterattacks of the high church party in the printers' shops before their appearance; second, that he perceived his task to be more or less exclusively to answer Samuel Parker rather than his more trivial sidekicks; and third, that he saw his answer as operating at a higher level than the first *Rehearsal Transpros'd,* as encroaching on the heroic genre of political theory; the phrase, "noble and high argument," with its Miltonic resonance, summoned up the *First* and *Second Defences of the English People,* the second of which Marvell had once studied "even to the getting of it by Heart" (*P&L,* 2:306). In fact, the second part of the *Rehearsal Transpros'd* did slightly less to defend the commonwealth era and the Good Old Cause than had the first. But what it offered instead was a theoretically coherent attack on the doctrines of monarchical absolutism, Erastianism, and enforced conformity that Parker had been advocating. Marvell's target was Parker, all 330 pages of him and counting—the *Reproof to the Rehearsal Transpros'd* finally came in at 528 pages—both because Parker was an immediate threat to the Nonconformists in the slippery circumstances of the early 1670s and because the challenge he had issued in the *Reproof* provided a perfect excuse for Marvell's reentry into the debate. His intended audiences, however, included Charles II, the largely intolerant Cavalier parliament, and the aristocrats who had been, more or less openly, patronizing Marvell: Anglesey, Buckingham, and, behind them in the shadows, Shaftesbury himself.

Between the appearance of the second edition of the original *Rehearsal Transpros'd,* probably in January 1673, and Marvell's letter to Harley of May 3, much had happened. The most important event was, of course, the king's formal withdrawal of the Declaration of Indulgence in his speech to the returned parliament on March 8, and Anglesey's aborted attempt to bring in a bill to exempt Protestant dissenters from the potentially reinforced penalties,[1] one of a series of such attempts from 1668 onward that were blocked by a majority determined to keep the sanctions in force.[2] It would

[1] See Historical Manuscript Commission, *Ninth Report,* Appendix 2 (House of Lords MSS), p. 25; cited by Douglas Greene, "Arthur Annesley, first earl of Anglesey, 1614–1686" (Ph.D. diss., Chicago, 1972), p. 87.

[2] For a benign account of the Commons' intentions and the effects of the Declaration's withdrawal, see John Spurr, *England in the 1670s* (Oxford, 2000), pp. 38–39, 42. But Marvell at this stage thought the Commons were hostile to toleration in general. One of the reactions Spurr quotes to the failure to pass such a bill was that of Marvell's

be hard to imagine that Anglesey's protection of Marvell, facilitated by his elevation to Lord Privy Seal on April 22, did not now extend to the *Second Part.*

In addition, the international ramifications of the local religious debate were beginning to become visible. At the opening of 1672 Dryden had dedicated his *Conquest of Granada* to James, duke of York, aligning him in advance with anti-Dutch policy, a move that would seem prophetic when the Third Dutch War was declared on March 17. In Easter term Peter Heylyn's son had reissued his father's rabid *Aerius Redivivus,* a hostile history of the Reformation in Europe.[3] It carried a provocative dedication to the parliament, urging them to maintain their legislation against protestant nonconformity at home.[4] During the summer of 1673, when Marvell was writing *RT2,* the duke of York resigned all his offices under the pressure of the Test Act, and by September 20 his marriage to the devoutly Roman Catholic Mary, duchess of Modena, had been celebrated in proxy. On November 3 Shaftesbury learned of the secret clauses in the Treaty of Dover, and less than a week later he was dismissed from the chancellorship and the Privy Council, partly at James's request. We can date the appearance of *RT2* very close to these events; its title page declared it to be a reply to two letters, the second "left for me at a Friends House, Dated Nov. 3. 1673."[5]

The rash of attacks on the original *Rehearsal Transpros'd* suggest political

---

correspondent, Sir Edward Harley himself, who wrote to his wife that the March adjournment had cast the bill into limbo: "The lord be gracious to those who find few friends in this world."

[3] Term Catalogues, 1:106.

[4] Peter Heylyn, *Aerius Redivivus, or the History of Presbyterians,* 2d ed. (London, 1672), Ai: "[This is] an History which in some measure confirms the Excellency of those Laws You have devised, and Sacred Majesty confirm'd, for the Protection of that Religion and Government You profess and stand for. The Beauty, Justice and Prudence of the Sanctions, will not a little appear in the ill usage of that Party, whose Rude humor and ungoverned Zeal is here represented."

[5] Inside the cover of Cambridge University Library Keynes T.3.31 is inscribed "William Dr Grey mei possessor December 20th 1673." Thomas Blount, who had been eagerly awaiting publication of *RT2* since August 6, 1673, when he wrote to Sir Edward Harley, "We were put in hope of Mr Marvels Reply, but it appeared not whilst I stayd in London," had to wait until January 11, 1674, before being able to write to Antony à Wood, asking, "What say your Academics to Rehearsal Transprosd 2d part, is it not bold?" Theo Bongaerts, *The Correspondence of Thomas Blount (1618–1679): A Recusant Antiquary* (Amsterdam, 1978), pp. 142, 145.

instigation, as had been the case in the 1590s when the bishops attacked by Martin Marprelate encouraged, if they did not actually commission, the pamphlets of the anti-Martinists. But if Gilbert Sheldon had organized the press attack on indulgence and encouraged Simon Patrick's *Friendly Debate,* there is nothing to connect the attacks on Marvell explicitly with the archbishop except Marvell's claim that Parker had organized them all. If we omit the first response, *Rosemary and Bayes* (1672) by Henry Stubbe, on the grounds that Stubbe attacked both Marvell and Parker, Marvell faced the following: the anonymous *S'too him Bayes,* and *A Common Place-Book Out of the Rehearsal Transpros'd; The Transproser Rehears'd,* now attributed to Samuel Butler; *Gregory, Father-Greybeard, with his Vizard off,* by Edmund Hickeringill; and Parker's own *Reproof to the Rehearsal Transpros'd.* All but the first of these were advertised in the Term Catalogues,[6] hence acquiring some measure of respectability. This threatened to turn a duel into a foxhunt. But Marvell would not, as he told Harley, allow himself to be distracted. Parker's book was, he thought, the rudest; it was also the biggest, at five shillings by far the most expensive, and advertised in the official *Gazette.* To the extent that Parker wrote as archdeacon of Canterbury, he would be seen as speaking on behalf of the conservative wing of the Anglican church on matters of broad ecclesiastical policy; whereas his other attackers had no social or clerical standing. Hickeringill, it is true, had been ordained at the Restoration, but he was a quarrelsome and litigious figure whose politics seem to have been highly confused.[7]

ARGUMENT AND LITERARY STRATEGY

As Marvell's letter to Harley had promised, *RT2* has an entirely different feel from *RT.* It is less a display of disconnected firecrackers and more a series of sinuously extended arguments, some theological, some political, though these were framed and interspersed with displays of the scatology, literary sophistication, and general high spirits that had made the original

[6] *A Common-place Book* was advertised for Hilary term 1673 (I:128); Parker's *Reproof* and *The Transproser Rehears'd* for Easter term (I:134 and 135); and *Gregory Father Greybeard* for Trinity term (I:142). Milton's *Of True Religion, Haeresie, Schism . . .* was also advertised for Easter 1673 (I:135).

[7] See Justin Champion and Lee McNulty, "Making Orthodoxy in Late Restoration England: The Trials of Edmund Hickeringill, 1662–1710," in *Negotiating Power in Early Modern Society: Order, Hierarchy and Subordination in Britain and Ireland,* ed. Michael J. Braddick and John Walter (Cambridge, 2001), pp. 227–48.

work an instant best-seller. As an act of character destruction, like Cicero's orations against Catiline, *RT2* had recourse to the time-honored and time-worn tactics of epideictic rhetoric; Parker would be demolished in terms of the categories of his parentage, his education, and his marriage, before Marvell turned back to his "works." Hence the devastating news that John Parker, Samuel's father, had been an eager supporter of the revolution and had profited considerably in consequence. And hence the endless jokes at Parker's expense about his "comfortable importance," explained by Marvell as his new wife, Mistress Pheasant.

As an answer, the *Second Part* also rose to the challenge (from Hickeringill) that the first part had been insufficiently scholarly in its citations and that its authorities were limited to John Hales's little pamphlet on schism and "Rushworth's orts."[8] With increasingly mortal aim, *RT2* marshaled its authorities, often the very same ones that Parker himself had mentioned, complete with edition and page references. A new system of marginal references (hard work for the printer) keyed Marvell's repartee in to the pages of his opponent's works; and where Parker had made the mistake of challenging the accuracy of Marvell's scholarship, the tactic proved rebarbative. Marvell would pick up a name that Parker had lobbed into the game and send it smashing back as an authority to refute the use that Parker had tried to make of it; or, to cite the fable of the Eagle and the Arrow that Marvell himself alluded to, the bird was pierced to the heart by an arrow feathered by himself. This happened, in particular, in relation to the emperor Julian, to his historian Ammianus Marcellinus, to the great continental theorist and theologian Hugo Grotius, and to Sir Francis Bacon. But Marvell also widened the field of his reading, informing himself about the history of the Council of Trent, the era of Archbishop Laud, Jewish rituals about accepting converts, and the biographies of all sorts of Parkers from the distant past to the Restoration present.

The heart of Marvell's argument occurs at pages 176–98 of the tract, pages 324–35 in this edition. Here he sets aside the gibing at Parker's ambition and the excesses of *his* argument for the magistrate's authority and turns to the central issues of seventeenth-century debates about church and state: what is the origin of government? what are its sanctions? how far should the secular power interfere with the inner life of conscience? what is the value, if any, of a national church or a universal religion? The issues that Marvell here strategically ignores (though he will turn to them in *Mr. Smirke* and the *Short*

[8] Edmund Hickeringill, *Gregory, Father-Greybeard,* p. 182.

Historical Essay) are: what are the grounds of belief? who, if anyone, has the authority to prescribe what men shall believe, or say they believe? and what, indeed, are the fundamentals of belief, the minimum conditions of agreement that permit oneself to call oneself a Christian?

Instead of embroiling himself in those still deeper questions, for which he perhaps had not yet acquired the polemical courage or knowledge, Marvell presents himself, brilliantly, as an orthodox adherent of the doctrine of the divine right of kings. Yet the further we read into his definition of this position, the more dangerously moderate and ironically nuanced it becomes. "The Power of the Magistrate does *most certainly* issue from the Divine Authority," Marvell wrote, sounding much like St. Paul, Calvin, and James I: "The Obedience due to that Power is by Divine Command, and Subjects are bound both as Men and as Christians to obey the Magistrate Actively in all things where their Duty to God intercedes not, and however [i.e., where it does] Passively, that is either by leaving their Countrey, or if they cannot do that (the Magistrate or the reason of their own occasions hindring them) then by suffering patiently at home, without giving the least publick disturbance" (p. 324; italics added). But here comes the first qualification: "But the modester Question . . . would be how far it is *advisable* for a Prince to exert and push the rigour of that Power which no man can deny him." This move from indubitable authority to a generous self-restraint is presented both as in the interest of the subject and the self-interest of the monarch: "Whoever shall cast his eye thorow the History of all Ages, will find that nothing has always succeeded better with Princes then the Clemency of Government: and that those, on the contrary, who have taken the sanguinary course, have been unfortunate to themselves and the people, the consequences not being separable." Calmly reversing the central doctrine of Machiavelli's *Prince,* Marvell then proceeded to insinuate another sort of Machiavellianism, whereby fundamental popular rights might conceivably be rendered obsolete by years of benevolent government: "I will not say what one Prince may compass within his own time, or what a second, though surely much may be done: but it is enough if a great and durable design be accomplish'd in the third Life, and, supposing an hereditary succession of any three taking up still where the other left, and dealing still in that fair and tender way of management . . . the very memory or thoughts of any such thing as Publick liberty would, as it were by consent, expire and be for ever extinguish'd" (pp. 324–26). The phrase "as it were by consent" prevents the careful reader from taking this outcome as truly desirable. And in the last stage of the argument Marvell (clearly separating himself from Hobbes)[9] adds to monarchical self-interest the *duty* of a Christian magistrate to govern in a Christian manner; for "where the Magistrate does clash with the rules and ends of Christianity, he does of consequence subvert his own power, and undermine his own Foundation" (p. 328) He thereby rendered his argument neatly circular.

In the rest of the tract Marvell shows with amazing (and sometimes tedious) persistence how and why Parker has taken it upon himself to give Charles II the opposite advice, placing him in a scandalous history of ecclesiastical greed and contentiousness that began under Constantine the Great. This theme anticipates the systematic coverage of primitive and imperial church history in the *Short Historical Essay*. But he also vouchsafed us information of great personal and literary value: his own theory of the ethics of controversy in matters of religion (pp. 236–41 of this edition); a cameo account of John Milton's career both before and after the Restoration, to defend him from the suspicion of having collaborated in *RT* (pp. 417–19); an account of how Parker had tried both to prevent the circulation of *RT* and to inhibit an effective answer to the *Reproof*, by lying about his own intentions (pp. 250–51); and proof that he himself was the translator of the 1672 Suetonius, the *History of the Twelve Caesars* sold by John Starkey, since his citations of Nero's and Caligula's histories are intimately related to that translation.[10]

THE AFTERLIFE OF THE *SECOND PART*

Despite its greater seriousness, *RT2* did not have the more general applicability of the *Short Historical Essay* and the *Account of the Growth of Popery and Arbitrary Government*, both of which were occasionally revived, quoted, or imitated by Whigs during the later seventeenth and eighteenth centuries.[11] The focus on Parker had been, after all, too effective to extend

[9] Contrast Jon Parkin's argument, in "Liberty Transpros'd: Marvell and Samuel Parker," in *Marvell and Liberty*, ed. Warren Chernaik and Martin Dzelzainis (Basingstoke, 1999), pp. 269–89, that Marvell was himself sympathetic to Hobbes.

[10] See Patterson, "A Restoration Suetonius: A New Marvell Text?" *Modern Language Quarterly* 61 (2000), 463–80.

[11] There is one important exception. William Disney, an ejected Nonconformist minister who was convicted of high treason and executed for printing and publishing

to other campaigns. Parker and Marvell lived on in Rochester's satire *Tunbridge Wells,* whose focus is society and polite (and impolite) letters, not politics:

> Listning I found the Cob of all this Rabble,
> Pert Bays, with his Importance Comfortable:
> Hee being rais'd to an Archdeaconry:
> By trampling on Religion's liberty,
> Was grown too great, and lookt too fatt and Jolly,
> To be disturb'd with care, and Melancholly,
> Tho *Marvell* has enough Expos'd his folly.[12]

Antony à Wood, whose now-classic account of the duel favored Parker's politics but gave Marvell the victory, seems not to attribute that feat to *RT2.* He described the duel as more well matched than most Marvell scholars can quite like; as:

> A perfect trial of each others skill and parts in a jerking, flirting way of writing, entertaining the reader with a great variety of sport and mirth, in seeing two such right cocks of the game so keenly engaging with sharp and dangerous weapons. And it was generally thought, nay even by many of those who were otherwise favourers of Parker's cause, that he (Parker) thro' a too loose and unwary handling of the debate (tho' in a brave, flourishing and lofty stile) laid himself too open to the severe strokes of his snearing adversary, and that the odds and victory lay on Marvell's side: Howsoever it was, it wrought this good effect upon our author, that for ever after it took down somewhat of his high spirit, insomuch that tho' Marvell in a second part replied upon our author's reproof, yet he judged it more prudent rather to lay down the cudgels than to enter the lists again.[13]

Monmouth's *Declaration* in June 1685, had in 1681 published two versions of an identical tract on political theory, *Nil dictum quod non dictum priius, or the case of the Government of England,* in which he silently adapts a long passage from Marvell's central argument in *RT2* (pp. 331–32 in this edition; cf. also Disney, pp. 3–4 and *RT2,* pp. 343–44).

[12] See *The Works of John Wilmot, Earl of Rochester,* ed. Harold Love (Oxford, 1999), pp. 50–51, 373. The first printed version of the poem appeared in Richard Head's *Proteus redivivus* (London, 1675; Stationers' Register, Nov. 10, 1674.)

[13] Wood, *Athenae Oxonienses,* ed. Philip Bliss (1820), 4:231. There were, however, two non-Parkerian replies to *RT2* : *An Apology and Advice for some of the Clergy, Who Suffer under False and Scandalous Reports. Written on the Occasion of the Second Part of the*

In fact, this was not true; Parker returned to the fight after Marvell's death in 1678, in his autobiographical *History of his own Time,* which was posthumously published by Parker's son in 1726, translated by Thomas Newlin in 1717, and reissued by the Whig publisher Edmund Curll in 1730 with the invidious title *Bishop Parker's History: or, the Tories Chronicle* and the stated intention of undermining Parker's reputation. At the ideological center of the *History* was Parker's rather well informed sketch of Marvell's career, which included a summary of the *First Anniversary* (still not generally admitted to be Marvell's); a long account of the *Account of the Growth of Popery and Arbitrary Government* (intended to refute it but unwisely giving its version of Restoration history further circulation); and most tellingly, a reprise of Parker's own antitolerationist arguments, which he now claimed to be more than ever justified by the events of the early 1680s. "Against these Encroachments of the King's Enemies," wrote Parker, following a diatribe against John Owen, "I, among others, became a Volontier, tho' too young, to handle Affairs of such great Moment." On the other side, "When . . . they could not find among all their Faction, one Man of Integrity, Learning, or Sobriety, who would undertake to defend their Cause, they sent this *empty Fellow* upon the Stage, who made Jest and Laughing-stock of all Things serious; and at the same time as they praised, they also despised the *merry Andrew.*"[14] It seems evident that Marvell's medicine still burned in the bishop's vitals. Ironically, his autobiography (and within it, his biography of Marvell) probably did more to remind his readers in Georgian England of the importance of Marvell's contributions to political history than to validate Parker's now-obsolete views.

On August 17, 1765, Harvard Library received a copy of the *Rehearsal Transpros'd: the Second Part,* in the 1673 edition, which had been sent to them by Thomas Hollis. On page 195, where Marvell began what I have identified as the heart of his argument—"The Power of the Magistrate does most certainly . . . "—one reader, and Hollis himself must be a prime suspect, had drawn in the margin a huge pointing hand, the only marginal intervention but one. Let us hope that this edition continues the Hollis tradition, of making the important accessible and intelligble.

Rehearsal Transpros'd: In a Letter to a Friend: And by Him Publish'd (London, 1674), and *Sober Reflections, Or, a Solid Confutation of Mr. Andrew Marvel's Works In a Letter Ab Ignoto ad Ignotum* (n.p. 1674).

[14] *Bishop Parker's History: or, the Tories Chronicle* (London, 1730), pp. 213–44, esp. pp. 228, 237.

THE TWO EDITIONS

Both the 1673 and 1674[15] editions announced themselves as "Printed for Nathaniel Ponder at the Peacock in Chancery-Lane" (see fig. 4). There is no sign of any official interference with either.[16] Indeed, Marvell was confident enough to have his name featured on the title page. The first edition of the *Second Part* (*73*) ran to 410 pages in quarto format, and the second (*74*), which was entirely reset in less spacious type and duodecimo format, to 376 pages. The motive for this resetting (without the threat or fact of confiscated forms) was probably less buyer demand (which for the second edition of *RT* had dictated trying to repeat the format, page for page, of the first edition) than a wish to forestall piracy: this time, Ponder would be the one to profit from the cheaper end of the market. Nevertheless, it appears that Marvell himself revised the text with considerable care; a most interesting fact that explains our reversing the decision of D. I. B. Smith to use the first edition as his copy-text.

There seems no question that *74* was intended to be an improved edition, though it was not announced as such. While some new mistakes are introduced, the majority of changes, and there are many, create new paragraphs intelligently, increase punctuation in the interest of clarity, slightly modernize spelling, add a missing marginal reference, delete a tautology, or (and this *is* remarkable) introduce new patterns of ironic emphasis through italicization, a project that must have driven Marvell's printer to distraction. "You" and "your" thus spring from the page in italics to emphasize Parker's egomania. In addition, there is a series of brief insertions. Smith took from these "the impression that Marvell is trying to finish off his opponent and leave no possibility of recourse" and noted that two instances raise "yet again, the tediously iterated charge that Parker was afflicted with venereal disease" (xxxi); but the variety of the revisions is greater than this suggests. Some

[15] All copies of the second edition *RT2* examined are dated 1674, with the exception of British Library C.115.n.27, which is dated 1673 (the title page is otherwise identical). This may genuinely indicate publication very late in 1673; since Ponder had opted for a duodecimo format for the second edition to thwart piracy, he would have been anxious to get it onto the market. However, it is also clear that copies of the first edition were still available at that time (see above, p. 209 n. 5). In view of this, 1674 has been adopted as the conventional (and probably actual) date of publication.

[16] This may not have been for want of trying. On July 15, 1673, Thomas Blount wrote to Wood concerning a rumor of "great searching the Printhouses for Marvels Reply to Parker, but cannot beleeve he wil give it so light a title, as a Whip for the Lambeth Ape, as is reported" (Bongaerts, *Correspondence*, p. 141).

instances seem to aim more at a useful or prudent precision. Thus when Marvell refers to Parker's having his *Reproof* advertised in the *Gazette,* a sign of his protection by the authorities, in *74* he adds the specific issue: "of the 15th of May, 1673" (p. 225). When he claims that "even the Clergy scruple" at the price of the *Reproof,* he restricts it to "the Clergy of his own Province." (p. 226) He changes "the Curate of Ikham" to "his own Curate of Ikham." (p. 230) When reviewing the history of Parker's publications, he changed "though he was resolved to run his head against a wall" to "though he was resolved, even in his first book, to run his head against a wall" (pp. 270–71).

Others seem merely afterthoughts. Attacking Parker's arrogant way of dealing with other writers, he inserted, "Nevertheless you tell Dr. Bathurst, You *had sufficiently convinced him how little the Vertue of Cato, and Honesty of Regulus, were to be valued*" (p. 402). This intervention required a return to Parker's *Censure of the Platonic Philosophy.* Some additions, on the other hand, play up the theatrical metaphors to which both contestants were now captive. To his charge that Parker's bad theology would "enervate the Grace and Work of Gods Spirit" Marvell added that it would "indeed . . . make a meer Play of Faith, that you seem to have nothing of a Divine, but from hence to deserve the name of Du-Foy, whom you in *p.* 11 of your *Reproof* have quoted" (p. 361). And after equating Parker and Buckingham's Bayes as too prolific with their plays, one for every day of the week, he adds "only you too have a seventh Play for Sunday" (p. 383). Reviewing Parker's own account of his early career, Marvell originally wrote, "you were *upon the very point of your departure to London*" and changed it in 1674 to "you were *upon the very point of your departure to* (the Scene of) *London,* and to play Bayes his part upon this present Theater" (p. 401). "This present Theater" is perhaps a reminder that the stakes are higher than personal antagonism, that the Buckingham/Dryden conflict had now acquired new political resonance, especially since Buckingham too had been dismissed from the Privy Council in January 1674. But apart from this nuance, none of Marvell's changes allude to the different circumstances and greater polarization of 1674.

Authorial revision of this minute, not to say picayune, nature is rare enough in the hurried world of seventeenth-century polemic to be itself a subject worthy of study. Smith had recorded substantial revisions as variants in his apparatus, but additions and deletions were not immediately visible in his text, nor was the new pattern of italicization retrievable. Nor had he registered typographically the feature of extensive marginal reference that Marvell had introduced for the *Second Part;* Marvell's own citations were invisibly merged with those of the editor in the endnotes. We have registered additions as between # #, and deletions (some of which were intentional, others printer's errors) as between ⟨ ⟩. Smith found a few press corrections in *73* and one important cancel, whereby a remark that Marvell had originally attributed to Thomas Tomkins during his doctoral examination was reallocated to his examiner. There are no new cancels in *74*.

FIRST EDITION

Title Page

THE/REHEARSALL/TRANSPROS'D://THE SECOND PART.// *Occasioned by Two Letters: The first/ Printed, by a nameless Author,/ Intituled,* A Reproof, *&c./The Second Letter left for me at a/Friends House, Dated* Nov. 3./1673. *Subscribed* J.G. *and/ concluding with these words;* If/thou darest to Print or Publish/any Lie or Libel against Doctor/*Parker,* By the Eternal God I/will cut thy Throat.//Answered by ANDREW MARVEL//*LONDON,/ Printed for* Nathaniel Ponder *at the* Peacock *in*/Chancery Lane *near* Fleet-Street, 1673.

Collation

8° [π]2, A–Z^8, Aa–Cc^8. 210 leaves paginated: [4] 1–65, 56, 67–134, 125, 136–238, 139, 240–319, 292, 321–414 [2] [=420]

Signatures

$(4)

Contents

[π] 1r: blank [π] 1v: between rows of hanging or standing acorns: *REPROOF,* p. 67/IF you have anything to object/against it, do your worst. You/know the Press is open./

Licensed the 1*st.*	*By the Author and /*
of *May,* 1673.	*Licenser of the* Ecclesi-/
	astical Polity.

[π] 2r: T.P.; [π] 2 v: blank, A1r: Half title under a double line: THE/REHEARSAL/TRANSPROS'D.//The Second Part.//Text begins; Cc7v: text ends.//*THE END.*//*ERRATA.* (with list); Cc8: blank.

Copies examined

B1	Bodleian Library: 8°.C.558 Linc.
B2	Bodleian Library: [MS] Ashm. 1585

B3 British Library: 1019.e.13
B4 British Library: G.19515
C1 Cambridge University Library: F.13.42
C2 Cambridge University Library: Keynes T.3.31
C3 Cambridge University Library: Peterborough D.5.14
C4 Cambridge University Library: Williams 509[2]
D1 Dr Williams's Library: 1024.E.6
D2 Dr Williams's Library: 3024.13.29
D3 Dr Williams's Library: 5614.G.10
D4 Durham University Library, Archives and Special Collections: ELCP.C73M
E Emmanuel College Library, Cambridge: S14.4.16
H1 Harvard: EC65.M3685.673r (Gift of Thomas Hollis)
L Lambeth Palace Library: H5136
O Oxford English Faculty Library: XK13.1[Reh] (formerly Rar.D235)
S1 Sion College Collection, Lambeth Palace Library: A69.3/M.36.4
S2 Sterling Library, University of London: [S.L.] I.[Marvell, A.–1672]
W1 Worcester College Library, Oxford: FF.1.10
W2 Wren Library, Trinity College, Cambridge: I.5.69
Y Yale, Beinecke Library: Ij M368.673, 1979.666

In all copies examined (with the possible exception of the eccentric C3, which requires separate investigation elsewhere), E5 (pp. 73–74) is a cancel. Smith mistakenly asserts (xxxiii) that E6 is also a cancel in all copies, but there is no evidence to support this claim, and evidence to the contrary in copies D4 and O, where E3 (pp. 69–70) and E6 (pp. 75–76) visibly form a conjugate pair. In most copies I2 (pp. 131–32) is also a cancel, changing the authorship of a remark from Thomas Tomkins to his examiner: see p. 291 of this edition. The original state can be seen in copies D1, E, S2, and Christ Church, Oxford: W.H.8.43.

SECOND EDITION

Title Page

Within a border of double rules; THE/REHEARSALL/TRANSPROS'D: //The SECOND PART.// *Occasioned by Two Letters: The first*

Print–/ed, by a nameless Author, Intituled A/Reproof, *&c./The Second Letter left for me at a Friends/House, Dated* Nov. 3. 1673. *Subscri–/bed* J.G. *and concluding with these words,*/If thou darest to Print or Publish any/Lie or Libel against Doctor *Parker*, By/the Eternal God I will cut thy Throat.// *Answered by* ANDREW MARVEL//*LONDON,/Printed for* Nathaniel Ponder *at the* Peacock *in*/Chancery-Lane *near* Fleet-Street, 1674.

Collation

12°: [π]², A-P¹², Q⁶. 188 leaves paginated: [4] 1–200, 221, 222, 203–57, 358–62, 263–72. [=376] (pp. 221–2 follow the pagination of the first edition).

Signatures

$ (5) [E3 printed with reversed E, G3 mis-signed G5, −G5, −L5, +P6, −Q4, −Q5].

Contents

[π] 1r: blank; [π] 1v: Between rows of upright and hanging acorns: *REPROOF.* p. 67./IF you have anything to ob-/ject against it, do your/worst. You know the Press is/open./*By the Author and/Licenser of the* Eccle-/siastical Politie./Licensed the 1st./of *May* 1673.; [π]2r: T.P.; [π]2v: blank; A1r: Half-title under a row of hanging acorns: THE/REHEARSAL/TRANSPROS'D.//The Second Part.//Text begins: Q6v: Text ends: between rules: *THE END.*

Copies examined

B5	Bodleian Library: Vet.A3.f.399
B6	British Library: C.115.n.27
B7	British Library: 1607/3406
C5	Cambridge University Library: Ely e.34
F	Folger Library: M883
H2	Harvard, Houghton Library: EC65.M3685.673rb (A)
W3	Worcester College Library, Oxford: L.R.1.21

Smith (xxxiv) noted press corrections in the inner form of M at pp. 279 and 287 (uncorrected state in W3) and to both forms of Q at pp. 362, 368, 369, and 371 (uncorrected state in B5, B7, F). In B6, the title page is dated 1673. In B5, p. 352 is misnumbered 452; in B6, M3 is signed M. H2 has MARVELL on the title page.

THE

REHEARSALL

TRANSPROS'D:

The SECOND PART.

Occasioned by Two Letters: The first Printed, by a nameless Author, Intituled, A Reproof, *&c.*

The Second Letter left for me at a Friends House, Dated Nov. 3. 1673. *Subscribed* J.G. *and concluding with these words,* If thou darest to Print or Publish any Lie or Libel against Doctor *Parker,* By the Eternal God I will cut thy Throat.

Answered by ANDREW MARVEL

LONDON,

Printed for Nathaniel Ponder *at the* Peacock *in* Chancery Lane *near* Fleet-Street, 1674.

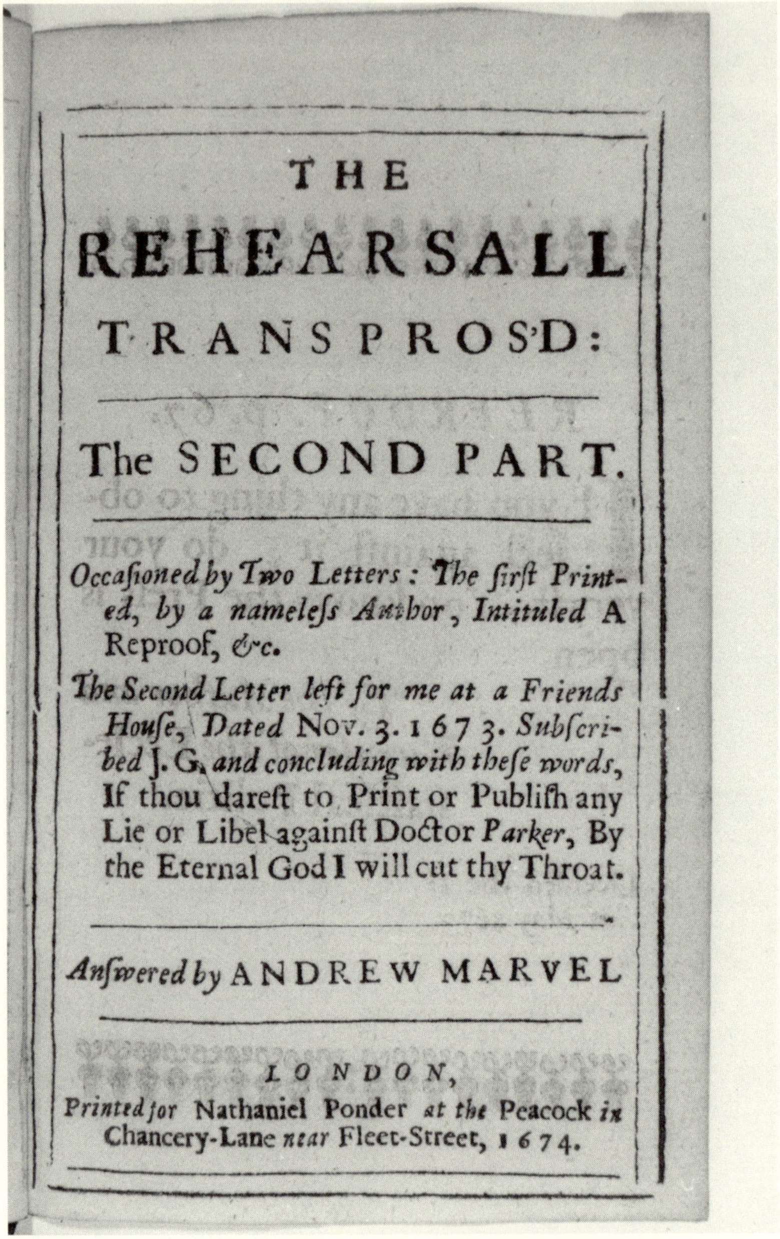

THE

REHEARSALL

TRANSPROS'D:

The SECOND PART.

Occasioned by Two Letters: The first Printed, by a nameless Author, Intituled A Reproof, *&c.*

The Second Letter left for me at a Friends House, Dated Nov. 3. 1673. *Subscribed* J. G. *and concluding with these words,* If thou darest to Print or Publish any Lie or Libel against Doctor *Parker*, By the Eternal God I will cut thy Throat.

Answered by ANDREW MARVEL

LONDON,

Printed for Nathaniel Ponder *at the* Peacock *in* Chancery-Lane *near* Fleet-Street, 1674.

Fig. 4. Title page of the second edition.

THE REHEARSAL TRANSPROS'D. *The Second Part.*

THe Author of the Ecclesiastical Polity (why not Doctor *Sermon?*)[1] doubts, with some reason, whether he has not in that Study *lost his understanding.*[2] To convince himself therefore and others of the contrary, he attempts to shew here at the beginning, that he not only knows as yet what he does, but remembers still the very circumstances of his actions. He tells me: *I had heard from him sooner had he not, immediately after he undertook my Correction, been preven-*[1]*ted by a dull and lazy distemper; but being now*[3] *recruited,*[4] &c. Sooner or later imports not, it comes much to the same account. No Naturalist has determin'd the certain time of a Mountains pregnancy, how long it goes before it be deliver'd: but one has told us what kind of Child it always produces.[5] And as for his dull and lazy Distemper, the Courtesie was no less superfluous to inform me of what most men have been long since fully satisfied upon undeniable Testimony. What is the World concern'd in the Revolutions of his health, or the courses of Physick that he runs through at Spring and Fall? Plutarch indeed gives us the Minutes of Alexander the Great's sickness after his last debauch;[6] and the Dutch Historian Aytzema is so punctual in the late Prince of Oranges malady, as even to Chronicle in Folio[7] what days he did *excernere Dura,* when *Foetida,*[8] and when *Faeces laudabiles.*[9] What then? Must it therefore follow that this Orange Doctor, by having commenc'd in this Princes Train,[10] is grown so considerable, that the *Temper of*

[*The last line of his Preface to the* Rep.]

[*Rep.* p. 1.]

[1] William Sermon (1629–79), physician to Charles II. His *Friend to the Sick* was published in 1673. Copy B4 has the marginal note: Dr. Sermon, a Quack of those days?

[2] *lost . . . understanding: Reproof,* "Preface," A4v.

[3] *now* 74] *new* 73.

[4] *had . . . recruited: Reproof,* p. 1.

[5] Mountain . . . produces: Horace, *Ars Poetica,* 1.139: *Parturient montes nascetur ridiculus mus* (The mountains labor and a ridiculous mouse is born).

[6] Plutarch . . . debauch: see *Lives of the Noble Grecians & Romans,* tr. Thomas North (London, 1657), p. 559.

[7] Aytzema . . . Folio: Lieuwe Van Aitzema (1600–69), Dutch statesman. See his *Notable Revolutions, beeing a True Relation of what hap'ned in the United Provinces in the years MDCL and MCCLI* (London, 1653), pp. 110–11, 114–15 (A, p. 25, #39).

[8] *Foetida* Ed.] *Faetida* 73, *Fatida* 74.

[9] *excernere . . . laudabiles:* "which days he passed hard faeces, when stinking, and when excellent."

[10] Doctor . . . Princes Train: i.e., Parker, who "had the degree of Doct. of Div.

his mind, the *Juncture of his Affairs,*[11] and the *State of his Body* should be transmitted to posterity? That after Ages must [2] read in what Moon his invention was fluent, and in what *Epocha,* costive?[12] That as in his late Preface he enter'd his *closer Importance*[13] upon Record, so in this voluminous Pamphlet his close Stool[14] too should be Register'd? But suppose he were of such Moment, he is too hard put to it, and but ill befriended, that he must do himself that Office. Was there not one true English Man left to help him? Ungrateful World, that when he has *lost his Labour and Understanding* in writing them an *Ecclesiastical Polity,* would not afford him some other Pen for his own Ecclesiastical History. But he is so self-sufficient, and an *At-all*[15] of so many capacities, that he would Excommunicate any Man who should have presumed to intermeddle so far within his Province. Has he been an Author? he is too the Licenser. Has he been a Father? he will stand too for God-father. Is he then to be marryed?[16] he asks his own Banes in Print. And now after he thinks himself cured, and in Wedding and Writing case, he cannot forbear nevertheless but he must be publishing his diseases. Had he Acted Pyramus he would have [3] been Moon-shine too, and the Hole in the Wall.[17] That first *Author of Ecclesiastical Polity,* Nero was of the same temper. He could not be contented with the Roman Empire unless he were too his own *Praecentor*;[18] and he in the same manner, out of meer Charity, when he apprehended Death, lamented only

[*The last line of Pref. to Rep.*]

---

confer'd on him at Cambridge [Nov. 26, 1670], at which time William Prince of Orange was entertained there." See Antony à Wood, *Athenae Oxonienses,* ed. Philip Bliss (Oxford, 1813–20), 4:227.

[11] *Juncture . . . Affairs: Preface to Bramhall,* A2.

[12] costive: constipated.

[13] *closer Importance: Preface to Bramhall,* A2.

[14] close Stool: enclosed chamber pot.

[15] *At-all:* in every way, extremely. Marvell's conversion of the adverb to a proper name echoes the character Sir Positive At-all in Thomas Shadwell's comedy *The Sullen Lovers, or The Impertinents.* Pepys saw the play on May 5, 1668, and learned that Sir Positive represented Sir Robert Howard. In the *Dramatis Personae* he was described as "a foolish Knight, that pretends to understand everything in the world, . . . so foolishly Positive, that he will never be convinced of an Error, though never so gross."

[16] Parker married Rebecca Pheasant in May 1673. The marriage becomes a running joke in *RT2.*

[17] Pyramus . . . Wall: an allusion to three characters in the farcical artisans' play in Shakespeare's *A Midsummer Nights Dream,* 1.ii, 5.i.

[18] *Praecentor:* chorus-leader.

the detriment that Mankind must sustain in losing so considerable a Fidler.[19] When a Man is once possess'd with this Fanatick kind of Spirit, he imagines, if a Shoulder do but itch, that the World has gall'd it with leaning on't so long, and therefore he wisely shrugs to remove the Globe to the other. If he chance but to sneeze, he salutes himself, and courteously prayes that the *Foundations of the Earth* be not shaken. And even so the *Author of the Ecclesiastical Polity,* ever since he crept up to be but the Weather-cock of a Steeple, he trembles and creaks at every puff of Wind that blows him about, as if the *Church of England were falling, and the State totter'd.*[20] And then, after Men are once come to mistake themselves as so necessary, it is no wonder if they impute it for a great Obligation, as oft as they condescend to give the Publick an account of their Privacies. [4] There is not any so undecent Circumstance of their life but they think it worthy to be committed to Paper, and, foul as it is, yet they forthwith send it away to the Printer. And now all Christendom doubtless has taken notice that *the Author of the Ecclesiastical Polity* has lain in of a dull and lazy distemper, and to be sure the Ecclesiasticks of his faculty have deeply Sympathized with his condition. The News will, after the rebound of some Months, reach Constantinople and Agra; and as soon as they hear of his recovery, the Mufti and Mulla[21] will certainly send to congratulate him. But however, he has methinks not dealt so kindly herein with his native Country, as their universal concernment for him might have deserved. For though indeed there must needs be a mighty profit upon the exportation of his Book, and those especially beyond the Line[22] will think it a great advantage to buy the account of his health at any rate with so large a Volume into the bargain; yet he might out of gratitude to our curiosity have advertis'd us at home the cheaper way, by the same Gazette #of the 15*th.* of May, 1673.# in which he cries his Book to make it vendible.[23] [5] Whereas the inserting it thus in so

[19] Nero . . . Fidler: the first of many allusions in *RT2* to Suetonius's *De vita XII Caesarum.* For Marvell's authorship of the 1672 translation of this work, published by John Starkey, see Patterson, "A Restoration Suetonius: A New Marvell Text?" *Modern Language Quarterly* 61 (2000), 463–80. For the Nero reference, see *The History of the Twelve Caesars* (London, 1672), section 49, p. 370.

[20] *Church . . . totter'd: Discourse,* p. 166.

[21] Mufti and Mulla: Muslim priests and theologians.

[22] beyond the Line: below the equator.

[23] Parker's *Reproof* was advertised in the *London Gazette,* no. 781. By adding the date in the second edition of *RT2,* Marvell not only helps to date his answer, but points to Parker's enjoyment of government support.

thick an *Octavo,* is a most palpable project upon Mens affections, and next to imposing his Book upon the Church-wardens of every Parish, and the Chapters of all the Cathedrals. As well as Men love him, yet they desire not that his Sickness should be as chargeable to the Countrey as a Visitation.[24] Nay, even the Clergy #of his own Province# scruple at the Price, and take it ill that as oft as their Arch-deacon comes abroad again in Print, they should be oblig'd in this manner to pay Procurations and Synodals.[25] But of all Men it falls most severely upon the Non-conformists, who having been exhausted with so many other penalties formerly, cannot so well afford to buy their Penance so dear, and take off his Books every year in Commutation.[26] 'Tis true, he has been kind to them, and to such a degree, that he hath done more service to their Cause by writing against it, than all their own Authors that ever writ for them. But that therefore being so contrary to his intention, the Accident diminishes the Courtesie. And if yet for *old acquaintance* sake they could be content to give somewhat for a *Book in some places erroni-*[6]*ous, in some places scarce sense, and of ill Consequence*; they compute that if *the Reproof to the Rehearsal Transpros'd in a Discourse to its Author by the Author of the Ecclesiastical Polity*[27] be of the same Nature, and at the same price, it is however better of the two to buy an English Bible with all its faults. He is return'd to be a *Precious Man* indeed, more precious than ever heretofore at the University; if since he arose to be *the Author of the Ecclesiastical Polity,* a poor Fanatick that has been of his intimacy cannot be inform'd how he does under the prodigal expence of Five Shillings.[28]

[Gregory p. 104. *concerning the English Bible.*]

He cannot sure take it unkindly if I enter into a further consultation of the Nature of his indisposition, and the remedies; seeing he has so voluntarily interessed me therein, and his Readers. For the Officious always spring game to the Curious. The Disease being as he relates so dull and lazy, I should think at first that it might have been a Lethargy, and whereas he imagines himself recruited, that he has only in order to a Cure (as is usual in that case) been cast into a Feaver. For he has forgot himself most

[24] Visitation: a visit by an ecclesiastical authority (especially a bishop or archdeacon) to examine into the state of a diocese.

[25] Procurations and Synodals: provision of or payment for entertainment for a visiting bishop or archdeacon by the parish.

[26] Commutation: substitution of one kind of payment for another.

[27] Polity 74] Policy 73.

[28] Shillings 73] Shilling 74.

extreamly, and [7] his whole discourse, as proceeding from a Man in the confines of two so contrary distempers, partakes all thorow equally of Stupidity and Raving.

But when I reflect further upon the Symptoms, and his description, it seems more probably to be the *Abelteria*,[29] a Greek discomposure, and to which those of his constitution are generally subject. The malignity of this affects the Mind rather than the Body, and therefore lies further beyond the reach of Physick. When once it takes a Man he is desperate, and there is no more possibility of his recovery; nor is that strange, it being the property of those that have it by how much they grow worse to conceive always that they are in a better Condition.

Some indeed will have it, that under those Terms of a dull and lazy distemper he calumniates a more active and stirring Disease, (as the Spleen and the Scurvy do oftentimes bear the blame of another infirmity) and that it is no Grecian malady, but derives its name from a Countrey much nearer.[30] But that *Distemper is so unsuitable to the Civility of his Education,* [8] *and the Gravity of his Profession,* that I question much whether it could be *so Clownish and Licentious* (bold though it be) *to accost* a Personage of his Figure and Character. Yet who knows after that new *Alliance* in the Year 1665. betwixt Nature and Divinity, that amorous season of his *Tentamina Physico-Theologica,* (if he were the Author) whether his Nature may not have given his Divinity the slip, and running its own random have met with some misadventure? For even then he had learnt how Aristotle Worshipped his Wench under show of Sacrificing to a Goddess. He inform'd us so early how Stilpo disputing before the Areopagites, that Minerva could not be a God, because she was a Woman, and therefore a Goddess; Theodorus somewhat smuttily ask'd him, whether he had seen her without her Shift.[31] And this re-party[33] of Theodorus he recommends there for so ingenious, that he ranks it among his Colours, why that Philosopher, who call'd himself God, should not be counted an Atheist; Though I can scarce

[Rep. p. 1]

[*Tent. Phys.* p. 2]

[*Tent. Phys.* p. 14.][32]

[29] *Abelteria:* transliteration of the Greek term for stupidity.

[30] much nearer: one of Marvell's frequent suggestions that Parker contracted the "French pox," syphilis.

[31] Stilpo . . . shift: this passage paraphrases and renders more bawdy Parker's Latin and Greek citation of Cicero's "Life of Stilpo" in *Tusculan Disputations,* book 1.

[32] p. 14 73, correctly] p. 12 74.

[33] re-party: repartee.

discern any more Wit or Theology in it then in his own Argu-[9]ment lately among a Knot of eminent Divines, the Women being present, that the rest of the Clergy-Mens Wives were but Dish-clouts, his own a Goddess; and they had been perfectly quit, had but Stilpo now *cap'd* Theodorus, by telling him that they were all however no more then needed to scowre his Mouth after so slovenly a comparison. In the same Book he demonstrates at large how impossible it was (though Epicurus[34] his Opinion) for Mankind to be produced at first from certain Vesicles or Pimples of the Earth. You would wonder to see how solidly and elaborately, with what *dint* of *Reason* he confutes so dangerous an Heresie, to the great instruction doubtless, and advantage of Sir John Hinton,[35] and Doctor Chamberlain.[36] Then he takes their Office out of their Hands, and proceeds immediately to read a publick Lecture of the Figure and Use of the Vessels of Generation, and more especially those of the Female. Like a forward Chick he pecks through Doctor Harvyes[37] Egg-shell, and tells us that most [10] famous Physician was not so cunning as he should have been in the chief Mystery of the seminal business. At last this blushing Gentleman, this ⟨very⟩ Picture of Modesty, in open terms undertakes to explain the pleasure annex'd to the Act of Procreation, and is so tickled with the imagination (presaging too perhaps, that it might ere long be his fortune to dine with a God, (so he stiles the Archbishop) and bed a Goddess, (so he calls his Mistress) that although he censures Lucretius[38] for speaking so broad, yet he cannot

[*Tent. Phys. from* p. 68. to p. 77. & p. 112.]

[*Tent. Phys. from* p. 99. *to* p. 108.]

[*Tent. Phys.* 106.]

[Repr. 227.]

[*Tent. Phys.* p. 108.]

[34] Epicurus: moral and natural philosopher (341–270 B.C.) who taught that the cosmos was created by accident, that there is no providential god nor life after death, and that the goal of the good life is pleasure.

[35] John Hinton: Sir John Hinton, M.D. (1603–82), royal physician and obstetrician.

[36] Doctor Chamberlain: either Peter Chamberlen, M.D. (d. 1631), famous obstetrician who attended the queens of James I and Charles I; his younger brother of the same name; or Peter the younger's son, also Peter (1601–83), physician to Charles II.

[37] William Harvey, royalist physician (1578–1657), who discovered the circulation of the blood. The work referred to here, however, is his last published work, *Exercitationes de Generatione Animalium* (London, 1651; trans. 1653), in which he described the growth of the chick within the hen's egg.

[38] Lucretius, Roman cosmological poet (c. 98–55 B.C.). Parker had cited *De Rerum*

refrain from using his own Words, *That 'twas so excessively sweet, as to be the solace not only of Mankind, but the Deities.* And all this stir is there made by the present *Author of the Ecclesiastical Polity,* in order forsooth to prove Gods providence, as if that could not be, or were not sufficiently evidenced without his *Gossiping* collections of naked Midwifery. Insomuch that one who understood not beyond his Latine, might justly doubt, whether by the *Tentamina*[39] [11] *Physico-Theologica* he meant indeed the Essays of his Divinity, or the Temptations of his Nature. Neither can it in Reason seem strange if the vigorous and frequent contemplation of such Objects transported him further, and her too as well as other Creatures might (to use his own Phrase) *out of that vehement and unbridled concupiscence rush in furias ignemque* thorow Fire and Water upon a dangerous experiment against the *Pimples of the Earth and* Paracelsus[40] his Limbeck.[41] For he himself in a succeeding Book (said to be his) *the censure of the Platonick Philosophy* confesses; *That if in any respect Virtue and Religion intrench upon the liberty of our Natures, 'tis in the Instances of sensuality, and that when the Man is divided from the Beast, and his Reason separated from the inferiour and bruitish appetites, then arise irregular and unreasonable desires,* &c. So that by his own acknowledgment, it is not impossible but the Man in him may at some time have been obliged to carry the brute[43] *a pick a pack.*[44] Only there is this difference betwixt his Beast and others; that [12] his mind, it seems, is more subject to irregular and unreasonable desires when abstracted within it self, whereas the Reason of other Men suffers most in conjunction with the inferiour and brutish

[#*Et Deus hunc mensa Deaque est dignata cubili.* See this Book, *p.* 262.#]

[*Hominumque Divum voluptas.*]

[*Tent. Phys.* p. 105.]

[*Tent. Phys.* p. 73.]

[*Cens. Plat. phil.* p. 211.][42]

Natura, 1.1 (*Crescebant uteri terrae . . . consimilem lactis*) in order to critique Lucretius's language.

[39] *Tentamina* 73] *Tentamini* 74.

[40] Paracelsus: great German physician and Neoplatonist (c. 1490–1541).

[41] Limbeck: alembic, vessel for distillation.

[42] Actually from Parker's *Account of the Nature and Extent of the Divine Dominion and Goodnesse* (1667), bound with *Censure.*

[43] brute 73] bruit 74.

[44] *a pick a pack:* on piggyback, on his shoulders.

appetites. So that although in the same Book he magnifies those spruce Gentlemen the Platonists, *as being professedly the most generous contemners of Women in the World,* and affirms, *that their amours* (for they were accus'd of Sodomy) *were not kindled by lust and petulancy, but were pure and cleanly enought to become Angels, and separated Souls*; though in the usual pompous explication of his own perfections he glories; *That he hath tasted less of sensual delights than he thinks any one placed in the said circumstances and capacities; for he hath hitherto scarce imploy'd any of his Senses but that of seeing*; notwithstanding all those preventive insinuations, I see no reason to trust him further than I would #his own# ⟨the⟩ Curate of Ikham,[45] with his Maid Mary Parker. But I rather suspect, ⟨that⟩ where he stops short in the career of a Sentence, *that he thinks nothing concerns him so much as those* [13] *designs that aspire to serve his dearest*---the rest was Bawdy. For though he were on the Rode to Canterbury, let any Female but cross his Way, 'tis odds that his Beast will stumble, and throw his Arch-deaconship in the Cart-rut, with his whole Tridentine[46] Portmantle[47] of Polity and Theology. Yet though I speak these things with some certainty, to evidence them to others would require a more difficult scrutiny. For whatsoever 'twas that befell him, he has been so concern'd of late to stop all Avenues, and every Cranny of Intelligence, that were he to pass through the discipline of sweating, there could not have been more strictness about the Doors and ⟨the⟩ Windows. And then his Physicians on the other side are shut up as close by the Obligation of their Faculty, having all of them sworn secrecy to Hippocrates.[48] Neither is it indeed at first sight probable that if he were so obnoxious to them, one of *so sweet a Nature* should so openly declare himself against the Nonconformists. Had he been cured by a Jew, so great a Prince as the *Author of the Ecclesiastical Polity* would surely, either out of his Clemency or his Wisdom, have been gracious to the whole [14] Tribe, and for his Doctors sake have at least conniv'd at their Synagogue. He is not the first that Phys. has

[*Cens. Pl. Phil.* p. 19.]

[*Cens. Pl. Phil.* p. 15.]

[*Cens. Pl. Phil.* p 123.]

[45] Marvell later mentions "Mr. Lee of Ikham," presumably Parker's curate. See pp. 254, 275, 310, 320, 375, 384 below.

[46] Tridentine: derived from the Council of Trent.

[47] Portmantle: portmanteau, suitcase, baggage.

[48] Hippocrates: the most famous physician of antiquity, born c. 450 B.C. Doctors still take the Hippocratic oath, which includes confidentiality.

whisper'd out of his Kingdom: And yet if he thought the matter once secured from discovery, I question much whether any other tie could hold him. For I know none so loose from all the restrictions of Humanity as some within his Girdle, and were there a Court of Faculties for that purpose he could not take out more ample dispensations from common Ingenuity and Gratitude. So that there could not have been more conformity betwixt the Person and the Disease, and an *Implacable Divine*[49] could never be better fitted than with that distemper which his Italian Author can tell him does sometimes make Truce, but never admits a Pacification. But he is I perceive a very *Secret one,*[51] in another sense then formerly, and perhaps did only publish his malady, the better to disguise it: So that I will not out of respect press this point further. If he should by giving so partial an account fail of a Cure, he is the more excusable; for it will have been the first time that his [15] Modesty did him prejudice. Yet this caution for humanity's sake I would leave with him; That he trust not too much to the Asses Milk in his *Hicringills Dispensatory*; for every one knows that if he have no better Specifick,[52] he will ever and anon be troubled with the Reliques.[53]

[*Rehearsal Comedy.* p. 17, 18.]

[*Fa tregua ma non mai pace.*][50]

[*Greg.* p. 119]

But whatever old mischief may possibly lurk in his Body; I am told by one, who pretends to the best intelligence, That this was a new Disease, which spread much through the Nation about last Autumn. I hear not that any dyed of it, and therefore its name is not yet read of in the Bills of Mortality. To be short, as I am certainly inform'd, he was sick of *the Rehearsal Transpros'd.* Then indeed the *Rehearsal Transpros'd* deserv'd a *Reproof,* for exceeding its Commission. I am sorry if that should occasion a distemper, which ⟨I⟩ ordered as Physick; the *Rehearsal Transpros'd* being too only a particular prescription in his case, and not to be applyed to others without special direction. But some curious persons would be licking at it, and most Men finding it not distastful to the Palate, it grew in a short time to be of common use in the Shops. I per-[16]ceive that it wrought a sensible alteration in all that took it; but varying in some for the better, in others for

[49] *Implacable Divine: Reproof,* p. 519.

[50] The phrase, perhaps from Aretino, has not been traced.

[51] *Secret one: Preface,* a1, a3, a5, b6v; *Reproof,* pp. 37, 47.

[52] Specifick: remedy, prescription.

[53] Reliques: recurrent symptoms.

the worse, according to the difference of their Complexions. Some were swoln up to the Throat, some their Heads turn'd round, and others it made their Hearts ake; but all these were but a few in number; most Men found only a little tingling in their Ears, and after its greatest violence, it discharged it self in an innocent fit of uncessant laughter. But the greatest harm it did was to the *Author of the Ecclesiastical Polity,* for whose good it was principally intended: For before he had half taken it, his spirits began to fail him, and it put him past, not only the *common drudgeries*[54] of Preaching and reading Prayers, but those other things too which he stiles *the innocent comforts of Humane life.*[55] So that he laid it by for a considerable time, and was resolv'd to have taken no more of it; finding it so contrary to his Nature. In that interval, his Humours being stir'd, the pre-domineering Choller in a short time diffus'd it self so through his Body Ecclesiastick, that it struck him into a deep Jaundice; and his Soul seemed to have set up a guilt[56] Vehicle of the new [17] Lacker.[57] The great little Animal was on a sudden turn'd so Yellow, and grown withall so unwieldy, that he might have past currant for the Elephant upon a Guinny.[58] For as he had long since foretold, *having been so inconsiderate as to write Books, and fallen so lately under the severe lash of one that knew him not,* it was his concurring misfortune to be now *exposed to the severer commands of those that knew him.* The cause was at present much altered from what in his Preface to Bishop Bramhall, and over and above the importunity of the Bookseller, he was now obliged to write in Canonical obedience. But his Yellow Coif[59] rendred him very unfit to appear in publick, and being troubled thus with the Jaundice, and under a necessity of exercising at the same time all the remainders yet left him of Reason, Wit or Invention, 'tis probable that he found indeed cause to complain of a dull and lazy distemper, and now too late repented, *that he had sold himself into so great a slavery.* However, having driven himself into that Condition, he must now needs go through [18] with his task; and therefore the time too being limited, he hastened to bring himself in plight by

[*Cens. Pl. Phil.* p. 1.]

[*Cens.* Pl. *Phil.* p. 1.]

[54] *common drudgeries: Defence,* "Preface," A6.

[55] *the . . . life:* ibid.

[56] guilt: golden, with a pun on guilty.

[57] Lacker: lacquer, glaze.

[58] Guinny: the golden guinea coin, worth twenty-one shillings.

[59] Coif: ecclesiastical headdress and/or bandage for the head.

such common remedies as were next to hand, writing too all the while by girds and snatches[60] hand over head. His other self Hicringill (who seems very well informed of all his distempers, and of this particularly) had told him that a Louse was good against the Jaundice,[61] and the *Author of the Ecclesiastical Polity*[62] himself had for all Events the *Sacrament of Lousiness* by him of his own preparation: So that this being much [*Rep.* p. 112.] easier to be procured then the Tribute of Fleas[63] was to be collected, there is no doubt to be made, but that he tryed the Vertue of this Medicine. And as the Tartars cracking the same Vermine with their Teeth, are used to wish solemnly, that they had their Enemies at the like advantage,[64] so methinks I see how he snapp'd them e're they got down, and ever #and# anon prayed betwixt the Teeth for the Nonconformists. But he had heard how his old acquaintance Doctor Rabelais, upon examination for his degree, answer'd, That if his Gargantua were sick, he would prescribe him *Pilulas* [19] *Evangelicas, ex centum libris Aloes & Myrrhae.*[65] He computed thence, that in his own case the Dose must be proportionable betwixt the Civil and the Ecclesiastical Giant. And if so, that though all Prisons should be depopulated, though Beggars-bush[66] pillag'd, though the *Phthiriases*[67] of all former persecutors revived, yet the quantity would not be sufficient; but as once the Incense of all Arabia was spent on one Funeral,[68] so the Lice of all the World must be consumed

[60] girds and snatches: sudden movements and grabs.

[61] Louse . . . Jaundice: *Gregory,* p. 93.

[62] *Polity* 74] *Policy* 73.

[63] Tribute of Fleas: cf. *RT,* p. 164 and note 688.

[64] Sebastian Münster, *Cosmographia Universalis* (Basle, 1559), p. 1060 (A, p. 25, #192).

[65] *Pilulas . . . Myrrhae:* evangelical pills, out of a hundred pounds of aloe and myrrh; the anecdote was traced by P. Legouis to *Les Historiettes* of Gedeon Tallemant de Réaux (1619–92): see *Études Anglaises* 6 (1953), 236–38; but this work, though compiled in the late 1650s, was not published until 1834–35. Legouis had to posit either that Marvell met Tallement de Réaux in France in 1656 or that they had a common oral source.

[66] Beggars-bush: a rendezvous for beggars, at a tree on the London road between Huntington and Caxton.

[67] *Phthiriases* 73] *Phthriases* 74; lousiness; a morbid condition of the body in which it is overrun by lice. It afflicted the tyrants Herod and Sylla. [S]

[68] Arabia . . . Funeral: The funeral was that of Poppaea, wife of Nero, whom he killed by kicking her in the stomach when she was pregnant. He then gave her an elaborate funeral (*publicae exsequiae*), in which her body was not burned but mummified with perfumes "according to the custom of foreign kings." See Tacitus, *Annales,* ed. G. Holbrooke (London, 1882), 16:6.21. Holbrooke notes that the incense consumed in these

upon his malady: But what he most considered was, That this must necessarily end in an utter dissolution of the Government of ⟨the⟩ *Phthirophagi,*[69] and that contrary to all good Ecclesiastical Polity, the *Presidents of the sacred Rites*[70] (for the other orders of Men 'twas less matter) should in reference to his cure be deprived of that *lean and slender subsistance* which was yet left them. This would have been a Sacrilege greater, because more universal than to have rifled the Louse out of St. Francis his Bosom.[71] So that upon this *Algebra* and Prospect, he desisted at last from the Lousie Diet, ⟨part out of his good Nature,⟩ part out of his Conscience, and partly out of Impossibility. And had he at the same time betaken himself in good earnest [20] to the *Extractum Apostoli*[72] of Faith, Hope, and Charity, as a *Succedaneum,*[73] (for even his second Rabelais, Doctor Hicringill, renders them equivalent to a Louse) he had been certainly cured both Mind and Body. But some doubt there is that his *Shop-Divines* have not #their# ⟨the⟩ right Composition of that medicine. However he was not now in case or disposition to take it; and the *Rehearsal Transpros'd,* which after many a grimasse he had now at last gulp'd down, had so terribly disorder'd him, that he had quite forgot there was any such remedy in the ancient *Praxis* of Christianity. But this Gentleman of *So tame,* if you will believe him, *and softly an Humour, of so cold a Complexion*: *that he scarce thinks himself capable of hot and passionate impressions*; he that is only offended at *them who will not suffer themselves to be embraced by those whose unbounded embraces would comprehend all,* and *quanquam alias praemitis sim*[74] *indolis,*[75] was altered beyond all imagination. I cannot determine whether I being but a

[*Greg.* 93.]

[*Rep.* p. 21.]

[*Pref. to Ec. Pol.* p. 1.]

[*Cens. Pl. Phil.* p. 25.]

[*Tent. Phys.* p. 109.]

---

ceremonies was more than the annual exportation of Arabia. Was Marvell also remembering *Macbeth,* 5.1.51–52: "All the perfumes of Arabia will not sweeten this little hand"?

[69] *Phthirophagi:* louse-eaters.

[70] Presidents . . . rites: *Preface,* e2.

[71] St. Francis: St. Francis of Assisi (1181–1226), whose concern for the creatures extended to lice and worms.

[72] *Extractum Apostoli:* the Apostolic extract; referring to the fact that Christianity reduced the Mosaic law to the basic elements necessary for salvation.

[73] *Succedaneum:* substitute.

[74] *praemitis sim* Ed., as in Parker] *praemitis sit* 73; *premitis sit* 74.

[75] *quanquam . . . indolis:* "although in other instances I am extremely gentle by nature."

[21] new unlicensed Practitioner, and the *Rehearsal Transpros'd* my first experiment, there might be some errour in the preparation, and it were too *strong of the Mineral,* or whether ⟨indeed⟩ it were #indeed# the extraordinary foulness of his Stomack. But it hath brought up such ulcerous stuff as never was seen; and whereas I intended it only for a *Diaphoretick*[76] to cast him into a breathing sweat, it hath had upon him all the effects of a Vomit, Turnep-tops, Froggs, rotten Eggs, Brass-coppers, Grashoppers, Pins, Mushromes,[77] *&c.* wrapt up together in such balls of Slime and Choller, that they would have burst the Dragon, and in good earnest seem to have something supernatural. Insomuch that he seems not so fit at present for the Arch-deacons Seat as to take his place below in the Church among the *Energumeni.*[78] But it is possible that after so notorious an evacuation, he may do better for the future; and it is more then visible that either his Disease or his Nature cannot hold out much longer. Therefore I shall not grudge from time to time to lend him my best assistance, though I hope that this Iteration will do his business, and carry off all the dregs of his di-[22]stemper. And now from what I have said hitherto, and that I may begin so far an accommodation betwixt us, I shall if he please recant and yield that the *asswaging his Concupiscence, and wreaking his malice, has been the highest Pinacle of his Ecclesiastical In-felicity.*

Having treated him in as short a method as so Chronical a malady would admit, I shall now be inforced to remove some dirt, that I may make my way cleaner to come at him: for otherwise there is no passing, but then I shall quickly have dispatch'd with him. He saith, *I have cowardly and dishonourably accosted him in such a Clownish and licentious a way of Writing as I knew to be unsuitable both to the Civility of his Education, and the Gravity of his Profession.* I thought I had in the close of my former book, and all thorow sufficiently satisfied him of the reasons and way of my proceeding with him: but seeing he hath it seems ⟨so⟩ soon forgot them (as Men willingly do, what it is grievous to remember) I shall now at more leisure refresh his memory, and deduce the order of my thoughts upon that and this occasion.[23]

[*Repr.* P. 1.]

[76] *Diaphoretick:* medicine to promote sweating.

[77] Turnep-tops . . . pins: a not very far-fetched parody of the ingredients for contemporary "cures"; William Sermon's *Friend to the Sick* (pp. 170–73) recommended as treatment for jaundice goat dung, eggshells, frogs, lice, and acorns.

[78] *Energumeni:* those who sat, as sinners, in the middle of the early church, as distinct from the narthex (for catechumens) or sanctuary (for priests).

Those that take upon themselves to be Writers, are moved to it either by Ambition or Charity: imagining that they shall do therein something to make themselves famous, or that they can communicate something that may be delightful and profitable to mankind. But therefore it is either way an envious and dangerous imployment. For, how well soever it be intended, the World will have some pretence to suspect, that the Author hath both too good a conceit of his own sufficiency, and that by undertaking to teach them, he implicitly accuses their ignorance. So that not to Write at all is much the safer course of life: but if a Mans Fate or *Genius* prompt him otherwise, 'tis necessary that he be copious in matter, solid in reason, methodical in the order of his work; and that the subject be well chosen, the season well fix'd, and, to be short, that his whole production be matur'd to see the light by a just course of time, and judicious deliberation. Otherwise, though with some of these conditions he may perhaps attain commendation; yet without them all he cannot deserve pardon. For indeed whosoever he be that comes in Print, whereas [24] he might have sate at home in quiet, does either make a Treat, or send a Challenge to all Readers; in which cases, the first, it concerns him to have no scarcity of Provisions, and in the other to be compleatly Arm'd: for if any thing be amiss on either part, Men are subject to scorn the weakness of the Attaque, or laugh at the meanness of the Entertainment. In conclusion, the *Author of the Ecclesiastical Polity* hath in his own particular very fully stated and comprehended this whole matter. For he saith ⟨here⟩ in his Preface to the Reader, that *if his Book have any effect* (I suppose he means any good effect) *he hath a double reward*; ⟨(that is both the publick and his private satisfaction); *but if it hath none*⟩ (that is impossible) *that then he hath his own reward*; (that is sure to be accounted none of the wisest) and indeed this Reward too is double; for if he fails of his design, he saith, *he must confess that he hath*[79] *lost* ⟨*both*⟩ *his Labour and his Understanding*. This is the common condition to which every Man that will Write a Book must be content with patience to submit.[25]

[*Pref. to Rep.* p. *penult.*]

[*Pref. Rep.* p. *ult.*]

But, among all the differences of writing, he that does publish an Invective, does it at his utmost peril, and 'tis but just that it should be so. For a Mans Credit is of so natural and high concernment to him, that the preserving of it better, was perhaps none of the least inducements at first to

[79] *hath* 74] *has* 73.

enter into the bonds of Society, and Civil Government;[80] as that Government too must at one time or other be dissolved where Mens Reputation cannot be under Security. 'Tis dearer than Life it self, and (to use a thought something perhaps too delicate, yet not altogether unreasonable) if beside the Law[81] of Murther, Men have thought fit, out of respect to humane Nature, That whatsoever else moves to the death of Man should be forfeit to pious uses, why should there not as well be Deodands[82] for Reputation? And this I intend not only of those who publish ignominous falshoods, to whom no Quarter ought to be granted, but even of such partly who by a truth too officious shall procure any Mans infamy. For 'tis better that evil Men should be left in an undisturbed possession of their repute, how unjustly soever they may have acquired it, then [26] that the Exchange and Credit of Mankind should be universally shaken, wherein the best too will suffer and be involved. It is one thing to do that which is justifiable, but another that which is commendable; and I suppose every prudent Writer aims at both: but how can the Author of an Invective, though never so truly founded, expect approbation (unless from such as love to see mischief at other Mens expence) who, in a World all furnished with subjects of praise, instruction and learned inquiry, shall studiously chuse and set himself apart to comment upon the blemishes and imperfections of some particular person? Such men do seldom miss too of *their own reward*; for whereas those that treat of innocent and benign argument are represented by the Muses, they that make it their business to set out others ill-favoredly do pass for Satyres, and themselves are sure to be personated with prick-ears, wrinkled horns, ⟨and⟩ cloven feet.

Yet if for once to write in that stile may be lawful, discreet or necessary, to do it a second time is lyable to greater Censure. Not so much because the After-meath seldom or never equals the first [27] Herbage;[83] (a Caution not unfit however for all Authors) as that by-standers will begin then to suspect, that what they look'd on first as an accident with some divertisement,

[80] the preserving . . . Civil Government: a witty adaptation of Thomas Hobbes's theory of the origins of government in each man's interest in preserving his life.

[81] Law 74] Laws 73.

[82] Deodands: in English law, a possession which, having caused the death of a human being, was forfeited to the Crown to be applied to pious uses. Cf. Marvell, *The Nymph complaining:* "E 'n Beasts must be with justice slain; / Else Men are made their *Deodands*" (ll. 16–17).

[83] After-meath . . . Herbage: the second mowing seldom equals the first.

do's rather proceed from a natural malignity of temper. For few Readers are so ill natur'd but that they are quickly tired with personal and passionate discourses; and when the contest comes to be continued and repeated, if they interess themselves at all, they usually incline #and# think that the justice lies on the weaker side. But whether the last appeal of Writers lie to the Readers, or to a Mans own ultimate Recollection, this Invective way cannot be truly satisfactory either to themselves or others. For it is a praedatory course of life, and indeed but a privateering upon reputation; wherein all that stock of Credit, which an honest Man perhaps hath all his age been toyling for, is in an hour or two's reading plunder'd from him by a Freebooter. So that whatsoever be the success, he that chances in these Contests to be Superiour, can at best (for that ⟨too⟩ is #too# disputable) be accounted of the two ⟨the⟩ less unfortunate. And certainly (as it was usual of old for any Man who had but casually acted in an [28] unlucky rencounter) he that hath had his Pen once in the Reputation of another, ought to withdraw, and disappear for some time till he has undergone and past through all the Ceremonies of Expiation.

But if the Credit of all Men whatsoever be, and ought to be so well guarded both by Nature, Law, and Discretion, the Clergy certainly of all other ought to be kept and preserv'd sacred in their Reputation. For they being Men of the same Spirit with others, and no less subject to Humane Passions, but confined within the regularity of their Function; It is indeed unmanly, whatsoever scuffle others may make among themselves, to vilifie or treat them with those affronts which nothing but the respect of Decency or Conscience could hinder them from resenting as well as others. But (which is more considerable) whoever too shall fix upon them an ill report, do's thereby frustrate the very effect of their Ministry in proportion. For though Baptism is not to be vacated by the contrary intention of him that officiates, yet few Men will or can be perswaded by his Doctrine, whose practice they conceive to be opposite. A [29] conversation differing from Doctrine is Spiritual Non-sence: Neither will Men believe by the Ear, when their Eye informs them otherwise. If an Artificer indeed make his Work fit for Mens wearing, 'tis sufficient: Or if he that Sells have good of the kind, Men inquire no further. No Mans Shooe wrings him the more because of the Heterodoxy,[84] or the tipling of his Shoo-maker. And a Billet[85] burns as well though bought of whatsoever Wood-monger: But the

[84] Heterodoxy 73] Hetrodoxy 74.

[85] Billet: piece of firewood.

Clergy being Men dedicate by their Vocation to teach what is Truth, what Falshood, to deter Men from vice, and lead them unto all virtue; 'tis expected from them, and with good reason, that they should define their opinion by their manners. And therefore Men ought to be chary of aspersing them on either account, but even reflect upon their failings with some reverence. A Clergy-man ought to have treble damages both for his Tithes and his Credit: and it were to be wish'd that with the same ease that their maintenance comes in from the fruits of Mens labour, they had too no less proportion out of the yearly increase of every Mans Reputation: the rest would thrive the better for [30] it. Their virtues are to be celebrated with all incouragement; and, if their vices be not notoriously palpable, let the Eye as it defends its Organ, so conceal the Object by Connivence.[86]

And yet nevertheless, and all that has been said before being granted, it may so chance that to write, and that Satyrically, and that a second time and a third; and this too even against a Clergy-man, may be not only excusable but necessary. That I may spare a tedious recapitulation, I shall prove all the rest upon the strongest instance, that is in the case of a Clergy-man. For it is not impossible that a man by evil arts may have crept into the Church, thorow the Belfry or at the Windows. 'Tis not improbable that having so got in he should foul the Pulpit, and afterwards the Press, with Opinions destructive to Humane Society and the Christian Religion. That he should illustrate so corrupt Doctrines with as ill a Conversation, and adorn the lasciviousness of his life with an equal petulancy of stile and language. In such a concurrence of misdemeanors what is to be done? Why certainly, how pernicious soever this must be in the example and consequence, yet [31] before any private man undertake to obviate it, he ought to expect the judgment of the Diocesan,[87] and the method of the Ecclesiastical Discipline. There was in the ancient times of Christianity a wholsome usage, but now obsolete, which went very far in preventing all these occasions. For whosoever was to receive Ordination, his name was first published to the Congregation in the same way as the Banes of those that enter into Matrimony: and if any could object a sufficient cause against him that was proposed, he was not to be admitted to the Ministry. He that would be a Preacher was to be first himself commented upon by the People, and in the stile of those Ages was said *Praedicari.*[88] But since that circumspection has

[86] Connivence: winking, blinking.

[87] Diocesan: he who is in charge of the diocese, i.e., the bishop.

[88] *Praedicari:* [fit] to be published.

been devolved into the single oversight of the later[89] Bishops, it cannot be otherwise, but some one or other may ⟨sometimes⟩ escape into the Church, who were much fitter to be shut out of Doors. Yet then if our great Pastors should but exercise the Wisdom of common Shepheards, by parting with one to stop the infection of the whole Flock, when his rottenness grew notorious; or if our Clergy would but use the instinct of other Creatures, [32] and chase the blown Deer[90] out of their Heard; such mischiefs might quickly be remedied. But on the contrary it happens not seldom that this necessary duty (which is so great a part of true *Ecclesiastical Polity*) is not only neglected, but that persons so dangerous are rather incouraged by their Superiors, and he that, upon their omission, shall but single out one of them, yet shall be exposed to the general out-cry of the Faculty, and be pursued with Bell, Book, and Candle,[91] as a declared and publick enemy of the Clergy. Whereas they ought to consider that by this way of proceeding, they themselves do render that universal which was but individual, and affix a personal crime upon their whole Order, and for want of separating from one obnoxious, do contribute to the causes of separation, justifying so far that Schism which they condemn. In this Case, and supposing such a failer of justice in those whose Province it is to prevent or punish, I ask again what is to be done? Why certainly the next thing had been to admonish him in particular as a Friend does his Friend, or one Christian another. But he that ⟨hath⟩ once Printed an ill Book, has thereby [33] condenc'd his words on purpose lest they should be carried away by the wind; he has diffused his poyson so publickly, in design that it might be beyond his own recollection; and put himself deliberately past the reach of any private admonition. In this Case it is that I think a Clergy-man is laid open to the Pen of any one that knows how to manage it; and that every person who has either Wit, Learning, or Sobriety, is licensed, if debauch'd to curb him, if erronious to catechize him, and if foul-mouth'd and biting to muzzle him. For they do but abuse themselves who shall any longer consider or reverence such an one as a Clergy-man, who as oft as he undresses degrades himself,[92] and

[89] later 73] latter 74.

[90] blown Deer: to blow is to cause the stomach of an animal to swell dangerously.

[91] Bell . . . Candle: referring to a form of excommunication which closed with the words, "Doe to the book, quench the candle, ring the bell."

[92] degrades himself: to degrade a priest was to formally deprive him of his office, a ceremony which involved removing his vestments. Cf. note 137 below.

would never have come into the Church but to take Sanctuary. Rather, wheresoever men shall find the footing of so wanton a Satyr out of his own bounds, the neighbourhood ought, notwithstanding all his pretended *capering* Divinity, to hunt him thorow the woods with hounds and horn home to his harbour.

How far and whether at all the *Author of the Ecclesiastical Politie* is culpable on these accounts, I must refer to the Readers judgment upon perusal of my first, and [34] this my second book, though I could much rather wish that Men would be at leisure to take the length of him out of his own discourses. But, had he not appear'd so to me, I should never have molested him, adventur'd my self, or interessed the Publick by writing in this manner. For I am too conscious of mine own imperfections to rake into and dilate upon the failings of other men; and though I carry always some ill Nature about me, yet it is I hope no more than is in this world necessary for a Preservative;[93] but as for the Clergy, the memory of mine own extraction,[94] and much more my sense of the Sanctity of their function, ingage me peculiarly to esteem and honour them. Insomuch that for their sakes I bear much respect even to their *poor* wives, of whom I may say (as Bishop Bramhall, comparing the Readers with the Preachers, and who understood both) that *if they come short* of other Women *in point of Efficacy, yet they have the advantage* of other Women *in point of Security.* And though I am not so inamour'd of them as to worship 'em for *Goddesses*; yet I am so far [35] from rejecting them as *Dish-clouts,* that what the *Author of the Ecclesiastical Politie*[95] affirms of the Clergy of the Church of England, *I dare averr* concerning their Wives, *That taking them under all their disadvantages, they are at this very time vastly the furthest off from being justly contemptible (to mention no other Order or Profession of Women) of any Clergymens Wives in the World. The pre-eminence is so evident that it clears the comparison from all possible suspition of being proud or odious.*

[B. *Bramh. Vind.* p. 160. & 161.]

[*Pref. to B.* Bramh 41.]

Being of this temper there could be no great appearance of my being over-forward to come out in Print in such a Stile against one of his cloath, unless

[93] ill Nature . . . Preservative: as, for example, vinegar. This whole passage is exceptional in Marvell, who usually tells us nothing of himself.

[94] mine . . . extraction: a reference to the fact that his father, Andrew Marvell, Sr. (1586–1640), was a clergyman, lecturer in Holy Trinity Church, Hull.

[95] *Author . . . Politie* 74] *Author of Eccles. Politie* 73.

upon some very extraordinary occasion. And such this occasion seemed to me, and so urgent and justifiable that it might absolve me in any Readers opinion. For this sharpness of Stile does indeed for the most part naturally flow from the humour of the Writer; and therefore 'tis observable that few are guilty of it, but either those that write too young, (when it resembles the acidity of juices strain'd from the fruits before they be matured) [36] or else those that write too old (and then 'tis like the sowrness of Liquors, which being near corrupting turn eager).[96] And both these are generally disrellish'd: or if Men do admit them for sawce, yet he must be very thirsty who[97] will take a draught of 'm; whereas the generousest wine drops from the grape naturally, without pressing, and though piquant hath its sweetness. And though I cannot arrogate so much as even the similitude of those good qualities to my Writing, yet I dare say that never was there a more pregnant ripeness in the causes. For having read one, two, three, and now four books of the same Author, and of the same subject, which was no less then that weighty matter of *Ecclesiastical Politie* and all its dependances, I observed first, that there was no name to them, a thing of very ill example. For every one that will treat of so nice and tender argument, ought to affix his name, thereby to make himself responsible to the publick for any damage that may arise by his undertaking. Otherwise, though he has a License in his pocket, or be perhaps himself the Licenser, it is but a more authoriz'd way of libelling; and it looks too like a man [37] that shall lay a train of Gun-powder, and then retire to some obscure place from whence after he has applyed his match, he may solace himself with the mischief: or though it be not so designed, yet the effect is not more probably to stop a flame than to propagate it, and instead of preserving, to subvert and blow up the Government: Whereas if Men were obliged to leave that anonymous and sculking method both of Writing and Licensing, they would certainly grow more careful what opinions they vented, what expressions they used, and we might have miss'd many books that have of late come out by the same authority, contrary to all good manners, and even to the Doctrine of our Church under which they take protection. Had there been no other cause but this, it might have sufficed, and when *Ecclesiastical Politie* march'd *Incognito,* and Theology went on mumming, it was no less allow-

[96] eager: sour, acrid.

[97] who 74] that 73.

[*Pref. to* Ec. Pol. p. 19. *Let the Author of the Friendly Debate be careful how he lays aside his Vizour.*]

able for any one to use the license of Mascarade[98] to[99] show him, and the rest of 'm the consequence of such practice.[38]

But besides this, when I perused his Books, and others of the same patern, I saw that they plainly incroached upon other mens vocations, and that a sort of Divines, among whom he always acted the highest parts, had clann'd together to set up above those of the King and Duke, a new Company of Comedians.[100] Such was their Dramatick and Scenical way of scribling, and they did so teem with new Plays perpetually, that there was no Post nor Pillar so sacred that was exempt, no not even the walls of Pauls[101] it self, much less the Temple-gate,[102] from the pasting up of the Titles. Insomuch that I have seen a Lacquey[103] that could not read, having been sent to take down the Play for the afternoon, has by mistake brought away the Title of a new Book of Theology. Yet if they did it well, they might perhaps in time get some custom; but alas those great men in the Pulpit how ridiculous do they appear on a Stage, and he that has all his life been cramp'd in a Reading pew at what a loss must he be when he comes to [39] tread in whatsoever Theater! They are so unfit to bear a part among any Civil and Judicious Company, that whatsoever place they may hold in the Church, I am confident they must make all their friends to be but received into the *Nursery*.[104] And had not Mr. Killegrew foreseen that they must of course

[*Pref. to* Ecc. Pol. p. 16. *many things are only design'd to set off his reasonings with a Comical humour and pleasantness.*]

[98] Mascarade: an assembly of people wearing masks or disguises.

[99] to 73] to to 74.

[100] King . . . Comedians: at the Restoration there were only two licensed theatrical companies, the King's, run by Thomas Killigrew, and the Duke of York's, run by William Davenant.

[101] Pauls: St. Paul's Cathedral, whose churchyard famously housed bookstalls and printing houses, while the nave of the church itself had been used for transactions, exchange of news, etc.

[102] Temple-gate: In 1672 a gateway designed by Sir Christopher Wren replaced an older structure marking Temple Bar, a historic barrier at the junction of the present Strand and Fleet Street.

[103] Lacquey: servant.

[104] *Nursery:* On July 23, 1663, Killigrew and Davenant were granted a license "to erect a third playhouse, as a nursery for training actors" (*CSPD,* 1663–64, p. 214). [S]

within a little time fall to dirt of themselves, he would ere this to be sure have trounced the *Author of the Ecclesiastical Politie,* for intrenching upon his Patent. But he knew they were below his neglect, and the *Pit* would quickly do their business, and not only hiss but palt[105] them off the Stage. And I, that had sate so long more quiet than all the rest of the Spectators, could not at last restrain my self from using also the liberty of the House, and revenging the expence of my time and money, by representing the *Author of the* Comedy call'd the *Ecclesiastical Politie* in that Farse of mine own, the *Rehearsal Transpros'd.*

Neither yet was this all that deserved reprehension in his Writings, He useth such a Ruffian-like stile, and upon which, to my knowledge, he peculiarly values himself, that any one would suspect he had travell'd and convers'd all his life time [40] either among the Nation of the *Bravo's* and *Filoux,*[106] or else had been educated in the Academy of the Venetian Galleys which he himself was in his second Book so apprehensive of, that he never rested until he had found in his third how to supply them with Slaves out of the Non-conformists. But I perceive since that men of his parts can arrive at those perfections sitting but in their Closets and over-hearing the Water-men which others after long Voyages and observation neither would nor could ever attain to. Then the Arrogance which runs through all his Books is insupportable, boasting proudly of himself, vilifying and censuring others to such a degree, that as I never heard any thing equal, so neither any thing like it but the Mountebanks[107] abroad, who after a deal of Scaffold Pageantry to draw audience, entertain them by decrying all others with a Panegyrick of their own Balsam: There is scarce any sort and rank of men ancient or modern, scarce any particular person, though of the most established and just reputation, but he does if he meet them not hale them into his way to invey [41] against them and trample upon them, nay even such as have but a Book, or two, or three before (perhaps a page, perhaps a line) been happy in his good opinion. And this he does for the most part in the most bitter manner that is possible: I know not whether I may properly call it Satyrical; but let it go so for once, for what he wants in wit he supplies however in good will, and

[*Cen. Plat. Phil.* p. 1.]

[*Ec. Pol.* p. 223.]

[105] palt: pelt.

[106] *Bravo's . . . Filoux:* villains and rogues.

[107] Mountebanks: itinerant quacks, who would advertise their products dramatically from a platform, hence the name.

where the Conceit is deficient, he makes it out always with railing. He scarce ever opens his mouth, but that he may Bite, nor Bites, but that from the *Vesicles* of his Gums he may infuse a Venom. Had he been but innocently dull, he might have been sure no man would have medled with him: But when there was no end of his buttering[108] one Book upon another, and he still writ worse and worse, with less vigour always, but more virulence, that perpetual grating did indeed set my teeth on edge, and I thought that even the most candid Readers would out of their equity not take it amiss, if at last he did by hearing ill himself, lose part of that pleasure which he had so frequently taken in traducing and speaking hitherto ill of others. For no man needs Letters of Mart[109] against [42] one that is an open Pirate of other mens Credit: and I remember within our time one Simons,[110] who rob'd always upon the *Bricolle,*[111] that is to say, never interrupted the Passengers, but still set upon the Thieves[112] themselves, after #that#, like Sir John Falstaff,[113] they were gorged with a booty; and by this way, so ingenious, that it was scarce criminal, he lived secure and unmolested all his days, with the reputation of a Judge rather than an High-way man.

But[114] my greatest incentive was, as I told him in my former Pamphlet, the perniciousness of the whole design of his Books; tending, in my opinion, to the disturbance of all Government, the misrepresenting of the generous and prudent Counsels of His Majesty, and raising a mis-intelligence betwixt Him and His People; besides his calumniating the whole foraign Protestancy, his stirring up of persecution against those at home, and his mangling even of Religion it self and Christianity: And to this purpose he suited befitting principles, and to those a Language as harmonious: seeming to have forgot not only all Scripture rules, but even all Scripture expressions; unless [43] where he either distorts them to his own interpretation, or attempts to make them ridiculous to others; Insomuch, that, of all the

[108] buttering: increasing the stakes every throw or game (slang).

[109] Letters of Mart: licenses to fit out armed vessels or privateers to raid enemy merchant ships.

[110] Simons: This ingenious pirate has not been identified. Copy Y has "Simms" in the margin in pencil.

[111] upon the *Bricolle:* on the rebound; a rare French import, used by Marvell also in *Third Advice to a Painter,* l. 76.

[112] Thieves 73] Thieve, 74.

[113] Sir John Falstaff: Shakespeare's rogue hero in *I Henry IV,* who robbed his friends of their previously stolen booty (act 2, scene 2).

[114] But: 74 introduces a new paragraph here.

Books that ever I read, I must needs say I never saw a Divine guilty of so much ribaldry and prophaneness. Which though it was a matter of such Decency to his undertaking, that I account it to have been even Necessary, yet in the whole I look'd upon it[115] as so uncanonical and impious, that it would bear an higher and more deserved accusation then that of Onias[116] the Son of Simeon the Just, for officiating in a Womans Zone instead of the Priestly girdle, and for the sacred Pectoral wearing his Mistresses Stomacher.[117] I must confess that when all these things centred together upon my imagination, and I saw that none of his Superiors offer'd to interpose against an evil so great in it self, and as to me appear'd so publick in the consequence and mischief, I could hold no longer, and I, though the most unfit of many, assumed upon him the Priviledge (if any such Priviledge there be) of an English *Zelote.*

Otherwise I indeed look'd upon him, whosoever he were, as a person in parts much my Superior, until the Cause as he [44] took and handled it, had depress'd and levell'd his understanding: neither could I ever discover before such an exuberance in mine own, either abilities, which I am sensible how mean, or yet in my inclination, that should tempt me from that modest retiredness to which I had all my life time hitherto been addicted. And truly after I had written, I had so slender an opinion of mine own performance, that I can attribute the acceptance which it found only to his favour, who had so handled the matter, that nothing could have come out at that time against him but must be assured of welcom. And that among the other more weighty causes by reason of his unspeakable arrogance beforementioned: a Vice so generally odious, that to repress it, is no less grateful; so that Lucretius might better have said that to be---*hominum divumque voluptas*;[118] there being scarce any spectacle more pleasing to God and Man

[115] it Ed.] not in 73 or 74.

[116] Onias: Onias IV, a high priest who fled from Jerusalem c. 154 B.C. (Josephus, *Antiquitates,* 12.3.1ff).

[117] Womans . . . Stomacher: The story is told in some detail in Babylonian Talmud Tractate *Menachot* 109b. Onias was tricked by his brother Shimei, who was jealous of his succeeding to the high priesthood, into wearing a gown and a girdle. Then he placed him near the altar, and said to his brother priests, "See what this man promised his beloved [his wife] and has now fulfilled? On the day in which I will assume the office of High Priest I will put on your gown and gird myself with your girdle'." At this his brother priests sought to kill Onias, who fled to Alexandria. We owe this information to the learning and kindness of Jason Rosenblatt.

[118] *hominum . . . voluptas:* see p. 229 above.

then to see the proud humbled. But could I have imagined that my Book could have had either so good or so ill a reception as it diversly met with, I have so much respect to those whom he calls the vulgar, and to whom he bids always Universal contempt [45] and defiance as a rout of Wolves and Tigres, Apes and Baboons, that I should however have bestow'd more pains upon it, I know not whether with better success. Yet the errours of that not being now revocable but by asking pardon of whosoever may have innocently mistaken my Book, and declaring, which I do, that if any thing therein do tend to the disparagement of the Church of England, I wish it unsaid as it was unthought, and do hereby utterly disclaim it; I took it to be part of my gratitude to go no more to Sea, having been sufficiently toss'd for one man upon the billows of applause and obloquy to put me in mind of a Shipwrack, which when the waves go high, may either way happen. And as to the *Author of the Ecclesiastical Polity* himself, whose person I was so far ignorant of, that I could only take aim at his errours, and much less could intend any other of that function, but those few who might assume to themselves his Character; I found nevertheless after the writing of that Book, that natural relenting of mind which most men feel after they have done an harsh, though necessary action. Insomuch, that [46] had it been in my power to have set him right again in mens opinions, as it was in his to #have# set himself wrong, I should have certainly done it. But for that, he and every one else may please to believe as they shall see occasion. But this however must be evident which follows.

[*Cens. Plat. Ph.* p. 34. and 35.]

Whereas I had in that Book, as is in that stile usual, intermixed things apparently fabulous, with others probably true, and that partly out of my uncertainty of the Author, and partly that if he pleas'd he might continue so; it seems however that I chanced to come so near his Form,[119] that it started him, and he thought fit to discover himself. Hereupon, and having understood what he was about, I thought it my duty, if possible, to break off this ruder intercourse for the future, and reduce the matter unto a more manly way of argument. I therefore took care to advertise him that I heard from several hands, That if in the answer intended there were any unjust and personal reflections, it would tend much to the disreputation of himself, and some persons whom he most esteemed, and that there was preparation made to that purpose. Upon this he sent me word, *That* [47] *if any Answer were intended, 'twas more then he was acquainted with, or would*

[119] Form: the nest in which a hare or deer lies low.

concern himself about; and assured me, my private reputation, nor no mans else, should ever be injur'd in publick by his consent.[120] I do not by quoting this answer of his pretend to sue his Word, to which he is no more a Slave than to the Venetian Galleys (such men being at liberty to comment upon their own as well as other Texts at[121] their pleasure). Nevertheless before this, and at that present time as well as ever since, I understood that he had sent out a general *Siquis*[122] thorow his own Province and the other, to make Inquisition concerning me. He voiced my Book all over as a most pernicious Engine bent against the whole body of the Clergy. And upon that pretence he summoned in all that ow'd suit and service to his Court, or the Church of England. The whole *Posse Archidiaconatus*[123] was raised to repress me, and great riding there was, and sending post every way to pick out the ablest Ecclesiastical Droles to prepare an Answer. Some came in daily as Voluntiers, and others were more mercenary. For certainly there was never such an hubbub made about a sorry Book; and, [48] since the day of ⟨St.⟩ Bartholomew,[124] there has not appear'd so great an expectation of an universal Donative.[125] Some one flatter'd himself with being at least a Surrogate;[126] another was so modest as to set up with being but a Paritor;[127] while the most generous hoped only to be graciously smiled upon, and well treated at a ⟨good⟩ Dinner: But the more hungry starvelings generally look'd upon it as an immediate Call to a Benefice, and he that could but write an Answer, whatsoever it were, took it for the most dexterous, cheap, and legal way of Simony.[128] So that, as is usual upon those occasions, there arose no small competition and mutiny among the Pretenders; and, it being

[120] *That . . . consent:* this passage is not in italics in 73.

[121] at 73] at at 74.

[122] *Siquis:* "if anyone . . ."; i.e., a public notice requesting information, usually about a crime.

[123] *Posse Archidiaconatus:* the archdeacon's (i.e., Parker's) police force.

[124] the day of St. Bartholomew: St. Bartholomew's day is August 24. It became notorious first in 1572, when many French Huguenots were massacred; but the reference here is to August 1662, when as a result of the new Act of Uniformity about two thousand nonconforming ministers were expelled from their parishes. Cf. *Third Advice,* ll. 243–44: "O Bartlemew, Saint of their Calender! / What's worse? thy Ejection or thy Massacre?"

[125] Donative: bounty, largesse.

[126] Surrogate: substitute (for an expelled minister).

[127] Paritor: apparitor, a summoning officer in an ecclesiastical court.

[128] Simony: the act, supposedly both illegal and a sin, of purchasing ecclesiastical office.

impossible to satisfie them all, many an one departed with a sad heart and dejected countenance, when their Answers would not pass muster. For it was not every Book that could now be admitted. 'Twas required upon this occasion to gain a License, that there should be some Wit more than ordinary, which most of them could not be at the expense of; some measure of Impudence, which few of them would pretend to; and above all such a proportion of Falsehood as might alone have supply'd the [49] other defects, and made their Books current; but scarce any of them would do it out of good Conscience. For that indeed was now the principal business, and the only argument that, as he had handled it, remain'd to this Cause; and therefore the *Author of the Ecclesiastical Polity* had alter'd his lodgings to a Calumny Office, and kept open chamber for all comers that he might be supplyed himself, or supply others as there was occasion. But, though he had been a little choice at first, the informations came in so slenderly, that he was glad to make use of any thing rather than sit out, and there was at last nothing so slight but it grew material, nothing so false but he resolved it should go for truth, and what wanted in matter he would make out with invention and artifice. So that he and his remaining Camarades[129] seem'd to have set up a Glass-house,[130] the Model of which he had observed from the height of his window in the Neighbourhood, and the Art he had been initiated into ever since from the Manufacture (he will criticize because not Orifacture)[131] of *Soape bubbles,* he improved by degrees to the mystery of making *Glass-drops,*[132] and thence in running [50] leaps mounted by these virtues to be Fellow of the Royal Society, Doctor of Divinity, Parson, Prebend,[133] and Arch-deacon. The Furnace was so hot of it self, that there needed no coals, much less any one to blow them. One burnt the Weed,[134] another calcined the Flint, a third melted down that mixture; but he him-

[129] Camarades 73] Camrades 74.

[130] Glass-house: In 1670 George Villiers, duke of Buckingham, opened a glassworks at Vauxhall, which would have been visible from Lambeth Palace.

[131] Orifacture: making with the mouth, instead of the hand; a comic nonce word. *OED* cites Marvell only.

[132] *Glass-drops:* Parker had mentioned glass drops in *Censure,* p. 44. Their manufacture was the subject of recent experiments by the Royal Society.

[133] Prebend: literally, a stipend paid to a canon of a cathedral or collegiate church; here a short form of prebendary, the stipendiary himself.

[134] Weed: seaweed, burned to make soda ash, or sodium carbonate, for glass manufacture. [S] Marvell's knowledge of the technology may have come from his relationship with Buckingham.

self fashion'd all with his breath, and polished with his stile, till out of a meer jelly of Sand and Ashes, he had furnish'd a whole Cupboard of things so brittle and incoherent, that the least touch would break them again in pieces, so transparent that every man might see thorow them.

In the mean time such care was used, that the License of my Book was recall'd,[135] and the *Rehearsal Transprosed* was dubb'd a Theological Book, only to bring it under the verge of that Jurisdiction, on purpose that it might be prohibited. It hath indeed been usual to degrade a Priest,[136] or scrape a shaven crown[137] to deface his character before he were deliver'd over to secular justice, But this was a strange and contrary method[138] to force a poor Book into Holy Orders, that so it might be subjected to censure and execution by the ordinary. This was an honour which [51] to my knowledge the poor Book neither affected nor deserved; though indeed it might have deserved it as well as the *Preface to Bishop Bramhall,* which occasion'd its Writing, and that 'tis true came out in state under the Title of a Theological Book in the Printed Catalogue[139] of that year, as several others do of the same nature. When he had thus provided that my Book should not speak for it self, and moreover used means, which having proved ineffectual I shall not particularize, to obstruct me from liberty of ever vindicating it for the future; it seem'd to him the most favourable season that ever was or could have been invented to keep his promise, and to publish his Answers to preserve *my private reputation.* For one Answer would not suffice; but therefore, to fit his ware for the purse and fancies of all Chapmen,[140] and to *ingratiate* not only the *Book-sellers* but the Pedlers; he order'd the matter so and digested it into several Volumes, that a man might buy a Groat,[141] Six pence, a Shilling, Eighteen pence, Half a Crown, or Five

[135] License . . . recall'd: see *RT,* Introduction, p. 33.

[136] degrade a Priest: see n. 92 above.

[137] scrape . . . crown: this detail of degradation was included in John Foxe's account of the ritual in *Acts and Monuments.* Marvell used the 1641 edition, 3:998–1000.

[138] a . . . method 73] a . . . ccontrary to method 74.

[139] Printed Catalogue: Between 1668 and 1709 John Starkey and Robert Clavell of the Stationers' Company published catalogues listing (and hence advertising) books published (with their prices) in each of the four legal terms or quarters of the year, Hilary, Easter, Trinity, and Michaelmas. These catalogues were licensed by Sir Roger L'Estrange, and their contents were therefore doubly authorized.

[140] Chapmen: pedlars or hawkers of books and pamphlets.

[141] Groat: worth four pence, this coin ceased to be issued in 1662. Cf. Robert Greene, *A Groatsworth of Witte* (1592).

Shillings-worth[142] of Theological Wit and Verity, as he saw occasion. The rest issued promiscuously; only before that which was to bear his [52] own character, and the other which was to be call'd Hicringills were divulged, he procured that I should be asked by good Authority whether the *Rehearsal Transpros'd* were of my doing, which I under my hand avowed. By this means he had gained however three points, as he imagined. The first, that he should thereby have some months time more to mature two such excellent pieces, which he intended as the Hercules Pillars,[143] and *Ne-plus-ultras*[144] of the Reason, Wit, Sobriety, Good-breeding and Orthodoxy of the Clergy of the Church of England. The next that he should now be able to take such certain aim at me, that he might every shot he made, hit me in the eye, or at least (for I have to do with a very critical adversary) in its Cavity, for I suppose his first arrow must have struck the eye out. And the last doubtless, that having let me know *that he would not concern himself*, and *assured me that my private reputation, nor any mans else should ever by him be injured in publick,* he might, now he[145] understood I was the professed Author, give by these Books so ample testimonial of his own Veracity. Though for some other reasons beside this last I rather con-[53]ceive it might have been more expedient for him not to have been so inquisitive of the Author, or at least after he had learnt it not to have taken that notice of me. Not that I assume to my self any of those lineaments wherewith he describes me; but however after I had owned the *Rehearsal Transpros'd,* whatsoever in either of his Books he reflects upon the Author, he must acknowledge as said by himself of me, and directed to me. At last when all other ⟨plots and⟩ clancular[146] contrivance[147] against me had failed him, these two Books also which he had kept in reserve, were in some hast Printed off; his day of Marriage too drawing fast on, which he intended to calender by a victory, and would perhaps have been deferr'd longer by the Friends, had he not first signaliz'd his prowess. So that now there were no

[142] Groat . . . Five Shillings-worth: Marvell alludes to the prices of his opponents' pamphlets, which were listed in the Term Catalogues: *A Common Place Book,* 6d; *The Transposer Rehears'd,* one shilling; *Gregory Father Greybeard,* 2/6d (i.e., half a crown); no price is listed in the Term Catalogues for the *Reproof to the Rehearsal Transpros'd,* but Marvell has already told us it cost five shillings.

[143] Hercules Pillars: the rocks on either side of the Strait of Gibraltar.

[144] *Ne-plus-ultras:* commands to go no further.

[145] he Ed.] be 73, 74.

[146] clancular: secret, clandestine.

[147] contrivance 74] contrivances 73.

less than half a dozen Answers out against me (not to mention several other Pamphlets wherein the Authors or Book-sellers by drawing in but by head and shoulders one line perhaps concerning the *Rehearsal Transpros'd,* or by naming it hoped to procure vent or better their livelyhood). He had thus got a *Sixiesme du valet*[148] in his hand already, and if he can but show three [54] more of the same Honour to make a *Quatorze,*[149] I am repiqued[150] inevitably and spoyl'd for a Gamster by a Dignitary much Superior to him of Lincoln.[151] There were no less than six *Scaramuccios*[152] together upon the Stage, all of them ⟨of⟩ the same gravity and behaviour, the same tone, the same habit, that it was impossible to discern which was the ⟨true⟩ *Author of the Ecclesiastical Polity.* I believe he imitated the Wisdom of some other Princes, who have sometimes been perswaded by their Servants to disguise several others in the Regal garb, that the enemy might not know in the battel whom to single.[153] But for my part though I know that several Gentlemen, and some of them Divines, are commonly named as the Authors of those Books, yet they are persons for the most part of more Candor, Learning, and good Judgment than that I should suspect the truth of it, or that they could possibly descend to so mean and contrary an undertaking. And even that *Gregory Greybeard,* which alone of all the six pretends to a Father, and to be writ by one that hath not only a Sir-name, but a Christen-name also, it sounds so strangely and unlike the name of any humane creature[154] that rather than so, it [55] seems[155] to me a word of

[148] *Sixiesme du valet:* in the game of picquet, a sequence of six cards of the same suit to the knave (strictly impossible since cards below seven are not included). [S]

[149] *Quatorze:* four aces, queens, knaves, or tens. [S]

[150] repiqued: If a player scores in hand alone thirty or more points before his adversary reckons anything, he gains a *repique* and adds sixty to his score. [S]

[151] See *RT,* p. 182 above, and n. 781; this passage depends for its bite on Parker's frequent gibes in the *Reproof* at Marvell as a gamester who had lost his patrimony playing piquet.

[152] *Scaramuccios:* cowardly boasters, stock figures of Italian farce; but the specific reference is surely to Tiberio Fiorilli (1608–94), whose Italian company was in England from April to September 1673. Cf. John Evelyn, *Diary,* ed. De Beer, 4:12). [S] Marvell mentions Fiorilli's second visit in a letter to Popple of July 24, 1675 (*P&L,* 2:320) and refers to the genre in both *Mr. Smirke* (vol. 2, p. 68) and the *Account* (vol. 2, p. 308).

[153] disguise . . . single: cf. Shakespeare, *I Henry IV,* act 5, scene 3.

[154] creature 73] creatures 74.

[155] it seems 73] it it seems 74.

Cipher, like the *Smectymnuus*[156] formerly of the Presbyterians, and so *Hicringill* to denote the Club of this whole party. But it is more probably by much the issue of the very same *Author of the Ecclesiastical Polity.* If it should be any other, 'tis a thing more remarkable than what is reported of the two learned brothers of St. Marthe,[157] who being Twins, and living to a great age, were so like one another, that they were not to be distinguish'd, but that one wore a Plain-band,[158] and the other a Ruff: nay, their minds had no less similitude; insomuch that, having with-drawn all day to study at any time on the same subject, when they come to compare at night they should find that they had light for the most part upon the same conceptions. For he that shall read the *Reproof to the Rehearsal Transpros'd,* and then this *Hicringill,* will discern so little difference in their expressions, humour and thoughts (such as no man else could have hit upon) as he must necessarily infer and conclude that they are the works of one and the same Artificer, and so much I can prove; that, if any one were not of his penning, yet all of them pass'd under his Inspection, [56] Approbation, or License. So that upon perusal of all those Books that have appeared in so many several shapes against me, first *Rosemary and Bayes,* then the *Common Places,* next the *Transproser Rehears'd,* fourthly *S'too him Bays,* afterwards the *Reproof,* and in fine, *Gregory Gray-beard*; I find plainly that 'tis but the same Ghost that hath haunted me in those differing Dresses and Vehicles.[159] Insomuch that upon consideration of so various an identity, methinks after so many years I begin to understand Doctor Donn's Progress of the Soul, which pass'd through no fewer revolutions, and had hitherto puzzled all its Readers.[160]

[156] *Smectymnuus:* an acronym developed for polemical purposes from the initials of a group of Presbyterian divines in the early 1640s; Stephen Marshall, Edmund Calamy, Thomas Young, Matthew Newcomen, and William Spurstow were challenging the Anglican theory of church government, especially as defended by Bishop Joseph Hall. The acronym is best known today for its use in Milton's antiprelatical *Apology against . . . the Remonstrant against Smectymnuus* (1642).

[157] learned brothers of St. Marthe: Louis (1571–1655) and Gaucher St. Marthe (1571–1649), twins noted through France for learning, piety, and extraordinary likeness. [S, from Pierre Legouis, *Philological Quarterly* 38 (1959), pp. 450–58.]

[158] Plain-band: simple collar, typical of the clergy; Marvell himself wears one in the Nettleton portrait.

[159] Vehicles 73] Vehicle 74.

[160] John Donne's *The Progresse of the Soule,* an enigmatic political allegory from the Elizabethan period of Donne's career. Marvell did not use the first edition of 1633, but 1635 (A, p. 40, #320) or one of the editions derived from it, all of which register, as 1633

For—*This Great Soul, which here amongst us now*
Does dwell, and—*to which Luther and Mahomet were*
Prisons of flesh, this Soul which oft did tear
And mend the wracks of th'Empire and late Rome,
[St. 7.] *And liv'd when every great Change did come.* [57]

[*St.* 9.] Did nevertheless fix it self at first in so mean condition as is scarce credible, in a chast and innocent Apple. But that being soon pluck'd, it betook it self into a Mandrake, and

To show that in Loves business he should still
A dealer be and be us'd well or ill,
[St. 15.] *His Apples kindle, his Leaves force of Conception kill.*

('Tis pity that his Curate of Ickham was not acquainted with its virtues.) From this it took its flight into a Sparrow, and lived a chirping life, as is there described,

Already this hot Cock, in bush and tree,
[St. 20.] *In Field and Tent, o'reflutters its next Hen,* &c.

From thence it dropp'd, I know not how, into a little Fish:
[*St.* 23.] after that, into another little Fish: and there learnt the Art
[*St.* 25.] of Tipling, which it practis'd [58] for some time in that
[*St.* 31.] moderate proportion. But next, in its third swimming
[*St.* 34.] leap, it pitch'd into a Whale, and grew up to be the great
Leviathan—*Now drinks he up Seas,*—

—*and ever as he went,*
[St. 32.] *He spouted rivers up*—

Immediately after this, the Soul by some misadventure dwindled into a Mouse, but a very busie Mouse, and of great design; So that

—*being late taught that great things might by less*
[*St.* 38.] *Be slain, to gallant mischief it doth it self address*:

and pick'd out no less opposite than an Elephant to buckle with,

[St. 39.] *Who foe to none, suspects no enemies,* &c.

---

does not, the reading "kindle" at l. 150. Smith thought Marvell was using a manuscript, because there are so many variants from the printed texts; but no more than was usual with Marvell's casual attitude to transcription.

and having crept up thorow his Trunk, was gnawing his Brain-strings asunder, but suddenly was crush'd under the ruines [59] of so great an adversary. In process of time it enter'd into a Wolf, and infested Abel's flock;

[*St.* 41.] *Abel as white and mild as his sheep were,*
Who, in that Trade of Church and Kingdom's there
was the first type—

[*St.* 42.] but being hindred by a vigilant Bitch, the Wolf corrupted her to his purpose; yet at last was taken in a trap and kill'd.
[*St.* 43.] But straight it enter'd into the young Lycisca,[161] that was new knotted, and the whelp[162] growing up was imploy'd by Abel in keeping the same Flock, but the Mungrel was not to be trusted, for partaking of both natures,

He as his Damme from Sheep drove Wolves away,
And as his Sire he made them his own prey.
[St. 45.] *Five years he liv'd, and cozened with his Trade*; [60]

and then coming at last to be discovered,

From Dogs a Wolf, from Wolves a Dog he[163] *fled:*
And like a Spy, to both sides false, he[164] *perished.*

The Soul being then at a loss, got admittance into an Ape, which being very facetious and full of Gambolls, grew into great favour with Madam Siphatecia:[165] but for some ugly tricks, and making too bold with his Mistresses *Apron,* he was with a great stone knock'd dead by Thelemite her Brother. After this Soul had passed thorow so many Brutes, and been hunted from Post to Pillar, its last receptacle was in the humane nature, and it housed it self in a female Conception, which after it came to years of consent, was Married to Cain by the name of Themech.[166] This was the sum of

[161] Lycisca: a dog engendered of a wolf and a bitch; the name of the bitch in Virgil, *Eclogues,* 3.18, and Ovid, *Metamorphoses,* 3.220. The word does not appear in Donne's poem.

[162] and the whelp 73] and by the whelp 74; *by* is redundant, caught from the line above.

[163] *he* 73] *h'* 74; printer misread an uninked *e.*

[164] *he* 73] *he he* 74.

[165] Siphatecia 73] Siphatetia 74.

[166] Siphatecia . . . Thelemite . . . Themech: embroideries on the biblical narrative,

that witty fable of Doctor Donne's, which if it do not perfectly suit with all the transmigrations of mine Answerer, the *Author of the Ecclesiastical Politie,* nor equal the Progress of so great a Prince, yet whoever will be so curious as himself to read that Poem, may follow the parallel much [61] further than I have done, lest I should be tedious to the Reader by too long and exact a similitude.[167] But if it do not quadrate[168] here, the resemblance will perhaps be more visible upon the examination of what remains to be consider'd next to the *Gravity of his Profession,* that is the *Civility of his Education,*[169] which he charges me by my former Book to have discomposed. For it is the interest of the Publick, especially he appealing to it upon this particular, that it should remain upon Record how Syllogistical a life his hath been to the Stile and Principles that he has managed and prosecuted.

Whoever shall go back to trace his Original, will quickly be at a stand, and[170] find themselves so soon involved in the Fabulous Age, that they will run astray and be benighted in his History before noon. They will find his Saturn to have reigned much later than William the Conquerour; or if, like a true born Arcadian, he derive himself from before the Moon,[171] it must be understood concerning the last Change. I cannot yet learn, though he hath imployed me long about it, who was his Grand-father: But, as modern as he must have been, 'tis the certainer Heraldry to [62] extract him from a *Vesicle of the Earth,* and let him go for the Grand son of a *Pimple.*[172] For no Prince how great soever begets his Predecessors, and the noblest Rivers are not Navigable to the Fountain. Even the parentage of the Nile is yet in obscurity, and 'tis a dispute among Authors whether *Snow* be not the head of his Pedigree.[173] I read indeed as long ago as in the Reign of Edward the

---

made sometime between the closing of the Old Testament narrative and the dispersal of the Jews under Titus and Vespasian. See H. J. Grierson, ed., *The Poems of John Donne,* 2 vols, (Oxford, 1912), 2:223–24.

[167] too long . . . a similitude: this late apology scarcely explains this astonishing digression into Donne's poem, for length unequaled in Marvell's canon.

[168] quadrate: square; i.e., match up.

[169] *Gravity . . . Education:* see *Reproof,* p. 1.

[170] and 74] & 73.

[171] Arcadian . . . Moon: Statius, *Thebaid,* 4:275. [S]

[172] *Vesicle . . . Pimple:* Marvell's running joke derived from the *Tentamina;* see p. 228 above.

[173] Parentage . . . Pedigree: Fresh discussion of this issue had been stirred up by Sir Peter Wyche's *Short Relation of the River Nile* (1669), including accounts of the source of the Blue Nile by Portuguese missionaries. In antiquity Ptolemy had argued that the

4th. concerning one Henry Parker, a Carmelite Friar, who having preach'd against the secular grandeur and pomp of the Clergy in those times, was forced to make a publick Recantation at Pauls-Cross.[174] But this is too obsolete: and though otherwise the Analogy might easily be propagated, yet I suppose the honest Monk kept to his vow of Continence: and besides, should the *Author of the Ecclesiastical Politie* descend from that Line, it would make too great a Solecism in his Scutcheon.[175] There was also in the latter end of Queen Elizabeth, and beginning of King James, one Robert Parker,[176] *the Author* of another kind of *Ecclesiastical Polity,* a Learned, but severe Non-conformist, who writ also the book *de Cruce,* for which he was forced to cross the Seas. [63] But neither can I find him to come within the proportion of time or Scale of his Genealogy. Therefore to come nearer, I find in the Reign of the late King Charles one Humphrey Parker, Yeoman, who together with Mr. Chancey, for opposing the Rails about the Communion Table at Ware, was sentenced to make a solemn submission and acknowledgment of his fault, as he did accordingly. There are several Arguments that might incline me to think the *Author of the Ecclesiastical Polity* is com'd of his Succession, and one particularly, because in the Record I read[177] that this Humphrey took a Journey upon this occasion into Northampton-shire, the seat of the Answerers Family. But that which seems to come nearest home to him and the Chronology of his Grandfather, is in the year 1640. in a Petition from the City of London and several

---

ultimate source was the melting snow on the Mountains of the Moon. [S]

[174] Henry Parker: a Carmelite friar of Doncaster, d. 1470. In 1464 he gave a reformist sermon at Paul's Cross, and after a lengthy imprisonment was forced to deliver a palinode at the same spot. The origin of this story is John Leland, ed. John Bale, *Catalogus Scriptorum Illustrium maioris Brytanniae* (Basle, 1557), p. 609 (A, p. 26, #231, 1559 ed.); but Marvell could also have read it in John Pits, *Relationes Historicae de Illustribus Britanniae Scriptoribus* (Paris, 1619), p. 660 (A, p. 30, #169 and p. 36, #64).

[175] Solecism . . . Scutcheon: error in his heraldry; presumably because Henry Parker, like the several other possible ancestors Marvell unearthed, had such opposite principles from Samuel's.

[176] Robert Parker: Puritan divine (1564–1614); See *RT,* p. 169 and n. 707 above.

[177] Record . . . I read: Charles Chauncey, clerk, late vicar of Ware County Hertford, and Humphrey Packer [*sic*] were brought before the High Commission on November 26, 1635, for opposing a communion rail at Ware. *CSPD,* Feb. 4, 1636. [S] Marvell's source, however, was John Rushworth, *Collections,* part II (1680), p. 316. Since both Rushworth and Marvell were dead when this part of the *Collections* was published, Marvell must have consulted it in manuscript in his old friend's house.

Counties to the then Parliament;[178] complaining among other things of Martin Parkers Ballads, in disgrace of Religion, to the increase of all vice, and withdrawing of People from reading, studying and hearing the Word of God and other good Books.[179] 'Tis not at all unlikely that this, as an hereditary provocation, hath stuck upon him ever [64] since, and that he swore at the Altar when he was but nine years old, to be avenged for this affront to his lineage. We see often that the signature of the Grand-father revives upon the child, and, as some Rivers diving for a while under ground, makes a Bridge of the Parents to spring up again at that interval. Hence doubtless hath proceeded all his peek[180] against the Non-conformists; hence that unquenchable *Nemesis*[181] against the City; hence it is that he hath taken upon him to defend in gross at this time the whole mass of enormities, right or wrong, then complained of in that Petition: all this mischief for a Ballad-makers sake of the kindred. The Duke of Muscovy indeed declared War against Poland, because he and his Nation had been vilified by a Polish Poet:[182] but the *Author of the Ecclesiastical Polity* would it seems disturb the peace of Christendom for the good old cause of a superannuated Chanter of Saffron-hill[183] and Pye-corner.[184] But though indeed

[178] Petition . . . Parliament: *The Humble Petition of Many of His Majesty's Subjects in and about the City of London, and several Counties of the Kingdom,* presented to the Long Parliament December 11, 1640. Marvell's source was again Rushworth, *Collections,* part III (1691), 1:93–96; and see n. 177 above.

[179] Martin Parker . . . Books: Rushworth, *Collections,* part III (1691), 1:94. Martin Parker, the ballad writer (1600–56), supported the monarchy and the Anglican bishops.

[180] peek: pique, ill temper.

[181] *Nemesis:* the Greek goddess of retribution; hence, retributive justice.

[182] Duke . . . Poet: see *Mercurius Politicus,* no. 204, May 4–11, 1654, p. 3476: "The Duke of Muskovy wrote Letters of late to the Q. of Sweden wherein he signified the cause of his Warr with the Pole. Two reasons he mentioned; one because a certain Poland Poet writing a Narration of former Warrs, wherein the Pole had the better, said they had beaten the Muscovite, with adding his Title . . ." [S]. Marvell, who would have been reading *Mercurius Politicus* with attention in 1654, and remembered the anecdote because of its featuring a poet, could also have found this in Anglesey's library (A, p. 74, bundle 158); he also recalled the story in the *Account* (vol. 2, p. 260).

[183] Saffron-hill: a street in the borough of Holborn running between Clerkenwell Road and Charterhouse Street, formerly a notorious area. [S]

[184] Pye-corner: see John Stow, *Survey of London* (1618), p. 706: "A place so called of such a signe, sometimes a faire Inne for receipte of Travellers, but now divided into tenements"; this is the first of several points in Farington Ward, including Smithfield and Bridewell, by which Marvell connects Parker to unsavory neighborhoods.

he doth not write his Books in the Smithfield Meetre,[185] yet they are all Blank Ballad,[186] and the subject and consequence *to the disgrace of Religion, the increase of all Vice, and with-drawing*[187] *people from reading, studying, and hearing the* [65] *Word of God, and other good Books* is exactly the same.[188] So that he may when he will put in for Letters of Administration in the Prerogative Court,[189] and enter his Claim too with the Heralds: for every one will yield him to be the next of kin to that Author; or let him but produce his own Writings, 'tis Evidence sufficient. If it should prove otherwise, the fault is in his own obscurity, that hath left all the Neighbourhood and me in the dark; and let him make what shift he will to procure himself a Grand-father, for I have taken pains enough, I am sure, to help him to one.

But however for that matter, let the worst come[190] to the worst, he had a Mother undeniably and probably a Father: Otherwise he would be shrowdly disappointed, and in a worse case then Prince Prettyman lamenting.

What Oracle this Secret can evince,
Sometimes a Fishers Son, sometimes a Prince:
[*Rehearsal Comedy* p. 27.] *It is a secret great, as is the world,*
In which I like the Soul am toss'd and hurl'd: [66]

And he might with good reason exclaim more pathetically—*Bring in my Father, why d'ye keep him from me? Although a Fisherman, he is my Father.*

Was ever Son yet brought to this distress,
To be for being a Son made fatherless?
[*Rehearsal Com.* p. 26.] *Oh you just Heavens! rob me not of a Father:*
The being of a Son take from me rather.

His Mother is said to have been an honest Yeoman's Daughter, and to have been his Fathers Servant, with whom she lived with good reputation, and

185 Smithfield Meetre: possibly refers to popular martyrological verse celebrating the Smithfield burnings of Protestants in Mary's reign. Cf. Thomas Brice (d. 1570), *A Compendium Register in Metre, containing the names and pacient suffryngs* (1559): "Peruse with pacience, I thee praye, / My simple style, and metre base."

186 Blank Ballad: we cannot find this term, obviously contemptuous, in use. Marvell may be inventing it on the analogy with blank verse, i.e., popular ballads that cannot manage rhyme.

187 *with-drawing* 73] *wish-drawing* 74.

188 is . . . same Ed.] 73, 74 italicize.

189 Prerogative Court: the court of an archbishop, for the probate of wills.

190 worst come 73] worst to come 74.

so ever since her marriage; except what disgrace may have reflected from her issue, which being her grief and misfortune ought not to be her scandal. But though he came of a good Mother, he had a very ill Sire.[191] He was a man bred toward the Law, and betook himself, as his best practice, to be a Sub-Committee man,[192] or, as the stile ran, one of the Assistant Committee in Northampton-shire. In the rapine of that employment, and what he got by picking the teeth of his Masters he sustained himself, till he had raked together some little [67] estate. And then being a man for the purpose, and that had begun his fortune out of the sequestration[193] of the Estates of the Kings party, he to perfect it the more, proceeded to take away their Lives; not in the hot and Military way (which diminishes always the offence) but in the cooler blood and sedentary execution of an High Court of Justice. Accordingly he was preferred to be one of that number that gave Sentence against the three Lords, Capel, Holland, and Hamilton, who were beheaded.[194] By this Learning in the Law he became worthy of the degree of a Serjeant, and sometimes to go[195] the Circuit till for misdemeanor he was Petition'd against.[196] But for a taste of his abilities, and the more to re-ingratiate himself, he printed in the year 1650. a very remarkable Book called *The Government of the People of England, precedent and present*

[191] ill Sire: John Parker, called to the bar in 1617, became a Welsh judge in 1647, and in 1648 was made a sergeant by parliament. He became a baron of the exchequer and M.P. for Rochester in 1654 and 1656. He lost his judgeship at the Restoration. Marvell's hostile minibiography contains details not in the old *DNB*.

[192] Sub-Committee man: Government by committee was typical of the republican and Cromwellian era, and hence the term became stigmatic. Cf. Sir Robert Howard's satirical play *The Committee* (1662).

[193] sequestration: temporary confiscation; a device used by the Long Parliament against "delinquents," those that had taken arms on the king's side. Cf. Marvell, *To . . . Lovelace,* ll. 29–30: "Some [say] you under sequestration are, / Because you write when going to the Warre."

[194] Capel . . . Hamilton: Arthur, lord Capel (b. 1610), joined with Henry Rich, earl of Holland (b. 1590), and James, duke of Hamilton and earl of Cambridge (b. 1606), led the renewed attack on the parliamentary forces that began the second civil war in 1648. They were executed for treason on March 9, 1649.

[195] to go 73] go to 74.

[196] Petition'd against: In 1648, "John Parker and others" occupied Forthampton, Gloucester, the home of the earl of Middlesex, who was currently under restraint. On June 20, 1648, the earl petitioned the House of Lords, and Parker and his companions were ordered before the House on a charge of breach of privilege and contempt. See *JHL,* 10:338. [S]

the same. Ad subscribentes confirmandum, Dubitantes informandum, Opponentes convincendum;[197] and underneath, *Multa videntur quae non sunt, Multa sunt quae non videntur.*[198] Under that ingraven, two Hands joyn'd with the Motto, *Ut uniamur,*[199] and beneath a Sheaf of Arrows with this Device, *Vis unita fortior*;[200] and to conclude, *Concordia parvae* [68] *res crescunt Discordia dilabuntur.*[201] A most Hieroglyphical Title, and sufficient to have supplyed the Mantlings[202] and Atchievments of the Family! By these Parents he was sent to Oxford, with intention to breed him up to the Ministry. There in a short time he enter'd himself into the Company of some young Students who were used to Fast and Pray weekly together, but for their refection fed sometimes on a Broth, from whence they were commonly call'd *Grewellers*: only it was observed that he was wont still to put more *Graves*[203] then all the rest in his Porrige. And after that he pick'd acquaintance not only with the Brotherhood at Wadham Colledge, but with the *Sisterhood* too at another old *Elsibeths,* one Elizabeth Hampton's,[204] a plain devout Woman, where he train'd himself up in hearing their Sermons and Prayers, receiving also the Sacrament in the House, till he had gain'd such proficience that he too began to exercise in that Meeting, and was esteem'd one of the *preciousest* young men in the University. But when thus, after several years approbation, he was even ready to have taken the charge not of an *admiring drove*[205] or *heard,* as he now calls them, but of a Flock upon him, by great misfortune, [69] the King came in by the miraculous providence of God influencing the distractions of some, the good affections of others, and the weariness of all towards that happy Restauration,

[197] *Ad . . . convincendum:* to confirm subscribers [to the Covenant], inform doubters, persuade opponents.

[198] *Multa . . . videntur:* Many things appear to be what they are not, many things are what they do not appear to be.

[199] *Ut uniamur:* let us be united.

[200] *Vis . . . fortior:* a force united is stronger.

[201] *Concordia . . . dilabuntur:* Small things grow by Concord and are scattered by Discord. Marvell quotes the pompous title page of John Parker's book in full.

[202] Mantlings: heraldic: drapery or scrollwork depicted behind an achievement.

[203] *Graves:* greaves, pork crackling.

[204] Elizabeth Hampton: With William Assheton (who also turned against his Nonconformist beginnings), Parker attended "the religious meetings in the house of Besse Hampton, an old decrepit laundress living in Halywell in the north suburb of Oxon." Wood, *Athenae Oxonienses,* 4:1820. [S]

[205] *admiring drove: Preface,* a3v, and *RT,* p. 136.

after so many sufferings to his Regal Crown and Dignity. Nevertheless, he broke not off yet from his former habitudes, and though it were now too late to obviate this inconvenience, yet he persisted, as far as in him was, that is by praying, caballing and discoursing to obstruct the restoring of the Episcopal Government, Revenues, and Authority. Insomuch that finding himself discountenanced on those accounts by the then Warden of Wadham,[206] he shifted Colledges to Trinity, and, when there, went away without his Degree, scrupling forsooth the subscription[207] then required. From thence he came to London, where he spent a considerable time in creeping into all Corners and Companies, Horoscoping up and down concerning the duration of the Government: not considering any thing as best, but as most lasting and most profitable. And after having many times cast a figure,[208] he at last satisfied himself that the Episcopal Government would indure as long as this King lived, and from [70] thence forward cast about how to be admitted into the Church of England, and find the High-way to her preferments. In order to this he daily inlarged, not only his Conversation but his Conscience, and was made free of some of the Town-vices: imagining like Muleasses King of Tunes (for I take witness that on all occasions I treat him rather above his quality then otherwise) that by hiding himself among the Onyons, he should escape being traced by his Perfumes.[209] Ignorant and mistaken man, that thought it necessary to part with any virtue to get a Living; or that the Church of England did not require and incourage more sobriety than he could ever be guilty of: whereas it hath always been fruitful of men, who, together with obedience to that Discipline, have lived to the envy of the Non-conformists in their conversation, and without such could never either have been preserved so long or after so long a dissipation have ever recover'd. But neither was this yet in his opinion sufficient: and therefore he resolved to try a shorter path which some few men have trode not unsuccessfully: that is, to print a Book, if that

[206] Warden of Wadham: Dr. Walter Blandford (1619–75), bishop of Worcester, warden of Wadham College, Oxford, 1659–65. [S]

[207] subscription: to take a degree required making a signed declaration of one's acceptance of the Thirty-Nine Articles.

[208] cast a figure: made an astrological prediction.

[209] Muleasses . . . Perfumes: Muleasses (*fl.* 1530) was ousted from the throne of Tunis by his son. Flying from defeat, he was "preserved by an old woman, who . . . hid him . . . under a great heap of garlicke," but was nevertheless taken captive, "nothing more bewraying him than his odoriferous perfumes." See R. Knolles, *The General History of the Turkes* (London, 1638), pp. 747–48. [S]

would not do, a second, if not that, [71] a third of an higher extraction and so forward, to give experiment against their former party of a keen stile and a Ductile[210] judgment. His first Proof-piece was in the year 1665. the *Tentamina Physico theologica*: a tedious transcript of his Common place Book, wherein there is very little of his own, but the arrogance and the unparallel'd censoriousness that he exercises over all other Writers, beside his undutiful inveying even then[211] against the *Vesicles of the Earth* for meer bubbles, as he did shortly after against his Fathers Memory, and in his Mothers presence before several witnesses, for a couple of *whining Phanaticks.* However he accounted it a safe Book, on all sides, it being of so trite and confessed an argument, that few judicious men would read it to examine the errours: and in so rough and scabbed a Latine, that a man must have long nails, and those sharper than ordinary, to distinguish betwixt the Skin and the Disease, the Faults and the Grammar. To omit his usual volume and circumference of periods; which though he takes always to be his chiefest strength, yet indeed, like too great a Line, weakens the defense, and requires too many men [72] to make it good. But the cause being against Atheism, he was secure that none would attaque him. For whether there be any Atheists is some controversie, and he is Compurgator[212] for most of 'm: or if there be such, yet they know the Bastions are all undermined and they should be blown up as soon as enter'd. But let him shew me any Atheist that he hath reduced by his Book, unless he may pretend to have converted some (as in the old Florentine Wars)[213] by meer tyring them out, and perfect weariness. In this Treatise however it was difficult for him to have hedged in the Nonconformists: only here and there he sprinkles a glittering ore, to give hopes of a vein underneath of such metal as might by a skilful hand be founded into any figure; and having shown as he thought sufficiently that he believ'd there was a God, he imagin'd that thenceforward, write what, and against whom he would, it might pass as indisputably; that all would be current which past his Touch-stone;[214] that as his Predecessor Midas turned into Gold whatsoever he touched,[215] so every thing by his handling should be

210 Ductile: flexible.

211 then 73] then then 74.

212 Compurgator: a witness to character, who swore along with the person accused.

213 Florentine Wars: probably the endemic feuds between the Guelfs and the Ghibellines in the early fourteenth century.

214 Touch-stone: a test or criterion of value.

215 Midas . . . touched: Midas, the legendary king of Phrygia. In return for the safe

transmuted to Orthodoxy. When he had Cook'd up these musty Col-[73]lections, he makes his first invitation to his *old Acquaintance* my Lord Arch-bishop of Canterbury,[216] who had never seen before nor heard of him. But I must confess he furbishes up his Grace in so glorious an Epistle, that, had not my Lord been long since proof against the most Spiritual Flattery, the Dedication only without ever reading the Book, might have served to have fix'd him from that instant as his Favourite. Yet all this I perceive did not his work, but his Grace was so unmindful, or rather so prudent, that the Gentleman thought it necessary to spur up again the next year with another new Book to show more plainly what he would be at. This he dedicates to Doctor Bathurst,[217] and to evidence from the very Epistle, that he was ready to renounce that very Education the Civility of which he is so tender of as to blame me for disordering it, he picks occasion to tell him: *to your prevailing advise, Sir, do I owe my first rescue from the Chains and Fetters of an unhappy Education.*[218] But in the Book which he calls, *a free and impartial Censure of the Platonick Philosophy,* (censure 'tis sure to be whatsoever he writes) he speaks out, and demonstrates himself ready and equipp'd to [74] surrender not only the Cause, but betray his party without making any Conditions for them, and to appear forthwith himself in the head of the contrary Interest. Which supposing the dispute to be just, yet in him was so mercenary, that none would have descended to act his part but a Divine of Fortune. And even Lawyers take themselves excused from being of Counsel for the King himself, in a Cause where they have been entertain'd and instructed by their Client. But so flippant he was, and forward in this Book, that, in despight of all Chronology, he could introduce Plato to invey against Calvin, and from the Platoniques he could miraculously hook in a Discourse against the Non-conformists. After this feat of activity he was ready to leap over the Moon: no scruple of Conscience could stand in his way, and no preferment seemed too high for

[*C. Pl. Ph.* p. 26, 27, 28, &c.]

return of Silenus, Dionysius granted him the (fatal) power that everything he touched would turn to gold. See Ovid, *Metamorphoses,* 11:90–193.

216 Arch-bishop of Canterbury: Gilbert Sheldon (1598–1677) was elevated to the see of Canterbury in 1663. Parker became his chaplain in 1667.

217 Dr. Bathurst: Ralph Bathurst (1620–1704), physician, poet, and theologian, president of Trinity College, Oxford, 1664–1704. [S]

218 *to . . . Education: Censure,* "Dedication," B2.

him; For about this time, I find that having taken a turn at Cambridge,[219] to qualifie himself, he was received within doors to be my Lord Arch-bishops other Chaplain,[220] and into some degree of favour: which, considering the difference of their humours and ages, was somewhat sur-[75]prizing. But, whether indeed in times of heat and faction the most temperate Spirits may sometimes chance to take delight in one that is spightful, and make some use of him; or whether it be that even the most grave and serious persons do for relaxation divert themselves willingly by whiles with a Creature that is unlucky, mimical and gamesome; so it was. And thence forward the nimble Gentleman danced upon Bell-ropes, vaulted from Steeple to Steeple, and cut Capers out of one Dignity to another. Having thus dexterously stuck his Groat in Lambeth Wainscot[221] it may easily be conceived he would be unwilling to lose it, and therefore he concern'd himself highly, and even to jealousie in upholding now that Palace, which if falling, he would out of instinct be the first should leave it. His Majesty about that time labouring to effect his constant promises of Indulgence to his people, the Author therefore walking with his own shadow in the evening took a great fright lest all were ago. And in this conceit being resolv'd to make good his Figure, and that one Government should not last any longer than the other, he set himself to write those dangerous Books which I have now to do with: wherein, [76] he first makes all that he will to be Law, and then whatsoever is Law to be Divinity. And I shall appeal to all Readers, and I hope make it good, that never in any age, by any man (that I may not say any Churchman) have there been published Discourses either so erroniously founded, or so foully managed, or of so pernicious consequence. In conclusion, this is that man who insists so much, and stirrops[222] himself upon the Gravity of his Profession, and the Civility of his Education: which if he had in the least observed in respect either to himself or others, I should, I could never have made so bold with him. And nevertheless, it being so necessary to represent him in his own likeness, that it may appear what he is to others, and to himself, if possibly he might at last correct his indecencies, I have not

[219] Cambridge: Parker was incorporated M.A. at Cambridge in 1667 and proceeded to D.D. in 1671. [S]

[220] other Chaplain: The other Chaplain was Thomas Tomkins. See p. 290 and note 365 below.

[221] Wainscot: wood paneling used to line the walls of a room.

[222] stirrops: mounts up in the stirrups.

committed any fault of stile, nor even this tediousness, but in his imitation. I have not used any harsh expressions but what were suitable to that Civility of Education which he practises, and that Gravity of Profession which he hath set up of: and even therein I have taken care, beside what my nature hath taken care for, to shoot below the mark, & not to retaliate [77] to the same degree; being willing, as I must yield him the preference for many good qualities, so in his worst however to give him the precedence. And yet withall that it hath been thus far the odiousest task that ever I undertook, and has look'd to me all the while like the cruelty of a Living Dissection, which, however it may tend to publick instruction, and though I have pick'd out the most noxious Creature to be anatomiz'd, yet doth scarce excuse or recompence the offensiveness of the scent and fouling of my fingers. Therefore I will here[223] break off abruptly, leaving many a vein not laid open, and many a passage not search'd into, nor read any further upon this Soul of the World, or prosecute afresh its allegory from the Apple, the Mandrake, the Sparrow, the Fishes, the Mouse, the Mungrel, the Ape, unto the day of Marriage,[224] but leave the Moral to the judicious. And I could here take advantage perhaps plausible[225] enough, to put a final conclusion to this whole book, for if a man hath taken off his railing, he hath therein answered his Argument. But if I have undergone the drudgery of the more loathsom part already, I will not defraud my self of what [78] is more truly pleasant, and remains behind the lighter burthen, the conflict with, if it may be so call'd his Reason. For his whole book is, according to his usual Address, a Letter to me, and it concerns my Civility to return an Answer to every part of it. He hath ask'd me many questions, and I take my self obliged to resolve them. And he hath promised me the Press shall be open;[226] neither would I therefore be behind hand with him in courtesie.

So[227] that I have now only three things of which he hath made it necessary that I caution the Reader. The first is not to be misled[228] by a pestilent way that he has of Youing me, and so making me an Epidemical[229] person,

[223] here 73] hear 74.

[224] Soul . . . Marriage: a reprise of Donne's allegory.

[225] plausible 74] plausibly 73.

[226] Press . . . open: *Reproof*, p. 67; and see the mock imprimatur to *RT2*.

[227] So: 74 introduces a new paragraph here.

[228] misled 73] missed 74.

[229] Epidemical: universal; i.e., by using the second person plural form of address, Parker has multiplied Marvell into a sect.

affixing thereby what hath ever, he pretends to have been said or done by any in the Cause of Non-conformity at any time to my account: although it never hath[230] enter'd into my Book or Imagination, and he had been more kind, if, as sometimes he does out of civility he had Thou'd me to the end of the Chapter. The second is not on the other part to impute any errors or weakness of mine to the Non-conformists, nor mistake me for one of them, (not that I fly it as a [79] reproach, but rather honour the most scrupulous:) for I write only what I think befits all men in Humanity, Christianity and Prudence towards Dissenters. The last is not to think that I am any such old Acquaintance[231] as he claims, to insinuate me of dis-ingenuity, for of our acquaintance I shall give account hereafter.

THat which gave me the first occasion of Writing was, as I have said formerly, his third *Crambe,*[232] of the same purulent[233] matter, and virulent stile, the *Preface to Bishop Bramhall*: and against that and its incomparable extravagancies[234] was my whole Discourse bent and levell'd. Only about the middle of mine I touch'd in passing upon some points of his other Treatises, that is, *the Power of the Magistrate, Conscience, Morality, Debauchery, Persecution,* &c. But he, whether by mistake or on purpose, turns my method quite backward, and, avoiding that which was direct for what is but collateral, begins in his second page, in his usual Military Metaphors of *Attack, Front and Rear,* &c. with the Ninety seventh of my Book. [80] This however, is an accident that hath befallen other great Commanders as well as himself. For his Ancient Friend, William the Conqueror, at the Battel of Hastings, had in the same manner the back of his Cuirasses placed before, by the error of him that put them on. The thing is ominous I doubt to the *Author of the Ecclesiastical Politie,* and assuredly (as the Duke then said) *This day his Fortune will turn, and he will be a King or nothing before night.*[235] Yet

[230] never hath 74] hath never 73.

[231] old Acquaintance: this phrase sums up Parker's reference to "ancient Friendship" and his claim that "You and I Sir have hitherto been good Friends," *Reproof,* pp. 81, 233; Marvell spurns the relationship in his later, scathing account, p. 418 below.

[232] *Crambe:* cabbage, particularly *crambe repetita,* cabbage served up again; i.e., distasteful repetition. [S]

[233] purulent: infected, suppurating.

[234] extravagancies 73] extravigancies 74.

[235] William the Conqueror . . . *night:* see Raphael Holinshed, *Chronicles* (London, 1587), 1:199 (misnumbered as 175); (A, p. 25, #63).

I will not decline the pursuit, but plod on after him in his own way, thorow thick and thin, hill or dale, over hedge and ditch wherever he leads; till I have laid hand on him, and deliver'd him bound either to Reason or Laughter, to Justice or Pity. If at any turn he gives me the least opportunity to be serious I shall gladly take it: but where he prevaricates or is scurrilous (and where is he not?) I shall treat him betwixt Jest and Earnest. That which is solid and sharp, being imp'd by something more light and airy, may carry further and pierce deeper, and therefore I shall look to it as well as I can, that mine Arrows be well pointed, and of mine own whetting; but for the Feathers I must borrow them out of his [81] Wing. Neither yet would I have this similitude improv'd to his disparagement: for he is a Bird of Prey, and an High-flyer,[236] and, though he hath lessen'd himself by the Height of his Place, he cannot certainly be other than an Eagle, and perhaps the same fate[237] may attend him.

First therefore, as to the Power of the Magistrate, he saith in gross: that *the Supream Government of every Common-wealth must of Necessity be Universal, Uncontroulable, Indispensable,*[238] *Unlimited, and Absolute in all affairs whatsoever that concern the Interests of Mankind and the ends of Government; as well in matters of Religion as in all other Civil concerns.* This is I confess pretty strongly worded, and drawn up doubtless by the advice of his Counsel Learned: But if these be terms unknown yet in our Law, we must refer it to the Supream Government *to define their signification.* However, if it be not Law, 'tis pity but it were so. 'Tis the very *Elixir Potestatis* and *Magisterium Domini*:[239] So fine a thing that no man living but would be inamour'd with it: For, wot ye well, it is a *Power* he saith [82] *established* of yore, at or before the beginning of the World, e're there was any such thing known or

[*Ec. Pol.* p. 27, 28, 35, &c.]

[*Ec. Pol.* p. 109.][240]

[236] High-flyer: in the late seventeenth and eighteenth centuries, one who supported lofty claims on behalf of the Church; an evangelical as contrasted to a moderate; Marvell's usage precedes the *DNB*'s first example, in 1680.

[237] same fate: In the fable of the Eagle and the Arrow, the eagle is killed by an arrow feathered with one of its own plumes. Not all collections of Aesop featured this fable; but see, for example, "Aquila," in *Fabulae Aesopi Graece ac Latine* (London, 1657), p. 114.

[238] *Indispensable* 73] *Indispensible* 74; i.e., not subject to special dispensations.

[239] *Elixir . . . Domini:* essence of power and rule of dominion.

[240] p. 109: actually p. 108.

thought of, as Periwigs or Glass-Coaches[241] *by the unalterable dictates of Natural Reason and Universal Practice and Consent of Nations.* Only in *the Jewish Common wealth for some peculiar Reasons of State,* (which he knows but will not tell us) 'twas for some time otherwise. But this [*Ec. Pol.* p. 32.] Power was *antecedent to Christ* himself, and it was so well [p. 35.] founded, that there was none, or very little need of the Authority of the Scripture in the Case, and therefore *the Scripture rather supposes then asserts this Jurisdiction.* Yet in our Saviours time, and for some while after there was such *a Posture of Affairs,* and *such an unhappy Juncture of Affairs* (how mechanically he expresses it?) that, while the Heathen Princes enjoy'd this Power by the [p. 37. p. 38. *Ecc. Pol.* p. 40] Antecedent Right of Soveraignty, and accordingly exercised it over Christians, 'twas also necessary to supply it among them *by Miracles of Severity.* But *when* [83] *once Christianity became the Imperial Religion, this Power began to resettle where Nature had placed it,* and so the World jog'd on, and *its Affairs were competently well Govern'd (though better or worse, according to the wis-* [p. 48.] *dom and vigilance of the several Emperors)* till the Bishop of [p. 54.] Rome, seeing this Power to be so rich and beautiful a Creature began to cast a sweet Eye on her, and, by the address of his constant sollicitation and courtship carried her sheer away from all the Princes of Christendom. So this Jewel of the Crown was for several hundred of years imbezel'd, till Henry the 8*th.* and other Princes found it again by chance in the ruines of an old Monastery at the Reformation. But *though the*[242] *Wisdom of the elder Ages had always practised this Power,* yet *since that Governors have not been thorowly in-* [p. 32.] *structed in its Nature and Extent, Government hath not been* [p. 58.] *rightly understood nor duely managed,* the Reformation *hath* [p. 229.][243] *not been able to resettle Princes in their full and Natural rights.* What will not the man deserve that can show them [p. 58.] better, and teach Go-[84]vernors a Receipt against so Chronical Negligence and Ignorance? *So little have Princes understood their*

[241] Periwigs or Glass-Coaches: periwigs were perukes and glass-coaches were those fitted with glass windows; hence, fashionable innovations of the late seventeenth century. Marvell reused this phrase in the *Essay,* vol. 2, p. 152.

[242] *though the* 74] not italicized in 73.

[243] p. 229; actually p. 223.

own Interests. So fatal has been their miscarriage. Send for a Physician e're they be all out of hope, and while there is yet some life in [p. 19.] 'm. But he will do well to make sure of his Fee beforehand, as those that sold the *Icterus,*[244] a Bird good against the Jaundise, hid it till they were pay'd, lest the buyer at first sight be cured. The Great Secret after all is, that *the Prince may, and hath Power to transfer the Exercise of the Priesthood upon another, and that he may if he please reserve it to himself.* Is this all? The notion is something new in- [p. 32.] deed; but he hath deduced it very well, and 'tis pretty probable: though I have known the time, and many others may remember it when it would not have been granted. I make account the *Author of the Ecclesiastical Politie* is sufficiently impowred by the whole Clergy, at least of England: and doubtless therefore His Majesty, among other Princes, will if he find it good and for his service accept the Donation, not much inferiour to that of Con-[85]stantine.[245] 'Tis a great piece of gratitude now in them, and 'twould have done well and more seasonably, had his late Majesty before the War been informed by them in this particular and the dependances. But I have some reason to be jealous that the *Author of the Ecclesiastical Politie* is not thus liberal without some design; that he hath some job or other to be done, and how Unlimited and Absolute soever he hath made and declared the Magistrate, there is some condition annex'd upon failure of which this Fiefe shall Reincamerate.[246] For he was of another opinion in his *Preface to Bishop Bramhall,* when he said *all Government does and must owe its quiet and continuance to the Churches Patronage.* Yes: there is another *Croisade* to be undertaken, and he hath [p. 30.][247] a project in his head to ingage all Princes in a war against Non-conformity, a second *Bellum Archidiaconale.*[248] For though he was resolved#, even in his first book,# to run his head against a

[244] *Icterus:* "A bird there is called in Greeke Icterus, of the yellow colour which the fethers carrie, which if one that hath the jaundise doe but looke upon, he or she shall presently be cured thereof; but the poore bird is sure to die for it." Pliny, *The Historie of the World,* trans. Philemon Holland (London, 1634), tom. II, bk. 30, ch. xi. [S] (A, p. 25, # 53).

[245] Donation . . . of Constantine: the alleged grant by Constantine of the city and territory of Rome to Pope Silvester and his successors; the "deed" was exposed as a forgery in the fifteenth century.

[246] Reincamerate: reannex to the pope's domain. [S]

[247] p. 30: actually, p. 59.

[248] *Bellum Archidiaconale:* archdeacon's war.

wall, and very ingeniously[249] professes there too, that *if he had spoke reason he ⟨had⟩ without any more ado carry'd the Cause, if he had not he was content to* [86] *lose his labour*; he intended not it should go so easily. But in that very first Book, while he was in the sweetest temper, in his natural serenity, and most benign inclinations, not heated or provoked by any Adversary; and before he had expected one minute what so strong a Reason, what so perswasive eloquence might have effected with the Non-conformists, joyn'd with that interest which he had so[251] many years been creating amongst them, even then at the same time he sounds another Trumpet then that in Sheere-lane,[252] to Horse, and hem in his Auditory. He proclaims them for meer dissenting[253] upon tenderness of Conscience, *Villains, Hypocrites, Rebels, Schismaticks, and the greatest and most notorious Hereticks.* He summons therefore the Magistrate to do his Office, that is to impose Ceremonies, which he owns to be indifferent, upon those that hold the contrary, with the severest Penalties, and the strictest Execution. What is this but to put Governors upon the Tenters,[254] to invent how possibly they may run their Subjects into Disobedience, and then to invent and apply the Tortures for their Disobeying? [87] As for the poor Subjects there is no help for them, but he gives them very excellent and Ghostly counsel to *abide their sad Fate* with Patience and Resignation; but instead of them he lays his Imposition now upon the Magistrate, and leaves him not so much as the Power to will nor chuse; but he must govern by the Laws of the *Author of the Ecclesiastical Politie.* He must[255] *scourge them into order.* He must[256] *Chastise them out*

[*Pref. Ecc. Pol.* p. 46.][250]

[p. 241. p. 273. p. 319.]

[249] ingeniously 74: ingenuously 73; the sentence could carry either word.

[250] p. 46: actually p. 36, or xxxvi.

[251] he had so 73] had been so 74.

[252] Trumpet . . . Sheere-lane: Shire (or Sheer) Lane, which connected Fleet Street with Lincoln's Inn Fields, was known as Rogues Lane in the reign of James I. See E. B. Chancellor, *Annals of Fleet Street* (New York, n.d.), pp. 1110–13. Midway along the lane was the Trumpet tavern, one of the oldest licensed houses in London. [S]

[253] dissenting 73] discenting 74.

[254] Tenters: stretching machines used in torture, as in "on tenterhooks."

[255] must 74] *must* 73.

[256] must 74] *must* 73.

of their peevishness, and Lash them into Obedience, There [*Ec. Pol.* p. 321.] *is no remedy, but the Rod and Correction. He* must[258] *re-* [p. 325.][257] *strain them with more rigour than unsanctified Villains. He* [p. 272.] must[259] *expose them to the Correction of the publick Rods and* *Axes.* Is this at last all the business why he hath been [p. 219.] building up all this while that Necessary, Universal, Uncontroulable, Indispensable,[260] Unlimited, Absolute Power of Governors; only to gratifie the humour and arrogance of an Unnecessary, Universal, Uncontroulable, Dispensable,[261] Unlimited and Absolute, Arch-Deacon? Still *must, must, must*: But what if the Supream Magistrate won't? Why, *must* again, eight times at least in [88] little more then one page, and thorow his whole book proportionably. This is (and let [⟨*Ecc. Pol.* p. 271⟩] him make a quibble on't if he please) like Doctor Rabelais his setting Julius Caesar to beat *Mustard*:[262] and just as worshipful an imployment, as if he should prefer his Majesty from his Kingdom and Whitehall to the Government of his Ancient Palace of Bridewell.[263] But Laws and Impositions he saith signifie nothing without Penalties, nor these without acting up roundly by rigorous Executions. Therefore that he might be true to his own principles, if the Supream Magistrate be disobedient, he hath provided against him too pretty severely. He hath denounced that in that case men deserve *to perish like Sardanapalus.*[264] That such a Prince *deserves to be King of the Night*;[265] and to conclude, he affirms that *Princes unless they will be resolute,* that is to do what he would have them, *they must not Govern.* 'Tis come to *Noli igitur*

[257] p. 325; actually p. 305.

[258] must 74] *must* 73.

[259] must 74] *must* 73. These four small revisions in 74 emphasize *must* by carefully reversing the italics.

[260] Indispensable 73] Indispensible 74.

[261] Dispensable 73] Dispensible 74.

[262] Julius Caesar . . . *Mustard:* In *Pantagruel,* book 2, Epistemon's account of what he saw in hell, it was Xerxes, not Julius Caesar, who was selling mustard; Caesar and Pompey were tarring ships.

[263] Ancient Palace of Bridewell: see John Stow, *Survey of London* (1618), pp. 747–48: "of old time the Kings house: for the Kings of this Realme have beene there lodged. . . But . . . this house became a house of correction . . . a Workehouse for the poore and idle persons of the Citie." [S] Anglesey owned the 1603 edition, p. 30, #13.

[264] *Defence,* p. 656. For Sardanapalus, see *RT,* p. 116 and n. 417 above.

[265] *deserves . . . Night: Defence,* p. 641.

[p. 271.] *regnare*:[266] They had need to take heed of him it seems, and how they behave themselves. But they may very well take all this kindly of him, and as an honour, for it is no less Authority than he exercises over God Almighty. For he [89] will have it that *God* must *too*[267] *of necessity have vested Princes in at least as much Power as was absolutely necessary to the Nature and Ends of Government.* And what the Authors ends are, we have and shall take occasion more particularly to examine hereafter. [*Ec. Pol.* p. 40.]

What needs there further for evidence in this matter, or if men would out of love to justice be more exactly inform'd, let them but read, if their patience will not last longer, the Contents at least of the several Chapters of his *Ecclesiastical Polity,* in this and the other matters. It is sufficient punishment for some Offenders to be placed in publick with their book, or its Title affix'd before them. But because he will not be satisfy'd with that, I shall presume so far on my Readers as to trace him thorow the Maze of what in the *Reproof* he would answer. He insults first because he saith I expose an innocent and undeniable Proposition of his, that the Magistrate hath such a Power as is before described, to govern and conduct the Consciences of his Subjects in affairs of Religion; and yet I say not a word in its confutation: but he forgets that where I quote that, I in the [90] very next line subjoyn thus, *And* pag. 22.[268] *he explains himself more fully: That unless Princes have Power to bind their Subjects to that Religion that they apprehend most advantagious to publick peace and tranquillity, and restrain those religious mistakes that tend to its Subversion, they are no better than Statues and Images of Authority.* And this I several times inculcated into him; but of this he takes not the least notice I warrant you: 'tis all hush'd. Is not this now a candid Reprover? But because I know he will hereupon be wriggling, I will shew him that these words cannot be interpreted otherwise by him than according to their first appearance and full latitude. He cannot mean it in matters of Ceremony, which indeed he ought to have kept to, but that the subject it seems turn'd into an argument, and led him further to confess and speak out what was in the bottom. For concerning Ceremonies he saith indeed, *That 'tis absolutely necessary that Governors injoyn matters of no great moment and consequence in*

[*Repr.* p. 3.]

[*Reh. Tr.* p. 97.]

266 *Noli . . . regnare:* "Do not rule therefore."

267 *God* must *too* 74] God too *must* 73.

268 pag. 22: actually p. 12.

themselves, thereby to avoid the evil that would naturally attend upon their being not [91] *injoyn'd: so that when they are determin'd, though perhaps they are of no great use to the Common wealth in themselves, yet they have at least this considerable usefulness as to prevent many great mischiefs that would probably follow if they were not determined*: A most memorable passage, and that deserves to be recorded as the full sum and state of the controversie. Yet he most ingeniously[269] professes that *All that concerns Religious Worship is no part of Religion it self, but only an Instrument,* &c. *and therefore though the Christians Laws command us by some exterior signs to express our interior Piety, yet they have no where set down any particular expressions of worship and adoration.* So also *All Rituals and Ceremonies and Postures and manners of performing the outward expressions of Devotion are not in their own Nature capable of being Parts of Religion.* And thus in many other places: So that he hath gained nothing by the first objection which he hath raised but a Proposition not so undeniable, nor very innocent, that the Prince hath Power to bind his Subjects to that Religion which he apprehends most advantagious, *&c.*[92]

[*Ec. Pol.* p. 322.]

[*Ec. Pol.* p. 99.]

[*Ec. Pol.* p. 206.]

His[270] next exception against me is very material, that I have quoted so many passages out of his book. It has I believe indeed anger'd him as it has been no small trouble to me: but how can I help it? I wish he would be pleas'd to teach me an Art (for if any man in the World, he hath it) to answer a book without, *turning over the Leaves* (for that in a former Answer offended him) or without citing the passages: In the mean time if to transcribe so much out of him must render a man as he therefore stiles me a *Scandalous Plagiary* I must plead Guilty: but by the same Law whoever shall either be Witness or Prosecutor, in behalf of the King, for Treasonable words, may be *indited*[272] for an High-way-man.[273]

[⟨*Repr.* p. 6.⟩][271]

[269] ingeniously 74] ingenuously 73.

[270] His: 74 introduces a new paragraph here.

[271] quoted . . . book: see *Reproof,* p. 6: "I believe it will be found against the Laws of the Stationers-hall, for your Book-seller to print so much of another mans Copy, after it is enter'd according to Order, without his leave and consent."

[272] *indited: Reproof,* p. 6.

[273] Law . . . High-way-man: See *Reproof,* p. 104, where Parker claims that Marvell cannot answer him "because no man can do it without bringing himself within the Statute of treasonable words." Marvell's twist is that a citizen who informs on another for treasonable words is as much a public nuisance as a highway robber.

After[274] this he asks me roundly whether I do seriously believe that his Majesty has no Power in matters of Religion. Let him first make good his own Assertions, which I have charged him with, and then I will tell him more of my mind; yet because he questions me of my Belief (which I believe he never yet did to any man in his own Parsonages, or either at Ickham or Chartham)[275] I do however count my self obliged to give him some answer, as much [93] as he can challenge of me; that is, I do most certainly believe that the Supream Magistrate hath some Power, but not all Power in matters of Religion. And particularly to advance so much further to our *Author of the Ecclesiastical Politie,* I do not believe that Princes have Power to bind their Subjects to that Religion they apprehend most advantagious. And I will give him a Reason too of this my Belief. He himself saith (and it is worthy to be taken good notice of) *that the Fanaticks of late have so imbroiled Christendom, that Christian Princes begin to be of a perswasion, that Christianity is an enemy to Government.* Now it is therefore to be presumed, that he is very conversant and intimate with all the Princes of Christendom. But I suppose that they reveal'd this secret of State to him only in confidence, for I never before heard of it in publick: and it is not so ingeniously[276] or prudently done of him to proclaim in Print the subject of a familiar discourse, and private conference with them. This sure will make Princes more cautelous[277] for the future, whom they chuse for their Ministers, and to believe that even he, [94] unless he be better at keeping a secret, is not so fit to be of their Privy-Counsel: no not in Affairs Ecclesiastical. But if it be so (as who dare controvert it after so authentical authority as the Author's of the *Ecclesiastical Politie*) that Princes are indeed perswaded that Christianity is an Enemy to Government, it is not so safe to acknowledge that they have Power to bind to what Religion they apprehend most advantagious. Especially if it should chance that so pliable a Gentleman should be at their elbow, who, out of excess of Conformity indulges the greatest Non-conformity imaginable. *We condemn,* saith he, *neither Turks nor Papists for their Forms and Postures of Adoration (unless they fall under one or both of the obliquities*

[*Ec. Pol.* p. 179.]

[274] After: 74 introduces a new paragraph here.

[275] questions . . . Chartham: One of the primary duties of a clergyman was to catechize the members of his parish; i.e., question them about the fundamentals of their belief.

[276] ingeniously 74] ingenuously 73.

[277] cautelous: cautious.

aforesaid.) Let them but address the same worship to its proper object, and we will never stand stiffly with them about their outward Rites and Ceremonies of its expression, but will freely allow them to conform to the significant Customs of their Countrey, as we do to those of ours. 'Tis most graciously done that his *We-ship* will allow them it: Will he not sound a Trumpet too when he has done to give 'm leave to go to din-[95]ner? In due time sure there will be an Hat for him to make him in requital the Cardinal-Deacon. But why will he not carry the good humour thorow, and be as merciful to his Neighbours? All abroad and nothing at home? There have been and are several Rites and Customs too in the Countries of England, which do neither countenance Vice, nor disgrace the Deity, and these dissenting people do address the same Worship to its due and proper Object. But (not to prevent my self) should he now, that is so clear as to matter of Ceremonies, be back'd at the same time with another Fellow-Prebend[279] of his no less Frank in Religion, who should tell the Princes that he abhors being a Papist as much as being a Presbyterian, and will as soon be a Turk, as he will either: what might become of us, if the Princes were satisfy'd of their own Power, and of these mens Discretion? It might breed no small alteration in the *affairs* of Christendom. For whatsoever the Papists be, there are many things to be said why the Turks is a very advantagious Religion.[96]

[*Def. Ec. Pol.* p. 286.][278]

[Dr. Pierce *against* Baxter. p. 167.][280]

Then he quotes his Majesties Declaration[281] to make good his---*making use of that Supream Power in Ecclesiastical matters, which is not only inherent in the Crown, but has been declared and recognized to be so by several Statutes and Acts of Parliament.* I honour the Quotation, and am come not long since from swearing religiously to own that Supremacy.[283] And it is surely the more valid for having received from the *Author of the Ecclesiastical Politie* this Confirmation. Only

[*Rep.* p. 3][282]

[278] p. 286 73, correctly] p. 289 74.

[279] Fellow-Prebend: Thomas Pierce (1622–91), prebendary of Langford Major at Lincoln, dean of Salisbury, president of Magdalen College, Oxford (1661–72). [S]

[280] Dr. Pierce *against* Baxter: William Pierce, bishop of Bath and Wells; his *The New Discoverer Discovered* was published in 1659.

[281] For the text of the Declaration, see A. Browning, *English Historical Documents 1660–1714* (London, 1966), pp. 387–88.

[282] p. 3: actually p. 7.

[283] Marvell had, as an officeholder, just taken the oaths required by the new Test Act of 1673 (25. Car.II. c.2).

it might have been wish'd that all his Books had not been writ directly counter to it, and under pretence of gratifying him with Titles he had not cut him out of the Exercise and Liberty of his Jurisdiction. But having in his *Ecclesiastical Politie* created himself Perpetual Dictator, *Nequid Res-clerica detrimenti capiat,*[284] and marching every where with four and twenty *Rods and Axes*[285] before him, he deputes the *Consul* to be indeed both his *Magister Equituum,*[286] and his *Pontifex Maximus,*[287] but all along speaks in the *Us* and ⟨the⟩ *We* of himself, and treats the good Civil Uncontroulable Magistrate with the *Must, Must,* to evidence his own rigorous Superiority. And in that only place where [97] he seems to give the Magistrate some little License, he doth it with so ill a grace, and stigmatizes both the Magistrate and the People with such a mark and Character, ⟨that⟩ 'twould put a generous Prince upon some deliberation, whether he were best to make use of an authority so ignominiously granted. For all that is to be obtained is this and in these terms. *Should any Prince through unhappy miscarriages in the State be brought into such straits and exigencies of affairs as that he cannot restrain the headlong inclinations of his Subjects without the hazard of raising such commotions and disturbances as perhaps he can never be able to allay, and so should be forced in spight of himself to indulge them their liberty in their fancies and perswasions about Religion; yet, unless he will divest himself of a more material and more necessary part of his authority, than if he should grant away his power of the* Militia, *or his Prerogative of ratifying Civil Laws; unless I say, he will thus hazard his Crown and make himself too weak for Government by renouncing the best part of his Supremacy, he* Must *lay an obligation upon all persons to whom he grants this religious freedom, to profess that* [98] *'tis matter of meer favour and indulgence, and that he hath*[288] *as much power to govern all the publick affairs of Religion as any other matters that are either conducive or prejudicial to the publick peace and quiet of the Common-wealth. And if they be brought to this Declaration they will but confess them-selves (to say no worse) turbulent and Seditious persons, by acknowledging that they refuse their obedience to those Laws which the Supream Authority has just*

[284] *Nequid . . . capiat:* cf. the consular formula: "Videant consules ne quid respublica detrimenti capiat" [S]; i.e., "Let the consuls see to it that the republic receives no harm."

[285] *Rods and Axes:* fasces; bundles of rods of elm or birchwood, and a single-headed axe, carried by Roman lictores as signs of magisterial authority.

[286] *Magister Equituum:* Master of the Horse.

[287] *Pontifex Maximus:* High priest.

[288] *hath* 74] *has* 73.

[*Ec. Pol.* p. 63, 64.] *Power to impose.* I know not whether all these Solemnities were duely observed in the late Declaration; or whether the failing in some of these Rituals may have render'd it less sacred. But our Authors concession here looks something like the Cardinal Antonio's suffrage, when he could not have his man chosen;[289] *Sia dunque Pamfilio Papa al nome del Diavolo.*[290] However this, such as it is, joyn'd with the former quotation does amount to some kind of Sanction, and the Parties concern'd may do well to consider of it.

He inquires next *whether I have never read or heard of any publick disturbances, under pretence of Religion.* Yes I have, and whosoever shall do so deserves to be severely punished. *Whe-*[99]*ther I have not* [*Repr.* p. 7] *heard of the merry pranks of John of Leyden and the Anabap-* [*Repr.* p. 8.] *tists of Germany.*[291] Yes, and they were handled as they deserved. Nay, moreover I have heard of the Anabaptists too of New-England, in a Book Printed in the year 1673. entituled *Mr. Baxter baptiz'd in Blood,*[292] which came out under the License of *the Author of the Ecclesiastical Politie*; being therefore as is to be supposed a Book of Theological nature. It was indeed a piece of Ecclesiastical History, which he thought it seems very fit *to reconcile to the present Juncture of Affairs, and recommend to the Genius of the Age: faithfully relating the Cruel Barbarous and Bloody Murther of Mr. Baxter an Orthodox Minister, who was kill'd by the Anabaptists, and his Skin most cruelly flea'd off from his Body.* And yet from beginning to end there never was a compleater falshood invented. But after

[289] Cardinal . . . chosen: Antonio Barberini (1607–71), brother of Urban VIII, was reluctantly persuaded to nominate Giovanni Battista Pamfili (1574–1655) as Innocent VIII. The story (without Marvell's Italian curse) is told in G. Leti, *Il Cardinalismo di Santa Chiesa,* 3 vols. (1668), 3:238–40. Marvell might have used the 1670 translation by G.H., p. 283.

[290] *Sia . . . Diavolo:* Then let Pamphilo be pope in the Devil's name.

[291] *Anabaptists of Germany:* In 1533–35 a group of Anabaptist refugees in Leyden attempted to set up a Kingdom of the Saints under the leadership of Jan Bockelson, i.e., John of Leyden. During the siege of the city they introduced polygamy and other excesses which discredited the whole movement.

[292] a Book . . . *Blood: Mr. Baxter Baptiz'd in Bloud, or, A Sad History of the unparallel'd cruelty of the Anabaptists in New England* (1673). This gruesome narrative of the murder of an orthodox minister by a sect was licensed by Parker. When investigated by the Privy Council and found to be completely false (*CSPD* 1673, p. 312) Parker had to notify the public (Bodley, MS Tanner 290, f. 202). The results of the exposure were published by John Darby, Marvell's printer for *RT,* as *Forgery Detected and Innocency Vindicated* (London, 1673). [S]

the *Author of the Ecclesiastical Politie* had in so many books of his own indeavour'd to harangue up the Nation into Fury against Tender Consciences, there could not have been contrived by the Wit of Man, any thing more hopeful to have blooded them upon the Non-conformists then such a Specta-[100]cle, and at the end of his Orations to flourish the Skin of an Orthodox Minister in this manner flea'd off by the Anabaptists. So that *Se non era vero fu ben trovato.*[293] And in good earnest I dare not swear but it was *the Author of the Ecclesiastical Polities* own handy-work. Several words I observe that he frequently and peculiarly makes use of in his other books, *Concerns, Villains, Villanies, Booby,* &c. but as for his *brisk and laboured periods,*[294] they may be traced every where. What say you to this for Example? *As the Profession of the Gospel is a most sacred thing, the Doctrine of the Gospel a most holy rule, the Author of our Religion an exemplar and pattern*[295] *of meekness: So when Christians renounce this Sacred Profession, lay aside this Holy Gospel, and abrenunciate*[296] *Christ the pattern of meekness, they soon become the most desperate Villains in the World.* (Ay: very truly said were it but rightly applyed.) Never in my life did I read any thing that more lively expresses and nicks the Energy of our Authors sense, or the rotundity and cadence of his Numbers: and so in many places more too long to be instanced. And indeed what reason could there be, what likelyhood [101] that any other man should go so far out of the way with such a book to him who was the most improper Licenser of things of that Nature? Unless he may have therefore been ⟨thought⟩ the most proper Licenser, because he had given so many Testimonies as books of his good inclination to such matters; and that (not only in History, but even in Doctrine too) he did not so nearly consider the Truth as the Interest. And therefore if perhaps he were not the Author, yet I dare undertake that when he came to the Licensing of that Pamphlet, he felt such an expansion of heart, such an adlubescence[297] of mind, and such an exaltation of spirit, that betwixt Joy and Love he could scarce restrain[298]

[*Bax. bap.* p 1.]

293 *Se . . . trovato:* if it is not true it's a great find; now proverbial, supposedly originating in a comment by Cardinal Ippolito D'Este on Ariosto's *Orlando Furioso* and quoted by Giordano Bruno, *Degli Eroici Furori* (1585). [S]

294 *laboured periods: Defence,* p. 240.

295 *pattern* 73] *patern* 74.

296 *abrenunciate:* renounce, repudiate.

297 adlubescence: pleasure; the *DNB* cites Marvell's usage here of this French word as the only English instance.

298 scarce restrain 74] scarcely refrain 73.

from kissing it. And this no man living can deny, that either if he thought there were any fault in it, he took care to correct and fit it for the Press with that advantage that it came out, or else he found it so satisfactory that it past his approbation without any amendment, and so transporting that he forgot to keep a Copy for his own justification. And truly had it not chanced that there was present and immediate proof upon the place to convict the Forgery as soon as published, it might pro-[102]bably have[299] had the effect for which it was designed. However no thanks to the Licenser, who either was also the Author, or the more criminal of the two; by how much the Licenser is always presumed to have the stricter inspection, the better judgment, and more honesty, and is therefore intrusted by my Lord Archbishop to give the stamp of publick authority. So that whereas this Author saith that, *had we but an Act of Parliament to abridge Preachers the use of fulsom and lushious Metaphors, it might perhaps be an effectual Cure of all our Distempers,* (what of the dull and lazy one too?)[300] *Let not the Reader smile at the odness of the Proposal.* (Neither? Is not that lawful before it come to be enacted, as certainly it will upon his recommendation?) [*Ecc. Pol.* p. 76.] I must rather say, that had we but an Act of Parliament to abridge Licensers from publishing falshoods, how sweet soever and lushious, and to command and enable them to authorize truth, there would be a sensible amendment in our modern History, Polity, and Theology. I know he will take it unkindly that this should be revived after, he will say, he hath given so ample satis-[103]faction for it in his testimonial to the contrary. But he may please to consider that this was since the late Act of General Pardon;[301] that it all happen'd since the writing of the Reproof; that he hath only given a Masterly Certificate as it were from a Justice of Peace, instead of making an humble Recantation as an Offender; that it is but the same Law which he every where would exact of the Nonconformists, and the same right which he does Mr. B. in the Preface to Bishop Bramhall. Had he but, as they say indeed, complemented[302] the Anabaptists on this occasion, so Printed it too, *That he esteem'd them to be the nearest to Truth of all the Dissenters from the Church of England,* it had been

[299] have 73] have have 74.

[300] dull and lazy one: a reprise of the joke of pp. 223, 224, 227, 232.

[301] Act . . . Pardon: i.e., an act of free and general pardon, indemnity and oblivion, 1660, 12 Car. II. cap. 11.

[302] complemented Ed.] he complemented 73, 74.

some sign of Penitence and Integrity, and amounted to some degree of Restitution.

From this of the Anabaptists, he falls as severely upon the word *Unhoopable,*[303] which I it seems used in representing his *Unlimited,* &c. But whereas I only threw it out like empty Cask to amuze him, knowing that I had a *Whale* to deal with,[304] and least he should overset me; he runs away with it as a very serious business, and so moyles[305] himself with tumbling [104] and tossing it, that he is in danger of melting his *Sperma Ceti.*[306] A Cork I see will serve without an Hook, and in stead of an Harping Iron, this grave and ponderous Creature may like Eeles be taken and pull'd up only with bobbing. What adoe he makes with Tubs, Kinderkins,[307] Hogsheads,[308] and their demensions![309] that you might suspect him first to have served as Gager[310] of the Lambeth brewing? I wonder that he should descend to so low imployment: but even that prudent Emperor Claudius publish'd an Edict[311] *de bene Picandis Doliis.*[312] And I perceive that a person of considerable Ecclesiastical Tunnage, did very lately *resemble the Church of England with its Ceremonies to a Vessel which* must *of* necessity *be composed of Staves, Hoops, Withs and Pins: but if the Pins were pull'd out, then of consequence the Withs slacken, the Hoops ungird, and the Staves fall asunder into confusion,*[313] so that you see the Trope of an Hoop is not so Apocryphal. And I should

[303] *Reproof,* p. 11.

[304] threw . . . deal with: see Sebastian Münster, *Cosmographia Universalis* (Basle, 1559), p. 852: "Cete grandia . . . conspiciuntur, quae naves evertunt nisi . . . missis in mare rotundis & vacuis vasis, quorum lusu delectantur, ludificentur." A woodcut shows a whale playing with barrels. [S] (A, p. 25, #192).

[305] moyles: moiles, fatigues.

[306] *Sperma Ceti:* the fatty substance found in the head and other parts of the sperm-whale, used for medicines and candles.

[307] Kinderkins: kilderkins; large casks containing from sixteen to eighteen old wine gallons.

[308] Hogsheads: very large cases, containing sixty-three old wine gallons.

[309] *Reproof,* p. 11.

[310] Gager: gauger; someone who measures, especially the depth of liquids.

[311] Emperor . . . Edict: see Suetonius, *The History of the Twelve Caesars,* p. 290: "He exhibited also twenty Edicts, or Proclamations, in one day; two of them to this purpose: the first, *That in respect there was like to be plenty of Grapes, all people should see their Vessels well pitch'd.*"

[312] *Doliis* 73: *Doltis* 74: *de bene Picandis Doliis:* re the pitching of wine-jars.

[313] *Discourse,* p. 166.

have thought that, if not out of respect to the Church of England; yet had it been only out of reverence to Cornelius his Tub[314] among the rest, it might have becom'd the *Author of the Ecclesiastical Politie* upon this occasion [105] to have been something more serious.

And no less does he intangle himself in another line of mine, weak enough I confess, yet though of but a single hair strong enough to land him. 'Tis where I chanc'd to say, that *he hath given* ⟨*here*⟩ *the Magistrate so infinite a power that it is extended to impotency as a streight Line continued grows a Circle.*[315] Here indeed I am hard put to it, and I begin too late to be sensible of my rashness in provoking so terrible an Adversary. But in good earnest I thought it enough when I wrote it, that in any small Segment of a great Circle the curvature is not perceptible,[316] but rectifies more by how much the Figure is extended. And at the same time I reflected, that if mine Author should carp at it (for I foresaw very well all the way where he would take hold, and where he would as soon eat his fingers) I would refer him as being an Ecclesiastical Mathematician to Cardinal Cusanus[317] his Treatise *de Docta Ignorantia,* p. 10. c. 14. where he might see in the Diagram: *Quod Infinita Linea sit Triangulus,* and p. 11. c. 15. *Quod ille Triangulus sit Circulus.*[318] But if this will not satisfie him, let him try conclusions with his own Girdle, which circumscribes somthing that is infinite. [106]

And no less considerable is that which he undertakes *to maintain that all Figures are Hoopable*:[319] and I on the contrary will defend that if he can make that good, he hath found out the Circle of the Quadrature.[320]

From hence he runs out into Plays, *designing,* as he told us his Friend did of the *Friendly Debate, to set off Reasonings with a Comical humour and pleasantness.* I must here acknowledge the defect of my reading. For Du

[314] Cornelius his Tub: a sweating-tub formerly used in the treatment of venereal disease. Cf. Thomas Nashe, *The Unfortunate Traveller* (1593), ed. R. B. McKerrow, *Works,* 5 vols. (Oxford, 1966), 2:228: "Mother Cornelius tub why it was like hell, he that came into it never came out of it." [S]

[315] *he hath . . . Circle:* cf. *RT,* p. 146 above.

[316] perceptible 73] preceptible 74.

[317] Cardinal Cusanus: Nicolaus Khrypffs, da Cusa, cardinal (1401–64).

[318] Treatise . . . *Circulus:* From the page references, Smith determined that Marvell used Cusanus's *Opera* in the Basle 1565 edition.

[319] *Reproof,* p. 14.

[320] found . . . Quadrature: see *RT,* p. 75 and n. 209 above.

[*Pref. Ec. Pol.* p. 16.][321] Foy[322] I have not heard of, and it might better have become him to have quoted instead of the *Conquest,*[323] the Arch-bishop of Granada.[324] But for what he recites out of the *Rehearsal*[325] and the Kings of Branford,[326] I understand it better, and seeing he is pleas'd to alter the Scene, I shall joyn with him, and try whether the humour of Bayes be so worn out that it may not give the Auditory a second dayes diversion. For indeed, 'tis too ceremonious and tiresom to repeat so often upon all occasions the *Author of the Ecclesiastical Politie,* and though I bear him great respect, yet I had rather of the two offend him than my Readers. He does indeed complain of it something pa-[107]thetically that I should have fix'd that name upon him, and in good earnest could I have yet in all this while have invented any name more consonant and agreeable to his Character, I would have chang'd for it. Neither did I at first make use of the *Rehearsal* so much in order to make merry with him as for a more publick and serious advantage. For having observed that he and others of his Coat did, for want either of Reading, Wit, or Piety, as oft as they would be facetious, make bold with the Scripture; thinking too perhaps that being so long acquainted they might be more familiar with it; I had a mind to show them by this example, that there was not so much need of Prophaneness to be ridiculous, or to take the Sacred Writings in vain; but that if they did but take up at adventure any book that was commonly read, known or approved of, they had the same and better opportunity than out of the Bible, to gather thence variety,

[321] p. 16: actually xiv.

[322] Du Foy: *Reproof,* p. 11; the valet in Etherege's *Comical Revenge or Love in a Tub* (1664). [E.D.J.]

[323] the *Conquest:* Parker, *Reproof,* p. 13, had unwisely cited Dryden's *Conquest of Granada* (1672), pt. 1 (1.i. 205–06): "Obey'd as Sovereign by thy Subjects be, / But know that I alone am King of me." The play was politically provocative. When published in February 1672 it carried a dedication to James, duke of York, attacking the Commonwealth and happily anticipating the Third Dutch War.

[324] Arch-bishop of Granada: Pedro Guerrero (d. 1576), archbishop of Granada 1546–76, leader of the Spanish delegates to the Council of Trent, and chief opponent there of the pope. [S]

[325] the *Rehearsal:* Buckingham's play.

[326] Kings of Branford: King Phys and King Ush, the two usurping kings in the *Rehearsal,* act 2; cf. *RT,* p. 200 above, and *Reproof,* p. 12.

allusion, and matter sufficient to make the people merry: and I hope I have attain'd my end in some measure. But beside this, I have now one Reason more and his own Authority to treat him under this Title, he having been since so [108] far in love with the name, as even to send to Colchester to procure him as much Bayes as would serve for a Facing.[327] One thing indeed he objects with some fading colour that there is an errour in Chronology, the Play of the *Rehearsal,* not having been made publick till after his first Book came out which yet is something excusable, seeing it was publish'd before his second or third, and to be sure however before mine. But you know Mr. Bayes, that you wanted not the opportunity to see it long before it was Printed, and that Comedy, as all judicious and lasting things ought, was long consider'd of e're it was thought fit to come abroad.[329] Had you follow'd the same example, and not divulged and promulgated your *Preface to Bishop Bramhall,* as you confess ⟨*before*⟩[330] *your thoughts were cool enough, or could possibly be so, to review or correct the indecencies either of its stile or contrivance,* had you *but had either leisure or patience to examine it,* all this labour might have been spared betwixt you and me, and I for mine own part should never have *tired either your self or the Reader.* But that I may be [109] quit with you for so weighty an *Emendatio temporum*;[331] have you not observed that your Hickringil or *Gregory,* though not published till after your *Reproof* foretells of it nevertheless, threatning what a vengeance

[*Repr.* p. 20][328]

[*Pref. B. B.* p. 2. *and* p. *last.*]

[327] Colchester . . . Facing: Colchester was a center for the manufacture of baize, a cloth used in facings. The pun also indicates Marvell's knowledge of Parker's everyday doings.

[328] p. 20 73, correctly] p. 30 74.

[329] opportunity . . . come abroad: Parker had foolishly complained that Buckingham's play was not relevant to his *Discourse* (1670) because it was not yet published. The play was advertised in the Term Catalogues (p. 111) on June 24, 1672. The first performance was December 1671; but Marvell implies that it had been circulating in manuscript long before. This confirms the rumor that the play had been ready for the stage in 1665, featuring Davenant, not Dryden, as Bayes. Davenant died in 1668, and the play was converted to the new circumstances of the 1670s.

[330] *before:* mistakenly omitted in 74.

[331] *Emendatio temporum:* the title of a book published in 1583 by the eminent but pedantic scholar J. J. Scaliger (1540–1609), on confusions in ancient chronology. John Owen owned the 1629 edition (p. 20, #51).

your Book[332] was impending over me? *That I must shortly be disciplin'd by another hand, advising me to say my Prayers, and tremble at the Rod that was coming upon me, except I thought it the wisest way to save the* Hang-man *a labour.* It is a Title[333] so honourable that I should scarce have adventur'd to give it him, but seeing he thinks fit to assume it, you may shift and divide it as you can betwixt you. This was I confess the most authentick way of Prophecy imaginable, it being fulfill'd before hand, but the worst piece of Chronology that ever I heard of. Indeed, Mr. Bayes, it appears to me very evident, that as I told you before this *Hicringill,* was your own book, and it was Licens'd too by your self, as certainly as *Baxter baptiz'd in blood.* The Strains and Recherches[334] are all along exactly the same with those of the *Reproof.* Read but for example in the very same page in answer to what I [110] say of the King of Polands being obliged to wear that Countrey habit. *For which unsufferable affront to his Majesties our Gracious Soveraign his Crown and Dignity Hereditary and not Elective, and at the good will either of People or Parliament, I leave him to be chastiz'd for this bold intrenchment and invasion of our Kings Prerogative and Title to his Crown.* Then read your *Reproof. This is an impudent intrenchment upon his Majesties Crown and Prerogative, for the Polish Kingdom being Hereditary and not Elective, and Parliament deals with their Kings as,* &c.[337] *Friend by your Politick Lectures you indanger your head,* &c. Was there ever such a double Pick-lock of the Law, to find out such a dangerous *innuendo*?[338] But thus those twin-books sympathize all thorow, although the *Reproof* was brought forth a considerable time before the other. Only, Mr. Bayes, as when in the *Rehearsal* you once *resolv'd* that for your *first Prologue you would come out in a*

[*Greg.* p. 196.]

[*Greg.* 196.][335]

[*Gregor.* p. 244.][336]

[*Repr.* p. 498.]

332 your Book Ed.] Book 73, 74.

333 Title: i.e., hangman.

334 Recherches: researches; or, as in French, far-fetched notions.

335 *Greg.* p. 196: in 73 and 74 wrongly placed before the next reference.

336 p. 244 73] p. 224 74: i.e., *RT,* p. 244; wrongly placed in 73 and 74.

337 Marvell or his printer has got this the wrong way round, thus making nonsense. Parker wrote "it is an impudent entrenchment upon his Majesties Crown and Prerogative. For the Polish Kingdome being Elective and not Hereditary . . ."

338 dangerous *innuendo: innuendo* was a term developed in the law of seditious libel; i.e., an injurious meaning alleged to be conveyed by words not themselves actionable. Marvell's usage is precocious.

long black veil with an huge Hangman behind you with a furr'd cap, and his Sword drawn; you could not [111] for a long time determine [*Reh. Com.* p. 7.] whether the *Reproof* or Hicringill should be *the Prologue* [⟨Ibid.⟩] *for the Epilogue, or the Epilogue for the Prologue*; whether your first or your second self should come formost. But having several things in your two books, some fit as you thought to be said in anothers person, and others in your own, you stood a great while thumming the Busk[339] of your *Comfortable Importance,* whether, whether, to divine which of these two should first be hatched, and *which leg should go first.* And from this irresolution and controversie arose [*Reh. Com* p. 30.][340] this most gross and yet most subtile errour in your Chronology, which would require another Scaliger[341] to reform it. The Case is parallel, and you were even so puzzled betwixt those two books as you were at Canterbury betwixt your two Capacities, how you should take place not only of others, but even of your self; whether as you were Arch-deacon, or as you were youngest Prebend: and, though an alternative had been more advisable, you determined that in all Enterviews with your self (which are not so frequent except in your Looking-glass) and in all publick [112] Solemnities among others, the Arch-deacon should both in Place and time have the Precedence.

Having I hope thus far done you right in matter of Chronology, I shall endeavour no less to satisfie you in point of Comedy, and your politick argument concerning the danger of a distinct jurisdiction in Civil affairs, and those of Conscience which you very weightily fetch from the two Kings of Branford. And therefore be pleas'd to accept as serious a Reply from the same Author; *to conclude Sir, the Place you fill has more then amply exacted the Talents of a wary Pilot, and all these threatning storms, which like impregnant clouds do hover o're our heads (when they once are grasp'd but by the eye of reason) melt into fruitful showres of blessings on the people.* Or if you have something to object against this, take your Answer from the [*Reh. Com* p. 12.] Kings themselves at their restauration; *Now Mortals* [*Reh. Com* p. 44.][342] *that hear how we tilt and carreer, With wonder will fear The event of such things as shall never appear.* For no less

[339] Busk: a strip of wood or whalebone in the front of a corset; hence the corset itself.

[340] p. 30 73] p. 40, incorrectly 74.

[341] Scaliger: see note 331 above.

[342] p. 44 73] p. 41, incorrectly 74.

causeless are the apprehensions which you raise up, Mr. Bayes [113] concerning Consciencious people under an equal Government.

I cannot now but take some notice of another argument, your threatning me here and in several other places with the loss of mine Ears, which however are yet in good plight, and apprehend no other danger, Mr. Bayes but to be of your Auditory. But it is no less then you have projected against all the Non-conformists, to the great prejudice of the Nation, in wasting so unseasonably so much good Timber to make *Whipping-Posts* for them and *Pillories.* This hath been a considerable part indeed of the *Ecclesiastical Politie,*[344] and doubtless a most effectual means of Conversion, and bringing men over to the Church of England. I cannot tell where you have learnt it, unless from the Wisdom and Piety of the Tartars, who in the year 1240. though they left upon every mans head one ear standing, yet fill'd no less than nine huge Sacks with the ears that they cut off of the Christians. But there is no peril as far as I perceive to either of us; for my Ears Mr. Bayes do not so much as [114] glow for all your talking of them, and I will secure yours at least upon one account for you are so far from running away like Evagrius for fear of a Bishoprick,[346] that much less will you like Ammonius cut off one of your Ears[347] to render your self uncapable of that Office.

[*Repr.* p. 25. 31.[343] 76.]

[*Del Rio.*[345] p. 144.]

[*Socr. l.* 4. c. 18.]

There follows one thing more which I know is personally intended to

[343] p. 31: actually p. 21.

[344] *Ecclesiastical Politie:* not italicized in 73.

[345] *Del Rio:* Martinus Antonius Del Rio, *Disquisitionum Magicarum* (Cologne, 1633), p. 144. Marvell's page reference shows that he used the 1633 edition, which, though not in Anglesey's library, was owned by John Owen (p. 23, #29).

[346] Evagrius . . . Bishoprick: Evagrius (c. 345–99) was one of the more important ascetical writers of the fourth century A.D. Theophilus of Alexandria had wanted to make him a bishop. For the anecdote, see Socrates, *Historiae Ecclesiasticae,* book 4, ch. 18. Marvell is already exploring early ecclesiastical history, for which, in the *Short Historical Essay,* he used the Greek and Latin edition of John Christophersen, first published in Louvain in 1569. Milton owned and used the 1612 Geneva edition.

[347] Ammonius . . . Ears: Ammonius Parotes ("earless"), one of the Tall Brothers. He accompanied Athanasius into exile in A.D. 341 and later became a hermit. Theophilus tried to make him a bishop also. The story is told by Sozomen, 6:30 (Christopherson, 3:155v–156). Marvell returned to this story in the *Essay,* vol. 2, p. 161.

me, but you have couch'd it so darkly, that at first I could my self scarce understand it. You tell of an Antique Medal,

[*Repr.* p. 27.][348] *On the Reverse whereof was graved*
Th'Alliance betwixt Christ and David.

and desire me to tell you in what Emperors time it was coyned. Why, it was as I remember in the year 1650. and of the *Government of the People of England precedent and present the same.* But if you would hereby insinuate any thing either concerning my self or my Father, I shall once for all unriddle in two or three lines the mystery of this your quotation, because otherwise such nodding reflections impress the Reader more effectually then [115] your more *brisk and laboured* Calumnies, which at other times you word more plainly, and vent more openly against us. This therefore is a greater errour in Chronology than your former; for as to my self I never had any, not the remotest relation to publick matters, nor correspondence with the persons then predominant, until the year 1657.[349] when indeed I enter'd into an imployment,[350] for which I was not altogether improper, and which I consider'd to be the most innocent and inoffensive towards his Majesties affairs of any in that usurped and irregular Government, to which all men were then exposed. And this I accordingly discharg'd without disobliging any one person, there having been opportunity and indeavours since his Majesties happy return to have discover'd had it been otherwise. But as to my Father, he dyed before ever the War broke out, having liv'd with some

[348] This couplet occurs in *Certain Verses Written By severall of the Authours Friends: to be reprinted with the Second Edition of Gondibert. With Hero and Leander the mock Poem* (London, 1653), p. 9. John Owen owned a copy (p. 30, #96). The British Library catalogue attributes the *Verses* to Denham, Buckingham, and others. There were at least three editions. Parker's allusion and Marvell's response are unintelligible unless one knows that the poem in which these lines occur is a satire against the Long Parliament and its imprisonment of Davenant for two years in the Tower. In the poem Davenant pulls out "an antique meddal" and gives it to his rescuers. Marvell, however, pretends there was a real medal coined to celebrate the founding of the republic, and recalls, by its title, the republican tract of John Parker, thereby defending his own father by reincriminating Parker's.

[349] until . . . 1657: Marvell is being disingenuous here. Parker, in his *History of his own Time,* knew that Marvell was the author of the 1654 *First Anniversary of the Government under O.C.,* however anonymous.

[350] an imployment: In September 1657 Marvell entered the office of John Thurloe as Latin secretary, at a salary of £200 per annum.

measure of reputation, both for Piety and Learning: and he was moreover a Conformist to the established Rites of the Church of England, though I confess none of the most over-running or eager in them.[351] I desire you, Mr. Bayes, to make my excuse to the Readers for having trou-[116]bled them so far with my private affairs, by your occasion. But whether they will so easily admit my excuse, for you I know not, you having by the servility of your performances since manifested, that, had you then been of age sufficient, you would not have declined a more homely imployment, which as you may read in Philip de Comines, another Oliver, a Barber, discharged under Lewis the Eleventh.[352] For the rest as to the Distich you have here quoted, whosoever was its Author, it might better have become your Divinity to have supprest so profane an Allusion;[353] but that, as I have told you before, and shall often have occasion, you have a singular snickering after Scripture Drollery. It may seem to some by the manner of your expression as if you had a mind to ascribe[354] it to me: but I resign all my interest in it to you and most men that are conversant about Town know very well who was the Author, who dyed some years since: and it may concern you, for some reasons not out of respect to be named, to take heed that you come not to resemble him in two of his Capacities.[355]

There remain still behind some Figures of Brass which you bestow upon me, as [117] *Colossus of Brass,* in requital to which I can only return you *Colosseros.*[356] *Brass upon Brass is false Heraldry*:[357] but Salt upon Salt is not. *Brazen Brow. Out-brazen. Brass-copper,* and I know not how many more of

[351] my Father . . . in them: see note 348 above.

[352] homely . . . Eleventh: see *The History of Philip de Commines,* trans. Thomas Dannett (3d. ed., 1665), p. 177: Oliver, barber to Louis XI, gained great influence with his master by regularly sucking his piles.

[353] so prophane an Allusion: a reference to the fact that the *Verses* are frequently scatological, and the mock version of *Hero and Leander* frankly pornographic.

[354] ascribe 73] subscribe 74.

[355] Author . . . capacities: Sir John Denham (1615–69), poet and satirist. He was cuckolded by the duke of York, went mad for a short time, and is supposed to have revenged himself by transmitting the pox. [S]

[356] *Colosseros:* see Suetonius, *History of the Twelve Caesars,* p. 248 (Life of Caligula): "A certain Gentleman called Esius Proculus, whose Father had been first Captain of his guards, was so personable a man, and so eminent for the tallness of his Stature, that he was called *Colosseros,* or the lovely *Colossus.*"

[357] *false Heraldry:* cf. *RT,* p. 60 and Bramhall, *Vindication,* p. 54.

the same Metal and Statuary.[358] I cannot possibly learn or imagine where you have improved your talent to such proficience, unless perhaps you have practised with a Modern Divine who is said to have appear'd not many years ago, and Preached in the Copper-Mines of Sweden.[359] And indeed such is your performance here all along, and much more hereafter when you treat concerning the most sacred arguments, that I suspect ⟨it⟩[360] is not all your own; but (though I shall not ⟨therefore⟩ call you *a Scandalous Plagiary*)[361] that you have attracted by force[362] of Phantasie some extraordinary Spirit to your Assistance. As Cicero said on another occasion,

---Multa quidem Ipse,
Multa sed & Daemon tibi suggerit.---[363]

So that I hope the Readers will in so unequal a contest assist me also, at least with their good wishes, and should I be worsted in such discourse, or rather abso-[118]lutely decline it, that yet they will not think the worse of me. Had he but wrote like a Man only, I might possibly have answer'd him: but where there appears something more then Humane in the business, I may well be excused.

But though in his Railing he is more than Man, he hath as moderate and reasonable a Reasoning as other Mortals: and that being therefore more proportionable to my weakness, I shall deal with as soon as I can find it; for it hath that advantage, that it is for the most part Invisible. But in the mean time I shall, to shew him how justly I might have declined all this trouble, quote him two Authors, the one Civil, ⟨the⟩[364] other Ecclesiastical, so nearly related to himself, and this Controversie that till he has answer'd them, I account my self under no obligation. The first his fellow-Chaplain Doctor Tomkins,[365] who in the last Act[366] at Oxford, the Question being,

[358] Marvell is citing a series of allusions by Parker to brass; *Reproof,* pp. 14, 17, 35, 21; Bramhall, *Vindication,* p. 57.

[359] Divine . . . Sweden: Later Marvell will refer to "your Fellow-Chaplain of the Copper-Mines" (p. 424). This implies that the Divine in question was Parker's fellow-chaplain to Gilbert Sheldon, Thomas Tomkins. See n. 365 below.

[360] a mistaken omission in 74.

[361] *Scandalous Plagiary: Reproof,* p. 6.

[362] force 73] fore 74.

[363] *Multa . . . suggerit:* "Many things you did by yourself, but many your Daemon suggested to you." We cannot find this in Cicero.

[364] the 73 cancel: 74 follows uncanceled version of 14.

[365] fellow-Chaplain Doctor Tomkins: Thomas Tomkins (1637–75) became chaplain

An summae Potestates Civiles gaudiant Potestate Clavium:[367] held it in the Negative, and being urged with all the testimonies and arguments to the contrary out of the *Ecclesiastical Politie#*, the Professor[368] was fain to help him out at a dead lift, disavowing# ⟨of this Author, did nevertheless disavow⟩[369] his authority in the face [119] of the whole Country and University in plain terms: *Non stamus hujus Authoritati.*[370] Now where two persons so eminent and equal in Learning, the two Say-masters[371] of Orthodoxy, and of whom all Theology must ask License, are of so contrary opinion in the very Fundamentals of Ecclesiastical Government, is it not time to have a general Vacation, and that all private Process should be respited till so dangerous a division betwixt the two *Pins of the Church of England,* be again cimented? The other is the supposed Father of the *Author of the Ecclesiastical Politie* (for as long as his Book is nameless, I can alwayes speak of him only at random) in that Tract beforementioned, *the Government of the People of England precedent and present the same.* It was writ to spirit men to subscribe to the Ingagement[372] *to be true and faithful to the Common-wealth as then established without a King or the House of Lords*: and there he asserts that, *Populus suo Magistratu prior est tempore, natura & dignitate: quia Populus Magistratum constituit & quia Populus sine*[373] *Magistratu esse potest sed Magistratus sine Populo non potest esse.*[374] Also out of another classical Au-

---

to Gilbert Sheldon ca. 1665, D.D. 1673. He was a zealous royalist and high churchman and was employed as assistant licenser of books. It was he who nearly refused to license *Paradise Lost* because he thought a simile about an eclipse of the sun was treasonable. In the same year, 1667, he published *The Inconveniences of Toleration,* a reply to John Humfrey.

366 the last Act: presumably Tomkins's examination for doctor of divinity.

367 *An . . . Clavium:* Whether the highest civil powers enjoy the power of the keys (i.e. excommunication).

368 the Professor: Richard Allestree (1619–81), provost of Eton and Regius Professor of Divinity at Oxford.

369 #the Professor . . . disavowing# 73 cancel] Smith cites two copies with this revision, which is followed by 74. The text of the canceled version, while it reattributes "Non stamus huius Authoritati" to Allestree, makes nonsense of what follows, where the "two Say-masters of Orthodoxy" are Parker and Tomkins.

370 *Non . . . Authoritati:* We will not stand on this authority.

371 Say-masters: arbiters.

372 Ingagement: The Engagement was an oath of loyalty which, on October 12, 1649, Parliament made obligatory for all officeholders. See *JHC,* 6:306–07.

373 *sine* 73] *sint* 74.

374 *Populus . . . esse:* "The people are temporally prior to their magistracy in nature and

thor, *Vindiciae contra Tyrannos,* he affirms: *Reges* [120] *sunt a Populo & sunt constituti causa Populi.*[375] More he undertakes to prove that the Kings of England had no Negative voice rightfully and by Law, but that it was contrary to the Law and their Oath at Coronation. And then *a fortiori,*[376] that the Lords neither can have any Negative upon the People. That Acts of Parliament may pass and be valid without consent of the Lords Spiritual:[377] and many other passages of an higher nature, if higher could be, which I cite not, least the very reading of them should prejudice the publick, that Book being the very Quintessence[378] of a Sub-Committee-man turn'd Serjeant at Law, and of the High-Court of Justice. It befitted our Author to have wash'd off the blood from his own Threshold before he had accused others: and no man is ingaged to answer his Necessary, Universal, Uncontroulable, Unappealable,[379] Indispensable,[380] Unlimited, Absolute Magistrate, as long as his own Father stands upon Record against him, and he *spends not so much as one Quibble in his confutation.*[381] Nevertheless I will supererrogate[382] and use all the means possible to find some more cleanly spot in him: though indeed he does all [121] over so wallow and coat himself in dirt, that he is almost impenetrable, and, unless his Skin were flea'd off like Baxters, there is no touching him without pollution.

He expostulates with me for *perverting the whole design of his Book.* What do I know the Designs that are managed betwixt him and his Book when they are together in Private? But when any discourse is made publick, it

[*Repr* p. 17. *and* p. 30.]

---

dignity: because the people constitute the magistracy and because people can exist without the magistracy but the magistracy cannot exist without the people"; see John Parker, *The Government of the People of England,* p. 1, citing Daneus (Lambert Daneau), *Politicorum Aphorismorum silva* (Antwerp, 1583), book I, chapter 4.

[375] *Reges . . . Populi:* "Kings derive from the people and are constituted for the people's sake"; see Parker, *Government,* p. 1, citing *Vindiciae contra Tyrannos* ("Edinburgh," 1579), quaestio 3. The *Vindiciae,* a famous antimonarchical text of Huguenot origins, variously attributed to Hubert Languet and Philippe du Plessis-Mornay, was one of Milton's favorites.

[376] *a fortiori:* from the stronger position (to the weaker).

[377] More . . . Spiritual: Parker, *Government,* p. 6.

[378] Quintessence 73] Quintessence 74; the fifth essence, in alchemical experiments.

[379] Unappealable 73] Unappearable 74.

[380] Indispensable 73] Indispensible 74.

[381] *spends . . . confutation: Reproof,* p. 3.

[382] supererrogate: to supererogate is to do or pay more than commanded or required.

must abide the common interpretation, and *Sit Liber Reus Testis & Judex.*[383] You know very well that, though no man ever spoke more perspicuously and fully then Calvin concerning the Obedience due to Magistrates, yet for one particular passage, *De Privatis hominibus semper loquor Nam si qui nunc sint populares Magistratus,*[384] ⟨&c.⟩ he is upon all occasions dress'd up by your self and others of your make as the bug-bear[385] of Princes. Therefore, Mr. Bayes, you should have done well #[*Rep.* 381]# to admonish your book, if it would needs be treating of Government, yet by his example to have learn't discretion and to weigh every word; for you cannot imagine what hurt a silly well-[122]meaning book may do in the world far from its intention: but if it have on the contrary a felonious intention, and not having the fear of God before its Eyes, as I doubt yours has not, you know then that it may do more mischief than you can ever make amends for. And this is all the matter depending betwixt your Book and me, for ought I can perceive by you. The contest is rather of the Truth of Fact than the Truth of Opinion; and a dispute rather of the Eye than the Understanding. Your Book hath said so and so concerning the Magistrate as you have seen in my former quotations. And now you come and would bear me down with more then ordinary confidence that your Book said no such thing, or else you understand its sense better then it self. Therefore pray let us see, Mr. Bayes, what you have to alledge: but in the mean time what have my Readers and I to do but to pity one another? I must quote all over again, and they read it all and you will affirm and deny; deny and affirm, without any regard to Truth or Honesty; and yet all this and more we must indure out of Love to Justice. But I hope at least, Mr. Bayes, that if I do convince ⟨you⟩ that the [123] quotations are right on my part, you will be so ingenuous as to put me upon no further trouble, but confess your Book misunderstood you and was in an errour. For if there be no fault in the Matter, why should you deny it?

You say that what you affirm'd of the Magistrates Authority to take upon

[383] *Sit . . . Judex:* "Let the book be both witness and judge of the accused." Cf. Plautus, *Trinummus,* 2.1.12: "*nisi hoc sic faciam . . . iudex sim reusque ad eam rem.*"

[384] *De Privatis . . . Magistratus:* Calvin, *Institutio Christianae Religionis,* 4:20:31: "I speak only of private men, for if popular magistrates [have been appointed to curb the tyranny of kings . . . I affirm that they fraudulently betray the liberty of the people"]. Calvin's important qualification of his own doctrine of passive obedience can be grasped only by those who complete the quotation.

[385] bug-bear: a sort of hobgoblin supposed to devour naughty children; hence, an imaginary terror.

him the exercise of the Priesthood, was only *as things stood in the bare state of Nature*: and, though you said the Magistrates Power was antecedent to Christ, *yet its continuance depends meerly upon his Confirmation, in that* (very politically said) *whatever Prince does not reverse a former grant confirms it.* Let us see how it is possible that these should either be your words or meaning. *The Priestly and the Royal Office in the first ages of the World, and for well nigh* 2500. *years descended together and upon the same person.* Then *this* same *Power, because it must be seated somewhere, can only properly belong to him in whom the Supream Power resides.* Then: *For he alone having authority to assign to every Subject his proper function, and among others* [124] *this of the Priesthood, as he may transfer the exercise thereof to another, so may he if he please reserve it to himself.* And therefore *this the Wisdom of the elder ages always practised.* Can there be any thing more plain under Heaven, then that you distinguish the elder times against these, and having done so, then assert that what was constant in those former times remains still the same, and that of necessity? But go on: *this* same *Power was firmly establish'd in the World by the unalterable dictates of* Natural *Reason and Universal Practice and Consent of Nations.* And then: *though in the Jewish Common-wealth for peculiar reasons of State, the two Offices of King and Priest were separated, yet the Power of the Priest remain'd subject to the other.* But this was only a present interruption: For then: *our Saviour at his birth came not to diminish the* Natural *rights of Princes,* so that all of them (for the Jewish Common-wealth was already dissolved by the Roman power, and by his coming) were reinstated certainly in the Royal and Priestly Office as before, *for he came not to set up any* [125] *new Models of Polity.* But however, *when Christianity had prevail'd long after to be the the Imperial Religion, then its Government began to resettle where* Nature *had placed it,* nay so far it went, that *therefore the Divine Providence did begin to withdraw, the miraculous power of the Church* (and you can tell us why too here, though the Jewish reasons of State for some peculiar reason you thought fit should be private;) *For the Necessity ceased, the Power of Miracles being now as well supplyed by the* Natural *and ordinary power of the*

[*Repr.* p. 23.]

[*Repr.* p. 27.][386]

[*Ecc. Pol.* p. 32. & 31.]

[*Ec. Pol.* p. 35.]

[*Ec. Pol.* p. 32.][387]

[*Ec. Pol.* p. 33.]

[*Ec. Pol.* p. 48.]

[*Ec. Pol.* p. 49.]

[386] p. 27: actually pp. 27 and 28.

[387] p. 32 73 correctly] p. 38 74.

Prince. And then came the Pope as you told us before, and then came the Reformation which was almost as bad it seems, for *though* [*Ec. Pol.* p. 54.][388] *it wrought wonderful alterations in the Christian world, yet it has not been able* (but you it seems have been able) *to resettle Princes in their full and* Natural[389] *rights in reference to the Concerns of Religion.* Now, Mr. Bayes, what is become of your Excuse, that you *affirm'd this Power in the bare state of Nature, but not under the* [*Ec. Pol.* p. 56.] *guidance* [126] *of Revelation, nor indifferently to all ages and periods of the Church under whatsoever positive Laws and different Institutions*? whereas your whole business has been to prove that Princes and mankind are herein still under the bare state of [*Repr.* p. 23.] Nature, though your Book perhaps did not intend it. But pray therefore Reprove your Book, Reprove even your *Reproof,* and if that will not serve, *take it under Correction*;[390] but if it prove incorrigible, I know not what course I should advise you to take with such a Rascal. For it hath said beside, *To what purpose should Christ grant Princes a new Commission, when this Power was already so firmly establish'd in the World by the unalterable dictate*[391] *of Natural reason,* &c. And this perhaps out of your Natural indulgence to your own book, you took no notice of. But by this means what becomes of that Confirmation of Christs which you speak of? For, as your book argues very strongly, it must have been either an Usurpation or impertinent. And whereas you say, *That* [*Repr.* p. 28.] *though the Magistrates were vested with an Ancient and Antecedent Right, yet its continuance, ever since our Saviour commenced this Empire,* [127] *depends meerly upon his Confirmation: in that whatsoever Prince does not Reverse a former Grant confirms it*; howsoever the Truth prove to be in Fact, yet it is not much obliged to your Argument. For that *who does not reverse a former Grant confirms it,* Supposes that the Power of Nature was equal, if not Superior, to that of our Saviour. For where a New and Superior Power is introduced all former Grants are null, unless they be expresly Confirmed. And so, if the Power of Christ were Superior to that of Nature, and he hath not positively Confirmed that Authority of the Civil

[388] p. 54, 73, 74] actually p. 49.

[389] Natural: throughout this passage Marvell accentuates Parker's use of "natural" by using roman type, not in the original, in order to show up a theme in Parker's thought.

[390] *take . . . Correction: Reproof,* p. 1.

[391] *dictate* 74] *dictates* 73.

Magistrate, it is absolutely extinguished, and the Magistrate hath no Power at all left him, but runs into a *Praemunire*[392] by exercising it. Beside you call the Original of the Magistrates Authority, the *Unalterable dictate of Natural Reason*:[393] so Christs Confirmation could have signified nothing. For what is unalterable is unconfirmable; and yet this too was in the state of depraved Nature. Nevertheless such is your inconsistence, that you own our Saviours Authority to be Superior. And it befitted you so to do, for, if you will be-[128]lieve him, *All Power was given him in Heaven and Earth.*[394] ⟨And he did not confirm it, and therefore he did confirm it.⟩[395] For *the Scripture,* you say, *rather supposes then asserts it,*[396] and *Every Prince not reversing a former Grant confirms it.*[397] ⟨This is your Argument.⟩[398] Nay, but further if you read *p.* 40. There is a solemn Renunciation, as full as could be drawn up by Counsel, of any Power of Christ in the whole matter, *We derive not therefore the Magistrates Ecclesiastical Jurisdiction from any grant of our Saviours; but from an antecedent right wherewith all Soveraign Power was indued before ever he was born into the World.* Here is an Ingagement with a witness, beyond that of 1650. Fathers nown Son.[399] And *will you be true and faithful to the Government establish'd, without Christ,* &c? And is #this# the Reproof then writ to prove *that the Government of England precedent to Christ and present is the same*? and *Ad subscribentes Confirmandum, Dubitantes Informandum, Opponentes convincendum*?[400] For in this I suppose 'twas not your Books fault only, but you and it were both of the same opinion; which is the reason that you say, *We derive it not*: that is, sure you and your Book. For if you meant it otherwise, you should have done [129] well to shew your Plenipotence[401] from all those that authorized you. However methinks betwixt You and your Book, you

[*Ec. Pol.* p. 34.]

[Ec. Pol. *p.* 40.]

392 *Praemunire:* a writ by which the sheriff is charged to summon an accused person.

393 *Unalterable . . . Reason: Discourse,* p. 35.

394 *All . . . Earth:* Matthew 28:18.

395 This apparently self-contradictory statement, presumably meant in mockery of Parker, was wisely omitted in 74.

396 *Scripture . . . it: Discourse,* p. 35.

397 *Every . . . it: Reproof,* p. 28.

398 This . . . Argument: also omitted in 74, to reduce tautology.

399 Fathers . . . son: a reprise of Marvell's account of Parker Sr. and his book, from the title of which he now proceeds to quote.

400 *Ad . . . convincendum:* see note 197 above.

401 Plenipotence: full authority.

might have had more wit then to have excluded any Grant of our Saviours, whatsoever, unless (as indeed you treat him like other Princes and *Crown'd heads,* only allowing him a Power something less than to others, and more moderate) you confine his everlasting Kingdom to the day of his Birth, and date his Dominion that is infinite from *Anno Domini & Anno Regni nostri primo.*[402] And now after all this, I leave it to the most candid or severest Reader to judge, whether for one in your case to affirm, *that you spoke of the Magistrates exercising the Priesthood in his own person, only in the bare state of nature*; and *that you did not make the Magistrates Power independent herein from Christ*; be not a flat contradiction to your self, and so outfacing to all ingenuity, that had you not first wash'd your face in Stygian water,[403] it were impossible for you to persist without blushing. And what detriment the Church of England might suffer upon this occasion, I leave it to themselves to consider. But I perceive some are wiser then some, and, though you were so forward [130] as to undertake this side of the Argument, yet it was so order'd betwixt you or somewhere else, that Doctor Tomkins should defend the contrary. For the Church of England is so intelligent, as not to trust all in one Doctors bottom:[404] but knows that it is good having two Strings to the Ecclesiastical Bow, that if one break the other may hold.

Neither, considering what you have thrown out upon this occasion, was it at all improperly said by me, That if the King might exercise the Priesthood in his own person, it was all the Reason of the world that he should too assume the Revenue. This, though it were the only passage in my whole book that could possibly be perverted to an ill sense in this matter, is by you and the rest of your *Scaramuccios*[405] invidiously applyed and aggravated both here and in many other places at large, as if it had been seriously intended by me for his Majesties assuming the Church Revenue. Whereas it appears to have been meant quite contrary, and only to represent your Malice in defaming the Government, or those persons eminently instrumental under his Majesty both in Church [131] and State, as if there were some such counsel or design on foot; and to show you how ridiculous your fear was (if it were not

[*Repr.* p. 22.]

[402] *Anno . . . primo:* in the year of our Lord and the first year of our reign; a monarchical formula.

[403] Stygian water: like the waters of the river Styx, infernal; and in Old Chemistry a name for nitrohydrochloric acid.

[404] bottom: foundation; vessel or tub.

[405] *Scaramuccios:* see note 152 above.

counterfeit) of any such matter, and to fright you something the more with your own argument. For indeed though you accuse me as if I put his Majesty in mind to violate his Coronation Oath for preserving the Rights of the Church, it was all that I said only to put you in mind, that, if the Magistrate may exercise the Priesthood in his own person, any such Coronation Oath was in it self invalid; as being contrary to the *unalterable dictates of Natural Reason*: and that, if he did exercise the Priesthood himself, he was by that Oath perjured, unless he himself also assumed the Revenue. For though you are pleasant, and say that by the same reason he may as well, because he is the Supream Civil Magistrate, assume the Revenues of the Laity; the argument holds not: forasmuch as the Ecclesiastical Maintenance is annex'd to the Function, and, this being extinguished, that devolves naturally upon the King; or, the King exercising the Function himself, the Revenue is so much the more due to him [132] and such other Lay persons as he shall depute under him in stead of the Clergy. But this being a thing so dissonant to mine own and other mens ordinary conceptions (though I shall shew you in a fitter place hereafter why you ought still to continue in the same opinion) I left you to be responsible for your own consequences; For that you may understand, Mr. Bayes, that I am none of those, that were I in capacity, could give any so pernicious advice, I tell you, and desire you hence forward to take notice of it, that I am so far from thinking enviously of the Revenue of the Church of England, that (though I will not as you do call that *Sacriledge* which makes up the estates of so many of the Nobility and Gentry of England, and of which the Church too hath its part, if it be Sacriledge,) that I think in my Conscience it is all but too little, and wish with all my heart that there could be some way found out to augment it. But in the mean time, (to tell you my heart, for what needs dissembling among friends?) I am inclinable to think, as the Revenue now stands, there is sometimes an errour in the Distribution. And for example, I think it is a shame that such a[406] one as you [133] should for writing of Political, flattering, persecuting, scandalous Books, be recompensed with more preferment, then would comfortably maintain ten Godly Orthodox and Conformable Ministers, who take care of the Peoples Souls committed to their charge, and reside among them. Whereas you, as being too great for your Sacred imployment, must be exercising it by your Spiritual Deputy or

[*Repr.* p. 24.]

[406] a 74] an 73.

Deputies, and one of them[407] so notorious, that, though married, it was his usual practice, under pretence of studying late at night for his Sermons, to lye with his Maid Mary Parker before-mentioned, and instead of instructing your Parish in the *Fruits of the Spirit,* he gave them an example of the *Works of the Flesh,* which *are these, Adultery, Fornication, Uncleanness, Lasciviousness,* &c. so far indeed excusable, if, as 'tis said, after he had finished the work, he attempted to administer something to undo it again, and make the fruit abortive. You in the mean time, as if you were an Exempt of the Clergy,[408] and as Parson can transmit over the Cure of Souls to your Curate, saunter about City and Countrey whither your gilt [134] Coach and extravagance[409] will carry you, starving your People, and pampring your Horses, so that a poor man cannot approach their Heels[410] without dying for't. I speak not of stale Anachronismes,[411] but of things that really happen'd all since the writing of your *Reproof,* and which deserve one better. For what reason can you alledge why you should gluttonize and devour as much as would honestly suffice so many of your Brethren that take pains in the word; like the great[412] Eater of Kent,[413] when you are either so unable or so *dull and lazy*[414] that you do not one mans labour? This is the great bane and scandal of the Church, that such Livings as more immediately belong to it should be the worst supplyed, and that you and some few Ingrossers[415] like you, should represent your selves by so ignorant and vicious Curates, men not fit to be mention'd in the same Collect;[416] and upon whom indeed the *Spirit of Grace* cannot descend but by *Miracle*: and while things are no better order'd, it is not strange at all if Non-conformity take root and spred further among Consciencious persons, nor that the Revenue of the Church, though in it self

[*Gal.* 5.19.]

[407] one of them: Mr. Lee of Ickham again.

[408] Exempt . . . Clergy: not subject to episcopal jurisdiction.

[409] extravagance 73] extravigance 74.

[410] their Heels 74] *their heels* 73.

[411] Anachronismes Ed.] Achronismes 73, 74; events from a wrong time period.

[412] the great 73] the the great 74.

[413] the great Eater of Kent: Nicholas Wood (d. 1630), who "would devour at one meal what was provided for twenty men." See Thomas Fuller, *Worthies of England* (1662), p. 86 (A, p. 26, #88).

[414] *dull and lazy: Reproof,* p. 1.

[415] Ingrossers: monopolists.

[416] Collect: assembly, collection; form of prayer in the Book of Common Prayer.

too slender, should ne-[135]vertheless appear too great and envious by the manner of Distribution. This is more then I should have said, had not you by your unseasonable discourses drawn it out of me, but however is intended principally to your self: though as long as the Church shall not think fit to repress such Writers it is unavoidable; but that some faults already too visible should be mention'd.

But to proceed: You say, *that I have upbraided you with ascribing an infinite jurisdiction to Princes without any regard to the Divine Laws, and that you give an Ecclesiastical authority to the Civil Magistrate absolutely Paramount to any other Jurisdiction whereas you meant it,* you say, *only in defiance to the claim of any other Humane Power.* What shall I answer in this case? Will you not remember that you say your *Power of the Prince is antecedent to Christ*; that it *was established such by the unalterable dictates of Natural reason*? That *God of Necessity must have given them such power*?[417] If it be antecedent to Christ, how is it accountable to him? If established by natural reason, does it not result only from man as a loose and free agent [136] however produced, and though from the *Vesicles of the Earth,* yet acting by Nature? and if God of necessity must give the Magistrate this Power, do you not make God accountable rather to him; and may ⟨not⟩ the Magistrate bring his action against the Deity *de Potesta imminuta,*[418] or accuse him *Laesae Majestatis*?[419] So that hereby the sum of your Doctrine appears to be (if without offence I may name it) that your Priestly and Uncontroulable Power of the Civil Magistrate is Antecedent to Christ, Contemporary to the World, nay at least Co-eternal, if not Preeternal, to God himself. And this is the more strongly confirm'd by your asserting, which I told you of, that the *Magistrate hath Power to bind his Subjects to that Religion that he apprehends most advantagious to publick Peace and Tranquillity*:[420] So that he may if he chuse his Religion, chuse his God too, unto whose Jurisdiction he will be accountable; and if he begin to think as you say he does, *That Christianity is an Enemy to Government,*[421] he may make use of Paganism. But still you clamour *that when you asserted the Soveraign Power to be Absolute, Uncontroulable, 'twas not to be understood so*

[*Repr.* p. 20.]

[*Repr.* p. 15. & 16.]

[417] *Power . . . power: Discourse,* pp. 34, 35, 40.

[418] *de . . . imminuta:* concerning his reduced power.

[419] *Laesae Majestatis:* of lèse-majesté, harming the sovereign authority.

[420] *Magistrate . . . Tranquillity: Discourse,* p. 12.

[421] *Christianity . . . Government: Discourse,* p. 178.

in regard to God.[422] (Why [137] then ⟨pray⟩ do not brave it and justifie your self at this rate, but make your submission humbly, and acknowledge your offence as an honest man should do.) And that, *when you said 'twas Absolute and Unlimited, no man, unless he would give his mind to misunderstanding, could understand it in any other sense, then that it was not confined to matters purely Civil, but extended its jurisdiction to matters of Ecclesiastical Importance,* (that is the word it seems in all senses, *Comfortable, Close, Ecclesiastical*) *upon which account alone you determin'd it to be Absolute, Universal and Uncontroulable.*[423] Why I perceive you did not, or would not observe what I had all the while been driving at, and of what I was all along jealous; that the thing would not end there, but that, as you had given to certain Uses, and for certain Valuable Considerations an Universal and Absolute Power to the Prince in Ecclesiasticals, so you would, if it were but out of Revenge, bestow the same upon him in Civils.

But you say: *there was never a man of such immodesty in the world to charge you with these things, whereas you know no Writer ancient* [138] *or Modern that hath so vehemently and industriously asserted the contrary, spending two whole Chapters in your first Book, to prove, that the Opinion of the Unlimited humane Authority was no less then rank Atheism and Blasphemy, and subverts the Power of all Government, and safety of all Societies.* Ay a very good man are you: hold you there. But I hinted to you once before, Mr. Bayes, that this writing forsooth against Atheism from the first hath stood you in very good stead, and under pretence of confuting Mr. Hobbs[424] (who I believe could explain himself as innocently as you have done) you #should# have usher'd in whatsoever Principles men lay to his charge, only disguised under another Notion to make them more venerable. Nay, in good earnest, I do not see but your *Behemoth*[425] exceeds his *Leviathan* some foot long, in whatsoever

[*Repr.* p. 21.]

[422] *that . . . God: Reproof,* p. 16.

[423] *when you said . . . Uncontroulable: Reproof,* p. 16; in this passage Marvell or his printer has lost control of the principle of italicization.

[424] Mr. Hobbs: Thomas Hobbes (1588–79), philosopher, author of *Leviathan* (1651), perhaps the most influential English work of political theory. In 1666 there were threats in parliament of an inquiry into Hobbes's religious views.

[425] *Behemoth:* Job 40:15; the other great beast to match Leviathan, the whale. Does this indicate Marvell's knowledge of the existence of Hobbes's *Behemoth,* a history of the civil war completed by 1668 but suppressed by Charles II? Alternatively, Marvell is alluding to the preface to Hobbes's *The Questions concerning Liberty, Necessity and Chance* (London, 1656), p. 20: "I can give them a fit Title for their Book: Behemoth

he saith of the Power of the Magistrate in matters of Religion and Civils; save that you have levyed the *Invisible Powers* to your assistance, the better to fright men out of their Wits, their Consciences and their Properties.[426] I have told you in my former Book that I do really believe you are no Atheist, and however I know you have so much wit as to [139] keep it to your self, though not perhaps to avoid some opinions, which if followed home, might in due time lead to it. But to what purpose is it, Atheism, or not Atheism, and what difference in the matter, if under pretext of Divinity an Uncontroulable Principle be insinuated and obtruded to the invasion of all the Rights of Mankind, and Priviledges of Reason: if an Unlimited and Absolute Power be challenged in things of Ecclesiastical as well as Civil, and of Civil as well as those of Ecclesiastical Consideration? and I think under one or other of these all are comprehended.

I have something a troublesome and unnecessary task herein if I were to deal with a person of ordinary ingenuity; for his Book is in Print, and I have also in Print charged this upon him, and nevertheless by this last Book he puts me again upon this double drudgery, to prove first that he said it, and afterwards to prove that he meant what he said. But, though I know this is only a piece of his Art, hoping to tire out the Auditory, not out of any belief of his own Innocence, yet a Guilty person ought not to be debarr'd from making the best of his own Case, [140] and I hope the Readers will, by his tedious evasions and tergiversations[427] in a thing so evident, be the rather provoked to do him Justice. Having therefore sufficiently witness'd his words, I shall now proceed to manifest his Intention. And to that purpose I shall alledge one or two material passages; the first in his first Book, *the Ecclesiastical Politie.*

He saith, *'Tis better to submit to the unreasonable Impositions of Nero and Caligula, then to hazard the Dissolution of the State.* What he means here by Dissolution of the State, he might have done well to have expressed: but what the unreasonable Impositions are, cannot be understood otherwise then either in matters of Religion or of Propriety, and how both these Emperors acquitted them-

[*Ec. Pol.* p. 215.]

against Leviathan." Compare the antiprelatical tirade in *The Loyal Scot,* ca. 1672–73: "And in a Baron Bishop you have both / Leviathen serv'd up and Behemoth" (*P&L,* 1:184).

[426] Properties 74] Proprieties 73.

[427] tergiversations: literally, acts of turning one's back (on earlier statements); reneging, equivocating.

selves on those two accounts, appears in their History.[428] For as to Nero,[429] beside his personal vices, which can scarce be imitated or parallel'd but[430] by Caligula, I will but succinctly mention how he behav'd himself to the Publick in the course of his Government. If men bequeath'd nothing to him by their last Wills and Testaments in token of [141] gratitude to the Prince, he confiscated the whole estate, and fined all Lawyers whatsoever by whose advice such Wills had been drawn. He decreed, that, though there were but one Informer, it should suffice to convict men of Treason, either for Words or Actions.[431] Whensoever he bestow'd an Office, he did it with these Instructions: *You understand what I have need of, and therefore let us make it our business, that no man may have any thing which he can call his own.*[432] Besides so many particular instances of Savage cruelty, he design'd to cut off the heads of all the Governors of Provinces. To poyson the whole Senate at a Dinner. To burn the City, and at the same time to turn out Wild beasts among the People to terrifie them from quenching the Fire.[433] A blazing Star appearing, he resolv'd to divert the *Omen* from his own head, by the Massacre of all the Nobility, and the most considerable persons in Rome. He did cause the city of Rome to be set on fire, and so carelessly that divers of his Officers, being taken with fire and flax in their hands, and in the very act, yet were let go for fear of offending him; and some houses not being so easily burnt, he took care to [142] have them beaten down with Engines.[434]

[428] their History: i.e., Suetonius, *The History of the Twelve Caesars.*

[429] Nero: Roman emperor A.D. 54–68; patron of the arts and music, his reign began well but ended in massive abuses.

[430] but 73] out 74.

[431] *History,* p. 348: "The first thing he decreed was . . . that their Wills should be void, and their Possessions confiscate, who had shown themselves ungrateful to their Prince in leaving him nothing; and that such Lawyers as had drawn or dictated the said Wills, should be finable and punish'd. That all words and actions should be brought within the Compass of Treason, if there was but any one informer to justifie the accusation."

[432] *History,* p. 348: "He never gave any man an office, but he had these words into the bargain; *You know what I need, and let us make it our business that no man may have any thing to call his own.*"

[433] *History,* p. 364: "His resolution was, to send persons into all the Provinces and armies to succeed, and massacre those which commanded. . . . To poison the whole Senate at an entertainment; to burn the City, and to turn out wild Beasts amongst the people, that so obstructing their quenching of the fire, their destruction might be more inevitable."

[434] *History,* pp. 357–58: ". . . he set [the city] on Fire so publickly, that several of his Officers being taken by the Consulares in their houses, as it were in the very act, with

And, though it was manifest how it was designed and[435] acted, he derived the crime of all this upon the innocent Christians.[436] He Sacrilegiously took the Donatives from the Temples and melted down the Images of the very Tutelar Gods of Rome to make money.[437] He contemned all Religions, and particularly is reckon'd to have been the first Persecutor of Christianity. He affirmed publickly, that *none of his Predecessors had known their own Power*:[438] the very same words in a manner, and spoke in the same sense as those of our Author, that *Governors have not been throughly instructed in the Nature and Extent of their Power*: and the other; *that no Nation hath rightly understood and duely managed Government, because*
[Ec. Pol. *p.* 58.] *they have not chain'd their Non-conformists to the Oare,*
[Ec. Pol. *p.* 223.] *and condemn'd them to the Galleys.* The Conclusion of this Tragedy is common: how Nero was by the Senate proclaim'd an Enemy to the State, and Sentenced to be punish'd after the Ancient manner; that is to be stripp'd naked, and his head held up with a Fork, till he were whipp'd unto [143] Death; but this by another death he prevented.[439] This is I suppose one, Mr. Bayes, of your *Uncontroulable Magistrates,* these his *Unreasonable Impositions,* and this your *Dissolution of the Government*; and you think 'twas better that this Nero had still reign'd then that Galba[440] should have succeeded. I would all of you that are of that mind had such Governors. And thus much concerning Nero.

Fire and Flax in their hands, they let them go without daring to meddle with them: There being certain Storehouses likewise about his *Golden Palace,* (which ground he desired to have) not being so easily burnt, because the Walls were of Stone, he caus'd them to be beaten down with his Engines of War."

[435] and 73] and and 74.

[436] Christians 73] Christian 74.

[437] *History,* pp. 348–49: "He spared not the very Temples themselves . . . melting down their Images of Gold and Silver, not excusing so much as the Images of the Tutelar Gods."

[438] *History,* p. 357: "He asserted publickly, *That none of his Predecessors had known their own power.*"

[439] *History,* pp. 370–71: ". . . reading . . . That he was declared Enemy to the State by the Senate, and . . . was to be sought after and punish'd according to Custom: He demanded what kind of punishment that was, and being told, that he was to be stript stark naked, that his head was to be held up with a Fork, and in that posture to be whipt to death [he stabbed himself]."

[440] Galba: Servius Sulpicius Galba (B.C. 3–A.D. 69); Roman emperor for about six months following Nero's suicide, he was himself assassinated.

But now as to Caligula[441] and his *Impositions,* What disposition he was of he manifested by his *wishing that all the People of Rome had but one Neck*:[442] beside that, he was used to *lament the unhappiness of his time, because it was not signaliz'd by any publick Calamity,* (as if there needed any other Calamity but his Government, and he himself had not abundantly supply'd the defect of any other misfortune) *whereas* said he, *the Reign of Augustus was felicitated by the defeat of Varus and his Legions, as Tiberius his was memorable for the fall of the Amphitheatre at Fidence,*[443] (in the ruines of which Twenty thousand men perish'd) *but my unfortunate prosperity will leave me in danger of being inglorious after death and forgotten.*[444] But he took good and effectual care to the contrary. He was [144] often heard to say, that he *would certainly reduce things into such a condition, that the Lawyers should not have any thing to say or do, but what he thought just and equitable*:[445] and he was as good as his word. The things may be seen in particular in his History: his whole Reign having been a Pandect[446] of Rapine and Tyranny, and his rule by which he proceeded, *that he might do what he pleas'd with whom he pleas'd*:[447] As to the *Sacred Rites and their Presidents,* take one instance. The Priest being ready to offer a Sacrifice at the Altar, he took upon himself, *according to the unalterable dictates of Natural Reason, to exercise the Priesthood in person,*[448] and having vested himself as in the Power, so too in the Sacerdotal habit, he took up the Mallet, and feigning to knock the Beast down, instead thereof struck down the Officer who stood by with

[441] Caligula: Gaius Caesar, nicknamed Caligula from wearing the soldiers' boot; Roman emperor A.D. 37–41.

[442] *History,* p. 244: "Being highly offended with the people for favouring his adversaries, he cryed out, *Would to God the people of Rome had but one neck.*"

[443] *Fidence:* i.e., Fidenae.

[444] *History,* p. 245: "Besides this he used frequently to complain of the unhappiness of his time, *Because not afflicted with any considerable calamity, to make it remarkable;* Lamenting *That the Reign of Augustus was memorable for the overthrow of Varus; Tiberius his, for the fall of the Amphitheatre at Fidenae, but such was his unfortunate prosperity, he was in great danger to be forgotten.*"

[445] *History,* p. 247: "And as to the Lawyers . . . he was often heard to say, *He would certainly bring things to that pass, that they should have nothing to say, but what he thought Equitable and Just.*"

[446] Pandect: a complete digest or abridgment.

[447] *History,* p. 243: "His Grandmother Antonia admonishing one day . . . *Remember* (says he) *I may do what I please, with whom I please.*"

[448] *according . . . in person:* references back to Parker's arguments.

the Knife.[449] Which should methinks be a sufficient caution unto Churchmen hereafter how they trust the Civil Magistrate with exercising the tools of the Priesthood. But this is nothing in respect of what follows. He commanded that the Statue of Jupiter Olympius among many others should be brought over from Greece, and their [145] heads taken off to place his[450] in the room of 'm. He seated himself often in the middle betwixt Castor and Pollux to be adored by the People. He built a temple to himself, and appointed Priests to his own Divinity: and even then there wanted not ambitious men, who by favour aspired to that Office, or purchased it by Simony;[451] upon any Ecclesiastical vacancy. The Sacrifices appointed for his own Worship, were Peacocks, Pheasants,[452] and all other the delicatest Fowl, and of greatest rarity.[453] He took upon him the Ensigns of all the Gods: the Lion from Hercules, the Caps from the Castors, the Ivy and Thyrsis[454] from Liber, the Caduceus[455] from Mercury, the Sword Helmet & Buckler from Mars, the Crown, Bow, Arrows and Graces from Apollo. He made love to the Moon, and pretended to her imbraces.[456] But more then this he commanded that his Image should be set up in the Temple at

[449] *History,* p. 246: "A Sacrifice being brought to the Altar . . . he came himself to the Altar in the habit of a Priest, and lifting up the Mallet as he would have knock'd down the Beast, he knock'd an Officer on the head which stood by with the Knife."

[450] place his 73] his place 74.

[451] Simony: see note 128 above.

[452] Pheasants: a subdued pun on Parker's marriage to Miss Pheasant.

[453] *History,* p. 235: ". . . he commanded, that the Images of those Gods which were in most esteem . . . and amongst the rest that of Jupiter Olympicus, should be brought from Greece, that their heads being taken off, he might place his own in their room . . . and altering the Temple of Castor and Pollux, into the model of a Portico, he plac'd himself oftentimes betwixt the divine Brothers, to be adored by all which came thither . . . he built a Temple, dedicated it to his own Divinity, and instituted Priests and Victims . . . The richest men of the City, either by bribery or favour, purchas'd the dignity of this Priesthood, according as vacancies fell. The Sacrifices which they offer'd were Peacocks, Pheasants, Numidian Hens, and other Fowls, the most rare and delicate could be got."

[454] Thyrsis: thyrsus, a staff or spear tipped with an ornament like a pinecone, borne by Bacchus.

[455] Caduceus: a wand with two serpents twined around it.

[456] *History,* p. 235: "When the Moon was in the Full, and shined bright, his custom was to call to her continually, and to invite her to bed to him, that she might taste of his embraces."

Jerusalem,[457] and that the Temple should be dedicated only to him, and he there to be worship'd under the name of the New Jupiter. He caused his Statues moreover to be placed in the Jews Synagogues to be there adored. Insomuch, that the great Grotius[458] does most accurately deduce and expound the 2 Thessalonians, 2 c. 3 and 4 verses[459] concerning [146] him (though differing therein from other Interpreters) and that St. Paul adventur'd to call him the *Son of Perdition, that is worthy to dye in the most miserable manner,* as he did afterwards, *and the Adversary, that is, the Enemy of God*: and that *his sitting as God in the Temple of God was to be meant of his command to erect his Image there, though it were not effected, yet however seeing he did his best to have it done.* And this, Mr. Bayes, is your other Magistrate, who *understood it seems the Nature and Extent of his Power*; and, as you would have Princes do, *made inflexible Laws under the severest Penalties, and acted up roundly to them.* [*Ec. Pol.* p. 21.] But when all people were weary of him, one Cassius Chaerea,[460] a Tribune of one of the Praetorian Cohorts, [*Ec. Pol.* p. 271.] for many affronts receiv'd from him, and among others that of giving Priapus and Venus for the Word,[461] undertook his death,[462] and so happen'd the Dissolution of his Government. Nevertheless I shall not decide here what submission was to be made either to Nero's or his Impositions; but only remember what your Doctor Heylin said concerning King Edward the sixth.[147] *It shall be left to the Readers Judgment, whether the King was either better studyed in his own Concernments, or seem'd to be worse principled in*

[457] Image . . . Jerusalem: as recorded by Josephus, *Jewish War,* 2.10.1 [S] Anglesey owned Josephus, *History of the Jews* (1640), p. 25, #44.

[458] Grotius: see *RT,* p. 63 and note 139 above. The work in question here is *Annotationes in Novum Testamentum* (Paris and Amsterdam, 1646), 2:678 (A, *Hug. Grotii Comment. Omnia in Vetus & Novum Test,* in 3 vols. [Paris and Amsterdam], p. 1, #25).

[459] 2 Thessalonians 2:3,4: "For that day shall not come, except there come a falling away first, and that man of sin be revealed, the son of perdition; who opposeth and exalteth himself above all that is called God, or that is worshipped; so that he as God sitteth in the Temple of God."

[460] Cassius Chaerea: see *RT* p. 163 and n. 682 above.

[461] the Word: an allusion to the practice of starting the Palatine games with a password from the emperor; see *History,* pp. 266, 268.

[462] *History,* p. 266: "Caligula in most opprobrious manner abus'd him, as wanton and effeminate; coming to him one while for the word, he gave him (by way of mockery) Priapus, or Venus."

matters which concern'd the Church. And in another place, *King Edwards death I cannot reckon for an infelicity to the Church of England, he being ill principled in himself, and easily inclined to embrace such Counsells.*[463] Neither will you I hope affirm that the loss of these two Emperors was any grievous Judgment upon the Roman Common-wealth, or a very sad affliction to the State of Christianity. This same Caligula was he that took so great affection to Incitatus, a fleet and metall'd Courser, that beside a Stable of Marble, a Manger of Ivory, Housing-cloaths of Purple, and a Poictrell of precious stones, he furnish'd him an house very nobly, and appointed him a family to entertain those who render'd visits to his *Equinity* and his *Hinnibility*[464] (words of yours on another occasion) and to treat such Guests as were invited, with the more magnificence. Nay, so far did he carry on this humour, that 'tis said, had he not been prevented, he [148] design'd to have made this race-horse Consul;[465] as fit however for that Office, as his Master to be Emperor. What pity 'tis, Mr. Bayes, that you did not live in that fortunate age, when desert was so well rewarded and understood, when preferments were so current! Certainly one of your Heels and Mettle would quickly have arrived to be something more then an Arch-Deacon. If an Horse had so great a Court, and so rich Furniture, and stood so fair for Election, what might not such an one as you have expected! Give me leave, Mr. Bayes, having been so long in your debt to requite and cap you with an *Ancient Distich*:[466] if I Thou you this once, it is not out of disrespect but only to repeat it the more faithfully. Had you then lived,

[*Heylin* Ref. p. 132.]

[*Heylin* Pref. Ref. p. 4.]

[463] your Doctor Heylin: see *RT* p. 79 above and note 231. The work in question here is *Ecclesia Restaurata, or the History of the Reformation of the Church of England* (1661), pp. 4[a2v], 132 (A, p. 2, #80).

[464] his *Equinity* and his *Hinnibility:* horsiness and capacity to neigh.

[465] *History,* p. 265: "Nay he was so exorbitant in his affection to a Horse he had, which he call'd Incitatus, that . . . his Stable was built of Marble, his Manger of Ivory, his Houshing-clothes [*sic*] of Purple, and a rich Collar of precious Stones which he wore for his *Poictrell;* he allow'd him a house very well furnish'd, and a Family to attend him, for no other end, but that such as were invited in his name, might be received and entertained with the more magnificence and elegancy; and it is reported, that he had a design to have made his Horse a Consul."

[466] *Ancient Distich:* a reference back to Parker's citation of an "Antique Medal," *Reproof,* p. 27.

Thou should'st have had a Silver Stye,
And she her self have pigg'd[467] *thee by.*[468]

So that there would have been no occasion for you to have coveted, as you do, your Neighbour Prebends House,[469] but you should have begun[470] at last, as Nero said, to dwell like your self, and have been installed in a Palace suitable to your Dignity.[471] But though those happy dayes are past and gone, you need not grumble; unless no-[149]thing will suffice you, and you are so ambitious of a fortune, that you cannot be content with the Spirituals of Simon Magus[472] and the Temporals of Caligula.

Hactenus, saith Grotius upon the same place: *Impium Principem descripsit, nunc venit ad Impium Doctorem*;[473] So that the field lies open (were it not against good Huntsmanship[474] to course two Hares at once) to run your Doctoral similitude here through your *Prote Ennoia*,[475] showing her self at so many windows; your Doctrines and deceits, tending *ut homines ad*

[467] *pigg'd:* lain close like pigs.

[468] *Thou . . . pigg'd thee by:* perhaps Marvell's revision of the nursery rhyme:

There was a lady loved a swine,
Honey, quoth she,
Pig-hot, wilt thou be mine?
Hoogh, quoth he.

I'll build thee a silver stye,
Honey, quoth she,
And in it thou shall lye.
Hoogh, quoth he.

[469] Neighbour Prebend: there were twelve prebends at Canterbury; perhaps Parker's envy was inspired by the most recent installation, that of T. Blomer in August 1673.

[470] begun 73: began 74.

[471] *History*, pp. 346–47: "He built a house which extended from the Palace as far as the Mount Esquilin . . . When this magnificent Structure was finish'd, . . . he approv'd it only thus far, as to say, *That at last he began to dwell like a man.*"

[472] Simon Magus: the origin of the term *simony;* in Acts 8: 9–24 he offered the disciples money to acquire the power of baptism.

[473] *Hactenus . . . Doctorem:* Grotius, *Annotationes in Novum Testamentum*, 2:681: "Thus far he has described an impious Prince, now he comes to an impious Doctor," commenting on 2 Thessalonians 2:8–9. [S]

[474] Huntsmanship 74] Huntmanship 73.

[475] *Prote Ennoia:* first conception.

flagitia impelleres aut in flagitiis detineres;[476] your attempting to fly with the assistance of two other Spirits.[477] But I will let all these things rest till another occasion shall offer, nor am I at present in humour to be too severe upon you. Only pray let me show you, Mr. Bayes, with how much reason you have recommended to the publick the Civil Magistrate Caligula, seeing you do so particularly resemble him. Who that shall but cast his eye upon you in your writings, can take any other representation of you, then that you have not only usurped the winged Bonnet from Mercury, the Thyrses and Ivy from Bacchus, the Bow[478] and Arrows and the Graces from [150] Apollo, the Lion from Hercules, the Sword, Buckler, and Head-piece from Mars; but that you have even stoln the Cerberus from Pluto, and the Snakes and Torches from the Furies? And though I will not strain it so high as that *you exalt your self above all that is called God in the Temple*,[479] yet it is notorious that you pretend to more *Worship* then belongs you in the Cathedral. Nor does it look otherwise when men see you crowd your self in between the Dean and the Senior Prebend,[480] then like Caligula's taking the middle between Castor and Pollux. 'Tis the same Imperial Spirit that makes you justle so for place, that out of your seeking for Pre-eminence, you have almost made a Schism in the Church of Canterbury: and it concerns Christian Princes to take care how you rise higher, lest the ancient Ecclesiastical Controversies be revived, to the *disturbance of the publick Tranquillity, and the Ends of Government.*[481] Then as Caligula had his Images in the Synagogues, so have you your Curates at Ickham and Chartham, for they *having no Power,* you know, *are no better than Statues and Images of Authority.* But Mr. Lee of Ickham in particu-[151]lar is so like you, that if both your heads were cut off and *Trans-pros'd* on each others shoulders, no man living but would take you one for the other. But to omit these, I shall, as in

[*Ec. Pol.* p. 12.]

[476] *ut homines . . . detineres:* Grotius, *Annotationes,* 2:682; "so as to drive men towards shameful behaviour or trap them in it"; commenting on 2 Thessalonians 2:10.

[477] your attempting to fly . . . Spirits: Simon claimed before Nero that he would fly with the assistance of his "angels," which he did, but Peter called upon the "angels of Satan" to let him go, and he fell to his death. *The Acts of the Holy Apostles Peter and Paul* [*Anti-Nicene Fathers,* 8:484.] [S]

[478] Bow 73] Bows 74.

[479] *exalt . . . in the Temple:* 2 Thessalonians 2:4.

[480] Dean and Senior Prebend: John Tillotson (1630–94) was installed dean on November 4, 1672. The senior prebend was John Castilion (1613–88). [S]

[481] *disturbance . . . Government: Discourse,* p. 12.

the case of Don Sebastian,[482] show by some more private marks of your body and mind, that though you might have imposed upon the Parthians for a Pseudo-Nero,[483] it is impossible you should be a Perkin-Caligula,[484] but the very Original. First he had a singular quality for which he admired himself, and gave it a peculiar name of *Adiatrepsia,* which was his unmoved constancy in assisting at, and looking upon the most horrid executions:[485] and no less is your unrelenting and undaunted resolution, in first condemning the Non-conformists to *the Galleys, the Pillories, the Whipping-Posts, the Publick Rods and Axes,*[486] and afterwards beholding the Execution with an extraordinary sedateness and judicial temper of Spirit. He had beside this a peculiar Antipathy which was the reason that it was made an hainous and capital offence in his reign to name but a Goat upon whatsoever occasion.[487] And the same aversion have you, if not to a greater height; insomuch that, I having but mention'd a Goat in my for-[152]mer Book, and under the disguised names too of *Crabe* and *Cabre,*[488] you do as good as accuse me of animating therefore the Subjects to Rebellion. He was moreover, as I told you, ingaged in a great intrigue of Courtship with the Moon, like that of your Camarade Bayes: *Where shall I thy true Love know, Thou pretty, pretty Moon? To morrow soon, ere it be noon, On Mount Vesuvio.* And you in like manner

[*Repr.* p. 210.]

[482] Don Sebastian: king of Portugal (b. 1554), supposedly killed at the battle of Alcacerquivir (1578). There were a number of accounts of his reappearance. He was supposed to be recognized by some "secret marks and tokens." See *A Continuation of the lamentable and Admirable Adventures of Don Sebastian* (1603). [S]

[483] *History of the Twelve Caesars,* pp. 375–76: "a person whose condition and quality was unknown, having the confidence to say he was Nero, twenty years after he was dead; his very Name was so gratefull to the Parthians, that they espoused his Quarrel."

[484] Perkin-Caligula: an allusion to Perkin Warbeck, a pretender who appeared in Ireland in 1491 declaring himself to be Richard, duke of York, younger son of Edward IV, supposedly murdered by Richard III in the Tower.

[485] *History,* p. 243: "There was nothing in his own nature he commended so much as (in his own words) his *adiatrepsian,* or unrelenting at the sight of Executions."

[486] *Galleys . . . Axes: Reproof,* p. 159.

[487] *History,* p. 260; The reason was that, except on his head, his body hair was "shagged and long. Whereupon . . . it was taken as a hainous and Capital offence . . . to name a Goat upon any occasion whatever."

[488] *Crabe* and *Cabre:* see *RT* p. 157 and note 659.

[*Reh. Com.* p. 51.] boast your self to be Married to a Goddess: but which of them 'tis I know not, for Selene[489] was adored under the figure of Minerva: but 'tis most probably Luna, for you courted her in the language of Bayes his Eclipse, but something more smutty, as I could rehearse to you from a good hand, were it not too broad for any mans mouth but yours, and that I would not have you blame me again for *betraying publickly the mirth and freedom of private conversation.*

[*Repr.* p. 244.] The last token of your Caligulism shall be the Sacrifices which he appointed of Pheasants and Peacocks to his Deity: and accordingly your Friend the *Author of the* [153] *Friendly Debate* hath sacrificed a *Pheasant,*[490] and I have sacrificed a *Peacock*[491] to your Divinity; and I hope it will be therefore henceforth and for ever to me propitious and favourable. Now that I have thus far represented in the persons of Caligula and Nero what it was that you meant in your former argument, and what those Impositions are which you instruct Princes to practice, and their people to submit to, I shall dismiss this Testimony, after I have mentioned one Imposition more of Caligula's, and indeed very laudable, which if you also will submit to, I would recommend to your graver consideration. He condemned those Authors, whose Writings gave no satisfaction to the publick, either to blur them over with a Spunge, or lick them out with their tongues; unless they rather chose to be disciplin'd with Ferulaes, in Commutation of Penance, or to be duck'd over head and ears in the next River:[492] a Punishment, which were it but for your incorrigible faculty of railing and scolding, you could scarce under so gentle a Government have avoided.

But to pass over, Mr. Bayes, from your Roman Empire, and come nearer home, [154] the second Testimony that I shall produce out of your own Book of the same Nature, shal be what you reply upon me concerning the Vicar of Brackley in Northampton-shire, your Countryman Doctor Sib-

489 Selene: Greek goddess of the moon.

490 your . . . *Pheasant:* presumably Simon Patrick married Parker and Miss Pheasant.

491 *Peacock:* perhaps a reference to the fact that Nathaniel Ponder, Marvell's bookseller, worked at the sign of the Peacock.

492 *History,* pp. 233–34: "He ordain'd a solemn Contention in Eloquence, both in Greek and in Latine . . . But for those who gave no satisfaction at all, they were condemn'd to expunge what they had done, whether with a Sponge, or their tongue, unless they would choose rather to be corrected with Ferula's, or plung'd over head and ears in the next River."

thorpe,[493] and who commenced Doctor much after the same manner that you did. His Sermon is extant in the History, and some *Heads* and *Points* of it I gave you in my first book as a *Pinn-paper* of your modern Orthodoxy, and the very *Flower* of your *Brann* (not of the Church of England, as you would suggest) in the Doctrine of some men in the late times concerning Impositions, and I shall here sift it after your grinding. Here in the *Reproof* you undertake to tell the story of that Doctors Sermon, which needed not for the Sermon is yet extant, beside what is legible in Arch-bishop Abbots Narrative;[494] but you ⟨also⟩ adventure #besides# to justifie it and Manwarings case[495] also, which you allow to be the same with Sibthorpes. But whereas you limit the matter to the indiscretion only of a single Country Vicar or so, I gave you those particular relations for an example of what was [155] then the Doctrine *a-la-mode*[496] at that time in most of your Pulpits, and which you here attempt to bring ⟨again⟩ in fashion. You defend that Loan and the carrying of it on in that manner, and if there were any illegal design of absolute Government promoted, you ascribe it to *the Impudence of the Members of Parliament,* to the *Assaults they then made upon the Royal Power by their bold and unreasonable demands*; to their *bringing things to that pass, that nothing must be done unless the King would either grant away all his power to them, or keep it all to himself*; to the *rudeness and insolence of their demands, so that the King must sometimes govern without them or not at all.*[497] And as to those persons and Members that were imprison'd for refusing the Loan; you say *they had forgot the respect they ought to their Prince, and the duty they ought to God*; that the *King was forced on those courses by the stubbornness of Presbyterian Parliaments*;[498] (No, Sir, it was by the Flattery of Archidiaconal Preachers) that as things then stood betwixt him and his Parliaments, *Punctilio's of Law were superseded; Their demands were disloyal and unreasonable*: all *good and ingenuous Subjects ought not to* [156] *have stood then so curiously upon Precedents and Nicetyes of old Custom.*[499] And in conclusion

[*From* p. 366. *to* p. 376.]

[*Repr.* p. 371.]

[493] Doctor Sibthorpe: see *RT,* p. 183 above, and note 792.
[494] Abbots Narrative: see *RT,* pp. 181 above, and note 775.
[495] Manwarings case: see *RT,* pp. 187 above, and note 821.
[496] *a-la-mode:* compare *Mr. Smirke; or, the Divine in Mode.*
[497] *the Impudence . . . at all: Reproof,* pp. 372–73.
[498] *they had forgot . . . Parliaments: Reproof,* p. 374.
[499] *Punctilio's . . . Custom: Reproof,* p. 375.

you determine *ex Tripode*[500] that *whatever that Parliament or the Refusers of the Loan were by the Laws of the Land, they were even then #the# most notorious Rebels by all the Laws of the Gospel.* It is worth taking notice more particularly, that the Parliament which you have thus qualified, was the Parliament 3° Caroli,[501] which I have heard by unprejudiced men to have been an Assembly of the most Loyal, Prudent, and Upright English Spirits that any age could have produced. Their actions are upon Record, and by them, not by your perishing and false glosses and relations, will posterity judge concerning them. And if we had no other effects and Laws from them but *the Petition of Right,*[502] it were sufficient to eternize their memory among all men that wear an English heart in their bosom. But it is too much for you to make their Process however, and to arraign a Parliament as Traytors by an Ecclesiastical Bill of Attaindor. *You dare,* you say, *determine them so.* 'Tis indeed like your fellow Bayes his Draw-can-Sir---[157]

[*Repr.* 376.]

You huff, you strut, look big and Stare,
And all this you can do because you dare.[503]

But I assure you, notwithstanding your complaint *of Ecclesiastical Laws, being in a manner cancell'd by the oppositions of Civil Constitutions,* 'twill never be well in England as long as that Doctrine holds that men though Loyal by the Laws of the Land, yet are most notorious Rebels by all the Laws of the Gospel. Here is Divinity indeed, not on Gods name I am sure, nor the Kings; whose then, you may consider. *You say indeed if Doctor Sibthorpe intermedled with the Kings Absolute Power of imposing Taxes without Consent in Parliament, he went beyond his own Commission.* But why might he not, Sir, as well as you?

[*Ec. Pol.* p. 20.]

[500] *ex Tripode:* from the three-legged stool; as used at Cambridge by a joker appointed to dispute with the candidates at Commencement.

[501] Parliament 3° Caroli: i.e. the parliament of 1628–29, the last parliament of Charles's reign before the eleven years of personal rule.

[502] *the Petition of Right:* passed by Parliament in 1628 forbidding the king to impose or to assess taxes without consent of Parliament. For the full text of the Petition, see www.britannia.com/history/docs/petition.html.

[503] *You huff . . . you dare:* Buckingham, *Rehearsal,* act 4, scene 1; identified in *The Key to the Rehearsal* (p. 23) as a parody of Dryden's *Conquest of Granada:* "Spight of my self, I'll stay, fight, love, despair: / And all this I can do because I dare" (part 2, 1.3.105–06). Parker himself cited the *Conquest,* p. 283 above.

[*Repr.* p. 370.] Where is your Commission, unless what he might not Preach, you have License to Print, and that alters the case? 'Tis it seems no matter for Manwaring, you say, for *his zeal in the Cause of Loyalty was punish'd with Preferments to defie the Pragmatical-ness of that Parliament,* and [158] so was Sibthorpe, and so you doubtless expect to be if you be not already sufficiently punish'd [*Repr.* p. 374.] with Preferments for the same merit. You will do well to Register your name in some Office of Address, or rather with the Clerks of both Houses; that if any new occasions[504] of Preferment should start, they may not escape you, nor you according to your deserts be forgotten. In conclusion, these kind of Sermons were not the least inducement of that Petition wherein I told you Martin Parkers Ballads were complain'd of; the very next Article but one being against *such as Preach'd that Subjects have no Propriety in their Estates, but that the King may take from them what he pleaseth, and that all is the Kings, and he is bound by no Law.*[505] In this Petition, though I find sundry things intermix'd which had been better[506] omitted, yet it is no wonder, if having this just cause of complaint, their pen being in their hand they dash'd out further then was fitting against the Clergy.[507] And now I hope I have pretty well evidenced that your Book hath said what it did say, and that you meant what you said, and it was but the self same design which both of you managed together. And yet, Mr. [159] Bayes, you think this is hard dealing, when you betwixt ranting and whining affirm this your Grand Thesis of the Unlimited and Absolute Magistrate, *to be so granted and undoubted a Truth that it is plainly ratified by the unanimous consent of all mankind. Nay* (inhumane!) *when a man has demonstrated its certainty from that unavoidable* [*Repr.* p. 9.] *influence that Religion always has upon the peace of #the# Kingdoms.* [⟨ib.⟩] *But when beside you have drawn up a brief and plain account of the parts, the coherence; and the design; when you have provided with equal care and caution too*[508] *against the inconvenien-*

[504] occasions Ed.] occasion 73, 74.

[505] *such as . . . Law:* "The Humble Petition of . . . the City of London," Rushworth, *Historical Collections,* part 3, 1:94, no. 10. As before, Marvell could have seen this privately in Rushworth's collection of documents.

[506] been better 74] better been 73.

[507] dash'd out . . . Clergy: the petition notes "A Particular of the manifold Evils, Pressures and Grievances caused, practised and occasioned by the Prelates and their Dependants." [S]

[508] *too:* not italicized in 73.

cies of both extreams; Unlimited Power on the one hand, and Unbounded License on the other: when the bounds you have proposed are so easie to be observed, and so unnecessary to be transgressed by all parties concern'd. That Governors only take care not to impose things certainly and apparently evil, and that Subjects be not allow'd to plead Conscience for disobedience in any other case: and when you have so carefully avoided all kinds of severity more then is absolutely necessary. Alas good Sir have you so, and nevertheless do they mis-[160]use you? Where is your Witness? But pray what are indeed these bounds that you have set? Let us consider; though when you had made the Magistrate once Unlimited, I know not whether he gave you leave again to set Bounds to him. But indeed they are as you say very easie. Only that he take care not to impose things certainly and apparently evil. But what things are so, you take not so much care to inform him. Oh! I have it: *He may command any thing in the worship of God that does not tend to debauch mens Practices, or their Conceptions of the Deity.* But I was of opinion that the Magistrate would think fit not only to refrain from imposing things certainly and apparently evil⟨, but that he would even have shun'd the Appearance of evil⟩:[509] I am sure, if he won't, his Subjects for their part ought both as men, and more as Christians, to follow that Maxime. But therefore in such weighty cases who shall be the Expositor, who the Judge betwixt People and Magistrate, one would have thought the Scripture should for good reason have decided a Case of Conscience. No it may as to matter of Obedience to the Magistrate; but as to the Magistrates Ecclesiastical Power of com-[161]manding, it has rather supposed it and Christ himself, being as you make him but Natures Successor, thought not fit to meddle with it. Why then we must have something else, *a Guardian of humane Nature,* (you know whence the word comes) to decide the business. In conclusion (though it be unusual, yet some precedents there are in the Roman Empire) you declare your self the Magistrate and Judge of all Controversies, without expecting the suffrages of the Prince or People. We are like to be well-govern'd then, Mr. Bayes, are we not think you all well taught and edified? Pray tell me first whether you be a Lawful Prince. But that is not so much matter neither: for some Usurpers because of the tenderness of their Title, have thought fit to carry with the greatest clem-

[*Repr.* p. 17.]

[*Repr.* p. 18.]

[*Ec. Pol.* p. 66.]

509 but . . . evil: the omission of this phrase in 74 is clearly in error.

ency and Equality to the people, and to make very good and wholsom Laws for the Publick. What yours are, I must intreat the Readers to see at least in the Contents of the seventh and eighth Chapters of your *Ecclesiastical Politie*: where you tell them strange Stories, and argue at a wild rate, and, knowing they were such Dunces as that they would not comprehend your reasoning, [162] you fall out upon your poor distressed Subjects, and Rogue and Rascal them in the most significant terms of Rebels, Traytors, ⟨Villains,⟩ Schismaticks, and the most notorious Hereticks, and, which you avow from the beginning of the Book to have been your design, you muster up all Christian Princes to Neronize and Caligulize them, unless they themselves the Princes will chuse for their omission to be Uilenspiegled[510] and Sardanapalized by you. But the Bounds which you boast your self to have so wisely and equally determined betwixt the Magistrate and the People are so inconsiderable and low, that any man may without weights leap plum over them. If any Subject do take that which is commanded to be apparently evil, he needs but, as I quoted you in my former Book,[511] consider that *if there be any Sin in the Command, he that imposes it shall answer for it, not the man whose duty it is to obey; for the Commands of Authority* (mark but here the[512] gradation of his capering Divinity) *will warrant my Obedience, my Obedience will hallow or at least excuse my action, and so secure me from Sin, if not from Errour.*[513] And in another place which I have since taken more notice of. *Publick Peace and* [163] *Tranquillity is a thing in it self so good and necessary, that there are very few actions that it will not render virtuous, whatever they are in themselves, wherever they happen to be useful and instrumental to its attainment.* Was there ever any man that writ of things of so high consequence, as to concern mens Reason, Honesty, and Salvation at so profligate and loose a rate! I will not be tedious, but those whole Chapters are such Stuff. You should have told us which actions were excused, and which were hallow'd, that we might have known how to shew them respect according to their several qualities. You should have caused the Magistrate to enter into good and sufficient security, and be bound in a round sum to save the

[*Ec. Pol.* p. 317.]

510 Uilenspiegled: duped, from Till Eulenspiegel, the fourteenth-century German folk hero noted for his roguery and practical jokes. [S]

511 quoted . . . former Book: see *RT*, pp. 93, 100 above.

512 mark . . . the: incorrectly italicized in 73.

513 *will . . . Errour:* incorrectly in roman in 73.

Subject harmless. And the Penalty of the Bonds should have differ'd, what in case he run the Subject only into Errour, and what in case of Sin, And the day too should have been expressed, although it had been but the Day of Judgment. And in the other place; if there be so few Actions that the Publick Peace will not render virtuous whatever they are in themselves, it had been kindly done of you, Mr. Bayes, [164] to enumerate them, and to have gratified our curiosity with shewing us the whole process and manner of the Transmutation. And no less arbitrary and conjectural is that expression concerning the Magistrates Power: *The same Providence that intrusted Princes with the Government of humane affairs, must of necessity have vested them with at least as much Power as was absolutely Necessary to the Nature and ends of Government.* You should have done well to have given us the Date when Providence intrusted the several Princes, and by what means it was brought about. You should have prescribed just how much power was intrusted, for ⟨if⟩ it were a *Depositum*[514] it is fit ⟨that⟩ there should be great exactness in order to account for it. But suppose Providence should have intrusted them with a little more Power then were absolutely necessary, whether or no would it have been absolutely Destructive? A small errour in the quantity leads on to great absurdities. Neither will the same proportion agree with all[515] Politick Bodies. The Turk, the Pope, the Emperour, the King of France, the King of Poland, and so on, are not all intrusted with the same [165] Power: but some of 'm have more, and some perhaps less then is absolutely necessary. 'Tis pity that you were not at the Admensuration,[516] and that you like Apollo did not order the Ballance of Government,[517] or fill the Cartridges and distribute them to each Magistrate according to his *Calibre.* Then whereas you say that Providence must of necessity have intrusted the Magistrate with at least as much Power as was absolutely necessary, you ought to have consider'd whether, according to your usual Exactness, Necessity upon Necessity *be not false Heraldry*: and when you add to the Nature and Ends of Government you should have exprest what those were; for Authors are very much divided about it; you say, Publick Peace and Tranquillity. Why

[*Ec. Pol.* p. 40.]

[514] *Depositum:* something entrusted for safekeeping.

[515] all 73] a 74.

[516] Admensuration: the apportionment of just shares.

[517] Apollo . . . Government: cf. Callimachus, "Hymn to Apollo," *The Works of Hesiod, Callimachus and Theognis,* trans. Banks (1856), p. 130: "And following Phoebus men are wont to measure out cities." [S]

but some, for the attainment of that, hold it to be Necessary that Subjects should have no Arms, others that they should have no Wealth, no Propriety, and a third that they should have no Understanding, no Learning nor Letters. You have indeed exprest your self in another place of the same Book that *there is no Creature so ungovernable as a wealthy Fanatick*:[518] Now you that say, *Princes must have at least as much* [166] *Power as is necessary to the ends of Government,* should also have weigh'd how much Wealth at least, and how much Religion at least was Necessary to make a man a *Wealthy Fanatick,* that Princes might have calculated better how to govern them. Whether a Dram of Wealth mix'd with a Pound of Conscience, or whether a Scruple of Conscience infused in a thousand Pounds a year do compound a Wealthy Fanatick. For otherwise there may be a great errour in the Dose of Government; and you may, even during your dull and lazy distemper, have had experience how Necessary it is to be exact in the preparation and quantity, though it were but of *Callimelanos.*[519] The word Fanatick is of a large acceptation. The Papists are Fanaticks; The Presbyterians, the Independents, the Anabaptists of New-England, and I know not how many more are Fanaticks. The Parliament 3° Caroli, that drew up the Petition of Right, and others that you mention, excluding that of Forty,[520] were Presbyterian, Fanatical, Puritanical, and Rebellious Parliaments. Who knows at this rate where Fanaticism will end, and whether, according to your notion, every man who has an estate, or who asserts propriety, [167] may not in a short time be deem'd a Fanatick; nay, whether ⟨you⟩ your self, that were formerly a Fanatick in point of Religion, may not now you are grown so wealthy, upon that account at least, turn Presbyterian? Moreover in your *Censure* too *of Platonick Philosophy,* when you first made courtship to *Ecclesiastical Politie,* but the Intrigue was not so avowed and publick, you have said: *Governors must keep their Subjects from sinking into too much Ignorance, or rising to too much Knowledge in matters of---*[521] (I wonder what this ⟨---⟩ should mean: it is not sure *of those designs that aspire to serve your dearest---*)[522] *for the former renders them salvage, which is apparently destructive to Government; the latter makes them proud, conceited, and zealous; that breeds*

[518] *there is . . . wealthy Fanatick: Discourse,* Preface, li.

[519] *Callimelanos:* calomel, or mercurious chloride, a drug used in the treatment of syphilis. [S] Copy B4 has here a cropped marginal MS note: "[Me]rcurius Dulcus . . . The Fre.Countrey"].

[520] of Forty: the Short or the Long Parliament.

[521] *Governours . . . of: Censure,* p. 219.

[522] *those . . . dearest: Censure,* p. 123; actually in the preface to its attached *Account.*

contempt of Governors, and sets them upon headless plots and designs of Reformation, that usually proceed to Rebellion, &c.[523] I see now that it is to be supplyed, *or rising to too much knowledge in matters of*---- Religion. You that do, as if it were in Rogation week,[524] perambulate the Bounds of Government, and leave them *so easie to be understood, and so unnecessary to be transgress'd,*[525] why would you here have conceal'd them, or was it that in this [168] manner you drew a Line betwixt the Prince and the Subject to serve ever after for their Boundary? Will you believe me? seeing you had blam'd me for saying that *you have extended the Princes Power to Impotency as a streight Line continued grows a Circle*;[526] when I saw this streight Line of yours, I took my Compasses and *divaricating*[527] them for experiment, I drew the Circular Line all along thorow it, that you could not see what was become of it, and without the least offence to the Figure upon either account. But here again, Mr. Bayes, or to use Chaucer's word for a change,[528] Mr. Limitour,[529] you are much out and too indefinite. You should if you would have said any thing to the purpose, have read a Lecture here to Princes upon the Centers of Knowledge and Ignorance, and how and when they Gravitate, and Levitate. But as you failed in the matter of Wealth and Fanaticism, and you did not instruct them how to know when their Subjects were fat or lean enough, when they were honest or dishonest enough; so you have here disappointed Governours extreamly, who would have been glad to have behaved themselves well, and to have ruled with good repu-[169]tation, that they are at an absolute loss to know how to diet their Subjects and to distinguish when their people are fools enough, and when wise enough, or how much ignorance would suffice a Reasonable man. But however upon this Survey, if the rule hold good that an Indefinite is equipollent to an Universal,[530] I collect from these two passages of yours last

[523] *for the . . . Rebellion: Account,* pp. 219–20.

[524] Rogation week: the Monday, Tuesday and Wednesday preceding Ascension Day.

[525] *so easie . . . transgressed: Reproof,* pp. 17–18.

[526] *you . . . Circle:* see *RT,* p. 146 above.

[527] *divaricating:* spreading apart; cf. *Defence,* p. 342 ("Divarications of the Nerves"), and *RT,* p. 122 above ("two fingers divaricated").

[528] Chaucer's word for a change Ed.] a Chaucer's word for change 73, 74.

[529] Limitour: a friar licensed to beg within certain limits. Cf. Chaucer, *Wife of Bath's Tale,* ll. 873–84: "For ther as wont to walken was an elf / Ther walketh now the lymitour hymself."

[530] Indefinite . . . Universal: In logic, a universal is applicable to or involves the whole of a class or genus. An indefinite has no mark either of universality or particularity (e.g.,

quoted, that you are pretty well satisfied that Providence having of necessity intrusted Princes with at least as much Power as is absolutely necessary to the Nature and Ends of Government, they ought for Peace and Tranquilities sake (for 'tis *Must* too in this out of your *Platonick Philosophy*) to keep their Subjects from Arms, from Letters, and from Propriety. For as you said formerly, *there are few actions* (whether of the Governour or of the People) *which that Nobler end of Publick Tranquillity will not render virtuous, whatsoever the actions be in their own nature.*[531] How others will judge of it I know not, or how far Princes will think ⟨that⟩ Expedient which you affirm necessary: but certainly if this course were once effectually taken, the whole year would consist of Halcyon Holy-dayes,[532] and the [170] whole world free from Storms and Tempests would be lull'd and dandled into a Brumall[533] Quiet.

Neither are you more distinct in the matter of Necessity, wherein, it being the Original from which you first derive all this Absolute and Unlimited Government, it behooved you if ever to have *shown your Heraldry.* For though Necessity be a very honourable Name of good extraction and alliance, yet there are several Families of the Necessities, as in yours of Bayes, and though some of 'm are Patrician, yet others are Plebeian. There is first of all a necessity, that some have talk'd of, and which I mention'd you in my former Book, that was pre-eternal to all things, and exercised dominion not only over all humane things, but over Jupiter himself and the rest of the Deities, and drove the great Iron nail thorough the Axle-tree of Nature.[534] I have some suspition that you would have men understand it of

"man is of few days"). "Equipollent" is used of propositions that express the same thing notwithstanding formal diversity. The phrase was used, however, by Sir Edward Dering in a speech to parliament on November 22, 1641, in a partial defense of episcopacy. Marvell would have found it in Rushworth, *Collections* (1659), part 3, 1:426: "Name the species of this Idolatry, that is introduced by the Bishops, that is (for indefinite propositions are aequipollent to universall) by all the Bishops, and by a *command* of theirs."

531 *there are . . . nature: Discourse,* p. 317.

532 Halcyon . . . dayes: fourteen days of calm weather, anciently believed to occur about the winter solstice, when the halcyon, or kingfisher, was brooding in a nest floating on the sea.

533 Brumall: the shortest day of winter.

534 necessity . . . Nature: Necessitas, in Orphic theology, the personification of absolute necessity, appears as the mother of the Moirai (Fates), as the wife of Demiurgus (Fashioner of the world), and mother of Heimarmene (Destiny). Her power is greater than that of the gods, and the world revolves around the spindle she holds in her

your self, and that you are that Necessity. For what can you be less or other who have given an Absolute and Unlimited Power to Princes, who have made Nature pre-existent to our Saviour, and pre-eminent, and have [171] therefore forced him to subscribe to its dictates, and confirm its grants, though to his own derogation and prejudice, who have obliged Providence to dispense Power to the Magistrate according to your good pleasure, and herein have claim'd to your self that Universal Dictatorship of Necessity over God and Man, though it were but *Clavi figendi causa,*[535] and to strike thorow all Government, Humane and Divine with the great Hammer? There is another which may be named the Necessity of the Neck, or Caligula's Necessity before spoke of; that is, that the whole body of the People should have but one Neck.[536] Do you mean this? for it is very useful and virtuous towards the attainment of *Publick Tranquillity and the ends of Government.* A third is the Necessity of the Calf, which in this Case would be very considerable to the Magistrate. For the Calves of the Legs being placed behind where they are altogether unuseful, it were necessary in some mens opinion, to place the Calf rather before for defence, lest men should break their Shins by making more hast then good speed. You may then reckon Necessity of State, to which in former times 'twas [172] usual to oppose Impossibility: and of kin to these is Necessity that has no Law, and that Necessity where the King loses his Right, that is, when nothing is to be had.[537] And lastly, there is one sort of men for whose sake there is a common Maxime establish'd, that there is an Absolute Necessity they should have good Memories.[538] I have thus far gratified your indefiniteness by this enumeration that you may hence forward pick and chuse a Necessity as you shall see occasion. And in the mean time, that I may furnish you with a Christen-name as well as a Sir-name, and set you up for an Author, you may please henceforward to write your self Mr. Necessity Bayes. But

---

lap. (See Plato, *Republic,* 616c.) Horace represents her as grasping huge nails (*Odes,* 1.35). [S]

[535] *Clavi figendi causa:* in order to drive in the nail; a reference to the *Dictator clavi figendi causa,* chosen to drive a nail into the temple wall. See Livy 7.3.3–8 (363 B.C.) and 8.18.12–13 (331 B.C.).

[536] Caligula's Necessity . . . one neck: see p. 305 above.

[537] These last two maxims are quoted from John Ray, *A Collection of English Proverbs* (Cambridge, 1670), p. 124, "Necessity hath no law," and p. 125, "Where nothing's to be had, the King must lose his right." The joke is in combining them. (A, p. 35 #84)

[538] common Maxime . . . Memories: cf. Quintilian, *De Institutione Oratoria,* 4:2.91: "Mendacem memorem esse oportere" (A liar needs a good memory). [S]

though the Necessity you speak of does more or less partake of all or most of those I have mention'd, it seems to me rather reducible to that of the Calf. That is to say, You do hereby seem to imagine, that Providence should have contrived all things according to the utmost perfection, or that which you conceive would have been most to your purpose. Whereas in the shape of Mans body, and in the frame of the world, there are many things indeed lyable to Objection, and which might [173] have been better if we should give ear to proud and curious Spirits. But we must nevertheless be content with such bodies, and to inhabit such an Earth as it has pleased God to allot us. And so also in the Government of the World, it were desirable that men might live in perpetual Peace, in a state of good Nature, without Law or Magistrate, because by the universal equity and rectitude of manners they would be superfluous. And had God intended it so, it would so have succeeded, and he would have sway'd and temper'd the Minds[539] and Affections of Mankind, so that their Innocence should have expressed that of the Angels, and the Tranquility of his Dominion here below should have resembled that in Heaven. But alas! that state of perfection was dissolv'd in the first Instance, and was shorter liv'd than Anarchy, scarce of one days continuance. And ever since the first Brother Sacrificed the other to Revenge, because his Offering was better accepted, Slaughter and War has made up half the business in the World, and oftentimes upon the same quarrel, and with like success. So that as God has hitherto, instead of an Eternal Spring, a standing [174] Serenity, and perpetual Sun-shine, subjected Mankind to the dismal influence of Comets from above, to Thunder, and Lightning, and Tempests from the middle Region, and from the lower Surface, to the raging of the Seas, and the tottering of Earth-quakes, beside all other the innumerable calamities to which humane life is exposed, he has in like manner distinguish'd the Government of the World by the intermitting seasons of Discord, War, and publick Disturbance. Neither has he so order'd it only (as men endeavour to express it) by meer permission, but sometimes out of Complacency.[540] For though it may happen that both the Parties may be guilty of War, as both of Schisme, yet there are many cases in which War is just, and few however where there is not more Justice on one ⟨side⟩ then the other. To repell an Invasion from abroad, or extinguish an Usurpation at home would not require a long consultation with Conscience. The Jews themselves learnt at last that 'twas lawful to

[539] Minds 74] Mind 73.

[540] Complacency: satisfaction.

fight a battel on the Sabbath-day, rather then submit their throats to the Enemy;[541] And had all Sectaries been of the opinion of some [175] Anabaptists and others, that all War is unlawful, they could have afforded matter rather of derision then disturbance. Nevertheless it is most certain, that Tranquility in Government is by all just means to be sought after, and it might easily be attain'd and preserv'd, did those that ⟨most⟩ pretend to it sincerely labour it. But Men have oftentimes, as I have partly show'd you in your own Doctrine, other Ends of Government, and that to compass them require other Means then will consist with so specious a Title. How should such persons arrive at their design'd port, but by disturbance? for if there were a dead calm always, and the Wind blew from no corner, there would be no Navigation. You will object perhaps, and I stand corrected, that though there should not be a breath of air, it might be performed by Galleys: and 'tis indeed the very thing proposed in your *Ecclesiastical Politie*, that you might be row'd in state over the Ocean of Publick Tranquility by the publick Slavery: But because you are subject to misconstrue even true English, I will explain my self as distinctly as I can, and as close as possible what is mine own opinion in this matter of the Magi-[176]strate and Government; that seeing I have blamed you where I thought you blame-worthy, you may have as fair hold of me too, if you can find where to fix your Accusation.

The Power of the Magistrate does most certainly issue from the Divine Authority.[542] The Obedience due to that Power is by Divine Command; and Subjects are bound both as Men and as Christians to obey the Magistrate Actively in all things where their Duty to God intercedes not, and however Passively, that is either by leaving their Countrey, or if they cannot do that (the Magistrate or the reason of their own occasions hindring them) then by suffering patiently at home, without giving the least publick disturbance. But the Dispute concerning the Magistrates Power ought to be superfluous: for that it is certainly founded upon his Commission from God, and for the most part sufficiently fortified with all humane advantages. There are few Soveraign Princes so abridged, but that, if they be not contented, they may envy their own Fortune. But the modester Question (if men will needs be medling with matters above them) would be how far it is ad-[177]visable for a Prince to exert and push the rigour of that Power

[541] Jews . . . Enemy: see Josephus, *The Jewish War*, 2.19.2. [S]

[542] Copy H1 (inscribed by Thomas Hollis) has here a large marginal pointing hand, indicating the importance of this section.

which no man can deny him; For Princes, as they derive the Right of Succession from their Ancestors, to they inherit from that ancient and illustrious extraction a Generosity that runs in the blood above the allay[543] of the rest of mankind. And being moreover at so much ease of Honour and Fortune, that they are free from the Gripes of Avarice and Twinges of Ambition, they are the more disposed to an universal Benignity towards their Subjects. What Prince that sees so many millions of men, either labouring industriously toward his Revenue, or adventuring their Lives in his Service, and all of them performing his Commands with a religious obedience, but conceives at the same time a relenting tenderness over them, whereof others out of the narrowness of their Minds cannot be capable? But if this gracious Temper be inconsistent with *the Nature and Ends of Government,* it behooves them to be aware, and by the rougher methods to provide for their own and the Peoples security. For though Princes are not, as in some barbarous parts of the world, sworn as 'twere upon [178] the Almanack, and violate their Coronation Oath, unless the seasons of the Year be very punctual, yet (abating only for any extraordinary accident from Heaven) they are responsible to him that gave them their Commission for the happiness or infelicity of their Subjects during the term of their Government. It is within their Power, depends upon their Counsels, and they cannot fail of a prosperous Reign, but by a mistaken choice betwixt Rigour or Moderation. But whoever shall cast his eye thorow the History of all Ages, will find that nothing has always succeeded better with Princes then the Clemency of Government: and that those, on the contrary, who have taken the sanguinary course, have been unfortunate to themselves and the people, the consequences not being separable. For whether that Royal and Magnanimous gentleness spring from a propensity of their Nature, or be acquired and confirmed by good and prudent consideration, it draws along with it all the effects of Policy. The wealth of a Shepheard depends upon the multitude of his flock, the goodness[544] of their Pasture, and the Quietness of their feeding: and Princes, whose dominion over Man-[179]kind resembles in some measure that of man over other creatures, cannot expect any considerable increase to themselves, if by continual terrour they amaze, shatter, and hare[545] their People, driving them into Woods, and running them upon Precipices. Nay even if this similitude were pursued to the

543 allay: alloy; a baser metal mixed with a nobler.

544 goodness 73] good 74.

545 hare: harass.

uttermost, and *the Absolute and Unlimited Power* over rational beings were so desirable as some, for their own sinister ends, will always be suggesting to Governors, there is not any so proper and certain way of attaining it, as by this softness of handling. If men do but compute how charming an efficacy one Word, and more one good Action has from a Superior upon those under him, it can scarce be reckon'd how Powerful a Magick there is in a Prince who shall by a constant tenour of humanity in Government go on daily gaining upon the affections of his People. There is not any Priviledge so dear, but it may be extorted from Subjects by good usages,[546] and by keeping them always up in their good humour. I will not say what one Prince may compass within his own time, or what a second, though surely much may be done: but it is enough if a great [180] and durable design be accomplish'd in the third Life,[547] and, supposing an hereditary succession of any three taking up still where the other left, and dealing still in that fair and tender way of management, it is impossible but that even without reach or intention upon the Princes part, all should fall into his hand, and in so short a time the very memory or thoughts of any such thing as Publick liberty would, as it were by consent, expire and be for ever extinguish'd. So that, whatever the Power of the Magistrate be in the Institution, it is much safer for them not to do that with the Left hand which they may do with the Right, nor by an Extraordinary what they may effect by the Ordinary way of Government. A Prince that goes to the Top of his Power is like him that ⟨shall go⟩ #goes# to the Bottom of his Treasure. And therefore it is very unadvisable however to put a great stress upon little things, and where the Obedience will not countervail the Experiment. It is like a Man that knits all his force to throw an inconsiderable weight: he both strains his arm with it, falls short and makes no impression; whereas he that chuses a just weight, does neither [181] find himself the weaker after he has deliver'd it, and reaches the length he aim'd at. And this I doubt has been the case in laying on so much load upon account of things at best only indifferent and ceremonious. But as it is the Wisdom and Virtue of a Prince to rule in this manner, so he hath that advantage that his safety herein is fortified by his Duty, and as being a Christian Magistrate, he has the stronger obligation upon him to govern his Subjects in this Christian manner. Even during the Law under the Mosaical dispensation, in that regal Chapter of the 17*th.* of

[546] usages 74] usage 73.

[547] one Prince . . . third Life: an ironic reprise of the criticism of monarchs in the *First Anniversary,* ll. 15–22: "For one Thing never was by one King don."

Deuteronomy, it is solemnly commanded that *when the King sits upon the Throne of his Kingdom, he shall write him a Copy of the Law in a Book out of that which is before the Priests the Levites, and it shall be with him, and he shall read therein all the dayes of his life, that he may learn to fear the Lord his God, to keep all the words of the Law, and these Statutes*[548] *to do them*:[549] that his heart be not lifted up above[550] his brethren,[551] *and that he turn not aside from the commandment to the right hand or to the left, to the end he may prolong his dayes in the Kingdom,* [182] *he and his children.*[552] And though our Saviour came to abrogate the Ceremonial part of the Law, yet this was so essential to the Magistrates duty, that he confirmed and establish'd it stronger by his Doctrine. He declares indeed, that those Christians *are blessed who are persecuted for Righteousness sake, and when men shall revile, persecute and say all manner of evil against them*:[553] but it does not therefore follow that the Magistrate by fulfilling that Prediction does gain any of the Beatitudes.[554] Rather he is invited to the contrary course, for as much as the Merciful are blessed, for they shall obtain mercy, and blessed are the meek for they shall inherit the earth.[555] And so, in the 13. to the Romans, where the duty of the Subject is so fully and excellently described, 'tis nevertheless as to the Magistrate said that *he is not,* (which is to say, he ought not to be) *a terrour to good works, but to the evil.*[556] Neither is it fair for any man to speak as though our Saviour had in a manner balked[557] the whole business of the ⟨Magistrates duty⟩ #Magistrate# intermixed with his jurisdiction. For whatsoever Christ did [183] generally dictate, unless where he speaks to men under the express capacity and notion of Subjects, is equally bound upon the Magistrate as well as the People. And where he denounces, *Woe to them that shall offend one ⟨of⟩ his little ones that believe in him, and who so doth it, that it were better for him that a Mill-stone were hang'd about his neck,*

548 *Statutes* 73] *Statutues* 74.

549 *when . . . them* 74] not in italics in 73.

550 *above* 74] *over* 73.

551 that . . . brethren] not in italics in 73, 74.

552 *and that . . . children* 74] not in italics in 73.

553 *are blessed . . . against them:* Matthew 5:10–11; not in italics in 73.

554 the Beatitudes: the blessed conditions enumerated by Christ in Matthew 5:3–11.

555 Matthew 5: 7, 5.

556 *he is not . . . to the evil:* Romans 13:3; not in italics in 73. This Pauline text was constantly cited during the seventeenth century in the debates about the limitations or otherwise on monarchical power.

557 balked: avoided.

and that he were drown'd in the Sea,[558] is said without reservation either to Prince or Subject. Neither where the Apostle Paul speaks of the *tribulation which God recompences to the troublers of Christianity,*[559] is there any exempt Jurisdiction to be pleaded. The Power of Princes is not improperly resembled and derived down by Paternal Authority, and that which a Master hath in his Family: and in the *6th.* to the Ephesians, where the rules are given of domestick obedience, yet both *Parents* are forbid too from *provoking their Children to wrath,* and *Masters* that they *do not threaten their Servants.*[560] Indeed although Christ did not assume an earthly and visible Kingdom, yet he by the Gospel gave Law to Princes and Subjects, obliging all Mankind to such a peaceable and gentle frame of Spirit as would [184] be the greatest and most lasting security to Government, rendring ⟨the⟩ people tractable to Superiors, and the Magistrate not grievous in the exercise of his Dominion. And he knew very well that without dethroning the Princes of the World at present, yet by the constant preaching of that benevolous and amiable Doctrine, by the assimiliating and charitable Love of the first Christians, and by their signal patience under all their sufferings and torments, all opposition would be worn out, and all Princes should make place for a Christian Empire. Neither therefore did he, or the Apostles, or the Primitive Christians that trode on in their steps, notwithstanding[561] their obedience to the Magistrate, intermit the declaring and propagating the whole Christian Doctrine in the doing of which, if I can express it so with decency, they did an act of the most direct and highest contumacy[562] and disobedience to those that then Governed. And so it did and alwayes will happen, that whereas Christianity is indeed most certainly the greatest Friend to Government, and takes [185] the greatest care, makes the best provision of any Doctrine whatsoever for the preserving of its authority; yet where the Magistrate does clash with the rules and ends of Christianity, he does of consequence subvert his own power, and undermine his own Foundation; not by any malignity that there is in the Religion, but by a distinct efficacy that it has in maintaining it self thorow all opposition. But when once Christianity had in this regular and direct way obtained the Soveraignty, Ecclesiastical persons in whose keeping the Counterparts of

[558] *Woe . . . Sea:* Mark 9:42; not in italics in 73.

[559] *tribulation . . . Christianity:* 2 Thessalonians 1:6; not in italics in 73.

[560] *Parents . . . Servants:* not in italics in 73.

[561] notwithstanding 73] nowithstanding 74.

[562] contumacy: obstinate resistance.

Christian Doctrine, and example are most properly deposited, began exceedingly to degenerate. For the former sincerity and devotion of the Teachers, joyned with their abstinence from riches or secular honours and imployments, had, as it will do always, render'd them in the opinion of others worthy of that which they most contemn'd and avoided, and by how much they fled, they were the more followed by a devout Liberality: And good reason it was that as the people did partake of their Spirituals, so they should[563] too of the Peoples Tem-[186]porals: neither could any plenty then seem envious, when the Donors saw them to be so good Stewards of what they gave them, converting little to their own profit, but dispensing the most part to pious and charitable uses. But in those days *Venenum*, as 'twas said, *infusum est Ecclesiae*[564] and Religion having brought forth Riches, the Daughter devoured the Mother.[565] Not that I think any reward can be too great for one that is faithful in the discharge of so sacred an Office, but those that can go upright under the load of wealth, make up the lesser number of mankind, and for the most part they that seek it more earnestly do the worst deserve it. Too many of that order did then begin to slight their own Function, although of all others the most eligible and worthy: consisting in the sweetness of a contemplative life, the inestimable care of mens Souls, a freedom from the common occasions of vice, and from the Mechanical drudgery of raking together a fortune. That which was an Office before, was now turn'd into a Benefice, and one would not suffice the Appetite, but they [187] introduced the Polygamy of Pluralities. Non-residence was so legal, that it was almost grown to a Science, and a man might have compil'd a Systeme of its several terms of Art and Distinctions. They follow'd the Courts of Princes, and intangled themselves in secular affairs, beyond what is lawful or convenient to the Sanctity of their Vocation: and from that unnatural Copulation of Ecclesiastical and Temporal together, have those Monsters of Practice & Opinion been begotten, with

[563] they should 74] should they 73.

[564] *Venenum . . . Ecclesiae:* "Poison was poured into the Church." According to a legent, Pope Sylvester I (d. 335) heard these words spoken from heaven on the occasion of the supposed Donation of Constantine. [S]

[565] Marvell is here following Milton, *Likeliest Means to remove Hirelings* (1659), *CPW* 7:279: "Which was foretold, as is recorded in ecclesiastical traditions, by a voice heard from heaven on the very day that those great donations and church-revenues were given, crying aloud, *This day is poison pourd into the church.* Which the event soon after verifi'd; as appeers by another no less ancient observation, *That religion brought forth wealth, and the daughter devourd the mother.*"

which the World has been ever since infested; They incumbred Christianity (that is the most short and plain Religion) with an innumerable rabble of Rites and Ceremonies; neglecting the sincere and solid for a Mosaical rubbish, that tends nothing to Edification, and which our Saviour had swept out of his Temple. They affected pre-eminence, and ruled their flock by constraint, Lording it over Gods inheritance. They rent the Universal Church in pieces, sometimes about the observation of a Festival,[566] other whiles about their scuffles for precedence. By degrees they bearded Princes themselves, and challenged so exempt a Jurisdiction, that it was re-[188]solved even the Concubines of Priests were not within the cognizance of the Civil Magistrate.[567] In conclusion, they let the reins loose to their own Covetousness, Ambition, Pride, Ignorance, Formality, and Contentions: and could never take up again. Insomuch that well-nigh ever since it has been more then half the business of Princes to regulate the brabbles and quarrels that have been unnecessarily sow'd by some of the Clergy; and they have brought the World to that pass that indeed it cannot longer subsist then Kings shall have and exercise an Ecclesiastical Supremacy as far as it can be stretched. And when the best Function was by these means the worst corrupted, so far have they been from returning to the good and ancient wayes of Christianity, that all their endeavours have bent to the establishing of their iniquity by Laws, and propagating it by the most indirect methods of humane Policy. They have strove constantly to make all Reformation, not only ridiculous but impossible; and to draw Princes into their Confederacy. Unto which end although they had accumulated the wealth of most Kingdoms into their [189] own Coffers, and grasped at all Jurisdiction, as oft as there was any fear of a Reformation, they have been very liberal again of Power and Treasure to dispose and inable the Magistrate to War and Violence. There have never been wanting among them such as would set the Magistrate upon the Pinnacle of the Temple, and showing him all the Power, Wealth, and Glory of the Kingdoms of the Earth, have proffer'd the Prince all so he would be tempted to fall down & worship

[566] the observation of a Festival: a reference to the quarrels as to when Easter should be kept, resolved by Constantine at the Council of Nicaea. Cf. *RT,* p. 131 and *Short Historical Essay,* vol. 2, p. 132. This whole passage anticipates Marvell's later, more comprehensive study of the decadence of the medieval church.

[567] Concubines . . . Magistrate: see Paolo Sarpi, *The Historie of the Council of Trent,* trans. Nathaniel Brent (1620), p. 82 [S]; Marvell probably used the 1640 edition (A, p. 1, #39).

them.[568] So that the Ecclesiastical Wisdom has resembled that after the Deluge, which having once wash'd the World clean from that filth of Luxury and Impiety that it had in so long a time been contracting, men thought it wonderful Politick, instead of trusting to Gods promise, and following Righteousness the only security against Gods judgments, to erect an impregnable Babel of Power, that should reach to Heaven.[569] But all such vain attempts are still by the Divine Providence turn'd into confusion. In the mean time Nations, it is true, have by this means been run up into Schismes, Heresies, and Rebellions, which are indeed crimes of the highest [190] nature, and of the most pernicious consequence; but do not in the least diminish, yea rather aggravate the guilt of those men who have always design'd to secure their own misdemeanors by publick oppression. For all Governments and Societies of men, and so the Ecclesiastical, do in process of long time gather an irregularity, and wear away much of their primitive institution. And therefore the true wisdom of all Ages hath been to review at fit periods those errours, defects or excesses, that have insensibly crept on into the Publick Administration; to brush the dust off the Wheels, and oyl them again, or if it be ⟨found⟩ advisable to chuse a set of new ones. And this Reformation is most easily and with least disturbance to be effected by the Society it self, no single men being forbidden by any Magistrate to amend their own manners, and much more all Societies having the liberty to bring themselves within compass. But if men themselves shall omit their duty in this matter, the only just and lawful way remains by the Magistrate, who, having the greatest trust and interest in preserving the publick wellfare, had need ⟨take⟩ care to redress in good [191] season whatsoever corruptions that may indanger and infect the Government. Otherwise, if the Society it self shall be so far from correcting its own exorbitances, as to defend them even to the offence and invasion of the Universality;[570] and if Princes shall not take the advantage of their errours to reduce them to reason; this work, being on both sides neglected, falls to the Peoples share, from which God defend every good Government. For though all Commotions be unlawful, yet by this means they prove unavoidable. In all things that are insensible there is nevertheless a natural force always operating to expel and reject whatsoever is contrary to their subsistence.[571] And the sensible but brutish

[568] Pinnacle . . . worship: cf. the temptation of Christ by the devil, Matthew 5:5–9.
[569] to erect . . . Heaven: Genesis 11: 3–4.
[570] Universality: the collective, the nation.
[571] subsistence: means of life.

creatures heard together as if it were in counsel against their common inconveniences, and imbolden'd by their multitude, rebell even against Man their Lord and Master. And the common People in all places partake so much of Sense and Nature, that, could they be imagined and contrived to be irrational, yet they would ferment and tumultuate at last for their own preservation. Yet neither do they want the use of Reason, and perhaps their [192] aggregated[572] Judgment discerns most truly the Errours of Government, forasmuch as they are the first to be sure that smart under them. In this only they come to be short-sighted; that though they know the Diseases, they understand not the Remedies; and though good Patients, they are ill Physicians.[573] The Magistrate onely is authorized, qualified, and capable to make a just and effectual Reformation, and especially among the Ecclesiasticks. For in all experience, as far as I can remember, they have never been forward to save the Prince that labour. If they had, there would have been no Wickliffe,[574] no Husse,[575] no Luther[576] in History. Or at least, upon so notable ⟨an⟩ Emergency as the last, the Church of Rome would then in the Council of Trent[577] have thought of rectifying it self in good earnest, that it might have recover'd its ancient[578] Character: whereas it left the same divisions much wider, and the Christian People of the World to suffer, Protestants under Popish Governours, Popish under Protestants, rather then let go any point of interessed Ambition. The Instances made by the

[572] aggregated 73] gregated 74; catchword=aggregated.

[573] For all Governments . . . ill Physicians: This whole passage was adapted by William Disney for his *Nil dictum quod non dictum prius Or the Case of the Government of England,* (pp. 2–3), published under two different titles in 1681. Disney was an ejected Nonconformist minister, later executed for publishing Monmouth's *Declaration.*

[574] Wickliffe: John Wycliffe (1323–84), English reformer, critical of the power and wealth of the church, founder of the Lollard movement, and translator of the Bible.

[575] Husse: John Huss (Jan Hus) (c. 1371–1415), Bohemian reformer, insisted on communion in both kinds, summoned for heresy before the Council of Constance, and burned.

[576] Luther: Martin Luther (1483–1546), leader of the German Reformation, focused his attack on indulgences, a position which developed into the doctrine of *Sola fide,* salvation by faith alone.

[577] Council of Trent: the beginning of the Counter-Reformation; initiated by Pope Paul III, who desired definition of doctrine, and by the emperor Charles V, who wanted reform of abuses in the church, the council had three stages, under three different popes: 1545–47, 1551–52, and 1562–63. Its effect was generally to increase the power of the papacy and to leave matters of doctrine and practice unchanged.

[578] ancient 73] ancients 74.

Emperour,[579] and by the King [193] of France,[580] with their Proposals for Reformation, the endeavours of sundry Great and Religious Prelates; and among the rest, the Arch-bishop of Granada,[581] whom I named on a former occasion, all came to nothing: and I wish our later Times did not furnish us with parallels of the same nature. What I have said thus far concerning the Ecclesiasticks, I have said with great regret; and it would be yet greater, did not the imputation upon such particular Persons, as are culpable on these accounts, set off the multitude of those that are commendable for the contrary with a fuller lustre. But as to our Church, as I wish that none therein could come within this reflection; yet truly there are not so many notorious defects in its Government, that any can suspect me to have directed this Discourse to those Reverend Persons that are the Guides of it; and who, if they would but add a little more moderation to their great prudence, might quickly mend what is to be mended; to the great quiet of themselves, and edification of the People.

In[582] this one Matter onely, of the Cere-[194]monial Controversie #(as it is managed)# in our Church, I must confess my want of capacity, which I have reason in all other things to acknowledg; And though indeed our Ecclesiastical Governours have the Law herein upon their side, it befitted them however to have seen that the Dispute should have been managed even on their part with more humanity: Which having been otherwise, has drawn me, as it might any Man else, beyond mine own diffidence, to say what I thought expedient. Even the Church of Rome, which cannot be thought the most negligent of things that concern Her Interest, does not, that I know of, lay any great stress upon Rituals and Ceremonials; so Men agree in Doctrine: Nor do I remember that they have Persecuted any upon that account, but left the several Churches in the Priviledg of their own Fashion. Insomuch that in the very Ritual of the Mass, the most religious part of their Worship, the Mosarabe Ceremonies[583] are allowed, where

579 Ferdinand I (1503–64), Holy Roman Emperor, had instructed the Council of Trent to reform the practices of the Roman church. For an account of the reforms he requested, see *A Review of the Council of Trent,* trans. G.L. (Oxford, 1638), pp. 61–62. [S]

580 King of France: Charles IX (1550–74).

581 For Pedro Guerrero, leader of the Spanish delegation to the Council of Trent, see p. 283 and note 324 above.

582 In: 74 introduces a new paragraph here.

583 Mosarabe Ceremonies: Mozarab is an Arabic word meaning "would be Arab." The Mozarabic liturgy was the national liturgy of the Spanish church till the Roman

formerly practised, in which Horses and Fencings are introduced, after the manner of the Moores, which Antonius of Valtellina[584] affirmed to [195] have a great Mystery and Signification in them, but that thereby that Mass so differ'd from the Roman, that no Italian would think it were a Mass, should he see it celebrated.[585] I have, as much as possible, disingaged my Mind from all Bias and Partiality, to think how or what prudence Men of so great Piety and Learning as the Guides of our Church could find out all along; it being now near an hundred and fifty years,[586] to press on and continue still impositions in these matters. On the Nonconformists part it is plain that they have persisted in this Dispute, because they have, or think they have the direct authority of Scripture on their side, and to keep themselves as remote as might be from the return of that Religion, from which they had reformed: Whereas on the other side, in the former times[587] Rigour was heighten'd with Rigour, and Innovation multiplyed by Innovation, that no man can conjecture where it would have ended. But whatever Design the Ecclesiastical Instruments managed, it is yet to me the greatest mystery in the World how the Civil Magistate could be perswaded to interess himself with all the severity [196] of his Power in a matter so unnecessary, so trivial, and so pernicious to the Publick Quiet. For had things been left in their own state of Indifferency, it is well known that the English Nation is generally neither so void of Understanding, Civility, Obedience, or Devotion, but that they would long ago have voluntarily closed, and fal'n naturally into those reverent manners of Worship which would sufficiently have exprest and suited with their Religion. And when things were carried on to an extraordinary height, by the Rulers of the Church, they suffered long, and even to extremity; which is as much as could by any Magistrate be expected, unless that too were made a Crime, and they must suffer for suffering. It's[588] true, at last men proceeded beyond the bounds of Christian Moderation and Patience; and there fell out those

---

liturgy was forced upon it at the end of the eleventh century; it still survives in Toledo. [S]

[584] Antonius of Valtellina: Antonio da Grossupto (in Valtellina) (d. 1570), Dominican, came to Trent in 1562 as theologue of the bishop of Vigeano, Maurizio Petra. [S]

[585] Insomuch . . . celebrated: see Sarpi, *The Historie of the Council of Trent,* pp. 548–49.

[586] near an hundred and fifty years: i.e., since the beginning of the Reformation in Europe.

[587] the former times: Marvell is probably referring to the tenure of Archbishop William Laud.

[588] It's 74] It is 73.

dismal effects,[589] which, if they cannot be forgotten, ought to be alwayes deplored, alwayes avoided.

To[590] conclude this matter thus far; there is no Command in Scripture that enjoyns the Christian Magistrate to lay any such Impositions: And that Promise, *that Kings shall be Nursing fathers to the Church,*[591] is so [197] far from warranting any such thing, that it rather implies the contrary; neither that they should so pamper the Clergy, and humour their weaknesses, as to forget that in our Church the National multitude is more properly included, and that as Nursing-Fathers they ought to be careful lest they overlay any of their Children.[592] Those therefore that ascribe an Absolute and Unlimited Power to the Magistrate, will not I hope deny them peremptorily, to proceed within the Bounds of their own Discretion. And if our Saviour has reserved some cases to his own Jurisdiction, as I shall treat hereafter, no Prince I hope will think it a diminution, but that rather he is thereby discharged, and eased of that part of Government wherein there would have been the most trouble, and can be the least advantage.

And that can be only in Case of *Conscience,* which is the second thing that in your pleasant and droling manner you have chose to insist upon. I have in some measure shown you, Mr. Necessity Bayes, how many absurdities you have incurred in managing the Absolute and Unlimited Ecclesiastical [198] Power of the Magistrate as well as Civil. That you may the more exalt that, you continue, as in your former Books, to revile and debase Conscience, so that you may put it out of Countenance,[593] and out of all good conceit with it self. *Most mens minds or Consciences,* you have said, *are weak, silly and ignorant things, acted by fond and absurd Principles.* You say, men talk of it as of *some distinct Puppet within*
[*Ec. Pol.* p. 7.] *them, or as if it were a Pope in their Bellies*; whereas
[*Repr.* p. 10 & p. 86.] *Conscience,* you say, is *an indeterminate thing, and has no more certain a signification than the clinking of a Bell, that is as every man fancies.* I understand Sir, what you mean; *As the fool*

[589] those dismal effects: Marvell's discreet description of the Puritan Revolution.

[590] To: 74 introduces a new paragraph here.

[591] *Kings . . . Church:* Isaiah 49:23.

[592] Nursing-Fathers . . . Children: Marvell is echoing Milton, *Means to remove Hirelings* (1659), *CPW* 7:279: "Constantine: who out of his zeal thinking he could be never too liberally a nursing father of the church, might be not unfitly said to have either overlaid it or choakd it in the nursing."

[593] put . . . Countenance: embarrass.

thinks, so the Conscience tinks.[594] Commend me to you, Mr. Bayes, for a good Conscience-maker. Who that were in his wits would trouble himself with a thing so inconsiderable? And yet the mischief is, that this is that by which every man must be excused or accused. But the good again of that mischief is, that this will have no effect till the Day of Judgment. In the mean time I take it, I assure you, to be [199] as serious a thing, as you would make it ridiculous; and what I fancy by it, is Humane Reason guided by the Scripture in order to Salvation. What you determine it to be, is to be seen more particularly in the third Chapter of your *Ecclesiastical Politie,* and summarily in the Contents: and you reproach me for representing it as if you there *confined the whole duty of Conscience to the inward thoughts of the Mind and its perswasions*;[595] and this (to avoid tediousness, and that I may not return your immodest answer) I shall refer to the Reader. If, as there you say, *the Inward Actions of the Mind, and Matters of meer Conscience* be made terms Convertible; if *Mankind have a Liberty of Conscience as far as concerns their Judgments, but not their Practices*; if *the Nature of Christian Liberty relate to our Thoughts, and not to our Actions*; if *Christian Liberty consist in the Restauration of the Mind of Man to its natural Liberty from the Yoke of Ceremonial Law*; I durst almost trust your self, though I have no great inducement to confide in you, with the arbitration betwixt us. For if the Inward Actions [200] of the Mind only be the Matters of meer Conscience, do you not confine the whole duty of Conscience to the inward thought and perswasions of the Mind? Or, if a man would help you over the Stile, and allow something to be Conscience that is not meer Conscience, do not you evacuate it again in saying, That men have a Liberty of Conscience as far as concerns their Judgements, but not their Practices? So that here is a second Commitment, and you have confined Conscience back again to the Inward Thoughts only and perswasions of the Mind. Nay even, if Christian Liberty consist in the Restauration of the Mind of Man to its Natural Liberty from the Mosaical Law, does not that too, according to your Doctrine here, dispense only with our Judgments, but our Practice is still, or may be bound up to the Observance of all the Mosaical Institutions. So that if you please you may keep the Lye

[*Ec. Pol.* p. 87.]

[594] *tinks* 73] *thinks* 74; Marvell revises the proverb, "As the fool thinks, so the bell tinks," referring to the superstitious (like Joan of Arc?) who hear spiritual advice in the sound of a bell. See John Ray, *A Collection of English Proverbs* (Cambridge, 1670), p. 91 (A, p. 35, #84).

[595] *confined . . . perswasions: Reproof,* p. 29.

to *your*[596] self, of which you are so liberal, or let it remain on the middle till it be decided whom it of right belongs to, and let him take it and make his best on't. But in this of the Jewish Law you are indeed very distinct, and as dogmatical [201, misnumbered 221] as a man would wish. For you say, that *if the Proconsul of Judaea should publish an Edict that all Christians shall submit to Circumcision out of regard to the eternal Obligation to the Law of Moses, that were a manifest violence to the freedom of the Gospel: but whatever else he may command, so he pretend not to any warrant of Divine Authority; whatever abuse it may be of his own power, it is no abuse of Christian Liberty.* So that *you*[597] do not determine that it would be so much as an abuse of his own Power, but *you* do determine, That, if he do command, not onely Circumcision, but whatsoever else, (how strangely comprehensive are those words!) it is no abuse of Christian Liberty. But *you* are so far in love with this Notion, that *you* say The *Mosaical Dispensation being Cancell'd by the Gospel, those indifferent things that had been made necessary by a Divine positive Command, return'd to their own nature, to be used or omitted only as occasion should direct.* So that here *you* plainly assert what *you* left disputable in the former passage, that the [202, misnumbered 222] Magistrate may, if he please, lawfully introduce and set up the Jewish Religion again among Christians. 'Tis a sad case in the mean time, and truly if our Saviour's Cancelling the Mosaical Law do but render the same indifferent, I am afraid that the confirming of the Magistrates Ecclesiastical Power, that you told us of, is not much better, and had no great validity. But I do not now wonder that *you* said it was in the power of the Magistrate to establish what Religion he took to be most advantagious: For I see *you* are an honest man of *your* word, and meant it in good earnest. He may command whatever he pleases. He may set up the whole Jewish Religion, as occasion shall direct. Whither[598] on Gods name will these Ceremonies of ours lead us at last, what shall we come to? I see there is nothing Divine or Humane, so unalterable or so Sacred, no Liberty that belongs to Men or to Christians that *you* are not ready to violate and prostitute to *your* own ends; and *you* will turn any thing, Jew or Heathen, and preach up others to it rather than lose a Speculation, or be foyl'd in an Argument. Whereas no Man hath devested [203] himself of any Natural Liberty as he is a Man, by professing himself a

[P. 413. *Defence.*]

[*Ecc. Pol.* p. 96.]

[596] *your:* not in italics in 73, and subsequently.

[597] *you:* not in italics in 73, and subsequently.

[598] Whither 74] Whether 73.

Christian, but one Liberty operates within the other more effectually, and strengthen themselves better by that double Title. Especially if *your* Rule hold in this case; *That our Saviour hath Confirmed what he hath not Reversed.* For as to this particular of the Mosaical Law, Christ has abrogated it for ever in perpetuity; and it must sure be a very pretty Doctrine this of *yours,* that so the Antecedent Necessity be taken away, the Magistrate may erect it again by a Subsequent. So in conclusion our Saviour has done just nothing, neither indeed could he by *your* Argument: And the Christian Subject being only at Liberty in his Judgment, is notwithstanding obliged in Obedience to conform to the whole Jewish Ceremonial, as oft as the Magistrate may think it expedient. But, I say, *you* ought to know and acknowledg that our Saviour has establish'd Christianity to indure till his second coming; and hath in the Institution of that Religion condescended, though he might have exacted both, to be himself treated without Ceremony, so that were supplyed [204] by Reality. For Christianity has obliged Men to very hard Duty, and ransacks their very Thoughts, not being contented with an Unblameableness as to the Law, nor with an external Righteousness: It aims all at that which is sincere and solid, and having laid that weight upon the Conscience, which will be found sufficient for any honest Man to walk under, it hath not pressed and loaded Men further with the burthen of Ritual and Ceremonial traditions and Impositions. For whether indeed they be so heavy as they appear to the Scrupulous, yet they are not so light to be sure as *you* would perswade Men; and most Creatures know when they have their just load, nor can *you* make them go if *you* add more. In conclusion, it is most certain that as our Saviour has exacted those Duties which are necessary with more declarative strictness from Christians, then was under any other Religion, and thereby bound the Conscience to a severer scrutiny within it self over all our performances; so hath he gratified them on the other part with larger Exemptions and Priviledges from things indifferent and unnecessary. And it is a gross abuse whoso-[205]ever strives to limit Christian Liberty only from the Jewish Ceremonial Law, which *you* too will hardly grant us. But whatsoever general Rules, Laws, and Precepts are given in Scripture, and more particularly in the New Testament, to direct the Magistrate in the moderation of his Power in things of this nature, do make up the great Charter of Christian Liberty, and they may justly plead it. 'Tis true, that the decision and punishment of those that shall transgress therein, if they be Supream Magistrates, is reserved to God's Tribunal; and the Appeal thither, which *you* almost laugh at, is the most proper: But the Law by which those that offend their weak Brother,[599] will then be proceeded upon, is very legible, both having been dictated by our Saviour himself, and by his Apostles. Yet though the Supreme Magistrate cannot be questioned, I am not at all doubtful but that he may punish any such Transgression in his Subalternals[600] and Substitutes: And if it would please God to inspire the hearts of Princes to curb that sanguinary and unchristian Spirit of those that for their own corrupt Ends make Government so uneasie [206] to Princes; so that we might once come to the experiment how happy a Prince and People might be under a plain and true Christian Administration; I believe all Men, and especially Princes, would be so satisfied, and in love with it, that they would make it Treason to give them any contrary Counsel.

But the occasion of all this medly and Hotch-potch[601] that you make in matters of meer Conscience, and of mixt Conscience, in the Liberty of Christians as to their Judgment, but not to their Practice, of the Magistrates Power to impose things by a subsequent, so he do it not by an Antecedent Necessity, is from your Ignorance of Divine and Humane things, which makes you jumble them so together that you cannot distinguish of their several Obligations. Or else it is *your* voluntary and affected perverting of your own knowledge, in the same manner as in Turkey they turn themselves so long giddy, till they can neither think nor see what is before them, and fall down in an extasie fit for Inspiration.[602] Or it is that *you* may thus contribute to *your* own Maxime, and, seeing *Governors must keep their People from sinking into too* [207] *much Ignorance, or rising to too much knowledge in matters of*--- to do your part in muffling them up to play before you at the Blind-man-buff[603] of Conscience. For whereas you quote out of the first of Peter 2.13. and 15. *Submit to every Ordinance of man for the Lord's sake, for so is the will of God, that with well doing you may put to silence the Ignorance of foolish men*; it appears, as if you had on purpose omitted what comes between in the latter end of the 13*th*, and the whole 14*th* verse: *Whether it be to the King, as Supreme, or unto Governors as unto them that are sent by him for the punishment of evil doers, and for the praise of them that do well*: and you

[*Defence.* p. 413.]

599 offend . . . Brother: Romans 14:21.

600 Subalternals: subalterns, lesser officers.

601 Hotch-potch 74] hoch-poch 73; medley, jumble.

602 Turkey . . . Inspiration: a reference to the famous whirling dervishes of Turkey.

603 Blind-man-buff: a game in which one player is blindfolded and tries to catch any of the others, who in the meantime push (buff) him about.

neglect in the 16*th* verse, *As free, and not using your liberty as a cloak of maliciousness,* the conclusion; *but as the Servants of God*: and *as Free* you Print in the common character[604] that men may not unless they look in the Bible discern that it is part of the Text. These are pretty little contrivances. But if this be consider'd in the whole, it seems to me that by *every Ordinance of man,* is not meant every Law of man, but the Governors themselves whether Supreme or Substitute. And that [208] submission not to be intended singly concerning an Active Obedience: For few men will offer to say that if Ordinances should be interpreted by Laws,[605] men ought so to obey *every* Law; for their duty is described *as free,* and *as the Servants of God*; so that whensoever those come to be contradistinguished, not Man, but God is to be obey'd. And therefore this Apostle, and so all the rest did actively disobey by Preaching the Gospel; and in particular Saint Paul perceiv'd another kind of *Necessity* then yours; *Necessity was laid upon him to preach the Gospel.*[606] And you may find in the 9*th* to the Hebrews that those *Ordinances* which you contend still to be lawful, are absolutely voided. For *the first Covenant also had Ordinances of Divine Service, and a worldly Sanctuary.* And v. 10. *it stood only in meats and drinks, and divers washings, and Carnal Ordinances imposed on them until the time of Reformation.* And you cannot, unless you shut your eyes, but discern Col. 2.14. that our *Saviour has blotted out the hand-writing of Ordinances, and taken it out of the way, nailing it to his Cross.* Neither in the 13*th* to the Romans, does it appear to me other-[209]wise than that therefore men ought not to contemn, contradict, resist the Magistrate, who indeed is the *Ordinance of God* according to that Text and others; but in the same place it is evident, that, as to active obedience to Governors in particular cases, the matter must be decided betwixt God and every mans Conscience. And I must still desire you to remember that by Conscience I understand Humane reason acting by the Rule of Scripture, in order to obedience to God and a Mans own Salvation. But you not content to have said, That the *Magistrate hath Power to make that a particular of the Divine Law which God hath not made so,* do avowedly and plainly make all Humane Laws that do not Countenance Vice, or Disgrace the Deity to be particulars of the Divine Law; and that to break any other Law then such, is a sin. And that *all Laws Civil as well as Ecclesiastical,*

[Ecc. Pol. *p.* 80.]

[604] in the common character: i.e., not in italics.

[605] by Laws: i.e., as Laws.

[606] *Necessity . . . Gospel:* I Corinthians 9:16.

equally oblige the Conscience, and upon pain of Damnation. So that hereby whatsoever is enacted on Earth is at the same time enacted in Heaven. Every Law carries along with it the pain of Excommunication. [210] Whatsoever the Magistrate binds on Earth, is bound in Heaven: and he delivers every man who transgresses in Cart-wheels, and the number of Horses in his Team,[607] or that buries not in Flannel,[608] over to Satan. There is no Christian Magistrate, but, if he thought the matter went so high, he would be very tender how he made Laws, and rather than multiply them to the damnation of his good Subjects, he would bear with many a Publick Inconvenience. But this desperate Maxime (though what I am going to say is unavoidable, yet I do it with reverence) does impose upon God's Conscience, that he must make that a Sin which was not so before the Magistrate commanded the Duty; it makes God to be the Magistrates Minister; and, whereas the Law-giver contents himself with the Penalty that the Law exacts in case of failure, nevertheless at the same time he obliges God to execute Damnation upon the Offender. I am almost confident that the Divine Justice would never have been thus far at the Magistrates beck, but that you have told God, that *he must of necessity grant him at least thus much Power*; and therefore I must [211] confess there is no help for it. Will you never be ashamed of this damning and damned Doctrine? It were better that all Uniformity had never been invented, than that it should be upheld by such Theology. But I will not fall into a further transport, seeing some allowance is to be given you, by reason of your ancient acquaintance, and your present friendship with the Nonconformists; which obliges you to do them all good offices, and therefore, like that Italian,[609] you would not do them an half-Courtesie, but contrive to kill their Bodies, and damn their Souls with one labour. Are there not many Customs that have gained the Force of Laws? Are there not many Persons that are ignorant of several

[607] transgresses . . . Team: "Proclamation for restraint of excessive carriages to the destruction of highways. In partial conformity with a proclamation of . . . 6 August 1622, it was commanded that no common carrier . . . should travel with any wain or cart which should have above two wheels . . . or be used above five horses." March 9, 1630. *CSPD,* 1629–31, p. 208. [S]

[608] Flannel 73] Flanel 74; On November 16, 1666, a bill was introduced into the House of Commons: "That no dead Person . . . be dressed or wrapped up for burial . . . in any Sort of Kind of Stuff whatsoever, except Flannel, or other Stuff made of Wool only." *JHC,* 8:650. [S]

[609] that Italian: possibly Pope Innocent III (1160–1216), who assimilated the crime of high treason against God to that of high treason against temporal rulers. [S]

Laws that are made? Are there not many Laws that by disuse are grown obsolete, and stand yet Unrepealed? What would you in this case advise God to do with poor Sinners? Will nothing serve but Hell-fire, or will you agree that there may be some gentler Limbo[610] prepared for them, where they may sweat out their guiltiness? It is impossible in such gross absurdities, but that a man should speak to the [212] quick, though never to desirous to treat of sacred things with due reverence. But moreover, whatsoever Obligations may be put upon Mankind, they are to be expounded by that great and fundamental Law of Mercy. And therefore it was that our Saviour, even in the case of Divine Positive Law, declared accordingly, and interpreted the meaning of, *I will have Mercy, and not Sacrifice,*[611] as a general dispensation in all things that come within that respect and consideration.

But[612] to proceed further, I say, with submission still to better Judgements, and especially to Superiors, that I conceive the Magistrate, as in Scripture described, is the Ordinance of God constituting him, and the Ordinance of Man assenting to his Dominion. For there is not now any express Revelation, no Inspiration of a Prophet, nor Unction[613] of that Nature, as to the declaring of that particular person that is to govern. Only God hath in general commanded and disposed men to be Governed; and the particular person reigns according to that right, more or less, respectively, which under Gods Providence, he or his [213] Predecessors have lawfully acquired over the Subject. Therefore I take the Magistrates Power to be from God, only in a Providential Constitution; and the nature of which is very well and reverently expressed by Princes themselves, *By the Grace of God, King of,* &c. but I do not understand that God has thereby imparted and devolved to the Magistrate his Divine Jurisdiction. God that sees into the thoughts of mens hearts, and to whom both Prince and Subjects are accountable, sees not as man sees, nor judges as he judges; but is his own Measure, and the first Rectitude. But for the Magistrate, it is surely sufficient, that God has fortified him with a Divine Law, that he may not be resisted: but his Administration is Humane, neither is it possible either for him to exact, or men to pay him more than a Civil obedience in those Laws which he constituteth. Otherwise it were in his power not only,

[610] Limbo: in Roman Catholic thought, a region on the borders of hell, to which are sent unbaptized infants and virtuous pagans who died before Christ's coming.

[611] *I will . . . Sacrifice:* Matthew 9:13.

[612] But: 74 introduces a new paragraph here.

[613] Unction: the action of anointing as a symbol of investing with an office.

as some, and Caligula for example, to decree that he is God, but even to be so. God surely, although it does for the most part, or ought to fall out that the same action is a sin against God, and a disobedience to the Humane Law, punishes [214] the Fact so far as he sees and knows in himself that ⟨it⟩ is sinful and contrary to the Eternal rule of Justice: but an Humane Law can create only an Humane Obligation; and unless the breach chance likewise to be against some express Divine Law, I cannot see but that the Offender is guilty not to God, but only to the Magistrate, and hath expiated his Offence, by undergoing the Penalty.

I should be very sorry to disseminate, in a matter so weighty, any Errour, nay, even an unseasonable or dangerous Truth; none being more desirous or more sensible of the Necessity of Publick Obedience. And therefore as I have consulted none to make them conscious or culpable of what mistake I may run into, so if any shall convince me of one herein, I shall ingenuously retract it. But if this appear to be sufficient in reason for the preserving of Government, 'tis probable that it will prove to be so likewise in fact, and that there is no further provision made for the Magistrate. I do suppose therefore that the true stress and force of Laws lies in their aptitude and convenience for the gene-[215]ral good of the People; and no Magistrate is so wanton as to make Laws meerly out of the pleasure of Legislation, but out of the prospect of some utility to the Publick. Few Subjects are so capable as to imagine any further Obligation; neither does that Opinion lean towards Atheism, but proceeds rather from an honourable apprehension concerning God; that he could not institute Government to the prejudice of Mankind, or exact Obedience to Laws that are destructive to the Society. Therefore, as long as the Magistrate shall provide Laws that appear useful in the Experiment, the whole People will stand by him to exact Obedience from the Refractory, and pursue them like a Common Enemy. But if it fall out otherwise, that the Laws are inconvenient in the practice, men are so sensible of that, and so dull in Divinity, that, should the Legislator persist never so much, he would danger[614] to be left in the Field very single; and should you, Mr. Necessity Bayes, inculcate *your* heart out, the Auditory would scarce be converted. Indeed how is it possible to imagine, and to [216] what purpose, that ever any Magistrate should make Laws but for a general advantage? and who again but would be glad to abrogate them when he finds them pernitious to his Government? And therefore it is very usual to make at first Probationary Laws, and for some term of years only;

[614] danger: render himself liable.

that both the Law-giver and the Subject may see at leisure how proper they are and suitable to the effect for which they were intended. And indeed all Laws however are but Probationers of time; and, though meant for perpetuity, yet, when unprofitable, do, as they were made by common consent, so expire by universal neglect, and without Repeal grow Obsolete. There is again beside the Convenience of a Law, another security in the Penalty. For because few Laws are so perfect or convenient, but that some man will out of a vicious temper or interest transgress them; the Penalties too of Pecuniary Mulcts,[615] or of Life, or Limme, or Liberty, and whatsoever else are necessary; and doubtless the Magistrate does therein hold the ballance of Justice, and weigh the punishment as near as may be, that it should be proportionable to the offence. And out of that care it is that Go-[217]vernors make the same fault sometimes Capital, other-whiles Pecuniary, other, Imprisonment, *&c.* but that, whatsoever it is, being once undergone, all men reckon that the Magistrate and Justice are satisfied. For indeed, how can humane Laws bind beyond the declared[616] intention of the Magistrate in them? They who obey them, find therein their Convenience and Reward; they who break them, the Punishment: and upon those two Wheels all Government hath turned. But to make all Obedience matter of Salvation, is a Note that I believe no Tyrant ever thought of: And it would be some trouble to calculate, when a Law is alter'd here upon Earth, and the same Offence shall one year be Capital, and the next year perhaps thought fit to be Finable; how far the Judicature of Heaven takes the same measures, as it is a sin, in the Damnation: Or, suppose the Crime be pardoned here, why should not the Malefactor plead it too in Heaven? Or how came it that *the Parliament 3° Caroli, whatsoever they were by the Laws of the Land, were notorious Rebels by all the Laws of the Gospel*? You say they are no Laws [218] unless they oblige the Conscience. It is no great matter however: For if they be not Laws, they are at least Halters; and the Obligation of that without Conscience will be sufficiently effectual. It was, you know, an Order in one Government, That he that proposed a new Law, should appear with an Halter about his Neck in the Assembly;[617] it being thought reasonable that he

[*Rep.* p. 376]

615 Pecuniary Mulcts: monetary fines.

616 declared 73] declarest 74.

617 one Government . . . Assembly: This was a custom in Locris. See Demosthenes, Oration 24, "Against Timocrates," 139–40. Loeb edition, trans. J. H. Vince (1930), p. 463. The allusion was common and had been made in the Commons on February 10,

should know his own Neck would be concerned as well as others in the Inconvenience. But for such an Ecclesiastical Law-giver as you, I know not what *Memento*[618] were competent, who bring in a Law that whosoever shall disobey any Statue, nay any by-Law, though he deserves not to be hang'd, nor to be fined ten pounds, yet shall in a trice, and the very same moment be damn'd. You should, before you thus confounded[619] all Humane and Divine Things together, have at least reflected upon Affairs nearer your understanding; To what purpose then have all those former Contests been managed; whether Episcopacy were *Jure Divino,* or *Jure Humano*?[620] Whether Residence in a Man's Living, were by Divine or by Canon Law? In which last Controversie the Arch-Bishop, [219] whom I minded you of at your Seige of Granada, determined it to be of Divine Obligation.[621] But the Pope said, That to declare that the Non-resident should incur the deprivation of the Benefice, would be a readier, way and much more effectual.[622] And that is indeed too experienced a Truth, That Humane Penalties do more powerfully affect Mens Obedience than Divine Obligations. But therefore as it is unlawful to palliate[623] with God, and enervate his Laws into an Humane only and Politick Consideration; so it is[624] on the other side unlawful and unnecessary, to give to Common and Civil Constitutions a Divine Sanction;

1668, ironically by those who opposed the entry of a bill for Comprehension. See Samuel Pepys, *Diary,* eds. R. Latham and W. Matthews, 11 vols. (Berkeley and Los Angeles, 1976), 9:60: "so furious they are against this Bill; and thereby a great blow either given to the King and presbyters; or, which is the rather of the two, to the House itself, by denying a thing desired by the King and so much desired by much the greater part of of the nation." For the bill and its sponsors, see John Spurr, "The Church of England, Comprehension and the Toleration Act of 1689," *English Historical Review* 104 (1989), 933–35.

618 *Memento:* as in *memento mori,* a reminder of death's inevitability.

619 confounded 73] confound 74.

620 whether . . . *Humano:* an issue raised at the Council of Trent. The archbishop of Granada (see above) held that bishops were *jure divino* and therefore independent of the pope. See Sarpi, *Historie of the Council of Trent,* p. 597. [S]

621 Arch-bishop . . . Obligation: "The Archbishop of Granata added . . . that the obligation of Residence was by the Law of God . . . When it shall be determined that residency is *de jure Divino,* all hinderances will cease of themselves; the Bishops understanding their duty, will think on their own conscience." See Sarpi, *Historie of the Council of Trent,* p. 487.

622 Pope . . . effectual: see Sarpi, *Historie,* p. 505.

623 palliate: to extenuate oneself.

624 it is 74] is it 73.

and it is so far from an owning of God's Jurisdiction, that it is an Invasion upon it. Now that I may more manifestly and further evidence, that, how horrid soever this Opinion be, which I object to you, yet I have not in the least aggravated your sense or words: it may be necessary, knowing what manner of Man I have to deal with, to press you, and instance a little closer in that one particular of the *Jejunium Cecilianum*[625] or the Wednesday Fast, in the 5° Elizabethae, to which purpose it is material that the original [220] Clause be cited. 'Tis thus; *And because no manner of Person shall misjudge of the intent of this Statute containing orders to eat fish, and forbear eating of flesh, but that the same is properly intended and meant Politickly, for the increase of Fisher-men and Marriners, and repairing of Port-Towns and Navigation, and not for superstition to be maintained in choice of Meats; Be it enacted, that whosoever shall by teaching, writing, or open speech notifie that any eating of Fish or forbidding of Flesh, mentioned in this Act, is of any Necessity for the saving of the Soul of man, or that it is the Service of God, otherwise than as other Politick Laws are and be, then that such persons shall be punish'd as spreaders of false News. This Act to last for ten years,* &c. Now upon consideration of what you maintain & quote out of a late Learned Prelate, whom you leave nameless, that you might have the honour of it; *Then the Law is no Law at all, and if it be not tyed upon the Conscience, it is no Sin to break it, and to keep it is no Duty*: And adding hereunto what you say [221] in the *Reproof*, upon this occasion; *I will challenge you and all your Party of Mankind to maintain that whoever*[627] *enacts a Law, with this Proviso, That it shall not bind in Conscience, enacts no Law; whether therefore the Clause were added by Cecil, or by the Parliament, I am not concerned, and though you should throw in the Queen, and Convocation, and all, I care not, I will declare that they were all miserably out in their Divinity*: I say, considering this, I am very jealous that neither your late Learned Prelate, nor You, ever read the Clause, but took it up at adventure. For there is not a word of Conscience in the whole Clause; and if you would mount what is said to mean Conscience, the Clause does not however exclude it, for it runs you see thus; *Or that it is the Service of God*

[Rastall.[626] 5. Eliz.c.5. p. 378.]

[*Ec. Pol.* p. 59.]

[*Repr.* p. 33, & 34.]

[625] *Jejunium Cecilianum:* see *RT,* p. 95 and note 307 above.

[626] Rastall: i.e., William Rastell, *A Collection in English of the Statutes now in Force* (1611), f.378.

[627] *whoever* Ed., as in Parker] whatever 73, 74.

otherwise then as all other Politick Laws are and be. Indeed at this rate you may say, and make what you please. But it is plain, that this Clause which is a part of the Act, and you call impertinent, was inserted with most exemplary and Christian prudence, to avoid not only apparent manifest evil, but the very appearance of evil, and to show [222] the perswasion of those times, though it prove so contrary to yours, that the Ordinances of Meats and Drinks were so abolish'd by our Saviour, that this Act could not concern men in their Salvation; and therefore too they made it but a Probationer, that the Subject also might have time to try the Convenience or Inconvenience. Therefore, Sir, I would advise you to go to your Statute-Book, and see whether the Act be continued or repealed; lest at any time you have incurr'd not only the Penalty of false News, *by Teaching, Writing and open Speech*; but lest you have unwittingly run your self into Damnation, according to your own Doctrine, by disobeying the Act. But as to your *throwing in the Queen and Convocation too, and that they were all wretchedly out in Divinity*: You might have considered whether Arch-Bishop Parker[628] were not there among them, who methinks how light soever all the rest were, might have weighed something in your Ballance. This however is according to your wonted bravery, Mr. Bayes, and, as your Camarade said of the Criticks, so Queen, Parliament, Convocation, when they are not of your mind, *have no more* [223] *wit in them than so many Hobby-horses*: and as Mr. Johnson replyed thereupon, *You have said enough of them in Conscience.* You are, it seems, your self the Man you mention in your Platonick Philosophy,

[Reh. Com. *p.* 8.]

Celsa qui mentis ab arce Despicis Errantes, humana Senacula ridens.[629]---

And you look down upon these *odd* Passages of Humane Laws, at the same time you make them Divine, as very despicable. Since you are come to be the *Cardinal*-Deacon, you look, as you say the Cardinals of Rome express it, upon all secular Affairs, as the *Undershrievalties*[630] *of this*[631] *Life,* with great *Sossiego*[632] and calmness. From what I have alledged of yours in

[C. Pl.Ph. *p.* 18.]

[*Ibid.*]

[628] Arch-bishop Parker: Matthew Parker (1504–75).

[629] *Celsa . . . ridens:* from Statius, *Silvae,* 2.2.131–32: "You who from the high citadel despise those who wander below, ridiculing human pleasures." Parker had absurdly used this to describe himself. In turning it against him, Marvell has substituted *senacula* (councils) for *gaudia* (pleasures).

[630] *Undershrievalties:* offices of the under-sheriff; see Parker, *Censure,* p. 17.

[631] this 74] that 73.

[632] *Sossiego:* Spanish for placidity.

this Clause, I hope it is evident, that you do maintain, not only that Statute, but all others to bind under pain of Damnation. What need I trouble my self in proving it out on you? 'Tis what you contend avowedly to make us believe. *God has annexed*, you say, *the same Penalties to disobedience to Man's* [224] *Laws as his own.* Henceforth I pray do not criticize so severely upon Calvin,[634] nor upbraid him with his *Horrendum Decretum*[635] of Divine Predestination: for at this rate you will make every Humane Law as horrible and terrible. Take heed of hooking things up to Heaven in this manner; for, though you look for some advantage from it, you may chance to raise them above your reach: and if you do not fasten and rivet them very well when you have them there, they will come down again with such a swing, that if you stand not out of the way, they may bear you down further than you thought of. I assure you I am sore afraid and very sorry for it, that not only you, but all your Clergy of England are in a way to be damned. For there is a Law that hath all the Force and Validity that any Ecclesiastical or Civil Constitution can carry among us, and something more to[636] boot, which was perhaps the reason that you said the Anabaptists were so much in the right: That is in the order of Publick Baptism in the Common-Prayer Book. For the words are these; *The Priest, if they shall certifie him that the Child may well indure it, shall* [225] *dip it in the Water discreetly and warily; but if they do certifie that the Child is weak, it shall suffice to pour Water upon it.* This is in a matter of no less moment than the Sacrament of initiation into Christianity: And *you* know very well what is nevertheless the Practice, and *you* have in *your* Doctrine informed us of the Consequence. Therefore, in my humble opinion, it were better for *you*, Mr. Bayes, to speak civilly of Princes, whensoever like Nursing-Fathers, or Nursing-Mothers, they speak tenderly of things relating to the Conscience and Salvation of their Subjects: though indeed either it seems they must themselves learn a new Divinity, or teach *you* better manners. And *you* would do well and wisely not to stretch, Gold-beat, ⟨and⟩ Wyer-draw Humane Laws thus to Heaven, lest they grow thereby too slender to hold, and lose in strength what they gain by extension and rarefaction. Reverend Mr. Hooker[637] ought to have serv'd *you* for a

[Ec. Pol. *p.* 260.[633]]

[633] p. 260 74 correctly] p. 20 73.

[634] Calvin: see *RT*, pp. 62, 68–73, 79 above.

[635] *Horrendum Decretum:* horrible decree.

[636] to 73] too 74.

[637] Mr. Hooker: see *RT*, p. 130 and notes 491, 494 above.

better example, who though he was willing to drive this Nail as far as it would go, yet having spent his whole eighth Book in sifting the Obligation of Humane Laws, concludes his whole *Ecclesiastical Politie* [226] with these Words; *Disobedience therefore unto Laws, which are made by the* Magistrate, *is not a thing of so small account as some would make it. However too rigorous it were, that the breach of every Humane Law should be held*[638] *a deadly sin. A mean there is between those Extremities, if so be we can find it out.*[639] You might have done wisely to have imitated his Modesty.

And[640] no less pernicious is all that you say further in this matter which I named *publick Conscience.* Forasmuch as you said, that, *in cases of Publick Concern mens wills and judgments are to be directed and determined by the Commands and Determinations of the Publick Conscience.*[641] She is a Lady doubtless of great Quality and Virtue, I should be glad to know her lodging and be better acquainted with her: though often it happens that there is little difference betwixt Publick and Prostitute. But she being very generous, *if there by any sin in her Commands, will her self answer for it,* and discharge you of all danger, *she will warrant your Obedience, and hallow, or at least excuse your Action.* Do what you will with her, *She will secure you from Sin, if not from Errour.* She *will render your Actions virtuous,* [227] *whatever they are in themselves.*[642] 'Tis the best Woman that ever was born. And further: *A Doubting Conscience must alwayes at least as much fright us from disobeying, as from obeying any humane Law.*[643] Ay, Private Conscience is a meer Trollop[644] to her, an old Beldam superannuate,[645] and a Bulbegger[646] fit to fright Children. These *at-leasts* are the very Spirit and flame of Casual Theology. Frighted at least as much on this side, and frighted at least as much on that side. What will become at this rate of the poor simple Doubter? He will be in as bad a Case as you when you were distracted betwixt your *Book-seller* and your *Comfortable Importance*: or like a Horse, he may stand and starve between two equal Hay-cocks; or hang in an *at-least* betwixt Heaven and Hell till the Day of Judgment. Nay, but to avoid

638 held 73, 74] Hooker wrote "made".

639 *Disobedience . . . find it out:* Hooker, *Works* (1666), p. 484.

640 And: 74 introduces a new paragraph here.

641 *in cases . . . Publick Conscience: Discourse,* p. 308.

642 *if there be . . . themselves: Discourse,* pp. 308, 331.

643 *a Doubting . . . Law: Discourse,* p. 287.

644 Trollop: slut.

645 Beldam superannuate: excessively old woman.

646 Bulbegger: a bogeyman, imaginary figure intended to scare.

that inconvenience, *if we would speak properly, the Commands of Authority perfectly determine & evacuate all doubtfulness and irresolution of Conscience*: So that now instead of what the Apostle said, *He that doubts is damned if he eat,*[647] the business is sheer alter'd, and if he doubts, he is therefore damned. And all your seventh and [228] eighth[648] Chapters of *Ecclesiastical Politie* swarm with such Affirmative and Imperative Divinity. So that you need not have astonish'd your self, when you find it ought[649] after long consideration, *that my Book was rather a Censure than a Confutation,* (yet that too others will judge of:) neither ought you to have taken it so ill though I had only *squirted,* as you call it, at your *Thesis* and Corollaries, unless you knew that Syringing had been, *if we would speak properly,* more suitable to your *Distemper.* But to conclude this Matter. Whatsoever *Villany* you say *there is in those mens Religion who distinguish betwixt Grace and Morality,* and how *Modern* soever that *Orthodoxy,* I am sure these opinions of yours are of an higher tincture: but because it is a Theology of your own begetting, 'tis reason to let you too[650] have the naming of it. But 'tis likely to prove a very wicked wretch, and should it grow up as in *Probability* at this rate, under your Instruction and Education, its Malice would soon supply its Age, and 'twill take very desperate courses: and what End it will come to you may easily imagine. I hope nevertheless that this Doctrine is yet an Alien in our Church, and therefore, if [229] for some notorious offence it come to its twelve God-fathers,[651] let it have however its Priviledge, and be tryed *per Medietatem Conscientiae.*[652] There is one thing more in your discussion of Christian Liberty concerning the Gnosticks,[653] whom you very frequently parallel #to# the Non-conformists; which, would I seek for new matter of mirth, or stir up fresh controversies, does adminster me abundant occasion. But I shall defer that till your Diagnosticks be better. For I am afraid you take that as you do many things else upon trust, and should you, upon further consultation with your Chronologers, discern that their Heresie began not till after the death of the Apostles, you would be shrewdly

[*Ec. Pol.* p. 287.]

[647] *He that doubts . . . eat:* Romans 14:23.

[648] eighth 73] eight 74.

[649] ought 73, 74] out?

[650] too 73] to 74.

[651] twelve God-fathers: Marvell seems to be merging baptism with trial by jury.

[652] *per Medietatem Conscientiae:* through the mediation of conscience.

[653] Gnosticks: mystical sects among the early Christians who claimed visionary knowledge.

disappointed to find your self guilty of the *Pseudonymos Gnosis,*[654] in that particular.

That[655] which in my former Book I call'd your third Play, of *Moral Grace,* you here act over again; but with so trivial levity that indeed I perceive I did you injury in calling it so, for I see it is but an old Farse new vamp'd. And truly here especially, but thorow your whole *Reproof,* it seems that you do not trouble your self so much [230] about the weight of the matter, as disquiet your mind with an Emulation of Wit, of which you ought to be a good Husband, for you come by it very hardly. Whether I have any at all I know not, neither, further than it is not fit for me to reject any good quality wherewith God may have indued me, do I much care: but would be glad to part with it very easily for any thing intellectual, that is solid and useful. Neither therefore do I at all complain or trouble my self, though I see you borrow or steal it before my face, and that you *turn* (with what felicity let others judge) *three parts of my own Book,* as you say you could, *upon me.*[656] Much good do you with it, I will never question you for't. But therefore when you should have been treating here with due gravity concerning the most serious Subject perhaps in all Christianity, you fall a mousing about the definition of a Quibble. You need not upbraid me with that which is the best of your Science, and I foresee within a few Pages that I shall discover you to be much better at it than I am, and that you ⟨are⟩ (if it be a Quibble it befits you) are a meer Word-pecker.[657] You have contrary to [231] all Architecture and good Oeconomy made a Snow-house in your upper Room: which indeed was Philosophically done of you, seeing you bear your head so high as if it were in or above the middle Region, and so you thought it secure from melting. But you did not at the same time consider that your Brain is so hot, that the Wit is dissolv'd by it, and is always dripping away at the Icicles of your Nose. But it Freezes again I confess as soon as it falls down, and hence it proceeds that there is no passage in my Book, deep or shallow, but with a chill and key-cold conceit you can ice it in a moment,

[654] *Pseudonymos Gnosis: Censure,* p. 88; Parker cites Colossians 2:8, but the main text for this much-disputed term is 1 Timothy 6:20: "avoiding profane and vain babblings, and oppositions of science falsely so called," a text which raised the question of whether Paul was already alluding to Gnosticism, since "oppositions" or antitheses later came to have technical meaning in that heresy.

[655] That: 74 introduces a new paragraph here.

[656] *turn . . . upon me: Reproof,* p. 226.

[657] Word-pecker: Marvell used the same pun in *To . . . Lovelace,* 1:19: "Word-peckers, Paper-rats, Book-scorpions."

and slide shere over it without scatches.[658] But, having done that, you shew your self mightily offended that I have upon this subject of Grace told you, that *if it be resolved into Morality, I think a man may almost as well make God too to be only a Notional and Moral Existence.*[659] I have told you that I foresaw every where at what you would be carping, so I did here, and nevertheless thought fit to express it so upon good deliberation: And could you now have held your Tongue you had heard no more of it, whereas now I am obliged frankly to satisfie you of my se-[232]veral Reasons. And 'tis first upon occasion of your *Tentamina Physico-Theologica* before mentioned, which you Dedicated to my Lord Arch-bishop; it being your first Address to Ecclesiastical Fortune, and an Essay by writing against Atheisme, to gain Authority to whatsoever Doctrine you should afterwards disseminate. I should not say what follows did I think I could thereby offend my Lord Arch-bishop, who having the oversight of this whole Church upon him, does, of course, and conscientiously doubtless, transmit such applicatory discourses to his Chaplains. So I suppose you bespoke Doctor Grigg[660] to make a favourable Report in your behalf, and give you, as he did, a Cast of his Office in the License. I must deduce the thing to make it clear to you. As soon as I open'd the Book at the Title, and saw the Authors name, if you be the same person, I met with *Typis A.M.*[661] but we two not being then acquainted, surely you could not prophesie that I should be the man that should Print you in so legible a Character in a first, and now this second Edition. Next after that *Venales*; which I could not reconcile either in Gender or Number but concern-[233]ing you and your Book, that henceforwards you were both alike Venal; you indeed, as in an Auction, to be Sold by Inch of Candle: Where? *apud Jo. Sherley.* Ay, there it was where you and your Book both lodged at one anothers expence. For whatever others

[658] scatches: wooden stilts put on to walk over dirty places.

[659] *if . . . Existence: RT,* p. 101 above.

[660] Dr. Grigg: Thomas Grigg (d. 1670), the licenser of *Tentamina,* which carried the following elaborate imprimatur: *Perlegi hanc Librum . . . In quo nihi reperio Fidei Ecclesiae Anglicanae aut bonis Moribus contrarium, multa vero, quae ingenio & eruditione non vulgari conscripta adversus Atheos . . . Tho. Grigg.* [I have read through this book . . . in which I find nothing contrary to the faith of the Church of England or to good customs, but much which is written, with uncommon wit and learning, against atheists.] Dated Feb. 15, 1664.

[661] *Typis A.M.:* Anne Maxwell, London printer 1665–75, seems likely; but Marvell is pretending they are his own initials.

are, you were then a meer *Shop divine* And did so nibble all his Library, and dirty them with your Thumbs, that the poor man had not one new Book left, but was fain to Sell them all at second hand. But where was his Shop? *Ad insigne Pelicani.*[662] A very Emblematical sign where you digged and pick'd your very Heart-blood[663] and Brains out to nourish your young *Tentamina.* Where was this? *in parva Britannia.*[664] You should have done well to have Printed us the Map of it; for I find it not in your Heylin, who mis-led you *on the South side of the Lake Leman.*[665] But, wherever you live, You will take a course to make it *little Britain.* This is not all: *Et apud Sam. Thompson,* to direct men further; and you were to be had at as many places as Buckworths Lozenges.[666] *In Caemeterio Divi Pauli*:[667] Bury him out of the way 'tis no matter: But, *ad In-*[234]*signe Capitis Episcopi,* at the Sign of the Bishops-head, there you are sure to be heard of.[668]

[*Repr.* p. 21.]

And,[669] to convince men that this was not all pure Chance, but there was something of Design and Wit in't, turn but over the Leaf and *you* meet full bob; *Reverendissimo in Christo Patri & Domino, Domino Gilberto, Providentia Divina, Archiepiscopo Cantuariensi, totius Angliae Primati & Metropolitana; & Augustissimo Principi, Carolo Secundo, Magnae Britanniae, Franciae, & Hiberniae Regi, a Secretioribus Consiliis.*[670] So here you *apud Jo. Sherley*

[662] *Ad insigne Pelicani:* at the sign of the Pelican.

[663] Emblematical . . . Heart-blood: In Renaissance lore, often expressed in emblem books, the pelican was believed to lacerate its breast with its beak and feed its young on the blood. Cf. *A Poem upon the Death of O.C.*, ll. 79–80: "Who now shall tell us more of mournful Swans, / Of Halcyons kind, or bleeding Pelicans?"

[664] *in parva Britannia:* in Little-Britain, a London street.

[665] your Heylin: Peter Heylin, *Cosmographie* (1657), p. 159 (A, p. 25, #51).

[666] Buckworths Lozenges: "Take notice that Mr. Theophilus Buckworth, the true Operator of the famous and long experienced Lozenges . . . hath now removed his dwelling . . . quantities of them [Lozenges] . . . are constantly to be had at Mr. Tho. Rooks . . . Mr. William Milwards . . . M. Place . . . Mr. Magnus," etc. etc. British Library Handbill, n.d. L.R.404.a4. no. 42. [S]

[667] *In Caemeterio Divi Pauli:* in St. Paul's Churchyard, where many booksellers had shops.

[668] The above details are from the title page to the *Tentamina,* of which Marvell makes foolish fun.

[669] And: 74 introduces a new paragraph here.

[670] *Reverendissimo . . . Consiliis:* "To the most reverend Father and Lord in Christ, Lord Gilbert, Archbishop of Canterbury, Primate of all England and Metropolitan; and in secret councils to the most august Prince, Charles Second, king of Great Britain,

in Parva Britannia, and my Lord Arch-bishop, *totius Angliae Primas,* and *Carolus Secundus Magnae Britanniae Rex,* are brought to an Enterview, and to set up a Triumvirate together. But I was at first surprized by your Marshalling and Commaes, not being able readily to distinguish whether it were not dedicated also to the King, and which of the two was the others Privy-Counsellor. Well, to proceed; *Nullus dubito quin mireris*[671] *pedibus tuis provolvi Recentem quendam Ignotae Frontis Clientulum*;[672] and well he might, for he knew not yet the height and breadth of your Forehead:[673] Had he, to
[235] remark it the better, it being so unknown, set a Brand upon it, it had been some courtesie to the Publick. *Et forsan obstupescis.*[674] 'Tis an uncivil Supposition, did *you* not since lessen it by affirming in your Hicringil; *Clerus Britannicus stupor*[675] *mundi* :[676] *Suppose, Mr. Bayes, you may suppose it seems what you please; I have nothing to do with your suppose: Suppose quoth a!---* But *you* intend to make him amends: *hominis fiduciam.*[677] This salves it indeed a little: For truly; if any thing in the World could rebate the vigour of so acute and solid a judgment, it must have stounded[678] him to reflect upon *your* Confidence, then in that Address, but much more in your latter Writings. But, *Qui faelicius litaturas sperarem studiorum Primitias quam si in summi Pontificis dextram libandas submitterem?*[679] Pretty well. *Tum quod animae germinantis impetum represserint quorum potius intererat tenella Conaminum germina radiis maturantibus inspirasse.*[680] The inspiring with Beams is a new

[Reh. Com. *p.* 7.]

France, and Scotland." Marvell now turns to eviscerating Parker's obsequious dedication. Unfortunately Parker's poor Latin caused considerable problems, both to his printer and to D. I. B. Smith.

[671] *mireris* 73] *mineris* 74.

[672] *Nullus dubito . . . Clientulum:* "I do not doubt but that you are surprised that a new client of unknown mien is prostrate at your feet."

[673] Forehead: Marvell is mocking Parker's use of *frontis* for general appearance.

[674] *El forsan obstupescis:* "And perhaps you are struck with amazement."

[675] *stupor* 73] *stuper* 74.

[676] *Clerus . . . mundi:* "The British clergy is the wonder of the world." Proverbial; quoted in *Gregory, Father Greybeard,* p. 45.

[677] *hominis fiduciam:* a fraction of a longer compliment.

[678] stounded: astonished.

[679] *Qui . . . submitterem:* "What more happy omens could I hope for the first-fruits of my studies than if I were to place them as an offering in the High Priest's right hand?"

[680] *Tum . . . inspirasse:* "The impulse of my growing spirit they then repressed who should rather have inspired the tender seeds with maturing beams."

Invention. But sweet germinating Soul, what was it did betide thee? Was it changed in the Cradle? Alas for't. [236] You were whimpring I doubt already, as you did afterwards to Doctor Bathurst, about *the Chains and Fetters of an unhappy* (yet civil) *Education.*[681] *Si vero jubare vestro afflentur*;[682] do you mean Sun-burning or Blasting?[683] *fiet forte* (suppose again, though it were *quod non est supponendum*)[684] *ut indies maturescant, dum tandem studia nostra ad meliorem frugem pervenerint.*[685] You found *Ecclesiastical Polities, Defences, Prefaces, Reproofs* even now stirring within you. *Ut plerumque solent Adolescentium partus minus vigoris & maturitatis adipisci.*[686] Do you mean it litterally? you do to be sure when you speak in the next line of enjoying *faelici genio & sorte,*[687] which was all you cared for, and which you promised your self, *tanti syderis aspectu*:[688] Take heed #that# you become not *syderatus,*[689] for that is worse than a Fanatick. *Sibi postulat Immensa Numinis Majestas*[690] *sacratissimos & prorsus Augustos Maecenates.*[691] Nay then I see you did indeed dedicate the Book both to my Lord Arch-Bishop, and the King, and in that precedence; or otherwise you have given my Lord a Title which he would not have thanked you for: But the whole Expres-[237]sion, had any one but you, Mr. Bayes, used it, is very Pedantical; for though you were scraping about for a Maecenas,[692] God to be sure stands not in need of one,

681 *the Chains . . . Education:* The "Dedicatory Epistle" of *Censure* to Ralph Bathurst.

682 *Si . . . afflentur:* "If indeed they are irradiated by your splendor."

683 Sun-burning or Blasting: See Psalm 121:6; a verse incorporated into the prayer book service for the churching of women. Marvell, however, was thinking of Milton's version in his *Apology . . . for Smectymnuus* (1642), where he inveighs against "impertinences" in the liturgy, "as those thanks in the womans Churching for her delivery from Sunburning and Moonblasting" (*CPW* 1:939), "moonblasting" being Milton's own word.

684 *quod . . . supponendum:* that which is not to be supposed.

685 *fiet forte . . . pervenerint:* "Let them by chance mature day by day, while yet my studies may attain to better fruit."

686 *Ut plerumque . . . adipisci:* "as the majority of adolescents are accustomed to achieve less strength and maturity."

687 *faelici . . . sorte:* "a happy genius and fate."

688 [*cui*] *tanti syderis aspectu*[*s faveat*]: "to whom such a heavenly aspect may be favorable."

689 *syderatus:* siderate, struck by a malign planet.

690 *Majestas* Ed., as in Parker] *Magistas* 73, 74.

691 *Maecenates* Ed., as in Parker] Mecaenates 73, 74; Sibi . . . Maecenates: "For him the immense Majesty of God appealed to the most sacred and indeed imperial patrons."

692 Maecenas Ed.] Mecaenas 73, 74; a generous patron of literature or art; from the historical patron of Virgil and Horace.

or however not of your chusing. But now your Theology thickens upon us: *Cum pro Aris dimicaverim cuius potius auxilia implorarem quam vestra, Venerande*[693] *Antistes, qui iis tanquam numen Tutelare praesideas.*[694] Here however you make my Lord indeed but a *Tanquam* Deity; but expect[695] a little. *Non video*[696] *cuius tantundem intersit ut Victor evadam, quantam summi Pontificis: Nempe si optimo numini imperium*[697] *abrogetur quid sequitur nisi protinus Maximo Pontifici abrogandum*[698] *esse?*[699] Really, Mr. Bayes, very closely argued, and from an efficacious Topick. But here you have made my Lord *Summus Pontifex,* and *Pontifex Maximus,* to the great disparagement of the other *Old Gentleman*[700] you speak of; but which is more, the pegging out[701] of the Prince, who might otherwise by your latter Law have pretended a Title to the Place, and exercised it in Person. Beside that, you have curtail'd *Optimus Maximus* from the Deity, and made him glad to go half with the Bi-[238]shop, lest he should leave him nothing. But at last it comes in plain terms: *Adeo res eadem sit de numine bene mereri atque de vestra Clementia*; which I can English no otherwise but thus; Insomuch that it is the very same thing to deserve well of God as of your Grace. That afterwards is pretty concerning your self: *Hosce Gigantum fraterculos non sat duxi expugnare nisi ut fabulantur superos,* &c.[702] making that what had been but fabled of the Gods, you had atchiev'd in good earnest. Had my Lord seen it, or had but Sir Francis Vere,[703] he would for certain have spit in your

693 *Venerande* Ed., as in Parker] *Vencerande* 73, 74.

694 *Cum . . . praesideas:* "When I shall contend on behalf of the altars whose aid shall I implore rather than yours, venerable Master, who presides over them like a tutelary deity."

695 expect: wait.

696 *video* Ed., as in Parker] *vide* 73, 74.

697 *imperium* Ed., as in Parker] *mipercum* 73, *impericum* 74.

698 *abrogandum* 73] *abregandum* 74.

699 *Non video . . . abrogandum esse:* "Nor do I see to whom it would be more important that I emerge as Victor, than the High Priest: indeed if the reign of God is to be abrogated, what follows but that of the High Priest must immediately be done away with."

700 *Old Gentleman:* God? Cf. *RT,* p. 190, "Old Gentlemen."

701 pegging out: confining or excluding, by marking a boundary.

702 *Hosce . . . superos:* "And I have not fully decided whether to subdue these little brothers of the Giants unless as it is fabled of the Gods . . ."

703 Sir Francis Vere: (1560–1609), general of the English troops in the service of the United Netherlands against Spain; the greatest English soldier of his generation. [S]

Mouth. But your last Collect[704] is something strange, praying for him; *ut sero tandem in Triumphantis Ecclesiae Gloriam & dignitatem* (that *dignitatem* comes off at last very poorly) *cooptetur.*[705] 'Tis true, better late than never; But to pray that it may be very late before a Man get to Heaven; hath, I confess, been done in the case of a secular Prince once by a Heathen Poet;[706] but was not so decent a piece of Chaplainship towards my Lord Arch-bishop. I see you write, Mr. Bayes, here after the Copy of Mr. Croxton,[707] and others in the former [239] times; *sanctissime Pater,* and *sanctitas vestra, spiritus sancti effusissime plenus; optimus Maximusque*[708] *in terris; Quo rectior non stat Regula & quo prior est corrigenda Religio.*[709] These were fine Complements to be bandyed among Ecclesiasticks. But what was in your mind, Mr. Bayes, to write this Letter, when a year after you appeal to Doctor Bathurst, *that it was he knew one of your greatest designs in this World to be one of the most unconcerned men in't*? You did it out of the meer abstracted generosity of your heart, and writ only your Letters Testimonial, in this manner on my Lord Arch-bishops behalf. For what I perceive you had by this breath only cool'd your own Porridge, and things were not as they should be, till upon further sollicitation you began to foresee & tell your friends *that you were exceedingly straitned in time*; and then a little after were all Cock-a-Hoop,[710] *upon the very point of your departure to London. My dearest Cuz. (where*[711] *you*

[*C.P.Ph.* p. 1.]

[704] Collect: a short prayer.

[705] *ut sero . . . cooptetur:* "that he might late at last be admitted into the glory and dignity of the Church Triumphant."

[706] secular . . . Poet: Horace on Augustus, *Odes,* 1.2.45. Marvell adapted the poem himself in a very early poem in praise of Charles I: *Ad Regem Carolum Parodia,* and used the very line he notes: "*serus in coelum redeas diuque.*" [S]

[707] Mr. Croxton: James Croxton, b. 1606, a favourite of Archbishop Laud, who recommended him to the earl of Strafford for preferment. H. Cotton, *Fasti Ecclesiae Hibernicae* (1850) 6:137–38. [S]

[708] *Maximusque* 73] Maximus qui 74.

[709] *sanctissime . . . Religio:* "most holy father, and your holiness, most full of the holy spirit; best and greatest on earth; by whom Rule could not stand more right and by whom Religion is first to be corrected." Marvell is quoting, fairly accurately, from William Prynne's attack on Laud after his execution, *Canterburies Doome,* (1646), p. 441. Prynne had cited these phrases as "the Pope's own Titles, . . . attributed to him in sundry Letters from the University of Oxford, [by] Master Croxton and others without control." [S]

[710] Cock-a-Hoop: crowing with exultation.

[711] *where* 73] were 74.

before us in the Sun-beams, buz.) From Trin. Col. Oxon, May 2. [240]

[*C.Pl.Ph.* p. 184. & p. 242.]

[*Reh. Com.* p. 36.]

Though you are so fertil, that when a man hath once begun, he can scarcely give over laughing: I have not forgotten, that my occasion of quoting this your Epistle, was, to to shew you might take it well I express'd your Notion of God so modestly; when, in the very Treatise where you confound Atheism from Pelion to Ossa,[712] from top to bottom; yet you would at the same time, for your own ends, Deifie a Person you had never seen, and worship an Unknown God. But you were so hungry at that time, that you would have ador'd an Onion, so it had cryed, *Come eat me.*

Another Reason why I said to you, that to resolve Grace into Morality, was almost the same as to make God a Notional and Moral Existence, was from a Passage I met with in your *Platonick Philosophy. From all which premises, we see that Gods Benignity, Goodness, and Beneficence, consist in a gracious Propensity to let forth the Communication of his fulness to his Creatures, which being lodged in the Divine Will, does not only suppose its freedom, but is also Subject to its Determination;*[713] *so that though it may encline, yet it cannot either command or destroy its liberty: because if it should, it would* [241] *not only interfere*---Here is indeed material intellectual Puff-past; Pinners-hall[714] has nothing like it. This is to shew how excellent you are at quoiting a Pea to stick upon the Point of a Needle. But what would, I know not what, not only interfiere with? Why, *not only with Gods Moral accomplishments, but it would withal be inconsistent with it self.* Gods Moral accom-

[*C.P.Ph.* p. 164.]

plishments! If it were an Oath, I should not think it binds me: But in the mean time methinks it has something in it bordering upon Blasphemy: But we Lay-men do not distinguish well when the Clergy blaspheme, and when they speak reverently.

712 Pelion to Ossa: two mountains in Thessaly, proverbial for great distance.

713 *Determination* 74] *determinations* 73.

714 Pinners-hall: *Reproof,* p. 102; See Neale, *History of the Puritans,* 2:562: "During this interval of parliament [in 1672], the declaration of indulgence continued in force, and the dissenters had rest; when the presbyterians and independents, to shew their agreement among themselves . . . set up a weekly lecture at Pinners'-hall in Broad-street, on Tuesday mornings, under the encouragement of the principal merchants and tradesmen in the city. Four presbyterians were joined with two independents to preach by turns, and to give it the greater reputation the principal ministers for learning and popularity were chosen as lecturers." Parker, of course, had mocked this development.

You perhaps, Mr. Bays, intended it very well and honourably, but you had talked your self round, and wanted a better word only: for I must confess 'twere proper enough to speak of the *Moral Accomplishments* of some young Gentleman at the Inns of Court that were upon his Preferment; but I do not remember to have heard it used ⟨at⟩ any time upon this occasion. I hope you see by this time that a man might at your rate of talking, have made God as well only a Notional and Moral existence. And to make the preaching of any other Doctrine ridiculous, you fall into such a desperate fit of Blasphemy, as I never heard any [242] man but your self; you indeed have it often. *The Nonconformists*[715] *Preachers,* you say, *make a grievous noise of the Lord Christ, talk loud of getting an interest in the Lord Christ, tell fine Romances of the secret Amours between the Believing Soul and the Lord Christ, and prodigious Stories of the miraculous feats of Faith in the Lord Christ.* Did ever Divine rattle out such prophane Balderdash! I [*Rep.* p. 56.] cannot refrain, Sir, to tell you that you are not fit to have Christ in your mouth. You talk like a Mountebank,[716] and seem to know so little of our Saviour, as if you had never convers'd but with Salvator Winter.[717] Is this our great Champion against Atheism? Is this he that tells young Gentlemen, *They are not acquainted with any Histories, unless that perhaps of the Follies and Amours of the French Court?*[718] *Alas young Gentlemen, you are too rash and forward: Your Confidence swells above your Understandings. 'Tis not for you to pretend to Atheism. 'Tis too great a Priviledge for Boys and Novices. 'Tis sawciness for you to be profane, and to Censure Religion, Impudence and ill Manners.* It were so indeed in the presence of so great an Artist. They ought to expect [*Pref. E. P.* from *p.* 22. to *p.* 45.][719] [243] till you have instructed them better in't, and set up an Academy and ⟨a⟩ publick Lecture to that purpose. What Distinction do you make betwixt the Amours of the French Court, and the secret Amours betwixt the believing Soul and

[715] Nonconformists 74] Nonconformist 73.

[716] Mountebank: see p. 244 and note 107 above.

[717] Salvator Winter: A notable mountebank, he claimed to have made an elixir that would cure anything. See *A Handbill extolling the virtues of a Medicine called Elixir, or Vegetable Spirit* (1664). [S]

[718] Perhaps the *Annals of Love, containing select Histories of the Amours of divers Princes Courts, pleasantly related. By a Person of Honor,* advertised in John Starkey's catalogue for February 1673.

[719] *they are not . . . ill Manners: Discourse,* xxxiii.

the Lord Christ? What betwixt the Feats of Faith in the 11th. to the Hebrews, and the Chivalry of *Don Belianis*[720] or *Don Quixote*?[721] What between the Romances of the Lord Christ, and those of the *Grand Cyrus* or *Cleopatra*?[722] None at all. *Tell me truly,* as you are wont to conjure me, *and by the tyes of ancient Friendship,* Was it not here that (as you told Dr. Bathurst) *the Recreation you took to frame your Thoughts and Conceptions into Words, did almost equal the Ravishing delight you derive from their first Births and Discoveries*?

[*C. P. Ph.* p. 3.]

It[723] is an uncomely thing to pass immediately from such foul expressions, into any discourse of so serious a Subject, without some more cleanly Transition; and a man had need wash himself first, before he handles any place of Scripture, after you have so bemired the Argument. 'Tis the fifth to the Galatians, where you had before expounded the Fruits of the Spirit to be meer Moral virtues, and the *Joy, Peace* and *Faith* [244] there spoken of, to be only *Peaceableness, Chearfulness,* and *Faithfulness*; as if they had been no more than the three Homiletical conversable Virtues, *Veritas, Comitas* and *Urbanitas.*[724] And truly you do so face me out in justifying this your Interpretation, that I was almost ready to have yielded it up, and confess my self in the wrong: Neither did I think it any thing extraordinary, if you had chanced once in your life to have understood a thing rightly, or for my self to have been more than once mistaken. But you do so insult and vociferate upon it, like one of your *bulkie* Princes, who had the Trumpet ready to sound whensoever he hit the Ball at Tennis, that I have a mind to try a little further, whether you were not in the Errour. In that of Faith you say, *That whatsoever other Acceptations it hath*[726] *in Scripture, 'tis to be ex-*

[*E. P.* p. 72. *Def.* p. 327. *Rep.* p. 320.][725]

[720] *Don Belianis:* a romance by G. Fernandez, trans. L.A., 1598.

[721] *Don Quixote:* see *RT,* p. 74 and note 202 above.

[722] *Grand Cyrus . . . Cleopatra:* i.e., *Artamenes or the Grand Cyrus,* by M. de Scudéry, trans. F.G. (1653); and *Cleopatra,* by G. de Costes de la Calprenède, trans. R. Loveday (1652). For the strategic popularity of these French romances among royalist circles in the 1650s, see Patterson, *Censorship and Interpretation* (Madison, 1984), pp. 194–97.

[723] It: 74 introduces a new paragraph here; in this case explicitly as a "cleanly Transition."

[724] three . . . *Urbanitas:* the three social virtues, Truthfulness, Courteousness, Urbanity.

[725] *Rep.* p. 320: actually, pp. 116–21.

[726] *hath* 74] *has* 73.

pounded here of Faithfulness, in opposition to the Perfidiousness of the Gnosticks; Peace, *of Peaceableness, in opposition to the Contentiousness of the Gnosticks.*[727] 'Tis great pity that you could not invent too, how Joy should mean Chearfulness, in opposition to the Melancholy of the Gnosticks. And you say, that *Faith here is reckoned up as one of the* [245] *Fruits of the Christian Faith, and therefore must be something distinct from it; and therefore can be nothing but the Virtue of Fidelity.* Whereas it is plainly enumerated as a Fruit of the Spirit of God here in the 22 Verse; and 'tis strange you should be so sleepy, as not have seen in the fifth Verse: *For we through the Spirit, wait for the hope of Righteousness by Faith*: but you had indeed a particular Reason to wink at that in this Controversie. And in the sixth Verse, *In Jesus Christ Faith only availeth which worketh by Love.* So that you have mis-interpreted the Place only out of love to your Notion; and by this pretence, to enervate the Grace and Work of Gods Spirit#; indeed to make a meer Play of Faith, that you seem to have nothing of a Divine, but from hence to deserve the name of that Du-Foy,[728] whom you in *p.* 11. of your *Reproof* have quoted#. For even Grotius too, who is of great Reputation with all men, and ought with you to have more Authority than ordinary, does in his Annotations[729] on this Text, expound Faith to be here *Aperta Professio verae Fidei,* an open Profession of the true Faith, *& opponitur Haeresibus.*[730] So that, if I might advise you as a [246] Friend, 'twere convenient for you to quit your Comment,[731] though being your own, it must needs be dear to you; and observe rather the Apostle's Rule in the last Verse of the same Chapter, *Let us not be desirous of Vain-glory, provoking one another, envying one another.*[732] But of al that you say in this business, nothing is more pleasant, then where arguing this matter, you say to[733] me, *If you have credit enough to borrow a Bible in the Neighbourhood, you will quickly find (if you can find the Epistle) that St. Paul is there describing the opposite effects between the Flesh and the Spirit; and there-*

[*Rep.* p. 121.]

[727] *That whatsoever . . . Gnosticks: Reproof,* p. 121.

[728] Du-Foy: see pp. 282–83 and n. 322 above.

[729] Annotations 74] Annotation 73.

[730] *Aperta . . . Haeresibus:* Grotius, *Annotationes in Novum Testamentum* (1646), 2:544, a commentary on Galatians 5:22 (A, p. 1, #25).

[731] Comment: commentary.

[732] *Let . . . another:* Galatians 5:26.

[733] to me 73] to to me 74.

fore as all the Fruits of the Flesh there reckoned up are Immoral Vices, so must all the Fruits of the Spirit there, opposed to them, be Moral Virtues. It follows not. For that those that speak distinguishingly of Grace, understand thereby an extraordinary Work of Gods Spirit, subduing their Wills, and heightning mens performances beyond the possibility of our endeavours. But no Fanatick, nor Un-fanatick ever doubted, but that men have pravity enough to be wicked, without any extraordinary assistance of some other Spirit. So that you argue, Men have sufficient Power of their own to do that which is Evil, therefore they [247] have sufficient *power* also of themselves by an ordinary influence, to do that which is Good and Adequate to Salvation. I deny not nevertheless, that some sins are so desperate, and of so high Malice and Contrivance, that no man could invent them out of his own Ingenuity, or practise them in his own Confidence, but must be strengthned thereto by supernatural Auxiliaries, and then indeed the Opposition you speak of betwixt Immoral Vices and Moral Virtues; or, as others, betwixt Sin and Grace, is more full, and runs parallel. And seeing you are talking of Gnosticks (but I have lately given you a caution about them, and I cannot find in History how the Gnosticks had already made an inrode upon the Galatians) Simon Magus, that goes for one of them with you, is one that mounted above the Humane pitch in his performances, and men *tell us prodigious stories of the miraculous feats* that he did, but it was by the extraordinary assistance of two Devils, one it seems not having been sufficient.[734]

[*Rep.* p. 118.]

But,[735] as to the main Controversie of the Non-conformists, distinguishing betwixt Grace and Morality, you only shew therein the Malice of your Wit: Whereas there is none of them but acknowledges Morality [248] to be absolutely necessary, and that without it Christianity is nothing; but however that to render men capable of Salvation, there is a more extraordinary influence of God's Spirit required and promised. You in the mean time make merry with it, and as in your *Reproof* (to shew your skill in Anatomy) you will have Conscience to be seated in the *Glandula Pinealis,*[736] ('twas civily done however that you placed it not in some other *Glandule*). So in

[734] Simon Magus: see p. 309 and note 472 above.

[735] But: 74 introduces a new paragraph here.

[736] *Glandula Pinealis: Reproof,* p. 87. Descartes believed that the pineal gland in the middle of the brain was the seat of the soul. See *Passiones Animae* (Amsterdam, 1650), Art. xxxi.ff [S] (A, p. 84, #210).

your *Defence,* you say, *It were an easie task for a Man that understands the Anatomy of the Brain, the structure of the Spleen and Hypochondria, the* Divarications *of the Nerves, their twisting about the Veins and Arteries, and the simpathy of the Parts, to give as certain and mechanical* ⟨*an*⟩ *account of all its Fanatick freaks and frensies, as of any Vital or Animal Function in the Body. The Philosophy of a Fanatick being as intelligible by the Laws of Mechanism, as the Motion of the Heart, and Circulation of the Blood; And there are some Treatises that give a more exact and consistent Hypothesis of Enthusiasm, than any Des Cartes has given of the natural Results of Matter & Motion.* 'Tis very well said, and what was to be expected from #such a# one as [249] you, of whose Philosophy and Religion the Mechanism is so visible in the *Tentamina,* concerning that *Sophism of Nature,* and the *vehemens & effraenata venerei coitus cupiditas & exquisitissima voluptas,* though there is a Maxime on the other side, *Omne Animal triste est post coitum, praeter Gallum Gallinaceum, & Sacellanum gratis fornicantem.*[738] But this Hypothesis of yours, confounding the extraordinary influx of God's Spirit for the Power of Nature, seems to arise from your being ill principled, and not well read in the Doctrine of the Church of England concerning Original sin, which you make *not to be a Crime, but an infelicity inflicted by God himself upon Mankind, as a Punishment of Adams Sin, and what is an Act of his* (that was God's) *will, can be no fault of ours.* We should be all engaged to you, would you carry this point thorow and make it good. And another reason of your Opinion, is, your too high conceit of mens good Works; as if, contrary to the stream of the Scripture, we could be thereby justified. For though you would make all the Party of English Nonconformists answer for one passage in Flacius[739] Illyricus,[740] *Bona Opera sunt* [250] *perniciosa ad Salutem;*[741]

[*Def.* p. 342.]

[*Tent.* p. 105.][737]

[*Def.* p. 198.]

[737] *vehemens . . . voluptas:* "that vehement and unruly desire of venereal coition and its exquisite pleasure."

[738] *Omne . . . fornicantem:* "Every animal is sad after coitus, except a dunghill-cock, and a lascivious chaplain." Marvell is adapting the commonplace, one of whose more common forms proposed as the exceptions a cock and a woman.

[739] Flacius 73] Flaccus 74.

[740] Flacius Illyricus: Matthias Flacius (1520–75), a controversial and extremist Lutheran reformer, opponent of the moderate Melanchthon.

[741] *Bona . . . Salutem:* Good works are dangerous to salvation.

[*Ec. Pol. p.* 74.] 'tis falsly imposed upon them by you; and 'twere well that you understood Flacius[742] himself rightly;[743] for whosoever shall, to the prejudice of our Saviours Merit, and debasing the operation of the Holy Ghost, attribute too much to his own natural vigour and performances, will be in some danger of finding his *Bona Opera perniciosa ad Salutem.*[744] For mine own part I have, I confess, some reason, perhaps particular to my self, to be diffident of mine own *Moral Accomplishments,* and therefore may be the more inclinable to think I have a necessity of some extraordinary assistance to sway the weakness of my belief, and to strengthen me in good Duties. If you be stronger, I am glad of it; and let every Man, after he has read and considered what we have of it in the Scripture, and what even in our Common-Prayer Book, take what course and opinion he thinks the safest. But this Controversie is of so high a nature that it overthrows your Maxime, that *all things disputable are little*: and the matter is so serious that it is not fit for you and me to treat of it in such a mixed and perfunctory Stile. You have already been answer'd upon this Subject by one,[745] who at least rivals [251] you in the Knowledg and Practice either of Grace or Morality. And as to your *challenge* to all the world *to produce any ancient Writer that has understood this matter otherwise then you have done*; if you will but have a little patience, I am told that it will be accepted and complyed with.[746] [*Repr.* p. 53.] Therefore I shall not at present oblige my self further to this dispute: and indeed, though what I could say might perhaps add not much weight or moment to the better understanding of it, yet neither on the other side do I think you a fit man to be discoursed with of such matters. For to what purpose should I make a secret of that which you make it your business to divulge & propagate among all, but especially female, Companies? Are not you the same *person* that says, *of all things in the World you would not make your Son a Preacher*? 'Twas seasonably and timely considered; *For 'tis better being drunk twice then making one Sermon.* Do not you

742 Flacius 73] Flaccus 74.

743 understood . . . rightly: Marvell, it seems, did not; at least John Owen had, in his response to Parker, observed that this was not the position of Illyricus, but rather that of Nicholas Amsdorf (1483–1565). See *Truth and Innocence Vindicated* (1669), p. 55.

744 *Bona . . . Salutem:* there is perhaps a pun here on *Opera,* in the sense of Parker's books.

745 by one: John Owen, in *Truth and Innocence Vindicated.*

746 complyed with: Richard Baxter contemplated an answer but was prevented by threats. *Reliquiae Baxterianae,* Part 3, p. 102. [S]

inveigh against the drudgery of that Sacred Office, to which nevertheless you have so many titles? But yet you say, *you can indure it pretty well, and it goes pleasantly off, when you have a company of handsom yong Women for your Auditory? but the old Jades do quite disgust you,* [252] *and they are mobled up*[747] *like so many Judges.* Are not you he that thinks it below your Dignity to step down to the Private Prayers in the family; and that, an honest Gentleman of your old acquaintance lodging with you in your chamber, left him to his Devotions, and told him you had in the mean while spent your time to as good purpose in reading of Plutarch? Do not you jeer the Women when they are serious and tell them; *You are troubled with sin I warrant you: 'tis nothing but some fond scruple the Minister has put into your head; let them learn of you, for you your self have not sinn'd this quarter of a year*? Is it not you that entertain them with a leading Narrative, of *a certain Lady that stray'd up into your Chamber, where you drunk her up to such an height till you had drunk her down, and lay'd her upon your*[748] *bed till you had recover'd her*? You told a Lady of better quality; that, *in case Popery were introduced, you would be one of the first to comply with it.*[749] What must others then do, think you, after your so illustrious example? Is not this, think you, *very edifying Doctrine for the White aprons*?[750] Yet, I assure you, I would not have told you of it, but that I have very good Authority for't. In the mean time therefore, if you will take my [253] advice, do not you intermeddle further in this dispute, but make friends as soon as you can both with Grace and Virtue: for, how inconsiderable soever you may imagine them at present, you may at some time or other stand in need of both their assistance. You draw into this brangle[751] too reverend Master Hooker,[752] though he is unconcerned in it, and you use his name continually as a piece of Inchantment only, that you understand not. For I have Commission to tell you that you said in good Company, *Hang Mr. Hooker's Ecclesiastical Politie; it was a long-winded Book, and you never had the patience to read it; but it was no matter, you would alwayes upbraid the Nonconformists with him, for you knew the Rogues had not read it neither.* And truly this is your usual practice and ingenuity as to other Authors.

[747] *mobled up:* have their heads and faces muffled.

[748] *your* 73] you 74.

[749] This whole passage seems to report oral gossip about Parker.

[750] *very . . . aprons: Preface,* a4v.

[751] brangle: brawl.

[752] Master Hooker: see *RT,* p. 130 and note 491 above.

The fourth thing, which I transiently objected to you, was your asserting that it was necessary to punish men more severely for their Errors in Religious Perswasions, then for their Immoralities and Debaucheries: and upon this you greedily fix, pretending to some advantage. You say, *That I have exhibited so foul a charge against you, without referring so much as to one* [254] *passage of yours to make it good, and that therefore I prove nothing at all, but that I have a bold face and a foul mouth; For We all know,* you say, (what *We* are you? I doubt you stand single, and no man else will vouch for you) *that you are not unskilful in improving the smallest and most inconsiderable advantages, that had you been furnish'd with any shadow of proof, you would #not#*[753] *have smother'd it,* &c. [*Repr.* p. 66.] Really I begin upon this your confidence to misdoubt my self, being very willing to believe that you had some reliques of Honesty, especially in a matter that would be manifest and evident to all men that would have recourse to my former Book. Hereupon I went to it my self. There I found: *Having thus inabled the Prince, dispensed with Conscience, and fitted up a Moral Religion for that Conscience; to show how much those Moral Virtues are to be valued,* p. 53. *of his Preface to the Ecclesiastical Politie, he affirms that it is absolutely necessary to the Peace and Happiness of Kingdoms, that there be set up a more severe Government over mens Consciences, and religious Perswasions than over their Vices and Immoralities*: and *p.* 55. of the same, *That Princes may with less hazard* [255] *give liberty to mens Vices and Debaucheries than their Consciences.* [*Reh. Tr.* p. 100, & 101.] Then again I find that I have quoted you, speaking of honest and well-meaning men, to have said; *So easie is it for men to deserve to be punished for their Consciences, that there is no Nation in the World in which were Government rightly understood, and duly managed, mistakes and abuses of Religion would not supply the Galleys with vastly greater numbers than Villany*; For that I cited your *p.* 223. and I immediately add, [*Reh. Tr.* p. 102.] *p.* 44.[754] of the *Ecclesiastical Politie,* he saith, *Of all Villains the well-meaning Zealot is the most dangerous.* Do I not by all this so much as refer to one passage of yours? And again, under the title of *Debauchery Tolerated,* (forasmuch as you advise in that *p.* 55. rather to tolerate that than Conscience) I refer in my *p.* 119. which is no great distance, to the very same Passages. And it had been needless to cite any more,

[753] *not* 74; a corrective revision, matching Parker's text] omitted in 73.

[754] *p.* 44: actually *Discourse,* Preface, liii; *RT* has p. 54.

[*Reh. Tr.* p. 119.] your Book being full and crawling all over with such expressions. And further (for having been desirous you should take notice of it, I have reminded you in several places) I find I [256] have objected the same to you, *and that you are contented the Nonconformists should be exposed to the Pillories, Whipping-Posts, Galleys, Rods and Axes; and moreover and above, to all other Punishments whatsoever, provided they be of a severer nature than those that are inflicted on men for their Immoralities,* &c. *So that although a man should be guilty of all those heinous Enormities, not to be named among Christians, beside all lesser Peccadillo's expresly against the Ten Commandments, or such other part of the Divine Law, as shall be of the Magistrates making, he shall be in a better condition, and more gently handled, than a well-meaning Zealot.* Is here again no Reference, so much as to one passage, no shadow of proof? [*Reh. Tr.* p. 125, & 126.] Gentle Reader, What shall we do with this Man, that puts us continually upon such tedious tasks in things so notorious? And you, Mr. Bayes, in what a miserable case are you, so distracted, that you know neither what to do, nor what you do! Whereas I told you there was a Maxime established for one sort of men, That 'tis necessary they should have good Memories. Yet such is my fate to have to do with such a man all along and thorow; insomuch [257] that, though I am no forward Undertaker, I think I can manifest to you when you are at leisure,[755] that in the *Reproof* (a book but of 528 pages) you are guilty of at least a thousand Falshoods: therefore I hope men will not be too forward to be imposed upon by you. But for my self, I am therefore so little moved with all the aspersions and ill language wherewith you have fraught your discourse, that I can only say your Tongue is not made of Bone: or that, whatever other Slave you be, which your self owned, [*C. Pl. Ph.* p. 1.][756] you are not (that I may suit you with a Cardinals phrase) a Slave of your word.[757] Whereas, next after this *Tentamen* of your veracity you taxt[758] me for saying, *'Tis demonstrable that for one War upon a Fanatick or Religious account, there have been an hundred occasioned by the thirst and glory of Empire; and more have*

[755] leisure 73] liesure 74.

[756] *Tongue . . . Bone:* Proverbial. Cf. Heylyn, *Cosmographie,* 1669, book 3, p. 224: When a king of Java "had broke promise with the Hollanders, and was challenged for it, he answered that *his tongue was not made of bone.*" [S]

[757] Slave . . . word: Copy B4 contains here a marginal MS note: Mazarine.

[758] taxt 74] tax 73.

sprung from the contentiousness and ambition of some of the Clergy: to give no less Essay of your Candor, you fall on turning and wresting[759] that, quite forgetting what follows, and was direct to the matter in hand; *but the most of all from the corruption of manners, and alwaies fatal Debauchery.* But [258, misnumbered 358] however you say, *if this were true, 'tis lamentable impertinent; for all the Wars that do concern our present debate, are Rebellions and not Invasions.* Who told you that? But 'tis probable Rebellions as well as Invasions have sprung from the same turbulence. I for my part left it applicable either way, and therefore, if it will do you any service, you may if you please add Rebellions too into the Scale, and I will submit it to be weighed by the Reader. And whereas you would confound my terms, as if it were all one, a War upon a Fanatick or Religious account, and a War from the Contentiousness and ambition of the Clergy; I suppose few that read it, besides your self, but will perceive that the Religious or Fanaticks are directly opposed there, and distinguished from the predominant Clergy. But as to your business of *Algebra,* and your computation of an hundred Wars, or an hundred and one, it is I confess very ingenious: 'tis worth my quoting; *if an hundred have been occasioned by thirst and glory of Empire, then if more by the ambition and contentiousness of the Clergy, there have been at least an hundred* [259; misnumbered 359] *and one of the last.*[760] As to this, be pleased to read that passage in your *Ecclesiastical Politie,* where you say; *'tis easie for one Commonwealth that has gained by Rebellion, to produce an hundred that it has hazarded, if not utterly ruined.* If you will first name me an hundred Commonwealths, I will joyn issue with you: and I will drop Clergy against Commonwealth, till one of us come at the end of our reckoning. You then cite me for having said on occasion of your greater rigour against Nonconformity then Debauchery, *that comparisons of Vice are dangerous*; which *jumps,* you say, *with as wise a Paradox of the Stoicks, that all Crimes are equal*: This of yours is a very strong consequence, and if it will hold I ask your pardon, for I assure you I did not intend it so. But, however, you can wring this against my known meaning; that of the Stoicks suits much better with a passage of your own formerly

[*Rep.* p. 70]

[*Reh. Tr.* p. 122.]

[*Rep.* 70]

[*Ec. Pol.* p. 216.[761]]

[*Rep.* p. 71.]

[759] wresting 73] resting 74.

[760] *if . . . the last: Reproof,* p. 70.

[761] p. 216 73, rightly] p. 215 74.

quoted; *that all Laws Civil as well as Ecclesiastical equally oblige the Conscience.* If they equally oblige the Conscience, a common understanding would [260; misnumbered 360] think that all Crimes are Equal. But as to the Hinge of the Controversie; that is, the danger to the publick, you affirming, that *Debauchery or Immorality rarely proves so dangerous, as either serious or affected pretenses of Religion*: (pity it were that serious pretenses should prove so.) Take but out at adventure any one Kingdom for instance, and work your Question upon it, I suppose you will find the contrary: But I know upon what ground and reason principally you maintain this Maxime. It is from your hatred and fear of Reformation; wherein you tread in the very foot-steps of Doctor Heylin and some others, who have deliberately applied themselves to vilifie, and make odious the Foreign, and even the English Reformation,[762] than which they could not have invented any thing more obliging to the Romish Church, and meritorious. For the Foreign Reformation was indeed wrought out of the Fire, and increased in those other Countries either by the Wars and Persecutions stirred up against it, or else did it self draw the Sword in defence of the just Civil Liberties (for it seldom can happen but that Tyranny in Religion introduces it self by an Invasion of Propriety.) [261; misnumbered 361] And therefore it was that our several Princes, and particularly King James, (who was conscientious and knowing as any man in that point) have ingaged both their Swords[763] and Pens,[764] both Reason of State and of Religion, not only their Publick but their Private Conscience in that quarrel: And if there must alwayes be Wars, I know no Cause more justifiable, nor any Design which were in Prudence more fitting to be still Prosecuted and Continued. Divers also of our Bishops, and eminentest Men in our Church, have appeared in the justifying of the Foreign Reformation. For otherwise, though Ours was indeed brought about something more peaceably, the Church of Rome, if we should single out our selves from other Protestants, would have found us more weak, if not more pli-

[*Rep.* p. 34.]

[*Rep.* p. 68.]

[762] Heylin . . . Reformation: in addition to his *Ecclesia Restaurata,* which was hostile to the Reformation, Heylyn's son had recently republished his father's *Aerius Redivivus* (1670), with a dedication to the parliament urging them to be severe on nonconformity (A, p. 26, #112).

[763] Swords 73] Sword 74.

[764] Pens: Marvell surely refers not to James's *Basilikon Doron,* Smith's suggestion, but rather to his *Apologie for the oath of allegiance,* published in 1609 with a letter to Cardinal Bellarmine.

able, and might urge the same, if not stronger and more efficacious Arguments against us. But you may at this rate of *the danger of serious pretences of Religion,* say in your usual confidence, that, whosoever our Princes were, and throw in King James too, and King Charles, and Parliaments, Bishops, and Convocations and all, you must and will declare that *they were miserably out in their Divinity.*[765] And upon the same [262; misnumbered 362] Reason and Apprehension it is, that you would be thus severe at home, and do raise this out-cry against Non-conformity in ballance to Debauchery; that you may thereby quench the good inclination of my Lords the Bishops, either as to a revisal of themselves, or moderation toward others; incense his Majesty against so estimable a part of his People; infuriate and inviperate[766] the Nation against peaceable Dissenters; and all to amuse men from observing, or to perswade them into the protecting of your own Irregularities. Hence it is that you say; *Tender Consciences, instead of being complyed with, must*[767] *be restrained with more peremptory and unyielding rigour, then naked and unsanctified Villany.* Hence; *If Governours would consider seriously, into what exorbitancies peevish and untoward Principles about Religion naturally improve themselves, they could not but perceive it to be as much their Concernment to punish them with the severest Inflictions, as any whatsoever Principles of Rebellion in the State.*

[*E. P.* p. 272.[768]]

Nay, once you appeal to Governours themselves (which is an extraordinary piece of civility in you) *to judge whether it does not concern* [263] *them, with as much vigilance and severity, either to prevent their Rise, or suppress their Growth, as to punish any the foulest Crimes of Immorality.* Tis something like the Story of Gondomar, this, who from the example of a Mother that whip'd her Girl before-hand, lest she should break the Pitcher, argued that Sir Walter Rawleighs Head should be cut off before he went to Guiana.[769] Indeed it is the very wisdom of Herod, who, lest there should a King be born among them, Massacred all the Children at Bethlehem. So they must be prevented, or so suppressed. As (and more then) any

[*E.P.* p.18.]

[*Ibid.*]

[765] *they . . . Divinity:* not in italics in 73.

[766] inviperate: create poisonous feelings in.

[767] *must* 74] in roman in 73, perhaps as an intentional reminder of the *must* sequence earlier.

[768] p. 272 73] p. 227 74, incorrectly.

[769] Gondomar . . . Guiana: we have not traced the source of this anecdote.

the foulest Immorality, as (and more then) any Principles of Rebellion. So here is a Law, That not to kneel at the Lord's Supper, shall be more Penal than Murther; not to wear a Surplice, more Criminal than Adultery; and to omit the Cross in Baptism, less Pardonable than Perjury. If this were once, as you would have it, Enacted, and that the whole Conventicle should forfeit their Lives and Estates, as in other cases of Treason; Do you think that *God has annexed the same Penalties* too here *to Disobedience to Man's Laws as his own*? You have already thrown in *Queen and Convocation and all*: But, if [264] you will maintain this Maxime, you must too throw in our Saviour and Apostles and all, and *declare, That they are no less miserably out in their Divinity.* But you imagine doubtless, and do not a little applaud your self for the Invention; that by the Doctrine of punishing Non-conformity more severely than the foulest Immorality, you have made your self the Head of a Party, and a World of People will clutter henceforward to shelter themselves under the Wing of your Patronage. I confess it is a great and brave undertaking, and which, I believe, none ever managed before, nor will be so hardy as to take it up again for the future: Let it be Ingraven on your Tomb. But perhaps nevertheless you may fail in your account, and, though you reckon your Function to be a Drudgery, and do in your Printed books debase, as much as you dare, the value of the Bible under the scornful name of *the English Bible*; and not only Satyrize the Non-conformists Sermons, but traduce all Preaching, and make it seem unnecessary, that so the Liturgy might be sufficient for Salvation; I believe you will find very few that will come up to you. For whether it be the Laity, there are not many of them such Libertines but they would be glad to [265] learn better, and once a Week to be told of their faults by an exemplary Teacher. And though you brave it like a Landlord, and that the *Clergy are possess'd by as good right of their revenue as any Seculars* (only it were to be wished that Benefices were hereditary) they have a rustick kind of opinion that you ought to do something for't, and that, whereas you have the Tythe of their labour, they should have the whole of yours. This perhaps you think unreasonable: but they think too worse, that you may well abide to give them good example; forasmuch as you are payed for living soberly and honestly among them, whereas they must be good at their own expence. And this is and hath been always their Clownish humour, that they may see somthing for their Money: neither are any almost so debauched that they will grudge their dues to a grave learned and pious Minister; but most think for such an one nothing is too much, and for the contrary nothing too little. This you think hard dealing here in your *Reproof*, and yet I assure you there it pinches. And moreover, though you would pre- [*Rep.* p. 339.] tend never so much to be the Landlord of your Living, [266] if you do not behave your self there as you should do, I think there is a very legal way to devest you of your Propriety, and there is a Trust reposed in some Persons to look to your manners. Neither on the other side are the Clergy so generally depraved that they need fly to you for Sanctuary: and I know many of them that con you little thank[770] for so scandalous a Doctrine. For those of them indeed that are among them debauched and immoral, there could not any thing more inveagling or more seasonable have been calculated. You have gained your self immortal renown, and how they chuckle and hug themselves and you for the invention. *It is a Crime in a Clergy man to be happy, nay to be a man. And if he will but be unkind and uncivil to himself, they will love him for that if for nothing else.* There spoke an Arch-Deacon! But you should not [*Rep.* p. 335.] serve yourself in such occasions of so equivocal and applicable expressions, lest ill use should be made of them beyond your intention. Who can tell whether the good Doctor at York last Shrove-Tuesday[771] were unkind and uncivil to himself. Your Curate of Ickham, when he laid with his Maid, [267] whether was not he kind to himself? And even you when you dissolved that precious Lady in good Sack at your Chamber, were not you kind to your self? And when you first got your *Dull and lazy Distemper,* were not you unkind to your self? Men are too prone to expound such passages to their own Inclinations: and some *Wag* may chance to write an History of the Clergies Kindnesses to themselves, and their Unkindnesses. Therefore let me request you, Mr. Bayes, the next time to define, how that Word *unkind to himself,* or *uncivil to himself* is to be understood properly for the future. But in good earnest, were it not for some that are unkind to themselves, you and your fellows would soon forfeit all the Clergies Reputation. But of all your Freaks upon this Subject of punishing Non-conformity beyond the foulest Immorality, there is none so capricious as the Declaration which you have without any occasion administred on my part, and with a boldness beyond all precedent

770 con . . . thank: acknowledge little gratitude to you.

771 good Doctor . . . Shrove-Tuesday: Dr. Lake (1624–89), then prebend of York, later bishop of Chichester. He objected to the noise of servants and apprentices interrupting divine service at York Minister on Shrove Tuesday 1673. In reaction they rioted and broke the windows of his house. *CSPD,* 1673, March 12, p. 36. [E.D.J.]

drawn up in his Majesties name. Yet seeing you are here so obligingly courteous to me as to promise me your License and the Liberty of the Press in these words *p.* 67. of your *Reproof,* thus: *If you, or he, or any Body* [268] *else have ought to object against* it, *you know the Press is open,* do your worst:[772] I accept the favour, and seeing your Declaration, I doubt, hath not so well been taken notice of, for want of the Character in which such Publick matters ought to be promulged,[773] I have in return of your Civility prevailed with my Printer to do you a cast of his Office. [269]

By the *Arch-Deacon.*

A DECLARATION

For the TOLERATING

OF

DEBAUCHERY.

BAYES R.

[Repr. *p.* 64]

Whereas ever since our happy Restauration, we have, out of our special zeal and care for the interest and security of the Church of England, executed with all severity all penal Laws against whatsoever sort of Nonconformists and Recusants; but yet finding, by the sad experience of 12 years, how ineffectual all forcible courses are either to reduce or restrain Dissenters; We think our self obliged to make use of that unhoopable Power, that is naturally inherent to us, not gran-[270]ted by Christ, but belonging to us and our Predecessors under the broad Seal of Nature, next and immediately before him. By vertue whereof we have and claim an absolute dominion, not only over the Consciences of all our Subjects, but over all the Laws of God and Man, so as to repeal or dispense with their Obligation, as shall from time to time seem good to our Royal Will and Pleasure. And therefore that we may obviate and prevent those mischiefs that are likely to befal our Kingdom from the sobriety and demureness of the Nonconformists; our Will and Pleasure is, to give a free and uncontroulable Licence to all manner of Vice and Debauchery; and of our Princely Grace and Favour we release to all our Loving Subjects the Obligation of the Ten Commandments, and all Laws of God, and Statutes of this Realm whatsoever contrary to the Contents of this our Declaration: And we require of all Judges, Justices, and other

772 do your worst: part of the original, and so should be in italics.

773 promulged: published or proclaimed.

Officers whatsoever, that the execution of all manner of Penalties, annexed to the Laws aforesaid, whether by Pillories, Whipping-posts, Gallies, Rods or Axes, &c. be immediately suspended, and they are hereby suspended. [271] From whence we hope, by the Blessing of God, to give some check and allay to the insolence of Fanatick Spirits, and by debauching our good People out of all tenderness of Conscience, to free our Kingdoms from those great and grievous Annoyances, wherewith they perpetually disturb our Government, and at last bring back all the advantages of peace and good fellowship, both to our Self and all our loving Subjects, &c.[774]

Given at Our Arch-Diaconal Court,
the first day of May, 1673.
GOD SAVE THE KING.
And----------the Inventor.

LONDON,
Printed for James Collins, at the Kings Arms
in Ludgate-street, 1673. [272]

The thing, Mr. Bayes, is very Judiciously drawn up by you: only I am surprized thus to see it conclude with an, *&c.* For it is true that I have heard in the former times of the *Etcaetera* Oath,[775] and there was another Dignitary, who like you penn'd Declarations;[776] yet I never saw before an *Etcaetera* Declaration. But I cannot comprehend by what License from his Majesty, or upon what occasion from me you have publish'd so daringly this Paper. For if you have any conceal'd criticism upon those words, *Debauchery Tolerated,* I explain'd what I menat by what I quoted out of you, and accused you nor further than what those words signified and Imported. And the Fact stood thus. His Majesty before his happy return transmitted hither a

[774] Whereas . . . Subjects: *Reproof,* pp. 64–66. Parker thought he was being ironic in parodying the king's Declaration of Indulgence; but Marvell makes the impropriety more visible by simply reprinting Parker's spoof in black letter.

[775] *Etcaetera* Oath: On May 29 1640, Convocation established an oath to be taken by all clergy and many of the laity in England: "That I A.B. doe sweare that I do approve the Doctrine and Discipline or Government established in the Church of England . . . Nor will I ever give my consent to alter the Government of this Church by Archbishops, Bishops, Deanes, and Archdeacons, &c. as it stands now established." Prynne, *Canterburies Doome* (1646), p. 40. In his impeachment, Laud was accused of responsibility for the oath. [S]

[776] another Dignitary: William Laud, whom Prynne constantly accused of unlawfully penning Declarations; e.g. *Canterburies Doome,* p. 128.

Gracious Declaration concerning Liberty to Tender Consciences, and hath ever since pursued it.[777] You, on the contrary, declare *p.* 55. before quoted,[778] and in many passages the same, *That Princes may with less hazard give Liberty to mens Vices and Debaucheries than to their Consciences.* But a Toleration or Indulgence to Conscience has been thought advisable. Do not you then maintain that a Liberty to Vice and Debauchery was the more advisable of the two? And was not this enough [273] to charge you in the terms of *Debauchery Tolerated*? But as for his Majesty, he had sufficiently manifested his judgment both of the one and the other by a Declaration of Indulgence to tender Consciences, and by a Proclamation against Debauchery:[779] so that you had little reason to raise so malapert[780] an allusion, and profane his name in a Mock-declaration, which indeed is your own and no mans else, and is not unsuitable to your Principles and Practice. Yet whatsoever mischief you intended by it, (for some you intend always) I am perswaded you were partly transported by the Ornament that you thought it would be to your Book; Nay, I do not think but you took it for a great piece of Wit, so great, that for its sake and two or three Speeches that you make for the Parliament men,[781] you writ the whole Book; or else I had scaped both *Reproof* and *Correction.* But because I have observed how careful you are to find out, before you attempt a great jump of wit, some convenient Rise, and you would not doubtless have penn'd so notable a Declaration without some Precedent; I cast about where to meet with it, and after a little searching, I found this in the *Caesares Juliani,*[782] where that Emperour[783] having undertaken [274] to Marshal his Predecessors under the Patronage

[777] ever since pursued it: Marvell is finessing the fact that Charles had been forced to withdraw the Declaration on March 8, 1673.

[778] quoted 73] *quoted* 74.

[779] a Proclamation against Debauchery: Charles II, *Proclamation for the observation of the Lord's day; and for the renewing a former proclamation against vitious, debauched and profane persons* (1663).

[780] malapert: presumptuous, saucy.

[781] *Reproof,* pp. 521–25; Marvell is referring to Parker's parody of his own parliamentary speaking habits.

[782] Julian, *Caesares,* in *Opera* (Paris, 1538), pp. 98–101, separately paginated; Marvell found this in Anglesey's library (A, p. 45, #32).

[783] that Emperour: Flavius Claudius Julianus, Roman emperor (361–63), was nicknamed Julian the Apostate, having converted away from Christianity to become an unusually sophisticated persecutor of Christians. Marvell will return to him in the *Short Historical Essay,* vol. 2, pp. 154–56. Julian was also remembered for his wit, of which the following text is presumably an example.

of some proper Deity, when he comes to Constantine does thus Satyrically represent him. *But Constantine not being able among all the Gods to find a Patern of his own Life, casting his eye about saw the Goddess of Luxury near him, and streight ran to her. She hereupon receiving him delicately and embracing him, trick'd him up in Womans cloaths, and conducted him to the Goddess of Intemperance, finding his Son returned,*[784] *and making to all Men this publick* Proclamation.

Let all Men take notice, of whatsoever condition and quality, whether they be Adulterers, or Murtherers, or guilty of any other Immorality, Vice, *or* Debauchery, *that hereby they are warranted and invited to continue boldly and confidently in the same, and I declare that upon dipping themselves only in this Water, they are, and shall be so reputed, pure and blameless to all intents and purposes. And moreover, as oft as they shall renew and frequent such other* Vices, Immoralities or Debaucheries; *I do hereby give and grant to them and every one of them, respectively, that by thumping his Breast, or giving but himself a pat on the Forehead, he shall thereupon be immediately discharged and absolved of all guilt and penalty therefore incurred, any* [275] *Law or Statute to the contrary notwithstanding.*[785]

This is in the 99*th.* Page of that Book, Printed at Paris 1583. to prevent any such accident for the future as that of the Epistle to Marcellinus;[786] for I am sensible of the great trouble I thereby gave you, though you have it recompensed by the great reputation you have acquired by your learned criticismes upon it. But good Mr. Bayes, surely you were hard set, that you had no body here to go to but Julian the Apostate for an Invention. Or however, if you had contracted some acquaintance or similitude with him, you could not have pick'd out a more unhappy instance for your imitation than this present. For, as he in this Proclamation ingratefully derides Constantine,[787] so do you traduce his Majesty by your Declaration, which

[784] *his Son returned:* There is no mention of Constantine's son in this passage. His sons do, however, appear on p. 41: "*Secundum ipsum & eius filii.*"

[785] *Let . . . notwithstanding:* It is impossible to derive this proclamation's text from Julian's Latin.

[786] accident . . . Marcellinus: for Parker's charge that Marvell is inaccurate in giving his scholarly references, and Marvell's refutation, see *Reproof,* p. 197 and *RT2,* p. 425 below.

[787] Constantine: Constantine I ("the Great"), Roman emperor, famous for his generosity to the early Christian church. He presided over the Council of Nicaea in 325. Marvell will himself qualify Constantine's reputation in the *Short Historical Essay,* vol. 2, pp. 126, 167.

deserves to perish with your Book: whereas he by his Proclamation against Debauchery hath sufficiently testified his judgment, and, as he hath resembled Constantine in his patience and industry toward composing (howsoever obstructed) the Ecclesiastical differences among us, so in his Largess and Munificence to the Church hath far exceeded him.

And this leads me directly to your fifth [276] Play, Mr. Bayes, of *Persecution recommended*: though I might perhaps more properly have call'd it a *Spectacle*, and exceeding whatsoever was exhibited at any time among the Romans, for cruelty. I had hereupon said, that, Julian *himself who was first a Reader and held forth in the Christian Churches, before he turn'd Apostate, and then Persecutor, could not have outdone you either in Irony or Cruelty*: and for the truth of that I refer to your whole *Ecclesiastial Policy*. You return me in answer to this passage; (for in my whole Book I have but this once mention'd him) *you bring the Emperour Julian upon the Stage as a more cruel and execrable Monster of Persecution than Antichrist or the Dragon himself, and you throw your slaver upon him with so much scorn and rudeness, that the People take him for as very a rake-shame*[788] *as Bishop Bonner,*[789] *or Pope Hildebrand.*[790] You are very Gentle, Mr. Bayes, and good-natured to extremity; which makes me the more wonder at this transport: for in your whole Book there are not above one or two like instances, and you have embraced no mans quarrel with more concernment and vehemency. [277] There must be somthing extraordinary in it. Had I then known that he was so old an acquaintance of yours as I find since in your *Platonick Philosophy*, or had I imagined that he was so near of kin to you, and one of your *Dearest Cuzzes*, I should perhaps, according to the rules of conversation, have spoke to him with more respect; but however I am cautioned sufficiently for the future. Especially seeing he has so ample Testimonial from you, *that he was a very civil Person, a great* Virtuoso, *and though somewhat heathenishly inclined, yet he had nothing of a persecuting Spirit in him against Christians, as*

[*Repr.* p. 73.]

[*Reh. Tr.* p. 124.]

[*Repr.* p. 73.]

788 *rake-shame:* one who covers himself with shame.

789 *Bishop Bonner: Reproof*, p. 73: Edmund Bonner (c. 1500–69), bishop of London, was restored to his bishopric at Mary's accession and became the chief instrument of Marian persecution.

790 *Pope Hildebrand:* Ibid.: Gregory VII (c. 1015–85) was marginally involved in repressing the heresy of Berengarius, but his reputation more generally was of a rigorous disciplinarian who ran an antisimony campaign.

may be seen at large in Ammianus Marcel.[791] l. 22. And you add immediately; *unless you will suppose, as he did, that there is no such effectual way of persecuting an established Church, as by suspending all Ecclesiastical proceedings against Schismaticks and Hereticks, and granting an unlimited, Universal Toleration.*[792] I do not suppose it, but you do; and it is one of the greatest arguments in your *Ecclesiastical Politie* against Toleration or indulgence. Therefore let us see what your Ammianus saith, *But when Julian observed that he was now free to do what he would, he reveal'd his secret design, and* [278] *by plain and absolute Edicts, commanded that the Temples should be open'd, Sacrifices offer'd, and the Worship of the Gods restored: and to strengthen the effect of what he had proposed to himself, he therefore called the Christian Bishops that were at odds with one another, and their divided people together into his Palace, admonishing them that laying aside their intestine quarrels, every one should boldly exercise without all disturbance his own Religion; which he therefore did, that this Liberty increasing their dissentions, he might be secured thenceforward against the unanimating*[793] *of the Christian people. For he had found by experience, that no Beasts were so cruel against man, as Christians for the most part are inveterate*[794] *against each other.* So it was then, and so you would still have it. But what have you gain'd by this Author? Under his Toleration they grew to a better understanding and Union; under his persecution they cemented still closer; and so it will alwayes probably succeed: whereas, in the former flourishing times, the Church was so miserably rent by the factions and contests of the then Bishops; and so was Julian's experiment, and so I hope will all others of that kind be, frustrated. [279] But further, does not your Ammianus tell you of *a most inhumane edict, and in respect to Julian's memory fit to be buried in perpetual silence, that no Grammarian or Rhetorician should presume to teach any Christian.* This he twice mentions with the same remark. Does he not tell you that *Apollo's Temple at Antiocha being burnt down,* whether by chance and Asclepiades the heathen Philosophers candle, or

[*Am.* l.22. p. 225.][795]

[*Am.* l. 25. p. 316. *&* l. 22. p. 239.]

[791] *Ammianus Marcel:* Ammianus Marcellinus (c. 327–c. 392), pagan Roman historian, accompanied Julian in his military campaigns and was generally admiring of him.

[792] *unless . . . Toleration: Reproof,* p. 73.

[793] *unanimating* 73] *unnaimating* 74 (B6, B7, C5, W3); corrected in reset inner form of M in Christ Church W.F.8.24, and copies B5, F, and H2.

[794] *inveterate:* embittered.

[795] *But when . . . each other:* From his page reference, Marvell is using the Latin text of Ammianus Marcellinus, *Res Gestarum* (Hamburg, 1609). [S]

otherwise, *he upon meer suspicion caus'd the Christians to be questioned and tormented more severely than usual, and commanded their great Church at Antioch to be shut up thenceforward.* He saith too, *that Julian left behind him there a turbulent and cruel Governour on purpose, affirming that he was not worthy of the Place, but the People deserved to be so handled*; So that this Author makes as much herein against your *great Virtuoso,* as could be expected from one that was no Christian, and in Julian's Service.

[*Am.* l. 22. p. 257.]

Let[796] this therefore serve as a return to you for my fifth *ad Marcellinum,* on which you spend so many pages; for this is your *Fifth Play,* you know, and this is your Marcelli-[280]nus: Only you have made him but Marcel, and have, out of a certain instinct, nibbled off the end of him, lest he should at any time fly in your face. But if upon occasion of this Marcellinus you had here too remembred St. Austin 18° *de Civitate Dei,*[797] you might have been better informed concerning your Julian. Or, if you will not admit him, would you but have given as much credit to Gregory Nazianzen,[798] or to Chrysostome,[799] and Nectarius,[800] and all the Ecclesiastical Writers of that time, as to Ammianus Marcellinus an Heathen Souldier, you could not sure have had so good an opinion of him. I have upon this occasion from you, made a Collection, whereby to manifest that during his short reign; there was by his means, and under his authority, as great, if not greater, ravage and cruelty exercised than in any of the former Persecutions: but I will not so far gratifie *your* ignorance or *your* falshood. You perhaps, because his is not reckoned among the Ten Persecutions,[801] thought there had been no

[796] Let: 74 introduces a new paragraph here.

[797] Augustine, *The City of God,* trans. J.H., 1640–2, book 18, ch. 52, p. 744: "Why are not Julians villanies reckoned amongst the ten? was he not a persecutor that forbad to teach the Christians the liberall arts?"

[798] Gregory Nazianzen: Saint, one of the four great fathers of the Eastern Church (329–89). He wrote two invectives against Julian. See *In Julianum Invectivae duae,* ed. H. Savile (Eton, 1610) (A, p. 7, #112).

[799] Chrysostome: St. John Chrysostom ("golden-tongued") (c. 345–407), most important of the Greek Fathers. His *Liber in Sanctum Babylam contra Julianum et Contra Gentiles* contains a long attack on Julian; see *Patrologia Graeca,* ed. Migne, 35:1857, col. 531. [S]

[800] Nectarius: patriarch of Constantinople following Gregory Nazianzen (d. 397). He too attacked Julian in a sermon; see *Patrologia Graeca,* 39:1863, col. 1826. [S]

[801] Ten Persecutions: The fifth-century historian Orosius numbered ten periods of Christian persecution under, respectively, the emperors Nero, Domitian, Trajan, Marcus Aurelius, Septimus Severus, Maximus, Decius, Valerian, Aurelian, and Diocletian.

more, neither in his time, nor Pope Hildebrands, nor Bishop Bonners, nor since. But I have truly a better esteem of your reading, and that all this comes from that good inclination you have to such matters; so that [281] you either sneer them off at the end of your Nose as old impertinent Stories, to jeer out our credulity; or do openly aver a known falshood in defence of Julian, for whom you have so great a friendship, and whose actions you approve of. But no man will think the better of your cause, for your justifying it by Panegyricks of Julian the Apostate, and Cardinal Granvel. The ripping up of Bellies, and tearing of mens Bowels; the whipping of Virgins, digging out their Eyes, pulling forth their Teeth, cutting off Hands and Tongues, breaking of Legs, boyling of Men in Caldrons, grilling them on Gridirons, roasting them on Spits, fricassing them in Frying-pans,[802] were but a small part of the Felicities of Julians Empire, *that* Virtuoso, *and who had nothing of a persecuting Spirit against Christians.* He was, I see, an excellent Cook for your Palate: and what Ragousts[803] had here been for you to have furnish'd the *Mazarines*[804] on your Table! you that can relish nothing less then Pillories, Whipping-posts, Galleys, Rods and Axes! 'Tis true nevertheless, that I find not any Edict of his against Christians: for his malice solaced it self in a more subtle way, by interpreting an old Statute about the viola-[282]ting of Temples; and under colour of that he proceeded against them, and caused them either to abjure their Faith, or quit their Estates; and if they chose the last, he subjected them notwithstanding to Death, and the most exquisite torments.[805] Truly, Mr. Bayes, you have a very notable face, and many men I meet very like you. Caligula before, how great a resemblance was there betwixt you? And now Julian, one would almost swear you were spit out of his Mouth. He set up a Nickname for the Christians, to make them out to be knock'd o' th' head: So do you give the Nonconformists the name of Fanaticks, as he them of Galileans;[806] but the great Galilean was too hard for him. Pray Sir, who are these Fanaticks? Most of them,[807] I assure you, better men than your self, of truer Principles than you are, and more conformable to the Doctrine of the

[802] The ripping . . . Frying pans: Nazianzen, *Contra Julianum, Patrologia Graeca,* ed. Migne, Tom. 35, col. 615. [S]

[803] Ragousts: stews.

[804] *Mazarines:* dishes for serving *ragousts;* perhaps with a pun on the name of Cardinal Mazarin.

[805] his malice . . . torments: Nazienzen, *Contra Julianum I,* 35, col. 630.

[806] Galileans: ibid., col. 599ff.

[807] them 74] 'm 73.

Church of England: only you by the advantage of some Knick-knacks,[808] have got the Ascendent over them, and left them in the lurch; so that now you have the priviledg to miscal, abuse, and triumph over them at your pleasure. And above all, the Pestilence of Julians wit and yours is incomparable, but betwixt you, there is not any more visible Token of a [283] mean Spirit, than to taunt and scoff at those in Affliction, and for a Man, by virulent jeers to exasperate and impoyson the wounds of his own giving. Such words are like chaw'd Bullets;[809] and as if it were not sufficient to shoot thorow, you invenom them with your Spittle. Neither is any torment to an ingenuous[810] mind so sensible as to be so insulted over, and for him that undertakes to be their Judg, to pelt them with such expressions of malice, as the condemned themselves, *in Curiae egressu,*[811] would not have used, though it were their priviledg. There is a certain civility due to such as suffer, and to bruise a broken Reed is inhumane. Nevertheless such was Julians practice; and when he seized the Estates of the Christians, it was, he said, but to discharge them of this worldly pelf, that being quit of such Baggage, they might march on to Heaven with better expedition. When he tormented them, he was not only a Reader, but a Preacher, and instructed them that it was their part only to be Patient under Affliction, for so Christ their King had commanded them.[812] And you in like manner point out the wealthy Fanaticks to the Magistrate as ungovernable Creatures; mark forth an hundred *Systematical-*[284]*Rat-Pushpin-Shop-Divines* for the publick vengeance; laugh at the calamities of the City when in ashes; interdict and embargue[813] all Traffick[814] till the Ceremonies be complyed with; and smile at *some that would be thought wonderfully grave and solemn States-men, who labour with mighty projects of Trade and Manufacture, while those things which you your self allow to be perhaps of no great use to the Commonwealth, are not submitted to.*[815] You tell a man, that if *he has not a good Conscience, yet he*

[808] Knicks-knacks: trifles.

[809] chaw'd Bullets: bullets rendered rough-edged, to tear the flesh rather than making a clean entry.

[810] ingenuous 73] ingenious 74; in this case the frequently varied spelling of this word(s) leaves the editor uncertain as to which to prefer.

[811] *in Curiae egressu:* on leaving the court.

[812] Julians . . . them: Nazianzen, *Contra Julianum I,* col. 631.

[813] embargue: lay under embargo, prohibit.

[814] Traffick: trade.

[815] *some . . . Manufacture: Discourse,* Preface, xxxviii. The rest of the sentence should not have been italicized.

has a brazen Wall; That *there is little difference betwixt a soft Head and a tender Conscience*; That *weakness of Conscience alwayes proceeds in some measure from want of wit*: Therefore that men should actively obey at all adventures, because *they have the publick Wisdom to warrant them, and their own Folly to excuse them*: You call the Scrupulous Dissenters so many *old Boys,* and would *have them lash'd out of their peevishness.* But why do I reproach you with these things, which I am perswaded, nay certain, that you take for an honour? I oblige *you* by the very repetition, and *you* clap and crow at the Wit and Malice of *your* Expressions. So some men find a second entertainment in the savouriness of their own Belches. Therefore I will not further gratifie *you* herein, or [285] nauseate the Reader: Your whole Book of *Ecclesiastical Politie* having been writ, not with a Pen but a Stilletto, and with an intention so un-Theological, that the Writer might not unjustly be tryed upon the Statute for stabbing. Methinks I discern now what secret impulse directed *you* in *your* learned Exercitations[816] concerning *Tintinnabulum*[817] and *Clangor*; though *you* knew it not, but *your* Bell like that in Spain, which forebodes no good, tinkled of its own accord, and rung it self backward.[818] You are indeed a meer *Tintinnabulum your* self; and, if with *your* leave I may transfer the Expression, though *you spoke with the tongues of Men and Angels, not having charity, you are become as sounding Brass, or a tinkling Cymbal.*[819] But whereas *you* are of a dimension small enough to hang in the Ear of an Hobby-Horse, yet *you* raise a noise and *Clangor* like the *Stentoro-Phonick*;[820] sounding the Trumpet of War, and ringing the *Tocsain*[821] of Persecution. Insomuch, that, not content to have Press'd and Muster'd up all the Princes of Christendom in *your* Service, *you* raise too the Ecclesiastical *Militia,* and the Train-bands of the Church in *your* Quarrel. *When mens Consciences,* you say, *are so squeamish, or so humorsome, as that* [286] *they will rise against the Customs and Injunctions of the Church they live*

[816] Exercitations: exercises.

[817] *Tintinnabulum: Censure,* p. 62, and *Defence,* pp. 445, 461; a small tinkling bell.

[818] that in Spain . . . backward: perhaps the miraculous bell of Vililla, which sounded of its own accord every time that religion was threatened. See Del Rio, *Disquisitionem Magicarum,* book 4, ch. 3, quaestione 2. [S]

[819] I Corinthians 13:1.

[820] *Stentoro-Phonick:* a speaking trumpet or bullhorn invented by Sir Samuel Morland (1625–95); see his *Description of the Tuba Stentorophonica an Instrument of excellent Use* (1671). [S]

[821] *Tocsain:* alarm bell; copy B4 has cropped marginal MS note: "Bell yt was [run]g at ye Paris [mass]acre. 1572."

in, She Must *scourge them into order, and chastise them, not so much for their fond perswasion, as for their troublesom peevishness.*[822] You will teach her to be a very Shrew if she will take *your* counsel. Was it not enough that *He must,* and *They must,* but *She Must* too? Suppose She has not a mind, and that She will not suffer *you* to wear the Breeches. You could have said no more to Her, had She been *your Comfortable Importance.* Really, if *you* be so masterful in the Church, I doubt *you* will learn to play reaks[823] at home. But if She find Her self not well, or not well used, I would advise Her to appeal to Julian; for he made a Law, That Women married should have liberty to divorce themselves from their Husbands.[824]

I have thus far instanced, that though *you* are not so great a Conjurer as Julian, yet it is not *your* fault if *you* have not been as severe a Persecutor. I come now to your sixth and last Play of *Push-pin Divinity.* For, as in all other things, so in this too you tread on Mr. Bayes his heels;[825] *Who, whereas every one makes five Acts to one Play, what does Me he, but make five Playes to one Plot; by which* [287] *means the Auditors have every day a new thing; and then upon Saturday, to make a close of all, (for he ever begins upon a Monday) he makes you up a sixth Play, that sums up the whole matter to them, and all that for fear they should have forgot it#; only you too have a seventh Play for Sunday#.*[826] So do *you* here recapitulate all *your* former profaneness, with some additions, pretending to represent the Nonconformists Divinity. The Expressions are *your* own, *Whether Conversion be perform'd in an instant, or whether it be divided into several Acts and Scenes? As first, The Work of Vocation is the Prologue. Secondly, This Vocation infuseth Faith, only say some; but Faith and Repentance say others; and then, Thirdly, this Faith must be Acted; so that it seems Believers may have Faith before they act it,* i.e. *they may believe before they believe. Fourthly, By this Act we apprehend Christ's Person, and by this apprehension we are united to him. Fifthly, From this Union proceed the Benefits, first of Justification, then of Sanctification,* &c.[827] These are I perceive

[*Reh. Com.* p. 33.]

[822] *When . . . peevishness: Discourse,* p. 321.

[823] reaks: pranks.

[824] Law: The "Julian Law" or *Lex Julia de adulteriis et de fundo dotali,* passed in 18 B.C., long before Julian, recognized the power of divorce in both husband and wife. [S]

[825] heels 73] heells 74; corrected on reset form M in Christ Church W.F.8.24, and copies B5, F, and H2.

[826] *only . . . Sunday:* Marvell's second thought; should not have been italicized.

[827] *Whether . . . Sanctification, &c.: Reproof,* p. 97.

what you call *the Scholastick Nothings of Faith and Justification.* You understand nothing but the Union of Benefices: these other things you laugh at as so many, ten real differences in the same thing. And yet, if one would call [288] over the Muster-role of your self, he should find near as many differences; and *you* would have been sorry that any of them should be omitted; Fellow of the Royal Society; Doctor of Divinity, Chaplain to my Lord Arch-bishop, Parson of Ickham, Parson of Chartham, Prebend of Canterbury, Arch-deacon of Canterbury &c. Yet methinks, if you be so delicate and scrupulous in a Tautology of Religion, as *you* pretend this to be, *you* ought to be eased in this Tautology of Livings and Dignities. Had *you* been well catechized in Bishop Usher's *Body of Divinity*;[828] or, because *you* will slight him as a *Systematical* Bishop, would *you* but once read Mr. Hooker's Life, *p* 17. or his Sermon of *Justification,*[829] p. 520.[830] *you* might, for his sake, if not for the Apostles, speak at least, if not think, more reverently concerning these Doctrines or Speculations.[831]

Then[832] you go on, *Whether the Word* ⟨*and*⟩ *Sacrament have onely a Moral Operation in the Conversion of a Sinner, as a Man draws an Horse to him by the sight of Provender, or a Hog after him by the ratling of Beans*;[833] and so on till *you* come to, *Blessed Apostle, shouldst thou but make a visit to the Christian World, how wouldst thou stand aghast to see such a vast body of* [289] *Modern Orthodox Faith framed out of thy writings,* &c? *How would it recover to thy memory all that gibberish in which thou wert so idely busie while thou satest at the feet of Rabbi Gamaliel?*[834] How came Saint Paul and you so well acquainted? I doubt you are not in a fit pickle to speak with him; and if he saw what you write it would recover to his memory his fighting with beasts at

[828] Bishop Usher's *Body of Divinity:* James Ussher (1581–1656), archbishop of Armagh, *A Bodie of Divinitie* (1645). Cf. *RT,* p. 56 above. In 1648 he offered Charles I a scheme for the reduction of episcopacy to presbytery (A, p. 2, #57).

[829] *Justification* 74: not italicized in 73.

[830] Mr. Hooker's Life . . . *Justification:* The 1666 edition of Hooker's *Works,* which Marvell is here citing, opened with Izaac Walton's *Life* of the author. *A Learned Discourse of Justification* appeared on pp. 511–36. Both passages are about the serious distinctions between faith and works in justification.

[831] Speculations 74] Seculation 73.

[832] Then: 74 introduces a new paragraph here.

[833] *Whether . . . Beans: Reproof,* p. 98.

[834] *Blessed . . . Gamaliel: Reproof,* p. 99; Rabbi Gamaliel I was president of the great Sanhedrin of Jerusalem. Paul, in Acts 22:3, boasted of having sat at his feet; i.e., studied with him. [S]

Ephesus.[835] What do you tell him of Gamaliel? 'tis a wonder you tell him not too, that *much Learning has made him mad.*[836] Blessed M. Bayes, that were brought up at the feet of Elizabeth Hampton,[837] should she but make a visit to Holywell,[838] and read those scandalous Volumes that you have written and published, she would go near, although she were bed-rid, to kick you: did she but see that so *precious* a young man, of her own Education, should in this manner stir up persecution, trample under foot the Graces of Gods Spirit, cry down the observation of the Lords Day, vilifie and mock the English Bible; *as not in every particular the Word of God, nor in any one thing the Words of the Prophets, nor of Christ, nor the Apostles; as a Book in some places erroneous, in some* [290] *scarce sense, and of dangerous consequences,* &c. that you should lead men off from searching the Scriptures, dispute against the work of Preaching, and sum up the whole duty of Man[839] (which an excellent though unknown Writer of our Church has done at another kind of rate,) in six Burlesque lines of Rhime-doggrel:

[*Hicr.* p. 95. to p. 103.]

[*Hicr.* p. 104. & 105. to p. 128.]

By the Liturgy daily pray,
So pray and praise God every day;
The Apostles Creed believe also,
Do as you would be done unto;
Receive the Sacrament as well as you can.
This is the Whole Duty of Man.[840]

And maintain that this Catch *is to be preferr'd before all the Sermons that have been preach'd for this* #36# ⟨*six and thirty years*⟩ *by the Nonconformists,* #*Rep.* p. 98.#[841] Did she but see these very passages

[*Hicr from* p. 262. to p. 272.]

[835] beasts at Ephesus: I Corinthians 15:32.

[836] *much . . . mad:* Acts 26:24.

[837] Elizabeth Hampton: see p. 261 and note 204 above.

[838] Holywell: the area in Oxford where she held her conventicles.

[839] whole duty of Man: perhaps Richard Allestree's *The Practice of Christian Graces Or the Whole Duty of Man . . .* (1658). For Allestree, see p. 291 and n. 368 above ("The Professor" who disappears from 74).

[840] By . . . Man: except for the last four words, this rhyme is printed in black letter, which was not the case in *Gregory Father-Greybeard.*

[841] *Rep.* p. 98: this is a marginal note in 73, p. 321, having got detached from p. 319 where it belongs. The typesetter of 74 assumed the phrase was part of the quote.

here, and how, under colour of some particular Author that does not please *you, you* run down and Baffle that serious business of Regeneration, Justification, Sanctification, Election, Vocation, Adoption, which the Apostle Paul hath, beside others, with so much labour illustrated and distinguish'd; and did she but perceive that you have done all this and worse, only *as a Horse* to gain *Provender,* or *like a Hog,* to procure [291] your self *Beans,* I dare say the good old Woman, (although she was not strait-handed to her ability) would grudge all the Oat-meal that you spent her in Grewel, and wish the Skellet[842] had boyled over.

But for *your desiring for the present, though you could be very large upon this Subject, that those who would be further satisfied in the Mystery, would repair to Pinne-makers-Hall, every*[843] *Tuesday about ten a clock in the forenoon*;[844] it is not the first Conventicle in *your* life-time that *you* have invited men to, though I suppose this now was only meant as a better direction to informers: but in return to the Wit of it, this being one of your most happy rencounters, you should have consider'd that the best part of *your* own *Push-pin Divinity* was fetch'd as far as from Aberford, a Town in York-shire, which subsists wholly on that Trade, and from whence *you* have furnish'd *your* self with Pins in abundance to set up with.

Thus at last, as you mock at men for *passing through so many Stages of Regeneration,* I have clamber'd as well as I could over these six Stages of your Theology. And I cannot but upon reflexion wonder, that so good a cause as that of Conformity could not be managed by better Doctrine and Ar-[292]gument. But certainly if any thing more material could have faln within the circuit of humane reason, or could that have been fitted up with a better stile or more polish'd language, we could not have failed of it. For you are it seems the last resort of Theological Understanding, and a man deservedly chosen out of the whole Body of the Clergy for this glorious enterprize. A man that, while I am writing these lines, is[845] proclaim'd, even under Doctor Tomkins[846] his *Imprimatur,* by another Mascarade-Divine, to be the[847] *Wonder of this Age,* and so you will be of the future. Give

[842] Skellet 74] Skillet 73.

[843] *every* 73, correctly] every 74.

[844] *your desiring . . . forenoon: Reproof,* p. 102.

[845] is 74] are 73.

[846] Doctor Tomkins: see p. 290 and note 365 above.

[847] the 74] *the* 73.

[*Free and Impartial Enquiry, &c.* p. 33.]

me leave therefore, Mr. Bayes, to sit in the Pit and clap my hands among the Herd of your humble Admirers.

I have thus far made good my former charge against *you,* and submitted partly to make my self the Defendant out of my Service to the Readers, and Candor towards *you,* but henceforward I shall take my liberty.[848] And now, when I look over the rest of your Book, it makes me very good sport to see you play more tricks than a Dancing Bear for the recreation of the Spectators. But you were afraid you should want com-[293]pany and therefore, instead of delivering Bills about, or being usher'd through the streets by the Bear-ward and his Musick, with the usual Ceremony, *you* have Printed a *Preface to the Reader*[849] even before my *Reproof, You have no other civility to request of the Reader, than only to desire him, That if he shall think what you have written worth his perusal, to read it over with an unprejudiced mind, and an ordinary attention.*[850] Ay, pray come in, pray come in Gentlemen; You shall have the rarest sport that ever was seen: Every man for his five shillings and welcom. Whether or no a man can think it worth his perusal before he has read it over, it had been more seasonable to advise men to an ordinary frugality, & an unprejudiced Pocket. The remainder of my business here with *you* is only to pick up and down *your* Flowers[851] of the Beargarden. But how to begin with *you,* or where to end, is unsearchable: for indeed there was never such a Book written, except those of *your* other Bayes; of which (*Reh. Com. Epilogue*)[852] 'tis excellently said;

If it be true that Monstrous Births presage
The following Mischiefs that afflict the Age,
And sad Disasters to the State proclaim;
Playes without Head or Tayl may do the same.[853][294]

The Empire of Atoms is more in order, and Chance it self has a better method. Therefore I shall be obliged to write too at adventure and sit by you, scumming off whatsoever comes uppermost, as it rises.

[848] take . . . liberty: i.e., cease rebutting Parker's arguments in order.

[849] *Preface . . . Reader:* not in italics in 73.

[850] *You have . . . attention: Reproof,* Preface, A4v.

[851] Flowers: as in flowers of rhetoric, especially fine passages.

[852] *Reh . . . Epilogue* 74] in 73, this appears instead as a marginal note.

[853] These lines from Buckingham's *Rehearsal* are printed in a tiny italic type.

You had deliberately discoursed from *p.* 47. to *p.* 54. of your *Ecclesiastical Politie,* to which I refer, against all Trade and Traffick in opposition to Non-conformity; and that, while it was not rectified, *to erect and incourage trading Combinations was only to build so many nests of Faction and Sedition*: and *you* had reckoned that the Non-conformists swarmed *most in great Cities and Corporations*; You had instructed men how Christ *whipped the Tradesmen out of the Temple.* Your whole Book was an Holoo[854] to Princes and all mankind to fall upon Tender Consciences with the severest rigour, and hereupon I said *'twas some sign of the Non-conformists peaceable temper that you were not Deified,*[855] and well I might say so. But *you* hereupon are in a terrible pelt that I have animated the Rabble against *you*; but *from me you fear no other weapon but a Spanish Fig,*[856] *or some more secret Italian dispatch.*

[*Rep.* p. 82.[857] & p. 110.]

No, no, set *your* heart at rest, Mr. Bayes, the very rabble are too judicious to [295] meddle with *you*; and *you* need not apprehend or be jealous of any unless it be the Caecilian Figs,[858] or those others which were used at the first institution of the ceremony of *il Fico,*[859] which *your* obsequiousness would have digested, from what place soever *you* had suck'd 'm.

There was another fear upon you, lest, having been so liberal to the Prince in Ecclesiastical matters, the Church should sue *you* for Dilapidations of its Power; wherein *you* have done just nothing, unless *you* had

[*Rep.* from p. 164. to p. 180.]

retracted the very words and things which I have justified upon *you,* and by one word of confession *you* might have saved your self and

[854] Holoo 74] Haloo 73.

[855] *'twas . . . Deified: RT,* p. 107; seriously misquoted.

[856] *Spanish Fig:* poison.

[857] p. 82 73, correctly] p. 62 74.

[858] Caecilian Figs: i.e., haemorrhoids; from Martial, 1.65.3: "*dicemus ficos, Caeciliane, tuos.*"

[859] first . . . *il Fico:* In 1116 Milan revolted from Frederick Barbarossa and insulted his wife, Beatrix. "To revenge this horrible affront, the Emperor besieged and forced the Town; adjudging all the people to die without mercy, but such as would undergo this ransome. Between the Buttocks of a skittish and kicking Mule, there was fastned a bunch of figs; one or more of which, such as desired to live must snatch out with their teeth . . . a condition which most of them accepted; and thereupon gave occasion to the custome used among the Italians: who when they intend to scoff or disgrace a man, are wont to put their thumb betwixt two of their fingers, saying *Ecco la Fico.*" Heylyn, *Cosmographie* (1657), book 1, p. 144. [S]

the Reader all this labour. But your proud heart would not come down. But *the Priestly and the Imperial Power,* you now say, #p. 178.#[860] *are both Supream in their several kinds.* The Priestly *is in its kind Supream, Universal, and Uncontroulable.* #p. 176.#[861] *Our Saviour deputed the Apostolical order or succession of Apostles* (in which *you* have some Interest) *to super intend the Affairs of the Holy Catholick Church.* These *may require obedience to their Constitutions, under pain of the Divine displeasure, and the lash of the Apostolical Rod.* [296] #p. 167, 168.#[862] I question it; if *you* will say, Christs Constitutions, you say right, but *yours* are *Et-caetera* Constitutions.[863] *When the exterminating sentence is passed upon the Offenders, it smites like the Sword of an Angel,* &c. *It cuts a man off from all the advantages of the Communion of Saints, and of our Saviours Incarnation: and that is a Capital Execution.*[864] Is it so? But at the Rates that our Excommunications are managed, and upon consideration for what matters they are inflicted, I doubt, and by what sort of persons they are issued, that there will be every day fewer men of your opinion. And many will think, if it be but an affair of *the Day of Judgment,* that the Non-conformists may abide the Tryal. But these discourses of yours, Mr. Bayes, have been the occasion that I have read several books over, which otherwise I should never have thought of; And wondring with my self, how it was possible that such a man as *you* should ever come to be intrusted with the Keys,[865] I met, in studying the point only as to your own particular, with some shrewd passages out of Arch-Bishop Cranmer, subscribed by his own hand. *In the Admission of Bishops, Parsons, Vicars, and other Priests, there are divers comely Ceremonies and Solemnities used, which* [297] *be not of necessity, but only for good order and seemly fashion: for if they were committed without such Ceremonies, they were nevertheless truly committed. There is no more promise of God, that Grace is given in committing the Ecclesiastical Office, than it is in committing the Civil. In the Apostles time there was no appointing of Ministers, but onely the uniform consent of Christian multitudes among themselves to follow the advice of such as*

[860] p. 178 74] in 73, this appears as a marginal note.

[861] p. 176 74] in 73, this appears as a marginal note.

[862] p. 167, 168 74] in 73, these are two separate marginal notes.

[863] *Et-caetera* Constitutions: see p. 374 and note 775 above.

[864] *When . . . Execution: Reproof,* p. 176.

[865] the Keys: The power of the keys, entrusted to Peter in Matthew 16:19, came to mean the power to excommunicate. Cf. *Short Historical Essay,* vol. 2, pp. 141–50.

God had most indued with the Spirit of Wisdom and Counsel. And when any were appointed or sent by the Apostles or others, the people did accept them; not for any Supremacy, Impery, or Dominion, that the Apostles had over them, but as ⟨*good*⟩ *people ready to obey the advice of good Counsellours. The Bishops and Priests were at one time, and were not two things, but one and the same Office in the beginning of Christ's Religion. Princes and Governours may make a Priest by the Scriptures, and that by the Authority of God committed to them, and so may the People also by their Election. In the New Testament, he that is appointed to be a Bishop or a Priest, needeth no Consecration by Scripture; for Election, or appointing thereto, is sufficient. It is not against God's Law, but contrary, they ought indeed so to do; and there be Histories that witness,*[866] *that some Christian Princes,* [298] *and other Lay-men unconsecrate, have done the same. They that be no Priests may Excommunicate also, if the Law allow thereunto.*[867] This from so excellent a Person, a most worthy Prelate, & most glorious Martyr, with other things of the like nature, from Authorities to you undeniable, have brought some odde thoughts into my head, how *you* came to be a Clergy-man, or what kind of Mungrel-creature *you* are: which was the reason I told *you,* that *you* for *your* part ought to have stood fast to *your* Maxime, that the Magistrate may exercise the Priesthood in his own person; though you have thought fit again in this Book to disown it.

[*Repr.* p. 23. & 22. & from *p.* 164, to *p.* 180.]

And then withal, reflecting as to your particular, who do so studiously oblige the Clergy by qualifying them for Political and Secular imployments, although there be many Constitutions (and I thought them Priviledges) against it; I begin to be of *your* mind, and that *you* are very capable of them great or small: And I acknowledg *your* humility, who being of so eminent parts, have not disdain'd nevertheless at first to exercise the Office of the Scavinger:[868] In good time *you* may make a further progress. [299]

You are offended at me for using *you* with so much familiarity, for *you* perceive that we are so *intimately acquainted, as if we had either rob'd Or-*

[866] *witness* 74] *witnesseth* 73.

[867] *In the . . . thereunto:* from Thomas Cranmer (1489–1556), archbishop of Canterbury (1533–53): "Seventeen Questions concerning the Sacraments," which Marvell had evidently read in manuscript, "subscribed by his own hand." See *Remains,* ed. Henry Jenkyns, 4 vols. (Oxford, 1833), 2:101–03. [S]

[868] Scavinger: scavenger; an officer whose duty it was to keep the streets clean.

chards or Lampoond the Court together. You best know what *you* are good at, but I have had so little society with *you,* except in *your* Books, that my ignorance may be excusable. But I suppose *you* spoke figuratively, and by *robbing of Orchards, you* understood Baldwins-Garden;[869] and by *Lampooning the Court, you* meant three-Crane-Court;[870] and *you* might have enlarged with Bonds Stables[871] and the Pall-mall;[872] for I perceive *you* have had some conversation there which *you* would count it uncivil to commemorate, but neither do I remember that I was ever there in *your* Company.

[*Rep.* p. 106.]

In the same Page *you* accuse me *with comparing his Majesty to a mad Horse, kicking and flinging most terribly.* 'Tis unkindly done of *you,* to say no worse: and to leave the Reader better possess'd against me, *you* quote not the place. The thing is below any answer, but to refer to the 110*th* page of my former Book being Horaces of Augustus.

I cannot omit, lest some should take it for an Expression of mine, what follows, for you seem to [300] have couch'd it so on purpose. *This is too like the stubbornness of your Shrew, that when she was duck'd over head and ears, stretched up the Symbols; or, as your Pin-divines would have it, the Sacraments of Lowsiness and Cuckoldry.* I have heard of some that have impoysoned with the Sacrament,[873] of another Emperor that had his Sir-name from the Font, Constantinus Copronymus, having marr'd it at his Baptism,[874] as did also Wenceslaus;[875] of

[*Rep.* p. 112.]

[869] Baldwins-Garden: an area running between Leather Lane and Grays Inn. As the site of a former religious building it had the privilege of sanctuary in civil processes and consequently was a haunt of criminals. [S]

[870] three-Crane-Court: Three Cranes Lane runs off Upper Thames Street; but Marvell is cleverly evading the charge that he had lampooned the royal court, as indeed he had, in *Last Instructions to a Painter* (1667).

[871] Bonds Stables: by Fetter Lane; another allusion to criminal haunts.

[872] Pall-mall: already a fashionable location for flirtatious "conversation." See Rochester, "Fragment of a Satire on Men," ll. 7–10: "To the pell Mell, Playhous and the drawing roome / Their Woemen Fayres, these Woemen Coursers come / To chaffer, chuse and ride theire bargaines home."

[873] impoysoned . . . Sacrament: Henry VII, German king and Roman emperor (1269–1313), was "supposed to be poisoned in the Chalice by a Frier at Benevent, a town of the Pope's." Heylyn, *Cosmographie* (1657), book 2, p. 407. Marvell evidently has Heylyn close at hand when writing this part of *RT2*.

[874] another Emperor . . . Baptism: Constantine IV (741–28), nicknamed Coprony-

Witches[876] that have imployed the *Hostia* in their Sorceries; and of Hereticks who have administred the Sacrament in the impurest Elements:[877] But I never read before of a Divine that had to such height improved the Invention. But for the Sacrament of *Lowsiness*[878] I have formerly reckoned with you; for the Sacrament of *Cuckoldry*,[879] cast up *your* own Accounts. I cannot imagine where *you* took the rise too of this jump of Wit, unless either from a Secular; Andronicus Comnenus,[880] who furnished an Horn-Gallery with a several Stags head for every mans Wife he had to do with: or, from an Ecclesiastick,[881] who was in former times like *you*, a Penner of Declarations, and fill'd a whole Trunk with the single Shooes of Women, such was his humour, with whom he had the same occasion; this man having chosen the [301] measure of the Wives Foot, the other of the Husbands Head, to remain as the Trophies of their Lasciviousness. This is, I know, only a Julianism, and you think, and are glad of the occasion, that as oft as you have to do with the Nonconformists, you have a liberty to speak prophanely, like those that will on purpose, Curse and Swear the rather in Civil Company. For I suppose you make thus bold with the Sacraments, because I mention'd an Argument not very weak on their part, that to institute and impose Ceremonies, was to make so many new Sacraments; forasmuch as our Church declares, *That they serve not only for decent Order, and godly Discipline, but they are apt to stir up the dull mind of man to the remembrance of his duty to God, by some special and notable significancy*

---

mus (from the Greek *kopros,* dung) "for that when he was baptized he bewrayed the Font." *Cosmographie,* book 2, p. 630.

875 Wenceslaus: Holy Roman Emperor (1361–1419). The anecdote of his baptism is untraced.

876 Witches 73] *Witches* 74.

877 Hereticks . . . Elements: probably the Nicholaitans: "Mans seed and menstruous blood were with them sacred, and used by the Gnosticks in their divine service." Alexander Ross, *Pansebeia* (1672), p. 188. [S]

878 *Lowsiness* 74: not in italics in 73.

879 *Cuckoldry* 74: not in italics in 73.

880 Andronicus Comnenus: (1110–85), Holy Roman Emperor. Heylyn, *Cosmographie,* book 21, p. 631, mentions that he was torn in pieces in a popular tumult, but does not include the Horn-Gallery.

881 Ecclesiastick: Previously Marvell had used Laud, unnamed, as the ecclesiastical penner of declarations; but this tale scarcely fits Laud.

whereby they may be edified.[882] And further, our Church defines a Sacrament, *an outward visible Sign of an inward spiritual Grace.*[883] And I added, *Our Author besides makes them by his Principle, when commanded, a new part of the Divine Law.*[884] But to this I do not find that in a very large and noisome Discourse *you* give any tolerable answer, but this jeer of *Sacraments of Lowsiness and Cuckoldry,* as in *your other*[885] [302] Book, that they cry *Sacraments, Sacraments,*[886] as if *you* had been swearing a Dutch Oath; save that *you* insist upon the old Answer still, that *Divine Institution is the only thing necessary to the Nature and Office of a Sacrament.* Whereas I think with submission, that by the same Argument, there can be no Idolatry in the World. For Idolatry is either worshipping a False God; or else the worshipping of a True God after a false manner. Now may *you* not as well say, That because there is but one true God, therefore man cannot adore a false one; because there is but one true Worship, men cannot practise Superstition; as because there are but two true Sacraments, men cannot devise new ones? And though the Church allows them not for Sacraments, You may remember the case of Julian's Souldiers at the burning of Incense.[888] It seems to me much the same, as if, because God made man upright, it were not possible for him to seek out many Inventions. But enough of this, onely I will furnish them[889] with one Argument more, though none of the weightiest, out of the *Rationale* of the *Common Prayer,*[890] which you ought not to have been ignorant of; the [303] Bishop instructing us, that the Collects are by some of the Ancients called *Sacramenta, either because their chief use was at the Communion, or because they were uttered* per Sacerdotem. At this rate there would

[*Repr.* from 180, *to* 204]

[*pag.* 186.][887]

[882] *That . . . edified:* see *Book of Common Prayer,* "Of Ceremonies."

[883] *an . . . Grace:* ibid., "A Catechism."

[884] *Our Author . . . Law: RT,* p. 150.

[885] *your other:* not in italics in 73.

[886] *Sacraments, Sacraments: Defence,* p. 447.

[887] 186 73, correctly] 85 74.

[888] Julian's . . . Incense: Julian imposed burning incense to Jupiter as a test of conformity to paganism. See Nazianzen, *Contra Julianum I,* vol. 35, col. 610.

[889] them: i.e., the Nonconformists.

[890] *Rationale . . . Prayer:* i.e., Anthony Sparrow (1612–85), theologian and bishop of Exeter, *A Rationale upon the Book of Common Prayer* (1672, first published 1657).

[*Rat.* p. 68.] indeed be *Sacraments, Sacraments*; I might pretend to be a shred of a Sacrament; the whole Liturgy would be so many Sacraments; nay your *Reproof*[891] might bustle to be a Sacrament, as being uttered too *per Sacerdotem.*

In many places of your Book, and sure you think it a lucky hit, you would fix upon me the old *Martin Mar-Prelate,* (in one page you do it four times).[892] Let me onely desire you as often to remember [*Rep.* p. 813.] Martin Parker, and your relation to him; for to my knowledg, if you do not make *Ballads to the Disgrace of Religion,*[893] you are a Singer of such Ballads; and if you be curious, I will at a more convenient time rehearse them to you.

You had said our Saviour in chasing the Sellers out of the Temple (Tradesmen you call them) had *put on, out of an hot fit of Zeal, a seeming fury and transport of Passion, and that he took upon him in that Action* [304] *the Person and Priviledg of a Jewish Zealot.* This I found fault with in my former [*Pref. Ep.* p. 7.[894] and *Def.* p. 152.] Book, #*p.* 324.#[895] and with good reason, if you would but consider that you say, *A well-meaning Zealot is the worst of all Villains.*[896] You still defend it here by the Examples of Phineas[897] and Elias;[898] and to have been *a Power, or at least a license for private persons to execute by publick authority notorious Malefactors, upon the place, without form and process of Law* #, Rep. *p.* 134#.[899] This Priviledg is very far fetch'd, and long discon-

[891] *Reproof* 74] not in italics in 73.

[892] *Reproof,* p. 113; both Parker and John Dryden saw the *Rehearsal Transpros'd* as the successor to the notorious Marprelate pamphlets, probably attributable to Job Throckmorton, that in the 1590s made effective mock of the repressive tendencies of some of the Elizabethan higher clergy.

[893] *Ballads . . . Religion:* see p. 258 and note 179 above.

[894] p. 7: actually p. v.

[895] p. 324 74] 73 has *Reh. Tr.* p. 324 as a marginal note.

[896] *A . . . Villains: Discourse,* Preface, xliii.

[897] Phineas: Numbers 10–11: "And the Lord spake unto Moses, saying, Phineas . . . hath turned my wrath away from the children of Israel, while he was zealous for my sake among them." Phineas had killed an Isaelite for consorting with a Midianite woman and stabbed "the woman through her belly"; often invoked as a precedent for religious zeal and political radicalism.

[898] Elias: i.e., Elijah, who, in I Kings 18:40, ordered the massacre of all the prophets of Baal.

[899] Rep. p. 134 74] 73 has *Rep.* p. 134 as a marginal note.

tinued, if from the time of Phineas and Elias until our Saviour, there were no new Claim enter'd. But really it seems to me, by this and some other passages, that you do not attribute much belief to the Miracles of our Saviour, among which perhaps this was one of the most remarkable. For, to omit other Authors, Grotius who ought to be of as much value with you as all the rest put together, interprets the Text thus; *Regni sui in hominum animos Specimen aliquod Christus dederat Asinorum accitu; Majus nunc & maxime admirabile edit in purganda aede paterna, nulla vi externa, sola Divina virtute venerabilis.*[900] *Our Saviour,* saith he, *had given an experiment of his Kingdom over the minds of Men by his sending for the Asses*; *He gives now a greater and most* [305] *admirable proof thereof by this cleansing of his Fathers house, which he did by the Majesty of his Divine Power, not of any external violence.*

I had quoted upon occasion Mr. Hales his Book of Schism,[901] And Doctor Stillingfleet[902] (who though yet living, deserves the honour to be already cited for good Authority) does the same, as I find since stiling him *as learned and judicious a Divine as most our Nation hath bred, in his excellent though little Tract of Schism*; and transcribes the same Passages. You hereupon laugh at me, for having said in his commendation, that he was a man *who had cleared himself from froath and groans.*[905] Had I been the Author of that expression, it was not at all ridiculous, but is very proper and significant, and founded upon a Latin classical saying.[906] But the best sport[907] is 'tis

[*Iren.*[903] p. 120.][904]

[*Rep.* p. 143.]

[900] *Regni . . . venerabilis:* Grotius, *Annotationes in Libros Evangeliorum* (Amsterdam, 1641), p. 353.

[901] Mr. Hales . . . Schism: see *RT,* p. 130 and note 496 above.

[902] Doctor Stillingfleet: Edward Stillingfleet (1635–99), later bishop of Worcester, currently a royal chaplain.

[903] *Iren.*: i.e., Stillingfleet, *Irenicum: A weapon salve for the Churches wounds* (London, 1662), a mediatorial contribution to the new Restoration church settlement (JO, p. 6, #143).

[904] 120 73, correctly] 20 74.

[905] *groans* 74] *groons* 73.

[906] Latin . . . saying: Columella, *De Re Rustica,* 12:20:8: "Omnem spumam musti cum faecibus expurgare." Cf. *RT,* p. 134 and n. 515 above; the rendering of *faecibus* (from *faeces*) as Hale's "growns" and Marvell's "groons" (versions of the now-obsolete word *groonds,* dregs) was polite but confusing to the printer. (Anglesey had a 1543 edition of Columella, p. 45, #56.)

[907] sport 73] sort 74.

Mr. Hales his own words in that same book; and though Mr. Hooker were *so long-winded an Author* that you never could read him, methinks you might have had the patience upon this occasion to have perused Mr. Hales his book of eight pages. But to amend the matter *you* say, *the loftiest thing that can be said of so great a man as Mr. Hales is, that he was neither a Mad-man nor a Fanatick.* [306][908] I yield,[909] Mr. *Bayes,* and instead of admiring *that Majesty and Beauty which sits upon the Forehead of Masculine Truth and generous Honesty,*[910] I will henceforward admire only the *maidenly modesty, & rosial blushes*[911] that bloom on *your* Cheeks and inhabit *your* Forehead. But this will not suffice: Mr. Hales *you* say too was a Socinian. I see *you* did not serve *your* Fanatick Prenticeship in vain. No man can tell you truth but he must presently be a Socinian. #No more Socinian than *your* self, Sir.# You have spent much paper in *your Defence,* to decipher the Fanatick deportment toward all Adversaries: but, whether it be theirs or no, I am sure *you* have learnt it to the height. *He has drop'd, you* say, *some loose passages in that Treatise, for which himself was then censured, and the Book is still, though the Author be pardon'd, because as he did not first publish it, so he afterward recanted it.*[912] Most judicially said, and in the language of the Tribunal. But who told *you* this fine Story? Doctor Heylin[913] I warrant *you;* for as for *your* self it appears *you* never read him. But if Mr. Hales of Schisme be too loose for *you,* will you be pleas'd to admit my Lord Arch-bishop of Canterburies Authority; that the Schism is alwayes the Crime of those who give the occasion.[914] But [307] if neither Mr. Hales, nor the late Lord Arch-bishop may be trusted in the matter, pray, Sir, inquire in the Shops for Copernicus *of Schisme,* if there be any such Treatise, for that Author would have been the most proper to have salved the *Phaenomena* either way.[915]

[908] *the . . . Fanatick: Reproof,* pp. 143–44.

[909] yield 73] yeild 74.

[910] *that Majesty . . . Honesty: Reproof,* p. 143, and *RT,* p. 134 above.

[911] *maidenly . . . blushes* 74] not in italics in 73.

[912] *He has . . . recanted it: Reproof,* p. 136.

[913] Doctor Heylin: in *Cyprianus Anglicus; or, the history of the life and death, of . . . William . . . Lord Archbishop of Canterbury* (1668), pp. 361–62. [S] (A, p. 26, #113).

[914] my Lord Arch-bishop . . . occasion: William Laud, *A Relation of the Conference between William Lawd . . . And Mr. Fisher* (1639), sect. 21, p. 133 [S] (A, p. 1, #30).

[915] that Author . . . either way: Copernicus (Nicolaus Koppernik) (1473–1543), astronomer. His *De Orbium Coelestium Revolutionibus VI* was published in Nuremberg in 1543; but the remark of being able to save the phenomena either way applies better to

You take occasion here and in very many other places of your book, to tax me partly upon Bishop Bramhall's account (and more of my Lord Arch-bishop Laud, Hugo Grotius, and others) as if I had traduced him under a seeming commendation. To this once for all. Had it not been for your Preface to Bishop Bramhal (which I will never pardon, because it drew me out into publick to be a Writer) I had never medled with him. But no man will fare the better or gain reputation by keeping you company: whereas you intrude your self upon men of the best authority, by their names to render your self considerable. In that Preface you stuff'd out the Bishop with such Bombast, *you* rung such an incessant peal of *In Laudem Thomae Bum, Bum, Bum, sine fine,*[916] that it would have made an Horse break his Halter. But now that I have wrought so good an effect, as to rescue him in some sort from *you,* [308] and that you have since (which looks prettily) Printed your *Preface* without his Book, I will not (though I have so fresh a temptation by your censure of Mr. Hales) further molest his memory, but let his life and death be buried together. And if I have in some historical passages writ too distinctly, I cannot ascribe whatsoever errour of that kind I may have committed, to any other cause than the reading of ill Books, which have perhaps vitiated my stile as well as others. For ever since you were to be sold at *Jo. Shirly's, Sam. Tompson's, Rich. Davis's, J. Martin's, James Collins's, Henry Hall's,*[917] *you* have so perpetually pester'd the Press with your own Books, and obstructed better Authors, that men have scarce had any thing else to read, and so your virulence has corrupted the Age you live in. For, as I instanced to you in my former Book, your malignant remark even upon Bishop Bramhal, that, *as far as the prejudice of the Age would permit him, he was an acute Philosopher*; I think it now pertinent to shew in some few examples more, how civil you are to your friends, and of consequence how generous to your Adversaries. First, for friend Galen.[918] *I confess that Galen gave a kind of* Specimen *in his* [309] *book* de usu Partium, *which though it is indeed a famous work, yet it is*

[*Rep.* p. 140.]

Galileo's *Dialogo . . . sopra il due massimi sistemi del mondo* (1633) (Anglesey owned the 1635 edition, p. 57, #126).

[916] *In Laudem . . . sine fine:* "in praise of Thomas Bum, Bum, Bum, without end."

[917] *Jo. Shirly's . . . Henry Hall's:* Parker's booksellers.

[918] Galen: Claudius Galenus (c. 130–c. 200), the most famous physician and medical writer of late antiquity; his *De usu Partium corporis humani* was published in Paris in 1528.

not so Divine as to be writ by Enthusiasme; but alwayes seem'd to me such a thing as might either be very much amended, or, much improved: which I do not say that I may extenuate Galen's commendation. No, I know you don't, just as *you did not publish your* Preface *to impair Mr. B's esteem in the least, but to correct his scribling humour, and for a warning to the Rat-Divines, and to show how the Bishop baffled him without condescending to his* Systematical *and* Pushpin *Divinity.*[919] Then Friend Harvy. *In whatsoever manner therefore Generation is performed, whether the Man do only,* &c.*(which excellent Doctor Harvy guesses at, but not so ingeniously*[920] *as he is wont.)* And yet you were not acquainted with your *Comfortable Importance.* Who next? *I wonder how Mercurius Trismegistus*[921] *cou'd Cousen those great Counsellors of Criticism, Lipsius,*[922] *the Scaligers,*[923] *&c. and I cannot but admire that Lipsius, Scaliger, Vossius,*[924] *nay, and Grotius too, so many clear-sighted men should understand the thing wrong, as if they did it on set purpose.* See more, *our Countrey-*[310]*men*[925] *Sanford or Parker, in a most learned book of Christs descending into Hell, which begun by Sanford, Parker finished, first attempted to accommodate, wrong and rashly, the Theological History of the Gentiles to the Sacred History:*[926] *but whoever was the first Author, the vener-*

[*Tent.* p. 77.]

[*Tent.* p. 106.]

[*Tent.* 189.]

[*Tent.* 188.]

919 *did not. . . . Divinity: Preface,* A8r–v.

920 *ingeniously* 73] *ingenuously* 74.

921 *Mercurius Trismegistus:* The philosopher Hermes Trismegistus was identified both with the Egyptian God Thoth and the Greek Hermes. He was supposed to have been the author of numerous esoteric writings, which were actually written in Alexandria in the third or fourth century A.D. They were known through the translation by Marsilio Ficino (Padua, 1494).

922 *Lipsius:* Justus Lipsius (1547–1606), Belgian scholar.

923 *the Scaligers:* Julius Caesar Scaliger (Della Scala) (1484–1558), philosopher and man of science; and his son Joseph Juste Scaliger, humanist scholar and rhetorician. His *Poetices* were published in 1561, the *De Emendatione Temporum* in 1583.

924 *Vossius:* Gerhard Johann Vossius (1577–1649), German scholar and theologian, friend of Grotius, one of the first to treat theological dogmas and heathen religions historically.

925 *men* 73] *man* 74.

926 *Sanford . . . Sacred History:* Hugh Sandford, Puritan divine, began an answer to Thomas Bilson on the Apostle's creed, relating to Christ's descent into Hell; he died after two years and Robert Parker (see p. 257 and n. 176 above) finished the work: *De Descensu Domini nostri Jesu Christi ad inferos* (Amsterdam, 1611). [S]

able Names of Scaliger, Selden,[927] *Bochart,*[928] *Vossius, ay and Grotius again brought it in reputation: so that every man that affects to be accounted a prime Philologer, sets up forthwith to accommodate of any fashion the Greek matters to the Hebrew; the Scabbado*[929] *of which affectation does so break out every day,* &c. but they got the Itch it seems first of Grotius and those other Scoundrels. 'Tis to be consider'd Mr. Bayes, that you are *the wonder of this Age,* so they must all subscribe to you, and carry your books after you. On: *I do* ⟨*not*⟩ *question but that great and honourable Person Picus Mirandula,*[930] *was a person of stupendious parts and learning: yet I am sure that those notions wherewith he made the greatest noise in the world, were but grand and pompous Futilities.* For the School-Doctors you abuse them at every turn; and I could away with it better but for one reason, which is, [311] that you say in the fifth Leaf of your *Preface*: It *was never any part of the Church of Englands design to exchange the old School-Doctors for Calvinian Systems and Syntagms*; so that it is not so handsomely said of 'm therefore, that *they are full of such stuff as makes fools stare, and wise men laugh.* But whereas I had hereupon said, *p.* 213. that you had owned the School-men for Authors of the Church of England's Divinity, you formally deny it, insulting with all your natural and acquired rudeness. It is not worth the Readers trouble to interess him in such a foolish brabble; but if any one please to take the pains to inspect your book again, as I have done and quoted the leaf on this occasion, the most he can say will be that you have Cheated me; but if you have done it so cunningly that it cannot be made out evidently, I am content to go by the loss. Yet for a collateral proof, how far to rely either upon your good Faith or good Memory in what you your self write, let him take one instance where you quote me in my page 120.

[*Tent.* 269.]

[*C. Pl. Ph.* p. 100.[931]]

[*C. Ph. Pl.* p. 68. *&* p. 93. *& Rep.* p. 201.]

[*Rep.* p. 200. & 201.]

[927] *Selden:* John Selden (1584–1654), jurist and antiquary. The work in question would have been *De Diis Syris* (1617).

[928] *Bochart:* Samuel Bochart (1599–1667), French scholar, protestant pastor at Caen, author of *Geographia Sacra* (1646). [S]

[929] *Scabbado:* scabies, scabby skin infection.

[930] *Picus Mirandula:* Giovanni Pico della Mirandola (1453–94), Florentine Neoplatonist. He attempted to reconcile the Christian mysteries with the Kabbalah. [S]

[931] p. 100; actually *Censure,* p. 96.

[*Rep.* p. 124.[932]] *Thus when you cite for your own convenience that passage, that Rebellion is as the sin of witchcraft, you are pleased* [312] *to add too; that this Text will scarce admit my interpretation; and yet you know no more what my interpretation would be, than you do what Witchcraft and Rebellion are.* You might have done me the favour, instead of saying, *I cite it for mine own convenience,* to have begun with my own words; *I will allow him that Rebellion is as the Sin of Witchcraft.* But that candor is not to be expected: Yet to show you that I know better what you write, and what your Interpretation would be than you do your self, pray read in your *Preface to Bishop Bramhall,* 32 Leaf; where you say; *The Clergy of England are as strongly principled against the hateful Sin of Rebellion, as against Witchcraft or Idolatry.* Then see the Text, 1 Sam. 15.25. *For Rebellion is as the Sin of Witchcraft, and Stubbornness is as Iniquity and Idolatry.* Now, Mr. Bayes, whether did I not at least guess shrowdly at your Interpretation? But you are excusable forasmuch as you confess'd in that *Preface,* both at beginning and end, *that you knew not what it would prove, not had leisure nor patience to examine whether it were Idle or not Idle.* Proceed, *I might have added to them the late grand dogmatical Master of Modern Orthodoxy, whose rude* [313] *dogmatizing has occasion'd as many Controversies in the Christian Church, as ever Manes*[933] *and Valentinus*[934] *did.* Had you told his Name it had been fairer; but by the project of that whole Book, it seems to be [*C. Pl. Ph.* p. 93.] Calvin. So, Mr. Bayes, he is sped: You have done his work that he shall never lift up his head again. Yet, *Lucian is every where so abusive, and bitter in his Satyrs against all sorts of Philosophers, that, if his mouth be any slander, they must have been a pack of the vilest Villains that ever breathed. Nevertheless,*[935] you say, *some have slander'd* [*C. Pl. Ph.* p. 6.] *Plato himself, together with Socrates, as guilty of that unnatural sin of the lustful Sodomites; which calumny had never gain'd any credit with us, had it not been reported by some of the Ancient Fathers; and yet it is too notorious to dissemble, that those Fathers were not only very careless in their relations concerning them, being apparently guilty of innumerable faults of memory, but also in many instances highly*

[932] p. 124 73, correctly] p. 142 74; actually *Reproof,* pp. 124–25.

[933] *Manes:* Mani (c. 215–c. 277), Persian, the founder of the Manichaean heresy.

[934] *Valentinus:* Valentinus, Egyptian of the early second century A.D., the founder of the Valentinian heresy.

[935] *Nevertheless:* not in italics in 73.

disingenuous;[936] *insomuch that I find no Prose-Writer agree so much with their reports as Lucian, whose main design it was to abuse every thing that was grave and sober.* Well spoke for your Clients, Mr. Bayes; ay, [314] and for your self too. For, *while you,* forsooth, *take only that most delightful prospect to behold others scrambling and aspiring to those things which you contemn and trample upon,*[937] *and while your palate is not surfeited and cloy'd with the same repeated relishes,* (for you were but newly come from your Grewel) *nor your eye quite weary of beholding the same repeated Objects,* #(you had not yet seen your *Comfortable Importance*);# *yet you could have been highly contented (upon the account of a Philosophick Curiosity) to leave this present Theater, that you might enter upon the next, for the delight of being entertained with a new Scene of things*; yet you handled it so, that by *p.* 242. you were *upon the very point of your departure to* #(the Scene of)# *London*#, and to play Bayes his part upon this present Theater#. Go on and prosper. But; *had the pristine Learning of Egypt been the same it was in latter*[939] *Ages, it had been as great a disparagement to Moses, as 'tis now justly reputed a commendation, that he was accomplished in all the Egyptian Learning, and had amounted only to this, That he was a vain, trifling, superstitious Fellow.* [315] Why so? You put it, Mr. Bayes, too hard upon Moses. For neither did you intend it as a disparagement to Bishop Bramhal, that *as far as the prejudice of the Age would permit him, he was an acute Philosopher.* Still: It *is not my design by representing the Primitive Sages as Fools and Dunces, to rob them of that esteem and veneration with which they have been deservedly honoured in all succeeding Ages.* That is more gentle where you say, *You might give account too of the mean abilities of Orpheus*[940] *and Pythagoras,*[941] *but that you delight not to speak*

[⟨*C. Pl. Ph.*⟩ p. 20. *&* 19.]

[C.Pl. Ph. *p.* 18. & *p.* 16.][938]

[C. Pl. Ph. *p.* 242. *&* *p.* 101.]

936 *disingenuous* Ed.] *disingenious* 73, 74.

937 73 has separate marginal note: *C Pl. Ph.* p. 18.

938 73 has separate note: *C. Pl. Ph.* p. 16; actually p. 15.

939 latter 74] later 73.

940 *Orpheus:* in Greek myth, a Thracian poet and musician who received the lyre from Apollo, thereby introducing music and poetry into the world.

941 *Pythagoras:* Greek philosopher and mathematician, sixth century B.C., who influenced Plato. He believed that the cosmos was mathematically ordered.

[*C. Pl. Ph.* p. 102.] [#C. Pl. Ph. *p.* 5.#]

too hardly of any Virtuoso's Ashes. #Nevertheless you tell Dr. Bathurst, You *had sufficiently convinced him how little the Vertue of Cato,*[942] *and Honesty of Regulus,*[943] *were to be valued.*# But to conclude; Whether do you handle our Saviour himself more softly? *And then if we look into our Saviours Life, the unparallel'd civility and obligingness of his Deportment seems to be almost as high an Evidence of the Truth and Divinity of his Doctrine as his unparallel'd Miracles were. For it is altogether unimaginable*[944] *that so sweet-natur'd a Person should be so base and* [316] *profligate an Impostor, as he must have been if he had been one.* And yet your self must, and do, avow, that he was not so sweet-natur'd to the Scribes and Pharisees, Matth. 23.15. *Wo unto you Scribes and Pharisees, Hypocrites, for ye compass Sea and Land to make one Proselite; and when he is made, you make him two-fold more the Child of Hell than your selves,* &c. and so in many other places. You know too ⟨that⟩ he was once in a very *hot fit of Zeal, and a seeming fury and transport of Passion.*[945] You say too, that *whereas the gentle and sweet natur'd St. John was his darling Disciple, you often find him checking Peter's rude and unmannerly Zeal.*[946]

[C. Pl. Ph.*p.*25.]

But by the way; where is it that you find it so often? I cannot find it more than once, which was when he rebuked him for cutting off Malchus his ear: neither is he there so severe upon him as you are to tax him of *rudeness and unmannerliness.* But once is not often. You, I doubt, trusted herein too much to your memory, and thought he had check'd his zeal four times, because the same thing is related by all the four Evangelists. I find indeed that our Saviour, John [21:]22. check'd Peter for inquiring what should be of John; and ask'd him *what is that to thee?* But here he reproved not his zeal but his cu-[317]riosity. And at another time, Mat. 14.31. when Peter, walking on the water began to sink, he blamed his want of Faith. And Mat. 16.23. Our Saviour said to him, *get thee behind me Satan, thou art an offence unto me, for thou savourest not the things that be of God, but the things that be*

942 Cato: Marcus Porcius Cato, d. c. 150 B.C.; the Roman censor, famous for his probity, moral rigor, and temperance.

943 Regulus: M. Attilius Regulus, Roman consul during the first Punic War. He was famous for keeping a promise to the Carthaginians to return into their hands if he was unable to negotiate a peace with Rome on their terms and was consequently tortured to death.

944 *unimaginable* 73] *unimagible* 74.

945 *hot . . . Passion:* see *RT,* pp. 201–02, and p. 394 above.

946 *whereas . . . Zeal: Censure,* p. 25.

of men. But this was *not*[947] neither because of Peters zeal, but the unseasonable care he had of our Saviours preservation. And I do not at present remember that he was check'd oftner upon whatsoever occasion. This mistake arises from reading of Plutarch, when you should be at your Bible and Devotions: and *the ravishing delight*[948] *you take in labouring your periods, and framing your own thoughts and conceptions into words,*[949] makes you forget the Text of Scripture. You were sure, and had some *Idea* remaining, that some-body was check'd; and so it were for zeal, (which was to your present purpose) it was not so much matter with you on whom it lighted. Whereas indeed I doubt it was that very John whom you oppose to Peter. For, Luke 9.54. he, because a Village of the Samaritans would not entertain our Saviour, would presently have *commanded fire from Heaven to consume them, as did Elias* (whom too you quoted for one of your *Zelotes.*) And [318] him indeed our Saviour severely rebuked for that zeal, telling him, *he knew not what manner of Spirit he was of.* And to this I might add Mark[950] 10.35. And Luke 20.20. Where the Mother of Zebedees Children, and the Sons #of# James and this John would first have covenanted with our Saviour, that he should grant them whatsoever they desired, and then made it the request of their Family, *that they two might sit, one at his right hand and the other at his left in his Kingdom*; for which he rebuked them, saying further, *Whosoever will be great among you shall be your Servant, and whoever will be the chief*[951] *of you shall be the Servant of all.* So that indeed I doubt you have rob'd John to pay Peter with his *rudeness and unmannerliness*; and in making it *often,* you have mistook thus the number of the Persons for the frequency of the time. But you may perhaps object, that this last of John was not a fault of zeal, but of ambition; nevertheless, because some mens zeal is only for preeminence, and thereupon they are often rude and unmannerly to their Betters, I thought it not unseasonable to put you in mind of it[952] on this occasion, that you might apply it to your self; and learn that being the Arch-deacon you ought instead of contend-[319]ing for Superiority over others *to be their Minister.*[953] But I pray *you* reflect seriously upon this *your* mistake, & hereafter either read the *English Bible* more carefully and *the*

[947] *not:* not in italics in 73.

[948] *delight* 73] *delights* 74.

[949] *the ravishing . . . words: Censure,* p. 3.

[950] Mark Ed.] Matth. 73, 74.

[951] *chief* 73] *cheif* 74.

[952] of it 73] of of it 74.

[953] *to . . . Minister:* Matthew 20:26; Mark 10:43.

words (but you will not allow them to be so) *of our Saviour and the Apostles,* or else, like a *Traditor,*[954] lay it by for good and all, as *a Book in some places erroneous, in some places scarce sense, and of dangerous consequences, when every pert, bold, and conceited Fellow takes upon himself to raise Doctrines and Opinions thence, contrary to the meaning of God in his Holy Word, and contrary to the Mind and Meaning of the Holy Ghost,* &c.

[*Hicr.* p. 104, 105.] But, to let these things be as they will, it is however too bold to say (but you durst not adventure further) that *the civility of our Saviours deportment was almost as high an evidence of the Divinity of his Doctrine, as his unparallel'd Miracles, otherwise he had been a base and profligate Impostor.* You ought not to put such things as these upon Cross and Pile so;[955] for ill use may be made of it, though it should be against your intention. [C. Pl. Ph. *p.* 25.] And really, had you writ as much of Mahomet as you have here done of Christ and Moses, you have put fair to be, as you have [320] been the second Author of *Ecclesiastical Politie,* so now, of the *Tre Grandi Impostori.*[956] So that you scc, I hopc, by this timc, if my Stile hath differently decipher'd the same person in different Circumstances, where I learn it, but have not yet attained the height of your Faculty.

You condemn me for having in my *p.* 309. mentioned the Reverend Bishop Andrews[957] his Form of Consecration of a Church or Chappel; which I might have done at large, and inserted something of History that depends upon it: but I did not, neither shall I now say any thing further, but only refer you to Arch-Bishop Parker, p. 85.[958] of his *Antiquitates Ecclesiae Britannicae,* where you may find what his Judgment was in this case of things of the very same nature. [*Rep.* p. 138]

I had said, *p.* 166. of my Book, That I could quote my Lord Verulam to

[954] *Traditor:* one of those early Christians who, in the great persecution under Diocletian, delivered up their sacred books in order to save their lives.

[955] Cross and Pile: from French *croix et pile,* the two sides of a coin. Marvell means "a thing and its opposite," heads *and* tails.

[956] *Tre Grandi Impostori:* a notorious satirical work, but not suppositious, as Smith recorded. There were two copies in Anglesey's library (A, p. 25, #70, p. 36, #110).

[957] Bishop Andrews: Lancelot Andrewes (1555–1626), bishop of Winchester. In *RT,* p. 194 above, Marvell had mentioned finding his *Form of Consecration of a Church or Chappel* on a bookstand, included in a copy of Anthony Sparrow's *Rationale.*

[958] p. 85: The 1605 edition used by Marvell (see p. 169 and note 708) has a diatribe by King Edgar against the decadence and luxury of the Church at p. 85.

your confusion: hereupon you tell me the *Quotation of my Lord Verulam would have been more to the purpose, or the Story of Pork, which you say I know, but I say I do not know; or however if I did, you might have had the manners to have told it for his Majesties sake, because he knows how to make use of it*; You think you put me hard to it. I am sorry that I [321] must trouble the Reader with such stuff, and these mean Contests *de Lana Porcina.*[959] But this is all the Fleece a Man can hope for in Sheering you. I had told you Sir, (there was not a word of His Majesty) in my *p.* 320.[960] alluding to your Tautologies, *That all the variety of your Treat is Pork, (you know the Story) but so little disguised by good Cookery, that it discovers the miserableness, or rather the penury of the Host.* Now here have you brought my *p.* 166. into conjunction with my *p.* 320.[961] that (which every man will discern) because my Lord Verulam was mentioned you might make a Quibble between[962] *Pork* and *Bacon.* Nor did I ever see a Quibble fetch'd at greater distance, or more cunningly carried. But in whatsoever you undertake, you are extraordinary, as (because I promis'd you before some Instances in your *Ecclesiastical Politie*) where you are informing the World concerning some *Sects of Men made up of Sanctified Fury,* &c. *Tois gar Presbuteroisin,*[963] &c. which was to make a Greek Quibble forsooth upon the Presbyterians, and of so many Ages ago. Whereas the good old Poet[964] never dreamed of any such thing, or such a Nation, and the Chrono-[322]logy and Geography of it varies as much as in the Play of Moses and Julius Caesar. A third Instance shall be in an Anagram you give us of Calvin; that is, *Culina*: though it be in two Languages that understand not one another, and the Man spent very little in his Kitchin, nor made Provision for it, but all went to his Study, and yet his whole Inventory at his death mounted not to above seventy pounds *Sterling.*[965] This may serve for a

[*Rep.* p. 155]

[*Ec. Pol.* p. 150.]

[959] *de Lana Porcina:* adapted from Horace, "Alter rixatur de lana saepe caprina" (Another often wrangles over a goatskin), *Epistolae,* 1.18.15; proverbial for squabbling over trivialities.

[960] *p.* 320 Ed.] *p.* 300 73, 74.

[961] Ditto.

[962] between 74] betwixt 73.

[963] *Sects . . . Presbuteroisin:* a pun on the Greek word for "elder."

[964] good old Poet: probably Homer, who uses *presbuteroisin, Iliad,* 15.204.

[965] Inventory . . . *Sterling:* See Theodore Beza, *Life of Calvin,* in Calvin, *Tracts,* trans. Henry Beveridge (Edinburgh, 1844), l.xvix–c: "He, whose whole effects, including the proceeds of his library which was well sold, scarcely amounted to 300 gold pieces. . .

Specimen or scantling of your Wit, and to shew how well you spent your time at both Universities: *Which I do not say by any means to diminish your just commendation*; for certainly none ever quibbled with greater *Enthusiasm.*

I shall, upon this occasion, take leave to digress a little further concerning Calvin and Geneva, to which you are every where a declared Enemy. The Town you might have spared, if not for his, yet for Sales his sake, the Bishop of Geneva;[966] whose Book was thought fit to be Licensed by your Predecessor Doctor Heywood:[967] though afterwards it was called in, and burnt by Proclamation, but the Doctor was *punished with Preferment.* But as to Calvin himself, it had been well that you had rather imita-[323]ted the incomparable Modesty and Candor of Reverend Mr. Hooker in all his Writings, and especially in this particular; but how should you imitate him, whom, notwithstanding your challenging and defying the Nonconformists with his *Ecclesiastical Politie,* it seems you had never read. *I think,* saith he, *that Calvin was incomparably the wisest Man that ever the French Church did enjoy, since it enjoyed him. Divine Knowledge he gathered not by Hearing or Reading so much, as by teaching others. For though thousands were Debtors to him, as touching Knowledg in that kind, yet he to none, but only to God the Author of that most blessed Fountain, the Book of Life; and of the admirable dexterity of Wit, together with the helps of other Learning, which were his Guides.*[968] And I find the Reverend Bishop of Durham, Doctor Morton, in his little Tract *de Pace Ecclesiastica,* had no less opinion of him. In that Tract the Bishop, as also Bishop Davenant, Bishop Hall,[969] and others do with

---

observed . . . 'If some will not be persuaded while I am alive, my death at all events, will show that I have not been a money-making man.'" [S]

966 Sales . . . Geneva: St. Francis of Sales (1567–1622), bishop of Geneva. His *Introduction to a Devout Life* (1609) was licensed but later withdrawn. In *Canterburies Doome* (pp. 186–88) Prynne made much of this episode, as an example of the scandals of the Laudian church.

967 William Heywood (1600–63), chaplain to Archbishop Laud and Charles I. He was petitioned against by his parishioners and attacked by Prynne as a "licenser of Popish Books."

968 *I think . . . his Guides:* Richard Hooker, *Of the Lawes of Ecclesiastical Politie* (1666): "A Preface to them that seeke . . . the *Reformation of Lawes and Orders* Ecclesiastical . . . ," B1v.

969 Morton . . . Hall: Thomas Morton (1564–1659), bishop of Durham; John Davenant (1576–1641), bishop of Salisbury; Joseph Hall (1574–1656), bishop of Norwich. Their opinions on church government were set forth in *De Pacis Ecclesiasticae Ra-*

singular Wisdom and Piety treat concerning reconciliation of Protestants among themselves: a Design much more probable and better timed, than that which was set up by others for the accommodating of our Church with the Roman. [324] There he saith, *Consulant illi, si placet, Lutherum Melanchthonem,*[970] *Jac. Andream Brentium;*[971] *Nos Calvinum Nostrum, Petrum Martyrum*[972] *& Zanchium*[973] *proferemus* (we will produce saith he our Calvin) *qui singuli in Ecclesia Christi veluti primae magnitudinis lumina fulserunt.* And he adds upon occasion in the next page, *Haec Calvinus tam pacate tam placide tamque indulgenter, ut jam non homo sed ipsa humanitas loqui videatur.*[974] It were endless to cite the testimonies of al sorts of men, not only of the Protestant, but of the Romish perswasion, concerning that excellent person: but indeed he needs no more certain commendation than that he is traduced and accused by you. And whereas you tax him as pragmatical and intermedling with other mens matters; what could he do otherwise, all the Learned men of Europe solliciting his approved Judgment in the most weighty occasions. Nor therefore could he avoid that general correspondence by Letters, of another stile I am sure than your Letters are, who are therefore offended at him. Though you might have remember'd that there were some Letters[975] too writ to him by Arch-bishop Parker. But the design of you and those of your Cast has been, and still it seems to continue, against [325] all the forraign Churches: and you are but Heylin

tionibus inter Evangelicos usurpandis Et de Theologorum fundamentali consensu (1634). Marvell is using the 1636 edition published at Amsterdam, pp. 3–4. [S]

970 *Melanchthonem:* Philip Melanchthon (1495–1560), German theologican and reformer, close friend of Luther, organizer and explicator of Luther's doctrines.

971 *Brentium:* Johann Brenz (1499–1570), Lutheran divine.

972 *Peter Martyrum:* Pietro Martire Vermigli (1500–62), Augustinian abbot who rejected Roman Catholicism, fled to Strasbourg, was invited to England by Cranmer, and in 1548 was appointed Regius Professor of Divinity at Oxford. [S]

973 *Zanchium;* Girolamo Zanchi (1516–90), converted to Protestantism by Peter Martyr, taught at the universities of Strasbourg and Heidelberg. [S]

974 *Consultant . . . videatur:* "Let them consult, if they please, Luther and Melanchthon, Jac. Andreas Brentius, we will produce our Calvin, Peter Martyr and Zanchius, who singly shone in the Church of Christ as if they were stars of the first magnitude." "Calvin [said] these things so peaceably, so calmly and so indulgently that it seems not a man speaking but humanity itself."

975 some Letters: There are no letters to Calvin in Parker's *Correspondence,* ed. Perowne and Bruce (1853). Strype notes a letter to Parker from Calvin in 1560, to which Parker apparently did not reply. *Life of Parker* (1711), p. 69. [S]

resuscitated, whose business it was by his scandalous Histories to blacken the whole Reformation; attributing (as Reverend Doctor Moulin[976] well expresses it) and *imputing the excesses that happened by the ordinary course of humane business unto Religion.*[977] And he did it to so good purpose, that I believe his Books have occasion'd among us the defection of more Protestants unto the Romish Religion, than any thing that themselves have writ in the points of Controversie. And this distance from all other of the Reformed Churches hath been and is held up by you and your party so studiously, that besides what has been writ against *them*[978] with all bitterness; they have even in cases of Extremity and Necessity refused to Communicate with them. Hence it is that you say in your *Preface*; *Therefore Reader I beg thy hearty prayers and endeavours for the Peace and Prosperity of the Church of England* (He had need when you do so dangerously interrupt it) *for when that is gone it will be very hard to find out another, with which, if thou art either honest or wise, thou wilt be over-forward to joyn Communion.*[979] And why so? Truly I know not unless it be for some more peculiar and Ceremonial perfection that our [326] Church may have attain'd to above others. And this indeed hath been alwaies magnifyed and esteemed to that height by those of your Bran and Leaven, that even our own Kings and Bishops have all along been Characteriz'd by them well or will, according as they promoted those matters or remitted them. As for Henry the Eight, he is a gone man, and his *Sacriledge*[980] will never be pardon'd even in his Successors. For Edward the Sixth, that miracle of Princes, *yet his death was none of the Infelicities of the Church of England.*[981] But might he not have lived to be wiser and better? But in the blessed Reign of Queen Mary (as in the Preface of the Oxford Statutes compiled in the time of Archbishop Laud) *Potiunte rerum Maria, inter incerta vacillans Statuta, viguit Academia, celebrantur studia, enituit disciplina, & optanda temporum faelici-*

[976] Reverend Doctor Moulin: Lewis du Moulin (1606–80), French born, moved to England and practiced medicine. In 1648 he held a professorship at Oxford but was ousted at the Restoration.

[977] *imputing . . . Religion:* perhaps an inexact memory of Du Moulin's attack on Heylyn in *Patronus Bonae Fidei in Causa Puritanorum contra Hierarchicos Anglos* (1672), p. 43.

[978] *them:* not in italics in 73.

[979] *Therefore . . . Communion:* Parker, *Preface,* e8v.

[980] *Sacriledge* 73] *Sacrilidge* 74.

[981] *yet his . . . England:* see above p. 308 and note 463.

tate (if it could be had again for wishing) *Tabularum defectus resarcivit innatus Candor, & quicquid legibus deerat*[982] *moribus Suppletum est.*[983] But then upon her death there came in an iron Age; *Terras Astraea*[984] *reliquit.*[985] For *Decurrente Temporum Serie,* that is in Queen Elizabeth and King James his times, *& Vitiis & Legibus pariter laboratum est*;[986] all was quite spoiled; yet sometimes she was Eli-[327]zabeth, and sometimes *old Elsibeth*[987] with you, thereafter as she behaved her self in the matter of Conformity. There in her *Quinto Eliz. she was miserably out in her Divinity.* And then in *Decimo Tertio* she did no better, when she was contented the Puritans should only subscribe the Articles of Doctrine. But at other times she was pretty tolerable. King James was more busie than belong'd him, when he writ a Letter to her in behalf of the Non-conformists:[988] but after he succeeded her in England he made amends. But he had a great fault nevertheless, that he was so uncivil to the Arminians, even to such a degree, as to stile Arminius *the Enemy of God,* Arminianisme *Heresie,* the Arminians *Hereticks and Atheistical Sectaries.*[989] For though in England he advanced the Episcopal Government, yet he had adhered to the Doctrine of Calvin, which you and your Tribe do so detest, that though a King please you never so well in matter of Conformity, yet unless he humour you too in Arminianisme or such devices, he cannot be assured of your good graces. And so it is too even as to the Bishops. Arch-bishop

[982] *deerat* 73] *deeret* 74.

[983] *Potiunte . . . Suppletum est: Corpus Statutorum Universitatis Oxon* (1634), S1v. "Praefatio ad Lectorem." [S] ("Mary, taking control of matters, wavering between uncertain Statues, was vigorous in the Academy, studies were celebrated, discipline shone forth, and in the wished-for happiness of the times she restored the innate clarity worn away in the regulations, and what was missing in the laws was supplied in the customs.")

[984] *Astraea* 73] *Austraea* 74.

[985] *Terras . . . reliquit:* Ovid, *Metamorphoses,* 1.150. The goddess Astraea was the last of the deities to abandon earth.

[986] *Decurrente . . . est: Corpus Statutorum,* S1v: "The process of time running on, defects and laws developed side by side."

[987] *old Elsibeth:* cf. *RT,* p. 168 and *Defence,* p. 483.

[988] King James . . . Non-conformists: In 1591 James I wrote to Elizabeth on behalf of the puritan John Udal (d. 1592) and Thomas Cartwright. Neal, *History of the Puritans* (1822), 1:414, 418. [S]

[989] *the Enemy . . . Sectaries:* James I, *Works* (1616), p. 355, "A declaration against Vorstius." [S]

Cranmer is subject to many exceptions. But Arch-bishop Parker was *a Prelate of great worth, and no less eminent in the Churches* [328] *cause.*[990] But Arch-bishop Grindal[991] *was a man of another Spirit, he having convers'd with Calvin and Beza abroad could not shake off their Acquaintance, or was as willing to continue it as they: when Bishop of London, he condescended to have a French Church set up in the City: when of York, he entertain'd correspondence with Zanchy a Divine of Heidelberge.*[992] An hainous crime! *Nay, but when he was Arch-bishop of Canterbury, he not only conniv'd at the Lectures, which were newly set up by the Puritans, but even incouraged them.*[993] A sad man was he! But then came Arch-bishop Whitgift,[994] who repar'd all that had run to ruine *by the negligence and remissness of some great Bishops,*[995] and by the zeal of the Grindalizing[996] Lecturers.[997] And yet this truly venerable Bishop could not escape censure too among you; for though he were right in Ceremonies, yet he was wrong in substance, and gave authority to the Articles of Lambeth,[998] which run point-blank against the Arminian Tenets. Therefore notwithstanding all his merits, he can scarce be forgiven. But Arch-bishop Bancroft[999] was a man I trow without exception. But then as misfortune would have it, Arch-bishop Abbot[1000] succeeds him, and *he was*

[990] *Prelate . . . cause:* Heylyn, *Aerius Redivivus: or The History of the Presbyterians,* 2d ed. (1672), p. 244. [S] (A, p. 26, #112)

[991] Grindal: Edmund Grindal (1519–83), archbishop of Canterbury, was suspended by Elizabeth in 1577 for refusing to suppress the "prophesyings," or puritan theological workshops.

[992] *was a man . . . Heidelberge:* Heylyn, *Aerius Redivivus,* pp. 244–45.

[993] *conniv'd . . . incouraged them:* Heylyn, *Aerius Redivivus,* p. 246; Marvell is paraphrasing rather than quoting.

[994] Whitgift: John Whitgift, archbishop of Canterbury after Grindal; see *RT,* p. 145 and note 584 above.

[995] *by the . . . Bishops:* Heylyn, *Aerius Redivivus,* p. 262.

[996] Grindalizing: ibid., p. 261.

[997] Lecturers 73] Lectures 74.

[998] Articles of Lambeth: nine Calvinist propositions maintaining the doctrines of Grace and Predestination compiled at Lambeth in 1595 by a committee under Whitgift. They were never authorized and strongly opposed by Elizabeth. [S]

[999] Bancroft: Richard Bancroft, archbishop of Canterbury: see *RT,* p. 125 and note 457 above.

[1000] Abbot: George Abbot, archbishop of Canterbury: see *RT,* p. 181 and note 775 above. Marvell had included in *RT* a section of Abbot's narrative of his troubles with Charles I and Laud.

too facil and yielding [329] *in the exercise of that great Office, and by his extraordinary remissness*[1001] *in exacting strict Conformity to the prescribed Orders of the Church in point of Ceremony, he seemed to resolve those legal Determinations to their first indifferency. And he brought in such an habit of Nonconformity, that the future reduction of those tender-conscienced men to a long discontinued obedience, was at the last interpreted an Innovation.*[1002] This is out of your Doctor Heylin, who goes down with you for Gospel, and is to you like Meat, Drink, and Cloathing. All this adoe must be made for things that profit nothing, (save that to you indeed they are very profitable) and according as great Princes or eminent Prelates are more or less ceremonious, so must they be ranked in your Calendar. By how much a man is more a Christian you account him the worse Bishop: and it is now grown, instead of the requisites in Scripture to that sacred Office, a sufficient commendation to have been *an admirable Ritualist.*

'Tis now time to return to our Pork and Bacon, but because you cry Pork Pork as often as any Raven, I will first to stay your Stomach, give you the story of the Pork, [330] and the rather to satisfie another friend of mine, who did me the favour to interpret it of his Highness the Duke of York, when he contented himself the former year with the homely fare of the Marriners at the Dogger-bank.[1003] It was at an Audience of the Embassadors of the Aetoleans and Antiochus, in the Council of Achaea, Quin-

[1001] *remissness* 73] *remisness* 74.

[1002] *he was too . . . Innovation:* Heylyn, *Aerius Redivivus,* pp. 383–84. Heylyn's stake in these matters was a result of his positions under Charles I and Laud, first as royal chaplain (1630), then as Laud's agent in harassing Bishop Williams. He was Laud's assistant in the Short Parliament and joined the king at Oxford, to become the author of the royalist newsletter, *Mercurius Aulicus.*

[1003] Duke of York . . . Dogger-bank: an ironic reference to the crucial shortage of victuals in the English fleet commanded by the duke of York in May 1665, during the Second Dutch War. The fleet was forced to return to Harwich for provisioning. See D. Hannay, *A Short History of the Royal Navy 1217–1688* (1898), p. 338; and cf. *Third Advice to a Painter,* ll. 327–32:

> See that the Men have Pay, & Beef, & Beere;
> Find out the cheats of the four-millioneer.
> Out of the very Beer they steale the Malt,
> Powd'r out of Powder, powder'd Beef the Salt.
> Put thy hand to the Tub: instead of Ox,
> They victuall with French Pork that has the Pox.

tius, the Roman General, being present.[1004] Antiochus his Embassadors boasted there very much of the potent Armies of their King; thundring out the hard names of Elymaeans, Cadusians, Medians, &c. of which they consisted: whereupon Quintius, to take off the wonderment and terrour, replyed; (and I will give you honest Philemon Holland[1005] for an Interpreter) *Now in faith this is mine Host of Chalcis up and down; a friendly Man I assure you, and a good Fellow in his House, and one that knoweth how to entertain his Guests, and make them very welcom. We went upon a time to make merry with him, and I remember it was at Midsummer, when the dayes are longest, and the Sun at the hottest. And as we wondred how, at such a season of the year, he met with that plenty of Venison, and such variety withal; the man nothing so vain-glorious as these Fellows are, smiled plea-*[331]*santly upon us, and said, We were welcom to a Feast of good Swine and no better: But well fare*[1006] *a good Cook my Masters, who by his cunning hand, what with seasoning it, and what with serving it up with divers Sawces, has made all this fair shew of wild Flesh, and the same of sundry sorts.*[1007] Thus, Mr. Bayes, have I reveal'd to you this great Mystery of Pork, of which you were so curious, and which tended only, as I told you, to show how jejune[1008] you were, who in all your matters, and even in that of railing, whereof you are most copious, and the best furnished; yet are forced to serve up to the Reader continually the cold Hashes of plain repetitions, to stuff out your Books and fill your Table. I hope I have with this stay'd your Stomach; and if you will but expect a little, I will too, in convenient time, bring in your Bacon.

You had, to make the Ceremonies go down better with the Nonconformists, said, *that 'twas no more for the Magistrate to impose them than to*

[1004] Aetoleans . . . Quintius: In 192 B.C. the Aetolians invited the Seleucid king Antiochus III (242–187 B.C.) to join them in taking control of all Greece, following the withdrawal of Roman troops. The Roman general and statesman Titus Quinctius Flamininus (c. 228–174 B.C.) was Rome's representative in negotiations at Aegium in Aechaea. [S]

[1005] Philemon Holland: Holland, known as "Translator-General" because of his assiduity in translating the classics, published his translation of Livy, *The Roman Historie,* in 1600. Anglesey's library contained the 1659 edition. See "Marvell and the Earl of Anglesey," *Historical Journal,* 44 (2001), 719.

[1006] well fare 73] welfare 74.

[1007] *Now . . . sundry sorts: The Roman Historie* (1659) book 35, p. 735. The point of the story is that Rome alone can provide all the military talents, and more, than the motley team assembled under Antiochus.

[1008] jejune: fasting, wanting in sustenance.

determine a new signification of words.[1009] For it is your great Art to make the Ceremonies at once stupendiously necessary and at the same time despicably little; both a Fly and a Whale: [332]

[Reh. Com. *p.* 40.] *In whose vast bulk, though store of Oyle doth lye,*
We find more shape, more beauty in a Fly.

This I made merry with, as of good reason. For it would raise a very great disorder in the World to boule-verse[1010] so, and overturn the signification of all words: for even in the name of your Function, if a man should but chance to lispe,[1011] it would make a dangerous alteration;[1012] but however to impose such contrary significations with the same penalties too, would make wild work, and pester the Nation with a whole swarm of Informers. But in that Debate, I instanced in Augustus Caesar, who was so shy of unusual words: And this you will needs have to be a notable mistake, because Julius Caesar compiled a Book *de Analogia,* forgetting that Suetonius describes at large Augustus his hereditary exquisiteness in that particular. *Those which delighted in new words, and those which affected old,* (apply it to Ceremonies) *he equally despised, both being alike contemptible*: Insomuch that it was reported, [333] he displaced a Consular Lieutenant for a Fault of Orthography.[1014] And if Orthography in Worship were now as strictly observed, perhaps your Spiritual Lieutenancy might run the same risk.

[*In vita Aug.* 86, & 88.[[1013]

I had chanced in my Book to speak of *Hudibras,* with that esteem which an excellent piece of Wit upon whatsoever Subject will alwayes merit.[1015] But you hereupon fall into such a Fit and Rupture of railing at me, that you have exceeded not only all the Oyster-women and Butter-whores, but even your self, pretending that I have done him some dishonour. Should I study

[1009] *'twas . . . words: Discourse,* p. 108.

[1010] boule-verse 73] boul-verse 74: to turn upside-down. Marvell's is the first and only use cited by *OED.*

[1011] lispe 73] lipse 74.

[1012] dangerous alteration: arse-Deacon, perhaps?

[1013] Despite the marginal reference to a Latin text, this is quoted exactly from *The History of the Twelve Caesars* (London, 1672), p. 133. Marvell seems to be going to some trouble to hide his recourse to this translation.

[1014] Fault of Orthography: *History,* pp. 135–35, section 88.

[1015] Wit . . . merit: an interesting comment, given Butler's intense satire at the expense of the Nonconformists.

a suitable return to you, I could not raise my self into more choler then to call you a *Jewel,* a *Glass-drop,* a *Tintinnabulum,*[1016] words that you with some sympathy delight in, and whose Heraldry is to be Pendant.[1017] As for you, I cannot restrain you of this liberty, who have wisely taken safeguard in the Ecclesiastical Function; and, fore-seeing betimes what occasion you might have, thought fit to Post your self up in Print, that *you are not valiant.*

[*C. Pl. Ph.* p. 15.] Only I could have for your own sake wished you had not call'd me Judas, lest so emi-[334]nent a Divine as you are should appear more concerned for Hudibras than for your Saviour. For the rest you may please to know, that, what-ever you have here said to me, cannot either diminish or increase my esteem for that Author.

You foam again as in the Falling-Sickness, because I had said that I thought God never intended the Clergy for Political and Secular Imployments, and you make it to be no less than Blasphemy. If they be so enamour'd of those drudgeries, and have deputed you to maintain it, much good may it do them and you. But why should you upon no more occasion tell me; *Fatuos & huius Terrae filios quod attinet (saith a Jewish Zealot) non magis nostro iudicio prophetare possunt quam Asinus & Rana.*[1018] *Asses and Todpoles may as soon expect the Impressions of the Divine Spirit, as such Dunces and Sots as you.*[1019] But these words of yours I suppose you pretend to be dictated by that Spirit. And further you say, *The* Ruac Hakodesh *dwell in such a distemper'd and polluted mind as yours! It may as soon unite it self to a Swine.*[1020] Ruack Hakodesh, Mr. Bayes, this is as your other Bayes has [335] it; *A Crust, a lasting Crust for your Rogue Critiques: I would fain see the proudest of them all but dare to nibble at this. If they do, this shall rub their Gums for'm, I promise you.* I doubt your *Ruac Hakodesh* is but at best a *Bath col.*[1021] But is not this of yours fine Language think you for an *A. Sac. Dom*?[1022] *O Seytang*[1023] *Aurang Olanda bacalay*

[*Rep.* p. 326]

[Reh. Com. *p.* 14.]

[1016] *Jewel . . . Tintinnabulum: Defence,* pp. 445, 461.

[1017] Pendant: hanging; or as applied to Parker, a dependant.

[1018] *Fatuos . . . Rana:* "In my opinion, it no more belongs to the foolish and the sons of this Earth that they can prophesy any more than asses and frogs."

[1019] *Fatuos . . . as you: Reproof,* p. 326.

[1020] Ruac . . . *Swine:* Ibid. *Ruac Hakodesh* is Hebrew for "Divine Spirit."

[1021] *Bath col:* Parker, *Censure,* p. 83; Hebrew for "Daughter of a Voice," the supernatural way of communicating God's will; or merely a rumor.

[1022] *A. Sac. Dom.:* archdeacon sacred to the Lord?

[1023] *Seytang* 73] *Seytagn* 74.

Samatay.[1024] To show you, Mr. Bayes, that I too have been sometimes conversant with the Jewish Zealots, I will tell you hereupon a Story out of one of them, that shall as yours be nameless. There was among the Jews a certain kind of People that were called *Proselytes,* which you may in English interpret *Turn-coats,* concerning whom was that expression that I quoted you before of our Saviour, Mat. 23.15. *Wo unto you Scribes and Pharisees, Hypocrites, for you compass Sea and Land to make a Proselyte, and when he is made, you make him two-fold more the Child of Hell than you your selves.*[1025] Now what I shall tell you of these men, I would not have you to misapply unto such Conscientious Persons, as have reunited themselves unto the Discipline of our Church; for I wish that all the Nonconformists rather could find reason to do in like manner: [336] but it relates particularly to your self, who, abandoning all Modesty and Christianity toward your former party, have defiled and dishonour'd the Church that has receiv'd you into protection. But concerning these *Proselytes* and Turn-coats it was that the Jews had that Maxime; *Proselyti & Paederastae impediunt adventum Messiae*:[1026] and again, *Proselyti sunt sicut Scabies Israeli*; that they were like a Scab or Leprosie to Israel. Therefore when a Proselyte was circumcised, they first catechized him about the sincerity of his Conversion; whether he did not do it, *ob adipiscendas Divitias,* to make his Fortune; *ob Timorem,* for fear of some inconvenience; or lastly, *ob Amorem erga aliquam Israeliticam,* Whether there were not some woman in the bottom of the business. For they had a shrewd suspicion of them, *Quod non periti essent Mandatorum, quodque inducerent Vindictas, atque insuper quod forte eorum Opera imitarentur Israelitae*:[1027] and therefore it was *quod Proselyti opus habebant Triumviratu,* and they would not trust them until three men had examined and taken care that all were right. And if it chanced that both the Man and the Wife [337] came together to be Proselytes, they were used to separate and keep them apart for ninety days, *ut diiudicari possit inter prolem in sanctitate*

[1024] *Seytang . . . Samatay:* This is the Malay of seventeenth-century Dutch missionary translators working in Ambon and other parts of E. Indonesia. It probably translates as "The Dutch devil persons fight with shit." Cf. n. 1156 below. We are indebted to Richard Richie and Waruno Mahdi for their help in solving this conundrum.

[1025] *Wo . . . selves:* see p. 402 above.

[1026] *Proselyti . . . Messiae:* "Converts and pederasts impede the coming of the Messiah."

[1027] *Quod non . . . Israelitae:* "because they might not have agreed to the rules and because they might plan revenges, and moreover because they might by chance counterfeit the works of the Israelites."

genitam.[1028] Nay, moreover there was a Baptisme peculiarly solemn before they could be admitted, and a great ceremonial *Rationale* by which it was to be administred. The whole body was to be dip'd *mersione una. Si, excepto apice minimi digiti, manebat adhuc in immunditia. Si quis capillosus admodum, omnem crinem capitis abluere necesse erat.*[1029] And there were many other scrupulous niceties in this washing. As for the Water; *homo Gonorrhaeus non mundatur nisi in fonte: Sed Menstruosa & Proselytus in Collectione aquarum.*[1030] But put case the same man were *Proselytus* and *Gonorrhaeus* too, though the Rabbies were very exact, I find not this decided; but it is easie to collect that he must have passed thorow both waters. They were so curious as to regulate what proportion too of water was sufficient, and the least quantity that could be allowed was, *Quatuor Seae aquarum* and the dimension, *Cubitus quadratus,*[1031] &c.[1032] Now, Mr. Bayes, I would gladly be satisfied whether you have been rightly and duly Proselyted according to these Cere-[338]monies, (for you know that the Jewish Ceremonies are not so abrogated but that the Pro-consul may re-establish them) but particularly have been drawn cross the River to Lambeth? has not so much as the top of your little finger escaped ducking? is there not one hair of your head but has been over head and ears in the River? All this ought to have been exactly observed, (especially considering how much filth you brought about you) else you are not a true Turn-coat, but remain still in your uncleanness. And you might have had the advantage, in traversing thus the water, to have catched some of the prophecying *Todpoles* you speak of. But really, there is

1028 *ut diiudicari . . . genitam:* "so that they could discern that their joint offspring were engendered in holiness."

1029 *mersione . . . erat:* "in one immersion. If the tip of the little finger was left out, he remained in uncleanliness. If he was very hairy, it was necessary to wash the whole head of hair."

1030 *homo . . . aquarum:* "a man with venereal disease was not allowed to be washed except in a fountain; but the menstruous and the convert in a reservoir."

1031 *Quattuor . . . quadratus:* "four large jars of water, of a square cubit in dimension."

1032 *Proselyti . . .* &c.: These comments about and rituals for the acceptance of converts to Judaism can be found in John Selden, *De Synedriis et Praefecturis Juridicis Veterum Ebraeorum,* ed. David Wilkins (London, 1726), I, cols. 1625–26. [Jason Rosenblatt] Marvell was not, however, quoting from the edition of Selden available to him, published in London by Jacob Flesher in three volumes, 1650–55 (A, p. 66, #47) where a less specific account of the rituals appears in vol. 1, pp. 25–27, so there must have been another source involved. Selden himself was using Talmudic sources. The relevant sections of the *Talmud* are "Yebamoth," 42 through 47, 109, and Tohoroth II, "Zabim."

your self and some few more such Proselytes to our Church, that are so impure Creatures, that before you had been admitted into it, *'t had*[1033] *been absolutely necessary* for you to have passed thorow this cold Water Ordeal.

You do three times at least in your *Reproof,* and in your *Transproser Rehears'd* well nigh half the book thorow, run upon an Author J.M.[1034] which does not a little offend me. For why should any other mans reputation suffer in a contest be-[339]twixt you and me? But it is because you resolved to suspect that he had an hand in my former book, wherein, whether you deceive your self or no, you deceive others extreamly. For by chance I had not seen him of two years before; but after I undertook writing, I did more carefully avoid either visiting or sending to him, least I should any way involve him in my consequences. And you might have understood, or I am sure your Friend the Author of the *Common Places*[1036] could have told you, (he too had a slash at J.M. upon my account)[1037] that had he took you in hand, you would have had cause to repent the occasion, and not escap'd so easily as you did under my *Transprosal.* But I take it moreover very ill that you should have so mean an opinion of me, as not to think me competent to write such a simple book as that without any assistance. It is a sign (however you upbraid me often as your old acquaintance) that you did not know me well, and that we had not much conversation together. But because in your 125. *p.*[1038] you are so particular *you know a friend of ours,* &c. intending that J.M. and his answer to Salmasius,[1039] I think it here seasonable to acquit my promise to you in giving the [340] Reader a short trouble concerning my first acquaintance with you. J.M. was, and is, a man of great Learning and Sharpness of wit as any man. It was his misfortune, living in a tumultous time, to be toss'd on the wrong side, and he writ *Flagrante*

[*Rep.* p. 191.[1035] 125.212.]

[1033] *t'had* Ed.] *'thad* 73, 74.

[1034] J.M.: John Milton.

[1035] 191 73, correctly] 101 74.

[1036] Author of the *Common Places:* i.e., the anonymous author of *A Common-Place Book Out of the Rehearsal Transpros'd* (1673).

[1037] he too . . . J.M.: *Common-Place Book,* p. 36.

[1038] 125 Ed.] 115 73, 74.

[1039] his answer to Salmasius: Milton's *Pro populo anglicano defensio (First Defence of the English People)* (1651), a reply to the *Defensio Regio* by Salmasius (Claude de Saumaise), who had been commissioned by Charles II, then in exile, to defend the claims of the English monarchy.

bello[1040] certain dangerous Treatises. His Books *of Divorce*[1041] I know not whether you may have use of; but those upon which you take him at advantage were of no other nature then that which I mentioned to you, writ by your own father; only with this difference, that your Fathers, which I have by me, was written with the same design, but with much less Wit or Judgment, for which there was no remedy: unless you will supply his Judgment with his High Court of Justice. At His Majesties happy Return, J.M. did partake, even as you your self did for all your huffing, of his Regal Clemency, and has ever since expiated himself in a retired silence.[1042] It was after that, I well remember it, that being one day at his house,[1043] I there first met you and accidentally. Since that I have been scarce four or five times in your Company, but, whether it were my foresight or my good fortune, I never contracted any friendship or confidence with you. But then it was, [341] when you, as I told you, wander'd up and down Moor-Fields Astrologizing upon the duration of His Majesties Government, that you frequented J.M. incessantly and haunted his house day by day. What discourses you there used he is too generous to remember. But he never having in the least provoked you, for you to insult thus over his old age, to traduce him by your *Scaramuccios,*[1044] and in your own person, as a School-Master, who was born and hath lived much more ingenuously and Liberally then your self; to have done all this, and lay at last my simple book to his charge, without ever taking care to inform your self better, which you had so easie opportunity to do; nay, when you your self too have said, to my knowledge, that you saw no such great matter in it but that I might be the Author: it is unhumanely and inhospitably done, and will I hope be a warning to all

[1040] *Flagrante bello:* in the heat of war.

[1041] Books of *Divorce:* Milton wrote four pamphlets advocating a change in the marriage law to permit divorce on grounds of incompatibility; the first and most important was *The Doctrine and Discipline of Divorce* (1643).

[1042] a retired silence: Marvell is being disingenuous. Not only had Milton, in the interim, published *Paradise Lost* (1667), but also a pamphlet of his own relating to the Declaration of Indulgence and its withdrawal: *Of true religion, haeresie, schism, toleration, and what best means may be us'd against the growth of popery* (1673). According to Milton's editors, he wrote it during the parliamentary session beginning February 4, 1673 (*CPW,* 8:411–12).

[1043] his house: in 1661–64 Milton lived in a house in Jewin Street, near Moorfields. See D. Masson, *The Life of John Milton* (1880), 6:452–53.

[1044] *Scaramuccios:* see p. 252 and note 152 above.

others, as it is to me, to avoid (I will not say such a Judas,) but a man that creeps into all companies, to jeer, trepan, and betray them.

But after this fresh example of Romantick generosity, and your John-like *Good nature,*[1045] you plunge over head and ears into History. That of Sibthorpe and Manwar-[342]ing, I had occasion before to speak of in better method. I shall therefore only renew your own request in your Epistle to the Reader, *that they would peruse it with an unprejudiced mind, and an ordinary attention,*[1046] and I shall leave the rest to their judgments. For I do not know but that you may have some peculiar dispensation to determine those in 3° Caroli to have been *most notorious Rebels,*[1047] notwithstanding that in the year 1667. this present Parliament resolved in the most solemn and judicial manner, by a concurrence of the Lords with the Commons, *that the judgment against them in* 5 *Caroli was illegal.*[1048] As to Manwarings particular, whose cause you take up with a remarkable concernment, I cannot but attribute it to some extraordinary correspondence of *Genius* betwixt you. His very name hath more influence and power upon you than Doctor Bathursts Talismans; and that very week that you uttered this History of Doctor Manwaring, comes out in[1049] the Gazette of the first of May (I know not by what sympathy) *The History and Mystery of the Venereal* Lues, *being a more new and ample discovery of that Disease, then yet hath been* [343] *extant, with the Medicines and Methods of Cure practised in Italy, Spain, Germany, Holland, France, and England, &c, By J. Manwaring,* Doctor of Physick.[1050]

[*Pref. to C. Pl. Ph.*]

You launch out into a Relation of the Conference too at Worcester-House,[1051] betwixt the Episcopal and the Nonconformist Divines, by His Majesties Commission. What is most to be taken notice of, is, that you say

[1045] John-like *Good nature:* a reference back to Parker's allusion to "*the gentle and sweet natur'd St. John,*" and Marvell's discovery of John's "*rudeness and unmannerliness.*" See p. 402 above.

[1046] *that . . . attention: Reproof,* "Preface," A4.

[1047] *most notorious Rebels:* ibid., p. 376.

[1048] this present Parliament resolved . . . *was illegal:* On November 23, 1667, the Commons resolved that the judgment of the Kings Bench in 1630 against Eliot, Holles, and Valentine had been illegal. On April 15, 1668, the Lords followed suit.

[1049] in 73] of 74.

[1050] *The History* . . . Physick: *London Gazette,* no. 777, April 28–May 1, 1673.

[1051] Conference . . . at Worcester-House: see *RT,* p. 62 and n. 133.

here and in several other places, that the Non-conformists had *nothing of Sin to object against those things from which they dissented.*[1052] I have heard to the contrary, that they did in eight, if not ten several instances, but it is not my business to enumerate either for them or you. Only I admire, I confess, that upon such an occasion they could not in any one thing be gratifyed, not so much as in forbearing the Lessons of the Apocrypha. Insomuch that, as many remember very well, after a long tug at the Convocation house about that matter, a good Doctor[1053] came out at last with great exultation, that *they had carried it for Bel and the Dragon.*[1054]

I cannot omit what it seems you thought necessary to be said in defence of your cause, that *none are better qualified for State-affairs then Church-men, and none have ac-*[344]*quitted themselves with greater art and success, and that things have rarely miscarried, but when their counsels have not been effectually followed (as you shall shew also in the cases of Cardinal Granvile and Arch-bishop Laud.)*[1055] Alas what needed you to have gone so far about, when your own Case all along, and even this your *Reproof* and this Parallel, are so pregnant a demonstration of their abilities? And you acquit your promise, where you say, *that the wise and resolute Ministry of Granvell was render'd not only successless but odious to the People. For as he was a man of extraordinary wisdom, courage, and fidelity, that sincerely pursued his Masters interest, faith-fully executed his commands, and kept up the height of his Authority; so being an* Implacable Divine *he saw to the bottom of the projects that were carryed on by the discontented Lords, and foresaw the tendency of Factions in Religion to Disorders and Seditions in the State.*[1056] I shall not suppose any one who

[1052] *nothing . . . dissented: Reproof,* p. 458.

[1053] a good Doctor: In the copy of *RT2* in Magdalene College, Oxford (N.18.26) there is a contemporary annotation: "Dr. Crowther Principall of St. Mary Hall, Oxford: and preb. of Worcester." Joseph Crowther (1610–89), chaplain to James, duke of York, became principal of St. Mary Hall in 1664. [S]

[1054] *Bel and the Dragon:* At the Savoy Conference of April 1661 the presbyterians asked "that no lessons be taken out of the apocryphal books" (Burnet, *History of My Own Time,* ed. O. Airy [1897], 1:319) and "charged the rubric and injunctions of the Church with eight things flatly sinful" Neal, *History of the Puritans,* 4:298. The conference ended without agreement, and Convocation subsequently revised the BCP even more to the dismay of the presbyterians, to the extent of adding a lesson out of Bel and the Dragon (Burnet, 1:325).

[1055] *none . . . Laud: Reproof,* p. 330.

[1056] *that the wise . . . State: Reproof,* pp. 511–12.

reads this book to have so little convers'd with the modern History, as not to gather hence how ready you are to make good your word to the Lady whom I mentioned, as to your Religion.[1057] But I have not yet heard of any Protestant, beside your self and the Recorder of Lon-[345]don,[1058] who hath of late years so publickly avowed the Inquisition, of which that Cardinal Granvell was the chief Patron and Instrument. And instead of that honorable character you give him, I shall refer you to Grotius, whom I chuse always to ply you with above all other Authors. *The Government of the Netherlands was in appearance in Margaret,*[1059] *but in effect, and as to the power, was only in Granvell in whom Industry, Vigilance, Ambition, Luxury, and Avarice, and all manner indeed of good and evil were remarkably visible,* &c.[1060] And therefore it is not the greatest instance of your prudence (whatsoever you thought in your *meer Conscience*) to take this publick *Liberty* of *dogmatizing*, and to pick out that Cardinal (whom I never thought of) to be the Precedent and Parallel of Arch-bishop Lauds administration.

I should after this do you injury, did I not take notice that whereas in your Preface to Bishop Bramhall, in the fifth leaf before you conclude, I told you that you spoke scandalously and with leering reflexion upon the Government and Ministers of State, you try with the best of your Skill to return it upon me. But so unfortunately, that, as alwayes, you sink [346] deeper and quag yourself in your Roman-Empire. *Were it possible,* say you (and I abhor to hear you) *that His Majesty should degenerate from the goodness*

[1057] the Lady . . . your Religion: a reference back to Marvell's claim (p. 365) that "You told a Lady of better quality; that, *in case Popery were introduced, you would be one of the first to comply with it.*"

[1058] the recorder of London: Sir John Howell, sergeant at law, recorder of London 1668–76. At the trial of the Quakers William Penn and William Mead for unlawful assembly, the jury, under great pressure to the contrary, acquitted them. See Marvell's letter to Popple (*P&L,* 2:318): "The jury not finding them guilty, as the Recorder and Mayor would have had them, they were kept without Meat or Drink some three Days, till almost starved, but would not alter their Verdict; so fined and imprisoned . . . The Recorder, among the rest, commended the Spanish Inquisition, saying it would never be well until we had something like it."

[1059] *Margaret:* illegitimate daughter of Charles V.

[1060] Grotius, *De Rebus Belgicis,* book 1. Smith cited *The Annals and History of the Low Country Warrs,* trans. T[homas].M[anley], 1665; but Marvell used a Latin edition and made his own, rather different translation, probably using the 1657 edition in Anglesey's library (A, p. 23, #124).

of his nature, as much as they say Nero did, and again, *these are the Sejanus's that you described.* It will not serve your turn this evasion. [*Rep.* p. 288.] 'Tis like mine Host in France, that when he swore *Jernie*[1061] *Dieu,* interpreted it of the *Dieu Bacchus.*[1062] You spoke not a word there of Nero or Sejanus, or that could be applyed to either; unless you can give us Nero's *Coronation-Oath,* or Sejanus his *cases of Conscience,* or at least instance in that Emperours *being canonized for a Saint and Martyr,*[1063] so that for the Wit and Chronology of the business this too is calculated for the Play of Moses and Julius Caesar.[1064] But for the discretion and loyalty of it, you might have long since answered, as for other passages, did either the *Rabble* or the *Statesmen* think you considerable; whereas indeed they reckon you (it seems) among that sort of men, who have a Priviledge to say any thing with impunity.[1065] But for the Long Parliament you have indeed an Ecclesiastical *Non obstante*[1066] to say what you will. I [347] shall only take up at one Passage: *To deal plainly with you, I have read most of the Long Parliament Speeches over, and, though I know you will chide me for calling a whole Parliament Coxcombes, yet it is better to call them so than worse. Yet this censure I dare pass upon them, without any suspicion of arrogance within myself, that they were for the most part no better than School-boyes Declamations,* &c. *all their discourses were much like yours, and accomodated to people that took Confidence for Reason, Nonsense for Mysteries, and Rudeness for Wit. Ay, Mr. Bayes, they wanted some* [*Rep.* P. 400.] *certain helps, helps for wit, which you Man of Art have thought fit to make use of. Ay, Sir, that's your position, and you do here aver, that no man yet the Sun ever shone upon, has parts sufficient to furnish out a Stage, except it be with the help of your Rules.*[1067] But I was misinform'd I perceive, who thought you might have call'd them all the names in the Rainbow but Coxcombes, and never heard them arraign'd of

[1061] *Jernie* 74] *Je venie* 73; *renie* 73 Errata.

[1062] *Jernie . . . Bacchus:* The meaning is "I abjure God"; *je renie* is therefore correct; but B's reading, *Jernie,* is more likely to be Marvell's intention, since it was a popular oath. [S] To interpret it "of the God Bacchus" means, of course, to renounce alcohol.

[1063] *being . . . Martyr: Preface,* E5v.

[1064] Play . . . Caesar: see *RT,* p. 199 above.

[1065] Priviledge . . . impunity: i.e., a court fool.

[1066] *Non obstante:* the first two words of a clause formerly used in statutes and letters patent, which conveyed a license from the king to do something notwithstanding any law to the contrary.

[1067] *some certain helps . . . Rules:* Buckingham, *The Rehearsal,* act 1, scene 1.

want of Wit, but by your Abundance. But that you may think altogether so meanly of them (though indeed who is the man, either in the former or this Age that is able to stand or appear before your profound Eloquence [348] and piercing judgment) let me refer you, although many others might be cited, to two Speeches of the Lord Falklands:[1068] the first concerning Episcopacy which begins, *He is a great stranger to Israel, who knows not that this Kingdom hath long laboured under many and great oppressions,* &c.[1069] The second Speech was to the Lords, at the delivery of the Articles against the Lord Keeper,[1070] and begins, *These Articles against my Lord Keeper being read, I may be bold to apply,* &c.[1071] And *if you think these worthy of perusal,* I shall expect your second opinion concerning the capacity and skill of those Gentlemen both in History and Oratory. But as for you, when Doctor Heylin's Divinity shall go for Orthodox, or his Praevarications pass for History, you may then, and not before, be reputed a Classical Author. And all the Canterbury Tales[1072] you have told in the *Reproof* will be Chronicle. There was just such another Italian acquaintance of yours, one Polidore Virgil, who coming into England, was dignifyed[1073] and distinguish'd like you, being made both a Prebend and an Arch-deacon; only you are not yet as he was, come to be Collector of the *Peter-pence,* but all in good time.[1074]

1068 Lord Falklands: Lucius Cary, 2d viscount Falkland (c. 1610–43), supported reformation of the church but opposed the abolition of episcopacy. He died fighting for the king. [S]

1069 *He is . . . oppressions: Speeches and Passages of this Great and Happy Parliament* (1641), p. 188. This powerful speech against the bishops was delivered on February 8, 1641. [S]

1070 Lord Keeper: John Finch, baron Finch of Fordwick (1584–1660), speaker of the Commons 1628–29, chief justice 1634, lord keeper 1640; noted for his brutality and the decision that ship money was constitutional. He was impeached by the Long Parliament, and Falkland led the attack on him.

1071 *These Articles . . . apply: Speeches and Passages,* p. 83; but Marvell could also have read this speech, delivered on January 14, 1641, in a pamphlet listed in Anglesey's library, "Lord Falkland's Speech against the Lord Finch," 1641 (A, p. 73, bundle 151).

1072 Canterbury Tales: from Chaucer's great work, but by this time often used disparagingly for cock-and-bull stories. There is, of course, also a pun on Parker's position as archdeacon of Canterbury.

1073 dignifyed 74] signifyed 73.

1074 Polidore Virgil . . . in good time: historian (c. 1470–1555); he came to England from Italy in 1501 as deputy collector of Peter's pence. In 1534 he published his *Historia Anglica,* a Lancastrian history of England written in the service of Henry VII, which was subsequently heavily criticized as incorporating mere legends.

This Gentleman did too, even as [349] you, oblige this Nation with a piece of History, which after he had writ he used a notable invention, which if you would but imitate and burn all the Records of the times you write of, it were the only way imaginable to make you authentick.[1075]

As you are officious in your own Stories, so you are very inquisitive and critical upon some that I have told you; and for a great space of your book you run out into such *Froath* and *Growns* and *Taplash* of Wit, that it deserves compassion. Insomuch that though men may perhaps believe that, as you your self affirmed, *you are not valiant,* yet there is some reason to doubt the truth of what you say in the same place, *that you are not miserable.* But you are more particularly concern'd to know who that Queen was, and of what Country, that gave so ridiculous a Town Seal.[1076] For wheresoever you can suspect any thing smutty underneath, you are wonderful curious to be thorowly informed. But I have already gratifyed you in Pork, and am not bound to nauseate the Reader to [350] comply with your ignorance. I will tell you who that tyrant[1077] was that demanded so many bushels of Fleas: It was John Basiliwich the great Duke of Muscovy, and it was of the Citizens of Muskow that he required it, fining them for Non-payment. But as for this Queen, it shall for certain reasons of State be a secret. Only, not to leave you wholly in the dark, if you please to speak with your Fellow-Chaplain[1078] of the Copper-Mines,[1079] he will inform you, for it is in that Kingdom. And if he do not satisfie you, if you please to resort to me, I will shew you the Medal[1080] of the City with that Device upon the Reverse of it.

[*Rep.* p. 401.]

[*C. Pl. Ph.* p. 15.]

[*Rep.* p. 503.]

[*Rep. p.* 503.]

'Tis more than time that I left scumming you, for I perceive 'tis all the

[1075] burn all the Records: In *De Antiquitate Cantabrigiae* (1574), Caius charged that Polydore Virgil "committed as many of our ancient and manuscript historians to the flames as would have filled a waggon, that the faults of his own work might pass undiscovered." Cited in Henry Ellis, ed., *Three Books of Polydore Vergil's English History* (1844), xxiii. [S]

[1076] that Queen . . . Seal: see *RT,* p. 164 above; copy B4 has a cropped marginal MS note: "Christina Q[ueen of] Sweden."

[1077] that tyrant: see *RT,* p. 164 above, and note 688.

[1078] Fellow-Chaplain: Thomas Tomkins.

[1079] Copper-Mines: Sweden was famed for its copper mines.

[1080] I will shew you the Medal: Marvell had been to Sweden with the earl of Carlisle in the mid-1660s and presumably had such a medal in his possession.

same stuff: and, should I continue, I should leave you nothing in the bottom; therefore I shall only take notice of two things more very remarkable. The one is concerning the quotation out of St. Austin, which I speak of from *p.* 209 to *p.* 214. of my former book: *Signa quum ad res divinas pertinent Sacramenta appellantur.*[1081] You had said, you would lay odds there was no such saying in St. Austin; and now, because your Answerer[1082] had said *sunt Sacramenta* in stead of *Sacramentae appellantur* (which therefore [351] you note in him as *a boldness with the Text for his own convenience, and an improvement beyond Modesty*)[1083] you think you are safe. But, good Mr. Bayes, whether or no doth an Arch-deacon *pertinere ad res divinas*? And pray tell me what is the difference betwixt saying that you are an Archdeacon, or you are called an Archdeacon? But because I wonder'd you could not find it when I my self had met with it, *Ep.* 5ta *ad Marcellinum.* You say, *you will not laugh at me, no, for I rather deserve to be scourged for so gross and impudent a falsehood: whereas (as fortune would have it) the Fourth is the last Epistle to Marcellinus that St. Austin ever writ, and if you had search'd after a Fifth Epistle to him, you might have pored till the day of Judgment.*[1084] Let all ingenuous men judge this matter. I quoted it only in the order of the Epistles, where the first to Marcellinus is the fifth Epistle. You say it should have been thus set down by me. *Ad Marcellinum: Epistola Quinta*: and that I quote it *Ep. Quinta ad Marcellinum.* I do not, but thus, *Ep.* $5^{ta.}$ *ad Marcellinum.* Mind first how falsely you have transcribed my quotation to fit it to your own turn; and then observe too, upon what a frivolous and mistaken [352] ground, and about how slight a matter, you molest the Reader: for, beside what here, there runs a repetition of this matter of Marcellinus, and others of less consequence, through the whole *Reproof.* But, Mr. Bayes, this business is not yet ended thus: I will save your *poring till the day of Judgment,* and help you to a Fifth Epistle of St. Austin too to Marcellinus. Take the Edition Lugduni. Anno 1561.[1085] and whereas you say that (*as fortune would have it*) *St. Austin never writ but four Epistles to Marcellinus*; this is but your usual misfortune, to hamper your self worse when you would dis-intangle your own errours. For his 5th. 7th. 158th. and 159th. are his four Epistles to

1081 *Signa . . . appellantur:* "Signs that pertain to things divine are called Sacraments."

1082 Answerer: John Owen, *Truth and Innocence Vindicated,* p. 280.

1083 *a boldness . . . Modesty: Reproof,* p. 198.

1084 *will not . . . Judgment: Reproof,* p. 197.

1085 Edition Lugduni . . . 1561: Augustine, *Omnium Operum,* 10 vols. in 16 vols. (Lyons, 1561–63); volume 2 contains "Epistolae" (A, p. 10, #1).

Marcellinus. But you will find there *p.* 1080. an[1086] 222d. Epistle, which is a fifth to the same person. It is noted so all along in the head of the pages, and the contents of it express before it begins: *longa & docta est haec Epistola, tractans de Baptismo parvulorum*[1087] *contra Pelagium* (Because it was against Pelagius,[1088] could you not or might you not see it?) *quem tamen clementer in hac Epistola tractat. Haec per examplaris vetustatem difficulter legi potuit, propter quod in aliquibus obscura est*[1089] (but not so obscure [353] but you might have discerned it.) You say you find none of the *Non-Conformists dirty Thumb-Nails in* ⟨*your*⟩ *Patrons Library.*[1090] But have not you, nor your poor *Leaf-turners*[1091] liberty to peruse the Volumes? Or is there a peculiar Reverence due to the Books in that place that no man does or may touch them? Or have you lost all your credit too *apud Jo. Shirley in parva Britannia*[1092] and is the *Pelican* grown hard-hearted? Could you but have reckon'd your five fingers you had not mistaken. But this proceeds from your bragging of Books (so usual with you) which you have not the patience to read over no more than your own; or having cast your eye on the *Index* you imagine you have read the Authour, for indeed here the *Index* points but at four Epistles, but the *Pollex* would have made them five.[1093]

[*Rep.* p. 195.]

The other passage of yours, and last which I purpose to recommend to the Reader, is indeed accompanyed with many extraordinary circumstances. It is not that wherein you accuse your Answerer to have given their degrees to Oliver and Ireton at Oxford,[1094] though it is notoriously known that it was a Bishop yet living who performed [354] that Ceremony.[1095]

[1086] an Ed.] and 73, 74.

[1087] *parvulorum* 73] *parvuloram* 74.

[1088] Pelagius: Pelagius (fl. 412–18), a monk who denied the doctrine of original sin and believed that Christ's influence was limited to instruction and example.

[1089] *longa . . . obscura est:* "This Epistle is long and learned, treating of the baptism of infants against Pelagius, whom [Augustine] always treats mildly in this Epistle. On account of its age, this is difficult to read, because it is obscure in some matters."

[1090] <*your*> . . . *Library:* i.e., Lambeth Palace library.

[1091] *Leaf-turners:* cf. *RT,* p. 148 above, and *Defence,* p. 54.

[1092] *Britannia* 73] *Britanni* 74.

[1093] *Index . . . Pollex:* a pun on the index finger, which points to items in an index to a book, versus the *pollex,* the thumb which actually turns the pages.

[1094] you accuse . . . Oxford: *Reproof,* p. 292; Owen was vice-chancellor of Oxford 1652–58.

[1095] Bishop . . . Ceremony: Edward Reynolds (1599–1676), vice-chancellor of Oxford

That is an untruth too slender to be taken notice of in a Book so pregnant as the *Reproof.* But it is the whole hinge it seems whereupon your design of writing has turned. For upon occasion of a certain *Declaration*[1096] *published,* as you inform, *after the Cheshire insurrection,*[1097] which you affirm to have been subscribed by your Answerer, and which you have kept in deck until this season; You pretend that you have dealt *so roundly,* as you call it, with him and the Party, and me too. Happy had it been for me that you had once understood how to speak truth. For had you not writ *so roundly*; I had never intermeddled in these matters, and so the *Reproof* too had been spared. However I have gain'd hereby so much learning as to know what is the Figure of Falshood, It seems 'tis Circular, and in your phrase, to speak *roundly*; and you have stretch'd it so till it is *Un-hoopable.* But I therefore shall answer you square. It is known, and ready to be proved by thousands, that the Declaration mention'd was not writ by your Answerer, nor any of his party; but by the Fifth-monarchy men,[1098] and its effect vented it self in that wild insurrection of Vennor.[1099] You your self, although you were not of so high a dis-[355]pensation, yet were at that time of Age sufficient, and stirring enough in your little Sphere to have understood it rightly. But it is a grievous thing to forego a falshood that is serviceable to the great design; and the *Ends of your publick Government will at least,*[1100] *excuse if not hallow,*

[*Rep. from* p. 422. *to* p. 426.]

1648–49. On May 19, 1649, Cromwell and Fairfax were created doctors of civil law. Wood, *Fasti,* ed. Bliss (1820), col. 152. Henry Ireton, parliamentary general and Cromwell's son-in-law, was not so honored. [S]

1096 *Declaration: An Essay toward Settlement upon a sure foundation, being a testimony for God in this perillous time by a few . . .* September 19, 1659 [Thomason Tracts, 669.f.21 (73)]. A John Owen's name headed the petitioners, but this was not Parker's Answerer. [S]

1097 Cheshire insurrection: a royalist uprising in Cheshire during August 1659, led by Sir George Booth (1622–84). It was to have been part of a general insurrection on behalf of the king, which failed. See Clarendon, *History of the Rebellion* (1720), part 2, 3:672–74. [S]

1098 Fifth-monarchy men: a fanatical sect who wished to bring about the Fifth Monarchy, as thought to have been prophesied in Daniel 2:44. During this period, Christ and his saints were to rule for one thousand years (Revelation 20:4). [S] Marvell excoriated this sect in *First Anniversary,* ll. 297–310.

1099 Vennor: Thomas Venner (d. 1661), a cooper and Fifth Monarchist preacher, led a plot against Cromwell's government in 1657; on January 6, 1661, he again urged his followers to overthrow the government and set up the Fifth Monarchy. He was captured and executed. [S]

1100 *least* 74] *last* 73.

the most Orbicular[1101] untruth. Hence it was that you were so forward to publish that book of *Baxter Baptized in Blood.*[1102] And hence now it is that, as your last reserve of slander and Malice, as you had essayed in the *Preface to Bishop Bramhall,* you throw this upon the body of the Non-conformists, upon me too, and your Answerer. Yet neither is this Declaration so mad as that which you have pen'd, *p.* 64, 65, 66. of your *Reproof,* in the stile and name of His Majesty, with a boldness of which I think no Age can bring a Parallel. But seeing neither that of *Baxter,* nor this attempt upon your Answerer and the Party, has had that bad effect which probably you had proposed, I shall not aggravate it further; but appeal to all Men, whether the world be well used, when such railing books, grounded upon voluntary and suborn'd suggestion and forgery, shall by publick Licence invade mens quiet, and disturb their modesty, and stir up a tumult [356] of writing; and yet, if any man shall but open his mouth to the contrary, and in defence of common ingenuity, the same person that invented or Licensed the falshood, shall have the priviledge likewise to prohibit the Truth and the Discovery. Only, Mr. Bayes, forasmuch as you do here avow that it was upon this occasion that you called for *Signal Marks, Acknowledgments, Recantations,* &c. and seeing this occasion chances to be no occasion, pray learn henceforward to be something more deliberate in your railing against the Non-conformists. Perhaps if you would use your incomparable *Suada,*[1103] and move them to Repentance in a Theological and Christian Language, they might be prevailed with. For truly it does befit all that have been accessory to the late mischiefs and crimes, to walk with great innocence and modesty, though after the State has set them right, the Church cannot of right, as you would have it, demand another Allegiance. But to think, that railing will do the work, or for men to hear themselves called *Traytors, Villains, Schismaticks, Hereticks,* and to have all mankind preach'd and hurangu'd up to extirpate them, for meer Non-conformity; and this by such a person as you (which makes their [357] suffering more infamous and odious to them) and for you to perswade them that all this is wholsome for them and the good of their Souls, and that therefore they should recant in your hands, it is just as if Rabshekah should pretend, when he threatned the men of Jerusalem they should drink their own Piss,[1104] that he prescribed

[1101] Orbicular: complete, rotund.

[1102] *Baxter . . . Blood:* see p. 278 and note 292 above.

[1103] *Suada:* persuasive eloquence.

[1104] Rabshekah . . . Piss: 2 Kings 18:27.

them a remedy for the Scurvy. Pray do but try a little Mr. Bayes, for experiment how you your self could away with this Recanting; if you were to disgorge all you had swallowed, and swallow all you had disgorged, it would make you I trow look very simply, and cast you into a Fit worse then of the *Miserere* or the Iliack Passion.[1105] Were you to recant all your false Doctrines, all your profanations of Scripture, all your Bear-garden and Billings-gate[1106] Railing and Scolding; Nay, were you to recant (and in good Conscience you ought to refund) for your estate got by Plunder, and Sequestration and High-Court of Justice.[1107] Were you to recant for all the Circles, Semicircles, Complements, and Segments in the *Reproof*; Were you but to refund to your Book-seller, for all those books that you were fain to give away to disperse them, and for that mutual *Gratification*, which you [358] were not asham'd, notwithstanding all your Dignities, to pillage him of before he could pay his Printer: I doubt the least of these would come off with an ill grace, and 'twould go very hard and aukwardly with you. But, because this may be too severe, you have here solemnly *protested that if your Answerer can convict you of any one Forgery, it shall not suffice to ask him forgiveness upon your knees, but you will make him a publick Recantation.*[1108] This thing of the Declaration, that it was subscribed by your Answerer, is a notorious and convict Forgery. Therefore do but now go to him, and kneel down on your knees, and ask his blessing, and make but a private Recantation, and I will say you are so far an honest man.

And now being so near a period I cannot but gratulate my good fortune, rather than my wisdom, that I have travelled such an Author through with no more extravagancy. 'Tis some kind of deliverance to have found my way so well when I was to follow an *Ignis Fatuus.*[1109] Had he thought fit to make use of my admonition, there had been no occasion for this intercourse. But seeing he has chosen it, I hope there are few persons of Candor who need strain their invention to supply my excuse; it being more [359] easie to justifie to others, than to delight my self with this kind of writing. And amongst the most Eminent, I hope my Lord Arch-bishop[1110] will not (if this be the man I take him for) misinterpret me. But that as he was once pleased to *thank me,*

[1105] Iliack Passion: also called *Miserere;* a painful intestinal obstruction.

[1106] Billings-gate: a fishmarket near this London gate, noted for vituperative language.

[1107] Sequestration . . . Justice: refers back to the career of Parker Sr.

[1108] *protested . . . Recantation: Reproof,* p. 426.

[1109] *Ignis Fatuus:* will-o'-the-wisp, a phosphorescent light hovering over marshes, deceptive to travelers.

[1110] Arch-bishop: Gilbert Sheldon, Parker's patron.

and acknowledge that I had done good service to the Church in detecting to him another Doctor[1111] so effectually, that he voluntarily subscribed never to come more within any Pulpit, although he is since *punished* with a Living of Three hundred pounds a year: so now his Grace will not take it ill that I have also discovered this man to him, the Tenure of whose Divinity is per *Saltum, Sufflum, & Pettum*;[1112] and whose Purse and Conscience, being link'd with the same Tyes, do make together the perfect Character of an, *&c.*[1113]

What remains, Mr. Bayes, is to serve in your Bacon, but because I would do it to the best advantage, I shall add something else for your better and more easie digestion. The first shall be your Ammianus[1114] Marcel. whom if you had, as I advised you, bit off at both ends, he could not probably have molested you. But in the *27th.* book, having described the contention of Damasus[1115] and Ursinus[1116] for Ecclesiastical preeminence, he adds; *These kind of men ought* [360] *indeed to be most sharply reprehended, who having obtained what they covet, are secure to be enriched with the offerings of the Ladies, and rowle about in Coaches, curiously drest up, and eat more delicately then Princes; whereas they might be truly happy, if neglecting the Grandeur and Ostentation of the City, which they make an excuse for their Vices, they would imitate in their manner of living, such Country Prelates; who eating and drinking moderately, clothing themselves homely, and looking humbly, recommend themselves thereby to the everlasting Deity, and those that truly worship him, as modest and pure persons.*[1117] Again, in his 21. book, giving the Character of Constantius, among other things he saith that, *He did confound the Christian Religion which is a perfect and plain thing,* Rem absolutam &

[1111] another Doctor: there is no trace of this intriguing incident in the sources for Marvell's biography.

[1112] *Saltum, Sufflum, & Pettum:* "dancing, whistling, and farting"; a servile act of vassalage for one's lord. [S]

[1113] Character of an, *&c:* The vogue for "characters," or satirical sketches of social and political types, often expressed itself in this phrase; cf. *The Character of a coffee-house, with the symptomes of a town wit.* April 11th, 1673; but cf. also *RT,* p. 172 and *Defence,* p. 1.

[1114] Ammianus Ed] Amminus 73, 74.

[1115] Damasus 74, correctly] Damascus 73.

[1116] Ursinus Ed] Ursicinus 73, 74.

[1117] *These . . . persons:* Ammianus Marcellinus, *Rerum Gestarum* (Hamburg, 1609), book 27, 3:14–15; p. 363. Marvell does not use Philemon Holland's translation (London, 1609), but Holland (pp. 307–08) gives the name as Ursicinus.

simplicem, *with a Grannamish*[1118] *and doating Superstition, and instead of composing with gravity the perplexed questions which he excited, he promoted them further with a strife of words; so that the Prelates, trooping it up and down on the publick Post-horses, and canterburing*[1119] *from Synod, as they call it, to Synod, whilest they indeavour to draw all Rites within their jurisdiction, there were* [361] *scarce any horses left to supply Travellers.*[1120] If this be for your service pray make use of it.

But lest you should say hereupon that your Ammianus was a Socinian, will you admit King James his judgment, who, after nineteen years experience tells the Parliament, *That the external Government appear'd well, Learned Judges, setled Peace, great Plenty, so that it was to be thought every man might have sat in safety under his own Vine and Fig-tree;*[1121] *yet he was ashamed, and it made his hair to stand upright to consider, how his people have in this time been vexed and poll'd by the vile execution of Projects, Patents, Bills of Conformity, and such like; which, beside the trouble of his People, have more exhausted their Purses then Subsidies would have done.*[1122] You see that a *bill of Conformity*[1123] (though it made not, in the phrase of your *Preface, an Archangel stare,*[1124] *yet it*) made a Kings hair stand an end.

But lest you should say King James was an Arminian,[1125] I shall now bring in my Lord Verulam,[1126] whom you cannot refuse, having so often call'd for him. And I the rather quote him because a wise man is as it were [362] eternal upon earth; and he speaks so judiciously and impartially, that it seems as if these very times we now live in had been in his present

1118 *Grannamish:* old-womanish.

1119 *canterburing:* a play on cantering and Canterbury.

1120 *He did . . . Travellers: Rerum Gestarum,* book 21, 16:18, pp. 218–19; Marvell here anticipates his sardonic translation of the account by Eusebius of the Council of Nice. Cf. *Essay,* vol. 2, pp. 131ff.

1121 *sat . . . Fig tree:* 1 Kings 4:25, an allusion to the peaceful reign of Solomon, to whom James liked to be compared.

1122 *the . . . done:* James I, speech to the Lords, 1621; Rushworth, *Historical Collections,* part I, (1659), 1:26.

1123 *bill of Conformity:* for the sake of this phrase, James's general irritation with the parliament goes without comment.

1124 *an Archangel stare: Preface,* b2.

1125 Arminian 74 corrected on inner form of Q in some copies] Arnunian 73; Armenian 74 uncorrected. See Smith, xxxiv.

1126 Lord Verulam: Sir Francis Bacon (1561–1626), lord chancellor under James, lawyer, philosopher, scientist.

prospect. There are two short Treatises of these matters, one begins p. 129. the other p. 180. of his *Resuscitatio.*[1127] Pray Mr. Bayes, let us both listen, for I assure you, before he has done, he will tell us many a wiser thing then is to be met with either in *Ecclesiastical Politie* or *Rehearsal.*[1128] "The Controver-
" sies themselves (saith he) I will not enter into, as judging that the Disease
" requires rather Rest then any other Cure. Neither are they concerning the
" great parts of the Worship of God, of which it is true; *Non servatur*
" *Unitas in Credendo, nisi eadem sit in Colendo.*[1129] Not as betwixt the East
" and West Church, about Images, or between us and the Church of Rome
" about the Adoration of the Sacrament, *&c.* but we contend about cere-
" monies, and things indifferent, about the extern Policy and Government
" of the Church. And as to these we ought to remember that the ancient
" and true Bounds of Unity are, one Faith, one Baptism, and not one
" Ceremony or Policy. *Differentiae Rituum commendant U-*[363]*nitatem*
" *Doctrinae.* The diversities of Ceremonies do set forth the Unity of Doc-
" trine, and *habet Religio quae sunt Eternitatis, habet quae sunt Temporis,*
" Religion hath parts which belong to Eternity, and parts which pertain to
" time. If we did but know the virtue of Silence and Slowness to speak,
" commended by St. James,[1130] and would leave the over-weaning and
" turbulent humors of these times, and revive the blessed proceeding of
" the Apostles and Primitive Fathers, which was in the like cases, not to
" enter into Assertions and Positions, but to deliver Counsels and Advices
" we should need no other remedy at all. *Brother, there is Reverence due to*
" *your Counsel, but Faith is not due to your Affirmation.* St. Paul was content
" to say, *I and not the Lord,*[1131] but now men lightly say, *not I but the Lord,*
" nay and bind it with an heavy denunciation of his judgments to terrifie

[1127] *Resuscitatio:* i.e., a collection of Bacon's smaller publications, ed. W. Rawley (Bacon's chaplain) in 1657. Marvell used the third edition (London, 1671), pp. 129 ff. The two tracts were *An Advertisement touching the Controversies of the Church of England,* written in 1589 in the first stage of the Marprelate controversy; and *Certain considerations touching the better Pacification and Edification of the Church of England,* presented to James at his accession and printed in 1604. In fact Marvell quotes only from the first pamphlet.

[1128] This long quotation from Bacon is set with marginal diples, the printer's recourse when there are quotations within quotations.

[1129] *Non . . . Colendo:* "Unity in believing is no use, unless it also be in drawing us together."

[1130] Silence . . . to speak: James 1:19.

[1131] *I and not the Lord:* 1 Corinthians 7:10: "I command, yet not I, but the Lord."

" the simple, whereas saith that wise man,[1132] *the causless Curse shall not* " *come.*[1133] The Remedies are first that there were an end made of this " immodest and deformed manner of writing lately entertained, whereby " matter of Religion is handled in the stile of the Stage. But[1134] to leave all " reverence and religious [364] compassion toward evils, or indignation " toward faults, and to turn Religion into a Comedy or Satyre, to search " and rip up wounds with a laughing Countenance, to intermix Scripture " and Scurrility sometimes in one Sentence is a thing far from the devout " reverence of a Christian, and scant beseeming the honest regard of a " sober man. Two principal causes have I ever known of Atheism; Curious " Controversie, and profane Scoffing. Now that these two are joyned in " one, no doubt that Sect will make no small progression. Job, speaking of " the Majesty and Gravity of a Judge, saith, *If I did smile they believed it* " *not*:[1135] that is, if I glanced upon conceit of mirth, yet mens minds were so " possessed with the Reverence of the Action in hand, as they could not " receive it. Much more ought not this to be among Bishops and Divines, " disputing about Holy things. Truly as I marvel that some of those " Preachers which call for Reformation (whom I am far from wronging so " far as to joyn them with these scoffers) do not publish some declaration, " in dislike that their cause should be thus sollicited; so I hope assuredly " that my Lords of the Clergy have no intelligence with this [365] inter- " libelling, but do altogether disallow that their Cause should be thus " defended. For though I observe in one of them many glosses, whereby " the Man would insinuate himself into their favours;[1136] yet I find it to be " ordinary that many pressing and fawning persons do misconjecture of the

1132 that wise man: Solomon.

1133 *the causeless . . . come:* Proverbs 26:2.

1134 Stage. But: Marvell here omits an important passage in Bacon which did not serve his present purpose: "Indeed, bitter and earnest writing may not hastily be condemned; for men cannot contend coldly and without affection about things which they hold dear and precious." The omission explains the "But."

1135 *If . . . believed it not:* Job 29:24.

1136 the Man . . . favours: The most likely candidate is A.L., whose *Antimartinus* was entered in the Stationers' Register on July 3, 1589. Bacon wrote his tract during the summer, preceding many of the most notorious anti-Martinist pamphlets, including Lyly's *Pappe with an Hatchet* and Nashe's *An Almond for a Parrat. Antimartinus* was not only licensed, but beautifully printed by George Bishop and Ralph Newbery. It defended the bishops and claimed to be working in the interest of the universities, the State, and the Church.

" humour of Men in Authority, and many times seek to gratifie them with " that which they most dislike. Nevertheless, I note that there is not an " indifferent hand carried to these Pamphlets as they deserve. For the one " sort fly in the dark, and the other is uttered openly. Next I find certain " indiscreet and dangerous amplifications as if the Civil Government," *&c.* For it is impossible to omit any thing in those excellent discourses, without apparent injury to the[1137] Author, and to the Reader. And that which makes them more pertinent is, that he does not spare neither the Non-conformists but gives them too their just charge; for neither then certainly, nor now, are they to be excused: though the unequal dealing used towards them doth justifie them the more, and hath not allowed place or leisure in this Book for me to particularize their failings. [366]

But least you should except against my Lord Bacon, as a Lay man, *not competent to judge of these Ecclesiastical matters in comparison with the Clergy, and who was but, as far as the prejudice of the Age he lived in would permit him, an acute Philosopher*; what say you to Doctor Stillingfleet in the Preface to his *Irenicon* from beginning to end? And in the Book it self from *p.* 117. to 123? I have made scruple to disguise[1138] the discourses of him and others,[1139] as some practise, to make them pass for mine own: and to quote them at length were unnecessary, being so easily found in the Author. But here in few pages you may find all that you have said with so many years labour, totally ruined.

But least you should reject Dr. Stillingfleet, as a Papist, may Bishop Usher, Dr. Hammond, Bishop Taylor, Chillingworth[1140] be allow'd of? I have them all ready at hand for you. But they are all I doubt *suspectae Fidei*, and you will believe none but your self. This is that which hath seduced you,

[1137] the 74] their 73.

[1138] I have . . . disguise: i.e., I am too scrupulous to disguise . . .

[1139] others 73] other 74.

[1140] Bishop Ussher . . . Chillingworth: a distinguished list of tolerationists from mostly unexpected circles. For Archbishop James Ussher, see p. 384 and note 828 above; Henry Hammond (1605–60), Charles I's almoner during his captivity, who on his deathbed was supposed to have exhorted his anglican colleagues not to persecute for religious difference; Jeremy Taylor, bishop of Down, a royalist whose *Liberty of Prophesying* (1647) was nevertheless used as a central tolerationist text in the Restoration, including by Marvell himself in *Mr. Smirke,* vol. 2, p. 108; and William Chillingworth (1602–44), who argued against persecuting for religion in his *Religion of Protestants* (1638) and was himself persecuted on his deathbed.

and because you preach'd over your notes of *Ecclesiastical Politie* in a private Congregation, without being interrupted, you imagined the whole world had been of that [367] mind, and 'twould pass for oecumenical[1141] Doctrine; Whereas I despair not of seeing yet by Gods goodness and the influence of his Majesty, upon the prudence and moderation of my Lords the Bishops, that if you still persist in your mischievous undertaking, you shall be but Simon Magus his sickle, to mow the whole field without any hand to manage it.[1142] It was in the latter end of Queen Elizabeth, after the long experiment of her Reign, that my Lord Verulam writ his first discourse I quoted, and his second at the coming in of King James, as Dr. Stillingfleet his[1143] at the restauration of His Majesty now reigning. But still at[1144] the beginning of the Reigns of our Princes, the proper seasons of redressing these Ecclesiastical matters, and of taking firm measures for their future government, some rub has been interposed unhappily that has thrown all of the Bias and so lost the Cast.[1145] Who is there that ever reads the Scriptures, unless he put on Ecclesiastical Spectacles, (and those too have a *Fly* ingraven upon them) but sees[1146] plainly what tenderness is due unto the scruples of Christians; that our Saviour hath taken Conscience into his immediate protection, and how conform-[368]able the Apostles were to his rule therein, both as to Doctrine and Practice? What English man, reflecting seriously, but must think it hard that a man be a Christian in Turky upon better conditions? that the French, Dutch, and the Walloons even at Canterbury,[1147] may serve God here more freely then our own Natives? that it shall be a Priviledge among us to be an Alien, while an home-born Subject

[1141] oecumenical: representing the whole Christian world.

[1142] Simon Magus . . . manage it: cf. N. Wanley, *The Wonders of the Little World,* ed. Johnston (1806), 2:270: "Clemens Romanus saith of Simon Magus . . . That he commanded a scythe to mow of its own accord." [S]

[1143] Stillingfleet his: on the outer form of Q in three copies "Stillingfleets" is corrected to "Stillingfleet his" and "is" is omitted.

[1144] still at 74, corrected copies] still is at, 73, uncorrected 74.

[1145] some rub . . . Cast: a metaphor from playing dice.

[1146] sees 73] set's 74.

[1147] French . . . Canterbury: on Elizabeth's accession, the Dutch and German Protestants, who had been welcomed by Edward VI, returned to England, and the queen restored their church and privileges. In 1561 the French Protestants were allowed to use a chapel beneath St. Anselm's tower in Canterbury. [S, citing Neal, *History of the Puritans* (1822), 1:136–37.]

must pay the Double-duty (nay forfeit his whole estate)[1148] for the Protestant Religion? What Christian can conceive how a man should lose his right to the Sacraments for dissenting from the Ceremonies? I think I objected that to you once, but you have never deigned,[1149] as far as I can observe, once to answer it. But who especially that as a wise man weighs, what it is to impose things unnecessary upon people obedient to all other Laws, can advise the continuance of such Counsels? For a Prince to adventure all upon it, is like Duke Charles of Burgundy, that fought three Battels for an Imposition upon Sheep-skins.[1150] For a Clergy-man to offer at persecution upon this Ceremonial account, is (as is related of one of the Popes) to justifie his indignation for his Peacock, by the [369] example of Gods anger for eating the forbidden fruit.[1151] But in you, Mr. Bayes, who are I know not well what, I look upon it as an effect of your madness, and only the *staring of an Arch-deacon.*

You say, *that most* wise men *were of opinion you should not answer me, only desire the world to compare it with your discourses: yet others,* ('tis uncivilly said both as to your self and them) *overpower'd you to this Reply, against the bent of your ⟨own⟩ inclinations.* What *others* was it? Was the Devil in you? Or were there *certain tyes upon you,* as Bayes saith, *that you could not be disingaged from? and you writ for the sake of some ingenious persons and choice female Spirits, that have a value for you? otherwise you would see'm all hang'd before you would ever more set Pen*

[*Rep. p.* 527.]

[1148] Double-duty . . . estate: An act of 2 & 3 Edward VI made any person refusing to set out tithes liable to pay double the value in the ecclesiastical court or treble in a commonlaw court. This act was enforced with great vigor, in particular against the Quakers, often leading to the seizure of estates. See A. Pearson, *The Great Case of Tithes* (1732). [S]

[1149] deigned 74, corrected copies] designed, 73, uncorrected 74.

[1150] Duke Charles . . . Sheep-skins: Charles the Bold, duke of Burgundy (1433–77) was defeated by the Swiss and killed. See *The History of Philip de Commines* (London, 1665), 3d ed., book 5, ch. 1, p. 110: "And for what quarrel began this War? forsooth for a load of Ships-skins taken by the Earl of Romont from a Swisser passing through his country."

[1151] justifie . . . fruit: The pope was Julius III (Giovanni Maria del Monte, 1487–1555). See J. Welsch, *Popery Anatomized,* 2d ed. (Glasgow, 1672), pp. 382–83: "Vergerius writes . . . when he missed a dish of cold peacock, . . . he vomit out most horrible blasphemy against God. And when one of his Cardinals answered, *Let not your Holinesse be offended at so light a matter.* He replyed, *If God was so angry for the eating of one apple, that he cast out our first parents out of Paradise; wherefore shal it not be lawful to me who is his Vicar, to be angry for a peacock, seeing it is far greater then an apple?*" [S]

to Paper. If I might advise you, Mr. Bayes, do so no more: for *I verily believe you have writ a whole Cart-load of things, every whit* [*Reh. Com. p.* 8.] *as good as this, and yet the insolent Rascalls turn them all* [*Reh. Com.* p. 15.] ⟨*back*⟩ *upon your hands again.* But do as you please, I have not paid you the Tythe[1152] of what I owe [370] you, but it lyes ready for you, when you please to send for it. You are a Blatant Writer[1153] and a Latrant;[1154] and for lesser crimes, though of the same nature, was Gnevoski, the Polander, sentenc'd to lye barking underneath the Table.[1155] You put me in mind of the Hollanders in Batavia, who, having spent their other Ammunition, charged with Excrements;[1156] the purity of the Savage Javaes could not abide it, but thereupon yielded them the Victory: neither does it become me to contend for it.

I will conclude in a short story, and more seasonable, because as your *Reproof,* it happen'd[1157] once at a Wedding.[1158] *#Et vous avez passé Monsieur par la Baviere.#*[1159] Wenceslaus the Emperor,[1160] Married the Duke of Bavaria's Daughter; the Duke, knowing the Emperours delights, brought along with him a Cart full of Jugling Conjurers, who playing their tricks, Zytho that was Wenceslaus his Magician, *accedens propius, artificem Bavarum cum omni apparatu protinus devorat (ore ad aures dehiscente) calceos duntaxat, quia luto obsiti videbantur, expuens: secessumque inde petens, ven-*

[1152] Tythe: tenth part.

[1153] Blatant Writer: from the Blatant Beast, the mad dog antagonist of Spenser's *Faerie Queene,* book 6, the symbol of slander.

[1154] Latrant: barking.

[1155] Gnevoski . . . Table: Smith could not trace this anecdote, and neither can we.

[1156] the Hollanders . . . Excrements: This episode appears in native Javan archives, regarding the perfidy of the Dutch in 1619, in deceptively building a fort at Jakarta, to become the town of Batavia. See T. S. Raffles, *The History of Java,* 2 vols. (Oxford, 1817), 2:154: "War then commenced, in which the Dutch were reduced to such an extremity that . . . as a last expedient, bags of the filthiest ordure were fired upon the Javans, whence the fort has ever since borne the name of *Kota tai.*"

[1157] happen'd 73, 74 corrected copies] hap-once 74 uncorrected.

[1158] Wedding 73] Weding 74.

[1159] *Et . . . Baviere:* "And you, Monsieur, have passed through the stage of la baviere"; for this insult, added as a second thought, Marvell combines knowledge of the treatment of syphilis with mercury, which causes *la baviere,* excessive salivation, with a double pun on *bavarder,* to engage in idle talk, and Bavaria, the scene of this last grotesque anecdote.

[1160] Wenceslaus IV (1361–1419), king of Bohemia and Holy Roman Emperor, married Joanna, daughter of Albert I, duke of Bavaria, in September 1370. [S]

trem insolita esca gravem in solium aqua plenum exonerat, Praestigiato- [371]*remque adhuc madidum Spectatoribus restituit passim deridendum, adeo ut caeteri quoque eius Socii a ludo abstinerent.*[1161] Whether I shall have the like success I know not (for truly our sport is much like it, and unfit for serious Spectators.) However I have spit out your dirty Shoon.

[*Del Rio. Mag.* p. 317.]

THE END. [372]

[1161] *accedens . . . abstinerent:* Del Rio, *Disquisitionum Magicarum* (1633), book 2, quaestione 30.i., p. 317: Zytho "coming close (stretching his mouth to his ears) devoured the Bavarian trickster with all his apparatus, spitting out only his shoes, because they looked covered in mud: seeking to depart thence, he relieved his stomach, overburdened with such unaccustomed food, in a tub full of water, and restored the conjuror, soaking wet, to the spectators, for their general derision, such that the rest of his comrades also abandoned the sport."

APPENDIXES

Appendix A

THE JUSTICE OF THE SWEDISH CAUSE AND THE DANGER OF THE PROTESTANT CAUSE INVOLVED THEREIN. "BY MONSR FREZENDORP." BRITISH LIBRARY ADD. MS. 4459.

Discovered by Hilton Kelliher, this manuscript records Marvell's longest known autograph manuscript, forty neatly transcribed pages of translation from a Latin political tract attributed to the Swedish envoy in England, Johann Frederick von Friessendorff. Kelliher dated the translation ca. January 1658, toward the end of Cromwell's Protectorate, since the translation is accompanied by a letter that mentions what must have been the second session of Cromwell's second parliament, between January 20 and February 4, 1658. The tract was aimed at persuading the Protector to lead his navy and that of Sweden against Holland and Spain and is related to a draft of a treaty to this end in Thurloe's hand, dated March 25, 1658.[1]

This translation therefore constitutes, if we except his correspondence, Marvell's first prose work. And work it was. At this period he was acting as Latin secretary in the office of John Thurloe, himself secretary to Cromwell's Council of State. Marvell's duties under Thurloe included translating correspondence and official papers from and into Latin. The translation, evidently merely a working document for policy discussions, is clumsy in the extreme and looks to be Marvell's phrase by phrase first response to the Latin text. It therefore testifies to his competence in Latin rather than to his later eloquence in English prose. Nevertheless, the spirit of the tract was clearly in harmony with his own principles, and phrases like "forcing

[1] See Hilton Kelliher, *Andrew Marvell Poet and Politician 1621–78* (London, 1978), p. 70, no. 57.

of mens Consciences in the matter of religion" and "the common Cause of religion and publick liberty" slip easily from his pen. Moreover, Marvell had been interesting himself in the history and politics of Scandinavia since 1653, when he wrote his Latin "Letter to Doctor Ingelo, then with my Lord Whitlock, Ambassador from the Protector to the Queen of Sweden," a poem already anticipating an alliance between England and Sweden (*P&L,* 1:104–07); and he was able to capitalize on this interest as secretary to the earl of Carlisle in his two-year-long embassy to Russia, Sweden, and Denmark, which began in 1663. Marvell's later tracts are peppered with references to Sweden and Poland. The tract is also interesting for its anti-Dutch polemic, which at this stage would have matched Marvell's own views, to judge from *The Character of Holland,* his own satire of 1653 (*P&L,* 1:100–03).

[f. 174v] It is known out of the Historyes what the domestical calamity of Sweden was before Gustavus the first under the tyrants of Denmarke the last of whome Christierne a monster of a man after his stupendious crueltyes and the shedding of rivers of most noble blood was cast as well out of Sweden as Denmark also. Therefore that first Gustavus one of the ancient nobility of Sweden being called unto that kingdome which he had deserved by his virtue vindicated purged and restored to its former glory his country that had been oppressed both with Popist and Danish slavery. And as for the contention with Denmarke after many battells he happily compos'd it upon condition that it should wholy renounce its pretensions to Sweden and that he should make a perpetuall confederacy And at home he setled the kingdome as hereditary whereas it had hitherto been free and elective. He having abjured the Popist religion for himselfe and all his posterity, under the penalty of losing the kingdome. Whence it came to passe that in the publick meeting of the States of the Kingdome, his eldest Sonn Erick was as the kings of Denmark had been depos'd for his tyranny and also Sigismund the Sonn of John the second, [f. 175] who being born of Katharine of Poland and by his mother (or whether by the command or connivence of his father is uncertain.) brought up in the Popish religion, for that cause, Stephen Bathor being dead without heires male in Poland was chosen to that kingdome against Maximilian of Austria, When he was obstinately determind to bring again the Popist superstition into Sweden nor would consent, which was desired, that his Son Vladislaus should be sent thither to be seasoned with the Protestant religion and upon that condition to receive the inheritance of his fathers kingdomes being by a publick Act of the States thereof by reason of his breaking of his Oath and his over-throwing of the fundamentall laws declared incapable of reigning the kingdome was by them conferred upon the third sonne of the said Gustavus, and Uncle of Sigismond, Charles the ninth, grandfather by the mothers side of that Charles who now reigneth. Hence arose the first warre with Poland.

Charles therefore hs affairs being composed by a renewed peace with Denmarke and Muscovia (such is the perfidiousnesse of both nations, as hath also appeared by a most late example) betook himselfe with so much greater force to that his hereditary and holy (for it was on account of religion) warre with Polande. Because Sigismund not onely prepared, sent into, restored ever and anon hostile armyes into Sweden [fol. 175v] and, towards the destruction of the nation, designed many things with diverse of the Papists but especially with those of the house of Austria and the Spaniards to whom he had interwove himself with a double and incestuous affinity to the detriment of this kingdome and of the whole protestant party and of all the borderers of the Baltique Sea into which he had a mind to bring the Spanish navyes but also did with his whole indeavour labour to divide the kingdome in itselfe with inward dissentions Wherefore the said Charles judged that it was best to carry the warre out of the bounds of his own kingdome that he might be securer at home. Which also he happily effected having seised upon the greatest part of Liefland and at length dying in the time of this most glorious warr transmitted to his Sonne Gustavus the Second, who afterwards was called the Great by reason of his atchievements, the inheritances of the Kingdomes and of this Warre also.

And he following his fathers stepps, having added Prusia to Liefland was now come so farre that although Sigismund was then if at any time most powerfull both in his own forces and those of the house of Austria with whom both by reason of affinity and neighbourhood he did perpetually communicate, he could either have thrust him out of his whole kingdome or at least compelld him to honourable and secure conditions of Peace had not his Piety more fervent for religion and the common Cause then for his own Country carryed the mind of that Heros another way. [176]

It fell out then that the Dane, after the Palatine had been beaten and put to flight, having undertaken the cause of the Protestants in Germany had fought unfortunately against the Austrians, had made a Peace with them more unfortunately, abandoning his Confederates and casting away all care of the Protestants that he might provide for his own safety, which he hath done hitherto by a most foule prevarication, from that time forward serving the interest of the house of Austria and sticking close to their counsells and so wholy exstinguishing the glory of the warre he had undertaken by surceasing it with a greater infamy. Concerning which in its place we shall speake further.

There had been amongst his Confederates the Dukes of Mecklenburgh a most ancient and royall family who being exposed to the cruelty of their most potent enemy when they could not contend by force, nor could effect any thing by entreaty were despoiled of their command dignity and all their goods and so driven into banishment: that a most noble province of Germany being first given for a prey afterwards for an inheritance to Wallenstein. Which power, as all his other, he insolently abusing would not contain himselfe upon Land but putting forth a Navy into the Baltick Sea, did not altogether vainly boast himselfe to be the Master and Lord of it. The tyranny and forcing of mens Consciences in the matter of religion being in the meane time both there and every where thorough all Germany most cruelly exercised. And all whatsoever Princes [176v] of our religion, after the Danes had deserted them, not daring once to mutter but even ready forthwith to be led in triumph by the houses of Austria. Who had resolved then at last to bring to effect that their Monarchy long since hammered betwixt them and the Spaniard. And verily they had done it unlesse by the direction of God taking pitty of his Church Gustavus had come upon them. So desperate in all probability was the busyinesse at that time. Gustavus therefore judged this a fit matter for his virtue although indeed joyned with very great danger. Yea he esteemed it more worthy then all those victoryes which he might now have won for the security of his family of his hereditary Enemy without any perill. Although beside that zele with which he was carrying for the preservation of Religion and the Publique liberty he had indeed both publickly and privately received many and intolerable injuryes from the house of Austria some of which we have expressed before, other are everywhere extant in the publicke declarations which did even extort from him the resolution of undertaking the German Warre. Wherefore according to all sound reason of the Politicks he esteemed it more safe to decide in the enemyes country and farthest from his own borders that warre which was framing against him in his own house by that new Lord as he callde himself of the Baltick. Hereupon therefore he made a truce with Poland seeing he could not have a Peace which he by all means sollicited (Concerning which you may see [177] the Justice of the Armes of Sweden a booke printed at Helmstad Anno 1655) for 26 years upon these conditions that the Polander should abstaine from his pretensions but from the title of Sweden especially in his Letters to Sweden and from the very least suspicion of hostility or any collusion with whatsoever enemyes thereof. And that during the Truce there should be a Treaty had concerning a perpetuall Peace. And to these conditions both partyes publickly ingaged France interposing this mediation.

Gustavus came into Germany not at all considering his own particular Succours every where religion oppressed restores the Dukes of Mecklenburgh and the Palatine vindicated the Saxon and Brandenburgh and many other Princes of the Empire though ever and anon struggling and against their own wills and many chiefe cities of the Empire from destruction and redeemed the publick safety of Germany both as to their bodyes and soules most gloriously with his own blood. After his death, Christina proceeding further not only vindicated and defended religion in the free parts of the Empire but also raisd up where it was oppressed and thrown down in the hereditary Provinces of Austria and gave Laws to Austria by degrees submitting it selfe. To how great good of the Church and profit and to how great consolation of lamenting Soules. So that unlesse the perverse counsells of some by a precipitated peace had come between our most pious intentions both Religion at this day should every where have been in good condition and a solid peace should have been fixed in all Europe [177v] concerning which seeing the books of all historians are full and the series of the busynesse is not yet gone out of our memory I will only point at the chiefe heads thereof.

The French and the Hollander had been among the considerable confederates of Sweden of whom the Hollanders by reason of a preposterous desire of Peace made their agreement apart with the Spaniard their confederates in vain admonishing them to the contrary. And to excuse them in some manner beside the Danes and the Princes of Germany spoken of before who had casst away the case of religion and publick liberty and made the victory every way more difficult to us, the kings of England were chiefely among those who abandoned both religion and their children and themselves and were therefore forsaken by God becaue they did not onely not succour the common Cause of religion and publick liberty but did also at home (whence they both could and ought to have succourd it abroad) therein insolently prevaricate. Neither in Sweden it selfe (for concerning France it is needlesse to speake seeing it is of another religion though in many things it hath carryed very well) were all things in this busynesse of Peace carryed according to the minds of the present king who being then Generalissimo in Germany did presse the Austrians at Prague the head and beginning of all the evills. And perhaps also the Queen, otherwise very good because she had been too flexible to the Spaniards hath experienced the hidden judgements and [178] vengeance of God upon her so that abusing her religion she of her own accord left the kingdome and surrenderd it to her Cousin germane by the Aunt one who would take more care of the publick.

. . . .

[fol. 189v] But we shall speake presently of the remedy when we have shak'd out the Cause of the Hollanders which onely remaines.

But whom should I liken them to. He who painted Mercury with wings seems to have expressed their nature who follow him. Let him that pleases looke upon the frontispice of the new built town-house of Amsterdam And he will see that the very stones speake concerning their disposition their mind their counsells. I will say it in a word all. Holland would be the Mistress of all commerces that so she may of all kingdomes. But whether she effect that by right or wrong it is all one to her, thinking that if right be to be violated then to obtaine Royalty. For whereas she was believ'd to plead the cause of Religion her selfe denyes that unlesse it be joyned with her own scope and profit. It is long that Holland hath propounded to it selfe the Commonwealth of Venice for a patterne and I know not whether in so little a time it hath exceeded it. So that what place Venice hath gotten among the Princes of Italy the same doth Holland hold among those of Europe. Concerning whom Holland may rightly say what Danozick of its Polanders that by their foolishnesse she is great. And because it knows how infirme power is that relyes not upon its own force as if she feared that the Daw would be laughd at when every bird comes for its feathers again hence is that turning and many-faced disposition.

For as at first it knew prittily how like Esops wren to hide her selfe under the wings of the neighbouring Eagles least she should become a prey to the hereditary Vulturs so since her feathers are grown and she hath learnd as they so to swim without bladders she always applyes her selfe to the weaker and as if she were cutting diamonds of those that are more potent, she [190] grinds the one with the other. Of which counsells the reason is that that of the losses of others with least charge to her selfe she may make her fortune. So what of late she did through Swedens side against Denmarke she now through Denmarks side against Sweden and by and by will be ready to do the same against England by whomsoever it be.

For England and Sweden it is that stand in her light and which she although her partners in religion though her Benefactors and though joyned to her in sacred Confederacyes yet hates worse then any Turke or Tartar and in hatred to them doubts not to joyne herselfe to the Dane and

Spaniard her ancient and hereditary enemyes and will reassume her hatred against these when she hath grinded and grated away those.

. . . .

192. . . . they point out the Brandenburger and the Dane as if they had been forsaken by us not we by them to defend the protestant religion. So they please themselves to cousin the world so to hold of England by their most exquisite deceits and calumnyes that among these things they may do their own busynesse. For that you may know that I do not speake vainly they set upon your Downing lately in Holland [insert: with those very words] by their publick ministers. Which Sinonian suttletyes that you may acknowledge and take heed of we intreat you in the name of God and the Truth. For lyes Howsoever they be specious do notwithstanding shine thorough and show their painting. Neither do we desire that we should you have you to favour our causes unlesse you find the truth to be on our sides although I doubt not that you do already know and believe it.

That we may in most lively colours returne this upon the Hollanders there is need of the story of Elias who answered ingenuously and truly to Ahab growing fierce in his wickednesse and asking proudly art thou he that troubles Israel. I do not trouble Israel but thou and the house of thy father while ye leave the precepts of the Lord and follow Baalim. Sweden dos not trouble Europe it dos not plant one warre upon another and gape after what is anothers: but pursues as farre as it may one and that a most necessary and pious warre for the true religion for the liberty of it selfe and all Europe with it undertook at home almost an age agoe still most constantly and to its eternall praise. But Holland Holland I say it is which having nothing of its own can not but by the ruine of others rise to that height which it designeth and therefore daily sows warres among Christian Princes that out of their carkasses it may make its harvest. Holland I say which every day and houre must seeke for its victualls and who hath onely that for its own which it can win from another. Which art how fortunately and ingeniously it exercises the penury of others and its treasures do witnesse. But what needs words. England it selfe will bear witnesse. Looke round about what it hath treated with France what with the [Swedes] what with the Spaniard unto your prejudice yea what in the midst of your own people and even at this day how smoothly it insinuates its poysons by what degrees it supplants your trades your liberty your counsells against the Spaniards and what not. Take notice [192v] I beseech you of their actions and examine them well and you will believe me.

Hitherto concerning the evills of Europe and the troublers of it. It remaines that we should add something concerning the remedyes which after God are in our hand and if they be with due caution applied to the Time are most easy. By how much the enemyes may be more they will trample upon and confound one another with their multitude their discords and the biting of their Consciences. There is no danger. Let there be foure hundreds of them against one Elias they are hirelings. They are servants of Baalim. Here is God and Gideon. Here is David and Jonathan. May I have leave to take up that most noble pair of friends as an omen and embleme of our friendship. For herein will consist both our own security and that of the afflicted Church of God if we do imitate them. But if we suffer our selves to be divided and deale apart we are both undone. Imagine that this were said by the oracle of Delphi. Tis an ancient devise of the house of Austria. Divide and Rule by which art only it hath hitherto grown to this stupendious greatnesse. You know by what art one Horatius overcometh three Curiacii. A double thred is not easily broken. If there be at any time friends equall among themselves or their Cause their Forces their Counsells not at all suspecting one another by reason of emulation or envy I durst set two such to fight with the whole world. But I Confesse I have never seen any between whom there is a greater agreement as to all these things then between Sweden and England Carolus and Oliver whether you consider their prudence their valour or all else that they seeme as it were a Paire chosen in Heaven and destind by the Fates themselves unto mutuall friendship. Come on therefore let us be Jonathan and David. Let us joyne Courage to Courage, Counsells to Counsells and in the name of God the God of battells & hostes let us make betwixt us speedily a Confederacy pious & holy for the honor of God for the safety of the Church for our Common Country for our Altars and our Hearths, as it is said, and that upon equall and brotherly conditions. This is the first and chiefe foundation of the whole matter which being once laid whatsoever is built upon it must have good successe. Let our Marke be the Austrian and Spanish faction and whosoever with them or for their sake do disturbe the quiet of Europe. This Standard as it were of publick liberty being once sett up streight all those will run to it whom if not the same piety yet the same hatred against the enemy will make confederates to our cause. Concerning France [193] and Portugal there is no doubt to be made. Many also of ours that is the Protestants who out of the slipperynesse of their own Councells or the perswasions of others or feare of the enemy or diffidence either of their own forces or our intention are yet faulty or stand wavering will forthwith come to so pious a Party. And though none of them should there is enough and more then enough of safeguard in God in our Concord and our Masculine virtue. Look upon that present warre which they alone beare up against so many which were impossible but that they have all so ready a Courage and so united a Counsell. Whence I would chiefly perswade that we might always have our forces joyned nor too farre dispersed and that we should set upon the very head of the busynesse Letting the rest alone for a while or at least suspending our hand. Something however more deliberately.

It is verily an excellent and most wholesome Counsell by which his Highnesse watches the Spanish navyes as the chiefe sinew of the Spanish affaires and which being once cut the whole bulk would easily come down. But I know not yet whether it doth enough answer the times and whether it be accommodated to the interest of England it selfe that I may say nothing concerning the Common Cause. Especially as long as the most cunning Hollanders whose present God is their ready mony and who would sell their very soules for a litle gaine by their cheating tricks do elude and in some manner make vain those things which were excellently designed. For indeed you seem to fish with a golden hooke and to weare out your selves more then you indamage them. Whence also the Spaniards by a most crafty counsell do hitherto oppose no forces against you that your charges may be the greater their damage and danger the lesse.

To conclude it seemeth credible the principall busynesse being effected that this most wholsome Counsell may be brought to effect farr more easily and with greater fruit the Navyes of all our confederates being joyned together the Command of them all being granted to England And in the meane time those expenses which England is at in the Navall warre which it maintains there would here finish all our busynesse.

Appendix B

THE LIFE OF CALIGULA CAESAR FROM *THE HISTORY OF THE TWELVE CAESARS, EMPERORS OF ROME* (LONDON, 1672)

Published by John Starkey, a well-known Whig and Dissenting bookseller, this anonymous translation was attributed to Marvell, in a seventeenth-century hand, in a copy in the Bodleian Library. Subsequent research has established that Marvell followed it closely when writing the *Rehearsal Transpros'd: The Second Part.* This strengthens the early attribution, which was plausible in itself. For a full argument about Marvell's authorship, and for the significance of Suetonius in late-seventeenth-century political culture, see Annabel Patterson, *Modern Language Quarterly* 61 (2000), 463–80. If he was the translator, Marvell worked from a combination of the Latin and the 1606 translation by Philemon Holland, which was by the 1670s linguistically archaic but still gave him considerable assistance. The selection here, about one-third of the *Life* of Caligula, is designed both to indicate the categories under which Suetonius organized his biography, a blend of the topical with the chronological, and to provide the full text of those sections in which, in the *Rehearsal Transpros'd,* Marvell was particularly interested.

9. The Sirname of Caligula was given him in the Camp, by the *Raillerie* of the Souldiers, because he was brought up amongst them in the habit of a Common Souldier; by virtue of which education he had contracted their affection so, that upon a Mutiny after the death of Augustus, his presence appeas'd them, when they were at the height of their fury: Nor could they possibly be quieted, till they understood he was to be sent away to the next City, lest he should be in any danger by their sedition; but as soon as they

understood that, repenting of what they had done, they stopt his Coach, excus'd their fault, and deprecated the displeasure he might have justly conceiv'd against them.

10. He accompanied his Father in his Expedition into Syria, from whence being return'd, his first residence was with his Mother, and (after her banishment) with his Great Grandmother Livia Augusta; who dying not long after, he made her Funeral Oration before the Rostra, though he was then but a youth, and in his *Praetexta*; from thence he went to his Grandmother Antonia, and afterwards when he was twenty years old, being sent for by Tiberius to Capreae, he assum'd the *Virile Robe,* and shaved his Beard the first time, both the same day, without the honour and solemnity which his Brothers had receiv'd upon the like occasion. When he was there, he was tempted by all tricks and designs to complain, or talk more freely then was allow'd; but he was too wise for them all, pass'd all by, as if he had forgot the misfortunes of his Family, and dissembled his own sufferings with incredible patience. In short, he demeaned himself towards his Grandfather, with so much obsequiousness, that it was said of him, and not without reason, *Never was there a better Servant, nor a worse Master.*

11. Howbeit he could not, even then, master his ill inclinations, but took delight to be present himself at all punishments and Executions. He disguis'd himself in the night, and ran up and down to Taverns and Brothel-houses, in a Perriwig and long Gown, that no body might discover him. He delighted passionately in Dancing, Musick, and such Arts as belong'd to the Stage; Tiberius willingly conniving, in hopes those Exercises might by degrees soften and mollifie the cruelty of his Nature, which the cunning old Prince had so perfectly foreseen, that he several times presaged, *That Caius lived for his destruction, and the ruine of them all; and that (in him) he brought up a Serpent for the People of Rome, and a Phaeton for the rest of the World.*

12. Not long after he married Claudilla, the daughter of M. Silanus, a Gentleman of antient extraction; and then being design'd Augur in the place of Drusus his Brother, before his investiture and inauguration, he was advanc'd to the Pontificate, with great shew of piety and good nature. As at that time there was no person at Court but himself, could make the least pretence to the Empire, (Sejanus being suspected already, and a while after destroy'd) he began to look about him, and to conceive some hopes of his succession; and that he might fortifie and confirm them the better, his Wife Junia being dead in Child-bed, he address'd himself to Ennia the Wife of Naevius Macro, then Captain of the Praetorian Cohorts, and having debauch'd her by frequent sollicitations, he swore to her, and promis'd her

Marriage under his hand, if ever he came to be Emperor: having by her means insinuated into the affection of Macro, as some think, he attempted Tiberius with Poyson; and having commanded his Ring to be taken off his finger, observing Tiberius to give some signs of resistance, he caus'd a pillow to be clapt upon his mouth, and stifled him with his own hands. An action that seem'd so cruel to one of his Freedmen, he could not forbear crying out; but he had as good have been quiet, for he caus'd him to be hang'd up immediately. Nor is it incredible, seeing there are Authors which affirm, that if he committed not that fact, yet he confess'd publickly that he designed it; and as a mark of his piety and good nature, he boasted, *That to revenge his Mother and Brothers, he went one time with a Dagger in his hand into Tiberius his Chamber, when he was asleep; but being touch'd with compassion, he threw away his weapon, and retired: that Tiberius saw him well enough, but durst neither examine nor revenge it.*

13. Having been known to most of the Provincials, and Souldiers, from his Childhood, and no less gratefull to the people of Rome, for the memory of his Father Germanicus, and in pity to his desolate Family, he arrived at the Empire to the satisfaction of all parties: In order to which, as he removed from Misenum, though he was in Mourning, and attended the Corps of Tiberius with great gravity; yet could he not forbear marching amongst the Altars, Sacrifices, and Torches which came out to meet him, being surrounded with an infinite number of people, testifying their joy by their acclamations, and calling him (besides other lucky names) *Sidus, Pullum, Puppum,* and *Alumnum,* their Star, their Chicken, their Child, and their Darling.

. . . .

15\. . . . With the same artifice and popularity he restor'd such as stood condemn'd, or banish'd, forgiving all past crimes, if there were any which remmain'd unpunish'd. All Registers and Records, relating any way to the proceedings against his Mother and Brothers, (lest their should be room left for fear, or apprehension in any of their Informers) he caus'd to be brought publickly into the Market-place; and having call'd the Gods to witness, that he had never read, nor so much as touch'd them, he threw them into the fire and burnt them. And this kindness which he hitherto had shewn them, was the reason he refus'd a Note which was offer'd him, tending to the discovery of a Conspiracy against him, alledging for his reason, *That he was not conscious of any thing might deserve the hatred of anybody*; and, *That he had no ears for Informers.*

16. He resolv'd to have cast the *Spintriae* or inventers of abominable recreations into the Sea, and when at last he was perswaded from that severity, he banish'd them from Rome. He suffer'd such as were curious to search for, and peruse the writings of Titus Labienus, Cordus Cremutius, and Cassius Severus, which had been prohibited and supprest by Order of the Senate, it being for his interest to have all passages transmitted to posterity. The establishment or Model of Augustus his administration, which had been neglected by Tiberius, he caus'd to be publish'd; He gave a free jurisdiction to the Magistrates, without reserving any appeal to himself. He took a strict view of the Gentry of Rome, taking away their horses before all people, when he found any of them guilty of any infamous wickedness: But for *peccadilloes,* and such persons as had but small offences to answer, he only past over their names as the rolls were dead, without further punishing them. To relieve the Judges who at that time were overlaid with the multitude of business, to the four before, he added a fifth *Decurie.* He endeavoured also to restore the antient manner of Elections of Magistrates by the suffrages of the people.

. . . .

20. . . . Amongst the rest he ordain'd a solemn Contention in Eloquence, both in Greek and in Latine; requiring those which were overcome, to give rewards to the Conqueror, and to make some Composition or other in his praise: But for those who gave no satisfaction at all, they were condemn'd to expunge what they had done, either with a Sponge, or their tongue, unless they would choose rather to be corrected with Ferula's, or plung'd over head and ears in the next River. . . .

. . . .

22. Thus far we have spoken of him as a Prince, hereafter we shall mention him no otherwise then as a Monster. . . . As he treated one night at Supper certain Kings, which were come to Rome, on purpose to pay him their devoirs, hearing them in controversie amongst themselves about the Nobility of their extraction, he interrupted them, and cry'd out in Greek, *Let there be but one Lord, and one King.* And he was once of the mind to have taken the Diadem immediately, and changed the Government into the form of a Kingdom: But being inform'd that he was already above the Dignity of all the Princes and Monarchs of the world, from that time forward he began to challenge the honour of a Divine Majesty. And indeed he commanded, that the Images of those Gods which were in most esteem, either for the Devotions perform'd unto them, or the Excellence of the

workmanship, and amongst the rest that of Jupiter Olympicus, should be brought from Greece, that their heads being taken off, he might place his own in their room. He enlarg'd and brought down one part of the Palatium, as far as the Market-place; and altering the Temple of Castor and Pollux, into the model of a *Portico,* he plac'd himself oftentimes betwixt the divine Brothers, to be adored by all which came thither; some were so profane as to salute him by the name of Jupiter Latialis. And it had been well if his impiety had rested here: But he built a Temple, dedicated it to his own Divinity, and instituted Priests and Victims, the most exquisite that could be thought on. In this Temple stood his Image in Gold, done to the life, habited in a Robe such as he wore himself. The richest men of the City, either by bribery or favour, purchas'd the dignity of this Priesthood, according as vacancies fell. The Sacrifices which they offer'd were Peacocks, Pheasants, Numidian Hens, and other Fowls, the most rare and delicate could be got, which they sorted, and Sacrificed daily by kinds. When the Moon was in the Full, and shined bright, his custom was to call to her continually, and to invite her to bed to him, that she might taste of his embraces. In the day time he would seem to talk privately with Jupiter Capitolinus, sometimes whispering to him, and then lending his his ear; sometimes he would speak aloud, and sometimes threaten him, as once he was heard in these words, *Ile send you packing into Greece.* At length overcome by the importunity of the Gods, who (as he told the story himself) did instantly desire his Company, he joined the Palatium to the Capitol, by a Bridge which he build over the Temple of Augustus; and a while after, that he might yet be nearer, he laid the foundation of a New House in the Court of the Capitol.

23. . . . He surprized his Brother Tiberius unawares, and commanded him to be killed by a Military Tribune. Silanus also his Father-in-law, he constrain'd to cut his own throat with a Raisor; and excusing himself in both, he alledg'd, that Silanus refus'd to go to Sea with him in a storm, with design to have seized upon the Government, if any disaster had happned to him; And that Tiberius for fear of being poisoned, had taken an Antidote, which he discover'd by his breath: whereas the truth is, Silanus could not endure the Sea, and Tiberius had only taken Physick for a Cough, which he had been troubled with long. And for his Unkle Claudius, he kept him alive as a subject only for his mockery and laughter.

24. He committed incest with all his sisters, and at all his great Feasts they lay with their heads in his bosome by turns, whilst his Wife was plac'd above. Of these Sisters (as it is verily thought) he deflower'd Drusilla when he was but a Boy, and was taken in Bed with her by his Grandmother

Antonia, in whose house they were brought up together. Afterwards she was married to Lusius Cassius Longinus, a Consular man, but he made bold to take her from him by force, and lived publickly with her, as she had been his own Wife, and being sick he appointed her Heir both of his Empire and Estate. When she died, he proclaimed a vacation of all Courts and proceedings in Law; and made it Capital for any man during that time, to laugh, bath, or eat with his friends. In short, not being able to comport himself in so sensible a loss, he left the Town on a sudden in the night, and passing in great haste thorow Campania, he went to Syracuse; from whence in as much haste he returned with his hair and beard all over-grown: Neither did he ever swear afterwards upon any occasion whatever, either in his Orations to the People, or Army, but *by the Divinity of Drusilla.* The rest of his Sisters he neither loved with so true an affection, nor used with so much respect, as persons whom he had prostituted to his own Catamites, which he made use of as an excuse for condemning them so easily in the case of AEmilius Lepidus, charging them with Adultery, and being privy to several Conspiracies against him. Nor did he only publish their dishonours that way, but he consecrated to *Mars the Revenger,* the three Daggers which they had prepar'd for his destruction, with a writing containing the whole Narrative of the Conspiracy.

. . . .

27. The cruelty of his nature appear'd yet more, by these actions following. Observing it very chargeable to feed the Wilde Beasts which were kept to be baited, he mark'd out several Malefactors to be given to them; for visiting his Prisons in person, he rang'd the Prisoners before him in a Gallery, and standing himself in the midst, he gave order to take away all, *a Calvo ad Calvum,* from such a Bald-pate (as he pointed to) to another, and throw them to the Beasts, without the least respect to the quality of their Crimes. A certain person having devoted himself to the Combate of the Gladiators for Caligula's recovery, he forc'd him to make good his Vow, was present himself when he fought at sharpes, and would not suffer him to retire till he had got the Victory, and all the people had interceded for his dismission. Another having vowed to dye upon the same condition, and being not over-forward in performing his promise, he caus'd him to be adorned with Herbs and Ribbands like a Victim, and in that manner to be delivered to the Boyes, who requiring the accomplishment of his Vow, as they hurried him along the streets, threw him at last down a Precipice, and killed him. Nay so great was his inhumanity towards several persons of good quality and Estate, that having mark'd them with hot Irons, he condemn'd them

either to the Mines, to the reparation of the High-wayes, to the Combate with Beasts, (shutting them up in close low places, where they were forc'd to crawle on all four, like the Beasts they were to fight with) or else saw'd them through the middle with a Saw. Nor was it for any weighty or grievous offence they suffer'd in this nature, but upon trifling occasions, as, if they had not lik'd any of his Shows, or had never sworn by his Genius. He constrain'd the Parents to be present many times, and assistant at the Execution of their own Children . . . He caus'd the Author of a Latine Farce, to be burnt in the midst of the Ampitheatre, only for a witty Verse which was capable of a double interpretation. . . .

. . . .

29. And if he was barbarous in his actions, he was little better in his words; He was wont to say, There was nothing in his nature he commended so much as (in his own words) his *adiatrepsian*, or unrelenting at the sight of Executions. His Grandmother Antonia admonishing one day; as if his disobedience had been nothing at all, *Remember* (says he) *I may do what I please, with whom I please.* Having a design to poison his own brother, and suspecting he used Antidotes, *How* (says he) *is there any Antidote against Caesar?* Having banish'd his Sisters, he threatned them, *That he had Swords as well as Islands. . . .*

30. He took great delight to kill people by degrees, not on a sudden, or at one blow, but with little and reiterated strokes, that according to his usual Expression, *They might be struck so, as they might be sensible of their death. . . .* In short, so unlimited and boundless was his inhumanity, he would often make use of that expression of the old Tragaedian, *Oderit dum metuant, Let them hate me as they please, so they do but fear me.* He upbraided the whole Senate at once, as the Creatures and dependants of Sejanus, or betrayers of his Mother, and Brothers; and producing such papers as he pretended was burnt, he justified the severity of Tiberius, as but necessary upon so many informations. The Gentry also he twitted in the Teeth with their too immoderate devotion to Spectacles, and Stage-plays. Being highly offended with the people for favouring his adversaries, he cryed out, *Would to God the people of Rome had but one neck. . . .*

31. Besides this he used frequently to complain of the unhappiness of his time, *Because not afflicted with any considerable calamity, to make it remarkable*; Lamenting *That the Reign of Augustus was memorable, for the overthrow of Varus; Tiberius his, for the fall of the Ampitheatre at Fidenae, but such was his unfortunate prosperity, he was in great danger to be forgotten*; in so

much that he many times wish'd for the destruction of some of his Armies, Famine, Pestilence, Fire, or some such opening of the Earth, as would swallow up a good lusty proportion of his people.

32. When he was even in his sports or entertainments, he used the same wildness both in his words and actions . . . A Sacrifice being brought to the Altar, and ready to be offered, he came himself to the Altar in the habit of a Priest, and lifting up the Mallet as he would have knock'd down the Beast, he knock'd an Officer on the head which stood by with the Knife. Falling suddenly into a great laughter as he was one night at Supper, the Consuls who sat near him, desired him mildly to know the reason, *For what think you* (says he) *but to consider that I can have both your throats cut, with the least nod of my head.*

. . . .

34. . . . It was once in his thoughts to have suppresst Homers works; *For why* (said he) *should not I have as much liberty as Plato, who banished him out of his Common-wealth.* He wanted not much also of throwing the Images and Writings of Virgil, and Titius Livius out of all Libraries, looking upon the first, *as a man of no wit, and as little learning*; and upbraiding the other, *with his verbosity and negligence in his History.* And as to the Lawyers (as if he meant to take away all use of their knowledg, and cunning) he was often heard to say, *He would certainly bring things to that pass, that they should have nothing to say, but what he thought Equitable and Just.*

. . . .

54. He took delight likewise in several other Exercises, which he practis'd most studiously: He was a Fencer, a manager of Chariots, Sung and Danc'd well; he fought well in Armes, and order'd his Chariot in the most difficult place of the Cirque. He suffer'd himself to be so far transported with Singing and Dancing, that even in the publick Shews, and Theatres, he could not forbear Singing along with the Tragedian, and imitating the Players by way either of correction, or applause. . . . He Danc'd also very frequently in the night, and being once in that humour, he sent for three persons which had been Consuls, out of their Beds, about three or four of the Clock in the morning: and whilst they were trembling in apprehension of some extremity, he plac'd them aloft upon a Scaffold, and then on a sudden with a great noise of Pipes and Castagnettoes, he came leaping out in a long Robe reaching down to his ankles; and at last dancing to the air of an excellent voice, he departed as he came. Yet this person, who was so docile and apt to everything else, could never by any art be taught how

to swim. The passion and kindness he had for such as he lik'd, was so indecently fond, that he kiss'd publickly Mnester the Mimick in the midst of a Play . . .

55. . . . His affection was so great to the party of Green Coachmen, that he supp'd ordinarily in their Stable, and lodg'd with them. To Cithicus a manager of Chariots, he gave at one time at a Collation, in the last Service amidst the Fruit, which they used to carry home, two millions of Sesterces. Nay he was so exorbitant in his affection to a Horse he had, which he call'd Incitatus, that the day before the Circensian Games, he was wont to give notice to the neighbourhood by his Souldiers, that they forbore making any noise for fear of disturbing him. Besides that, his Stable was built of Marble, his Manger of Ivory, his Houshing-clothes of Purple, and a rich Collar of precious Stones which he wore for his *Poictrell*; he allow'd him a house very well furnish'd, and a Family to attend him, for no other end, but that such as were invited in his name, might be received and entertained with the more magnificence and elegancy; and it is reported, that he had a design to have made his Horse a Consul.

56. In the midst of these extravagancies, several persons were inclin'd to assassinate him, whilst others were remiss for want of opportunity; but two Conspiracies having been discover'd a third was perpetrated by the correspondence of two persons, who communicated their design with the most considerable Freed-men, and Officers of his Guards; who embrac'd it the more willingly, because they found themselves named (though falsly) as partakers in another Conspiracy, and perceiv'd they were not only suspected, but hated by him. . . . It being resolv'd to attaque him during the Palatine Games, as he went out of the Theatre to Dinner, Cassius Chaerea Tribune of one of the Praetorian Cohorts, desired the first part in the Action, in revenge of the continual affronts he receiv'd from him; for though he was ancient, and well stricken in years, yet Caligula in most opprobrious manner abus'd him, as wanton and effeminate; coming to him one while for the word, he gave him (by way of mockery) *Priapus*, or *Venus*: And when he address'd himself to him, to give him thanks for any thing, he thrust out his hand for him to kiss, but it was alwayes in a most obscene and immodest form.

. . . .

58. What fell out afterwards, is reported two several wayes; some say, that whilst he was in discourse with these Boyes, Chaerea came behind him, and with his Sword gave him a mortal blow on the back part of his head, giving him these words as he was striking, *Hoc age, Think upon this*; after which

another of the Tribunes call'd Cornelius Sabinus, one of the Conspirators likewise, ran him clear through the body. Others say, that the Centurions who were privy to the design, having removed the multitude from about him, Sabinus went to him, as usually, for the word, and that Caligula giving him, *Jupiter,* Chaerea cry'd out, *Accipe ratum, Take it sure*; and as Caligula look'd behind him, Chaerea cut off his Jaw at one blow, and struck him to the ground; where, as he lay along tumbling and gathering up his limbs, he cry'd out several times, *He was still alive*; but the rest of the Conspirators fell in, and dispatch'd him with thirty wounds, their words amongst themselves being, *Repete, To him again*; in which some of them were so zealous, they ran him into the very Privities . . .

. . . .

60. What the condition of those times were, any one may collect from these very particulars; upon the first report, his death was not believ'd, it being suspected to be given out by himself, to discover the affections of the people towards him. Neither had the persons engaged in the Conspiracy, designed any other body to succeed him: The whole Senate was so unanimously dispos'd to their ancient Freedom, that the Consuls would not call them at first into the Ordinary Court, because it was call'd Julia, but convented them in the Capitol. Some were of opinion, to abolish the very memory of the Caesars, and to pull down their Temples. And it is particularly remarkable, that all the Caesars whose first names were Caius, died by the Sword, from that very Caius who was kill'd in the dayes of Cinna.

Appendix C

"THE KING'S SPEECH"

On March 1, 1675, Girolamo Alberti, Venetian secretary to the Doge and Senate, included in a long letter on current English church politics the following report: "A mock discourse is circulating in the squares which purports to be the king's speech at the next session of parliament giving the mob ideas most prejudicial to the Court. The lads who hawk about the streets the order in Council and the proclamation have the audacity to shout 'Declaration of his . . . Majesty for sweetmeats for the parliament.'" (See *CSPD Venetian* 1675, p. 366.) This speech, which survives in twelve manuscripts,[1] none of which is in Marvell's hand, was ascribed to Marvell in *Poems on Affairs of State,* vol. 3 (London, 1704), where it appeared in print for the first time. The various manuscript versions differ considerably in small and not so small ways, making collation impractical. We chose to print the version that appears in Ms. Bodleian Don. B8, which seems closest both to Marvell's satirical style and to Charles II's indolent speech patterns. Bodleian Ms. Don B. belonged to Sir William Haward, knight of the Privy Chamber to Charles I. It contains most of Marvell's satires[2] and dozens of later painter poems. It therefore has a certain authority.

The mock-speech explicitly parodies that of Charles II on March 8, 1673 (also recorded in this manuscript at ff. 388–89), in which he agrees not to act on the Declaration of Indulgence and asks for a supply to prepare a fleet for the summer for "the Safety, Honour, & interesse of England." The mock-speech also responds

[1] See Peter Beal, *Index of English Literary Manuscripts* (London and New York, 1980), pp. 66–67.

[2] Significantly, it dates "The Statue at Charing Crosse" to 1675 (f. 525).

to the chancellor's long speech at the same time (ff. 398–404), which mentions the stopping of the Exchequer (f. 402), as well as the suspicions raised in the country by the Declaration (ff. 398–404).

A pretended libellous Speech prepared for his Matie in February 1674/5 to be spoken to both Houses att the meeting of the parliamt on ye. 13th of April following.

My Lords, & Gentlemen,

I told you last meeting, ye Winter was ye fittest tyme for businesse, & truely I thought soe, till my Lord Treasurer[3] assured mee, that ye Spring is ye best Season for Sallets, & Subsidyes. I hope therefore, that Aprill will not prove such an unnatural Moneth, as not to afforde some kinde Showers, to refresh my parched Exchequer, that gapeth for want of them.

But some of you may perhaps thinke it dangerous, to make mee too rich, but doe not feare it, I promise you faithfully, whatever you give mee, I will alwayes want, & although in other things my word may bee thought, but slender Security, yet in that you may rely on me that I will not breake it.

My Lords, & Gentlemen,

I can beare my owne straites with patience, but my Lord Treasurer doeth protest to mee, that ye Revenue, as it now standeth, will not serve him, & mee too; one of Us must pinch for it, if you do not helpe Us. I must speake freely to you, I am in incumbrances, for besides my Mistresses in present Service, my Reformado Mistresses lye hard upon mee. I have a pritty good Estate, I confesse; but Gods-Fish I have a great charge upon itt. here is my Lord Treasurer can tell you, that all ye Money designed for ye next Summers Guard must of necessity be applyed to ye next yeares Cradles, & Swadling Clothes; what shall wee doe for Ships then? I onely hint it to you, for that is your businesse, & not mine: I know by experience, I can live without them. I lived ten yeares abroad without Ships, & had never better health in my life: but how you will doe without them I leave to your selves to judge, & therefore mention that onely by ye Bye, I do not insist upon itt.

There is another thing I must press more earnestly, which is, that it seemes a good part of my Revenue will fayle in two, or three yeares, except you will be pleased, to continue it. I have now to say

[3] Treasurer: Thomas Osborne (1632–1712), earl of Danby.

for itt, pray why did you give mee soe much, as you have done, except you resolve to give on as fast, as I shall aske you? The Nation hates you already, for having given soe much, & I shall hate you now, if you do not give mee more: so if you do not sticke to mee, you will not have a freind left in England. On the other side, if you will give me the Revenue as I desire, I shall be enabled, to doe those things for your Religion, & Liberty, that I have had longe in my thoughts, but cannot effect them without a little more money, to cary mee through in itt. Therefore looke to it, & take notice, that if you doe not make me rich enough, to undoe you, it shall lye att your doores, for my part I wash my hands of itt: but that I may gaine your good opinion, ye best way to it is, to acquaynt you with what, I have done, to deserve it out of my Royall Care of your Religion, & your property.

For ye first, my late Declaration is a true picture of my mynde; he, that cannot in that, as in a Glasse, see my Zeale for ye Church of England, doeth not deserve any further satisfaction; for I declare him willfull, & not good-natur'd. Some may perhaps be startled, & say, how comes this sudden change? To that I reply in a Word. I am a Changeling; I thinke, that is a full answer. But to convince Men further, that I meane, as I say, there are these Arguments.

1. I tell you soe, & you know, I never broke my word with you.
2. My Lord Treasurer sayth so, & you know, he never told a Lye.
3. My Lord Lauderdaile[4] will undertake for mee, & I should be loath by any Act of mine, to forfeit ye Creditt, he hath with you. If you desire more instances of my Zeale, I have them for you. For Example; I have converted all my Naturall Sons from popery, & I may say without vanity, it was my owne worke, & much more peculiar to mee, than ye getting of them. It would doe your hearts good, to heare how prittily little George[5] can reade already ye psalter;[6] they are fine children, God blesse them, *& like me in their understanding.* But as I was a saying, I have, to please you, given a pension to your Favourite the Lord Lauderdaile, not so much, that I thought, he wanted it, as that I knew, you would take it kindly. For ye same

[4] Lauderdaile: John Maitland (1616–82), earl of Lauderdale and Charles's chief minister in Scotland.

[5] George: George Fitzroy, earl of Northumberland (b. 1674), Charles's youngest son by Barbara Palmer, duchess of Cleveland.

[6] ye psalter: Marvell implies that the bastard children of Cleveland and the king are being brought up as Roman Catholics. Cleveland herself converted to Catholicism in 1663.

reason I have made Carwell[7] a Duchesse, & marryed her Sister to my Lord of Pembroke.[8] I have att my Brothers request sent my Lord Inchiqueen, to settle ye protestant Religion at Tangier:[9] I have made Crew[10] Bishop of Durham, & att ye first word of my Duchesse of Portesmouth Brediocke[11] Bishop of Chichester. I doe not know for my part, what Factitious men would have: sure I am, that none of my predecessors ever did any thing like this, to gaine ye good will of their Subjects. So much for your Religion.

Now, as for your property, my behaviour to ye Bankers[12] for a publique instance, & that proceeding about Mrs. Hyde,[13] & Mrs Sutton[14] for a private one are very convincing Evidences, that it will bee needless, to say any more.

I must now acquaynt you, that by my Lord Treasurers advice, I have made a considerable retrenchment upon my Household Expences in Candle, & Charcoale, & I doe not intend, to stop there, but will with your help looke into ye late Imbezlements of Kitchin-Stuffe, of which [by ye way] upon my Conscience neither my Lord Trea-

[7] Carwell: Louise de Keroualle (1649–1734), duchess of Portsmouth, who replaced Cleveland as the king's premier mistress in 1674.

[8] On Wednesday, December 19, 1674, Marvell wrote to Sir Henry Thompson, "You have heard doubtlesse that the Duchesse of Portsmoth has 10000 li a yeare settled out of the Wine Licenses . . . Her sister was on Thursday married to the Earle of Pembroke he being prity well recoverd of his Clap" (*P&L,* 2:336).

[9] Lord Inchiqueen: William O'Brien (1638?–92), second earl of Inchiquin, who succeeded his father, Murrough O'Brien, as earl on September 9, 1674. Early in 1674 he was appointed captain-general of the king's forces in Africa, and governor and vice-admiral of the royal citadel of Tangier (part of the dowry of Catherine of Braganza). O'Brien's father had converted to Catholicism in 1657, which may explain the sneer.

[10] Crew: Nathaniel Crew, bishop of Durham, Cleveland's uncle.

[11] Brediocke: Ralph Brideoak (1613–78), personal chaplain to the king.

[12] the bankers: Marvell refers to Charles's notorious stop of the Exchequer of January 1672, which suspended payments on government loans and caused great financial distress to the City bankers. Cf. *Account,* vol. 2, pp. 253–54.

[13] Mrs. Hyde: Sir Robert Viner's stepdaughter Bridget Hide, aged twelve, had been secretly married to a Mr. Emerton. Danby wished her to marry his son, Lord Dunblane. When Parliament met in January 1675, Danby was accused of pressuring the clergyman who had officiated at the marriage to deny it, and of having bribed Viner to consent. See Marvell's letter to the Hull Corporation of April 24, 1675, which condemns this "detestable and most ignominious story" (*P&L,* 2:150).

[14] Mrs. Sutton: This may be an error for "Emerton," the reading in BL MS. Add. 34362 and Princeton, Robert H. Taylor Collection (Files). The syntax implies there was just one scandal in question, not two.

surer, nor my Lord Lauderdaile are guilty, I speake my Opinion, but if you shall find them dabbling in ye businesse, I tell you plainely, I leave them to you, for I would have the world to know, I am not a Man to bee cheated.
My Lords & Gentlemen,

I desire you, to beleave of mee, as you have found mee, & I doe solemnly promise, that whatever you give mee, shall be especially managed with the same Conduct, Thrift, Sincerity, & Prudence, that I have ever practised, since my happy Restauration.

Index